THE PAPERS OF WILLIAM WOODS HOLDEN

William Woods Holden. Photograph of engraving from North Carolina Collection, University of North Carolina at Chapel Hill.

The Papers of William Woods Holden

• Volume 1 •

1841-1868

Horace W. Raper
Editor

Thornton W. Mitchell
Associate Editor

Raleigh
Division of Archives and History
North Carolina Department of Cultural Resources
2000

ISBN 0-86526-292-6

CONTENTS

List of Illustrations ix
Foreword xi
Acknowledgments xii
Introduction xv
Editorial Method xxxiii
List of Papers Printed in this Volume xxxv
Abbreviations of Sources Cited xlv

The Papers of William Woods Holden 1

Index 447

ILLUSTRATIONS

William W. Holden (ca. 1870) . . . . frontispiece

David S. Reid . . . . following page 200
John W. Ellis
Stephen A. Douglas
John C. Breckinridge
Zebulon B. Vance
Andrew Johnson
Jonathan Worth
William A. Graham
Joseph W. Holden
Louisa Virginia Harrison Holden

FOREWORD

Among the political leaders who have left their mark on the history of North Carolina during the Civil War and Reconstruction era, perhaps none has been more misunderstood and vilified than William Woods Holden. Born of humble origins in Hillsborough, North Carolina, in 1818, Holden became an important political influence as editor of the Raleigh *North Carolina Standard* and leader of the antebellum state Democratic Party. Also an attorney who practiced only a short time, he served in the North Carolina House of Commons in 1846-1847 and held other minor state offices. Although labeled a secessionist, he, in fact, supported the Union until after the firing on Fort Sumter, when he endorsed North Carolina's secession.

During the Civil War, Holden continued to publish the *Standard* and became an out-spoken critic of the Confederate government. In 1863 he launched a movement for a negotiated peace with the Federal government and ran for governor on a peace platform in 1864 but was soundly defeated by the incumbent Zebulon B. Vance. Immediately following the war, Holden served briefly as North Carolina's provisional governor under President Andrew Johnson's mild plan of reconstruction, which did not provide for the safety and rights of former slaves. But when the so-called Radical Republicans in Congress gained control of Reconstruction in March 1867, he supported their program to guarantee political and civil rights for African Americans in the South. He helped organize the Republican Party in North Carolina and in 1868 was elected governor.

As North Carolina's chief executive, Holden labored to govern the state under the changes required by the provisions of Congressional Reconstruction—which included the ratification of the Fourteenth Amendment to the U.S. Constitution, the establishment of a new state constitution, and the election of new state and local officers and representatives to Congress—before North Carolina could be readmitted to the Union. By late July the state's legislators and voters had carried out those important requirements, and Congress had approved the new state constitution and seated two new Republican senators from North Carolina. The Tar Heel state was back in the Union. But Holden still faced a multitude of resistance and hostility from members of the state's Conservative Party, who wanted to regain political power by preventing white and black Republicans from voting and holding office. As the year of 1868 came to a close, the governor increasingly had to contend with the growing terror and lawlessness of the Ku Klux Klan, which had arisen during the recent elections and continually resorted to violence and ultimately murder to keep newly enfranchised blacks and their white Republican allies from the polls.

In volume one (1841-1868) of *The Papers of William Woods Holden*, editor Horace W. Raper and associate editor Thornton W. Mitchell have skillfully selected, edited, and annotated a series of documents that provide significant insight into the enigmatic Holden from the time he rose to power as leader of the pre-Civil War Democratic Party until the end of the first six months following his election as North Carolina's governor during Congressional Reconstruction. Horace W. Raper, professor emeritus of Tennessee Technological University and an authority on Holden, received his A.B., M.A., and Ph.D. degrees from the University of North Carolina at Chapel Hill. Among his publications are a number of articles and book reviews in the *North Carolina Historical Review*. In 1985 the University of North Carolina Press published his book *William W. Holden: North Carolina's Political Enigma*. Thornton W. Mitchell received an A.B. and an A.M. from Stanford University and a Ph.D. from Columbia University. He retired as North Carolina State Archivist in 1981 after a career of forty years in archival and records management. He is a fellow of the Society of American Archivists and is also a certified records manager. He edited *Norton on Archives: The Writings of Margaret Cross Norton on Archival and Records Management* and is the author of *The State Library and Library Development in North Carolina* and *North Carolina Wills: A Testator Index, 1665-1900*. His articles have appeared in the *North Carolina Historical Review*, and in 1974 he and his wife, Memory F. Mitchell, shared the Robert D. W. Connor Award for the best article in the *Review*.

Joe A. Mobley
Historical Publications Administrator

September 2000

ACKNOWLEDGMENTS

With a project that has been in preparation for several years, the editors acknowledge the assistance they have received from many individuals and organizations. The principal source of documents relating to William Woods Holden is the North Carolina State Archives, Division of Archives and History, and the staff of the Archives Search Room has been helpful in many ways. Thanks is expressed particularly to Mary J. Rogers, George Stevenson, and C. Edward Morris, Search Room supervisors, and the members of their staffs, particularly Russell Koonts and Debra A. Blake. Another major source is the Special Collections Library, Duke University, Durham, which has custody of papers relating principally to the Holden family. Mattie Russell, Robert Byrd, Linda McCurdy, and William Erwin of that library have been generous in making material available. Many of the materials in the Southern Historical Collection, Wilson Library, University of North Carolina, Chapel Hill, contain letters written by Holden, and its staff has been more than helpful in locating documents. Special thanks is due J. Isaac Copeland, Carolyn Wallace, Timothy Pyatt, directors of that collection, their staff members and particularly Richard A. Shrader for their unfailing assistance. Administrators and staff of the Historical Publications Section, Division of Archives and History, helped ensure completion of the project. Special thanks is expressed to administrators Memory F. Mitchell, Jeffrey J. Crow, and Joe A. Mobley for their guidance, and to Trudy M. Rayfield and Gail Elliott for their technical assistance. Thanks also is due to the Library of Congress, Washington, D. C., and the Department of Special Collctions, University of Chicago Library, for permission to quote from collections in their custody.

Editor Horace W. Raper's work was materially aided by the Tennessee Technological University Faculty Committee on Research with financial and teaching assistance, particularly in transcribing and copying a multitude of documents. The assistance of the committee is gratefully acknowledged.

Finally, both editors found unlimited support from their respective families. Mrs. Betty B. Raper, Stephen W. Raper, and Edward Raper were constant supporters during the years that this project was pursued. Mrs. Memory F. Mitchell was supportive in the final stages of the project. Without the unfailing support of these family members, this volume in all probability would not have appeared.

Horace W. Raper
Thornton W. Mitchell

INTRODUCTION

William Woods Holden was one of the most controversial political figures in nineteenth-century North Carolina, particularly in the period of Congressional Reconstruction that followed the Civil War. He was, in addition, probably North Carolina's most maligned politician during and after his public career. Impeached and removed from office, he was later vilified by Conservatives, a group of implacable anti-Republicans who later coalesced into the Democratic Party. Throughout much of North Carolina's history since Reconstruction, Democratic politicians, historians, and others have disparaged Holden. J. G. de Roulhac Hamilton, in his partisan *Reconstruction in North Carolina*, claimed that "The governor was much more interested in party politics and personal advancement than in good government. . . . For party reasons he was ready to overlook any lack of honesty. . . ."[1] Thomas Dixon, Jr., in one of his novels glorifying the Ku Klux Klan during Reconstruction identified the "Provisional Governor" as a "writer of brilliant and forceful style" who, after defeat in the election of 1865, "began his schemes of revengeful ambition."[2] Even an icon like the prominent politician William A. Graham, a contemporary of Holden, condemned him for his "morbid partisanship."[3]

Holden has been the subject of three biographies and of several articles in the *North Carolina Historical Review* and other professional journals. Edgar E. Folk and Bynum Shaw, *W. W. Holden: A Political Biography*,[4] was based largely on Folk's dissertation at Peabody College and deals principally with Holden's career as a newspaper man. Horace W. Raper, *William W. Holden: North Carolina's Political Enigma*,[5] was based on Raper's dissertation at the University of North Carolina, Chapel Hill. William C. Harris, *William Woods Holden: Firebrand of North Carolina Politics*[6] is the most recently published. In addition, late in his life Holden allegedly dictated *Memoirs of W. W. Holden*[7] to his daughter Mary and completed the task immediately prior to a major stroke which completely disabled him. It quotes extensively from letters and editorials and consists principally of a defense of Holden's public career. It is unfortunate that Holden was not able to edit the *Memoirs* himself.

William Woods Holden was born near Hillsborough, North Carolina, on November 24, 1818, to Priscilla Woods and Thomas Holden, who were not married. Little is known of his early childhood, but when he was six or seven years old, his father's wife took him into their home where he was raised with other Holden children. When William was nine or ten years old, he became an "irregular" apprentice in the office of Dennis Heart, Whig editor and publisher of the *Hillsborough Recorder*, where he remained for about six years. After brief periods as a printer in Milton, North Carolina, and in Danville, Virginia, he returned to Hillsborough to work as a clerk in a store. During that time, he wrote several articles for the Raleigh *Star*, and after about a year he applied for and received a job as a typesetter at that paper. Holden had very little formal education, but he claimed he read the "standard authors" widely. In October 1836 he arrived in Raleigh.[8]

Acting largely on his own, Holden read law and was licensed as an attorney on January 2, 1841. He appears to have practiced law in and around Raleigh for nearly two and a half years; but in June 1843, he purchased control of the *North Carolina Standard*, the organ of the Democratic Party in the state, and thereafter devoted his career to newspaper editing and writing and to politics.[9]

Holden had become a member of the Democratic Party State Executive Committee by 1846, and, accordingly, he participated in the selection of James B. Shepard as the party candidate for governor.[10] Holden, himself, became a candidate for public office, and in 1846 he was elected to the House of Commons as a representative from Wake County.[11] Holden's record in the legislature was not outstanding, and in 1848 he announced that he would not seek reelection.[12]

By 1848, however, Holden was deeply involved in the affairs of the Democratic Party in the state. He made the arrangements for a successful convention at which Senator Stephen A. Douglas was the principal speaker, and he actively participated in the unsuccessful campaign of David Settle Reid for governor in that year.[13] Concerned because of the provisions of the Wilmot Proviso, Holden intensified his efforts on behalf of the Democratic Party in 1850. Reid was again chosen as the candidate for governor; although he originally declined, he eventually accepted the nomination and was elected.[14]

Toward the end of 1850, Holden came to realize that the slavery issue threatened the survival of the Union, although he did not acquiesce in the Compromise of 1850.[15] Reid was again nominated for governor in 1852, and in June, Holden attended the national convention of the Democratic Party in Baltimore. He originally endorsed the candidacy of James Buchanan for president, with Stephen A. Douglas as his second choice; but he supported Franklin Pierce following his nomination.[16]

On June 20, 1852, Holden's wife, Ann Augusta Young, died, survived by her husband and four children, the youngest only four months old. This child, Henrietta, was named for Mrs. David S. Reid.[17]

With Reid unable to succeed himself for another term as governor, Holden sought a candidate and settled on John Willis Ellis, then a judge of the superior court, as the best prospect. Throughout 1853, he urged Ellis to allow his name to be offered to the Democratic convention, telling him on October 26: "I write you briefly to apprize you of the fact that, so far as I can hear and judge, *You will be the next Democratic nominee for Governor.*" On December 10, however, in a letter that

Holden published in the *Standard* on December 17, Ellis declined to become a candidate and effectively took himself out of the race.[18]

For the next two years, Holden appears to have devoted himself principally to the affairs of his printing business and to the *Standard*. In September 1854, he announced that he had obtained the services of Frank I. Wilson, former editor of the *Salisbury Banner*, as associate editor in charge of the printing and publishing department.[19] By the end of the following year, however, he found it necessary to appeal to his subscribers to pay their accounts, which were approximately $4,000 in arrears.[20]

Although Holden did not attend the 1856 Democratic Party convention in Cincinnati, he enthusiastically supported the candidacy of James Buchanan for president. He feared the election of John C. Fremont, the Republican candidate, and he had little use for Millard Fillmore, candidate of the Know-Nothing Party.[21]

It was in 1858 that Holden's political career came to a major turning point. Having been a power in the Democratic Party for many years, in 1858 Holden sought election as governor of North Carolina. On February 15, 1858, the Wake County Democratic Convention nominated him for governor. Despite the endorsement of Holden by other county conventions, John Willis Ellis of Rowan County was nominated by the state convention at Charlotte on April 14, 1858. Although disappointed, Holden endorsed the Ellis nomination, which, he promised, "will receive my cordial and active support."[22] Holden congratulated Ellis on his nomination and appears to have labored diligently for his successful election.[23]

It was later in 1858 that Holden suffered another crushing defeat. U. S. senator Asa Biggs had resigned to accept appointment as a federal district judge, and Thomas L. Clingman had been appointed to succeed him, subject to election by the General Assembly in 1858. In addition, the term of David S. Reid as U. S. senator expired in 1858, and two senators would be elected when the legislature reconvened. Although Clingman had worked to ensure his reelection, the process was complicated when Holden entered the race. Former governor Thomas Bragg was also a senatorial candidate, and in the first ballot in the General Assembly he received forty votes to Holden's thirty-six and Reid's eighteen. The Reid supporters then voted for Bragg on the second ballot, and he was elected senator.[24]

Holden denied, however, that he had sought election as a U. S. senator to "punish" those who opposed his nomination as governor at the Charlotte convention. He also denied that he was willing to sacrifice the "harmony and integrity" of the Democratic Party. He concluded: "I earnestly desire the harmony and the continued success and prosperity of the Democratic party. I will sacrifice anything and every thing which a man of honor ought to sacrifice, to promote and preserve harmony. . . ."[25]

With the election of 1860 approaching, Holden resumed the sole editorship of the *Standard*, although Frank Wilson continued as an employee in the business department. Holden noted editorially that the "*Standard* has uniformly reflected my opinions, and I consider that I was responsible for every thing it has contained, or failed to contain. . . ." He also noted that the election of 1860 was "near at hand"

and that he regarded it "as the most important since the government was formed, since its result is most probably to determine whether the government shall continue to exist."[26] Two weeks later, he repeated his belief in the significance of the 1860 election and expressed the belief that the great interests at stake could be preserved only by the ascendancy of the Democratic Party. He claimed he would do his full part in maintaining Democratic principles and in protecting North Carolina from the "aggressions of the black Republicans."[27]

In April, 1860, Holden was a delegate to the Democratic convention in Charleston, South Carolina. He wrote to his wife: "All is yet uncertainty. No one can predict who will be the nominee." He felt the North Carolina delegates would vote for Robert Mercer Taliferro Hunter of Virginia initially, although he favored the candidacy of Joseph Lane of Oregon or John C. Breckinridge of Kentucky.[28] North Carolina delegates did not join the delegations of other states who left the convention in a dispute over the party platform provisions on slavery, but Holden recognized the threat. He later told Thomas Goode Tucker: "From what I saw and heard at Charleston I am convinced that the leaders of the seceders . . . are disunionists *per se*." Although he consistently voted against Stephen A. Douglas at Charleston, he expected to vote for him at the adjourned convention at Baltimore.[29]

Holden attended that convention in July, but he did not bolt it as did other North Carolina delegates. With the Democratic Party split, one wing nominated Stephen A. Douglas for president, and the opposing wing nominated John C. Breckinridge to head its ticket. In July the *Standard* endorsed Breckinridge on the grounds that Douglas was a partisan candidate of the North, while Breckinridge represented the interests of the South.[30]

With the secession of South Carolina and other southern states, the General Assembly called for a vote for a convention in February, 1861, to take North Carolina out of the Union. Holden was a candidate as a delegate in the proposed convention, but he opposed secession and urged the voters of Wake County to preserve the Union and to vote against holding the convention. He and other Unionists were elected, but the proposal for a convention was defeated. In May, however, after President Lincoln called for troops to suppress the southern states, Holden became a candidate for the second proposed convention, and he proclaimed that he would vote for secession from the federal union and would vote to join the Confederate States.[31]

With North Carolina a member of the Confederacy and faced with an election for governor in 1862, on June 4, 1862, Holden proposed the name of Zebulon B. Vance for that position. Holden proclaimed: "We need just such a man in the office at this time." [32] Vance was elected, but by the end of 1862 Holden began to express dissatisfaction with the governing elements of the Confederacy, claiming that only the original secessionists had received appointments and that Unionists were branded as traitors. He urged that conservative men should be placed in office and that conservative principles and counsels should direct the ship of state.[33]

The year 1863 was fateful both for the Confederacy and for North Carolina. The loss at the Battle of Antietam and the issuance of the preliminary Emancipation Proclamation in September, 1862, had effectively ended the possibility of foreign intervention in favor of the South. The disasterous defeats at Vicksburg and Gettysburg in mid-1863 confirmed that fact and proved without doubt the superior power of the Federal army. The loss at Vicksburg and the presence of the Federal navy on the Misssissippi River split the Confederacy, some of the states of which had been lost to the Union army. The U. S. naval blockade of Confederate ports continued to tighten the grip of Union forces. In North Carolina, conscription, the fear of slave insurrection, inflation, shortages, battlefield losses, and the fact that the eastern part of the state was occupied by the Union army contributed to a significant loss of enthusiasm for the war.[34]

In July, 1863, Holden came out editorially in the *Standard* for peace, thus sparking the peace movement in the state. He noted that from the beginning of the war the Federal army had gained territory in the South, which had lost Missouri, Maryland, Kentucky, Tennessee, the Mississippi valley, Texas, Louisiana, Arkansas, and portions of other states. "We are," he claimed, "weaker to-day than when he [General Lee] crossed the Potomac into Maryland." He further claimed that the Confederate army was exhausted but he felt the war would continue, with five million whites unable to conquor twenty million whites. "It is time," he said, "to consult reason and common sense, and to discard prejudice and passion." The time had come, he stated, to seek peace or to risk the consequences of a military defeat.[35] Subsequent letters to the *Standard* from Caldwell and Montgomery counties indicated strong support for his position.[36] Holden thus became identified as the spokesman for the peace movement in North Carolina.

It was for this reason that, on the evening of September 9, 1863, members of the Second and Twenty-Ninth Georgia Regiments then passing through Raleigh mobbed and destroyed the office of the *Standard*. According to Holden, the damage would have been more severe if Governor Vance and Raleigh mayor William H. Harrison had not intervened. Type was poured into the street and several forms of type were pied, but the presses were not damaged. The next morning, some of Holden's friends retaliated by destroying the plant of the Raleigh *State Journal* , which opposed Holden; and Vance, Holden, and others prevented damage to the office of the *Raleigh Register*. Several days later, another attempt to mob the *Standard* office by the Fourth Alabama Regiment was prevented. Holden accused the Davis administration of favoring secessionist partisans in both military and civilian appointments, thus leading to the Union or peace meetings in North Carolina. Holden made it a clear that he stood firmly for peace. "I am told if I talk for peace while our brave soldiers are fighting for it, I am aiding and comforting the enemy. If this be so, when will the time come to talk for it?"[37]

That Holden's stand for peace was the motivation for the attack on the *Standard* was made clear by Lt. Col. Eli M. Seago, Twentieth Georgia Regiment, when he returned a package of paper with the comment: "They believe you to be opposed to our cause, and desire to betray us into the hands of the enemies of our peace, our property, and our independence."[38] Because troops were still passing through Raleigh, Holden found it expedient after the mob attack on the *Standard* to seek refuge outside the city for his personal safety.[39]

Late in 1863 or early in 1864, Holden broke with Vance over the issue of the peace movement. In a letter to his future son-in-law Calvin J. Cowles, a Wilkes County Unionist, he reviewed the reasons for this action. In August, 1863, Vance visited the Confederate administration in Richmond, at which time Holden was convinced he had joined the "Destructives." Vance then wrote a lengthy letter for publication condemning the peace movement which, at Holden's urging, was submitted to former governor William A. Graham, who subsequently recommended that it be toned down. The letter was not published. In February, 1864, Vance delivered a speech in Wilkesboro, at which he strongly opposed the peace movement and threatened coercion by Confederate troops should North Carolina vote to leave the Confederacy.[40] As a result, on March 2, 1864, Holden announced that he was a candidate for governor in the 1864 election. "If elected," he promised, "I will do everything in my power to promote the interests, the honor and the glory of North Carolina, and to secure an honorable peace."[41]

Holden was decisively defeated in the 1864 election, receiving only 14,491 votes or about 20 percent of 72,561 votes cast.[42] He was, however, "neither dismayed nor depressed by the result of the recent election in this State." He made it clear that he had not abandoned his quest for peace, arguing that every means should be used to "obtain an armistice, so as to transfer the great questions in dispute between the two sections from the smoke of the battle-field to the calm, clear atmosphere and diplomacy in the civil councils, where alone, in the end, these questions must be settled."[43]

The great questions to which Holden referred were, in fact, decided on the battlefield; and the Civil War virtually ended on April 17 and 18 with the surrender of General Joseph E. Johnston at the Bennett farmhouse west of Durham Station. Union General William T. Sherman had occupied Raleigh on April 13, and four days later, Holden proclaimed: "Mr. Lincoln has made good his declaration that he would 'hold, occupy, and possess' the forts and other property of the United States, and that he would enforce the laws of the nation." A week later, Holden editorially endorsed the moderate presidential plan of reconstruction, which involved appointment of a provisional governor, a convention to dispose of slavery and to establish a new state government, and election of members of Congress to take their seats in December, 1865.[44]

On May 9, President Andrew Johnson, who had succeeded to the presidency following the assassination of Abraham Lincoln on April 15, summoned Holden to Washington to "confer . . . in reference to North Carolina affairs." Holden delayed his departure in order to address a Union meeting in Raleigh on May 11, but on May 13 he left for Washington after assuring the president that a "large majority of the people are delighted on immediate emancipation and are ready for civil government as soon as it can be conveniently established."[45] Holden was accompanied by several supporters including state senator Robert P. Dick; at the same time, a group consisting of David L. Swain, Bartholomew F. Moore, and William Eaton, Jr., went to Washington to oppose the president's plans, particularly in regard to the appointment of a provisional governor.[46]

Despite this opposition, on May 29, 1865, President Johnson appointed Holden provisional governor of North Carolina with "all the powers necessary and proper to enable the loyal people of the State of North Carolina to restore said state to its constitutional relations to the federal government. . . ."[47]

As provisional governor, on June 12, 1865, Holden issued a proclamation announcing that a convention would be called as soon as practicable to alter or amend the state constitution and to provide for the election of a governor and members of the legislature. Provision would be made for election of members of the U. S. House of Representatives. He also announced that he would appoint justices of the peace, and that he would provide for superior courts of oyer and terminer to dispose of criminal cases. The justices of the peace were authorized to hold courts for the transaction of business that did not require trial by jury and also to appoint sheriffs and clerks. The provisional governor would appoint state directors and state proxies in the corporations in which the state held interest. Holden invited "the loyal people . . . to resume with cheerfulness, and with confidence in the future, their accustomed pursuits. . . ." He also addressed the recently freed slaves: "It now remains for you, aided as you will be by the superior intelligence of the white race, and cheered by the sympathies of all good people, to decide whether the freedom thus suddenly bestowed upon you, will be a blessing to you or a source of injury."[48]

Within a few days, Governor Holden encountered another serious problem. The president's amnesty proclamation of May 29 provided that no person could be appointed to any office unless he could subscribe to an oath in which he swore that he had not participated in or subscribed to thirteen categories of activities that represented support of the Confederacy. The oath requirement prevented Robert P. Dick, who had been appointed a judge of the federal district court and many others from qualifying for appointment. This problem was brought to the attention of President Johnson, but it severely limited Governor Holden's ability to appoint qualified persons.[49] By the middle of July, he had been able to appoint about 3,000 magistrates and mayors and commissioners of towns. County courts had been organized, and he was ready to call a convention. His plan called for the convention to assemble on October 2, with the amended constitution to be submitted to the voters on November 20. Assuming that the constitution would be ratified by the voters, an election for governor and members of the legislature could be held on December 15 or 20 so that regular government could be inaugurated on January 1, 1866.[50]

The election for delegates to the convention was set for September 21, 1865, and justices of the peace were directed to administer the oath prescribed in President Johnson's amnesty proclamation of May 29, 1865. Each oath was to be certified by two justices of the peace.[51]

Although Reconstruction appeared to be progressing smoothly, some problems developed. The New York *Tribune* reported that pardoned rebels in North Carolina were defiant and disloyal and were depending on the new government to authorize repayment of the state debt incurred during the war. President Johnson responded by suggesting that reports that provisional governors were showing preference to former rebels was weakening his reconstruction policies.[52] Holden denied that he had favored former rebels and claimed he had been careful to prefer and to appoint Union men and those who wanted to restore the authority of the federal government.[53]

While attempting to reestablish the judicial system, Governor Holden encountered yet another problem. The existing laws of the state did not permit the testimony of freedmen or free persons of color in cases in which white persons were concerned, and the military authorities would not permit former slaves to be tried in courts in which their testimony could not be heard. All such cases were required to be tried in military courts, and Holden was concerned that freedmen would be at a disadvantage in the counties that were not within the direct authority of the military. In a compromise worked out with Maj. Gen. Thomas H. Ruger, commanding the Department of North Carolina, judges were permitted to arrest all persons who violated the law and either to require bail or to lodge offenders in the county jail, subject to the orders of the military commander of the district in the cases of freedmen.[54]

The convention called by Governor Holden in his proclamation of August 8 met in Raleigh in October, and by overwhelming vote abrogated the secession ordinance, declaring it null and void, and reaffirming the ratification of the United States Constitution in 1789 and the adoption of amendments to it. The convention also abolished slavery and involuntary servitude other than that resulting from conviction of crime. But, Holden informed President Johnson, the convention in all probability would "ignore" the rebel state debt. The convention also provided for the election of governor, members of the General Assembly, and members of Congress on November 9, 1865, with the legislature to meet on November 19.[55]

The convention did not so readily reach a decision in regard to the debt incurred by North Carolina as a member of the Confederacy. Holden apparently thought that action on the debt would be taken promptly without devisive debate, but concern over the financial solvency of the state and the condition of the common schools' Literary Fund, which had been invested in war-time state securities, led some members to oppose repudiation. Holden immediately appealed to President Johnson, noting that if the debate continued, the work of reconstruction would be seriously affected. Johnson replied immediately that "Every dollar of the debt created to aid the Rebellion against the United States should be repudiated finally and immediately." Holden referred the president's message to the convention, which promptly repudiated the debt and committed future legislatures not to pay any of it.[56]

Even before the convention adjourned, political maneuvering in anticipation of the campaign for governor began. On October 14, fifty-one members of the convention petitioned Holden to permit his name to be offered to the voters as a candidate for governor in the ensuing election. In accepting the nomination, Holden pledged if elected to "promote the prosperity and the happiness of North Carolina, and to secure her return at the earliest possible moment to her place in the federal Union."[57] Four days later state treasurer Jonathan Worth told Holden that he had decided to allow his friends to offer his name as a candidate for governor in the forthcoming election. Worth did not intend to campaign for the position, and he hoped that the "friendly, personal and official relations" between him and Holden would not be damaged.[58]

Although Holden felt "morally" certain of his election, he asked President Johnson for a public statement of his support. Holden felt that the rebel debt interest in the state was opposed to him, and that a powerful effort was being made to rally the old Whig Party against him. He told the president that if he were to be defeated, opposition to the Johnson administration would be immediate. Johnson, however, declined to intercede.[59] In the November election, Holden was decisively defeated, receiving only 44 percent of the 58,348 votes cast. He carried thirty-four counties located principally in the western and the northeastern parts of the state. [60] In a telegram that was written by R. J. Powell, the North Carolina representative in Washington, Johnson expressed regret at Holden's defeat, cautioning that the election results damaged the prospect of the state's restoration and warning that the legislature should repair rather than increase the difficulties under which the state had already placed itself.[61]

The legislature responded to the implied threat in the Johnson telegram by ratifying the Thirteenth Amendment to the Constitution. That amendment abolished slavery.[62] And on December 23, 1865, Secretary of State William H. Seward, by direction of the president, relieved Holden of his post as provisional governor of North Carolina and directed him to turn over the papers and property of the state in his possession to the governor-elect.[63]

In January 1866 the disappointed Holden resumed active control of the *Standard* and watched from Raleigh the struggle between President Johnson and the Radical Republicans over reconstruction of the southern states. In July, Holden went to Washington, where he met with the president and others. He asked President Johnson to write a letter in response to one from him in which the president would reaffirm support for Holden's service as provisional governor and enable the "Conservatives" to regain control of the state government.[64] President Johnson did not do so, and from that point onward Holden abandoned the president and turned toward the Republicans supporting Radical Reconstruction.

On September 20, 1866, a Union convention met in Raleigh at which Holden delivered the principal address in which he charged that the "spirit of sincere loyalty" demanded by the president had been ignored by the electorate. He claimed that the president's reconstruction plan had been "marred and destroyed by malcontents and traitors at this end of the line." The president's plan having failed through the treachery and selfishness of politicians, the only alternative was the congressional plan based on ratification of the so-called Howard Amendment, which became the Fourteenth Amendment to the U. S. Constitution. Holden claimed that President Johnson supported the amendment, and he further claimed that the only way to restore the Union was by acceptance of the amendment.[65]

The convention formed the Union Party and nominated Alfred Dockery for governor. It endorsed a platform calling for ratification of the Howard Amendment. Not only was Dockery defeated by Governor Worth, but a strong Conservative majority was elected to the legislature, which, when it met, rejected the Fourteenth Amendment.[66]

Holden, meanwhile, had visited Washington, where the *Sentinel* charged that he had advised Radical Republican Thaddeus Stevens on a bill to reorganize the southern states on the basis of white and Negro suffrage. Holden admitted he and others had met not only with Stevens but with Radical Charles Sumner and others and that he was convinced that if the South did not accept the Howard Amendment the reconstruction that would follow would include Negro suffrage, confiscation of property, and "many other evils."[67] Toward the end of the year, Holden, with North Carolina Unionists John Pool, Ceburn L. Harris, James F. Taylor, and David A. Jenkins visited Washington where they met with Stevens, who asked them to draft a bill "to establish civil government in North Carolina, and to enable it to resume its former relations" to the Union. The bill called for election of a convention to write a new state constitution that would be acceptable to Congress. Whites previously eligible to vote could take part in the election, as could blacks who were literate and owned $100 worth of real property. To qualify for the convention, a delegate had to swear that as of March 4, 1864, he had opposed the rebellion and had desired the success of the Union. March 4, 1864, was the day after Holden's candidacy for governor in the campaign against Vance was made public, and the oath based on that date would ensure that Holden supporters would control the convention. Although the bill was introduced, it was lost in the movement toward the more severe reconstruction acts passed early in 1867.[68]

Having embraced Congressional Reconstruction and having parted from the Conservatives, Holden turned his attention to the establishment of the Republican Party in the state. That took place at a convention held in Raleigh on March 27, 1867, at which time Holden was chosen as chairman of the party executive committee. At about the same time, severe reconstruction acts were passed by Congress over President Johnson's veto. Under that legislation, the southern states were divided into military districts and each state was required to hold a convention, with membership elected by universal male suffrage, which would write a new constitution guaranteeing the rights of blacks to vote and to hold office. Ratification of the Howard Amendment was also a prerequisite for readmission to the Union. Maj. Gen. Edward R. S. Canby, commanding the district of North and South Carolina, ordered an election on November 19 and 20 to approve a convention and to choose delegates. Not only was the convention approved by the voters, but the Republicans elected

107 of the 120 delegates. The constitution written by the convention which met January 14, 1868, was approved by a large majority in a vote April 21-23, and at the same time new officials for the state government were chosen. Coincidentally, the imposition of Congressional Reconstruction and the establishment of the Republican Party saw the formation not only of the Union League but also of the Ku Klux Klan in North Carolina.[69]

Holden had been nominated for governor as a candidate of the Republican Party when it met in convention in February, 1868, and he was elected with a majority of fifty-five percent of the votes cast over the Conservative candidate.[70] North Carolina, however, was still controlled by the commander of the military district of North and South Carolina created by the Congressional Reconstruction Acts of March, 1867, although it had met all of the requirements of that legislation but one; Holden, therefore, was "appointed" governor by General E. R. S. Canby who also removed Gov. Jonathan Worth, and Holden took the oath of office on July 1, 1868.[71] On July 2 the General Assembly, which had been called into session a day earlier, ratified the Fourteenth Amendment and North Carolina was eligible for readmission to the Federal Union.[72]

In his inaugural address delivered July 4, 1868, Governor Holden reviewed the features of the new state constitution that had been adopted the previous April. He made it clear, however, that that constitution "must be administered by its friends and supporters." He promised that there would be no social recrimination and he reaffirmed his commitment to education, although he advocated the separation of schools for whites and blacks. He urged the immediate organization of the militia in order to ensure that the laws were faithfully executed and that peace among the people was preserved. He also strongly advocated the payment of the interest on the state debt in order to enable North Carolina to borrow money for internal improvements. He promised to keep constantly in view the welfare of North Carolina and concluded by asking that "the future of our beloved state [may] be as bright and as glorious as the last seven years have been disasterous and unhappy."[73]

On July 13 Holden announced that he had sold the *Standard* to Messrs. N. Paige and Company, acknowledging that he was parting with "an old and valued friend." The purchasers were actually a group of Republicans headed by Milton S. Littlefield, whose name appeared later in 1869 in the masthead of the paper as publisher. The paper sold for $15,000.[74]

Although ratification of the Fourteenth Amendment permitted North Carolina to reenter the Federal Union, it also presented Governor Holden with a major problem. Section three of the amendment effectively barred any person who had formerly taken an oath to support the Constitution of the United States but had engaged in "insurrection or rebellion" from holding federal, state, or local office until pardoned by Congress. Holden took the position that until elections could be held under the recently adopted state constitution, all local offices were vacant and that it was his responsibility to appoint persons to fill them.[75] Not only did he find it difficult to find candidates for some offices, but several of his appointments to local office faced resistance from the persons they displaced, and some of the newly appointed sheriffs required military support from the federal army in order to take office.[76]

In a special message to the General Assembly on July 17, Governor Holden repeated his request for the immediate organization of the state militia in order to ensure the prompt execution of the laws. He asserted that it was the intention of the opponents of the government to overthrow it on the grounds that it was not constitutional, and he found it essential that he have the power to sustain the authority of the state against all assaults and to maintain the peace. The existence of a militia would enable him to install officers where their appointment had been resisted and to support them in the performance of their duties.[77] The General Assembly responded on August 17 by creating the militia of North Carolina, consisting off three divisions, for the purpose of preserving the peace and enforcing the laws. The detailed militia was limited to 6,000 men and was to be used only for the purpose of executing the laws and suppressing opposition to their enforcement.[78]

Within a few weeks of his inauguration, Governor Holden began to receive complaints from around the state about the activities of white supremicist, night-riding, terrorist organizations identified collectively as the Ku Klux Klan. Patterned to some degree on the Klan initially organized in Tennessee, it consisted of persons committed to the principle of white supremacy and to an effort to reinstate the old order and to return to the conditions of life prior to the Civil War. It opposed the African American vote, which was finally written into the United States Constitution with the Fifteenth Amendment, and the Republican Party, which it considered to be planning to guarantee political and legal equality to blacks and which was responsible for Radical Reconstruction. Because Governor Holden was a Republican, the Klan strongly opposed his administration. The Klan first appeared in the spring and summer of 1868 in Wilmington, where there had been racial unrest during Holden's term as provisional governor.[79] By the middle of August 1868 there were reports of Klan activities in Halifax and Warren Counties, and in Gates as well as Sampson.[80] Two months later there were similar complaints from Granville, Brunswick, and Wayne Counties.[81] Of greater significance, in view of later developments, were racial riots in Yanceyville and Milton, Caswell County, that were inspired by masked and hooded members of the Ku Klux Klan.[82] By the end of the year, Governor Holden had reason to believe that the Klan was rampant in that county.[83] The initial problems would be magnified within the next two years.

At the end of the Civil War and immediately thereafter, railroads in North Carolina were in serious disrepair, and the state began to issue bonds to repair and overhaul them. But by 1868, concern for internal improvements led the convention that met in January to launch a program to assist financially new and extended railroads. The convention authorized the incorporation of six railroads and granted more than $2 million to finance the completion of five of them. Most of the money went to the Wilmington, Charlotte, and Rutherfordton

Rail Road, the Chatham Rail Road, and the Western North Carolina Rail Road[84] When the General Assembly met in July, it granted $2 million to the Chatham Rail Road Company, $300,000 to the Williamston and Tarboro Railroad Company, loaned the Northwestern Rail Road Company $10,000 per mile for each section of five miles surveyed and located, and separated the Western North Carolina Rail Road that ran west from Salisbury into eastern and western divisions.[85]

By the end of the year, Governor Holden reported to the General Assembly that the state debt incurred principally for internal improvements amounted to $19,209,945 with an additional $4.5 million in bonds committed but not yet issued. The interest due on that debt amounted to $1,032,596, and the state did not have sufficient funds in the public treasury to pay it. In fact, persons who held state bonds began to question the ability of the state to meet its obligations.[86]

In addition, the bonds issued on behalf of the Chatham Rail Road Company had been challenged, and in 1871 the Supreme Court ruled that the legislation that authorized them was void.[87]

As Holden approached the end of the first six months as elected governor of the state, he received an increasing number of complaints about threats of violence that were made against blacks, the Union League, Republicans, and northerners who had come to North Carolina to help freedmen as they adjusted to emancipation. The threats were not localized, but came from Halifax County, Chapel Hill and Orange County, Bertie County, Chatham County, Northampton County, Fayetteville, Carteret County, and Wayne County. They were sufficiently widespread that Holden on at least one occasion called on the federal army to send a detachment to maintain peace.[88]

Equally disturbing were consistent reports that weapons were being brought into the state and were being secreted by the Conservatives. There were reports from New Hanover County and also from New Bern that guns had been received and hidden.[89] Holden, concerned about the reported accumulation of firearms, brought the matter to the attention of Maj. Gen. Nelson A. Miles, commander of the North and South Carolina Military District. The governor reported that arms had also been received in Charlotte, and he asked General Miles to use federal troops to maintain peace and to support the state government if it were challenged. General Miles had also received reports of arms coming into the state, and he agreed that the federal military would be used to maintain the laws, if needed.[90] Governor Holden found it necessary, however, to issue a proclamation on October 12 warning against the use of violence against the existing government and promising that it would be maintained. He considered resistance to the laws to be treason, and he promised that any effort to prevent the voters from going to the polls would be forestalled by the federal military.[91]

In the presidential election of 1868, Governor Holden enthusiastically supported Gen. U. S. Grant; and, following Grant's election, compared him to George Washington and Abraham Lincoln.[92] Holden, however, was never as close to Grant as he had been, early in the administration, to Andrew Johnson. Holden apparently had some aspirations for a position in the administration, and in December John Pool, then a United States senator from North Carolina, asked him about his desire for a cabinet position.[93] Whatever Holden's ambitions may have been at that time, his response to Pool's inquiry is not known, and Grant never offered him a cabinet position.

As 1868 came to an end, Governor Holden faced many difficult problems. As significant as they may have appeared at the time, they were insignificant when compared to those he would face in the next two years. The finances of the state, railroad scandals, and excesses of the Ku Klux Klan would bulk large in the affairs of the Holden administration during 1869 and 1870.

[1] J. G. de Roulhac Hamilton, *Reconstruction in North Carolina* (New York: Columbia University Press, 1914), 413.

[2] Thomas Dixon, Jr., *The Leopard's Spots: A Romance of the White Man's Burden, 1864-1900* (New York: Doubleday, Page & Co., 1902), 36.

[3] J. G. de Roulhac Hamilton, Max R. Williams, and Mary Reynolds Peacock, eds., *The Papers of William Alexander Graham*, 8 vols. (Raleigh: Division of Archives and History, 1957-1992), 8: 184.

[4] Edgar E. Folk and Bynum Shaw, *W. W. Holden: A Political Biography* (Winston-Salem: John F. Blair, 1982).

[5] Horace W. Raper, *William W. Holden: North Carolina's Political Enigma* (Chapel Hill and London: University of North Carolina Press, 1985).

[6] William C. Harris, *William Woods Holden: Firebrand of North Carolina Politics* (Baton Rouge and London: Louisiana State University Press, 1987).

[7] *Memoirs of W. W. Holden* (Durham: Seeman Printery, 1911). Because of the condition of Holden's health, the extent of his participation in the "dictation" of the *Memoirs* may properly be questioned. William K. Boyd, who edited the *Memoirs* for publication, stated in his introduction that they were written between November, 1889, and March, 1890. Dr. Eugene Grisson, former superintendent of the insane asylum at Raleigh and a longtime friend of Holden's, in a deposition dated February 24, 1894, stated that Holden had a stroke in 1887 that caused general paralysis and a cerebral hemorrhage in January, 1889, that destroyed his mental powers. Deposition of Dr. Eugene Grissom, February 24, 1894, in Estate of W. W. Holden, Wake County Estate Records, North Carolina State Archives.

[8] Harris, *William Woods Holden*, 8-10.

[9] *North Carolina Standard* (Raleigh), May 31, 1843.

[10] Lindley S. Butler, ed., *The Papers of David Settle Reid*, 2 vols. (Raleigh: Division of Archives and History, 1993-1997) 1:163.

[11] W. W. Holden to James M. Bullock, June 10, 1846, Edward Vernon Howell Papers, Southern Historical Collection, Wilson Library, University of North Carolina at Chapel Hill; John L. Cheney, Jr., *North Carolina Government, 1585-1979: A Narrative and Statistical History* (Raleigh: North Carolina Department of the Secretary of State, 1981), 316.

[12] *Standard*, January 19, 1848.

[13] Butler, *The Papers of David Settle Reid* , 1: 225-226, 229.

[14] Butler, *The Papers of David Settle Reid*, 1: 237-240, 264.

[15] W. W. Holden to A. W. Venable, December 24, 1851, Abraham Watkins Venable Papers, Southern Historical Collection, Wilson Library, University of North Carolina at Chapel Hill.

[16] Noble J. Tolbert, *The Papers of John Willis Ellis*, 2 vols. (Raleigh: State Department of Archives and History, 1964), 1: 114-116.

[17] Butler, *The Papers of David Settle Reid*, 1: 399-400.

[18] Tolbert, *The Papers of John Willis Ellis*, 1: 127-129.

[19] *Standard*, September 9, 1854.

[20] *Standard*, October 27, 1855.

[21] *Standard*, September 12, 1856.

[22] *Standard*, February 17, 1858, April 21, 1858.

[23] Tolbert, *The Papers of John Willis Ellis*, 1: 187-188.

[24] Butler, *The Papers of David Settle Reid*, 1: xlvii-xlviii.

[25] *Standard*, October 20, 1858.

[26] *Standard*, November 2, 1859.

[27] *Standard*, November 16, 1859.

[28] W. W. Holden to "My dearest Wife," April 22, 1860, William Woods Holden Papers, Special Collections Library, Duke University, Durham. Holden married Louisa Virginia Harrison, his second wife, on March 7, 1854. Wake County Record of Marriages, 1851-1857, 1862-1866, North Carolina State Archives.

[29] W. W. Holden to Th. Goode Tucker, May 19, 1860, Stephen A. Douglas Papers, Department of Special Collections, University of Chicago Library, Chicago.

[30] *Standard*, July 18, 1860.

[31] *Standard*, February 27, 1861, March 2, 1861, May 8, 1861.

[32] *Standard*, June 4, 1862.

[33] *Standard*, November 21, 1862.

[34] E. Merton Coulter, *The Confederate States of America, 1861-1865* (Baton Rouge: Louisiana State University Press, 1950), 355-358.

[35] *Standard*, July 17, 1863.

[36] *Standard*, August 18, 21, 1863.

[37] *Standard*, October 2, 1863.

[38] *Standard*, October 23, 1863.

[39] W. W. Holden to Edward J. Hale, September 14, 1863, Edward Jones Hale Papers, Private Collections, North Carolina State Archives.

[40] W. W. Holden to C. J. Cowles, March 18, 1864, William Woods Holden Papers, Private Collections, North Carolina State Archives. The Vance letter referred to is printed in Frontis W. Johnston and Joe A. Mobley, eds., *The Papers of Zebulon Baird Vance*, 2 vols. to date (Raleigh: Division of Archives and History, 1963-), 2: 241-247. Governor Vance's Wilkesboro speech was published in the *Standard*, April 20, 1864.

[41] *Standard*, March 3, 1864.

[42] Cheney, *North Carolina Government, 1585-1976*, 1401.

[43] *Standard*, August 12, 1864.

[44] *Standard*, April 17, 24, 1865.

[45] Andrew Johnson to W. W. Holden, May 9, 1865, Andrew Johnson Papers, Library of Congress, Washington, D. C. (microfilm copy in D. H. Hill Library, North Carolina State University, Raleigh); W. W. Holden to President Johnson, May 13, 1865, Andrew Johnson Papers.

[46] J. M. Schofield to President Johnson, May 13, 1865, Andrew Johnson Papers.

[47] *United States Statutes at Large*, 13:1866, 760-761.

[48] Proclamation by William W. Holden, Provisional Governor, June 12, 1865, William Woods Holden Papers, Private Collections, North Carolina State Archives.

[49] W. W. Holden to the President, June 29, 1865, Andrew Johnson Papers.

[50] W. W. Holden to the President, July 24, 1865, Andrew Johnson Papers.

[51] Proclamation by William W. Holden, Provisional Governor, August 8, 1865, William Woods Holden Papers, Southern Historical Collection, Wilson Library, University of North Carolina at Chapel Hill.

[52] New York *Tribune*, quoted in Raleigh *Daily Sentinel*, August 10, 1865; Andrew Johnson to Wm. W. Holden, August 22, 1865, Andrew Johnson Papers.

[53] W. W. Holden to the President, August 26, 1865, Andrew Johnson Papers.

[54] *Standard*, September 20, 1865.

[55] W. W. Holden to the President, October 6, 7, 1865, Andrew Johnson Papers.

[56] Harris, *William Woods Holden*, 188-190.

[57] *Standard*, October 18, 1865.

[58] Jonathan Worth to Govr Holden, October 18, 1865, Jonathan Worth Papers, Private Collections, North Carolina State Archives.

[59] W. W. Holden to the President, November 4, 1865, Andrew Johnson to W. W. Holden, November 5, 1865, Andrew Johnson Papers.

[60] Cheney, *North Carolina Government, 1585-1976*, 1402-1403.

[61] Andrew Johnson to W. W. Holden, November 27, 1865, Andrew Johnson Papers.

[62] W. W. Holden to the President, December 1, 1865, Andrew Johnson Papers.

[63] William H. Seward to W. W. Holden, December 23, 1865, Provisional Governors Papers, North Carolina State Archives.

[64] W. W. Holden to the President, July 11, 1866, Andrew Johnson Papers.

[65] *Standard*, September 26, 1866.

[66] Harris, *William Woods Holden*, 207-210.

[67] *Standard*, October 10, 1866.

[68] W. W. Holden to "My dear Wife," December 9, 1866, William Woods Holden Papers, Private Collections, North Carolina State Archives; Harris, *William Woods Holden*, 210-212.

[69] William S. Powell, *North Carolina through Four Centuries* (Chapel Hill and London: University of North Carolina Press, 1989), 388-395.

[70] Cheney, *North Carolina Government, 1585-1979*, 1403.

[71] Harris, *William Woods Holden*, 242-244; E. Merton Coulter, *The South during Reconstruction, 1865-1877* (Baton Rouge: Louisiana State University Press, 1947), 119-120.

[72] Cheney, *North Carolina Government, 1585-1979*, 783-784.

[73] Inaugural Address of Governor W. W. Holden, July 4, 1868, Governors Letter Books, North Carolina State Archives.

[74] *Standard*, July 13, 1868; deposition of Ida H. Cowles, February 20, 1904, in "F. L. Mahler & Wife, et als, *v.* W. R. Henry & Wife, et als," in Estate of W. W. Holden, Wake County Estate Records, North Carolina State Archives.

[75] W. W. Holden to Maj. Gen. E. R. S. Canby, July 16, 1868, Governors Papers, North Carolina State Archives.

[76] See, for example, William D. Haywood to William H. Harrison, July 14, 1868, Governors Papers, North Carolina State Archives, in regard to the mayor and commissioners

of Raleigh; see also W. W. Holden to Maj. Gen. E. R. S. Canby, July 15, 1868, Governors Papers, North Carolina State Archives, in regard to the sheriff of New Hanover County.

[77] W. W. Holden to the General Assembly, July 17, 1868, Governors Papers, North Carolina State Archives.

[78] *Public Laws of North Carolina, July, 1868*, ch. 22.

[79] Allen W. Trelease, *White Terror: The Ku Klux Klan Conspiracy and Southern Recosnstruction* (New York: Harper & Row, 1971) , 68-70.

[80] See Henry W. Paschall to W. W. Holden, August 18, 1868, John W. Hofler to W. W. Holden, August 22, 1868, Affidavit of Duncan Holmes, August 25, 1868, all in Governors Papers, North Carolina State Archives.

[81] See Silas L. Curtis to W. W. Holden, Ooctober 11, 1868, E. M. Rosafy to W. W. Holden, October 15, 1868, and John Robinson to W. W. Holden, October 30, 1868, all in Governors Papers, North Carolina State Archives.

[82] See W. J. Dawes to Jacob F. Chur, August 22, 1868, and September 8, 1868, both in Governors Papers, North Carolina State Archives.

[83] G. T. F. Gannaway to W. W. Holden, December 28, 1868, Governors Papers, North Carolina State Archives.

[84] *The Constitution of the State of North-Carolina Together with the Ordinances and Resolutions of the Constitutional Convention Assembled in the City of Raleigh, Jan. 14th, 1868* (Raleigh: Joseph W. Holden, Convention Printer, 1868), ch. 3, 17, 19, 20, 30, and 49.

[85] *Private Laws of North Carolina, July, 1868*, ch. 14, 15, 24, and 26.

[86] W. W. Holden to the General Assembly, November 17, 1868, and W. W. Holden to the General Assembly, December 11, 1868, Governors Letter Books, North Carolina State Archives; John A. Griswold to W. W. Holden, August 11, 1868, and Lewis Johnson to Holden, September 7, 1868, Governors Papers, North Carolina State Archives.

[87] *A. J. Galloway v. D. A. Jenkins, Treasurer, and The Chatham Rail Road Company, North Carolina Reports* 63 (1871): 147.

[88] Nelson A. Miles to W. W. Holden, Ocotober 27, 1868, Governors Papers, North Carolina State Archives.

[89] Affidavit of Henry Baker, September 24, 1868, and Jno. V. Sherard to W. W. Holden, October 7, 1868, Governors Papers, North Carolina State Archives.

[90] W. W. Holden to Nelson A. Miles, October 7, 1868, and Miles to Holden, October 9, 1868, both in *Standard*, October 9, 1868.

[91] Proclamation of W. W. Holden Governor of N. C., October 12, 1868, Governors Letter Books, North Carolina State Archives.

[92] *Standard*, November 9, 1868.

[93] John Pool to W. W. Holden, December 13, 1868, Governors Papers, North Carolina State Archives.

EDITORIAL METHOD

The documents currently known to exist in the public and private papers of William Woods Holden number in the thousands. The principal repository for these materials is the State Archives, Division of Archives and History, Raleigh. That facility houses five major collections pertaining to Holden: the Governors Papers as provisional governor, the Governors Letter Book as provisional governor, the Governors Papers as elected governor, the Governors Letter Book as elected governor, and a small collection of his personal and business papers. In addition, the Special Collections Library, Duke University, Durham, has a collection of letters from Holden, principally to members of his family. The manner in which other major repositories of private papers processed those materials made it possible to find many letters that were written by Holden to various correspondents, although unfortunately, he seemed rarely to keep the letters to which he was responding. Because of the large number of documents not included in this volume, it was not feasible to calendar them.

The most difficult task in editing a collection of papers of a significant historical figure is the problem of selecting the documents to include. Any selective process is of necessity subjective, but Holden's role in the antebellum political history of North Carolina and in the difficult Reconstruction period has dictated some standards that the editors have followed. Papers were selected relating to Holden's actions in building the Democratic Party before the Civil War; his role in the peace movement; his service as provisional governor in 1865 during Presidential Reconstruction; his actions as elected governor, particularly in relation to the construction of railroads and to efforts to control the Ku Klux Klan. In addition, materials relating to Holden's role as a family man have been included, as have a few documents of general interest or of some significance, such as a letter concerning the North Carolina swamp lands and a request for the return of the Great Seal of the state.

The editors have made transcriptions principally from manuscript sources. Important letters were frequently printed in the *Standard* for which the originals were not retained, and some of these printed documents have been included. Holden for a period of twenty-five years was editor of the *Standard*, and some of his editorials, particularly during the Civil War, have also been included. The *Standard* was published at various times as a weekly, semi-weekly, tri-weekly, or daily newspaper, although the differing intervals rarely overlapped. When material from the *Standard* or another newspaper is included, the date of the issue in which the document appeared is shown immediately under the name of the paper.

Some documents have previously been printed in volumes relating to other significant historical figures, particularly the *Papers of John Willis Ellis*, published by the Department of Archives and History in 1964, and the *Papers of David Settle Reid*, published by the Division of Archives and History in 1993 and 1997. Holden's addresses to the General Assembly, which have been printed in *Legislative Documents* published by the State of North Carolina, are not contained herein.

It should be noted that the Governors Papers occasionally include drafts in his own handwriting of letters that Governor Holden subsequently sent. If a document from Holden is indicated as being located in the Governors Papers (A&H:GP), it probably was a draft but is not so indicated.

The Holden papers have been transcribed and reproduced as exactly as feasible, although a few editorial adjustments appear throughout the volume in order to assist the reader. Margins, indentation, and placement of elements have been standardized. Governor Holden rarely misspelled either a word or a name, but if he did it was silently corrected or a misspelled name was corrected in a footnote. Some of the people who wrote him were illiterate, and in such cases the spelling has not been corrected. Punctuation obviously intended to end a sentence has been replaced by a period, although most long dashes have been retained. [*Sic*] has been used sparingly only to indicate words that were repeated in error ("the the" for example). Superscript letters have been brought down to the line. [*Illegible*] indicates the few words that could not be deciphered and such terms as [*torn*] appear where appropriate. All notes follow immediately after the document to which they refer.

William W. Holden frequently made endorsements on the back of letters indicating the response he wanted to make. This was especially true during his service as provisional governor and elected governor. Because many of these indicate the nature of the response to be made, these have been placed, with the designation [*Endorsed*], immediately at the end of the document to which the endorsement relates. Enclosures have been indicated with the heading [*Enclosure*] and have been placed immediately after the correspondence they accompanied.

In his correspondence, Holden frequently referred to individuals only by surname, or by surname and title such as Col. or Mr. In such instances, the person is further identified by a footnote. If a person was referred to by initials or by given and surname and had previously been identified, he was not further identified. Only rarely was it impossible to identify a person referred to in the correspondence.

The editors originally intended to issue the papers of William Woods Holden in a single volume, but as the work of preparing them for publication moved into the documents dated in the middle of 1869, it became clear that the original plan was not feasible because of the large number of items selected. For this reason, the decision was reached to publish two volumes, each of which would be self-standing with an introduction and index, and it was agreed that the first volume would end with 1868. The second volume to be issued later will begin with January 1869 and will conclude in 1887 before the stroke and the later cerebral hemorrhage which completely disabled Governor Holden.

LIST OF PAPERS PRINTED IN THIS VOLUME

1. WWH to Thomas Ruffin, February 3, 1841
2. WWH to William A. Jeffreys, April 14, 1843
3. *Standard* Editorial, May 31, 1843
4. WWH to William A. Jeffreys, March 9, 1844
5. Romulus M. Saunders to Editor of the *Standard,* May 6, 1844
6. Joseph D. Ward for the *Standard,* May 22, 1844
7. John W. Cunningham to the Editor of the *Standard,* June 19, 1844
8. Louis D. Henry for the *Standard,* July 14, 1844
9. WWH to David S. Reid, October 30, 1844
10. WWH to David S. Reid, May 24, 1845
11. John H. Wheeler to WWH, December 10, 1845
12. Greene W. Caldwell to Democratic State Committee, January 20, 1846
13. Democratic State Committee to James B. Shepard, March 17, 1846
14. James B. Shepard to Democratic State Committee, March 17, 1846
15. WWH to David S. Reid, March 20, 1846
16. WWH to James M. Bullock, June 10, 1846
17. WWH to David S. Reid, December 8, 1847
18. WWH to Weldon N. Edwards, March 12, 1848
19. WWH to Abraham W. Venable, March 12, 1848
20. WWH to David S. Reid, April 19, 1848
21. WWH to David S. Reid, June 23, 1848
22. WWH to David S. Reid, August 6, 1848
23. WWH to Henry T. Clark, June 21, 1849
24. WWH to David L. Swain, August 1, 1849
25. WWH to David S. Reid, June 1, 1850
26. David S. Reid to WWH, June 24, 1850
27. WWH to David S. Reid, July 7, 1850
28. WWH to David S. Reid, July 10, 1850
29. WWH to Weldon N. Edwards, July 15, 1850
30. Thomas Ruffin, Jr., and Others to WWH, July 16, 1850
31. WWH to David S. Reid, July 19, 1850
32. WWH to David S. Reid, July 24, 1850
33. WWH to David S. Reid, August 7, 1850
34. WWH to David S. Reid, December 1, 1850
35. WWH to David S. Reid, January 7, 1851

36. WWH to Abraham W. Venable, April 16, 1851
37. WWH to Abraham W. Venable, December 2, 1851
38. WWH to Abraham W. Venable, December 29, 1851.
39. WWH to Calvin H. Wiley. December 29, 1851
40. WWH to John W. Ellis, January 8, 1852
41. WWH to Abraham W. Venable, January 13, 1852
42. WWH to John W. Ellis, January 26, 1852
43. WWH to Abraham W. Venable, February 7, 1852
44. WWH to Abraham W. Venable, March 10, 1852
45. WWH to Abraham W. Venable, March 26, 1852
46. WWH to Abraham W. Venable, May 16, 1852
47. WWH to John W. Ellis, June 16, 1852
48. WWH to Abraham W. Venable, July 8, 1852
49. WWH to Thomas Settle, Sr., July 13, 1852
50. WWH to David S. Reid, August 10, 1852
51. WWH to Abraham W. Venable, August 11, 1852
52. Hezekiah G. Spruill to WWH, October 29, 1852
53. WWH to Thomas Settle, Jr., June 18, 1853
54. WWH to John W. Ellis, October 26, 1853
55. WWH to John W. Ellis, September 27, 1853
56. WWH to John W. Ellis, December 10, 1853
57. John W. Ellis to WWH, December 10, 1853
58. Thomas L. Clingman to WWH, June 30, 1854
59. WWH to Subscribers and Friends, September 9, 1854
60. WWH to William D. Cooke, May 19, 1855
61. W. Greene Duke to the Editors of the *Standard*, June 4, 1855
62. Lawrence O'Bryan Branch to WWH and Frank I. Wilson, June 18, 1855
63. "An Appeal to my Subscribers," October 27, 1855
64. WWH to Weldon N. Edwards, February 2, 1856
65. WWH to Thomas Settle, Jr., February 13, 1856
66. David S. Reid to WWH and Frank I. Wilson, July 18, 1856
67. WWH to Calvin H. Wiley, August 19, 1856
68. WWH to John W. Ellis, January 19, 1857
69. WWH to David L. Swain, January 24, 1857
70. WWH to Calvin H. Wiley, July 3, 1857
71. WWH to Laura Holden, April 4, 1858
72. WWH to John W. Ellis, April 19, 1858
73. WWH to Democratic Party of the State, April 16, 1858
74. WWH to John W. Ellis, May 4, 1858
75. WWH to John W. Ellis, May 5, 1858
76. WWH to John W. Ellis, May 18, 1858
77. WWH to John W. Ellis, June 1, 1858
78. WWH to Laura Holden, August 6, 1858
79. WWH to John W. Ellis, August 6, 1858

80. WWH to the Democratic Party of North Carolina, October 18, 1858
81. Editorial in the *Standard*, January 22, 1859
82. WWH to the Readers of the *Standard*, November 2, 1859
83. Editorial in the *Standard*, November 10, 1859
84. DeWitt Clinton Jones to WWH, March 3, 1860
85. WWH to Louisa Holden, April 22, 1860
86. WWH to Louisa Holden, April 24, 1860
87. Letter from the Editor, April 28, 1860
88. WWH to Calvin H. Wiley, May 9, 1860
89. WWH to the Public, May 17, 1860
90. WWH to Thomas Goode Tucker, May 19, 1860
91. WWH to Stephen A. Douglas, June 1, 1860
92. Editorial "The Presidency," July 18, 1860
93. William L. Saunders to WWH, July 18, 1860
94. WWH to William L. Saunders, July 19, 1860
95. Thomas L. Clingman to WWH, July 22, 1860
96. WWH to Louisa Holden, August 30, 1860
97. WWH to Louisa Holden, September 1, 1860
98. WWH to Daniel M. Barringer, September 2, 1860
99. Marcus Erwin to WWH, January 11, 1861
100. Editorial "Union Men to the Polls," February 27, 1861
101. Editorial "The Result in this State," March 2, 1861
102. WWH to the Voters of Wake County, May 2, 1861
103. WWH to the Voters of Wake County, May 6, 1861
104. WWH to Louisa Holden, July 8, 1861
105. WWH to Mrs. L. H. Holden, September 22, 1861
106. WWH to the Public, December 6, 1861
107. WWH to William A. Graham, January 1, 1862
108. Cornelius H. Coffield to the Editor of the *Standard*, February 6, 1862
109. William H. Thomas to WWH, May 10, 1862
110. Editorial, "Candidate for Governor," June 4, 1862
111. WWH to Zebulon B. Vance. August 10, 1862
112. WWH to J. Johnston Pettigrew, October 28, 1862
113. Peter F. Pescud to WWH, October 28, 1862
114. WWH to Robert B. Gilliam, November 19, 1862
115. Editorial "The Duty of the Conservatives," November 21, 1862
116. WWH to Edward J. Hale, November 21, 1862
117. C. W. Wooley & E. G. L. Barringer to WWH, January 22, 1863
118. Editorial, "Peace—When shall we have Peace?" July 17, 1863
119. For the Standard, July 28, 1863
120. S. H. Christian for the Standard, August 19, 1863
121. E. M. Seago to WWH, September 9, 1863
122. WWH to E. J. Hale, September 14, 1863
123. WWH to the Public, October 1, 1863

124. WWH to E. J. Hale, October 7, 1863
125. WWH to Thomas Settle, Jr., December 22, 1863
126. WWH to the People of North Carolina, March 2, 1864
127. WWH to Calvin J. Cowles, March 18, 1864
128. WWH to the Public, April 18, 1864
129. Jonathan Worth to WWH, April 23, 1864
130. WWH to the Conservatives of North Carolina, May 19, 1864
131. WWH to Calvin J. Cowles, July 19, 1864
132. WWH to Calvin J. Cowles, July 29, 1864
133. Editorial, "The North-Carolina Standard," August 12, 1864
134. Robert P. Dick to WWH, August 20, 1864
135. Robert P. Dick to WWH, February 24, 1865
136. G. W. Blount and Others to WWH, April 29, 1865
137. WWH to G. W. Blount and Others, May 2, 1865
138. Andrew Johnson to WWH, May 9, 1865
139. Speech to Union Mass Meeting at Raleigh, May 12, 1865
140. WWH to Andrew Johnson, May 12, 1865
141. WWH to President Johnson, May 13, 1865
142. Editorial, May 15, 1865
143. Robert P. Dick and Others to Andrew Johnson, May 26, 1865
144. William H. Seward to WWH, May 29, 1865
145. Proclamation by the President, May 29, 1865
146. R. L. Patterson to WWH, June 8, 1865
147. W. H. Eddins to WWH, June 10, 1865
148. R. W. King to WWH, June 10, 1865
149. D. H. Hill to WWH, June 11, 1865
150. Calvin H. Wiley to WWH, June 12, 1865
151. Proclamation by the Governor, June 12, 1865
152. WWH to President Johnson, June 13, 1865
153. WWH to Major General Schofield, June 16, 1865
154. Jonathan Worth to WWH, June 16, 1865
155. WWH to R. L. Patterson, June 18, 1865
156. Zebulon B. Vance to WWH, June 18, 1865
157. A. M. Waddell to WWH, June 18, 1865
158. WWH to Robert M. Henry, June 19, 1865
159. James Speed to WWH, June 19, 1865
160. WWH to William H. Seward, June 19, 1865
161. James Speed to WWH, June 21, 1865
162. WWH to Major General J. D. Cox, June 22, 1865
163. J. D. Cox to WWH, June 23, 1865
164. I. Hubley Ashton to WWH, June 23, 1865
165. W. Hunter to WWH, June 24, 1865
166. WWH to R. M. Henry. June 26, 1865
167. WWH to Major General J. D. Cox, June 26, 1865

168. WWH to the President, June 27, 1865
169. WWH to the President, June 29, 1865
170. WWH to the President, July 4, 1865
171. Joseph S. Cannon to S. D. Wallace, July 4, 1865
172. Robert P. Dick to WWH, July 6, 1865
173. William H. Seward to WWH, July 8, 1865
174. William H. Seward to WWH, July 10, 1865
175. J. A. McMannin to WWH, July 10, 1865
176. Mayor and Commissioners of Wilmington to WWH, July 12, 1865
177. St. John E. S. Skinner to WWH, July 14, 1865
178. WWH to Mayor & Commissioners of Wilmington, July 15, 1865
179. WWH to Major General Ruger, July 15, 1865
180. WWH to the President, July 17, 1865
181. WWH to Reubin Swann, July 19, 1865
182. WWH to Dr. Edward A Crudup, July 20, 1865
183. WWH to the Attorney General, July 22, 1865
184. WWH to the President, July 24, 1865
185. WWH to Major General Ruger, July 227, 1865
186. Thomas H. Ruger to WWH, August 1, 1865
187. Mayor and Commissioners of Wilmington to WWH, August 3, 1865
188. Joseph S. Cannon to R. R. Bridgers, August 4, 1865
189. Lewis Hanes to Major General Ruger, August 4, 1865
190. Andrew Johnson to WWH, August 7, 1865
191. Proclamation, August 8, 1865
192. WWH to the President, August 10, 1865
193. Tod R. Caldwell to Andrew Johnson, August 18, 1865
194. Andrew Johnson to WWH, August 22, 1865
195. John Mc. Davis to WWH, August 25, 1865
196. WWH to the President, August 26, 1865
197. WWH to William Dennison, August 28, 1865
198. George W. McLelland to WWH, August 30, 1865
199. Andrew Johnson to WWH, August 30, 1865
200. WWH to Major General Ruger, August 30, 1865
201. WWH to William R. Albright, August 31, 1865
202. WWH to Justices of Peace of Yadkin County, September 13, 1865
203. Calvin H. Wiley to WWH, September 14, 1865
204. WWH to Major General Ruger, September 14, 1865
205. Thomas H. Ruger to WWH, September 14, 1865
206. R. C. Badger to Anderson Mitchell, September 14, 1865
207. Hugh McCulloch to WWH, September 16, 1865
208. WWH to Calvin H. Wiley, September 18, 1865
209. WWH to the President, September 21, 1865
210. Andrew Johnson to WWH, September 21, 1865
211. George G. Meade to WWH, September 22, 1865

212. WWH to the President, September 25, 1865
213. WWH to the President, October 2, 1865
214. WWH to R. J. Powell, October 5, 1865
215. WWH to the President. October 5, 1865
216. WWH to the President, October 6, 1865
217. WWH to the President. October 7, 1865
218. R. J. Powell to WWH, October 7, 1865
219. WWH to the President, October 7, 1865
220. Convention Delegates to WWH, October 14, 1865
221. WWH to the President, October 17, 1865
222. WWH to Convention Delegates, October 17, 1865
223. Andrew Johnson to WWH, October 18, 1865
224. WWH to Edwin G. Reade, October 18, 1865
225. Jonathan Worth to WWH, October 18, 1865
226. WWH to the President, October 20, 1865
227. WWH to the President, November 4, 1865
228. Andrew Johnson to WWH, November 5, 1865
229. WWH to the President, November 6, 1865
230. E. G. Reade to WWH, November 11, 1865
231. William H. Seward to WWH, November 11, 1865
232. Joseph S. Cannon to the President, November 13, 1865
233. William A. Graham to WWH, November 14, 1865
234. Joseph S. Cannon to Jonathan Worth, November 15, 1865
235. William H. Seward to WWH, November 18, 1865
236. William H. Seward to WWH, November 21, 1865
237. R. J. Powell to the President, November 26, 1865
238. Andrew Johnson to WWH, November 27, 1865
239. WWH to the President, November 27, 1865
240. WWH to the General Assembly, November 30, 1865
241. WWH to the President, December 1, 1865
242. R. J. Powell to the President, December 1, 1865
243. WWH to the President, December 4, 1865
244. WWH to Andrew Johnson, December 6, 1865
245. WWH to the President, December 9, 1865
246. Proclamation, December 9, 1865
247. William H. Seward to WWH, December 23, 1865
248. WWH to William H. Seward, December 23, 1865
249. WWH to Jonathan Worth, May 21, 1866
250. WWH to the President, July 11, 1866
251. WWH to the President, August 1, 1866
252. WWH to James S. Harrington, September 3, 1866
253. Speech "To the People of North Carolina," September 20, 1866
254. WWH to James E. O'Hara, October 3, 1866
255. Editorial, "W. W. Holden's complicity with Thad Stevens," October 10, 1866

256. WWH to Louisa Holden, December 9, 1866
257. WWH to Louisa Holden, February 11, 1867
258. Kemp P. Battle to WWH, February 16, 1867
259. WWH to John Sherman, February 23, 1867
260. W. D. Whitted to WWH, March 22, 1867
261. R. M. Henry to WWH, March 26, 1867
262. George S. Boutwell to WWH, June 18, 1867
263. Benjamin F. Butler to WWH, June 19, 1867
264. Petition, July 8, 1867
265. T. J. Candler to WWH, February 22, 1868
266. William Gibbins to WWH, May 4, 1868
267. William B. Rodman to WWH, May 5, 1868
268. John Pool to WWH, May 9, 1868
269. Louis V. Caziere to WWH, May 16. 1868
270. Bryon Laflin to WWH, June 15, 1868
271. Proclamation, June 15, 1868
272. John W. Stephens to WWH, June 20, 1868
273. Friends of the U. L. A. to WWH, June 24, 1868
274. Ed. R. S. Canby to WWH, June 29, 1868
275. Jonathan Worth to WWH, July 1, 1868
276. Ed. R. S. Canby to WWH, July 3, 1868
277. Inaugural Address of WWH, July 4, 1868
278. WWH to the President, July 4, 1868
279. Charles Dewey to WWH, July 7, 1868
280. Benjamin W. Ivey to WWH, July 7, 1868
281. Charles B. Mallett to WWH, July 8, 1868
282. Edmund L. Pemberton to WWH, July 8, 1868
283. Ed. R. S. Canby to WWH, July 9, 1868
284. George Dixon to WWH, July 12, 1868
285. WWH to Patrons and Friends of *Standard*, July 13, 1868
286. WWH to Col. G. A. Williams, July 14, 1868
287. William D. Haywood to William H. Harrison, July 14, 1868
288. WWH to Ed. R. S. Canby, July 14, 1868
289. J. W. Schenck, Jr., to WWH, July 15, 1868
290. WWH to J. W. Schenck, Jr., July 15, 1868
291. WWH to Ed. R. S. Canby, July 15, 1868
292. Ed. R. S. Canby to WWH, July 15, 1868
293. Ed. R. S. Canby to WWH, July 15, 1868
294. WWH to Ed. R. S. Canby, July 16, 1868
295. Ed. R. S. Canby to WWH, July 16, 1868
296. WWH to the General Assembly, July 17, 1868
297. W. F. Henderson to WWH, July 17, 1868
298. WWH to Col. George A. Williams, July 17, 1868
299. Col. George A. Williams to WWH, July 18, 1868

300. Ed. R. S. Canby to WWH, July 22, 1868
301. WWH to Col. George A. Williams, July 25, 1868
302. Jonathan Worth to WWH, July 29, 1868
303. WWH to the General Assembly, August 4, 1868
304. John H. Everitt to WWH, August 5, 1868
305. William H. Porter to WWH, August 13, 1868
306. Solomon Pool to John Pool, August 15, 1868
307. John A. Griswold to WWH, August 17, 1868
308. E. L. Pemberton to WWH, August 17, 1868
309. Henry W. Paschall to WWH, August 18, 1868
310. Solomon Pool to John Pool, August 19, 1868
311. Pinkney Rollins to WWH, August 21, 1868
312. John W. Hofler to WWH, August 22, 1868
313. John E. Cook to WWH, August 22, 1868
314. James Pace to WWH, August 22, 1868
315. W. J. Dawes to Jacob F. Chur, August 22, 1868
316. John H. Everitt to WWH, August 24, 1868
317. WWH to Charles B. Mallett, August 25, 1868
318. Affadivit of Duncan Holmes, August 25, 1868
319. WWH to Major General George C. Meade, August 25, 1868
320. John W. Stephens to WWH, August 29, 1868
321. Tod R. Caldwell to WWH, August 30, 1868
322. Charles B. Mallett to WWH, September 1, 1868
323. Lewis Johnson to WWH, September 7, 1868
324. W. J. Dawes to WWH, September 8, 1868
325. Miles Welch to WWH, September 12, 1868
326. WWH to Major General George C. Meade, September 14, 1868
327. R. C. Drum to WWH, September 15, 1868
328. Robert M. Douglas to C. M. Farris, September 21, 1868
329. F. W. Liedtke to WWH, September 22, 1868
330. Speech by Governor Holden, September 23, 1868
331. Affidavit of Henry Baker, September 24, 1868
332. John Patterson to WWH, October 3, 1868
333. Jacob F. Chur to WWH, October 5, 1868
334. P. Ridenhour to WWH, October 6, 1868
335. John V. Sherard to WWH, October 7, 1868
336. WWH to Nelson A. Miles, October 7, 1868
337. Nelson A. Miles to WWH, October 9, 1868
338. J. W. Schenck, Jr., to WWH, October 10, 1868
339. Silas L. Curtis to WWH, October 11, 1868
340. Proclamation by WWH, October 12, 1868
341. WWH to James I. Moore, October 14, 1868
342. E. M. Rosafy to Robert M. Douglas, October 15, 1868
343. A. W. Fisher to WWH, October 16, 1868

344. Robert M. Martin to WWH, October 16, 1868
345. Samuel McD. Tate to WWH, October 19, 1868
346. Victor C. Barringer to WWH, October 20, 1868
347. WWH to Sheriff of Cumberland County, October 24, 1868
348. John Reilly to WWH, October 27, 1868
349. Nelson A. Miles to WWH, October 27, 1868
350. John Robinson to WWH, October 30, 1868
351. William W. Cawthorne to WWH, October 31, 1868
352. John H. Everitt to WWH, November 1, 1868
353. Benjamin Satterfield to WWH, November 3, 1868
354. R. M. Henry to WWH, November 4, 1868
355. William J. Laird to WWH, November 9, 1868
356. Speech by Governor Holden, November 9, 1868
357. Hanibal D. Norton to Jacob F. Chur, November 12, 1868
358. Affidavit of Jacob Pass, November 14, 1868
359. Oscar Eastmond to WWH, November 14, 1868
360. John H. Everitt to WWH, November 15, 1868
361. WWH to the General Assembly, November 17, 1868
362. WWH to Hanibal D. Norton, November 17, 1868
363. William D. McCallum to WWH, November 25, 1868
364. George W. Swepson to WWH, November 27, 1868
365. WWH to the General Assembly, November 28, 1868
366. WWH to the Sheriff of Warren County, November 30, 1868
367. WWH to the Sheriff of Robeson County, November 30, 1868
368. Baltzer and Taaks to WWH, December 2, 1868
369. WWH to the Sheriff of Robeson County, December 2, 1868
370. James W. Alston to WWH, December 3, 1868
371. William J. Doughty to WWH, December 5, 1868
372. William H. Doherty to WWH, December 8, 1868
373. Alexander H. Jones to WWH, December 9, 1868
374. Jere Smith to WWH, December 10, 1868
375. William M. Coleman to WWH, December 10, 1868
376. WWH to the General Assembly, December 11, 1868
377. John Pool to WWH, December 13, 1868
378. Richard H. Bennett to WWH, December 17, 1868
379. Certified Statement, December 19, 1868
380. Baltzer and Taaks to WWH, December 20, 1868
381. J. T. Schenck to WWH, December 20, 1868
382. W. D. Whitted to WWH, December 20, 1868
383. WWH to Lewis Bond, December 22, 1868
384. F. W. Ahrens to WWH, December 24, 1868
385. Harriet J. Moore to General Miles, December 28, 1868
386. G. T. F. Gannaway to WWH, December 28, 1868
387. R. Beverly Frayser to WWH, December 28, 1868

ABBREVIATIONS OF SOURCES CITED

A&H:Conway	Katherine Clark Conway Collection, Private Collections, North Carolina State Archives, Division of Archives and History, Department of Cultural Resources, Raleigh
A&H:Douglas	Robert Martin Douglas Papers, Private Collections, North Carolina State Archives, Division of Archives and History, Department of Cultural Resources, Raleigh
A&H:GLB	Governors Letter Book of William W. Holden as Governor, North Carolina State Archives, Division of Archives and History, Department of Cultural Resources, Raleigh
A&H:GLB(Prov)	Governors Letter Book of William W. Holden as Provisional Governor, North Carolina State Archives, Division of Archives and History, Department of Cultural Resources, Raleigh
A&H:GP	Governors Papers of William W. Holden as Governor, North Carolina State Archives, Division of Archives and History, Department of Cultural Resources, Raleigh
A&H:GP(Prov)	Governors Papers of William W. Holden as Provisional Governor, North Carolina State Archives, Division of Archives and History, Department of Cultural Resources, Raleigh
A&H:Graham	William Alexander Graham Papers, Private Collections, North Carolina State Archives, Division of Archives and History, Department of Cultural Resources, Raleigh
A&H:Hale	Edward Jones Hale Papers, Private Collections, North Carolina State Archives, Division of Archives and History, Department of Cultural Resources, Raleigh
A&H:Holden	William Woods Holden Papers, Private Collections, North Carolina State Archives, Division of Archives and History, Department of Cultural Resources, Raleigh
A&H:Jeffreys	William Andrews Jeffreys and Family Papers, Private Collections, North Carolina State Archives, Division of Archives and History, Department of Cultural Resources, Raleigh

A&H:Reid	David S. Reid Papers, Private Collections, North Carolina State Archives, Division of Archives and History, Department of Cultural Resources, Raleigh
A&H:Pettigrew	Pettigrew Papers, Private Collections, North Carolina State Archives, Division of Archives and History, Department of Cultural Resources, Raleigh
A&H:Swepson	George W. Swepson Papers, Private Collections, North Carolina State Archives, Division of Archives and History, Department of Cultural Resources, Raleigh
A&H:T&C	Treasurers and Controllers Records, North Carolina State Archives, Division of Archives and History, Department off Cultural Resources, Raleigh
A&H:Vance	Zebulon Baird Vance Papers, Private Collections, North Carolina State Archives, Division of Archives and History, Department of Cultural Resources, Raleigh
A&H:Wiley	Calvin H. Wiley Papers, Private Collections, North Carolina State Archives, Division of Archives and History, Department of Cultural Resources, Raleigh
A&H:Worth	Jonathan Worth Papers, Private Collections, North Carolina State Archives, Division of Archives and History, Department of Cultural Resources, Raleigh
Chi:Douglas	Stephen A. Douglas Papers, Department of Special Collections, University of Chicago Library, Chicago, Illinois
DU:Clark	Henry Toole Clark Papers, Special Collections Library, Duke University, Durham
DU:Holden	William Woods Holden Papers, Special Collections Library, Duke University, Durham
LC:Johnson	Andrew Johnson Papers, Manuscript Department, Library of Congress, Washington, D. C. (Microfilm copy in D. H. Hill Library, North Carolina State University, Raleigh)
NCHR	*North Carolina Historical Review*
SHC:Barringer	Daniel Moreau Barringer Papers, Southern Historical Collection, Wilson Library, University of North Carolina at Chapel Hill
SHC:Cowles	Calvin J. Cowles Papers, Southern Historical Collection, Wilson Library, University of North Carolina at Chapel Hill
SHC:Ellis	John Willis Ellis Papers, Southern Historical Collection, Wilson Library, University of North Carolina at Chapel Hill

SHC:Graham	William Alexander Graham Papers, Southern Historical Collection, Wilson Library, University of North Carolina at Chapel Hill
SHC:Holden	William W. Holden Papers, Southern Historical Collection, Wilson Library, University of North Carolina at Chapel Hill
SHC:Howell	Edward Vernon Howell Papers, Southern Historical Collection, Wilson Library, University of North Carolina at Chapel Hill
SHC:Ruffin	Thomas Ruffin Papers, Southern Historical Collection, Wilson Library, University of North Carolina at Chapel Hill
SHC:Settle, Jr.	Thomas Settle, Jr., Papers, Southern Historical Collection, Wilson Library, University of North Carolina at Chapel Hill
SHC:Settle, Sr.	Thomas Settle, Sr., Papers, Southern Historical Collection, Wilson Library, University of North Carolina at Chapel Hill
SHC:Swain	David Lowry Swain Papers, Southern Historical Collection, Wilson Library, University of North Carolina at Chapel Hill
SHC:Venable	Abraham Watkins Venable Papers, Southern Historical Collection, Wilson Library, University of North Carolina at Chapel Hill
SHC:Wiley	Calvin Henderson Wiley Papers, Southern Historical Collection, Wilson Library, University of North Carolina at Chapel Hill
Standard	*North Carolina Standard* (Raleigh)

THE PAPERS OF WILLIAM WOODS HOLDEN

Holden to Hon. Thomas Ruffin, Sr. SHC: Ruffin

February 3, 1841

Hon. Thomas Ruffin[1]

Sir: I received a letter from my Father, a few days ago, from which I take the liberty of transcribing the following passage:

"I wish you to present to his Honour, Judge Ruffin, a renewal of my warmest affections, for the kind and liberal manner he manifested toward you in your examination; and any act of kindness in future will be greatly appreciated and remembered by his humble friend.

Tho: W. Holden"[2]

I have been disappointed in the expectation I entertained of locating in Western Carolina; and shall remain in the city, at all events, until I obtain a license in the Superior Courts.[3] In case of a vacancy, may I be pardoned in presuming to ask the Office of Reporter to the Supreme Court? Being a practical printer, and engaged in the office at which the Reports are statedly printed, I should be enabled to give to them my undivided attention; and I would most confidently, but respectfully, assure the Honourable Court, that no pains should be spared, in the event of my appointment, to Report the decisions with accuracy and fidelity, and to enhance, if possible, the typographical beauty and elegance of the work.

I hope the kindness of your heart will pardon the liberties I have taken on this occasion.

With great respect
Will: W. Holden

[1] Thomas Ruffin, chief justice of the North Carolina Supreme Court. *Dictionary of North Carolina Biography*, s.v. "Ruffin, Thomas."

[2] Thomas W. Holden, William W. Holden's father and a prominent gristmill operator in Hillsborough, Orange County. "Notes taken by E. E. Folk at Interview with Mrs. Henry Murdock, April 29, 1930" in William Woods Holden Papers, Private Collections, North Carolina State Archives.

[3] Holden had been licensed to practice as an attorney and counsellor at law by the North Carolina Supreme Court on January 2, 1841. See "Certificate of Admission to Practise as an Attorney and Counsellor at Law" in William Woods Holden Papers, Special Collections Library, Duke University, Durham. The certificate is signed by Chief Justice Thomas Ruffin, and associate justices Joseph J. Daniel and William Gaston.

Holden to W. A. Jeffreys, Esq. A&H: Jeffreys

Raleigh, April 14, 1843

My dear Jeffreys:[1]

I left Franklin County Court somewhat earlier than I expected, and was prevented from bidding you farewell, as I should have done. But, between friends I am persuaded, all apologies of this sort are unnecessary. I shall always remember with unmingled pleasure my visit to you. You are indeed pleasantly situated, and I make no doubt realize as much happiness as you can well desire.—The matter about which we were speaking, to wit, the House of Commons, has engaged my mind in some degree since I saw you, and I have come to the determination to become a candidate, provided my pretensions should meet the approbation of the people. I am thoroughly democratic in my sentiments; and have been for some time; and I should consider it a singular stroke of good fortune in my behalf, to be able to act in any honorable way, as an instrument in advancing the peculiar principles and policies of the democracy of Wake County.—The constitution, I believe, requires that a member of the House shall have possessed for the space of twelve months an estate in land in fee—this I have not.[2] Can you put me in a way to obtain an hundred acres? I am not able, at present, to pay a high price for land, especially when it would be of no material use to me. Would it be improper to accept a conveyance, and pass my note therefor—both to be repassed, whenever it might be judged proper? I should have no objection, however, to paying $1 per acre for poor land, for I could not ask any other for that price. I expect in two or three years to own any quantity of land; but you know I must have some for present purposes.—There is some talk here of placing a new Editor at the head of the Standard. I have been applied to to edit a Calhoun Journal, but have declined. Some of the party speak of placing Busbee[3] at the helm of the Standard-ship; but it won't do. Busbee is too compliant—too servile towards Haywood;[4] and too aristocratical in his pretentions. We must prevent it, if possible.—I have not talked with our mutual friend, Shepard[5] about it; but I am certain as to the light in which he will view it. Indeed, if Busbee were at the head of any democratic print, he would not scruple, in my opinion, to take strong sides against Shepard, and against us also, not through patriotic motives but from feelings of envy. Our course is clear. We must move *right on*, unmindful of the scoffs of the proud, and undaunted by the threats of the profligate. *Politicians by trade* must be put down; and the people consulted, obeyed and honored. We are young now; but let us be friends. We are boys, comparatively; let us labor to show ourselves *men*.

I hope, Jef, to hear from you frequently. Take whatever steps you think best to introduce my name to the people about Rolesville, and be assured that your generous confidence will never be betrayed.

Please write forthwith. Any commands you may have here will be cherrfully attended to.

Very Truly your friend,
W. W. Holden

W. A. Jeffreys, Esq.

[1] William Andrew Jeffreys, Raleigh merchant, member, state Senate, representing Franklin County, 1844-1845. John L. Cheney, Jr., ed., *North Carolina Government, 1585-1979: A Narrative and Statistical History* (Raleigh: Department of the Secretary of State, 1981), 313.

[2] Par. 6 of the 1776 Constitution provided that each member of the House of Commons shall have possessed for six months not less than 100 acres of land in fee. Cheney, *North Carolina Government, 1585-1979*, 812.

[3] Perrin Busbee, Wake county lawyer, A.B., U.N.C., 1837; reporter, North Carolina Supreme Court, 1852-1853; clerk, House of Commons, 1848-1851; president and member of the Council of State, 1852. Cheney, *North Carolina Government, 1585-1979*, 178, 316, 318; Daniel Lindsey Grant, *Alumni History of the University of North Carolina* (Durham: General Alumni Association, 1924), 89.

[4] William Henry Haywood, Raleigh lawyer, A.B., U.N.C., 1819; member, House of Commons, 1831 and 1834-1836; speaker of the house, 1836; member, United States Senate, March, 1843, to July, 1846. *Dictionary of North Carolina Biography*, s.v. "Haywood, William Henry, Jr."

[5] James Biddle Shepard, lawyer, A.B., U.N.C., 1834; A.M., 1838; appointed U. S. district attorney, 1839, but soon resigned; represented Wake County in state Senate, 1842-1843, and in the House of Commons, 1844-1845; unsuccessful candidate for governor as nominee of the Democratic party in 1846. *Dictionary of North Carolina Biography*, s.v. "Shepard, James Biddle."

Standard
May 31, 1843

The undersigned, in assuming the Editorial control of *The North Carolina Standard*, announces to the numerous friends and patrons of that print, and to the public, that no change will take place in its political principles. He is, and ever has been, a Democratic Republican of the School of '98 and '99; and in his new vocation will labour, with whatever diligence and intensity his feeble abilities will permit, to uphold and perpetuate the great doctrines of that School. He is a democrat, as well in feeling and in principle, because the members of the democratic party have always approved themselves the friends and supporters of equal rights; because they have ever been, and are now, the advocates of the *many* against the *few*; because, whilst they yield to the Federal Government the exercise of its acknowledged and undoubted Constitutional powers, they at the same time guard with peculiar vigilance the freedom sovreignty and independence of the respective States; because they regard the people as the true and the only source of the legitimate power, and believe, to the fullest extent, in their capacity for self-government; because it is a principle universally recognized in their political creed that public men are the *servants* and not the *masters* of the people; and because, in his opinion, the important public measures advocated at present by the democratic party are eminently calculated to augment the public prosperity and welfare.

The undersigned is opposed to all taxation, whether direct or indirect, beyond what is necessary to supply the public wants; and he would be glad to see the public expenditures cut down to the lowest standard consistent with a vigorous and healthful administration of public affairs. He is opposed to costly splendour of State or National Administration. He is opposed to a National Debt in any form whatever, unless its creation be unavoidable. He is opposed to a National Bank, on grounds both of expediency and constitutionality. He is opposed to a distribution of the proceeds of the sales of the Public Lands, especially when they are indispensable to the support of government. He is opposed to the present high Tariff, believing, as he does, that it is based on protective principles, that it operates as a bounty to the manufacturing interests, and imposes unequal and oppressive burdens especially upon the Southern States. He is opposed to the dangerous and unjust principles involved in the late Bankrupt Law. He is opposed, utterly opposed, to the proposition that the General Government should assume the debts of the States. He is opposed to any alteration or modification of the Veto Power. And in fine, he is opposed to all the projects, measures and principles of the modern Whig Party.

In striking from the columns of the Standard (as he shall do next week,) the name of Mr. Van Buren[1] as the Democratic Candidate for President, the undersigned desires it to be distinctly understood that he takes no stand in opposition to the pretentions of that great and patriotic Statesman. No man can be more deeply impressed than he is with a sense of Mr. Van Buren's high character and distinguished public service; and no man will go farther, in advocating his claims to the Presidency, should the voice of the Democratic party, in Convention assembled, be given in his favour. But the democratic party has other men in its ranks equally distinguished, whose claims upon the country are certainly entitled to equal consideration and regard; and, whilst the undersigned is disposed, nay, even desirous, as the conductor of a democratic press, to afford to the friends of each and all of those gentlemen who have been spoken of by the democracy of the country in connection with the Presidency, the fullest and amplest range for discussion and for mutual consultation, he must be permitted to persevere in the course he has marked out for himself of pledging his support to no man in advance. He is willing to abide the decision of a Democratic National Convention; and whatever his personal preferences may be, he would be the last man to permit them to conflict with the performance of the duty which he owes to his party and to the country.

The undersigned has thus given, very briefly and imperfectly, however, a general outline of his political opinions and of the principles by which he is determined to be guided in his Editorial course. He cannot hope to bring to the performance of the task before him the experience and ability which characterized the career of his highly respectable predecessor; but he promises to exert himself to the uttermost, and, planting himself upon the broad platform of just and imperishable principles, he assures his friends, the democratic party and the public, that he will shrink from no responsibility which, as the conductor of a public press, he may be summoned to assume.

TERMS

Three dollars per annum, payable *in advance*

The Standard will be sent for one year to Clubs at the following rates:

For five dollars, two copies; for ten dollars, four copies; for twenty dollars, ten copies. Any person procuring and forwarding five subscrivers, with the Cash ($15) will be entitled to the Standard one year free of charge.

The undersigned most respectfully solicits his democratic friends throughout the State to assist him, as far as they can, in enlarging and strengthening his Subscription list.

William W. Holden

May 31, 1843

[1] Martin Van Buren, U. S. senator; secretary of state; vice-president, 1833-1837; eighth president of the United States, 1837-1841; candidate for the nomination as president of the Democratic Party in 1844, but withdrew in favor of James K. Polk. *Dictionary of American Biography*, s.v. "Van Buren, Martin."

Holden to W. A. Jeffreys, Esq. A&H: Jeffreys

Raleigh, March 9, 1844

W. A. Jeffreys, Esq.[1]

My dear Jeffreys:

Your kind favor of the 7th has been received. I regret most deeply that I cannot be at Rolesville. My engagements are such as to prevent it. I shall, however, endeavor to be there during the campaign. I have just seen our friend Shepard.[2] He will go to-morrow to Orange Superior court, but says he is sorry he cannot be at Rolesville. His course has been misunderstood. This is for your private eye, to be used discreetly, but with firmness and assurance. He is looking to Congress, in case of Judge Saunders[3] getting an appointment, and he desired, in writing his late letter, to be placed in a condition to run for a seat in that body. *He will, however, run for the Legislature, on the Commons ticket, if nominated by the County Convention.* This his friends should understand, in order that they may know what course to adopt.

I hope you will be here at April Superior Court. I am anxious to see you, and have a talk about matters and things.

Excuse this short and imperfect letter, for I am greatly pressed. (Let nobody see this.)

Sincerely yours,
W.W. Holden

[1] William Andrew Jeffreys.

[2] James Biddle Shepard.

[3] Romulus Mitchell Saunders, lawyer; member, U.N.C. board of trustees, 1819-1864; elected to House of Commons, 1815, 1818-1820, serving the last two years as speaker; member, state Senate, 1816; member, U. S. House of Representatives, 1821-1827; North Carolina attorney general, 1828-1833; judge of superior court, 1835-1840; member, U. S. House of Representatives, 1841-1845; minister plenipotentiary to Spain, 1846-1849; member, House of commons, 1850-1853. *Dictionary of North Carolina Biography*, s.v. "Saunders, Romulus Mitchell."

R. M. Saunders to the Editor of the Standard *Standard*
May 6, 1844

To the Editor of the Standard:

As it has been publicly charged, that a portion of the democratic members of Congress have been engaged in an intrigue to influence and control the Baltimore Convention against the nomination of Mr. Van Buren,[1] as the democratic candidate for the Presidency; and as I understand I am considered as one of the "traitors in the camp," I desire my constituents shall know the part I have acted, that they may be prepared to decide as to the justice of the charge, so far as I am concerned. I had attended no caucus, signed no paper, with the view of operating against Mr. Van Buren for the Presidency. I have interchanged opinions freely with our democratic friends in Congress, and have uniformly declared against the policy of setting aside Mr. Van Buren, as I considered his nomination had been fixed by the party. But I have at the same time have said, I could see no impropriety in the delegation from each State acting for themselves; and as the members of Congress were in the daily receipt of letters from their constituents, they could communicate any information they might receive, to their own delegation to the Convention; that I presumed all who desired success to the cause, would not object to information from any source; that, as to the charge of caucus dictation, both whigs and democrats were in the weekly if not daily—or rather nightly— practice of holding caucuses; that while the delegates might be "fresh from the people," they certainly could not object to any additional information, judging themselves of its nature. Being myself an alternate delegate, and notified by my principal that he could not attend, I desired information for my guide. I now state, as the result of my conference as matters at present stand: *That in the twenty-one States, in which the democratic party claim as having any reasonable prospect of success, a majority of the democratic delegations representing those States will say that, with Mr. Van Buren as the Presidential candidate, we cannot carry more than SEVEN;—that with a fresh candidate, of sound democratic principles, we should have an equal and even a better chance, than our opponents, in carrying the other FOURTEEN States.* If what I have thus stated and done, be treason to the people, then I am a traitor. But I take the occasion to say to those who are prating so offensively about traitors, that, in the matter now agitating the public, *Arnolds* may be found in the field; and it will not be difficult in deciding who they are.

R. M. SAUNDERS[2]

Washington City, May 6, 1844

[1] Martin Van Buren.
[2] Romulus Mitchell Saunders.

J.D.W.[ard] for the North Carolina Standard — *Standard* May 22, 1844

For the North Carolina Standard

Texas and the Presidency

Mr. Holden: I have been, as you well know, a fast friend of Mr. Van Buren's; but circumstances have recently occurred to prove to me that he is not the proper candidate for the Democratic party to rally upon. I arrive at this conclusion from the fact, that Mr. Van Buren differs so widely from the mass of the Democratic party upon the question of the *immediate annexation of Texas*, that I cannot possibly hope that we can succeed with him, or any other candidate who will take such broad grounds against it. I copy a production from a Northern Whig paper, to show what are the feelings of the Whigs in that section of the country in relation to the accession of Texas and what means they imploy to intimidate the South: "If the blood hounds are to be let loose, we will select the hunting ground and the game. Our people, if they are to fight at all, will fight, not for Texas, nor for California, nor for Oregon, nor for any other such *bagatelle, but for* Canada. When slave-holding Texas is annexed to the American Union on the South, in defiance of Northern sentiments, and Northern rights, we will annex the non-slaveholding Canadas on the North—law or no law, treaty or no treaty, Constitution or no Constitution." These sentiments have been adopted by the National Intelligencer, with its English Editor at its head.

This shows, that this is a question between the abolitionists and the non-abolitionists—between the people of the South, (and the West, who depend upon the Southern market for a consumption of their agriculture products;) both of which unite in expressing the opinion in favor of the immediate annexation of Texas, and that Democratic candidate who is in favor of it, as is shown by the recent expressions of members of Congress on the subject, from information derived from their constituents. I repeat, that it is a question, between this class of the community, and those who entertain the sentiment contained in the above quoted production.

It is then a struggle to maintain the institutions of the South—to ascertain whether England should obtain a footing on our Southern frontier, which may enable her to abolish slavery in the United States, and thus prevent us from competing in the articles of Cotton and Sugar with her East and West Indian slaves, and finally by thus destroying the great market of American manufactures, make us mere tributaries to her. The fanaticism of abolition, together with the opinions of those who wish to avail themselves of the aid of those men in the coming Presidential election, has prevented the American people from being unanimous in their opinion of the immediate annexation of Texas, so essentially necessary is it to the interests of all portions, and all sections of the United States. All the true patriots of the country see this; and freed from any sinister motives they have come out openly and boldly, in favor of the immediate annexation. Your own able and worthy Representative, General Saunders,[1] has boldly come out upon this subject, and is sustained, by such men as the venerable Jackson,[2] "Old Ironsides," (Commodore Stewart,)[3] Senator Walker,[4] C. J. Ingersoll,[5] and many other distinguished men, besides, the entire Democratic delegation from Indiana, and the mass of the members of Congress, who came here, with a full determination to run no man but Mr. Van Buren. They have been compelled from the strong expression of public feeling in regard to this question, to come out publicly, and declare that Mr. Van Buren cannot be elected.

In advance of the opinion of Mr. Van Buren upon this subject, the leading Democratic papers expressed their feelings in favor of the annexation. "The Richmond Enquirer," "The Globe", "The Plebian", all the Democratic papers, contained arguments strongly in favor of it. Can we go back now, and say that the whole Democratic party were wrong in this matter, and that the Whigs who are always opposed to the extension of the principles of liberty, with Henry Clay at their head, are right; and the Democratic party were wrong, merely, because one man of the party chooses to endorse it? All the Democratic papers, and leading Democrats (with the exception of the Globe, which came out more strongly in favor of immediate annexation, than any other paper) show no disposition to pursue this course.

The Democratic party was not organized to elevate any man; but for the purpose of securing equal rights to all. It matters therefore not, who is the man it may select, provided he is one who will carry out the principles of the party. The Whigs have now nominated Henry Clay for the Presidency. He is well known to be in favor of a system, that will rob a majority of the community, to enrich a favorite few. Our object is to place before the people, a candidate who can prevent him from becoming the President, and fastening upon us this odious system. I am well convinced that no man opposed to the annexation of Texas can accomplish this, and therefore am willing to give up my first choice in favor of any Democrat, who has already shown himself friendly to the annexation of Texas, this being the absorbing question, provided I know he is right upon the other great principles, and measures of the Democratic party—opposed to a Bank of the United States, a protective Tariff, and the distribution of the public lands, etc.

J.D.W.[6]

Washington City, May, 1844

[1] Romulus Mitchell Saunders.

[2] Andrew Jackson.

[3] Charles Stewart, naval officer; commanded *U.S.S. Constitution* in War of 1812; naval commissioner, 1830-1832; created "Senior Flag Officer," 1859. *Dictionary of American Biography*, s.v. "Stewart, Charles."

[4] Robert James Walker, U.S. senator from Mississippi, 1835-1845; secretary of the treasury under President Polk, 1845-1849. *Biographical Directory of the American Congress, 1774-1971*, s.v. "Walker, Robert James."

[5] Charles Jared Ingersoll, member, U.S. House of Representatives from Pennsylvania, 1813-1815, 1841-1849; U. S. judge for district of Connecticut. *Biographical Directory of the American Congress, 1774-1971*, s.v. "Ingersoll, Charles Jared."

[6] Joseph D. Ward, member, House of Commons representing Onslow County, 1832-1833; assistant secretary, 1835 Constitutional Convention. Cheney, *North Carolina Government, 1585-1979*, 299, 817.

Jno. W. Cuningham to the Editor of the Standard *Standard*
June 19, 1844

To the Editor of the Standard:

Cuningham's Store
June 8, 1844

Dr. Sir: Through your paper of the 31st ult., I note a solicitation on the part of "Many Democratic Voters" of the tried and true county of Person, to become a candidate for a seat in the next Legislature.

Suffer me to say, Sir, that the communication was as unexpected as gratifying, as I have never sought, coveted, or even entertained an idea of political advancement; and even now, were I left to consult the true bent of my own inclination, I should most unhesitatingly decline; but with the present crisis, and your very flattering communications before me, I should feel myself guilty of a morbid ingratitude to decline.

To these aspirants for the seat, by whom I have been honored by thus constituting me the centre of harmony, I return my thanks.

My feeble state of health at the time the communication reached me, prevented an earlier response.

With much regard, etc

Your obedient servant
Jno. W. Cuningham[1]

[1] John Wilson Cuningham, planter and political leader; A.B., U.N.C., 1840; member, state Senate, 1852 to 1860; elected to House of Commons, 1844; member of the secession convention from May 20, 1861, to November 1, 1862; member, state Senate, 1866-1868, 1872-1874, 1876-1877, and 1881; member of convention of 1875. *Dictionary of North Carolina Biography*, s.v. "Cunningham, John Wilson"; Grant, *Alumni History*, 146; Cheney, *North Carolina Government*, 1585-1979, 825, 314, 319, 322, 324, 325, 334, 453,457, 460, 387.

H. for the North Carolina Standard *Standard*
July 24, 1844

Mr. Holden: There was a barbeque gotten up on Saturday, the 13th instant, at Hayesville, Franklin county, by the citizens of the neighborhood, to which a general invitation was given, and particularly to the whig candidate for Elector, Mr. Robert B. Gilliam,[1] who attended with aids in considerable force, and was evidently intended to have imposing effect, for all or most of the leading Whigs of the county were in attendance as it seemed by concert. And doubtless they expected to carry the day as their own. But some few democratic friends learned that A. W. Venable,[2] the democratic candidate for Elector for the District, was expected in the train from Raleigh where he had been in attendance at the Supreme Court, and they posted off to Stanton's,[3] and on the arrival of the train met Mr. Venable and prevailed upon him to go to Hayesville, to which place they carried him to the great gratification of his democratic friends, and, as appeared, to the discomfiture of the whigs who expected to have the day to themselves. Mr. Venable and Mr. Gilliam soon arranged the order of debate—Mr. V. to speak first, and the time allotted one hour and a half to each. Here I take great pleasure in premising that the courtesy if these two gentlemen to each other, which was in character with their usual urbanity, gave great pleasure to all present.

Mr. Venable filled his hour and a half by a most able argument, in which he exposed in the clearest terms the inconsistencies of Mr. Clay, who he asserted, and which he proved, had been on both sides of every great question or upon the fence, and might be given as authority for or against any and every measure. Mr. Venable exposed and laid fair to view the inconsistencies and unsoundness of the principles of Mr. Clay, in such strong and glowing colors, as to leave no doubt, upon the minds of the unprejudiced, of the impropriety of making him the head of this great nation.

Mr. Gilliam replied for two hours; and, considering the badness of his cause, he did tolerably well. He was, however, very cautious not to reply upon the Bank question; and he ran over other subjects superficially, to get at anecdotes to decoy off the popular attention from his inability to do a bad cause better justice. His courtesy and gentlemanly deportment, however, were conspicuous.

The time, one hour and a half, was too short for Mr. Venable to discuss various subjects which he left untouched, promising his friends at an after-time to meet them again for that purpose; and he has fixed Tuesday the 13th of August to meet them at Franklinton, to make another address to the people. I congratulate the democratic party upon the selection of Mr. Venable as their candidate for Elector; because his great fund of sound intelligence, which he delivers with an ease and elegance, I may say elegance, which carries conviction to every unprejudiced mind, ably fits him for the canvass which he has undertaken, and which we are prepared to say he discharges with an energy which entitles him to our particular gratitude.

H.[4]

July 14, 1844

[1] Robert Ballard Gilliam, lawyer; A.B., U.N.C., 1823; A.M., 1826; member, House of Commons, 1836-1840, 1846-1848, 1862; speaker, 1848 and 1862; member, 1835 convention; judge superior court, 1863-1865 and 1867-1868. Grant, *Alumni History*, 220.

[2] Abraham Watkins Venable, lawyer and politician; Democratic presidential elector in 1832 and 1836; elected to first of three terms as a member of the U. S. House of Representatives in 1846, but defeated in 1852 because of opposition to Compromise of 1850; member, Secession Convention, 1861; member, Confederate States Provisional Congress, 1861. *Dictionary of North Carolina Biography*, s.v. "Venable, Abraham Watkins"; Cheney, *North Carolina Government, 1585-1979*, 386, 388, 824.

[3] Now known as Kittrell, town in southwest Vance County. William S. Powell, *The North Carelina Gazetteer* (Chapel Hill: University of North Carolina Press, 1968), 266.

[4] Probably Louis Debonair Henry, lawyer and legislator; member, House of Commons, 1821, 1822, and 1830-1832; member, Council of State, 1834 and 1835; Democratic candidate for governor, 1842; delegate to Democratic National Convention, 1844. *Dictionary of North Carolina Biography*, s.v. "Henry, Louis Debonair."

Holden to Hon. D.S. Reid A&H: Reid

Raleigh, Oct. 30, 1844

Hon. D.S. Reid[1]

My dear Sir:

Yours of the 26th has been received. The tickets have been sent as you requested, and I hope they will reach you in good time.

Your letter in reply to mine[2] enclosing the forged letter was received. I hold this forgery over the head of its author, and justice to Dr. Williamson[3] may yet call it out. I wrote to the P.M. at Wentworth, who informed me that he knew no one by the name of "Thomas A.H. Hughes."

The democrats hereabouts are wide awake and full of enthusiasm. Listen for *thunder* from Edgecomb! From all quarters we have assurances of an increased vote. Orange will poll a powerful vote. So our friends there inform me. Wake will also do her duty, and Cumberland promises 500 majority for Polk and Dallas. Indeed the Cape Fear counties are all ready and panting for action. Upon the whole we have much cause for hope for N. Carolina. I may be too sanguine, but it does seem to me that the election of Col. Polk is placed beyond a reasonable doubt.

Be pleased to send me all the returns you can get, as soon as possible.

Truly yours
W.W. Holden

[1] David Settle Reid, member, state Senate; member, U.S. House of Representatives, 1843-1847; nominee for governor, 1848; elected governor for two terms beginning in 1850; member, U.S. Senate, 1854-1858. *Dictionary of North Carolina Biography*, s.v. "Reid, David Settle."

[2] Not extant.

[3] Not identified, but probably physician Robert Paine Williamson of Roxboro, A.B., U.N.C., 1823; A.M., 1827. Grant, *Alumni History*, 679.

Holden to Hon. D.S. Reid A&H: Reid

Raleigh, May 24, 1845

Hon. D.S. Reid,

My dear Sir:

Your esteemed favor of the 20th has been received. Mr. J.J. Wheeden, my agent, who hands you this, you will find to be intelligent, gentlemanly, and a sterling democrat. He goes to collect for me, and to get all the subscribers he can for the Standard. I am happy to say, that he is entitled to the fullest confidence. He is a good writer, and can give me weekly, accounts of the discussions in your District, and you will oblige me by giving him, when convenient, the leads and main points in your speeches.

There is nothing of interest here. The late years news is good; but of course you get the review, and know all about it. Things are just so with Clark[1] and Toole,[2] but I learn that Mr. C. will distance him, notwithstanding Mr. Stanly[3] has given in his decision to Mr. T. Stanly has personal spite against Clark.

Again thanking you for your kind words in behalf of the Standard, I remain

Truly yours,
W.W. Holden

[1] Henry Selby Clark, A.B., U.N.C., 1828; member, House of Commons, 1834-1836; member, U.S. House of Representatives, 1845-1847; lawyer. *Dictionary of North Carolina Biography*, s.v. "Clark, Henry Selby"; Grant, *Alumni History*, 111.

[2] Henry Irwin Toole, lawyer; A.B., U.N.C., 1828; A.M. 1839; editor of the Wilmington *Aurora*. Grant, *Alumni History*, 625.

[3] Edward Stanly, lawyer; member, U.S. House of Representatives, 1837-1843; member, House of Commons, 1844-1848, serving both sessions as speaker; attorney general of the state, 1847-1848; reelected to the U.S. House of Representatives, 1849-1851; appointed military governor of North Carolina by President Lincoln in 1862, resigned in January, 1863. *Dictionary of North Carolina Biography*, s.v. "Stanly, Edward."

Jno. H. Wheeler to Holden *Standard*
December 24, 1845

Newton, Catawba County, N.C.
10th December, 1845

W.W. Holden, Esq., Editor "Standard"

Sir: You will see from the "Lincoln Courier" and "Mecklenburg Jeffersonian" that the democratic party of this county had a meeting on yesterday to appoint delegates who will attend the Convention on the 8th of January next, in your city.

The meeting war large, respectable and enthusiastic. Many delegates were appointed, and the name of the Hon. Charles Fisher,[1] of Rowan, was recommended as the choice of the democracy of Catawba. Be assured that this region of our State will be fully and faithfully represented in the Convention; and whoever it may select as the candidate for Governor will receive a firm, warm and manly support.

My name has been, in a remote degree, by the public Press and private letters, connected with this important post. I am not insensible to the kindness of my friends, or the confidence of my country; but you are aware, as one of my personal friends, that when last winter I retired from the Treasury Department of our State, it was my desire to seek repose for a while, in the quiet retreat of private life. This, and the strong and conclusive indications of public sentiment in this section for another, leads me to take this occasion to say thus publicily to you that it is not my desire that my name be considered among those from whom a choice is to be made.

From my own personal observation on a circuit of Courts in this section of our State; from a recent journey from my native District (the Edenton) to the mountains; and from other sources, I am convinced that the Hon. Charles Fisher, of Rowan, is the choice of our western democracy.

Other names have been presented in communications to your paper, from the west, but no observant politican can say that they have met any response from the great mass of the people. The eye of public opinion in this section seems almost exclusively directed to Mr. Fisher; and he would be a doubtful friend to the cause, who would endeavor to divert it. In this Congressional District particularly, by his late gallant and exciting contest, has he endeared himself to the democratic party. It is well known in our State that by the Legislature of 1842 (ill-starred so far as this District is concerned) this "Gibraltar of democracy," the old Mecklenburg District, was darkened by the shadow of federalism. In it, as now organized, Gen. Harrison beat Mr. Van Buren 1790 votes, and Mr. Clay received 862 votes more than Mr. Polk who was born in it; and the present member (Hon. D.M. Barringer)[2] made an easy transit from the Legislature that passed the bill to the House of Representatives in Congress. Last summer we nominated Mr. Fisher to lead our forces on the seemingly impregnable majority—sustained, too by a candidate in office, who had been faithful to those who elected him, with personal claims that few could resist, and with address and ingenuity that none could excel; yet, such was the power of Mr. Fisher's elequence, such the energy of his character and the suavity of his demeanor, that he was only defeated by twenty-six votes! Not only to this District is he well known, but to the whole western part of North Carolina, as a member of the House of commons, a laborious and faithful advocate of their views and interests.

Some of our Eastern friends have suggested that his opinions and courses will be subjected to severe attack from our political oppenents. Who or where is the man in whom the democracy confide, that they will not attack? Did they spare, in the last campaign, the talented, amiable, and lamented Hoke?[3] Were our candidates "as chaste as ice and pure as snow," he would not "escape their calumnay." To be attacked by the poisoned Press of their party, will be the best passport to the public confidence; to be praised by it or their leaders, is a certain sign of a want of firmness or political integrity.

I have seen Mr. Fisher but once since his campaign in our District. He is now absent from home, and I do not know whether he will accept the nomination; but with him for our standard-bearer, the west will present a strong and undivided front.

But we go for "principles, not men," and whatever candidate the Convention may select—whether it be Mr. Fisher, or from among "the unterrified democracy" of Edgecomb, or the sound republican region of Caswell, or the pure land of Macon, or the blue hills of Burke, or elsewhere—we of the West will unite with the democracy of our State, shoulder to shoulder, to elect the nominee, and rescue the "Old North State" from her unnatural alliance that she has recently had with abilition Vermont and federal Massachusetts, and place her, as in the days of yore, in the company of her democratic neighbors Virginia, South Carolina and Tennessee.

I am very sincerely,
Your faithful friend,
Jno. H. Wheeler[4]

[1] Charles Fisher, lawyer; elected to state Senate in 1818; member, U.S. House of Representatives, 1819-1823, 1839-1841; member, House of Commons 1821-1823, 1826-1831, 1833, and 1836, serving as speaker in 1830 and 1831. *Dictionary of North Carolina Biography*, s.v. "Fisher, Charles."

[2] Daniel Moreau Barringer, lawyer, congressman, minister to Spain; A.B., U.N.C., 1826; member, House of Commons, 1829-1835; member, convention, 1835; member, U.S. House of Representatives, 1843-1849; minister to Spain, 1849-1853; member, House of Commons, 1854-1855; member U.N.C. Board of Trustees, 1832-1868. *Dictionary of North Carolina Biography*, s.v. "Barringer, Daniel Moreau"; Grant, *Alumni History*, 35-36.

[3] Michael Hoke, lawyer and politician; member, House of Commons, representing Lincoln County, 1834, 1835, 1836, 1838, and 1840; U.N.C. trustee, 1838-1844; unsuccessful Democratic nominee for governor, 1844. *Dictionary of North Carolina Biography*, s.v. "Hoke, Michael."

[4] John Hill Wheeler, lawyer and diplomat; A.B., George Washington University, 1826; A.M., U.N.C. 1828; member, House of Commons, 1827-1831, 1852; minister to Nicaragua, 1854-1857. *Dictionary of North Carolina Biography*, s.v. "Wheeler, John Hill."

G.W. Caldwell to Democratic State Committee *Standard*
January 28, 1846

Charlotte, N.C., Jan.20, 1846.

North Carolina Democratic State Committee:[1]

Gentlemen: I had the honor, on the 16th instant, to receive your letter of the 10th informing me that the Democratic Convention which assembled at Raleigh on the 8th, had unanimously nominated me as the Democratic candidate for the office of Governor of North Carolina in the coming contest.

Highly impressed as I am with this honor, which has been conferred on me, much to my surprise, and however desirous I may be under such a flattering inducement to comply with the demand of my party—yet I am constrained by ill health and the condition of my private matters to decline the nomination.

In taking this resolution, I am not unconscious of its great delicacy, but I beg you to do me the justice to believe that I was driven to it after the most serious consideration by circumstances as you must perceive of absolute necessity.

Believing that the withholding of my name will be productive of no inconvenience to the union or harmony of the party, I ask you to accept my most profound acknowledgements for the very flattering matter in which you have been pleased to make the coummunication, and to believe me gentlemen,

Very respectfully,
Your most ob't. servant,
G.W. Caldwell[2]

[1] The committee consisted of William A. Avery, of Burke; John W. Ellis, of Rowan; Calvin Graves, of Caswell; Robert P. Dick, of Guilford; Robert Strange, of Cumberland; Gabriel Holmes, of New Hanover; Weldon N. Edwards, of Warren; Louis D. Wilson, of Edgecombe; Thomas Bragg, Jr., of Northampton; Perris Busbee, of Wake; Gaston H. Wilder, of Wake; and William W. Holden, of Wake.

[2] Greene Washington Caldwell, lawyer and physician; member, House of Commons, 1836-1841; member, U.S. House of Representatives, 1841-1843; superintendent, U.S. Mint, Charlotte, 1844-1847; member, state Senate, 1850-1852. *Dictionary of North Carolina Biography*, s.v. "Caldwell, Greene Washington."

Democratic State Committee to James B. Shepard *Standard*
March 18, 1846

Raleigh, March 17, 1846

James B. Shepard, Esq.

Dear Sir: At a Meeting of the Democratic State Committee of North Carolina, held this day, you were nominated by a majority of the committee as the Democratic Republican candidate for Governor at the ensuing election.

Permit us, Sir, to add the hope that you will accept this nomination, tendered as it is under the most encouraging circumstances for the democratic cause, and in the well-founded belief that perservance and vigorous exertion in the present contest, must be crowned with the happiest results.

Democratic State Committee

James B. Shepard to Democratic State committee *Standard*
March 18, 1846

Raleigh, N.C.
Tuesday, March 17th, 1846

Gentlemen: Your letter informing me of my nomination as the democratic candidate for Governor of North Carolina, has been received. In January last, when in Newbern, I received a letter from a friend requesting me to accept such a nomination. To that request I returned a prompt and decided negative; on two occasions subsequent (as some of the Committee well know) I desired that my name might not be connected in any manner with the distinguished office of Governor; but being since privately and publicily called on and now urgently solicited (by the Committee appointed by the late Convention to act for the party) to become the standard bearer of our noble principles, I cannot longer hesitate. I accept therefore, the nomination so cordially and politely tendered, and shall use every exertion to defeat the policy and measures of the Federal party.

It is entirely unnecessary at this time to mention my views on any subject of State or National interest, as they may be familar to every section of the Commonwealth. With zeal, activity, and energy, we can and will be triumphant; and here permit me to congratulate the Democracy upon the success of all the leading measures of the administration. The admission of Texas into our glorious Union and the adjustment of the Tariff, upon equitable principles, during the present session of Congress, cannot fail to redound to the honor of the Democratic party. On the currency, the controversy concerning Oregon, and questions of State policy, and indeed all others, I deem it quite useless now to expatiate, because they will be examined at length in my discussions before the people. With sentiments of high regard and esteem,

Your ob't. Servant,
James B. Shepard.[1]

[1] In the 1846 election, William A. Graham was elected with 43,486 votes to Shepard's 35,627 votes. Cheney, *North Carolina Government, 1585-1979*, 1399.

Holden to Hon. D. S. Reid A&H: Reid

Raleigh, March 20, 1846

Hon. D. S. Reid

My dear Sir:

You will have seen, by the Standard, that the committee have at length decided, and that Mr. Shepard[1] is the nominee. Mr. Leak,[2] who is desirious of running, was fairly treated by the Committee, his name having been most respectfully considered; but now, that a majority has declared against him, he surely cannot be so selfish and unmanageable as to attempt to plunge the party into the perils of schisms and divisions. Indeed, while the matter was under consideration, he wrote letters to me, which were, to say the least, offensive in their tone; but all this has been passed over, for the sake of harmony; and last night I wrote to him in the kindest manner, informing him of the action of the Committee, and that I should support Mr. Shepard, as I would have supported him, had he been the Nominee. I hope he may be induced to yield; but if he holds on, he cannot get 100 democrats to back him.

Mr. Shepard is in high spirits. He will start in a few days for the East, and will canvass vigoriously until the day of election. He will attack Gov. G.[3] in the East and in the West upon the Rail Road debts—and in the East I feel confident he will make heavy inroads upon the Whig party. Consider, if you please, that in 1840 William A. Graham beat William B. Shepard for Senator; consider the feeling this aroused in the East against Gov. Graham, and the strong personal popularity of W. B. Shepard, and the certainty that he will not oppose his brother, and the probability rather that he will support him; consider also, that this is a section of the State where our friend Biggs[4] set the ball so gloriously in motion; and consider that in Tyrell and Craven our Candidate has Whig relations of great influence, and who will doubtless favor him considerably, and you will have some idea of his strength in the East. Besides, he is a bold and vigorous young man, full of enthusiasm and bent on success.

I will write more at length hereafter. I hope you will do all you can for him in your District.

Your Oregon Speech will appear in the next standard. Please let me hear from you.

Yours truly,
W.W. Holden

[1] William Biddle Shepard.

[2] Walter Francis Leake (Leak), lawyer and textile manufacturer; member, U.N.C trustees, 1846-1868; member, House of Commons, 1831-1832; member, state Senate, 1832-1833; delegate to Democratic National Convention, 1844; delegate to 1861 secession convention. *Dictionary of North Carolina Biography*, s.v. "Leake, Walter Francis."

[3] William Alexander Graham, lawyer and planter; A.B., U.N.C., 1824; LL.D., 1849; member, House of Commons, 1833-1836, 1838-1841; speaker, House of Commons, 1838-1841; member, U.S. Senate, 1840-1843; governor, 1845-1849; U.S. secretary of the navy, 1850-1853; member of secession convention, 1861; member, Confederate states senate, 1864. *Dictionary of North Carolina Biography*, s.v. "Graham, William Alexander."

[4] Asa Biggs, lawyer and politician; member of the 1835 constitutional convention; member, House of Commons, 1840-1843; member, state Senate, 1844-1845, 1854-1855;

member, U.S. House of Representatives, 1845-1847; member, U.S. Senate, 1855-1858; U.S. district judge, 1858-1861; member of 1861 secession convention; Confederate States district judge, 1861-1865. *Dictionary of North Carolina Biography*, s.v. "Biggs, Asa."

Holden to J. M. Bullock, Esq. SHC:Howell

Raleigh, June 10, 1846

J. M. Bullock, Esq.[1]

My dear Sir:

I have just sent you per Mail to Lynesville copies of the Journals for 1840 and 1842, and regret to say that copies for '38 and '44 cannot be obtained. Doubtless Mr. Stone[2] and Mr. Eaton[3], who were members at the last session, have the Journals for 1844, and will loan them to you on the campaign. The price of those sent is $2 per copy, which I paid to Mr. Lemay[4] —the other dollar I placed to your credit. If I should be able to procure the other copies in time, I will send them to you.

I am pressing the State Debts, and that bid of Gov. Graham [5] for the Rail Road. These are the strong points, and will have this legitimate effect. The War with Mexico will, in my opinion, operate in our favor, especially if we should get another splendid victory about the middle of July. It is important , too, to state the fact that Mexico will be held responsible for the *expenses* of the War.—I think we shall carry the Legislature, and I shall be pleased to hear of your election.

Mr. Shepard,[6] I learn, is doing extremely well in his campaign. I entertain no doubt of his election, provided the party put forth their full strength.

Truly you friend,
W.W. Holden

[1] James M. Bullock, represented Granville County in House of Commons, in 1844-1847, 1854-1861. Cheney, *North Carolina Government, 1585-1979*, 314, 315, 323, 324, 326, 328.

[2] Jonathan M. Stone, represented Granville County in House of Commons, 1842-1847, 1866-1867. Cheney, *North Carolina Government, 1585-1979*, 312, 314, 315, 335.

[3] William Eaton, Jr., lawyer and legislator; A.B., U.N.C., 1829; trustee, U.N.C., 1838-1868; member, House of commons, 1838-1841, 1850, 1854, 1856; attorney general, 1851-1852; represented Warren County at 1865 convention. *Dictionary of North Carolina Biography*, s.v. "Eaton, William, Jr."

[4] Thomas J. Lemay, editor and publisher of the Raleigh *Star*. *Dictionary of North Carolina Biography*, s.v. "Lemay, Thomas J."

[5] Governor William A. Graham.

[6] James Biddle Shepard.

Holden to Hon. D. S. Reid A&H:Reid

Raleigh, Dec 8, 1847

Hon. D. S. Reid

My dear Sir:

Yours of the 26th was duly received. I was glad to hear from you, and was much pleased with the Resolutions of the Rockingham Meeting. We shall expect you, by all means, at the Convention.

The general impression among our friends seems to be, that January, or even February, would be too early. March or April has been mentioned; and I find, on reference to the Almanac, that fewer Courts will be in session about the 1st of April than any month in the year. Besides, the weather will then be open, and favorable for travelling. The Whigs will probably hold their Convention early in February. We always lose by long campaigns. The adversary has full time to rally—to bring out his crossroad politicians and merchants—to circulate his documents and "revolutionary Circulars"—and to put his presses—two to one to ours—full to work. A short campaign—a Chapultepec fight is the sort for us.

I see that the Whigs are getting pestered already, since Rayner[1] begged off, on account of sick head ache! and his Arkansas farm! The Roanoke Republican of a late date, gives it to Gales[2] in fine style, on account of his cold and his *business-like* notice of Col. Joyner;[3] Dr. Hill,[4] of Brunswick, is understood to be anxious to run; Gen. Dockery's[5] "great firmness of purpose and strenth of intellect" inclines him the same way; and to cap the climax, I see that a writer in the last Wilmington Commericial gravely brings forward the Hon. Richard Hines.[6] But after all the generallizing, and snarling, and scrambling for an office which they have only by a pitiful four thousand majority, they will settle down on some one, and support him with a savage determination.

We ought to make our Convention as imposing and as powerful as possible. Let us kindle the fire here by the aid of strong hands and stout hearts, and keep it burning until Federalism is consumed.

I see that the Whigs of the House have done the deed! Winthrop,[7] a Wilmot Provisionist is the speaker. I have not seen the vote, but I presume all our Whig Delegation voted for him. This is a base betrayal of the South, but they will be sustained here by the Register, Badger[8] Clique; and I verily believe these men would support, for the two highest offices in the land, Webster[9] and Corwin.[10]

I have not as yet seen the Message, but we shall probably get it today.

Mr. French,[11] the former Clerk, is said to have been reelected.

Let me hear from you soon, and let me know, *in confidence*, what our friends in Rockingham think of a National Convention and the Presidency. When I get more time I will write you at length on this subject.

Truly yours,
W.W. Holden

[1] Kenneth Rayner, legislator and Whig party leader; member of the 1835 convention; member, House of Commons, 1835, 1836, 1838, 1845 to 1851; member, U.S. House of Representatives, 1839-1845; member, state Senate, 1854-1855; unsuccessful candidate for U.S. vice-president, 1848. *Dictionary of North Carolina Biography*, s.v. "Rayner, Kenneth."

[2] Weston Raleigh Gales, editor of the *Raleigh Register*; member, House of Commons, 1836-1837. *Dictionary of North Carolina Biography*, s.v. "Gales, Weston Raleigh."

[3] Andrew Joyner, legislator and army officer; trustee, U.N.C., 1836-1856; major and lieutenant colonel in North Carolina volunteer regiments in the war of 1812; member, state Senate, 1835-1852; speaker, 1838, 1840, 1846. *Dictionary of North Carolina Biography*, s.v. "Joyner, Andrew."

[4] John H. Hill, physician; member, House of Commons, 1850-1851. Grant, *Alumni History*, 282.

[5] Alfred Dockery, farmer and legislator; member, House of Commons, 1822; member of 1835 convention; member, state Senate, 1836-1845; member, U.S. House of Representatives, 1845-1847, 1849-1851; member of the 1865 convention; identified by title "General" but did not serve in armed forces. *Dictionary of North Carolina Biography*, s.v. "Dockery, Alfred."

[6] Richard Hines, lawyer; member, House of Commons, 1824; member, U.S. House of Representatives, 1825-1827. *Dictionary of North Carolina Biography*, s.v. "Hines, Richard."

[7] Robert Charles Winthrop, member, U.S. House of Representatives, from Massachusetts, 1840-1859; speaker of U.S. House of Representatives, 1847-1850; member, U. S. Senate, 1850-1851. *Biographical Directory of the American Congress, 1774-1971*, s.v. "Winthrop, Robert Charles."

[8] George Edmund Badger, superior court judge and U. S. senator; trustee of U.N.C., 1818-1844; member, House of commons, 1816; superior court judge, 1820-1825; appointed secretary of the navy, 1841; member, U.S. Senate, 1846-1855; member of secession convention of 1861. *Dictionary of North Carolina Biography*, s.v. "Badger, George Edmund."

[9] Daniel Webster.

[10] Thomas Corwin, member, U.S. House of Representatives from Ohio, 1831-1840; governor of Ohio, 1840-1842; member, U. S. Senate, 1845-1850; secretary of the treasury, 1850-1853; member, U. S. House of Representatives, 1859-1861. *Biographical Directory of the American Congress, 1774-1971*, s.v. "Corwin, Thomas."

[11] Benjamin B. French of New Hampshire, clerk, U. S. House of Representatives, 1843-1849. *Biographical Directory of the American Congress, 1774-1971*, 139, 143, 147.

Holden to Hon. W. N. Edwards A&H:Conway

Raleigh, March 12, 1848.

Hon. W. N. Edwards[1]

My Dear Sir:

Your esteemed favor of the 7th was duly received. I concur with you that it is our duty as Southern men, as it will be my pleasure, to vindicate Mr. Buchanan[2], and your letter of the 25th December shall appear in the next Standard.

I have just received letters from Dancy,[3] Venable,[4] and Wheeler.[5] The latter writes me that Leake[6] addressed a letter to a Western friend (Mr. Lander)[7] in which he declines to canvass the State. If this be so, Leak is out of the question, as of course, if we have a Candidate at all, the State must be canvassed. I know three men in the State who, I believe, could carry it against Mr. Manly,[8] to wit, Weldon N. Edwards, of Warren, Calvin Graves,[9] of Caswell, and James C. Dobbin,[10] of Cumberland. What do you think of that? I know your aversion to this sort of thing, and I fear you will think me entirely out of the way in making and pressing the proposition; but if you *could* consent to take the field, and canvass the State thoroughly, in my opinion victory would be certain. Mr. Graves *will not* run. This I know. Whether Mr. Dobbin would or not, I cannot say—I heard once that he would, and then again McRae[11] assured me he would not. Dobbin is one of our strongest men. Amiable, gentlemanly, kind, admitted to be so by the opposite party, and able, he would not only carry the full strength every where, but you know how *clannish* the Cape Fear people are—they would stick to him like leeches. Still, I think you would make the *best* run of any man in the party, and I hope you will consider the whole matter again.

Mr. Venable thinks the State can be carried, and he seemed determined to do all in his power to effect this glorious result. It is *certain* that the nomination of Mr. Manly has occasioned in the East deep and wide-spread dissatisfaction; and Mr. Manly himself will prove a weak Candidate on the stump. All we need is, *peace*, a strong Candidate for Governor, and Clay in the field again.

Mr. Dancy writes me that our friends in Edgecombe and Nash think of appointing *County* Delegates to Baltimore. That, it seems to me, would not do, as the Convention could not recognize Counties, and the Delegates, after all, would have to hail from the District. I think the suggestion in the last Standard, of four principals and four substitutes, will satisfy Edgecombe and Nash.

The Resolutions of your County Meeting are capital. They breathe the right spirit, and they hit the mark every time. We shall look for a large Delegation from Warren—our friend, Mr. Baskerville[12], will, I hope, by all means be present.

It would indeed afford me a great deal of pleasure to see you, and I would certainly avail myself of your kind invitation, but the truth is I am tied down here, and besides, I have had a swollen jaw for weeks, and now have it, occasioned by cold. As I pass to Baltimore, or return, I hope to have the pleasure of calling on you.

Be pleased to let me hear from you often. Present my best wishes and regards to Mr. Baskerville, and accept for yourself assurances of the sincere esteem with which I am

Truly Your Friend,
W. W. Holden

[1] Weldon Nathaniel Edwards, planter, state senator, and congressman; represented Warren County in House of Commons, 1814 and 1815; member, U.S. House of Representatives, 1815 to 1827; member state Senate 1827 to 1852, serving as speaker

in 1850 and 1852; member of the 1835 convention; elected chairman of secession convention of 1861. *Dictionary of North Carolina Biography*, s.v. "Edwards, Weldon Nathaniel."

[2] James Buchanan, fifteenth president of the United States; member of the U.S. House of Representatives, 1821-1831; member of U.S. Senate, 1834-1845; secretary of state, 1845-1849. *Dictionary of American Biography*, s.v. "Buchanan, James."

[3] William Francis Dancy, lawyer; A.B., U.N.C., 1841; member, House of Commons, 1846-1848. Grant, *Alumni History*, 150.

[4] Abraham Watkins Venable.

[5] John Hill Wheeler.

[6] Walter Francis Leake.

[7] William Lander, lawyer; member, House of Commons, 1852; district solicitor, 1853-1862; member of the 1861 secession convention; member, Confederate House of Representatives, 1861-1863. *Dictionary of North Carolina biography*, s.v. "Lander, William."

[8] Charles Manly, lawyer and governor; A.B., U.N.C., 1814; A.M.; secretary-treasurer, U.N.C. board of trustees, 1821-1849, 1851-1868; governor, 1849-1851. *Dictionary of North Carolina biography*, s.v. "Manly, Charles."

[9] Calvin Graves, lawyer and farmer; member of the 1835 convention; member, House of Commons, 1840-1845; member, state Senate 1846-1849, serving as speaker in the 1848-1849 session; U.N.C. trustee, 1844-1868. *Dictionary of North Carolina Biography*, s.v. "Graves, Calvin."

[10] James Cochran Dobbin, lawyer; A.B., U.N.C., 1832; member, U.S. House of Representatives, 1845-1847; member House of Commons, 1848-1851, serving as speaker 1850-1851; appointed secretary of the navy by President Franklin Peirce, 1853-1857. *Dictionary of North Carolina Biography*, s.v. "Dobbin, James Cochran."

[11] Duncan Kirkland McRae, lawyer and diplomat; graduate of College of William and Mary; member, House of Commons, 1842-1843; U.S. consul to Paris, 1853-1857; unsuccessful candidate for governor, 1858; colonel, fifth N.C. Regiment, 1861-1862. *Dictionary of North Carolina Biography*, s.v. "McRae, Duncan Kirkland."

[12] Probably George D. Baskerville, Warren County planter. Patrick Hamilton Baskerville, *Genealogy of the Baskerville Family* (Richmond, Va.: Wm. Ellis Jones' Sons, Inc., 1912), 68.

Holden to Hon. A. W. Venable SHC:Venable

Raleigh, March 12, 1848

Hon. A. W. Venable

My dear Sir:

Your esteemed favor of the 8th was duly received. I was glad to hear from you. Of course your communication to me will be considered confidential. I hope you will write the articles you speak of—I shall be much obliged to you for them, especially as my varied duties keep me constantly at hard labor. Please write a plain hand, and punctate.

I agree with you, that with proper efforts we can carry the State in the ensuing elections. Mr. Manly[1] will prove a weak Candidate, and in addition to this it is *certain* that the dissatisfaction in the East at his nomination is deep and widespread. All we need is a peace, a strong candidate for Governor, and Clay in the field again. You allude to Leak[2] and ask me how I think Dobbins[3] would do for Governor. Leak, if he really desires to run, seems entitled to the track: but Wheeler[4] informs me that Leak has written a letter to a Western friend, in which he declines to canvas the State. That, you know, won't do. If we are to have a candidate, a canvas from May till August is indispensable. Whether Dobbins would run or not, I do not know, *but he is one of our strongest men*; and I believe a better nomination could not be made. Our friends in all parts of the State are in motion, and the best spirit prevails. I think we shall have a full and spirited Convention. Can't you make it convenient to be present?

The Democracy of Martin County (you will see the meeting in the next Standard) have nominated Gen. McKay[5] for Vice President.

I should be glad to hear from you often. Please ask my friend Daniel[6] why he does not write?

Truly yours,
W.W. Holden

[1] Charles Manly.

[2] Walter Francis Leake.

[3] James Cochran Dobbin.

[4] John Hill Wheeler.

[5] James Iver McKay, lawyer and congressman; appointed U.S. district attorney for North Carolina, 1817; member, state Senate, 1815-1818, 1822, 1826, and 1829-1830; member, U.S. House of Representatives, 1831-1849; active in militia affairs and frequently addressed as "general," although he had no military experience. *Dictionary of North Carolina Biography*, s.v. "McKay, James Iver."

[6] John Reeves Jones Daniel, lawyer and congressman; A.B., U.N.C., 1821; A.M., 1831; member, House of Commons, 1831-1834; North Carolina attorney general, 1834-1841; member, U.S. House of Representatives, 1841-1853. *Dictionary of North Carolina Biography*, s.v. "Daniel, John Reeves Jones."

Holden to Hon. David S. Reid A&H:Reid

Raleigh, April 19, 1848

Hon. David S. Reid

My dear Sir:

I suppose, of course, that the committee to inform you of your nomination have written you, and that ere this you have received their letter. I have just received a letter from our mutual friend, Dobbins[1], of Cumberland, He is much pleased at your nomination. He feels assured that you will "run well," and he says he will "take care of you" in his part of the State. About a month ago I received a letter from Col. Biggs[2] espressing his desire to see you nominated, and, in addition to this, I *know* that your nomination has given universal satisfaction to the party. You will start with no enemies and no prejudices to encounter, and, if you follow Manly[3] up and hold him to the fires, you will defeat him.

We had a most enthusiastic convention. The Speech of Douglas[4] was the greatest popular effort I ever heard, and Houston[5] sustained himself well. the view taken by Douglas of the boundary question is *unanswerable*. Have you a copy of his last speech on the subject in the Senate? You will find it very valuable.

You will see by the Register that Mr. Manly has made his Eastern appointments, and is about starting on his campaign. Of course you will follow him up as soon as possible. Now is the time to visit the East. We hope to see you here at the earliest day possible, when we can talk the matter over, and you can make your arrangements more fully.

You have hard work, but a brilliant path before you. If you succeed, you will achieve a reputation second to that of no man in the State, and the Union will know you; if you fail, you will fail with honor, and elevate yourself in the estimation of your party.

Truly yours,
W.W. Holden

[1] James Cochran Dobbin.

[2] Asa Biggs.

[3] Charles Manly.

[4] Stephen Arnold Douglas, member, Illinois House of Representatives, 1836-1837; judge, Illinois state supreme court, 1841-1843; member, U.S. House of Representatives, 1843-1847; member, U.S. Senate, 1847-1861; unsuccessful Democratic Party candidate for president, 1860. *Biographical Directory of the American Congress, 1774-1971*, s.v. "Douglas, Stephen Arnold."

[5] Sam Houston, member, U.S. House of Representatives, 1823-1827; governor of Tennessee, 1827-1829; member, Texas constitutional convention, 1835; President, Republic of Texas, 1836-1838, 1841-1844; member, Texas Congress, 1838-1840; member, U.S. Senate, 1846-1859; governor of Texas, 1859-1861. *Biographical Directory of the American Congress, 1774-1971*, s.v. "Houston, Sam."

Holden to Hon. David S. Reid A&H:Reid

Raleigh, June 23, 1848

Hon. David S. Reid

My dear sir:

I have sent papers to you at different points, and hope you have received them.

Col. Biggs[1] and Judge Strange[2] have been here for a week, in attendance on the Supreme Court. They are both in high spirits, and think your chances of the best character. Biggs says his part of the State shall be throughly organized, and that the largest vote possible will be polled for you. The Suffrage question is still working well. We continue to hear of changes in your favor, but none from Manly.[3] In Chatham I learn that you will gain—in Johnston, Greene, Franklin, Granville, Orange, and I *know* in Wake. I am doing all I can. Busbee[4] and McRae[5] are *thoroughly aroused*, and will do their duty. The truth is, the enthusiasm is all on our side. The attempt of the Feds here to get up extra feeling for Taylor,[6] will signally fail. If we can only elect you, the State is sure for Cass[7] & Butler.[8] I send this letter to Asheville, and enclose a letter from Mr. Dobbins[9], the only one I have as yet received for you. Please write me from Ahseville, and let me know at what point to address you hereafter.

Rest assured that we will do our best for you here. If you continue to gain you will defeat Manly. God grant it!

Your friends here send their respects and best wishes. Go ahead! Hoping to hear from you soon, and wishing you good health and success I am Truly Your Friend,

W.W. Holden

[1] Asa Biggs

[2] Robert Strange, Jr., lawyer, judge, and senator; member, House of Commons, 1821-1826; judge, North Carolina Superior Court, 1826-1836; member, U.S. Senate, 1836-1840. *Dictionary of North Carolina Biography*, s.v. "Strange, Robert, Jr."

[3] Charles Manly.

[4] Perrin Busbee.

[5] Duncan Kirkland McRae.

[6] Zachary Taylor, twelfth President of the United States; appointed 1st Lieutenant 7th Infantry, 1808; breveted major general in War with Mexico; Whig Party candidate for president, 1848. *Dictionary of American Biography*, s.v. "Taylor, Zachary."

[7] Lewis Cass, unsuccessful Democratic Party candidate for president, 1848; military and civil governor of Michigan, 1813-1831; secretary of war, 1831-1836; member, U.S. Senate, 1845-1857. *Biographical Directory of the American Congress, 1774-1971*, s.v. "Cass, Lewis."

[8] William Orlando Butler, unsuccessful Democratic Party candidate for vice-president, 1848; member, U.S. House of Representatives, 1839-1843; major general of volunteers during war with Mexico. *Biographical Directory of the American Congress, 1774-1971*, s.v. "Butler, William Orlando."

Holden to [David S. Reid] A&H:Reid

Raleigh, August 6, 1848

My dear Colonel:

The ball opens gloriously! If you have held up and gained in the Counties to be heard from in proportion to these given below, you are elected by a signal majority. These are all we have as yet received:

	Reid	Manly
Wake	1293	991
Wayne	1089	260
Johnston	814	720
Lenoir	254 maj.	
Martin	546	339
Moore	499	294
Nash	900	65
Samson	692	530
Cumberland	1023	578
Franklin	638	290
Greene	100 maj.	
	7848	4067
	4067	
Hoke's majority in	3781	
the above counties	2821	
	960!	

What do you think of that? In Northampton you have beaten Manly[1]—what maj[ority] I know not. Graham[2] beat Hoke[3] there about 150 votes. We have gained a commoner and Senator in Northampton—one Commoner in Johnston—a Senator in Franklin—two Commoners in Orange—a commoner in Person; and we have lost a member in Granville, and two in Halifax. We gave you a *gain* of 109 here in Wake. At the Raleigh box we gained 50, and at this box you got the *highest* vote ever given to any Candidate for Governor, and Manly the *lowest*. Wake, Wayne, Johnston, and Moore have done gloriously. the rumor is that Manly has lost 100 in Chatham. A Telegraphic dispatch from Mr. Dobbins[4] informs us that you gained in Robeson and Bladen. In 48 hours more we shall know enough to say with certainity. Many Whigs here give up. You never saw such long faces and heard such groaning! Free Suffrage—beg your pardon—*equal* Suffrage is a humbug—is it?[5]

You have no doubt lost some in Warren and Granville; but if you keep on as you have commenced, you are certainly elected.[6]

I write in great haste, surrounded by excited and joyous friends. By the next mail I will send you nearly all the returns.

Truly Yours,
W.W. Holden

[1] Charles Manly
[2] William Alexander Graham
[3] Michael Hoke
[4] James Cochran Dobbin.

[5] Reid had agreed to accept the nomination on the condition that "Free Suffrage"—abolition of the requirement that only owners of fifty acres of property could vote for state senators—would be an issue. All taxpayers could vote for governor and members of the House of Commons, but more than 100,000 voters could not vote for state senators. William S. Powell, *North Carolina through Four Centuries* (Chapel Hill and London: University of North Carolina Press, 1989), 300-305.

[6] Holden's forecast of victory was premature, with Manly defeating Reid by 854 votes—Manly with 42,536 votes to 41,682 for Reid. Cheney, *North Carolina Government, 1585-1979*, 1399.

Holden to Col. Henry T. Clark DU:Clark

Raleigh, June 21, 1849

Col. Henry T. Clark[1]

My dear sir:

Your last esteemed favor came duly to hand. I feel much gratified that my articles on the Slavery question meet your commendation and the approval of the Edgecomb Democracy. The truth is, the hour has come! If we back now and again, as the Whigs unfortunately wish us to do, resistance hereafter, even for compromise purposes, will be impossible. So far as I am concerned I shall strive to do my duty. You see the Freesoil platform on which the Register and Times have placed themselves. They are looking ahead. They know, now more certainly after Benton's[2] infamous conduct and speech, that the Wilmot Proviso[3] will pass the next Congress, that Taylor[4] will approve it; and they are preparing the minds of their readers for it in time. What baseness—what humiliation! What treachery and deception! As a just God lives and disposes of the affairs of nations—as the American people possess common sense and reason, to say nothing of common honesty, such a course of policy must and will be blasted.

It appears to me, from all I can learn from various quarters, that our prospects in this State were never better. Caldwell[5] must, I think, Succeed; and Lane's[6] chances are of the first water. Person[7] *may* triumph, but that is more doubtful. Outlaw,[8] admitting as he does the Constitutionality of the Proviso, has a heavy load to carry; but then he has a strong majority to fall back upon. Of Venable's[9] election by an increased majority I have not the slightest doubt.

The death of Mr. Polk,[10] of which you have no doubt heard, is a very great calamity to the American Democracy. Judged by his deeds, as well as by his success as a statesman, which has been achieved by honest means, no man deserves to stand higher than he in history. He has left his mark, in characters which will never go out, on the age in which he lived.

I hope that by this time your health is restored, and that you will find time between this and August to give me some Nos. on the Slavery question.

Our town enjoys good health—neither, Small Pox nor Cholera among us. I should be glad to hear from you often

Truly yours,
W.W. Holden

[1] Henry Toole Clark, lawyer and governor; A.B., U.N.C., 1826; member, state Senate, 1850-1861, speaker in 1861; became governor on death of John Willis Ellis, 1861-1862; member, state Senate, 1866. *Dictionary of North Carolina Biography*, s.v. "Clark, Henry Toole."

[2] Thomas Hart Benton, member, U.S. Senate from Missouri, 1821-1851; member, U.S. House of Representatives, 1853-1855. *Biographical Directory of the American Congress, 1774-1971*, s.v. "Benton, Thomas Hart."

[3] Wilmot Proviso was a proposal added to an appropriation bill to provide funds to facilitate negotiations with Mexico and adopted in the House of Representatives that neither slavery nor in voluntary servitide would exist in land obtained from Mexico. *Dictionary of American History*, s.v. "Wilmot Proviso."

[4] President Zachary Taylor.

[5] Greene Washington Caldwell.

[6] William B. Lane, Randolph County; member, House of Commons, 1835-1841; member, state Senate, 1848-1855. Cheney, *North Carolina Government, 1585-1979*, 1248-1249.

[7] Samual Jones Person, lawyer; A.B., U.N.C., 1843; member, House of Commons, 1848-1850, 1854; judge, superior court, 1854-1858. Grant, *Alumni History*, 488.

[8] David Outlaw, lawyer; A.B., U.N.C., 1824; member, House of Commons, 1831-1834, 1854-1858; member, U.S. House of Representatives, 1847-1853; member, state Senate, 1860, 1866. *Dictionary of North Carolina Biography*, s.v. "Outlaw, David"

[9] Abraham Watkins Venable.

[10] James Knox Polk, eleventh president of the United States. He died in Knoxville, Tennessee, on June 15, 1849. *Dictionary of North Carolina Biography*, s.v. "Polk, James Knox."

Holden to Hon. D. L. Swain SHC:Swain

Raleigh, Aug. 1, 1849

Hon. D. L. Swain[1]

My dear Sir:

I regret the mistake in publishing Tables Nos. 1 and 2; but it is shown by their re-publication that the fault was "the Printer's." I sent slips of your letter of to-day to both the Register and Star on Monday morning, as early as they were ready, but I presume they could not well make room in their issues to-day. They will publish, however, and so will, of course, the Times.

Your letters have attracted general attention, and must effect much good to the cause.[2] I have heard them spoken of by numbers as able, highly interesting, and to the point. I trust, Sir, you will continue them.

Thus far, the subscriptions here to the Road are small; not more than $20,000. Wake county ought to subscribe at least $100,000. If we get $50,000, judging from present indications, we shall do remarkably well. There is a lamentable deadness here, in regard to it, so far as subscriptions are concerned. Men who ought to take thousands put down Hundreds; but we shall hope on, and therefore work on. The losses herefore incurred by our citizens by the Gaston Road, is the great drawback.

Very truly yours,
W. W. Holden

[1] David Lowry Swain, Lawyer, governor, and educator; member, House of Commons, 1824-1829; superior court judge, 1830-1832; elected governor, 1832, 1833, 1834; delegate from Buncombe County to 1835 constitutional convention; president of U.N.C. from 1835 to 1868. *Dictionary of North Carolina Biography*, s.v. "Swain, David Lowry."

[2] Swain was supporting the North Carolina Railroad from Goldsboro through Raleigh to Charlotte. Efforts were made to charter a road from Charlotte to Danville, Virginia, with a connection to Columbia, South Carolina. Eventually, a compromise was effected, and the North Carolina Railroad was chartered in 1849. Powell, *North Carolina through Four Centuries*, 288-290.

Holden to Hon. D. S. Reid A&H:Reid

Raleigh, June 1st, 1850

Hon. D. S. Reid

My dear Sir:

Yours of May 25th was duly received by last nights' mail; and you will receive this, if at home, on Tuesday morning.

I have read and *re-read* your confidential letter, but cannot, for my life, perceive that your reasons for declining are conclusive. So far as the Trusteeship is concerned, that argues but little. It is easy to understand how that was done. Hassell[1], was elected by his being an "iron-side" Baptist, and there being no such person in the Board, and the others were chosen because they were *here*, and they or their friends directly sought it. I know your friends, or those really your friends, stood by you. I regret that your name was even brought forward for it; and if the result had been foreseen, it would not have been. But this, I repeat, proves nothing. You are the strongest man with *the masses* ever presented to the people, and the leaders *dare not* oppose you, or even appear indifferent. I know it.

Just look, if you please, at the condition of things. Both the Mountain Banner and the Asheville News, Whig papers, are *pledged against* Manly[2], and for "State Reforms." Also, the Whigs of Buncombe, who have just had a meeting. In addition to this, I shall publish a Communication next week, headed "who shall be the Nominee?" and pressing your name from a well-informed Rutherford Democrat, who assures me that you will beat Manly in Rutherford 500 votes. John Gray Bynum[3] is running for the Senate in that County *against* Manly: and in Halifax and Granville the Whigs are disorganized, and cannot get candidates. Besides, Clay has just attacked Taylor[4] in the strongest terms, and Whigs in this State *must* divide between the two. Several Whig papers have already denounced Taylor; and next week the Raleigh Star will denounce Stanly,[5] the North State Whig, and the Raleigh Times, in the fiercest terms. These things, all together, may not indeed give you any *Whig* votes, but they *must* produce lukewarmness in the Whig ranks—divisions and heartburnings, which cannot fail to *diminish* Manly's vote. For the last two months I have carefully kept back from the Standard all evidences of Manly's unpopularity, in the hope that he would again be the candidate; there is now no doubt that he will be; and I have all these evidences filed away, to be used as soon as he is nominated.

So far as the Central Road is concerned, you have taken, in your letter to me, *the right ground, and the very ground which I have all along told our friends you would take*. Allow me to assure you that though Raleigh is for the Road, you are the first choice of every Democrat here; and Maj. Nixon[6] B. B. Smith[7], and others of our friends, who recognize the true ground in regard to the Rail Road, prefer you. They say, and truly, that your election, under the circumstances, could not injure the Rail Road Democrats, who have nothing more to ask in the way of appropriations, while it would give confidence to the anti-Rail Road Democrats, because they could trust you on the subject. Gen. Saunders, [8] I know, is warmly for you; and but a few days since he sent word to our friend D.,[9] by Judge Strange,[10] not to think of running, for that he would be inevitably and disastrously defeated. All the Rail Road men ask of you is, what you had written me. I know it. I can speak for them; and besides, being for the Road, I have a right to require them, by every honorable consideration, to sustain you. They will do it, almost, if not quite, unanimously. Again; If you will run, you are obliged to get the same vote, at least, you got last year west of Raleigh, and I think you will increase it. *Eight or ten Counties in the centre might have elected you before, by polling their full strength.* With you in the field, I shall call on these Counties by name, point to the vote , and *prove* to them what they can do; and I will address every leading man in them in relation to his duty. These leading men know these facts, and they will be *bound* to do their duty towards you.

It is not necessary that you should stump the State at all. You have done it once. You are universally known as Manly's former competition, *and as the author of Equal Suffrage*. All you will have to say, will be, that you and the Governor have already stumped the State once, and that, while you are willing to do it again, so far as the time will allow, *you await the movements of* "*His Excellency.*" This will throw the blame on him of leaving his duties here.

In regard to the Nashville Convention, that is a dead question. *I knew four weeks ago, that you were opposed to it*; or rather, that you thought it inexpedient now; but what of that? We are all for union at the proper time; and in going for it I but yielded to the will of the majority, and did not dream of proscribing any one. Saunders occupies the same position you do in regards to it; *and so does strange now.* All you will have to do, in this regard, if you accept, is to endorse the Resolutions of the Convention. In regard to Clay's Compromise and Taylor's plan, you need not advocate either; but you might say, if *compelled* to choose, that you would take Clay's plan. In your letter of acceptance, you might enforce Equal Suffrage—go for Judges, &c. by the people, and in regard to "State Reform" generally called for by the Buncombe Whigs, you might say that you were for "State Reform," and would, if elected, cheerfully co-operate with the Assembly in bringing it about. *Manly could not say that, without condemning his own party*, which has had the State government fourteen years.

You will see in the last Standard that a number of the Counties have called upon you to take the field. You are unquestionably the first choice of the party. At our meeting here, Mr. Shepard [11] offered a Resolution nominating you, which would have passed by acclamation; but Messrs. Busbee[12] and McRae[13] interposed. It was not withdrawn, however, until they had said that you were clearly entitled to the field, *and that they were for you, in preference to any one else*, provided you would consent to run. They opposed the Resolution on the ground that it would savor of Central dictation. If you run, Wake will do better for you than she did before.

I write the universal opinion of our friends here when I say you are, by far, the strongest man, and that your election is certain. I have not conversed with a single Democrat who speaks otherwise; and Whigs have told me you would certainly beat Manly. so far as I am concerned, I am for you against the world; and if you will consent to run, I will omit neither expense, nor labor, nor pains, so far as they will go, to ensure your success. I will publish the Standard twice a week from the convention until the election, and labor for you, *with an assurance of triumph*, day and night.

I shall withhold your letter intended for publication, until I hear from you. If you receive this at home, you can write me by return mail. I shall also drop you a note to Chapel Hill, by some friend going to Commencement; but if you received this on Tuesday at Reidsville, you can reply so as to reach me, at farthest, on Sunday night, the 9th. That would be in time for the Standard of the 12th. But if you receive this Tuesday morning, and then start for Chapel Hill, *be sure to come to Raleigh before you return.* Should you utterly decline to run, I shall, of course, publish your letter with a heavy heart; but I sincerely hope you will reconsider the matter, and agree to take the field. There are many things which I could tell you, if here, which would give strength to the views already advanced in this letter. All you have to do, as I wrote you before, is to allow us the use of your name, and to serve as Governor. Messrs. Wilder,[14] Smith-, Shepard, Nixon, and the entire party here, joins me in this appeal.

Hoping for a favorable reply, but your friend always, happen what may.

Truly Yours,
W. W. Holden

P. S. The Wake Resolutions I drew myself. They embody the very views you take about the Central Road. No reasonable man can take any other view of it. It would be madness to make either the Central road or the Nashville Convention a test. I have never done so; but directly the contrary.

During the last two months I have made it a point to converse with Democrats here from various parts of the State in regard to the Governorship. I suppose I have talked with not less than fifty. They *all* assured me that *you* were the first choice of the party in their respective sections, and that your election is regarded as certain.

I have now given you facts, in a hurried and broken manner. Think over the matter most seriously, and do the best you can for your friends and your party.

But what if you are beaten? Is it a disgrace? And if the time for a canvass is limited, or if there is no canvass, that is not your fault; your party made it so. But if you succeed, as you must, what an honor for a young man to redeem poor old Whig-ridden North Carolina!

Yours,
W. W. H.

P. S. again. If you consent to run, you can so inform me, and I can announce the fact in the Standard of the 12th, that though you are are not anxious about it, *you are in the hands of your friends;* and I can also authoritatively state the same to the members of the Convention.

W. W. H.

I have seen several friends since writing this. They all concur with me in opinion. for the first time in fourteen years, the Democratic party would go into the contest with *confidence*. They did not have this confidence. They did not have this confidence before, because they had been so often defeated, and did not know what you could do. While writing the Whig paper printed in Edenton has come to hand. The Editor, in pressing W. B. Shepard's nomination, says: "No nomination can be made which will be more unsatisfactory to the Whigs of this District than that of the present incumbent. It is not necessary to explain the causes of this dissatisfaction—suffice it to say, it *exists*, and *that to no small extent*." This is one evidence out of dozens, East and West, that I might give you.

W.W.H.

[1] Cushing Biggs Hassell, merchant, educator, and clergyman; merchant in Williamston, 1831-1837; pastor of Skewarkey and Spring Creek Primitive Baptist Churches; moderator of Kehukee Primitive Baptist Association from 1852 until his death; trustee of U.N.C.; local official of Martin County; delegate to 1875 constitutional convention. *Dictionary of North Carolina Biography*, s.v. "Hassell, Cushing Biggs."

[2] Charles Manly.

[3] John Gray Bynum, lawyer; A. B., U.N.C., 1833; A.M., 1836; member, state Senate, 1840, 1850, 1852; member, House of Commons, 1854. Grant, *Alumni History*, 91.

[4] President Zachary Taylor.

[5] Edward Stanly.

[6] Jere Nixon, probably Jeremiah Nixon, promoter of the North Carolina Railroad, progressive farmer, and promoter of the State Fair. Elizabeth Reid Murray, *Wake: Capital County of North Carolina*, 1 vol. to date, (Raleigh: Capital County Publishing Company, 1983), 1:261, 292, 295.

[7] Benjamin B. Smith, wealthy Raleigh merchant. 1850 U.S. Census population Schedule, North Carolina: Wake, 346 (microfilm).

[8] Romulus Mitchell Saunders.

[9] James Cochran Dobbin.

[10] Robert Strange, Jr.

[11] James Biddle Shepard.

[12] Perrin Busbee.

[13] Duncan Kirkland McRae.

[14] Gaston Hillary Wilder, lawyer and railroad president; A. B., U.N.C., 1838; A.M., 1843; member, House of Commons, 1842-1847; member, state Senate, 1854-1857; president, Raleigh and Gaston Railroad, 1858-1861. *Dictionary of North Carolina Biography*, s.v. "Wilder, Gaston Hillary."

David S. Reid to W. W. Holden, Esq. *Standard*
July 3, 1850

Reidsville, June 24, 1850

Sir: The Raleigh Register of the 22d instant, in relation to my nomination, and my vote on the Bill to establish a Territorial government in Oregon, applies the following language to myself and the Democratic party:

> "Yet they ask the people of North Carolina to cast their votes for a man who surrendered their rights and honor and opened the citadel to free soilers and abolitionists—aye, to sustain David S. Reid, whose name stands recorded upon the journals of the House of Representatives in favor of the same Bill with the Wilmot Proviso shining forth as its most prominent feature! What a monument of infamy to him is this vote, and what a moanument of inconsistency of Locofoism is his nomination!"

Now I pronounce the charge that I have at any time or in any way voted for the Wilmot Povisio, as *utterly false*. I desire this architect, who intends to erect a monument of infamy to me, shall be branded with his true character, that the public may understand him.[1]

When the bill to establish a Territorial Government for Oregon was before Congress, it contained a clause inhibiting slavery in that Territory. I had to vote for the bill with that provision, or against giving the people of that Territory a Government. although I believed that in entering in to the Missouri Compromise the South had conceded too much to the North, yet as that Compromise had long been acquiesced in, I did not feel disposed to disturb it; and being anxious to establish a Government for the protection of our citizens in that distant Territory, I, in company with a large number of Southern members, whom I know to be as ardently attached to the institutions of the South as any men in the Union, voted for the bill. Oregon lies north of the Missouri Compromise line, and the bill only inhibited slavery in that Territory. The Wilmot Provise inhibits slavery in the Territory both north and south of that line. This I conceive to be a broad distinction. Why did not the Editor charge me with voting for the Wilmot Proviso in the annexation of Texas? The annexation Resolutions contained a Proviso inhibiting slavery in that part of Texas which lies north of the Missouri compromise line. All the Democratic members from the South, and some of the Whigs, voted for these Resolutions with the Proviso, and they were approved by the Democratic party at the South. Yet, according to the Register, all who voted for or approved the annexation of Texas, were in favor of the Wilmot Proviso.

Very respectfully,
Your ob't. servant,
David S. Reid

To. W. W. Holden, Esq.

[1] Seaton Gales, editor; A. B., U. N. C., 1848; editor of the *Raleigh Register* from 1848 to 1856, when the paper was sold. *Dictionary of North Carolina Biography*, s. v. "Gales, Seaton."

Holden to Hon. David S. Reid A&H:Reid

Raleigh, July 7, 1850

Hon. David S. Reid

My dear Sir:

Your letters from Wentworth and Germanton were both received in due course of Mail. The information that Manly[1] had come out against the black basis, astounded us all. I wrote forthwith to Bayne,[2] Fulton,[3] Robinson,[4] and Gulick[5] and other friends. The Whig leaders in the East will deny it. I have written to Mr. Ruffin[6] at Wentworth, to have a statement of the fact made out and signed by Whigs and Democrats for publication. If the people of the East, Centre, and South, are convinced of the fact, Manly must lose thousands. Indeed, if he were to go to such Counties as Pitt, Beaufort, &c. and advocate the white basis he could not get one vote in ten in his own party. He must lose by it in the East, and it cannot affect you in the West. A baser demagogue than Charles Manly never lived. Give it to him.

Your address is well received. I have sent off a number of extra copies of the Standard containing it, and am now sending out the Address in all directions in handbill form. There are some ten Counties in this region that gave Mr. Polk 1000 votes more than they gave you. These votes you will get now. Manly's position on the basis will give you the full vote in Warren and other Counties. Your friends here are all confident, and doing their duty. I have got Clarke,[7] Shepard,[8] Nixon[9] and others to write to friends in all directions. The Feds are dismayed. They see the handwriting on the wall; and Manly's course on the basis question is regarded as evidence of his desperation. I shall *rake* him from this time forth in the hottest and heaviest style.

I learn that Clay has again denounced the President[10] and Cabinet as a "miserable Cabal," and held them up to the general scorn. We have had no Northern Mail for two days, but as soon as I receive his Speech I will send it to you. You can exterminate Manly on his endorse[ment] of Taylor's "line of policy" and the New Mexico outrage. The Feds here do not pretend to defend Taylor. They denounce the Cabinet, and are silent about Taylor. "Buenta Vista" has lost its charm.

You will see I have given it to Manly about his "negro Senators," and next Wednesday I shall have a list of charges against him which I shall keep standing.

Things are working admirably. You are obliged to beat him. There are Whigs here who give it up.

You ought to get 500 votes in Wilkes, now that our friend Stokes[11] and the volunteers are back; and I think you must gain considerably, even on your last vote, from Caswell to Ashe. You will gain at least 100 in Person—100 in Orange and Alamance—100 in Warren, and also in Franklin, Edgecome, Onslow, &c.

I shall write you next at Morganton, and send to that point your papers, &c.

Our friend Avery[12] writes me that Manly has made a fatal mistake in not going to Rutherford. It is best for you not to go there. You might stir them up and make them vote against you. Let the medicine work.

With my best wishes for your health and success.

I am Your Friend
W. W. Holden

[1] Charles Manly

[2] William H. Bayne, editor of *The North Carolinian*, Fayetteville.

[3] Samuel Fulton, editor of the *Argus*, Wadesborough.

[4] William Robinson, editor and proprietor of the *Goldsboro Patriot*.

[5] William B. Gulick, editor of the *New Bern Republican.*

[6] Thomas Ruffin, Jr., lawyer; A. B., U.N.C., 1848; member, House of Commons, 1850-1851; district solicitor, 1854-1860; superior court judge, 1861-1862; judge, North Carolina Supreme Court, 1881-1883. *Dictionary of North Carolina Biography*, s.v. "Ruffin, Thomas, Jr."

[7] William John Clarke, soldier and state official; A.B., U.N.C., 1841; A.M., 1844; major, Twelfth U. S. Infantry during War with Mexico; unsuccessful Democratic candidate for Congress, 1849; state comptroller, 1850-1855; Confederate army officer during Civil War; original commander of state military force, 1870; superior court judge, 1870-1874. *Dictionary of North Carolina Biography*, s.v. "Clarke, William John."

[8] James Biddle Shepard.

[9] Jere Nixon

[10] Zachary Taylor

[11] Montfort Sidney Stokes, military officer; naval officer, 1829-1839; officer during Mexican War; member, Council of State, 1850-1851; colonel during Civil War. *Dictionary of North Carolina Biography*, s.v. "Stokes, Montfort Sidney."

[12] William Waightstill Avery, lawyer; A.B., U.N.C., 1837; member, House of Commons, 1842, 1850, 1852; trustee, U.N.C., 1850-1857; member, state Senate, 1856, serving as speaker; reelected 1860; member, provisional Confederate Congress, 1861. *Dictionary of North Carolina Biography*, s.v. "Avery, William Waightstill."

Holden to Hon. D.S. Reid A&H:Reid

Raleigh, July 10, 1850

Hon. D.S Reid

My dear Colonel:

Gen. Taylor[1] died last night at 35 minutes past 10. His disease was Cholera Morbus. Of a truth "God rules in the earth as well as in the armies of Heaven!

Fillmore,[2] the Abolitionist, is now in the seat of Washington! I enclosed you his famous Buffalo letter, in which he goes the fill Abolitionist stripe. Gov. Manly will answer that he wrote a letter during the campaign, taking back his opinion in relation to the internal slave-trade; but he only said that, as the Supreme Court had found such a law unconstitutional, he yielded the right to enact it. He did not say that he had changed his mind and was *opposed* to such a law. On the other points, I am certain Gov. Manly cannot show that he ever said anything. He is an Abolitionist; and not only that, but one of the *champions* of Protectionism, and for a National Bank.

Manly's opposition to the Federal basis falls like a bomb shell on the middle and East. I wrote at once to Fulton, Gulick, Bayne, and Robinson;[3] and you will see that I have put the points strongly in the Standard today. The Register evades and denies. Your friends here are in the finest spirits. They regard your election as certain. Neither the Vagrant Law, (they used the same thing two years since,) nor the Oregon bill can affect you. The minds of the people are already made up. Manly also used the federal population matter against you two years since, and you nevertheless gained votes in the West!

The elements are getting hot here, but Whigism will collapse now,–now that blow after blow falls upon it, like an exploding steamboat.

Forward and onward! Your friends here will leave no effort untried, and you must succeed.

Yours in haste
W.W. Holden

[1] President Zachary Taylor.

[2] Millard Fillmore, thirteenth president of the United States; member, U.S. House of Representatives, 1833-1835, 1837-1834; vice-president of United Sates, 1849-1850; succeeded to presidency on death of Zachary Taylor; defeated for renomination, 1852; defeated as National American candidate, 1856. *Dictionary of American Biography*, s.v. "Fillmore, Millard."

[3] Samual Fulton, William B. Gulick, William H. Bayne, William Robinson, editors of newspapers supporting the Democratic Party.

Holden to Hon. W. N. Edwards A&H:Conway

Raleigh, July 15, 1850

Hon. W. N. Edwards[1]

My dear Friend:

I would have written you earlier, but I have been awaiting a letter from you or our friend Baskerville,[2] who was here a short time since. I am glad to hear that you are in the field in Warren, and from my heart I wish you success. I cannot doubt your triumph. I feel sure of it.

I sent you, a Mail or so back, a copy of the Raleigh Star, containing an account of the Salem discussion. I wanted you to have the facts in a *Whig* paper, so the Feds could not deny it. I assure you that Gov. Manly *has* taken ground in the next against the basis of representation. The account in the Star *admits* it, so far as the Senate is concerned, and it is notorious is in favor of distributing the School money according to white population. You have now an opportunity of turning your batteries on Manly with deadly effect. Col. Reid is *sound* on all these points. A Western man, he is opposed to touching the basis, and he is meeting Manly every day on these very points. He proposes what he regards as the right of all the voters in the State in a republican government—to vote for all the officers who sit upon their lives and their property—he advocates the *extension* of the right of Suffrage to the mechanics, the merchants, the artisans, and the business men generally; and he is then charged by Gov. Manly and the Whig presses as being *responsible* for *their* attempt to upset the basis of representation! As well hold the Christian Religion on the Blessed Goddess of Liberty responsible for the crimes committed in His name! Col. Reid stands now where he did two years since. His Address to the people of the State speaks for him.

If the Eastern and middle Counties poll their full strength, we shall *certainly* elect him. Warren gave Polk 810 and Reid only 630. The full vote will be out this time. Let me beg you to give him at least 800. That increase may elect him, and Warren, I am sure, will never regret the deed. He flings himself into the breach against Manly's wild and ruinious pro-positions—let Warren, ever true to the faith, and the glorious land of the immortal Macon,[3] show her devotion *to her own interests* and to Democracy now!

You will see I have published the Address of 1833, at Col. Little's[4] request. If I can serve you, or the course in Warren in any way, it will afford me great pleasure to do it. Whatever position you may occupy, nothing shall divide us; and I shall hail your election with as much gratification as if you were the strongest Equal Suffrage man in the State. It is no test of Democracy. We can agree to disagree about it.

Please to ponder on the hurried and very free manner in which I have written. Hoping to hear from you soon. I am, as ever

Yours,
W. W. Holden

[1] Weldon Nathaniel Edwards.

[2] George D. Baskerville.

[3] Nathaniel Macon, statesman; member, state Senate, 1781-1786; member, House of Commons, 1790; member, U.S. House of Representatives, 1791-1815, serving as speaker from 1801 to 1807; member, U.S. Senate, 1815-1828; presiding officer, constitutional convention, 1835. *Dictionary of North Carolina Biography*, s.v. "Macon, Nathaniel."

[4] George Little, Wake County; merchant in partnership with William D. Haywood in Haywood, Little & Co.; aid-de-camp to Governor Vance; U.S. marshal, 1845-1861; state commissioner of immigration; secretary and president, North Carolina Land Company. *Raleigh News*, November 3, 1876.

Thomas Ruffin, Jr., and others to Holden *Standard*
July 20, 1850

Wentworth, July 16, 1850

Mr. Holden—Sir: Understanding that it is doubted, if not denied, by some, that Gov. Manly in his Speech at this place came out in favor of the *White Basis* for representation, we, the undersigned, who were present on that occasion and heard him, do certify that he then declared most distinctly and unequivocally that *he was in favor of "abolishing the present black or federal basis and instituting a white basis in its stead.*" He called upon Col. Reid to know what were his views of this subject; to which the Colonel unhesitatingly replied, that he was opposed to any change whatever in the mode of apportioning our representatives, and especially so at this particular juncture. Gov. Manly then emphatically announced himself in favor of the change, and proclaimed that he was a better friend to *Equal Suffgrage* than his opponent.

Some whose signatures are hereto annexed are Whigs, and have therefore no wish to injure Gov. Manly or his election; but they deem it to be the duty of all men, be they Whigs or Democrats, to give the truth to the world whenever doubts have arisen in relation to the position and views of him who may be a candidate for office, and especially on a subject so intricate and important as this.

We heard Gov. Manly on the occasion referred to with our own ears, and are willing to testify to it; and should it be denied we pledge ourselves to produce the certificates of fifty as respectable men as the world contains.

We are not ambitious of appearing in the public papers, but should it be necessary in order to establish the truth, we consent that this may be published.

Yours, &c.
T. B. Wheeler
Joseph S. Robinson, Jr.,
E. W. Hancock,
J. W. Ellington,
T. Ruffin, Jr.

Holden to Hon. David S. Reid A&H:Reid

Raleigh, July 19, 1850

Hon. David S. Reid

My dear Colonel:

I write you in haste, under high steam pressure. The Standard for to-morrow is just out, and I send you some copies by this Mail. I fear that my Foreman made a mistake, and sent the bundles of the 13th and 17th to the wrong places—the 17th to Morganton, and the 13th to Asheville. I have therefore sent you, to-day, a copy of the 17th; and I have written to the P.M. at Waynesville to forward to Franklin in case you pass the former place before these arrived.

Our friend Ivey[1] came down from Rockingham, just in time, last evening, bringing me the "Proof" against Manly on the basic matter. The Eastern Feds were denying and swearing—and it falls, of course, like a bomb-shell in their midst. Manly must lose, to say the least, *hundreds* by it in the East. Leading Feds here admit his defeat in private conversation, and many of the Whig masses give it up.

The charge of Federalism against him stings his friends here, but I have *proved* it on him. If that was unpleasant, what will they say to the proof about the basis matter?

Go ahead! The glorious East will do her full duty. You will gain in Warren, alone, 200 votes—and the same in New Hanover, Samson. I have written largely to our friends, and expect to do more of it.

I could write you more, but the Mail is about to close. You shall hear from me again at Franklin by Sunday's Mail.

I regard your success as certain! Hurrah for—the "People's Candidate"!

Your Friend,
W.W. Holden

[1] Probably Stendon Ivey, a teacher in Rockingham County in 1850. 1850 U.S. Census Population Schedule, North Carolina: Rockingham, 107 (microfilm).

Holden to [David S. Reid] A&H:Reid

Raleigh, July 24, 1850

My dear Colonel:

A *private* letter has been received from Gov. Manly, addressed to Mrs. Manly, in which he says: "Tell Chas. (meaning his son.) he may assure Robateau (the Times Editor,) that the story about my having come out for white population as the basis for representation, is *false*. My views are set forth in my printed Speech, and I take no course inconsistent with the positions and declarations therein made." This is taken, word for word, from the letter. You will see that in the Standard of to-day I have used it against him. His son called to get me to state that his father *denied*, and I took down the words. I considered it best to pursue this course, as they would have raised a terrible cry of imposter, and have gotten, perhaps, some sympathy in the surrounding counties; and I knew the letter had been received, and a denial would be made to-day in the Register. His denial, made in *this* way, makes the case much worst for him. It exposes him to the contempt of his friends everywhere; and it would do him no good now, even if his name were signed to it, with explanations. Ten to one against him–impartial men every where will decide against him.

If you get this in time you can use the words, quoted against him, at Murphy.

Your prospects are still brightening. *All* our friends here are firm in the belief that you will be elected. I have not the slightest doubt of it; and I should not be surprised if your majority were between four and five thousand. The enthusiasm for "Reid" is greater in this region than it was ever known to be before for any candidate. A few days, however, will decide.

I will send you the returns as fast as I receive them. Please send me all you get.

Truly yours
W.W. Holden

P.S. I have mailed you a letter at Murphy. A request of James Fulton, Esq. of the Wilmington Journal. I presume it refers to the basis matter. He has the *proof*, however, before now, as it was in the Standard of the 20th. Now that Manly has denied, I have no doubt that our friend Ruffin[1] will produce his "*fifty*" men to confirm his statement.

Gov. Manly's letter is dated Wilkesborough. If the election were only two weeks further off, you could beat him still more disasterously.

I learn that our friends in Chatham are betting *on your carrying that* County, and also on Gen. Cotten[2] being, the foremost man in the Commons!

Gen. Saunders[3] is *raking* Manly on the basis question, and doing his best for you. The communication in today's standard, signed "Marattoch" if from our friend Col. Biggs.[4] He says you will gain 75 in Martin. Hurrah!

[1] Thomas Ruffin, Jr.

[2] Richard Carney Cotten, member, House of Commons 1816-1818, 1822, 1824, 1833-1836, 1850-1857; adjutant general, 1857-1859. Cheney, *North Carolina Government, 1585-1979*, 183, 1094.

[3] Romulus Mitchell Saunders.

[4] Asa Biggs.

Holden to Hon. David S. Reid A&H:Reid

Raleigh, Aug. 7, 1850

Hon. David S. Reid

My dear Sir:

You have swept everthing before you. It is indeed a triumph, glorious and unprecedented. The Standard of to-day, which I have sent you to Salisbury, contains all the news up to this morning. The vote in Craven, Onslow, Jones, and person, is as follows:

	R	M
Craven	541	609
Onslow	715	186
Jones	182	221
Person	577	329

In Carteret Manly's maj. is about 60. You can explain out the gains and losses for yourself.

Your majority cannot, I think, fall below 3,000, and it may be 4,000.[1] The Feds here are surprised and thunderstruck. We take it quietly, and just as if we expected it all along.

I should like to have time to write you more at length, but will do so when I think you have reached home. I congratulate you on the very high position you now occupy.

In haste, Yours as ever,
W.W. Holden

[1] Reid's majority was 2,744, with the final tabulation showing 45,058 votes for him, with 42,314 votes for Charles Manly. Cheney, *North Carolina Government*, 1585-1979, 1399.

Holden to Hon. D.S. Reid A&H:Reid

Raleigh, Dec. 1, 1850

Hon. D. S. Reid

My dear Gov:

No nominations have yet been made for Treasurer or comptroller. The Canvas called on Friday night was not full, on account of the rain, and one is called to-morrow night to decide finally. Hinton[1] and Collins[2] will both get some Democratic votes! Clarke,[3] I think, is *certain* for Comptroller, and Wheeler[4] is the strongest for Treasurer. If he should be nominated he will be elected. Though some of our friends—McLean[5] among them—"swear" they will *not* support him. It is impossible to say who will be Treasurer.

The Slavery Committee is still at work. I understand they have decided, by a vote of 9 to 5, that a State has a right to secede. It is impossible to say what will be done on this question. Two things, however, are certain, if action is had—The late "adjustment" will *not* be approved, and it will be emphatically answered that if the fugitive-slave law is not enforced, the State will take steps to dissolve. This question gathers danger every hour. Nothing but the Providence of God, which guided and shielded Washington, can save the present Union. I have just read the Message of the Governor of South Carolina. It is a calm, strong, *decided* document. He *dispairs*, but he does not say that south Carolina will or ought to go off by herself. He speakes of her destiny as common with that of her Southern sisters. He recommends a day of Humiliation and Prayers to the Almighty, for blessings and guidance in the midst of trouble, which has been opposed by the Legislature! You will come into office at a time of general anxiety, and heavy, very heavy will be the responsibility which you must incur. I have no doubt you will acquit yourself well.

Next week the two Houses will get fairly under way. I will write you again by Wednesday's Mail.

Mr. McGorman[6] at my request, will send you in a day or so, copies of the Treasurer's and Comptroller's Reports.

I have seen the rough sketch of the *next* Governor at Mr. Brown's[7] room. It will be a good likeness. Brown cannot be surpassed.

If I should get a copy of the President's Message in time, I will send it to you by Wednesday's Mail.

Truly Yours,
W.W. Holden

[1] Charles Lewis Hinton, member, House of Commons, 1820-1821, 1832; member, state Senate, 1827-1830, 1833; state treasurer, 1839-1843, 1845-1852; trustee, U.N.C., 1832-1860. Grant, *Alumni History*, 285.

[2] William F. Collins, comptroller, 1836-1851. He was defeated for reelection in 1850. Cheney, *North Carolina Government, 1585-1979*, 182,197.

[3] William John Clarke.

[4] John Hill Wheeler.

[5] Archibald D. Mclean, member, House of Commons, 1864-1865; member, state Senate, 1865-1867. Cheney, *North Carolina Government, 1585-1979*, 331, 332, 335.

[6] Not Identified.

[7] William Carl Browne, Jr., painter; travelled throughout the South painting portraits in the 1850's; after the Civil War, opened a studio on Fayetteville Street, Raleigh; credited with designing North Carolina state flag. *Dictionary of North Carolina Biography*, s.v. "Browne (Brown), William Carl, Jr."

Holden to Hon. D. S. Reid A&H:Reid

Monday Morning [Jany 7, 1851]

Hon. D. S. Reid

My dear Sir:

I ought to have written you last evening, according to your request.

You desired my opinion, finally, about the Boards. It seems to me, after some reflection, that it would be as good a plan as any to appoint Alfred Jones[1] and R. P. Dick[2] on the Litera[r]y Board, and put Mr. Bragg[3] on the other Board with Mr. Graves.[4] Locality, if the right sort of a man can be found, amounts to nothing. Dick and Bragg are both very suitable for these posts, and if you should prefer Dick, or any one else (a Democrat) from a distance, I know of no one of the Whigs of this County who would do better than Alfred Jones.

I have written this at your request, but hope you will do as it may seem best to you, without reference to my opinion. You know much more about the whole matter than I do, and have no doubt given to it a good deal of anxious consideration.

Your Friend,
W.W. Holden

[1] Alfred Jones, member, Council of State, 1830-1834. Cheney, *North Carolina Government, 1585-1979*, 175.

[2] Robert Paine Dick, lawyer and jurist; A.B., U.N.C., 1843; A.M., 1847; U.S. District attorney, 1853-1861; member, state Senate, 1864-1865; justice, North Carolina Supreme Court, 1868-1872; U.S. district court judge, 1872-1898. *Dictionary of North Carolina Biography*, s.v. "Dick, Robert Paine."

[3] Thomas Bragg, lawyer and governor; member, House of Commons, 1842-1843; governor, 1855-1859; member, U.S. Senate, 1859-1861; attorney general of the Confederate States, 1861-1862. *Dictionary of North Carolina Biography*, s.v. "Bragg, Thomas."

[4] Calvin Graves.

Holden to Hon. A. W. Venable SHC:Venable

Raleigh, April 16, 1851

Hon. A. W. Venable

My dear Sir:

Your esteemed favor of the 3d was duly received, and you will see that I have announced you in due form for Congress[1]. My position in relation to this District was and still is such that I could not say any thing Editorially, but you and my readers know what estimate I place upon your public course. I shall rejoice in your election, and shall stand by you amid all trials, so long as you stand forward, as you have done, for the constitution and your native land. You have richly earned your position, and long may you keep it in the hearts of your friends and in the eyes of the country.

My impression is, that Gen. Daniel[2] will have opposition. There will be no Convention, but in all probability Shepard,[3] Busbee,[4] or Wilder[5] will oppose him. Either would probably defeat him.

I fully concur with you in your views as to the Presidency. It is time enough yet; hence, I have been silent. We have this State, and by prudent management, we shall hold it almost indefinitely. Reid[6] is winning golden opinions, and constantly adding to personal strength.

With many wishes for your happiness, I am

Truly Your Friend,
W.W. Holden

[1] Venable was reelected to the Thirty-Second Congress.
[2] John Reeves Jones Daniel.
[3] James Biddle Shepard.
[4] Perrin Busbee.
[5] Gaston Hillary Wilder.
[6] David Settle Reid.

Holden to Hon. A. W. Venable SHC:Venable

Raleigh, Dec. 2, 1851

Hon. A. W. Venable

My dear Sir:

Yours of the 12th has been received, and would have been answered earlier but for the pressure of unavoidable engagements.

I confess I was surprised at the Caucus "Compromise" movement. the question has been settled! *The Union had been saved*, and behold the people's Representatives were called upon to come forward and save it again. The Union must indeed be cheap to be thus put in market and bid up and down according to the caprice and whims of ambitions politicians. I have read your letter with much attention, and also your Resolutions, which you sent me. You were right; and you can say to these "Union saving" gentlemen that there is at least one Editor, as sound a Democrat as ever trod the earth, who *never will*, so help him God, vote a "cheerful" acquiescence on that "Compromise." Portions of it I approve—portions of it I never will.[1] I will, however. stand by it for the sake of peace and the Union, and I will stand by it in good faith and in expressive of acquiescence in it, and binding our Northern friends to stand honestly by the fugitive slave law; but if a movement of this sort is to open anew the wounds of the country, or to be products of no benefit, why let it not be made.

You will see an article in the Standard of today in relation to the ensuing campaign. We have no occasion to be in a hurry. We are gaining by repose. Whigism here is in a dying condition—it will make a desperate effort next Summer, but it will avail nothing.

I am thankful that Foote[2] has left Washington. God grant he may never return! Such men have done us more injury than all Whigism and Federalism combined.

I am always glad to hear from you, and hope you will write freely, and especially when you have information of an important nature. The truth is you are the only member from whom I get information as to passing events. Rest assured that I am always what I was.

Truly Your Friend,
W. W. Holden

P.S. I wish to obtain the services of a reliable *Telegraphic* correspondent. Can you point out the man and get him to write me as to his terms, &c.?

[1] In regard to the so-called compromise of 1850, Holden had commented: "Our position in relation to the so-called 'Compromise' is known to our readers. We were opposed to the admission of California at the time she was admitted, to the Texas boundary bill, and to the bill abolishing slave trade in the District of Columbia; but we were in favor of the Territorial bills and of the fugitive slave law." *North Carolina Standard*, December 10, 1851.

[2] Henry Stuart Foote, member, U.S. Senate from Mississippi; elected governor of Mississippi, 1852. *Biographical Directory of the American Congress, 1774-1971*, s.v. "Foote, Henry Stuart."

Holden to Hon. A. W. Venable SHC:Venable

Raleigh, Dec. 29, 1851

Hon. A. W. Venable

My dear Sir:

Your last letter, mainly in relation to Kossuth,[1] has been received. I wrote you a few days since, but you had not received my letter when you last wrote.

I had written an article, before I got your last, which you will see in the next Standard. I have observed the extraodinary court paid to Kossuth by the Abolitionists; but so far as I could gather the facts from the papers, I could not see that they had acquired any influence over him. He has certainly borne himself with great shrewdness and tact. His intervention doctrine is, however, out of the question. We cannot undertake a crusade against Russia for Hungary, nor can we involve ourselves in European wars in behalf of any people. The feeling here is changing—Kossuth's proposition to involve us in war, is universally opposed. My article of Wednesday you may take as a fair expression of the feelings and opinions prevailing now.

You ask me who I prefer for the Presidency, Douglas[2] or Buchanan?[3] I like them both personally. I consider them both sound on the great question, and they are both good Democrats. As at present advised I believe this State will vote for Mr. Buchanan in Convention; if he should fail to get the nomination, I believe Judge

Douglas would be voted for next. This is, of course, mere belief. I believe either would be elected; but I do not think Gen. Cass, [4] Gen. Butler[5], Gen. Wood,[6] or Gen. Houston[7] would make much headway in the South. I do not expect to be a Delegate to the Convention, but only as spectator.

We shall carry this State next Summer, like a storm; and I think we shall be able to cast the Electoral vote for the Democratic nominee. Whigism here is sadly hacked. It will never make another successful fight.

This Kossuth business will all come right. He will return to Europe in a few weeks, and the feeling he has evoked will go to sleep until again aroused by an actual struggle in Hungary. We must keep clear of this war-feature. The people will not approve it. Judge Douglas took a good view on the matter. He went as far as it was prudent to go, and Gen. Cass went a little too far.

I shall always be glad to hear from you.

Truly Yours,
W. W. Holden

[1] Lojos Kossuth, Hungarian patriot and leader of the 1848-1849 Hungarian revolt; after the revolution was crushed, Kossuth visited the United States, seeking intervention. He received a tumultous welcome but very little money. When the enthusiasm waned, he returned to Europe. Thomas A. Bailey, *A Diplomatic History of the American People*, 6th ed. (New York, Appleton-Century-Crofts, Inc., 1958) 272-274.

[2] Stephen Arnold Douglas.

[3] James Bucnanan.

[4] Lewis Cass.

[5] William Orlando Butler.

[6] Fernando Wood, member, U.S. House of Representatives from New York, 1841-1843, 1863-1865, 1867-1881; mayor of New York City, 1855-1858, 1861, 1862. *Biographical Directory of the American Congress, 1774-1971*, s.v. "Wood, Fernando."

[7] Sam Houston.

Holden to C. H. Wiley SHC:Wiley

Raleigh, Dec. 29, 1851

To C. H. Wiley[1]

My dear sir:

Yours of the 14th has been received. I have read and reflected upon it, and must say I doubt the practability of your plan in regard to the Reader.[2] You would find, in the first place, that the Counties, after your offer had been made to them, would move with provoking slowness; and in the second place, the Literary Board could do but little if any thing connected with your work, unless authorized by law. Your true course, it strikes me, is to sell your present edition, prepare another with care and faithful revision, as you propose; and then await the action of the Legislature. That body, at its next session, will in all probability take five or ten thousand copies. You will have friends who will press the proposition, that is, to authorize the Literary Board to subscribe for the copies; and my opinion is the proposition will succeed. I can assure you that every member of the Literary Board, so far as I know, is friendly to your work, and would be gratified to see it in general use.

I showed your letter to the Governor,[3] and he told me he would write you soon.

Wishing you the most complete success in your literary labors, and all personal prosperity and happiness, I am

Your friend,
W. W. Holden

[1] Calvin Henderson Wiley, educator; A.B., U.N.C., 1840; A.M., 1845; member, House of Commons, 1850-1852; state superintendent of common schools, 1853-1865; trustee, U.N.C., 1874-1887. *Dictionary of North Carolina Biography*, s.v. "Wiley, Calvin Henderson."

[2] In 1851, Wiley published *The North-Carolina Reader* for use in the schools of the state. The reader was published in eight editions between 1851 and 1874. Powell, *North Carolina through Four Centuries*, 305-307.

[3] David Settle Reid.

Holden to John W. Ellis SHC:Ellis

Raleigh, Jan. 8, 1852

To John W. Ellis[1]

My dear Ellis:

Yours of the 9th December came duly to hand. I was glad to hear from you, and would have replied ere this, but for the pressure of numberless engagements.

Politically, things are going on handsomely. The Slavery question I regard as settled, but we have gained and will gain, in the long run, by our Southern Rights, or rather State's Rights position, which grew out of it. Strong government, and no municipal or State's rights, means, in Austria, *absoluteism*—here it means *consolidation*. The old fashioned Democratic Republicans of 1798-'99, have been, and their successors are now, the saviors of the public liberties and of the Union. When I say I regard the Slavery question as settled, I only mean to say that the "Compromise" is to be regarded as a *finality*. I agree with you that the agitation will be revived, and that Slavery is, in all probability, a doomed institution. Should this turn out to be the case, the Southern people will have themselves to blame for the result.

Your allusion to our friend Wheeler's book is received in the best possible spirit.[2] The truth is, I had no idea that the little criticism I indulged in would be particularly noticed, or that Wheeler would complain. He had done so, however, in strong terms. His book *has* merits, and is valuable—it ought to be in the hands of every North Carolinian. This I said in the article referred to, for the twentieth time: but then you know there is something due to the Press, as well as to History. It *is* inaccurate in style, much of it in bad taste, and but little good grammar in it. I spoke of all this tenderly, and with no disposition to mortify his feelings or to injure the sale of his work. It is useless for me to attempt to point out to you the defects of the work—you have no doubt observed them. I hope the Colonel will realize a handsome sum from his labors, and that he will receive all the credit he deserves as an author.

I should like very much to have a long chat with you, but I suppose you will not be here until the Spring.

We shall have a warm but decisive contest next Summer. We shall no doubt get the Legislature and the Governor, and then a hard struggle for Senator. *Who* he will be is difficult to predict, but my opinion is that Old Hunkerism will not "Come it." This is between us. I should like to see you in the Senate, but more of this hereafter.

W. W. Holden

[1] John Willis Ellis, judge and governor; A.B., U.N.C., 1841; member, House of Commons, 1844-1848; judge, North Carolina superior court, 1848-1858; elected governor 1858; reelected 1860. *Dictionary of North Carolina Biography*, s.v. "Ellis, John Willis."

[2] The reference was to John Hill Wheeler's *Historical Sketches of North Carolina, from 1584 to 1851*, published in 1851. In a review in the *North Carolina Standard* of November 19, 1851, Holden had stated: "It is due to candor to state that the style is, in many instances, inaccurate and defective, and that, in some respects, the best taste has not been displayed; but we are not disposed to criticize the work, or to find fault with the manner of its execution."

Holden to A. W. Venable SHC:Venable

Raleigh, Jany. 13, 1852

A. W. Venable:

My dear Sir:

Yours of the 6th has been received. You will see in the Standard of tomorrow an article headed "the Presidency," written mainly on account of what your last letter contains. I have heretofore published great deal in regard to Mr. Buchanan[1] and Gen. Cass,[2] and I was only giving Judge Douglas[3] a hearing. I was doing it solely for party advantage, and not for his advancement personally. I agree with you and Messrs. Ashe[4] and Clingman,[5] that my province is to support the nominee, if sound upon the great question; and to abstain scrupulously from expressing any preference. This I have done; but I must either publish speeches by Buchanan,

Douglas, and others, as they are made, in order to let my readers see for themselves where and what they are; or I must say nothing, so far as that goes, about them. The article to which I refer explains and embodies my position on the subject; and it is but a repetition of what I said some six or eight weeks since. I am obliged to you for the frankness with which you have written on the subject. The idea of "dictator" has no effect on me. I know what you have written was sincerely said, and communicated from the best motives. If friends cannot confer, suggest, and advise, there is an end to confidence between them. I think you will find that I will not commit any of our friends, or our party, to any particular man or direction. We have got Federalism now just where we want it, and if we make no mistakes, and if we should not be over-confident in our strength, we shall utterly demolish it.

Please do me the favor to show this to Messrs. Ashe, Clingman, and Daniel.[6] I have received the copy of the Globe you sent me, and will publish your Kossuth remarks in Saturdays's Standard. We do not entirely agree, but you are of course entitled to be heard, and shall be.

Could not our friend Cooke[7] act as a Telegraphic Correspondent? Or, if he cannot, please get some to write me on the subject, who will.

Truly Yours,
W. W. Holden

[1] James Buchanan.

[2] Lewis M. Cass.

[3] Stephen Arnold Douglas.

[4] William Shepperd Ashe, lawyer, congressman, railroad president; member, state Senate 1848-1851, 1858; member, U.S. House of Representatives, 1849-1853; became president of Wilmington and Weldon Railroad in 1854, serving until 1861; member of secession convention of 1861. *Dictionary of North Carolina Biography*, s.v. "Ashe, William Shepperd."

[5] Thomas Lanier Clingman, lawyer and political leader; A.B., U.N.C., 1832; member, House of Commons, 1835; member, state Senate, 1840; member, U.S. House of Representatives, 1843-1845, 1847-1858; member, U.S. Senate, 1858-1861; brigadier general in the Civil War. *Dictionary of North Carolina Biography*, s.v. "Clingman, Thomas Lanier."

[6] John Reeves Jones Daniel.

[7] Not identified.

Holden to John W. Ellis SHC:Ellis

Raleigh, Jany. 26, 1852

My dear Ellis:

Yours of the 12th has been duly received. You ask whether it is not best to postpone asking for the State's subscription to the N. C. road until after the election. I think so, decidedly. Some difficulty may arise; and even if there should be none, there are some in our ranks who are so hostile to the Road that the bare act by the Governor of subscribing, will either render them lukewarm or array them against him. By all means let it be postponed.

I concur with you, most heartily, in your Kossuth[1] views. I dislike the manner in which the Abolitionists cling about him, but he is not to blame for that. He has no part nor lot with them, having emphatically repudiated all connexion with parties or sects. The truth is, the Seward gang is the *smartest* gang North—that's the secret. They got the start in New York, and they seem likely to hold it. And "Gov. Seward"[2] is a great man in Washington City. Cass,[3] Houston,[4] Badger,[5] and others are on the best terms with him; and, after all, they abuse him only in the abstract. If he be indeed what they say he is, he ought to be avoided and treated personally as an incendiary and scoundrel. But Kossuth—what an Orator! How the heart leaps and the blood tingles under the influence of his rich and lofty tones! More than any man, living or dead, does he fill my idea of *Genius*. God prosper his cause—no other power can!

Douglas[6] is constantly gaining ground. He is *the* strongest man in some localities, while in nearly all portions of the country he is the second choice after either Cass or Buchanan;[7] and this latter presents him in his most dangerous attitude towards other aspirants. The nomination lies between him and Buchanan.

I was in dead earnest in regard to the Senatorship. Mr. Dobbin[8] will be held up to succeed Reid[9] as Governor; and Reid may succeed Badger in the Senate, but next time will be the great struggle, and some new man will, in all probability, be brought out and elected after a long fight among the most prominant aspirants. I believe you present more elements of strength than any other young or new man; and hence I wrote you as I did. I think we shall have to call on Jno. Hoke[10] after Dobbin serves his four years as Governor; but Mr. Dobbin *may* desire to be Senator, and if he should, he will stand a strong chance for the nomination. I think he will be here next Winter as Senator from his County. Your present position is certainly a safe and no doubt an agreable one—if you are patient you will go up higher on the Bench; but I would not advise you to leave it for any political office of less dignity or importance than the Senatorship.

Bragg[11] and Biggs[12] are both here, looking well; and McRae[13] and Strange[14] have just left. By the way, we had a *scene* here a short time since. Syd. Smith, [15] of Chatham—formerly of Orange—was here, drunk, and attended the Governor's Levee. For some cause or other he has a spite against W. H. Haywood, Jr.;[16] and during the Levee he attempted to pull Haywood's nose. He was quickly "hustled" out. Haywood bore it very well; but for a day or two after Smith went about swearing he would whip Haywood, and speaking of him as a scoundrel, &c. Haywood got a stick and went to look for him, and at Yarboroughs his son Edward joined him. While standing in Yarboroughs piazza or portico, Smith came out and advanced towards Haywood. Some words passed, when Haywood struck him with his stick, and his son Edward pushing him aside, collared Smith, threw him down, and choked him. Smith was then about half drunk, and had been so for a week. He was not hurt. His friends came for him and took him home.

The Governor's Levee went off remarkable well. Every one was pleased. He had a fine band of Music, and dancing till two o'clock.

Hoping to hear from you soon, I am

Truly Your Friend
W. W. Holden

John W. Ellis Esq.

[1] Lajos Kossuth

[2] William Henry Seward; member, New York state Senate, 1830-1834; governor of New York, 1838-1842; member, U.S. Senate, 1849-1861; secretary of state, 1861-1869. *Biographic Directory of the American Congress, 1774-1971*, s.v. "Seward, William Henry."

[3] Lewis M. Cass.

[4] Sam Houston.

[5] George Edmund Badger.

[6] Stephen Arnold Douglas.

[7] James Buchanan.

[8] James Cochran Dobbin.

[9] David Settle Reid.

[10] John Franklin Hoke, lawyer and legislator; A.B., U.N. C., 1841; captain, 12th U.S. Infantry Regiment during Mexican War; member, state Senate, 1850-1854, 1863; member, House of Commons, 1860, 1865; colonel, 23rd regiment of North Carolina Infantry during Civil War. *Dictionary of North Carolina Biography*, s.v. "Hoke, John Franklin."

[11] Thomas Bragg.

[12] Asa Biggs.

[13] Duncan Kirkland McRae

[14] Robert Strange, Jr.

[15] Sidney Smith, member, House of Commons, 1846-1847, representing Orange county. Cheney, *North Carolina Government, 1585-1979*, 315.

[16] William Henry Haywood, Jr.

Holden to Hon. A. W. Venable SHC:Venable

Raleigh, Feb. 7, 1852

Hon. A. W. Venable

My dear sir:

Yours of Jan. 26th has been received. You will have seen that I have published your Speech about the Census Printing.[1] I fear it will not do you any good. If delivered three months since, it might have been better; but there is a very strong feeling now among the Democrats for union and harmony; and besides, *the masses of the party do not know and understand, as we do, the position occupied by the Union newspaper.*[2] They look upon it as the organ, and though they have doubts as to the propriety of its course on one question, still they do not like to see it attacked. Take care of your constitutents, *of yourself*, of the South, and of the Union. We all live, more or less, by party; and you know from observation, when one loses hold upon his party, how difficult it is to regain it. I write this frankly, because I am your friend.

I do not hesitate to say, however, that *it is wrong* to give the Union the Census Printing because it is the organ, or is so considered. It would be wrong in the Whigs, and it is equally wrong in the Democrats. What! has it come to this that parties are to reward presses by giving them public jobs, at "reasonable" prices, without competition—is this to happen, and no voice to be raised against it? I would give the Union office the preference, but not the monopoly. If they would do it on as fair terms, and as well, as any respectable Whig office, I would let them have it; and I would do this because, all things being equal, I would stand first by friends. Of course I am not advising you, but speaking on the subject more in the abstract than otherwise.

You know my opinion of the Union on a single question. I have not changed it. It has uniformily persisted in declaring that Secession is claimed by its advocates as a "*Constitutional*" right, though it has been told a thousand times that it is wrong in so doing; and in addition to this it never has, and I suppose never will, tell its readers the difference between threatened Secession by South Carolina in 1832, and the abstract right as now claimed by Southern Democrats. But all this and more might be forgotten, if that paper would cease to puff that fellow Foote,[3] and Gov. Cobb,[4] and would let the Slavery question alone.

You will see that I have got a Telegraphic Correspondent. I do not wish a letter-writer.

Wishing you a smooth sea, and much happiness in your voyage political, I am

Truly Your Friend,
W. W. Holden

[1] On January 24, 1852, Venable delivered a speech in the House of Representatives objecting to awarding a contract for the printing of census material to the *Washington Union*, a Democratic newspaper. Holden reprinted the speech in full in the *Standard* on February 7, 1852.

[2] The *Washington Union* was a Democratic newspaper of which Andrew Jackson Donelson was the editor, 1851-1856; and Robert Armstrong was the proprietor, 1845-1854. *Dictionary of American Biography*, s.v. "Donelson, Andrew Jackson" and "Armstrong, Robert."

[3] Henry Stuart Foote, senator; member, U.S. Senate from Mississippi, 1847-1852; governor of Mississippi, 1852-1854; member of Southern convention, Knoxville, 1859. *Biographical Directory of the American Congress, 1774-1971*, s.v. "Foote, Henry Stuart."

[4] Howell Cobb, lawyer; member, U. S. House of Representatives from Georgia, 1843-1851, 1855-1857; speaker, 1849-1851; governor of Georgia, 1851-1853; secretary of the treasury, 1857-1860; major general in Confederate army. *Biographical Directory of the American Congress, 1774-1971*, s.v. "Cobb, Howell."

Holden to Hon. A. W. Venable SHC:Venable

Raleigh, March 10, 1852

Hon. A. W. Venable

My dear Sir:

You will have perceived that we are holding meetings in all parts of the State, and making preparations for an active campaign. The very best spirit prevails among the masses of the party , and I have no doubt we shall sweep this State and hold it for good and all, provided the action of the Baltimore Convention is satisfactory.

We hear rumors that the party is divided at Washington—that this and that portion of it is arranged against this and that man—and that, in fine, we are not likely to have harmony or success, if the leading men at Washington are to be relied upon to secure it. The "Union" cries harmony! harmony! day and night, and yet all the while its columns are teeming with allusions to Foote[1] and Cobb,[2] Quitman[3] and Davis,[4] and Jere Clemens,[5] and so on. If he desires harmony, *why not be silent, and let harmony ensue?* That paper reminds me of a bully on the Court-green, who rushes into the crowd, crying "men, don't fight!" at the same giving every man he meets a clip over the head. For the sake of the cause and of the country, let us have done with disputes, and make ready, as one man, for the *desperate conflict* that awaits us. Let the Union turn its battles on the enemy, and do execution there.

By the way, I see that Mr. Breckinridge[6] is quite severe in his remarks on Judge Douglas.[7] His defence of Gen. Butler[8] would have been better, if it had been *really* a defence, and not, as it is to a great extent, an attack. Evil and evil only can result, if we fail to harmonize; and the only sure way to attain this end, is to be silent as to the past, improve the present, and prepare to grasp the future.

Rest assured that I take a lively interest in all your movements. I do not assume to lecture you, but I am speaking generally, and I say what I *know* to be the feelings and wishes of the masses. I consider it my duty, as your friend, to keep you informed as to public feeling, and hence I write thus. Here is an iron determination in the hearts of the Democracy in this region to have no more strife and divisions, if they can prevent it, and to abide the action of the Baltimore Convention. That sentence embraces everthing. I should be glad to hear from you.

Truly Yours,
W. W. Holden

[1] Henry Stuart Foote.

[2] Howell Cobb.

[3] John Anthony Quitman, member, Mississippi House of Representatives, 1826-1827; chancellor of state, 1828-1835; member, Mississippi state Senate, 1835-1836; governor of Mississippi, 1850-1851; member, U.S. House of Representatives, 1855-1858. *Biographical Directory of the American Congress, 1774-1971*, s.v. "Quitman, John Anthony."

[4] Jefferson Davis, graduate of U.S. Military Academy, West Point, N.Y.; member, U.S. House of Representatives from Mississippi, 1845-1846; served in Mexican War; member, U.S. Senate, 1847-1851. 1859-1861; secretary of war, 1853-1857; president of Confederate States, 1861-1865. *Biographical Directory of the American Congress, 1774-1971*, s.v. "Davis, Jefferson."

[5] Jeremiah Clemens, member, Alabama House of Representatives, 1839-1841, 1843-1844; member, U.S. Senate, 1849-1853. *Biographical Directory of the American Congress, 1774-1971*, s.v. "Clemens, Jeremiah."

[6] John Cabell Breckinridge, member, Kentucky House of Representatives, 1849; member, U.S. House of Representatives, 1851-1855; vice-president of United States, 1857-1861; member, U.S. Senate, 1861; Confederate secretary of war, 1865. *Biographical Directory of the American Congress, 1774-1971*, s.v. "Breckinridge, John Cabell."

[7] Stephen Arnold Douglas.

[8] William Orlando Butler.

Holden to Hon. A. W. Venable SHC:Venable

Raleigh, March 26, 1852

Hon. A. W. Venable

My dear Sir:

Yours of the 16th has been duly received. Your letters always give me pleasure, and at a time like this they are especially acceptable. I find that we agree in the main upon the points touched in your last, but you seem to be under some misapprehension as to what I said about the Baltimore Convention. what I meant to say was, that the party in this State, so far as I could judge, would support the nominee, provided, of *course*, he be sound upon the fugitive-slave law and stand on the old platform. We are a unit in this State—every man is for harmony, conciliation, on honorable terms, and against further and bitter controversy as between Buchanan, Douglas, Cass, Butler, &c. But suppose Gen. Cass[1] should be nominated! and I judge he is gaining strength—what then? Undoubtedly the masses, that is the bulk of the party in this State, would support him. I should, though I should regret his nomination. His nomination would be your misfortune, not your fault. You understand me. You can do more quietly to avert this than you can publicly. *This* State will undoubtedly vote first for Buchanan, and next for Douglas; but I do not think it good policy to express a preference at our State convention. Judge Strange[2] will, however, in all probability, be presented as the first choice of the State for Vice President.

I see they have had a strong time in the Virginia convention. Wise[3] is for Buchanan as you know, and it appears he commenced the disturbance. No harm will come of it, however. I observe by the way, that Gen. Cass has had the bad taste to refer twice in the Senate, to the term "old fogy."

Our meetings are going forward finely—we shall have a full and enthusiatic Convention. Reid[4] will run, and will beat the field by from 3 to 5,000. Kerr,[5] whom you know pretty well, will probably be the Whig candidate. The Whig divisions on the Convention business may be patched up, *but cannot be cured*. The Feds will enter the campaign disorganized, and this will cripple them not only with reference to the Governor, but will ensure us the Assembly. With prudence and hard work the State is ours for years to come.

It strikes me, from all I can gather, that we shall have to call an extra session in the State to arrange the Electoral Districts. If the Senate Report should be adopted, and precedent should be adhered to, a called session will be indispensable. The Legislature might, however, be convened in September, so as to enable it to dispatch all the public business, and go home by Christmas. I should like to hear from you on this point. When will Congress probably adjourn?

Truly Yours,
W.W. Holden

[1] Lewis Cass.

[2] Robert Strange, Jr.

[3] Henry Alexander Wise, lawyer; member, U.S. House of Representatives, 1833-1844; minister to Brazil, 1844-1847; governor of Virginia, 1856-1860; brigadier general in Confederate army. *Biographical Directory of the American Congress, 1774-1971*, s.v. "Wise, Henry Alexander."

[4] David Settle Reid.

[5] John Kerr, Jr., unsuccessful Whig Party candidate for governor, 1852; member, U.S. House of Representatives, 1853-1855; member, House of Commons, 1858-1860; judge, Superior Court, 1862-1863, 1874-1879. *Dictionary of North Carolina Biography*, s.v. "Kerr, John, Jr."

Holden to Hon. A. W. Venable SHC:Venable

Raleigh, May 16, 1852

Hon. A. W. Venable

My dear Sir:

I must snatch time to give you an succinct account of our Convention.

We had 42 Counties and 102 Delegates. I never witnessed greater enthusiasm. Saunders,[1] Dobbin,[2] Rencher,[3] Dick,[4] and Reid[5] made admirable, telling Speeches and every man went home *confident of victory*. The Resolutions, I think, will please you.

The Delegates to Baltimore are all Buchanan[6] men, but Douglas[7] is their second choice. the feeling was nearly unanimous for Buchanan as the *first* and Douglas the *second* choice. I saw no Cass[8] men, but there was one or two ardent Lane[9] men.

I think Lane would be the *third* choice of this State. Edwards[10] beat Dick, a Douglas man, only three votes in Caucus; and McRae,[11] the President, is a Douglas man. No rivalry whatever between the friends of the different candidates. I expect to attend the Baltimore Convention, and shall therefore soon have the pleasure of seeing you. Should be glad to hear from you.

Truly Your Friend,
W.W. Holden

[1] Romulus Mitchell Saunders.
[2] James Cochran Dobbin.
[3] Abraham Rencher, lawyer and legislator; A.B., U.N.C., 1822; member, U.S. House of Representatives, 1829-1839, 1841-1843; charge d'affaires to Portugal, 1843-1847; president, Democratic State Convention, 1854; governor of Territory of New Mexico, 1857-1861. *Dictionary of North Carolina Biography*, s.v. "Rencher, Abraham."
[4] Robert Paine Dick.
[5] David Settle Reid.
[6] James Buchanan.
[7] Stephen Arnold Douglas.
[8] Lewis Cass.
[9] Joseph Lane, native North Carolinian; first elected to Indiana legislature, 1822; governor, Territory of Oregon, 1848-1850; Oregon delegate to Congress, 1850-1859; member, U.S. Senate from Oregon, 1859-1861; unsuccessful Democratic Party candidate for vice-president, 1860. *Dictionary of North Carolina Biography*, s.v. "Lane, Joseph."
[10] Weldon Nathaniel Edwards.
[11] Duncan Kirkland McRae.

Holden to Hon. John W. Ellis SHC:Ellis

Raleigh, June 16, 1852

Hon. John W. Ellis

My dear Ellis:

I found your kind and interesting letter among others on my return from Baltimore. I am obliged to you for the list of Subscribers. I have forwarded the papers, and herewith enclosed your recpts in each case.

We had a stormy time and a glorious issue at Baltimore. It would be impossible, in the limits of a letter, to give you any idea of the scenes. They were worthy, in every respect of the "unterrified and unconquerable Democracy." Our Delegation went first, of course, for Buchanan,[1] and afterwards Dick,[2] Caldwell,[3] Wheeler[4], McRae,[5] and myself did all we could for Douglas,[6] aided in a way by Saunders[7] and Dobbin;[8] but we found the combinations too strong for the present against the "little Giant." Venable[9] made himself conspicuous in our Delegation by his opposition to Douglas—he poisoned the minds of several of our friends, by his one-sided statements, against him. But the "new man" only awaits the current of four years—as that *presses* into an ebbtide he will roll in on the flood. Pierce's[10] location is the best possible on that account—next time the great valley of the Mississippi *will* be heard, and who but Douglas will tower then as now above all competitors in that noble region? Let Douglas, therefore, "suffer and be strong."

I know you will be pleased with the platform. The nomination for President was made about two o'clock on Saturday, amid wild excitement; an adjournment then took place to 4, when the Vice President[11] was nominated; and then at about 5 we had the platform. It was read in a clear, loud voice by B. B. French,[12] and when he came to the Slavery portion the hurrahs were tremendous and long-continued. That portion was called for again, again read, and then again we had the same end cries of gratification and Joy. Gen. Saunders then moved the "previous question"—it was put and carried; and then the vote was taken on the Resolutions *en masse*. The ayes were "like the sound of many waters," and there were eight or ten noes from among the Ohio Delegation, when occasioned general laughter. I write you this particularly, because efforts are being made by the freesoil and NY presses to produce the impression that the Resolutions were not adopted. These presses *know they are lying* in making these efforts.

I can assure you, as a friend and as a lover of the Union and the rights of the States, that, so far as I could Judge—and I observed closely and heard a great deal—*the vast majority of the Democracy of the free States are sound upon the fugitive-slave law*. I talked with the New Hampshire, Connecticut, and Pennsylvania Delegates; and they assured me they were in favor of giving us *all* our Constitutional rights; and having fought down the Freesoilers at home, they *demanded* as a measure of protection to themselves at home that the fugitive-slave laws should be endorsed.

I heard Soule[13] and Wise.[14] The former is a most accomplished orator, and the latter is a genius and talks like a thunderstorm, when fully aroused.

I heard from our friend Reid[15] at Elizabethtown. He was in good spirits; but we shall have to work, or rather *I* shall, as in 1850. The Feds are making desperate efforts and will resort to all kinds of rascalities; but the people—the farmers are fine, and *they* are the men whose votes tell at the ballot box.

But I tire you with all this. You will be here in July, when I shall have the pleasure of seeing you; and in the meantime I should be glad to hear from you.

Mrs. H. and family are all well;[16] and we hope soon to get into our new *Democratic* house, where I hope, time and again, to have the pleasure of your company.

Your Friend
W.W. Holden

[1] James Buchanan.
[2] Robert Paine Dick.

[3] Greene Washington Caldwell.

[4] John Hill Wheeler.

[5] Duncan Kirkland McRae.

[6] Stephen Arnold Douglas.

[7] Romulus Mitchell Saunders.

[8] James Cochran Dobbin.

[9] Abraham Watkins Venable

[10] Franklin Pierce, member, U.S. House of Representatives, 1833-1837; member, U.S. Senate, 1837-1842; elected fourteenth president of the Unites States, 1852. *Biographical Directory of the American Congress, 1774-1971*, s.v. "Pierce, Franklin."

[11] William Rufus Devane King, legislator; member, House of Commons, 1808-1809; member, U.S. House of Representatives, 1811-1817; member, U.S. Senate representing Alabama, 1819-1844, 1848-1852; minister to France, 1844-1846; elected vice-president of the United States, 1852. *Dictionary of North Carolina Biography*, s.v. "King, William Rufus Devane."

[12] Benjamin B. French.

[13] Pierre Soule, member, Louisiana state Senate, 1845; member, U.S. Senate, 1847, 1849-1853; minister to Spain, 1853-1855. *Biographical Directory of the American Congress, 1774-1971*, s.v. "Soule, Pierre."

[14] Henry Alexander Wise.

[15] David Settle Reid.

[16] Ann Augusta Young Holden died suddenly on June 20, 1852, survived by her husband and four young children. *Raleigh Register*, June 23, 1852.

Holden to Hon. A. W. Venable SHC:Venable

Raleigh, July 8, 1852

Hon. A. W. Venable

My dear Sir:

Your late kind letter came duly to hand. I thank you for the sympathy felt and expressed for me under my unutterable bereavement. I have realized for the first time that all words and forms of grief and unavailing; nothing sustains me, but a sense of duty to those behind, and an unshaken confidence in God and the assurance of meeting her hereafter.

If the President's message and accompanying documents have been printed, please send a copy to Capt. John Berry,[1] Chapel Hill. He has consented to run for the Senate, and wants an official copy of the last Report of the Secretary of the Treasury. I have written him that I would request you to send it to him.

I have no time just now to particularize, but will say, generally, that we shall sweep the State for both Governor and Legislature. I cannot be mistaken. All my letters are that way, and most enthusatically so. Clingman's[2] friends in the mountains are doing their full duty. We shall gain in both East and West.

By the way, one of the best documents you could send to the State now would be Toomb's Speech.[3]

I will write again soon.

Your Friend
W.W. Holden

P. S. Please say to Mr. Outlaw[4] that I shall do him the justice to make some extracts from his speech in the Standard of the 14th. Say to Daniel[5] and other friends to flood the State with documents; or to the Democratic Committee to do so. North Carolina's portions of money for the cause will be forthcoming in due time through our Committeeman, Mr. Buxton.[6] If I had documents *already franked, I could send them from this point to great advantage*. Please attend to this.

W. W. Holden

[1] John Berry, builder and politician; member, state Senate, 1848-1852, 1864-1866; member, House of Commons, 1862; member of the Orange Guards, after which the title "Captain" was always given him. *Dictionary of North Carolina Biography*, s.v. "Berry, John."

[2] Thomas Lanier Clingman.

[3] Robert Augustus Toombs, lawyer; member, U.S. House of Representatives, representing Georgia, 1847-1853; member, U.S. Senate, 1853-1861; brigadier general, Confederate States army, 1861-1863. *Biographical Directory of the American Congress, 1774-1971*, s.v. "Toombs, Robert Augustus."

[4] David Outlaw.

[5] John Reeves Jones Daniel.

[6] Ralph Potts Buxton, lawyer; A.B., U.N.C., 1845; trustee, U.N.C., 1868, 1879-1887; superior court judge, 1865-1880; unsuccessful Republical Party candidate for governor, 1880. *Dictionary of North Carolina Biography*, s.v. "Buxton, Ralph Potts."

Holden to Hon. Thomas Settle SHC:Settle, Sr.

Raleigh, July 13, 1852

Hon. Thomas Settle[1]

My dear sir:

Your esteemed favor of the 29th June was duly received. My sorrow for the death of my dear wife may be mitigated, but not forgotten. The performance of duty will, however, relieve my mind of the pressure upon it; and my hope as to the life hereafter will make this appear short, and the years as they pass not altogether dreary, because of the blessed relaities to which, I humbly trust, they may bear me and the dear children; for, after all, the next is the *real* life, and this but a realm of uncertainities and shadows.

I have not heard from our friend Gov. Reid[2] for a week or so, but expect a letter by to-night's mail. His prospects here, and in the East are good and brightening. I entertain *no* doubt of his triumphant re-election. I hear constantly of Democratic or Reid or Pierce gains, but of no Casses.

Be pleased to say to my friend, Mrs. Reid, that her kind and consoling letter was received, and read with mournful pleasure. Say to her that the children are well; and that little *Etta* is especially hearty, and grows rapidly. Sally is very attentive to her, and appears to be strongly attached to her. She has an abundance of milk for both children.[3]

Be pleased, Sir, to present my respectful regards to your family, and acept asssurance of my high esteem.

W. W. Holden

[1] Thomas Settle, lawyer and judge; member, House of Commons, 1816, 1826-1827; speaker, 1827; member, U.S. House of Representatives, 1817-1821; superior court judge, 1832-1854. *Dictionary of North Carolina Biography*, s.v. "Settle, Thomas."

[2] David Settle Reid.

[3] Four small children survived their mother's death: Laura, Joseph William, Ida Augusta, and Henrietta. Henrietta, an infant, was named for Mrs. David S. Reid and was usually referred to as Etta.

Holden to Hon. D. S. Reid A&H:Reid

Raleigh, Aug. 10, 1852

Hon. D. S. Reid

My dear Sir:

Knowing your anxiety to hear from the elections, I drop you some items in relation thereto. We have Heard from the Counties of Caswell, Person, Granville, Bertie, Hertford, Northampton, Craven, Jones, Richmond, Lenoir, Greene, Martin, Brunswick, Iredell, Stanly, Washington, Pasquotank, Perquimins, Chowan, Davidson, Davie, Duplin, Edgecombe, Franklin, Guilford, Halifax, Johnston, Lincoln, Moore, Mecklenburg, Nash, New Hanover, Onslow, Orange, Pitt, Robeson, Rowan, Rutherford, Randolph, Sampson, Surry, Forsyth, Wake, Warren, Wayne—54 in all. In these Counties Mr. Kerr[1] gains, 2,107, and you gain 3,300, making your clear gain 1,193. Your majority, I think, must reach 5,000. You have lost but 52 votes in Washington—Reid 297, Kerr 247; and we have saved the Commoner, Phelps,[2] in that County. You have gained 78 in Chowan, 16 in Perquimins, and 70 in Gates. You have gained 109 in Richmond, 89 in Iredell, and 63 in Jones, and lost 68 in Stanly, 28 in Brunswick, and 31 in Pasquotank, and 10 in Greene. These are returns not included in those of the Standard, which you will receive by this mail. I will keep this letter open until we receive the Western Mail to-night, Tuesday.

You will see you have lost in Caswell. I am glad Mr. Williamson[3] is beaten. In Person we have lost a Commoner,[4] and there is no doubt of a loss in Perquimins and Chowan. Wilson[5] was beaten 11 votes and Johnson 32.[6] If we have lost in Wilkes and Buncombe, we shall be in a bad box, unless we have gained in Carteret, or Caldwell, or Davie, or Macon. The Whigs claim a loss of two in Surry, which I doubt, and also two in Stokes, which is highly improbable. Dr. Mills,[7] you will see, is beaten. We have no news from Camden and Currituck, but I have my fears. Craven and Jones have done nobly; but our losses in Johnston, Orange, and Lincoln, and Person, to say nothing of Bladen and Robeson, are totally inexcusable. The rumor here is that we have gained a Commoner in Tyrrell! The Commons is in great doubt, but we are sure of the Senate by four, and quite sure, I think, of a majority on joint ballot.[8]

Your triumph is indeed a brilliant one. The Feds here, who were so bitter but a few days ago, now hang their heads and say Free Suffrage did it. They have been foiled only for the moment. Politically, they deserve no quarter.

By the way, I made another good guess as to the Wake vote, though I did not publish it. Several days before the election I made out the supposed vote for yourself, Kerr, Saunders, Wilder, and Allen.[9] I gave you 1560 votes in Wake—you got 1561, but I missed considerably in every other calculation. I gave Kerr, for instance, 1043—he got 1102. The Sheriff's election came in one of defeating us generally in the County. But for that I feel sure we should given you 100 gain.

I am worn down and exhausted by the labors of the campaign, but I shall get better as soon as I can get enough sleep. My children are well, and little *Etta Reid* especially. She has not been sick an hour.

Your friends here expect you soon, and will be glad to see you. Please let me know what day you will arrive.

Please present my kindest regards to Mrs. Reid and Judge Settle's family, and accept for yourself, Sir, assurances of my unalterable attachment and friendship.

Yours,
W. W. Holden

P.S. Our news by the Western Mail is not so full as I expected. We have lost a Commoner in Wilkes, also in Buncombe—also in Stokes. Joel F. Hill[10] beaten. No news from Caldwell or Macon; we have not gained in Davie. You have lost 43 in Stokes, 21 in Cabarrus, and your loss in Surry is not 291, as first reported, but 165. Your clear gain is still 1200, not counting Buncombe, where it is thought you have gained over 200. The news from the great West comes in with provoking slowness. I fear we have lost the Legislature on joint ballot. As matters now stand, we have certainly lost the Commons.

Yours,
W. W. Holden

[1] John Kerr, Whig candidate for governor.

[2] Charles Phelps, Washington County; member, House of Commons, 1833-1835, 1852. Cheney, *North Carolina Government*, 1585-1979, 301, 302, 322.

[3] George Williamson, Caswell County; member, state Senate, 1850-1851, 1874-1875, 1879-1880. Cheney, *North Carolina Government*, 1585-1979, 1088.

[4] Charles S. Winstead, Person County; member, House of commons, 1850-1851, 1881; member, state Senate, 1860-1861, 1864-1866, 1868-1870. Cheney, *North Carolina Government*, 1585-1979, 1241-1242.

[5] Thomas Wilson, Perquimans County; member, House of Commons, 1850-1851; member of 1865 constitutional convention. Cheney, *North Carolina Government*, 1585-1979, 832, 1239.

[6] L. J. Johnson, Chowan County, Democrat, defeated by Hugh Collins, Whig, by 32 votes. *North Carolina Standard*, August 16, 1852.

[7] Columbus Mills, Rutherford County; member, state Senate, 1846-1847, 1854-1857, but defeated by John G. Bynum in 1852; member council of state, 1852-1854, 1858-1860. *Dictionary of North Carolina Biography*, s.v. "Mills, Columbus."

[8] The final vote showed the state Senate composed of 28 Democrats and 22 Whigs; while the House of Commons had 58 Democrats and 62 Whigs. On a joint ballot by means of which all officials were elected, there were 86 Democratic votes and 84 Whig votes. *North Carolina Standard*, August 18, 21, 1852.

[9] Romulus Mitchell Saunders, Gaston Hillary Wilder, and W. A. Allen were elected to the House of Commons in Wake County.

[10] Joel F. Hill, Stokes County; member, House of Commons, 1854-1859, Cheney, *North Carolina Government*, 1585-1979, 1275.

Holden to Hon. A. W. Venable SHC:Venable

Raleigh, Aug. 11, 1852.

Hon. A. W. Venable

My dear Sir:

You will find in the Standard of today all the returns, except a few items which I now give you. We have a rumor that we have a commoner in Tyrrell, and contrary to my calculations, the Whigs have just admitted that we have gained a Commoner in Carteret. I am afraid this latter is too good to be true. I received a letter by the last mail, from Thos. J. Pasteur,[1] giving up the Commoner in that County. The Whigs have thus far gained 16 and we 8. If we have gained in Cartaret, or in Tyrrell, or in Beaufort and Hyde, as rumored—or in Currituck and Camden, or in Macon or Caldwell, we shall tie them on Joint ballot; if not in these counties, we shall not on Joint ballot, &c. At any rate, *we have them* in my opinion, in any event, for if pressed we can fall back on the anti-Scott Whig members elect. We shall know all about it in a few days. The returns in this State come in, as you are aware, with provoking slowness. I intended to print an extra this morning with the final results, but the returns were so confused and doubtful, and withal so unsatisfactory in some respects that I concluded to postpone it. You will see that we have lost the Assembly, if at all, by bad management in *Democratic* Counties! Person, Lincoln, Bladen, Robeson, Johnston, Orange—such Counties electing Whigs!

Reid's election is sure by from four to five thousand majority. His clear gains, thus far, is some 1200 in 56 Counties, the heavy loss in Rutherford included.

Please show this to our friends in Washington.

Truly Yours,
W. W. Holden

P.S. I have no news from Buncombe, but fear Erwin[2] is beaten for the Senate.

We are certain of the Senate by at least 4 majority. This will give us a strong check as to the Senatorial and Congressional Districts; and no Scott Whigs whatever the result may have been, can be elected to the U.S. Senate.

[1] Thomas Jefferson Pasteur, Craven County; member, state Senate, 1835, 1840-1845; collector of customs at New Bern, 1845-1849. Grant, *Alumni History*, 476.

[2] Marcus Erwin, Buncombe County, lawyer; member, House of Commons, 1850-1851, 1856-1857; member, state Senate, 1860-1861. Cheney, *North Carolina Government*, 1585-1979, 1070-1071.

H. G. Spruill to Holden A&H:Holden

Plymouth. Oct. 29, 1852

W. W Holden

My dear Sir:

On my way from Raleigh I was attacked with chills & fever, which lasted for sometime—I have, until within a few days, been so unwell as to attend to but little business; which is the excuse I will offer for not complying with your request, at an earlier period.

You requested me to give my views of the value & extent of the swamp land owned by the Literary Board. As regards the reclaimed lands owned by the Board & represented on the plat in the Executive Office, no correct estimate, under present circumstances, can be formed of their value, or availability as funds. Experience has taught me, that the policy of draining Swamp Lands by the State, unaided by private capital & enterprise, is, at best a doubtful one. That a large portion of these lands are very valuable, there is no doubt. They are covered with the finest growth of timber, (juniper & principally cypress) which is now becoming scarce & in demand, and after the Cypress timber is off, will be more valuable for clearing, because more easily cleared. The fertility of the soil cannot be doubted, indeed, it cannot be excelled, by the lands around any of the adjacent lakes. Another portion of these lands, is called priarie, having no timber, & originally no growth of any kind. Its adaptation to agricultural purposes has been doubted by many experienced persons. These lands are certainly under going a change, being now, I learn, covered with a fine thrifty growth, which has sprung up since the Canals were cut. My opinion is that these will be valuable, in a few years.

I have remarked that, no estimate could be formed of the availability as funds, of these lands, *under present circumstances*. I will now proceed to give the reasons. 1st The value of the timber & the value of the Land for agricultural purposes is admitted by all; and the land would be sought for & purchased at its value; but a portion of best timbered land, is claimed by the Albemarle Land Company, and buyers are deterred from purchasing by the fear of litigated suit, with an established & wealthy company. The claim set up by this company is not believed to be a valid one, and the Literary Board have determined to take the proper steps to test the title.

2nd As regards the selling these lands for agricultural purposes. Even after the main Canals have been cut, it requires much labor & expense to bring the lands into cultivation; and while there is such a demand for the labor of able bodied negro men, in getting timber, & working on Rail Roads, as now exists, & must exist for several years to come, it is not probable that those commanding such labor, will devert it from these profitable employments to clearing Swamp lands

When the title to these lands shall have been settled; when the tide of emigration, (which for a few years has been checked) shall have ceased to rob our state of its energy & wealth; when the timber in the Swamps, shall have been worked up (& it cannot last very many years longer); and when our negro population shall have increased, to the amount it must increase in a few more years; then, these, and all the Swamp lands susceptible of drainage must be brought under the hand of the Cultivator. The high lands are nearly all cleared up and much of it worn out; labor must be employed; & these lands must open the only field which this section of the state presents.

By the Act of 1836, all the Swamp lands in the State are conveyed to the President & Directors of the Literary Fund. The construction placed on this act; (& doubtless the correct one) vests in the Board *all* the Swamp lands, as well those unreclaimed, by the Board, as those that are. Prior to this act these lands were subject to entry at 10 & 5 cents per acre. The amount & value of these lands I have no data to form an opinion from—nor do I believe it possible to form any correct or well defined opinion of them. The labor exposure, & expense of these Swamp surveys, is very heavy. All these lands are generally supposed to be covered by old Patents (many of which are not well defined). There is no way of arriving at any conclusion, about their extent or value, except by surveying out all these old Patents, which would cost more than the lands would be worth.

Conflicting interests among the owners of these Patents, often exposes, the want of title to pieces or portions of these swamps. Surveys are made, by the owners of these conflicting titles, and, as many of these old patents, were not made on actual survey, & as many of them were a much larger quantity of Land, than the number of acres purchased from the State; there, is, not unfrequently, found parcels not covered by old Patents.

Frequent applications were made to the Literary Board to purchase these parcels of Swamp land; and, as a means of preventing, any fraud, & to ensure uniformity, the Board adopted & published a set of regulations for the sale of them.

Actual survey must be made—the land must be valued by competent and disinterested judges, to be appointed by the Clerks of the County Courts, and the valuation to be made on oath, before a Justice of the Peace or Clerk. It was believed, that by adopting this plan the interest of the Board would be protected & no land sold for less than its nominal value. No sale, of any of these Swamp lands, has been made by the board, except when these regulations have been strictly complied with.

In pursuance of an act passed at the Session of 1850-51, Entitled "An Act concerning a Turnpike road from Lake Pungo to the Town of Plymouth in Washington County" The Board proceeded, to let out, at public auction, before the Court House Door in the Town of Plymouth, on the 2nd day of October 1851 the building of said Road—The sum of $5000 was appropriated, and the Board entered into a contract with Charles Latham,[1] H. H. Waters[2] & J D Windley,[3] to build 6 1/4 miles and 5 yards of said road, for the sum appropriated, ($5000), which was the last bid, made therefor. The contract was thought, at the time to be a very favorable one for the Board, and the accounts of the contractors shew that they have suffered a heavy loss by it. The contractors have reported to me that they have finished the Road, and have discharged there hands, (which indeed they were compelled to do, by the lateness of the season). I have been in hopes that my health would permit me to go & examine it, but I find that I am not able to go, and have today appointed some gentlemen of high character, & in whose judgment & honesty I can rely, to go examine the Road, and report to me, I expect, in a few days to present to his excellency & the Board, the final report. The contractors will want their money.

The whole road by actual survey made by J. T Phelps,[4] including the road from the head of the Pungo River road is 9 1/4 miles The length of the Road contracted for & made by Messr Latham, & Co is 6 1/4 miles & 5 yards (say 6 1/4 [miles] which leaves to be made—3 miles) The work that has been done will be valueless, without the road is completed and the expenditure of $5000 will be thrown away. The several Acts & Resolutions which have been passed by the Legislature, shew that the object was to complete the road, in order to afford accessibility to the public lands—To stop now would be worse than folly—by finishing the work, one of the great obstacles in the way of the sale of these lands will be removed, as they will be easily got to, & entirely accessible; and a great public work will have been accomplished, which will be of vast benefit to those visiting these lands, & the public at large—

All the Acts passed on the subject, seem to contemplate that these improvements shall be made by the funds from the sale of these lands—The following statement will shew that there are funds in hand from the sale of these lands, to complete the Road

By statement on the Journal of the Board made 22 Aug 1851 it appears, that, there had been sold of the swamp lands in May /47 to the Amt with Int recd. of $6724.51

And in June 1849	3581,91
	$10306.42
There had been expended on Road, (route around the Lake, found to be impracticable & abandoned	3268,75
	$7037.67
Amt for Pungo Road, under Act of 1850	5000.00
Ral. on hand-	$2037.67
There has been sold by the Board of other Swamp lands, since 1 Oct 1851—to the amt of	1221.67

There are large bodies of land, which have been reclaimed, or vastly benefited, by the Canal & road, and I submit, whether under the 8th Section of 67 Chapter of the Revised Statute, those lands ought not to be assessed. This cannot properly be done, before the Road is finished—An equtable contribution would afford enough to complete the Road or nearly so—

I submit *whether his Excellency should not recommend, in the Report, an appropration to complete the Road*.

I have, my dear sir, thrown together, in rather a desultory manner my veiws of that portion of the duty of the Board, which has come under my supervision—If you can gather any thing from them to aid you I shall be gratified—

I am ashamed of the length of my communication.

I have the honor to be
very Resy
H. G. Spruill[5]

[1] Charles Latham, Washington County sheriff. 1850 U.S. Census Population Schedule, North Carolina: Washington, 106 (microfilm).

[2] Hardy H. Waters, Washington County farmer. 1860 U.S. Census Population Schedule, North Carolina: Washington, 069 (microfilm).

[3] Jacob D. Windley, Washington County farmer. 1850 U.S. Census Population Schedule, North Carolina: Washington, 071 (microfilm).

[4] John T. Phelps, local surveyor in Washington County. State Board of Education, Literary Fund, Minutes, Letters, Reports, etc., 1848-1853, September 24, 1852, North Carolina State Archives.

[5] Hezekiah G. Spruill, member, Literary Board; member, House of Commons, representing Tyrrell County, 1831-1832; member, state Senate, representing Tyrrell County, 1836-1843; member, 1835 constitutional convention; Washington County planter. State Board of Education, Literary Fund, Minutes, letters, Reports, etc., 1848-1853, April 18, 1851, North Carolina State Archives; Cheney, *North Carolina Government, 1585-1979*, 1289; 1850 U.S. Census Population Schedule, North Carolina: Washington, 101 (microfilm).

Holden to T. Settle, Jr., Esq. SHC:Settle, Jr.

Raleigh, June 18, 1853

My dear friend:

I trust you will pardon me for not writing you before this. I was much obliged to you for your sketch of the discussion between Boyd[1] and Puryear.[2] I received a letter by the last Mail from Boyd. He is aroused and in good spirits. Judging from the tone of his letter he must be elected. It will be very important to get out a full vote in Rockingham. Dr. Shaw's[3] prospects are not so good as Boyd's, but he may nevertheless be elected. Leeke[Leake][4] it is said, will run Ashe[5] closely, but I cannot believe it. In this District we are likely to have a Convention, in which event both Venable[6] and Lewis [7] will probably be set aside. Many of my friends have been pressing me to accept the nomination but I *do not deserve it*. As the matter stands the chances are very, very against Venable.

I have no doubt you are making progress in your studies. Bear in mind that it is better to know a few things well, than a great many imperfectly. Most of our young men go to the bar at too early an age. A lawyer, to succeed, must know human nature as well as law. "The proper study of mankind is man."

The Governor and Mrs. Reid are well, and the child, Davy, was better last evening. He is a fine boy.

It will always give me pleasure to hear from you, and if I can be of any service to you here in any way, please let me know it.

Yours Truly,
W. W. Holden

T. Settle, Jr., Esq.[8]

[1] George Dillard Boyd, legislator and merchant; member, House of Commons, 1840-1841; member, state Senate 1842-1847, 1852-1859. *Dictionary of North Carolina Biography*, s.v. "Boyd, George Dillard."

[2] Richard Clanselle Puryear, planter; member, House of Commons, 1838-1839, 1844-1847, 1852; member, state Senate 1849-1851; member, U. S. House of Representatives, 1853-1857; delegate to Confederate Provisional Congress. *Dictionary of North Carolina Biography*, s.v. "Puryear, Richard Clanselle."

[3] Henry Marchmore Shaw, physician and Confederate army officer; medical education at University of Pennsylvania; member, state Senate, 1851; member, U.S. House of Representatives, 1853-1855, 1857-1859; colonel, Eighth Regiment, North Carolina Troops. *Dictionary of North Carolina Biography*, s.v. "Shaw, Henry Marchmore."

[4] Walter Francis Leake.

[5] William Shepperd Ashe.

[6] Abraham Watkins Venable.

[7] Augustus Marion Lewis, lawyer; member, House of Commons, 1856; trustee, U.N.C., 1879-1893; officer, Confederate States army. Grant, *Alumni History*, 363.

[8] Thomas Settle, Jr., A.B., U.N.C., 1850; member, House of Commons, 1854-1859; speaker, 1858-1859; trustee, U.N.C., 1856-1874; associate justice, North Carolina Supreme

Court, 1868-1871, 1872-1876; unsuccessful Republical Party candidate for governor, 1876; U.S. District Court judge in Florida, 1877-1888. *Dictionary of North Carolina Biography*, s.v. "Settle, Thomas, Jr."

Holden to Hon. J. W. Ellis SHC:Ellis

Raleigh, Sept. 27, 1853

My dear Ellis:

Your very kind favor of the 5th, dated Plymouth, was duly received.

Every thing here is quiet and dull. We were startled and grieved by the death of our friend Busbee,[1] who was confined but a few days. He returned from Morganton in apparently fine health—had a chill on Monday evening, and died on Friday evening. I learn from Mrs. Taylor[2] and Mr. Lacy[3] that he was ready for the change. A few hours before he died he rallied and spoke in calm and impressive tones to his wife. He told her that his only cause of sorrow was leaving her and his little boys—that he had no fear of death, but hoped he would be saved through the merits of Jesus Christ. His death is indeed a great loss to us all. He was the most popular man we had, and could have defeated Venable[4] by two thousand majority. He would have run but for his Reportership. P. H. Winston[5] and Maj. Clarke[6] and S. F. Phillips[7] and Q. Busbee[8] are applicants for the Reportership. I incline to think that Phillips and Busbee will be appointed. The office can be made to pay for two to three thousand dollars; the State's subscription of 140 copies paying for the printing, about $1200 per annum.

I apprehend but little if any loss to our cause from the *land distribution question*. Venable is defunct. His course after the election has completed his destruction. He attended our last August Court, in the hope of getting encouragement for a new paper here, but most of his supporters advised him against it. He denounced Mr. Dobbin[9] and Gov. Reid publicly at Yarboroughs, and afterwards denied it. I saw his letter to Maj. Wilder[10] denying it, and the Major's reply *fixing the facts upon him*! He was disgruntled because he thought Mr. Dobbin had some agency in appointing McGowan[11] Route Agent, and because he had heard that Gov. Reid had *expressed* himself in private against his election. I am convinced, upon the whole, that Venable is as deficient in moral as he is in political principle. I am awaiting the message of the President[12] in December, in the hope that he will take some good ground on the land question; and shall say as little as possible on the subject until then. He can so manage the question, I am certain, as not to lose by it.

I have seen a number of Sheriffs and others lately from various parts of the State, and I find a general and ardent wish that John W. Ellis should consent to run next time for Governor. Rives,[13] of Chatham, and Rushing,[14] of Union, are especially anxious that you should be the candidate. Of course this is a matter for your own serious consideration. Of your election I have not the shadow of a doubt; indeed I believe we shall be able to elect any one who may be nominated. Dr. Columbus Mills and Avery[15] and Col. Bower,[16] and W. H. Thomas[17] have also been spoken of. It is *unnecessary*, I know, that I should assure you that no man would exert himself more for you than I would. I should like to hear from you on the subject—of course in the strictest confidence.

We can also carry the Assembly, in case we have union and good organization. The Federalists, however, will make a strong fight—their all depends upon the result. It is supposed here that they will run Gen. Dockery[18] for Governor. Danl. M. Barringer is probably their strongest man.

With many wishes for your happiness and prosperity, I am

Truly Your friend
W. W. Holden

Hon. J. W. Ellis

[1] Perrin Busbee

[2] Not identified.

[3] Probably Dr. Drury Lacy, Jr., pastor of the Raleigh Presbyterian Church from 1836 to 1855; president of Davidson College, 1855-1860. *Dictionary of North Carolina Biography*, s.v. "Lacy, Drury, Jr."

[4] Abraham Watkins Venable.

[5] Patrick Henry Winston, lawyer and public official; member, House of Commons, 1850, 1854-1855; president, Council of State, 1864; member of 1865 constitutional convention. *Dictionary of North Carolina Biography*, s.v. "Winston, Patrick Henry."

[6] William John Clark.

[7] Samuel Field Phillips, lawyer; A.B., U.N.C., 1841; A.M., 1844; member, House of Commons, 1852-1854, 1864-1865; speaker, 1865; auditor of public accounts, 1862-1864; trustee, U.N.C., 1864-1868; member, 1865 constitutional convention. Grant, *Alumni History*, 493.

[8] Quentin Durward Busbee, lawyer; appointed Supreme Court reporter, 1853. Grant, *Alumni History*, 89

[9] James Cochran Dobbin.

[10] Gaston Hillary Wilder.

[11] Patrick McGowan, Wake County; U.S. mail agent. 1860 U.S. Census Population Schedule, North Carolina: Wake, 295 (microfilm).

[12] President Franklin Pierce.

[13] Robert E. Rives, Chatham County; member, state Senate, 1856-1857. Cheney, *North Carolina Government* , *1585-1979*, 324.

[14] Darling Rushing, Union County; member, House of Commons, 1856-1857. Cheney, *North Carolina Government*, 1585-1979, 325

[15] William Waightstill Avery.

[16] George Bower, Ashe County; member, state Senate, 1812-1817, 1848-1855; member, House of Commons, 1842-1843. Cheney, *North Carolina Government, 1585-1979*, 1053.

[17] William Holland Thomas, legislator; white chief of Eastern Band of Cherokees; member, state Senate, 1849-1861; colonel, Sixty-ninth North Carolina Regiment. *Dictionary of North Carolina Biography*, s.v. "Thomas, William Holland."

[18] Alfred Dockery.

Holden to Hon. Jno. W. Ellis SHC:Ellis

Raleigh, Oct. 26, 1853

My dear Sir:

Yours, from Hertford, was duly received. I was glad to hear from you, and to learn that your health has been good while on your Circuit.

I write you briefly to apprize you of the fact that, so far as I can hear and judge, *You will be the next Democratic nominee for Governor*. This, of course, is only for *you*; and I give it as the result of all my inquiries and suggestions on the subject. I have seen many of our friends during the past two months, and heard from others, and am, therefore, prepared to form an opinion. I pledge you my word, buttoned on hard labor and unfaltering faith, that you will be elected. I do not think you ought to decline, or that you can do so. But I hope to have the pleasure of seeing you on your return from your Circuit, when the matter can be more fully and freely discussed.

Mr. Clingman[1] passed through here a few days since on his way to Washington. *He is all right*.

Truly Your friend
W. W. Holden

Hon. Jno. N. Ellis

[1] Thomas Lanier Clingman.

Holden to Hon. Jno. W. Ellis SHC:Ellis

Raleigh, Dec. 10, 1853

My dear Ellis:

Yours of the 1st has been received, and, you must pardon me for saying, it has given me some concern. I have read it most attentively, and I think I appreciate your position and somewhat embarrasssing circumstances that surround it. It is natural that you should feel more or less annoyed by misrepresentations of your views on distribution, to say nothing of feeling on the part of aspirants; and this especially, as your whole course in the matter has been unselfish, and has looked, as I honestly believe, to the success and welfare of the party. Still you are, to a considerable extent, the property of that party and of your friends; as a public man you can, expect little exemption from anxiety; and the "angry strifes" to which you allude, are but the crucibles in which the pure gold is brought out. If you *can*, with any sort of Justice to your private interests, consent to accept the nomination, I think you ought to do it; and then, if you have doubts, serious doubts and apprehensions on the subject, still do it, trusting to your own strong arm, to that good fortune which seems to have crowned you from the start, and to that power above all, which *is* about and around all honest public men, who strive to serve their fellows and to be useful in their day and time. Nor would the four years be lost. Your powers would in the mean time be expanding and enlarging, and you would be able to "redeem the time." And besides, is it not a high distinction to have your name enrolled for all time with the leading minds which have preceded you? But you have thought of all that, and more. There can be no doubt that you are the first choice of the party. I speak from what I have heard, *and* letters received; but a day or two ago, Whitmell Stallings, of Gates[1] wrote me to do all I could to *induce* you to accept, for he regards you by far the strongest man in his section of the State. The eye of the party is upon you; and after the nomination there would be but one impulse and one voice. So far as I am concerned, I would labor for your success as I did for that of Reid;[2] and what I say to you is said by one, who, though ardent and enthusiastic, yet knows something of North Carolina politics—and that is, you would go through with a shout of triumph and of rejoicing from the seashore to the blue mountains of the West. There is no doubt of it. If, however, your purpose to decline is final, then I think the party ought to be apprized of it in some way. But if you are only in serious doubt, let me beg you to let the matter stand, at least for the present. A month hence will do as well as now, and by that time your feelings and views may undergo some change. If I were to make an announcement of your declination to be considered of those from whom a nomination was expected to be made, I should have to do so "by authority." Let me hear from you again soon on the subject. I shall, so far as I am concerned, do in the matter what you shall finally suggest or desire; but I shall pen any such articles as that withdrawing you from the field with reluctance and deep regret. Think of it all again and again, and write me freely, as before, on the subject.

Truly Your Friend
W. W. Holden

Hon. Jno. W. Ellis

[1] Whitmel Stallings, Ashe County; member, House of Commons, 1831-1833, 1835-1841; member, state Senate, 1842-1847. Cheney, *North Carolina Government*, 1585-1979, 1142-1143.

[2] David Settle Reid.

John W. Ellis to Holden *Standard*
December 17, 1853

Salisbury, Dec. 10, 1853

Sir: Late numbers of the Standard and other papers have brought my attention communications connecting my name with the next canvass for Governor of the State; and without any evidence that this feeling is general in its character, I must be permitted to express my disposition upon the subject, lest further silence should be construed into an acquiescence, on my part, in these suggestions.

I certainly feel obliged to those gentlemen who have thus honorably associated my name with the first office of the State; but, for reasons uninteresting to the public, yet of controlling influence with me, I must request that public attention will henceforth be exclusively confined to other gentlemen whose names have already or may hereafter be mentioned in the same connection. Both the position of candidate and the office itself, have duties appertaining, to the execution of which I am not in a situation to devote my labors.

In conclusion, permit me as a citizen, to express my appreciation of your efficient advocacy, as a public journalist, of questions of general interest; and especially, such prudent, yet energetic measures, as tend to develope the vast natural resources of our much cherished State.

Very respectfully, yours &c
John W. Ellis

W. W. Holden. Esq.

T. L. Clingman to Holden *Standard*
July 8, 1854

House of Representatives,
June 30, 1854

Sir: A late number of the Raleigh Register charges that I have gone over to the "Locofocos,"[1] and that in consequence, there is a bargin that Gov. Reid and myself are to be chosen Senators. A similar statement has been made, I think, in the *Star* and some other papers. It is well known that I am not in the habit of noticing the falsehoods that are issued from time to time by such organs. If I take a different course on the present occasion, it is not because I think it necessary to defend myself, much less Gov. Reid, from such an allegation, but for a different purpose. I do not addresss this note to any one of those papers; because they have been for years in the habit of publishing misrepresentations and falsehoods against me, while they have carefully abstained from publishing my own speeches and letters that would refuted their allegations, and therefore I have no room to suppose that they would willingly give place to any statement of mine.

I may remark in passing, that for many years they have asserted that I have gone over to the Democrats, &c. These declarations were particularly vehement when I took a stand against Gen. Scott,[2] and they professed great joy that I had taken open ground against them, &c. During the last contest for Congress in the State, I was classed as a "locofoco" candidate. It is true, however, that as soon as the election was over, as on former occasions, they claimed me as whig member, there by admitting that the public had no faith in their assertions. Some weeks since, in the classification of the votes on the Nebraska bill, I was set down as a "locofoco." They now affect to have suddenly ascertained that I had, for a consideration of political advantage to myself, joined the Democratic party; or at least agreed to cooperate with them in the Senatorial election. These editors ought, at least, to admit the falsity of their former charges, before they can expect to obtain forgiveness and credit to their present one.

If I was formerly indifferent to their attacks, I have still more room to be so from their late conduct.

While hypocritically professing friendship for the Nebraska bill, they have insidiously, and in the most cowardly manner, made war on the measure. Nay more. They have assailed the brave and patriotic men of the North, who, amid all the storms of fanaticism and sectional denunciation, have firmly and gallantly marched forward and carried the bill, exhibiting as much courage and magnaminity as was ever shown on the bloodiest battle field. Well knowing that every strong whig from the free States was against the measure, and that it was supported by the administration and a majority of its Northern friends, they nevertheless gave all the "*aid and comfort*" they could to the former, and made war on the latter. Yes, during the great struggle to restore the South to equality in the Union, they have been de-nouncing the generous men of the North who came to our aid, because they were not able sooner to pass the bill, by reason of the fierce opposition of Those whigs whom they were praising and defending. Professing friendship for the measure, they still helped its enemies, and railed at its friends, because of the difficulty they found in overcoming the opposition.

During our revolutionary struggle, what would have been thought, if a professed Whig paper, that had continued to praise the British army and assailled our ally, France, because she did not sooner put an end to the war; and that had abused Lafayette and his gallant comrades, because they could not at once drive the British out of America? And yet the conduct of such a journal would not have been in anywise more ignominiously base, than the course of the papers I have referred to. They must meet with contempt and degradation whenever truth and honor have fame.

With restpect to the Senatorial position, it is known that at the last session of the Legislature a large majority of the Democratic members voted for me for that station. To these gentlemen, and to my friends among the whigs, and to others of both parties, who stood ready to vote for me if another ballot could have been had,

I am ever ready to express my sense of obligation. I trust that no act of mine, either as a public man or in the walks of private life, will ever cause any one of these gentlemen to regret his past friendship. If there be other persons who are in doubt as to my position, I refer them to my acts and speeches as a public man. As to whether any contingency will arise in the future, that will place me before the public for such a station, it would be unbecoming on my part to express an opinion. Should I ever, at any time, be so fortunate as to obtain the position of Senator, my elevation will not be owing to intrigue or combinations with any one, but to a belief in those making the election that the interest and honor of the State could be safely confided to my keeping.

Very respectfully,
T. L. Clingman[3]

W. W. Holden, Esq.
Editor of the Standard

[1] Originally a term used to refer to a faction of the Democratic Party known as the Equal Rights Party but later used by opponents to refer to all Democrats. *Dictionary of American History*, s.v. "Loco Foco Party."

[2] General Winfield Scott, Whig Party candidate for president in 1852. *Dictionary of American Biography*, s.v. "Scott, Winfield."

[3] Thomas Lanier Clingman, a Whig Party member of the House of Representatives.

Holden "To my Subscribers and Friends" *Standard*
September 9, 1854

I have made arrangements, by which I have secured the services of Frank I. Wilson, Esq.,[1] late Editor of the Salisbury Banner, as Associate Editor of the Standard and as the business partner of the establishment. Mr. Wilson will have charge, after the 1st of November next, of the printing and publishing department, and will also write for the paper as occasion may require. This will leave with me the principal Editorship; and being thus exempt from the heavy labors incident to the printing and publishing department, I will have more time to devote to study, and will be thereby enabled, perhaps, to render the Standard more useful to its friends and more acceptable to its readers generally. This is an arrangement which I have desired for some time to effect; and indeed it had become almost indispensable, owing to the increased subscriptions and business of the establishment.

Mr. Wilson is well known to the Democracy of the State as a consistent and unflinching Democrat, and as a forcible and effective writer. I esteem myself fortunate in having secured his services. He joins to fine abilities as a writer, habits of industry and labor, and of attention to buiness, seldom found in the same individual. My friends, I doubt not, when they shall come to know him as well as I do, will cordially concur in the estimate I have formed of his character and services.

I have been engaged for more than eleven years in publishing the standard. I took charge of it at a period when the signs were not favorable to Democratic success; but I have had the gratific t ion of recording in these columns, since then, many glorious Democratic triumphs, and of rejoicing with friends over the useful and beneficent results of these triumphs to North Carolina and the Union. I trust that, in my sphere of labor, I have done my duty. That I have made mistakes and committted errors, I am free to confess; but I have constantly striven to do what I believed to be right, and have, at any rate, adhered to principles without regard to men. I have uniformly regarded it as my first duty, as a Democratic Editor, to adhere under all circumstances, to the great principles of the Democratic party, to the rights of the States, and to a strict construction of the federal Constitution as the only course for preserving the Union of the States itself as it was established, and as its founders intended it should be administered; and secondly, to insist upon organization in the party as indispensible and as the only means of carrying out its principles. Nor have I been indifferent to the prosperity of North Carolina. I have the gratification of knowing that the Standard has been the decided advocate of Common Schools, of internal improvements, and of all the measures calculated to advance our mining, agricultural, and commercial interests; and that it was among the first, if not the very first, next to Gov. Reid, to take ground for the great principle of equality between free white men at the ballot-box. The course of the paper, I scarcely need say, will not be changed. It will continue to be a defender and exponent of Democratic principles—the unwavering advocate of organization in the Democratic party; and devoted to such measures as shall give promise of bringing out the resounces and of adding to the prosperity and glory of our beloved State.

To the friends who have stood by me through the labors and strifes of eleven years, and who have sustained me and honored me with their confidence far beyond my merits, I take this occasion to return the homage of my most hearty thanks and gratitude. My highest ambition shall be to retain such friends, to make more friends of the same genuine stamp, and to prove myself worthy of their support and confidence.

W. W. Holden

[1] Franklin Inge (Frank) Wilson, lawyer and newspaper man; co-editor and editor of the Rutherfordton *Mountain Banner*, 1848-1853; published Salisbury *Republican Banner*, 1853-1854; associate editor of the *North Carolina Standard*, 1854-1859; published *Ad Valorem Banner* in Raleigh, 1860 until his death in 1865. *Dictionary of North Carolina Biography*, s.v. "Wilson, Franklin Inge (Frank)."

Holden to W. D. Cooke, Esq. *Standard*
May 26, 1855

Raleigh, May 19, 1855

Dear Sir: Yours of the 17th has been received. You request me to "state the circumstances under which" Mr. Gales[1] and myself called upon you "to execute" for us "the printing of the Laws of the State for the session of 1852."

I have no hesitation in stating my recollections of the circumstances referred to. Mr. Gales and myself were the successful budders for the Laws, the Journals, and the printing for the Legislature of 1854. As you had a power press, and as neither of us had one at that time, and as the press-work of the Laws was heavy, we applied to you to ascertain on what terms you would print the Laws for us. It may have been, for I am not certain, that we proposed to pay you a sum to be agreed upon for the press work, we setting the type and preparing the forms; but at any rate we could not come to an agreement with you—and so, as we were content with the Journals and the printing for the session of 1854, we relinquished our bids for the Laws, and the Secretary of State, gave the printing thereof to Mr. Wesley Whitaker, Jr.,[2] whose bid was the next lowest to ours. The Laws were then printed at your office at the Asylum. You did not bid, as I understand, for any of the public printing.

Very Respectfully,
W. W. Holden

W. D. Cooke, Esq.[3]

[1] Seaton Gales.

[2] Wesley Whitaker, Jr., Wake County; printer. 1850 U.S. Census Population Schedule, North Carolina: Wake, 277 (microfilm).

[3] William Dewey Cooke, educator and publisher; principal, North Carolina Institution for the Deaf, 1845-1860; engaged a printer and installed a press at the school, publishing various newspapers and journals. *Dictionary of North Carolina Biography*, s.v. "Cooke, William Dewey."

W. G. Duke to Standard Editors *Standard*
June 9, 1855

Graham, June 4th, 1855

Editors Standard:-Enclosed you will find two dollars, for which send me the weekly Standard to Big Falls, Alamance County N.C.

I joined the Know Nothings some time in December last. I was induced to do this from representations of those in whom I had confidence, who assured me that it was not a Whig nor a Democratic measure, but entirely a national party. I now believe it to be anything but a national party. I have now withdrawn, and would earnestly advise all to do and do likewise, and I hope the Democratic party will receive an erring brother back into the fold again.

You can publish this if you choose.

W. G. Duke[1]

[1] W. Green Duke, Alamance County; farm laborer. 1850 U.S. Census Population Schedule, North Carolina: Alamance, 069 (microfilm).

L. O'B. Branch to Messrs. Holden & Wilson *Standard* June 20, 1855

Raleigh, June 18th, 1855

Messrs. Holden & Wilson:–I understand I am represented to have advocated in my speech in Raleigh, the exclusion from the State of all persons born at the North. That is precisely the opposite of what I did say. One of my arguments against the Know Nothings is, that if they succeed in excluding foreigners on the ground that they compete injuriously with our mechanics and other laboring classes, the next thing we hear of, will be an attempt by the same or some similar party, to exclude all persons not born in the State, and particularly those born at the North; that, such an attempt to build up a Chinese Wall around the State, would be ruinous to every class in the State, and to none more so, than to our mechanics. I said that if being a skillful, industrious, and economical mechanic, was to be established as a sufficient reason for excluding a man from the State, a clamor could be raised against our Northern born mechanics with far more ease, because one of them was a more formidable competitor than half a dozen foreigners, in as much as the foreigner generally brings with him a trade that our people do not take to.

I everywhere warn the Northern born man against countenancing Know Nothingism, lest its exclusive policy may soon seek to embrace them in its proscritions. I need hardly say that I deprecate any such policy, and it is one of the strongest objections I have to Know Nothingism that the spirit it engenders and the prejudices it appeals to, will not be content with the victims it is now pursuing.

Yours very respectfully,
L. O'B. Branch[1]

[1] Lawrence O'Bryan Branch, lawyer; A.B., Princeton, 1838; president of the Raleigh and Gaston Railroad Company, 1852; member, U.S. House of Representatives, 1855-1861; brigadier general, Confederate army, killed at Antietam. *Dictionary of North Carolina Biography*, s.v. "Branch, Lawrence O'Bryan."

"*An appeal to my Subscribers*" *Standard*
October 27, 1855

Gentlemen: about two months since I appealed to all of you to pay up your subscriptions, and to pay in advance; and I sent at the same time, to three hundred and fifty of you, accounts amounting to over four thousand dollars. If this four thousand I have received only two or three hundred dollars!–and but few others have responded.

I feel quite sure that I have the best list of subscribers in the State. Nineteen–twentieths of them are entirely able, as they are no doubt willing, to pay but from procrastination and neglect, and a want of what is deemed a suitable opportunity, they do not pay, and very many of them are in arrears. The main profits of my arduous and constant labors, I feel constrained to state, are from advertising and job work–and this with a weekly and semi-weekly list fully equal together to four thousand weekly subscribers. I cannot afford to lose thousands of dollars every year by this failure on the part of my subscribers; and if they are not much more prompt in their payment in the future, I shall be compelled, after the close of next campaign, *to adopt the cash system*—to send the none without the cash in advance, and stop the paper as soon as the time paid for has expired. Just think of it!—I have been sending, for example, for four or five years, some thirty copies of the Standard to one County, and have not received from these subscribers as much as money as would pay for the paper used in printing for them! The same is true as to several other Counties, but I have not yet cut these delinquents off, because it is highly important to the Democratic cause that the Standard, or some other Republican paper, should be circulated in these Counties.

What I ask is this: That *every* subscriber to the Standard, who knows or believes that he is due for it to any amount, will at once forward the money—a sum certain if he knows the amount, or near the amount—and if not certain of the sum due, such amount as he may consider right and proper; and in all cases receipts will be immediately returned in the paper, showing the time paid for. If every subscriber will do this, the receipts which will be returned will enable all to see how they stand; and then each one can take a new start, with a determination (having filed away his receipt for future reference) to pay always in advance—a custom, we beg leave to add, much better than the existing one or any other for both subscriber and publisher. There is little if any risk in sending money by mail. Enclose the amount in the presence of a Postmaster, or some other witness, or have the Postmaster register the letter as containing money—pre-pay the postage, and I will be responsible after that. This is a plain and easy mode; and every one who is able and disposed to pay—and who cannot call at the office, or send by some friend—will avail himself of it.

If compelled, as above stated, to adopt the cash system, the Standard's circulation would in all probability, at once fall off at least one thousand. This is matter for reflection among my friends in all parts of the State, who have, as I have, and as we all have, the cause of Democracy so much at heart.

It is painful for me have to write thus. I should be deeply mortified to be considered a *dun*, or as unreasonable, or importunate in dealing with my subscribers—to many of whom I owe so many thanks and so much gratitude. I have spoken plainly, but nothing is further from me than a disposition to irritate or offend any one; and I feel sure that the necessity which I regarded as existing for making this appeal, has occasioned me more anxiety and unpleasantness of feeling than it will to any one whom it is addressed.

This appeal is, of course, not intended for such as have already paid in advance.

If this call should be responded to, as I have a right to expect and as I trust it will be, I shall be thereby cheered in my labors, and enabled to incur more pecuniary outlays and sacrifices for the cause during the ensuing campaign; but if disappointed, one source of consolation will be that I am already somewhat accustomed to it; and I shall continue, whatever may happen to devote all my energies to my readers, and to the great and glorious party which has so honored and sustained me beyond my merits.

W. W. Holden

October, 1855

Holden to Hon. W. N. Edwards A&H:Conway

Raleigh, Feb. 2, 1856.

Hon. W N. Edwards[1]

My dear Sir:

Your esteemed favor of the 22nd was duly received. Dr. Hawkins[2] called and paid your account. Your account stands thus: Weekly Standard from 1st of June 1849 to 1st Nov. 1850, when the Semi-Weekly commenced, $4.25. You are credited $15.75 on Semi-Weekly, up to November 1854; which, together, makes $20, as per my receipt, enclosed by you to me, and herewith returned. Is not this right?

I concur with you entirely in your views in relation to the House. Let them resign, and return to the people—but will they do it? In the earlier days of the Republic such a spectacle was never presented. Still, I apprehend nothing very serious. The States—the States! they are taking care of the people. And besides, my friend, I am no canter, and not superstitious—but I verily believe that *Almighty God* takes care of this Republic, and that He will save it amid all its trials, and make it in the end a wonder, and a glory, and an all-pervading blessing to the nation. The work of the immortals of '76—the hopes of all good men, every where, and the earnest prayers of millions, are not to be blasted and destroyed. I believe that the spirit of the loftiest patriotism which speaks out in the President's Message, meets a response from a vast majority of the American people; the crisis will perish, accursed, and the Republic will endure. May God grant it! You, Sir, are approaching the limit assigned to mortal life. When the summons comes to you, you can look back over a long course of honorable service, and feel that, if you have made mistakes, you have never *deliberately* done wrong; in that moment this reflection, added to the love of friends, will be sweet to you—but to survive the Republic would send a pang to your heart which would be felt above and beyond all such refining and blessed influences. But I cannot trust myself to write this.

Be assured I shall always be happy to hear from you. We have differed honestly on one question, now nearly settled—but upon all others we are together.

Truly your friend,
W. W. Holden

[1] Weldon Nathaniel Edwards.

[2] William Joseph Hawkins, physician and railroad official; A.B., William and Mary College, 1840; University of Pennsylvania medical department, 1842; president, Raleigh and Gaston Railroad, 1855-1875; trustee, U.N.C., 1881-1891. *Dictionary of North Carolina Biography*, s.v. "Hawkins, William Joseph."

Holden to Thos. Settle, Jr. Esq. SHC:Settle, Jr.

Raleigh, Feb. 13, 1856

My dear Settle:[1] Yours of the 10th was duly received. We had some conversation with Mr. Ruffin[2] in relation to Ratliff.[3] He takes the same view of the matter which you do, and in that view we entirely concur. We attached but little importance to his letter anyway; and his apology, which you enclosed, is certainly ample. I am satisfied.

I would write to Gov. Reid if I thought a letter would reach him in Rockingham. If at home, please present him my warmest regards. I trust Mrs. Reid and children are well. Gov. R. in a late letter was kind enough to inquire especially, in Mrs. Reid's name, about her little namesake, "Etta." Please say to her that she is a lovely child, and very intelligent. She is remarkably blessed with health. She frequently speaks of Mrs. R., and invariably insists that Davy Reid is her "sweetheart." She has any number of dolls, and all kinds of names for them. Revering and loving, as I know you do, your parents, and good boy as you have been, you will never fully know what parental affection is, until you have children of your own.

Mr. Ruffin, while here, paid your subscription for you, and has probably ere this handed you your receipt. The $5 you sent is, therefore, subject to your order, and will be either returned or applied as you may direct.

I send herewith an order on Messrs. Smith and Raines.[4] If convenient, please receive the money for me, but do not go to much trouble about it.

We shall expect to see you at the State convention. We hope to see a full delegation from Rockingham. Let me hear from you when convenient.

Truly Your friend,
W. W. Holden

Thos. Settle, Jr. Esq.

[1] Thomas Settle, Jr.
[2] Probably Thomas Ruffin, Sr.
[3] Not identified.
[4] Not identified.

David S. Reid to Messrs. Holden & Wilson *Standard*
July 30, 1856

Washington City, July 18, 1856

Messrs. Holden & Wilson:—I have recently received letters from various points in our State, informing me that the Hon. James Buchanan is charged by the political friends of Mr. Fillmore[1] with having voted for the Bankrupt law of 1841. To save the trouble of answering these enquiries separately, I have written this letter for publication, giving a statement of facts as I find them.

At the time this act was passed Mr. Buchanan was in the United States Senate, and on July 24, 1841, he is recorded as voting against the passage of the Bankrupt bill. See Senate Journal for that session, page 115. On the same day Mr. Buchanan made a speech against the bill. See Appendix to Congressional Globe for that session, page 205.

On February 25, 1843, Mr. Buchanan is recorded as voting for the repeal of the Bankrupt law. See Senate Journal for that session, page 229.

When the pact passed Mr. Fillmore was a member of the House of Representatives, and on August 18, 1841, he is recorded as voting for the Bankrupt bill. See House Journal for that session, page 378. Mr. Fillmore made a speech in favor of the passage of the bill, August 16, 1841. See Appendix to Congressional Globe for that session, page 480.

On January 17, 1843, Millard Fillmore is recorded as voting against the repeal of the bankrupt act. See House Journal for that session, page 215.

It will, therefore, be seen that Mr. Buchanan did not vote for the Bankrupt law, but that Mr. Fillmore did; and moreover, that Mr. Buchanan voted *for the repeal* of the law, while Mr. Fillmore voted *against the repeal.*

The ensuing Presidential election will be the most important that has ever taken place since the adoption of the Federal Constitution; and as there ought to be no difference of opinion among the people of North Carolina upon the great issue involved, it is to be regretted that a large party are engaged in a course calculated to prove disastrous to the interests of the South and fatal to the principles of the Constitution. The larger number of those who support Mr. Fillmore are no doubt actuated by pure and patriotic motives; but we must remember that this fact will not render their course, if it succeeds, the less fatal in its consequences to the country. The error may be discovered too late to repair the injury it inflicts.

Every one who has taken the pains to make an impartial inquiry in regard to the state of political parties and the tone of public sentiment, must know that the contest is between Mr. Buchanan, the candidate of the Democratic Constitutional party on the one side, and Mr. Fremont,[2] the black Republican abolition candidate on the other. No candid well informed man will venture to express the opinion that Mr. Fillmore stands any chance to be elected by the people. Every vote, therefore, given for Mr. Fillmore weakens Mr. Buchanan and strengthens Mr. Fremont. The Know Nothing party of the North has been absorbed by the black Republicans, and if the Southern Know Nothings should, by carryig a few Southern States for Mr. Fillmore, succeed in throwing the election into the House of Representatives, then what have we to expect? Could we reasonably hope that a sound man would be chosen by a body which has elected a black Republican of the deepest dye as its Speaker, and has thus far cast every important vote in favor of that party? It is true that in choosing a President the House votes by States, but that does not make the prospect of success more favorable at this time.

I repeat, the contest is between Mr. Buchanan and Mr. Fremont. Those who prefer the former to the latter and desire to preserve the rights of the States and maintain the Constitution, ought to vote for him, regardless of former political association. I am gratified to know that hundreds—including the masses as well as the politicians—who have not heretofore acted with the Democratic party, taking the proper view of the subject, have determined to sacrifice party for the good of the country, and are giving a cordial support to Mr. Buchanan.

Mr. Fremont is a purely sectional candidate representing a party held together by the one idea of inveterate hostility to the domestic institutions of the South, and we have nothing to hope from him. On the other hand Mr. Buchanan is the candidate of a national party; he is a pure man, a statesman of wisdom and experience, and will administer the government according to the principles of the Constitution.

The deepest interest is felt by the Constitutional men of the North and of the South in regard to the result of the August election in our State; and I am sure she will neither disregard her own interests nor disappoint their expectations.

The result of the North Carolina elections has often been to me, as you well know, a source of peculiar pride and satisfaction; but I can assure you that I have never before felt so deep a solicitude for the triumph of the Democratic party for the reason that we have never had so much staked upon the issue.

Very respectfully, &c.
David S. Reid

[1] Millard Fillmore, president of the United States, 1850-1853; American Party candidate for president, 1856.

[2] John Charles Fremont, explorer; member, U.S. Senate from California, 1850-1851; unsuccessful Republican Party candidate for president, 1856. *Biographical Directory of the American Congress, 1774-1971*, s.v. "Fremont, John Charles."

Holden to Hon. C. H. Wiley A&H:Wiley

Raleigh, Aug. 19, 1856

Hon. C. H. Wiley[1]

My dear Sir: Yours of Aug. 11 has been received. I feel much flattered by the position assigned me at the next Common School Convention; yet I fear it will not be in my power to attend. The time fixed, the 21st Oct. is so near that of our State fair, and I shall have so many engagements, that I fear it will be impracticable for me to leave the City. Under these circumstances, I trust I will be excused. My heart is in the cause, and I am most anxious for its success. At the Convention of 1857, should I be spared, I hope to be able to attend in person and throw in my mite. Meantime my paper is open to the cause; and I should be pleased to have from your pen, at an early day, just such an Editorial as you would like to have in the Standard on the subject. Let me her from you in time in this respect.

I regret to inform you that your Journal is not yet out. It provokes me, I assure you, as much as it must you. but, during the late hot weather, we found it impossible to make progress with it. Our rollers melted, and the new ones we cast would not work. Now, however, we are fairly under way again. the excitement of the election, too, operating on the office hands, retarded the work; and we have had at the same time, a number of small jobs from the Capitol and the Railroads—regular customers—which we are obliged to do.

I can only promise that I will urge the work to the utmost.

With many wishes for your personal happiness, and the continued progress of Common Schools

I am Your Friend,
W. W. Holden

[1] Calvin Henderson Wiley.

Holden to Hon. J. W. Ellis SHC:Ellis

Raleigh, Jan. 19, 1857

My dear sir: Your recent kind letter was duly received, and I regret I could not find time to reply to it sooner. I am always glad to hear from you, and to know that you are well and prospering. I can never forget the seasons of intercourse between us in years long gone—not *long gone*, after all, for that would make you a middle-aged, unmarried man. I have just been through the Journals of 1846, looking up the facts about the "Mexican Preamble"—and the examination brought many things, long asleep in memory, to vivid recollection. You will notice the results of these labors in the Standard of Wednesday.

The Legislature has done little thus far. It is doubtful whether any Bank will be chartered, except the old State Bank, with a charter not materially different from that passed two years ago. I do not think the stockholders will accept this; especially as the Cape Fear Bank, which accepted a similar one, is now praying amendments at the hands of this Legislature. The Legislature may, just before adjourning, extend the charter under which the State Bank is now working, for five or six years—but this is doubtful. Caldwell's[1] scheme cannot pass.

As to internal improvements but little will be done. The Western Extension will be aided, in all probability—but nothing will be done, I fear, for developing the Coal Fields. The taxes will have to be increased about one hundred thousand dollars; and this, as you may well imagine, has a powerful effect on the minds of the members. I think it highly probable, however, that some measure of relief will be devised and adopted for the Atlantic and N.C. Roads.

As the session approaches its close the interest of those having measures before it increases, and the lobbies are pretty well thronged with "members"—the most anxious being those having in charge the Cape Fear and Deep River interest.

I have looked for you during the session, thinking you might find it convenient and agreeable to spend a few days in the City. I should be glad to see you.

You will observe that our friends in the Commons have voted down the proposition to elect judges and magistrates by the people. This was the result of caucus determination, predicated on the ground that it was advisable to take no new steps for Constitutional reform until the Free Suffrage measure shall have been fully perfected. Besides, the movement by the opposition, was no doubt for party capital.

Looking ahead four years, I have serious fears that the black Republicans will succeed in the Presidential struggle. The future is indeed gloomy. The indications are that Mr. Seward[2] will almost surely carry New York, Pennsylvania, and Ohio; and the lesser free States stars, with one or two exceptions, must follow in such a train. God defend and preserve the Republic!

Truly your friend,
W. W. Holden

Hon. J. W. Ellis

P.S. Mr. Wilson has duly credited you for. . .[torn]sent for the S. W. Standard

[1] David Franklin Caldwell, businessman, editor; member, House of Commons, 1848-1861; member, state Senate, 1878; private in the Confederate army; elected to U.S. House

of Representatives, 1868, but disqualified; interested in building and financing North Carolina Railroad. *Dictionary of North Carolina Biography*, s.v. "Caldwell, David Franklin."

[2] William H. Seward.

Holden to Hon. D. L. Swain A&H:Holden

Raleigh, Jan. 24, 1857

My dear sir: Your esteemed favor of the 21st has been received. I thank you for your kind allusion to my election as a Trustee of the University. I esteem it a high honor, and unworthy as I may be of it, I trust I shall never be wanting in zeal and sincerity of purpose in my efforts to advance the University and the cause of education generally. I have the consolation of knowing that I did not seek the office, but that it came to me without the slightest effort on my part. Pending the election, which has excited some feeling, I did not mention the subject to any one. Such places, especially, should never be sought.

Your letter to Mr. Avery[1] was submitted by him to the Senate, and printed and placed on the tables of members this (Saturday)evening. Soon after, the Committee which had had the subject in charge, reported the bill which had passed the Commons, and recommended its passage. I have had some conversations on the subject with Mr. Avery, Mr. Cameron[2], and Gov. Manly;[3] and the hope is entertained that the measure may be arrested in the Senate. Mr. Cameron will doubtless make a strong showing for the University when the bill comes up.

It is to be regretted that the explanatory or declaratory law was introduced. The University was already in possession of the escheated property, without question. The Literary Board had proposed no steps on the subject; nor would it have done so. But the introduction of the bill in the Commons was a temptation too strong to be resisted; and the proposition to amend by giving the escheats to the Common Schools was adopted by a vote of two to one. Without streneus efforts and a full explanation of the facts, the bill may also pass the Senate. It has taken its regular place in the calender of that body, and may not be reached before the last of next week. The two Houses, it is now thought, will most probably adjourn sine die on Monday week, the 2d February.

Very Truly Yours,
W. W. Holden

Hon. D. L. Swain

[1] William Waightstill Avery.

[2] Paul Carrington Cameron, planter, railway and road builder; member, state Senate, 1856; promoter of North Carolina Railroad; director of Raleigh and Gaston Railroad. *Dictionary of North Carolina Biography*, s.v. "Cameron, Paul Carrington."

[3] Governor Charles Manly.

Holden to Rev. C. H. Wiley SHC:Wiley

Raleigh, Friday 3 July, 1857

My dear Sir: I returned home from Warrenton last evening. Your absence was deeply felt and regretted, yet, all things considered, we did well.[1] Our friends, Messrs. Ogburn[2] and Cole,[3] will give you full acounts. Wednesday evening and Thursday I was too unwell to take much part in the proceedings, and I do not even know what was finally done on the Educational Journal. Mr. Cole and myself were on the Committee on the subject. *Something must be done*. The Association must have an organ that will go to the 3,500 districts of the State.

The Convention was, upon the whole, successful. The best and most hopeful spirit prevailed. This great cause must and shall go forward.

The Convention kindly determined to publish my address.[4] Mr. Ogburn, I believe, has the manuscript. Please see him on the subject, and ask him to inform me how it was finally decided to publish it. If in pamphlet form, and I print it, it will cost nothing, but the paper and actual outlay for setting it up. I trust you are nearly well. Let me hear from you.

Truly yours,
W. W. Holden

Rev. C. H. Wiley

[1] Holden had reference to the state educational convention, a complete account of which was published in the *Standard*, July 8, 1857.

[2] Edmund D. Ogburn, Guilford County; member, House of Commons, 1846-1847. Cheney, *North Carolina Government, 1585-1979*, 1153.

[3] Christopher C. Cole, one of the editors of the *Greensboro times*.

[4] The Holden speech was printed in the *Standard*, August 5, 1857. In it he compared the status of education in North Carolina with both northern and southern states, and showed that between 50,000 and 60,000 white children in the state never attended school.

Holden to Miss Laura Holden A&H:Holden

Raleigh, April 4, 1858

My dear Daughter: this is a beautiful Sabbath morning. The atmosphere is clear and pleasant, the trees are putting on their garments of green, the flowers are bursting into life and beauty, and the birds are singing in the copses and fields. The church bells are ringing, and many persons are going to the house of prayer. A deep religious feeling is manifesting itself here, as elsewhere in the country. Some twenty of the pupils of St. Marys I learn, are soon to be confirmed by Bishop Atkinson[1]. Nothing, my dear child, gives me greater satisfaction than to know that you are living with reference to the next life. Religion is a matter of principle—not cold and formal, but lively, earnest, and of the heart. It consists in "ceasing to do" or think evil, and "learning to do well." It is no matter of whim or fancy, to be thought of to-day and forgotten to-morrow; but it should be a part of our daily lives, always paramount, and manifesting itself in all we say or do. You grieve over your ungovernable temper; but do not despond with reference to this, for you are yet quite young, and patience and trust in God will enable you to overcome this evil. Be patient and forbearing, and you will thus form a habit of self-control which will accompany you always, and which will be to you and to all around you the source of constant satisfaction. This infirmity of temper is common to us all. I was so myself when young, but have to a great extent overcome it. Learn to know yourself, and when you have learned that you will know much of the thoughts, the wants, and the disposition of others. If in the ordinary intercourse of life you are kind to others, preferring their comfort to your own, they will in most cases act in the same way towards you; for the law of kindness is stronger than the law of dislike and selfishness.

Your examination will take place, you say, about the last of May. I feel sure you will prepare yourself to fill your part in it with credit.

Your Ma's health is improving. She sends her love. The rest of the family are all as well as they usually are.

Let me admonish you to keep your mind free of "love thoughts" and "nice young men." Not one young man in five is worthy of the affection of a pure minded young woman. You do not know them as I do. Above all, look at their moral character. A disobedient son, a spendthrift, a "fast young man" will never make a good husband. You are not yet sixteen. It will be time enough two years hence to think of being married. Now-a-days our boys are men, and our girls are women. This is wrong, and in some instances ruinous to both soul and body. Life is a reality. Common sense is the best sense. We must look at the world as it is, and not in the light of fancy or passion. Remember that those who marry are wedded for life, and that they must bear with each other's foibles and infirmities. The romance of it soon passes away. Happy are those in whom esteem and sincere respect and affection succeed to romance, imagination, and passion! Let me also admonish and urge you to keep no thought of this sort from me and your mother. Never think of engaging your thoughts or affections upon any one until you know thoroughly who he is, or until you consult one of us in relation to his habits and his character.

So you see I have written you along letter. All I have said is the expression of pure affection. I desire most ardently to see all my children happy here and saved hereafter. I may not have much to give them; but if they should be well educated and should be moral, just, courteous, honest, industrious, gentle and yet spirited when occasion really requires it, I will esteem this as infinitely better for them than dollars and cents.

Your affectionate father,
W. W. Holden.

To Miss Laura Holden

Salem Female Academy,
Salem,

[1] Thomas Atkinson, third Episcopal bishop of North Carolina. *Dictionary of North Carolina Biography*, s.v. "Atkinson, Thomas."

Holden to Hon. J. W. Ellis SHC:Ellis

Raleigh, April 19, 1858

My dear Sir: Permit me to congratulate you on your nomination at Charlotte, and to say that I am prepared to do all I can to promote your success as the nominee of the Democratic party.

I know nothing of the plans or calculations of the opposition, but should not be surprised if they were to get out a candidate. In that event, or indeed in any event, I presume you intend thoroughly to canvass the State. If I can aid you in any respect, please let me know it.

We had a large and spirited *ratification* meeting here on Friday evening last. We expect to form a Democratic Club for the campaign.

I have no disposition to complain. My nature is to look on the bright side. I bow to the decision of the Convention, and shall work for the party with as much ardor as I should have worked for myself. I trust that your majority will be a signal one, and that your administration will be creditable to yourself and beneficial to the whole people of the State.

Very Truly Yours
W. W. Holden

Hon. J. W. Ellis

Holden to the Democratic Party of the State *Standard*
April 21, 1858

TO THE DEMOCRATIC PARTY OF THE STATE

The delegates of the Democracy, in Convention at Charlotte, have nominated for Governor, John W. Ellis, of Rowan. It is a good nomination, and will receive my cordial and active support. Such an appeal, I feel sure, is not necessary; but as I was voted for in that Convention, and lest my position and feelings should be misunderstood and misconstrued, I appeal to all my friends, in every portion of the State, to go as I do, heartily and entirely for this nomination. The nominee is worthy; and besides, brother Democrats, we owe it to ourselves, to our principles, and to the cause of a Constitutional Union, to present a solid front to the common adversary. Men die and pass away like the dew of the morning; but principles are co-existent with time, and must be maintained without regard to men.—Let the preferences and the passions of the hour have no sway over the great cause which is so dear and so important to us all.

To my friends from every portion of the State, who stood by me at Charlotte, and who urged my humble name for the nomination for Governor—and especially to the gallent and indomitable Democracy of the mountain Counties—I tender the homage and the thanks of a grateful heart.

W. W. Holden

Raleigh, April 16, 1858

Holden to Hon. J. W. Ellis SHC:Ellis

Raleigh, May 4, 1858

My dear Sir: Your favor has been received. I will look up all the documents I can, and send them to you by the next or succeeding mail. I have never seen, but I have heard of the letter of Mr. McRae[1] to which you refer, devouring Mr. Clay[2] and distribution. I will find it if I can. The most assailable point in his character, so far as distribution is concerned, is his action in the Baltimore Convention of 1852. He was on the Committee on Resolutions for this State, and of course voted for the resolution declaring distribution unconstitutional. This was *after* his "kick-up," as Cantwell would say, in the State Convention of 1852.

I shall prepare and publish soon a cheap pamphlet on distribution—to contain also a sketch of Mr. McRae, the State Platform, and a sketch of your public life. I will put them at cost, so as to ensure a wide circulation.

Col. Biggs[3] was no doubt confirmed as Judge to-day. Mr. Clingman[4] will, I feel sure, be appointed his successor.

You will see Mr. McRae's letter in the Register of to-day. It is somewhat ingenious, but very answerable. I thought it best not to publish it, though requested to do so, until I could find room for comment.

Truly Yours
W. W. Holden

Hon. J. W. Ellis

[1] Duncan Kirkland McRae, distributionist candidate for governor, 1858. Distribution proponents supported distributing public lands or the proceeds of their sales to the states.

[2] Henry Clay, Kentucky; member, U.S. Senate, 1810-1811, 1831-1842, 1849-1852; member, U.S. House of Representatives, 1811-1821, 1823-1825; speaker, 1811-1814, 1815-1820, 1823-1824; unsuccessful nominee for presidency 1824, 1832, 1844. *Biographical Dirctory of the American Congress, 1774-1971*, s.v. "Clay, Henry."

[3] Asa Biggs.

[4] Thomas Lanier Clingman.

Holden to Hon. J. W. Ellis SHC:Ellis

Raleigh, May 5, 1858

My dear Sir: I have just written a reply to Mr. McRae's[1] letter, which will appear in the Standard of Friday. I have given in that article several of the resolutions which you want, and some facts in relation to Mr. McRae as a public man, which may be of use to you. I could not find the letter of his to which you refer. Probably it appeared in the "*Signal*" of 1843-4.[2] I have no file of that, but Col. H. T. Clark,[3] of Tarboro has. Suppose you write him to look, and also for anti-distribution Editorials.

I will copy in Tuesday's paper Mr. McRae's speech on taking the chair as President of the Convention in 1852; also, some extracts from my notice of his speech in reply to Mr. Kerr,[4] in 1848, at Franklinton.

Mr. Courts[5] is getting up some documents for you, which he will send soon. If I can lay my hands on anything I may deem useful, I will send to you at once on your campaign. Enclosed you will find resolutions of Democratic Conventions.

Very Truly Yours,
W. W. Holden

Hon. J. W. Ellis

[1] Duncan Kirkland McRae.

[2] Holden probably referred to the *Democratic Signal*, a weekly newspaper published in Raleigh in 1843-1844.

[3] Henry Toole Clark.

[4] John Kerr, Jr.

[5] Daniel William Courts, legislator and state treasurer; A.B., U.N.C., 1823; A.M., 1832; U.N.C. trustee, 1832-1839, 1846-1868; member, House of Commons, 1831-1833, 1836, 1846, 1848; member, state Senate, 1850, 1864; state treasurer, 1837-1839, 1852-1863. *Dictionary of North Carolina Biography*, s.v. "Courts, Daniel William."

Holden to Hon. J. W. Ellis SHC:Ellis

Raleigh, May 18, 1858

My dear Sir: Your favors dated Monroe and Wadesborough have been received. I was glad to hear from you. You are "getting the hang of the schoolhouse" and will have no cause, I am sure, to regret your efforts before the people. McRae[1] had the advantage in the outset, being in trim, his mind imbued with all the questions, and his whole soul set upon the issue. My correspondents write me privately that at both Monroe and Wadesborough you got the advantage of him, and maintained yourself admirably.

I have sent you by this mail to Fayetteville some documents which I trust will be of use to you. First, the Standard of to-morrow, containing Bennett's Land Bill[2], and the substance of Hunter's graduation bill[3]; second, Mr. Cobb's[4] speech on Morrill's[5] bill donating lands for agricultural purposes and colleges; third, the speech of Robbins,[6] with an official table, the very thing, I take it, which you might want; fourth, Green's Report[7], which I thought you might not have; fifth, the *Observer* of 11th February, containing an account of Mr. McRae's speech in Fayetteville, from which you will see his position then in relation to Kansas and Judge Douglas.[8] By the way, Morrill and Robbins are both black Republicans; and these are the men we are called upon to *beg* for "our share."

Mr. McRae is a bold campaigner, and our plan is to put him all the time on the defensive. His denunciation of taxation, though not so intended, can be shown to be a sort of preparation of the hearts of the people for repudiation; his opposition to Kansas with Lecompton places him side by side with the black Republicans and against the administration; his censures upon Gov. Bragg[9] for appointing Clingman[10]; and upon the President for appointing Biggs,[11] places him among our enemies and in front of the disorganizers; and his intention is, if he can secure a balance-of power party in the Legislature, to throw his whole influence against the party here, against our Northern brethren, in favor of Douglas and the new party now forming for 1860, and of course against the administration and the Democratic party generally. I have just *conversed* with our friend the Governor on all the points, and he requests me to say to you that that the true policy is to charge on Duncan—to catechize him—to crowd him—to put him and keep him on the defensive. He knew that you were doing this, but still the importance which we both attach to it will justify, as we know you will pardon, a suggestion of this kind.

The Circular which Mr. Branch[12] has just issued to his constituents, will do much good, and he informs me that it will be thickly circulated. I will publish it in the next Standard. My pamphlet will be out in a few days. As you suggest, I will devote a part of it to the question of taxation. That question will affect us somewhat, but it can be met; and besides, Mr. McRae himself, by his course on Kansas, is diverting the minds of the people from it. Important as it is to many of them, they nevertheless regard their rights and their equality in the Union, as more important.

When will your next appointments be published? I would respectfully suggest the importance of your speaking here and in Johnston. We will do our best for you in Wake, but still I would be glad if you could visit us and speak.

I have thus written you freely, and brokenly, too, amid the pressure of calls and business incident to our Court week.

Go ahead, and be of good cheer. You will beat him largely. All the signs are that way. The opposition will not all support him, and his vote from our ranks must be small.

Very Truly Yours
W. W. Holden

Hon. J. W. Ellis

[1] Duncan Kirkland McRae.

[2] Henry Bennett, New York; member, U.S. House of Representative, 1849-1859. *Biographical Directory of the American Congress, 1774-1971*, s.v. "Bennett, Henry."

[3] Robert Mercer Taliaferro Hunter, Virginia; member, U.S. House of Representatives, 1837-1843, 1845-1847; speaker, 1839-1841; member, U.S. Senate, 1847-1861; candidate for president, 1860; Confederate secretary of state, 1861-1862; member, Confederate Senate, 1862-1865. *Biographical Directory of the American Congress, 1774-1971*, s.v. "Hunter, Robert Mercer Taliaferro."

[4] Howell Cobb

[5] Justin Smith Morrill, Vermont; member, U.S. House of Representatives, 1855-1867; author of land grant bill to promote colleges of agricultural and mechanical art; member, U.S. Senate, 1867-1898. *Biographical Directory of the American Congress, 1774-1971*, s.v. "Morrill, Justin Smith."

[6] George Robbins Robbins, New Jersey; physician; member, U.S. House of Representatives, 1849-1855. *Biographical Directory of the American Congress, 1774-1971*, s.v. "Robbins, George Robbins."

[7] James Stephen Green, Missouri; member, U.S. House of Representatives, 1847-1851; member, U.S. Senate, 1857-1861. *Biographical Directory of the American Congress, 1774-1971*, s.v. "Green, James Stephen."

[8] Stephen Arnold Douglas.

[9] Governor Thomas Bragg.

[10] Thomas Lanier Clingman.

[11] Asa Biggs.

[12] Lawrence O'Bryan Branch.

Holden to Hon. J. W. Ellis SHC:Ellis

Raleigh, June 1, 1858

My dear Sir: On my return from Salem I found your favors awaiting me, and would have replied sooner but for the pressure of numerous engagements.

Your statements as to your volunteering and as to the communication signed "Delta," are just such as I expected. These things cannot affect you. It is hardly necessary, it seems to me, to allude to them now; but it may be necessary during the campaign, to refer to the facts connected with your volunteering. I infer from the reports of the discussions, that Mr. McRae[1] is not using these points; and I presume he will not. In deed, I am gratified to see the courtesy exhibited on both sides, and I trust it will continue. It is onerous enough to have to canvass the State, without the superaddition of unkind and acrimonious words.

I have lately visited Salem, and had many opportunties of collecting public sentiment. My candid opinion is that Mr. McRae has been losing ever since the campaign commenced, and you have, of course, been gaining. Duncan has a bad cause, and a shattered and depressed opposition to depend on. Besides, though superior in mere action, he is deficient in judgment and tactics. Our friends, where I have been, and all from whom I have heard, are in good spirits. You will get 300 majority in Forsythe; while Mr. McRae, in the judgment of Mr. Anslem Reid[2] and others, cannot poll more than 1200 votes.

The Democrats of Forsythe will probably run Mr. Masten,[3] the old member and Mr. Fries.[4] In Franklin, Green[5] for the Commons again, and young Lankford[6] for the Senate. We shall have some trouble, I fear, in Chatham. I am glad to see McDowell[7] out in Bladen. That most probably secures that Senatorial district. I think the chances are that we shall have the Legislature by at least 30 on joint ballot.

I am glad to hear that your voice is improving. the labor of the campaign is likely to be beneficial to your health.

I should be glad to hear from you often, and to co-operate with you in any way suggested for the advancement of the cause.

Very Truly Yours
W. W. Holden

Hon. J. W. Ellis

[1] Duncan Kirkland McRae.

[2] Ansolem Reid, Guilford County; farmer. 1860 U.S. Census Population Schedule, North Carolina: Guilford, 242 (microfilm).

[3] John Masten, Forsyth County; member, House of Commons, 1856-1859. Cheney, *North Carolina Government, 1585-1979*, 1135

[4] Francis Levin Fries, textile manufacturer; member, House of Commons, 1858-1859. *Dictionary of North Carolina Biography*, s.v. "Fries, Francis (Franz) Levin."

[5] William F. Green, Franklin County; member, House of Commons, 1856-1861. Cheney, *North Carolina government, 1585-1979*, 1138.

[6] Menalcus Lankford, lawyer and planter; A.B., U.N.C., 1847; member, state Senate, 1858-1859. Grant, *Alumni History*, 353.

[7] Thomas David Smith McDowell, planter; A.B., U.N.C., 1843; member, House of Commons, 1846-1851; member, state Senate, 1852-1855, 1858-1859; member, Confederate House of Representatives, 1861-1864. Grant, *Alumni History*, 388.

Holden to Miss L. H. Holden DU:Holden

August 6, 1858

My dear Daughter:

Your welcome letter of Tuesday has been received. We were very glad to hear from you, and to learn that you were so well pleased with the Select class.

We expect to start in the morning for Beaufort. Your Ma[1] and Mary,[2] your Aunt Lotty[3] and Mrs. Marriot[4] will go with me. I expect to remain some eight or ten days. Write to me at Beaufort, Carteret, N.C. The letter will reach me in less than two days, though Beaufort is some 260 miles from Salem.

The election is just over, and as you may well suppose I have been much engaged seeing friends, hearing the result, &c. Mr. High[5] is re-elected sheriff of Wake by a decided majority. The Democrats have carried the State, as was expected, by a large majority.

I feel it is not necessary that I should advise you as to the importance of affection to your studies. I believe you will do the best you can, and leave no duty unperformed. Rest assured that we all remember you constantly and love you, and pray for your continued health and happiness.

Affectionately Yours,
W. W. Holden

Miss L. H. Holden[6]

[1] Louisa Virginia Harrison Holden, Holden's second wife, whom he married in 1854.

[2] Mary Eldridge Holden, the first child born to Holden and his second wife.

[3] Not identified.

[4] Not identified.

[5] William High, Wake County; sheriff. 1860 U.S. Census Population Schedule, North Carolina: Wake, 354 (microfilm).

[6] Laura H. Holden, eldest child of Holden and his first wife; student at Salem Female Academy.

Holden to Hon. J. W. Ellis SHC:Ellis

Raleigh, Aug. 6, 1858

My dear Sir: The Standard of to-morrow will give you all the news I have. We have gained in the Legislature, and lost also, but not so as to affect us. The Legislature must be Democratic by from 40 to 50. *Your* majority will be a glorious one—perhaps 20,000.

We have given you 880 majority in Wake—the largest ever given to any man.

I expect to leave for Beaufort in the morning, where I will be for a week or two.

I regret our losses in Johnston and Craven. Bad management in the latter, and the popularity of Willis Sanders[1] in the former. I learn that your vote is a fine one in Wayne, Dublin, Craven, Lenoir, etc.

Very Truly Yours
W. W. Holden

Hon. J. W. Ellis

[1] Willis Henry Sanders, Johnston County; A.B., U.N.C., 1843; member, House of Commons, 1852-1853, 1858-1859. Grant, *Alumni History*, 544.

"To the Democratic Party of North Carolina" *Standard*
October 20, 1858

I deem it my duty to notice publicly over my own name the following charges which have recently been originated and circulated against me:

First, It is charged that I am exerting myself to "punish" (that is the word used) those who opposed my nomination for Governor at Charlotte.

Secondly, It is charged that I am seeking a Senatorship in the Congress of the United States, and that I will continue to do so at a sacrifice of the harmony and integrity of the Democratic party.

Thirdly, it is charged that I wrote, or suggested, or advised, or instigated the articles which have recently appeared in the *Warrenton News* in relation to "Federal and State appointments."

In relation to the first charge I may say that no Democrat in the State gave to John W. Ellis a more active support than I did; and that the columns of the *Standard* will be examined in vain for any evidence of injustice or unkindness towards his friends. Nor has my course been different, nor will it be different as a man. I have no resentments of this kind to gratify, nor have I exerted, nor will I exert myself to "punish" or injure those who opposed me at Charlotte. This charge, unjust and unfounded as it is, may temporarily furnish some little capital to some office seeker, who thinks quite as much of his own interests as he does of the harmony and integrity of the party; but all good Democrats will see through it sooner or later, and treat it with the silent indifference it deserves.

In reply to the second charge I say that I am not seeking a Senatorship; and that my feelings have always been subordinated, as they always will be, to the harmony, the prosperity, and the integrity of my party. No man will say that I ever approached him on the subject of a Senatorship, or that I ever even intimated that I was a candidate for Senator. On the contrary, I have uniformly informed my friends that I was not a candidate, and would not seek the place. Moreover, I have always done justice both in the *Standard* and in private conversations to others who have been spoken of for the Senatorships; and I have said nothing of them or about them, which, if imparted to them, should in the slightest degree interrupt the friendship that exists between us.

There are a few persons in North Carolina professing to be Democrats, who are really Aristocrats, and who will never forgive me for consenting to the use of my name for Governor. Of course these persons have their dependents, who echo what they say. If I were to say, what I so not choose to say, that in no event would I accept a Senatorship, *they* would be gratified, and charges like those to which I am now replying would no longer be made. It was my lot to be born in humble circumstances, to an inheritance of ignorance and poverty, and to be brought up to a mechanical trade; and there are some who would "punish" me on account of my origin, and because I had the energy and the ambition to struggle upwards in life, who, if they had been born in the condition in which I was, would have been there yet. Proud towards the proud, and humble among the humble, I have never cringed to a rich man because he was rich, nor slighted a poor man because he was poor. Nor have I ever played the demagogue, seeking to array one class of society against another. I have been the friend, both as an Editor and as a man, of *all* interests and *all* classes in North Carolina, from the college in which those who have means are educated, to the common school, where the "children of the people" are cared for and educated by the State. Unpretending as was my origin, I thank God that he has given me a disposition to live my State, and my whole State with the affection of a son; and though others have served her with far more efficiency and ability than I have, yet none have laid upon her altar the offerings of a more loyal or patriotic heart.

In reply to the third charge I state that I neither wrote, nor suggested, nor advised, nor instigated the articles referred to in the *Warrenton News*.—During the fifteen years I have been at the head of the *Standard*, I have never assailed a recognized Democrat, and have never failed, when the occasion required it, to defend and vindicate Democrats and the Democratic party against the attacks of the opposition. I have never advised others to do what I would not do myself, and I have never assailed any one covertly or in the dark. No man is my friend who hesitates for a moment as to whether I would instigate privately what I would not do myself publicly, or who would leave the impression, by insinuation or otherwise, that I was capable of a hidden or an unmanly deed. I am not responsible for the course of the Editor of the *Warrenton News*,[1] and I will take no part in a controversy between Democrats. It is true the Editor of that paper is my friend, and was at one time a Clerk in my office; but I paid him his salary as he earned it, and nothing more, and he is under no greater obligations to me of any kind than I am to him.

It is sufficient to say that I approved, both as an Editor and as a man, of the appointment of Senator Biggs[2] as Judge; of the appointment of Mr. Clingman[3] as Senator; of the appointment of Mr. Page[4] as Secretary of State, to fill the unexpired term; and that when Mr. Cooke[5] was appointed Postmaster at Raleigh, it was stated in the *Standard* that he was well qualified for the post, and that his appointment would give general satisfaction to our citizens. I have made no charge of corruption against Gov. Bragg[6] and our congressional delegation, nor do I for one moment believe any such charge; though candor requires me to say that I have always disapproved, and do yet disapprove of the custom by which members of Congress *substantially* appoint to Federal office. I was among the first to suggest the name of Thomas Bragg for Governor in 1853; I have been associated with him as a member of the Literary Board from his inauguration to the present time, as I was with Gov. Reid[7] during both his terms; and I have given to Gov. Bragg's administration, and still give to it, a cordial and unwavering support. Under the circumstances, as the Editor of the *Register*[8] had copied the articles referred to from the *Warrenton News*, it was perhaps natural and proper that the Governor should request the former to say "that no member of the Congress ever requested, either orally or in writing, Gov. Bragg to appoint Mr. Clingman to the vacancy made in the Senate by the resignation of Mr. Biggs." But if the Governor had made the request of me, I would have gone further and borne my testimony to his integrity as a public servant, and would have re-published the article which appeared in the *Standard* when Mr. Clingman was appointed, in which the appointment was approved, and Mr. Clingman spoken of in the highest terms.

In relation to the delegation in Congress I may add that some of them have honored me with their intimate personal friendship, and for all of them I entertain friendly feelings. I rejoiced at their success over the opposition in August last, and I have joined in no attacks upon them at any time or of any kind whatsoever. So far as Mr. Branch,[9] our immediate Representative, is concerned, many of my friends in this community know that I was among the first to suggest his name for Congress in 1855, though I had understood he had voted for Mr. Venable[10] in 1853; and from that time until this I have done him justice both in the *Standard* and in private conversations. I have always been his friend. I am not his enemy now, nor do I expect to be. If I shall conceive it to be my duty as one of his constituents, or as the Editor of a Democratic journal, to complain of his course, I will do so publicly and openly on my own responsibility, and not by indirection or privately through another person.

What then? I am censured because I do not defend these gentlemen through the columns of the *Standard* against the stricture of the Warrenton *News*. I do not say they censure me, because I do not know the fact, and they have not approached me on the subject; but this community is full of the rumor that I *am* censured in various quarters, because I do not repel these attacks of the *News*. I cannot do it, and I am presumed to know something of my duties. When the State officers at the Capitol and our delegation in Congress were assailed a month or two since by the *Register*, they were promptly defended by the *Standard*, as they always will be, if in the right, when assailed by the opposition. But I cannot engage in a controversy between Democrats. To do so would only add fuel to the flame, while it would gratify the opposition, as may be plainly inferred from the tone of the *Register*. The Editor of the *Warrenton News* and those gentlemen in Warren and elsewhere who are sustaining him in his course, have neither abandoned principle nor infringed organization; and they hold themselves, and are held by others, to be as good Democrats as those whom they assail. Who made me a judge between them? Who commissioned me to decide questions of this sort? Who armed me with the power to defend one portion of the party and put another portion under ban? What right have I to engage in a controversy which is rather personal than political, and which concerns office and place more than it does principle? I regret the controversy, but I have had and will have no part in it. It is not so serious, after all, as some suppose; and if it should increase and threaten injurious consequences, *the Democratic people will themselves command the peace*. For my part I earnestly desire the harmony and the continued success and prosperity of the Democratic party. I will sacrifice anything and every thing which a man of honor ought to sacrifice, to promote and preserve harmony; and I will go as far, now and hereafter, as he who will go farthest, to render the party a unit, and to make it, and the prosperity of our beloved State, paramount to all other considerations.

My Democratic friends will bear me witness that I am not in the habit of addressing them on matters personal to myself. Under the circumstances, I could not in justice to myself have said less. This is the second Card which I have published during my fifteen years of public life. My first one was an appeal in April last to my friends to support Judge Ellis for Governor. They *did* support him with an enthusiasm and thoroughness which both he and I will always gratefully remember.

W. W. Holden

Raleigh, Oct. 18, 1858

[1] William A. Walsh, formerly of Petersburg, Virginia, editor of the *Warrenton News*. Lizzie Wilson Montgomery, *Sketches of Old Warrenton, North Carolina* (Raleigh: Edwards & Broughton Printing Company, 1924), 179.

[2] Asa Biggs.

[3] Thomas Lanier Clingman.

[4] Rufus H. Page was appointed secretary of state November 10, 1857, and was reelected November 19, 1858. He served in that office until November 25, 1862. Cheney, *North Carolina Government, 1885-1979*, 181.

[5] George T. Cooke, postmaster of Raleigh. 1860 U.S. Census Population Schedule, North Carolina: Wake, 296 (microfilm).

[6] Thomas Bragg.

[7] David Settle Reid.

[8] John William Syme, newspaper editor; editor of the Petersburg, Virginia, *Petersburg Intelligencer*; member, Virginia Assembly, 1845-1850; purchased Raleigh *Register*, December, 1856; ceased publication August, 1864. *Dictionary of North Carolina Biography*, s.v. "Syme, John William."

[9] Lawrence O'Bryan Branch.

[10] Abraham Watkins Venable.

Standard
January 22, 1859

The Senior Editor of the *Standard* has no reply to offer to the remarks of Mr. Turner,[1] submitted to the Senate a few days since.[2] He will not condescend to engage in a war of words with a person who substitutes vituperation for argument, and low epithets for that dignified language which we expect from a Senator. He has no respect for Mr. Turner, and no disposition even to think of him. He will not be at the emotional expense even of conceiving and entertaining contempt for the Senator from Orange. As Uncle Toby said to the fly, he can very quietly say to Mr. Turner: "Go thy way, poor creature—the world is large enough for both thee and me."

[1] Josiah Turner, Jr., editor and militant foe of reconstruction; member, House of Commons, 1852-1854; member, state Senate, 1858-1860; member confederate House of Representatives, 1864-1865; director, North Carolina Railroad, 1866 and 1867, president, 1867; purchased Raleigh *Sentinel*, 1868, serving as editor until 1876. *Dictionary of North Carolina Biography*, s.v. "Turner, Josiah, Jr."

[2] Turner had been editorially rebuked by the *Standard* for a disorderly performance in the state Senate, and had accused him of buying his election with "barbecue and whiskey, etc." Turner than attacked Holden on the floor of the Senate, causing this comment by Holden. For an account of the affair, see *Standard*, January 19, 1859.

TO THE READERS OF THE STANDARD

Standard
November 2, 1859

With this number I resume the sole Editorship of the *Standard*, Mr. Wilson,[1] my associate, having of his own account retired. I take pleasure in bearing testimony to his worth as a man, and to his soundness and integrity as a Democrat. Nothing in the slightest degree unpleasant has occurred between us during the five years he has been associated with me; and though he has occasionally written the paper, giving me important aid in his capacity as Associate, yet the *Standard* has uniformly reflected my opinions, and I consider that I was responsible for every thing it has contained, or failed to contain, since the time I took charge of it in June, 1843.

The business of the office will in future be conducted in my name, the firm of Holden & Wilson having ceased by limitation. I have engaged the services of Mr. Wilson in the business department, who will manage for me in my name.

The business of editing and conducting a newspaper like the *Standard*, is by no means easy or very pleasant. It requires patience, forbearance, a sense of justice towards both political friends and opponents, a constant and inflexible devotion to principle without regard to men, incessant vigilance, and, if I may add, almost incessant labor. It is not for me to say to what extent I have succeeded, if I have succeeded at all, in this business. My course is before my party and public,—it is for them to say whether it had been correct, or of any service to the country. One thing, however, I *know*: I have been true to Democracy and to North Carolina.

I have no pledge to make as to the future, for the plain reason that I expect to perform my duty to my readers and to my party as I have heretofore performed it. The contest in 1860 is near at hand. I regard it as the most important since the government was formed, since its result is most probably to determine whether the government shall continue to exist. I have no fears as to the result of the next elections in North Carolina. I think the Democrats will carry their Governor and the Legislature as heretofore, and that the state will cast her electoral vote and the Legislature as heretofore, and that the State will cast her electoral vote for the nominee of the Charleston Convention. But I hold that a man should always "show his faith by his works," and therefore, for my part, I expect to labor as energetically and as resolutely as if the result were in doubt. The Democratic party of the State cannot hope to maintain ascendency without effort. It is sometimes more difficult to retain power than it is to obtain it. Let all, then, determine to *work* as we worked in 1848 and in 1850; let us do this, and the motley crew of "the opposition" will give way and go on before us, as they did when Reid triumphed under the banner of Democracy and Free Suffrage. I trust that my Democratic friends generally will exert themselves somewhat to increase the circulation of the *Standard*. If we expect to succeed, we must lay the documents with the facts and arguments before the people.

W. W. Holden

[1] Franklin Inge Wilson (Frank).

Standard
November 16, 1859

The political contest of 1860 will be the most exciting and important that has ever taken place in this country. On its result may depend the existence of the Union itself. Great interests are at stake; and those interests, in the opinion of the undersigned, can be protected and preserved in no other way than by the continued ascendency of the Democratic party. To preserve this ascendency should be the aim of every friend of the Constitution and Union. The undersigned expects to do his full part, in his humble way, in maintaining Democratic principles, and in protecting North-Carolina from the aggressions of the black Republicans.

In addition to the Presidential contest, elections will be held for Governor and members of the Legislature in 1860. The *Standard* will be found, as heretofore, in the thickest of the contest, expounding and maintaining Democratic principles and supporting the candidates of the Democratic party. It will also be found at all times true to North-Carolina, her mental, physical, and moral interests. The latest news on all subjects will also be regularly given. In a word, neither expense nor labor will be spared to render the *Standard* a readable, useful, and reliable Democratic paper.

The undersigned most respectfully appeals to his friends to aid him in increasing the circulation of the *Standard*.

The terms of the *Standard* are as follows:—Weekly, $2 in advance; Semi-Weekly, $4 in advance. The Weekly paper will be sent to clubs at the following rates:—Six copies one year for $10—ten copies for one year for $15.

W. W. Holden

Raleigh, N.C., Nov. 10, 1859

D.W.C.J. for the Standard *Standard*
March 3, 1860

Mr. Holden: I wish to express a few thoughts in regard to the "crisis" that is now upon us.

1. If Seward[1] or any of his associates who has endorsed Helper's book[2] be elected, I am in favor of resistance.

2. The very fact of the black Republicans running Seward, or any of his stripe, for President, would be an open declaration of war upon the South. And in that event, even before the election, I would go for a National Convention, as suggested by Gov. Letcher in his inaugural.[3]

3. Encourage volunteer companies by contributions until the Legislature meets. That body should give substantial aid in equipping and fostering volunteer companies, and putting in their hands the best and most approved arms. Let the South be well armed, and the Union is safe. A good supply of Sharpe and Minnie rifles in the hands of brave and exasperated volunteers in the South, will command respect, and check the whirlwind of Abolition fanaticism.

4. Let us wear and use home-made manufactures; and instead of buying silks and broadcloths, let us buy guns and powder for our volunteers.

5. I am for the Union as long as I can be with honor. As a last resort, I am for secession, peaceably if we can—forcibly if we must.

I agree with you that the South, though much exasperated, as she has cause to be, should be careful to take no rash or hasty step—none from which she would have to recede. But let her take the right course, and firmly pursue it.

D.W.C.J.[4]

Davidson County, N.C.

[1] William Henry Seward.

[2] Hinton Rowan Helper, *The Impending Crisis in the South: How to Meet It* (New York: A. B. Burdick, 1859).

[3] John Letcher, governor of Virginia, 1860-1864. His inaugural speech was printed in the *Standard*, January 14, 1860.

[4] DeWitt Clinton Johnson, Davidson County; lawyer; one of founders of Bank of Thomasville. M. Jewel Sink & Mary Green Matthews, *Pathfinders, Past and Present: A History of Davidson County, North Carolina* (N.P.: N.C., 1972), 325.

Holden to Louisa Holden DU:Holden

Charleston, Apl 22, 1860

My dearest Wife:

I arrived here on Friday to dinner, feeling not very well, owing to being up all night, but I am now very well indeed. On the way it was cool, and my overcoat was comfortable, but as we neared Charleston the sky cleared and the weather became quite warm. I am now writing in a public room in the Charleston Hotel, in the midst of "noise and confusion." The thing here is not so great as was expected, owing no doubt to the rumors which prevailed about high prices, &c. but still there are a great many persons. Charleston is indeed a noble City. I do not wonder that the South Carolinians are proud of it. It is equal in size and population to Baltimore, and constantly gaining. The Hotel at which I am staying is conducted in the best manner, and I have every comfort I could desire. The table is superior in every respect. Every thing you can think of in the way of fowl, meats, vegetables, and dessert are before you. All our delegation are stopping here, and they are all here except R. L. Patterson,[1] N. M. Long[2] and Capt. John Walker.[3] By the way Mrs. Walker passed up the Road on Thursday with me to Charlotte.

The weather is very warm, and it appears to be midsummer here. Vegetation is fully out. I am glad I brought my thin coat. I am staying in a room with Avery,[4] J.W.B. Watson,[5] Gen. T.J. Green,[6] and W.S. Ashe.[7] We are having a very pleasant time. I went last night to see and hear Mrs. Julie Dean Haryse in Lucretia Borgie. It is great acting. She is certainly a remarkable woman.

The convention will assemble to-morrow. All is yet uncertainty. No one can predict who will be the nominee. The contest is between Breckinridge,[8] Lane,[9] Hunter,[10] and Douglas,[11] but someone not named may be the fortunate person. I incline to think our delegation will vote the first time for Hunter, though I would prefer Lane or Breckinridge. Douglas *may*, after all, be nominated. The manner in which he is pursued and persecuted by the Administration of Mr. Buchanan,[12] and the extreme bitterness of the far Southern States against him are addiing to his strength & creating a sympathy for him.

I will telegraph every day to Mr. Wilson,[13] so that the news may be known in Raleigh, and I will write to you again on the 24th. I sincerely hope that we may be through by Friday. If so, I can be at home Sunday. But do not be anxious about me. I am well, and doing well. I think of you and the dear children often, often, as well when in crowds as when alone. I trust you are all well. Though absent but for a few days, still I long to see you, and to be with you again. You will know every day by my dispatch to Mr. Wilson, that I am alive and well.

Your devoted and affectionate husband,
W. W. Holden

[1] Rufus Lenoir Patterson, manufacturer; A.B., U.N.C., 1851; owned and operated several textile mills; member of conventions of 1861 and 1865; director and supporter of railroads. *Dictionary of North Carolina Biography*, s.v. "Patterson, Rufus Lenoir."

[2] Nicholas M. Long, Halifax county; member, Council of State, 1856. Cheney, *North Carolina Government*, 1585-1979, 179.

[3] John Walker, Mecklenburg County; member, House of Commons, 1840-1841; member, state Senate, 1842-1845, 1854-1855, 1860-1861. Cheney, *North Carolina Government*, 1585-1979, 1201-1202.

[4] William Waightstill Avery.

[5] John William Bryan Watson, Johnston County; planter; member, state Senate, 1862. Grant, *Alumni History*, 650.

[6] Thomas Jefferson Green, Warren County; planter; member, House of Commons, 1826; brigadier general, Texas army; major general, California militia. *Dictionary of North Carolina Biography*, s.v. "Green, Thomas Jefferson."

[7] William Shepperd Ashe.

[8] John Cabell Breckinridge.

[9] Joseph Lane, Oregon; major general in War with Mexico; governor of Oregon Territory, 1849-1850; delegate to Congress from Oregon, 1851-1859; member, U.S. Senate, 1859-1861; unsuccessful candidate for vice-president, 1860. *Biographical Directory of the American Congress, 1774-1971*, s.v. "Lane, Joseph."

[10] Robert Mercer Taliaferro Hunter.

[11] Stephen Arnold Douglas.

[12] President James Buchanan.

[13] Franklin Inge Wilson (Frank).

Holden to Louisa Holden DU:Holden

Charleston, April 24, 1860

My dear Lula: This is Tuesday evening. The convention has adjourned till tomorrow morning, and I seize the first opportunity to write you. It is impossible to say what day we will adjourn, but I think by Friday evening. If so, I will reach home Saturday evening.

We have not yet voted for President. all at present is uncertain. Our State will vote for Hunter[1] first, and afterwards for Breckinridge[2] and others.

I am passing my time quite pleasantly, though I would much prefer to be at home. We have good quarters and good entertainment. I feel better now than I have for a long while, and am thus satisfied that all I require for good health is exercise.

I think of you very often, in the throng, in the Hotel, in my room, every where, your sweet face and kind voice are remembered. Tell the dear children that I bear them all in mind.

Mr. Delany[3] is here, looking quite well; besides many North Carolinians. In this respect I feel at home. The throng has considerably increased, but is by no means as large as was expected.

Good-bye,
W. W. Holden

[1] Robert Mercer Taliaferro Hunter of Virginia.

[2] John Cabell Breckinridge of Kentucky.

[3] Not identified.

Letter from the Editor *Standard*
May 9, 1860

Charlston, April 28, 1860

The Convention has just adjourned (at ten P.M.) until Monday Morning. The Platform is still under discussion, no vote for President having been taken. The report of the committee on resolutions, made on Thursday, was discussed and then recommitted. The committee reported again today, in substance, what was reported on Thursday; the previous question was called and put, and so on Monday morning the vote will be taken without debate on the resolutions. After the resolutions shall have been adopted, the Convention will commence to vote for President.

The majority report was made at first by one majority by States, and the second time by three majority. It undoubtedly embodies the true doctrine on the subject of slavery, but differs from the views of many of our Northern friends, in that they believe it asserts the doctrine of Congressional protection to slavery in the Territories. This is not intended. The *government*, and not Congress, is called upon to protect slave property in the Territories. The minority report, presented by a majority of the non-slaveholding States, refers to the difference of opinion or construction between the North and South on the Cincinnati platform, and after re-affirming that platform, it proposes to abide the action of the Supreme Court on the subject. The Convention has been addressed with much ability on both sides. Northern Democrats declare that they are ready and willing to give us all our rights on the subject of slavery both in the States and Territories; that they oppose, detest, and most earnestly desire to crush the black Republican organization, and thus preserve the Constitution and the Union; but that, if crippled by Congressional protection and a distinct repudiation of what we call "squatter sovereignty," they will not be able to sustain themselves at home. This is the opinion of a large majority of the Northern Democracy; but a portion of the Pennsylvania delegation, and California and Oregon think and act differently. On the other hand delegates from Alabama, Arkansas, Mississippi, and Florida declare that if the minority report shall be adopted they will retire from the Convention; and they will certainly do so if the Cincinnati platform, pure and simple, and nothing else, shall be adopted. I have no idea that they will be sustained in this movement by the Democracy of their respective States. It is *for them*, however, to act as they may deem it to be their duty to act, leaving the national Democracy to pursue the "even tenor of their way," determined on victory under all circumstances and against whatever apparent odds.

Mr. Lander[1] is the Chairman of our delegation, and Mr. Avery[2] the Chairman of the committee on Resolutions. This latter is a high honor for our State. Mr. A. has sustained himself ably in the discussion. Mr. Moore[3] was our committee-man on organization; Mr. Bridgers[4] on credentials and qualifications of members; Hon. Bedford Brown[5] is a Vice President from our State: Mr. Humphrey[6] a Secretary from our State; Mr. Hargrave[7] on the committee raised on the national Executive

Committee; and Mr. Holden has been selected by the delegation as the national committee-man for the next four years.

We *may* get to a vote on Monday for President; and I think that on Tuesday we will nominate. North Carolina will vote first nine votes for Mr. Hunter[8] and one vote for Mr. Douglas[9]—the latter vote by Mr. Dick.[10] Douglas will probably poll the highest vote on the first ballot. Our State will vote for Mr. Breckinridge[11] after Mr. Hunter, if the latter should fail to be nominated; then most probably for Gen. Lane;[12] then most probably for Mr. Dickinson;[13] and then——. These, of course, are my own opinions, except as to the first vote. That has already been determined.

We have had several exciting scenes in the Convention, but no bitter feeling has been exhibited. Generally the members are good humored, and the approach to discord (though there is necessarily confusion now and then in so large a body;) are promptly checked by the President, Hon. Caleb Cushing,[14] who presides with consuminate ability.

Several meetings have been held by the delegates from Texas, Alabama, Mississippi, Florida and Arkansas. The Leading spirits are Yancey,[15] of Alabama, Glenn,[16] of Mississippi, and Burroughs,[17] of Arkansas. North-Carolina declined to recognize officially this movement, but some of her delegates attended one of these meetings with the view of pouring oil on the troubled waters. Among these, the Hon. Bedford Brown was called upon, and addressed the meeting. While contending for all the Constitutional rights of the South, he admonished the meeting against precipitate or hasty action, and warned the South not to demand Congressional protection for slavery in the Territories. His remarks were able and to the point, and imbued with true doctrine; yet as I state to show the temper of these Southern delegates, the most opposite sentiments and the most extravagant declarations, uttered by speakers before and after Col. Brown addressed the meeting, were vehemently applauded.

If the convention adjourns, as I hope it will, on Tuesday evening, I expect to reach home on Thursday morning.

W.W.H.

[1] William Lander.

[2] William Waightstill Avery.

[3] William Armistead Moore, lawyer and judge; colonel and commander of Fifth Regiment of North Carolina militia; member, House of Commons, 1869-1870; judge of superior court, 1871-1879. *Dictionary of North Carolina Biography*, s.v. "Moore, William Armistead."

[4] Robert Rufus Bridgers, lawyer and railroad official; A.B., U.N.C., 1841; member, House of Commons, 1844, 1856-1860; member, Confederate House of Representatives, 1862-1865; president, Wilmington and Weldon Railroad. *Dictionary of North Carolina Biography*, s.v. "Bridgers, Robert Rufus."

[5] Bedford Brown, farmer and legislator; member, House of Commons, 1815-1818, 1823-1824; member, state Senate, 1828-1829, 1842-1843, 1858-1864, 1868; member, U.S. Senate, 1831-1840. *Dictionary of North Carolina Biography*, s.v. "Brown, Bedford."

[6] Lott W. Humphrey, Onslow County; member, House of Commons, 1854-1857; member, state Senate, 1858-1861. Cheney, *North Carolina Government, 1585-1979*, 1223-1224.

[7] Samuel Hargrove, Davidson County; member, state Senate, 1846-1847, 1850-1852. *Cheney, North Carolina Government, 1585-1979*, 1121.

[8] Robert Mercer Taliaferreo Hunter.

[9] Stephen Arnold Douglas.

[10] Robert Paine Dick.

[11] John Cabell Breckinridge.

[12] Joseph Lane

[13] Daniel Stevens Dickinson, New York; member, state Senate, 1837-1840; lieutenant governor, 1842-1844; member, U.S. Senate, 1844-1851; elected attorney general of New York, 1861. *Biographical Directory of the American Congress, 1774-1971*, s.v. "Dickinson, Daniel Stevens."

[14] Caleb Cushing, Massachusetts; member, state House of Representatives, 1825, 1833, 1834, 1845-1846; member, state Senate, 1827; member, U.S. House of Representatives, 1835-1843; minister to China, 1843-1845; U.S. attorney general, 1853-1857; minister to Spain, 1874-1877. *Biographical Directory of the American Congress, 1774-1971*, s.v. "Cushing, Caleb."

[15] William Lowndes Yancey, Alabama; planter and editor; member, state House of Representatives, 1841; member, state Senate, 1853; member, U.S. House of Representatives, 1844-1846; member, Confederate States Senate, 1862-1863. *Biographical Directory of the American Congress, 1774-1971*, s.v. "Yancy, William Lowndes."

[16] Probably David C. Glenn, lawyer; attorney general of Mississippi in 1850; secessionist leader and member of Mississippi secession convention. 1850 U.S. Census Population Schedule, Mississippi: Hinds, 134; William L. Barney, *The Secessionist Impulse: Alabama and Mississippi in 1860* (Princeton, N.J.: Princeton University Press, 1974), 309-310.

[17] Not identified.

Holden to Rev. C. H. Wiley SHC:Wiley

Raleigh, May 9, 1860

My dear Sir: I write to know if it will be convenient for you to be present in Raleigh on Wednesday the 23rd of May, to aid in forming an Educational Association for this County. The spirit is up here, and the friends of the cause would be greatly gratified to have the benefit of your personal presence and counsel. Please let me hear from you at once.

When I see you I will give you a full account of the Charleston Convention. I regard the Union as in imminent peril. It must be saved, if at all possible.

In haste, Truly Yours,
W. W. Holden

Rev. C. H. Wiley

Holden to the Public *Standard*
May 19, 1860

I understand the statement is in circulation in certain portions of the State that I have "*farmed out*" the *Standard* office to Mr. Frank I. Wilson, and that my control over the *Standard* is only nominal, and not real. Certainly no intelligent person who is unprejudiced can believe this statement, as my name appears in every issue of the *Standard* both as Editor and Proprietor; but, since the uninformed may be imposed upon by it, and in order to leave designing and unscrupulous persons no room for their misrepresentations, I have thought it my duty to contradict, as I do most emphatically, the statement referred to. On the 1st November, 1859, when Mr. Wilson retired from the Editorial department of the *Standard*, I said:

> "The business of the office will in future be conducted in my name, the firm of Holden & Wilson having ceased by limitation. I have engaged the services of Mr. Wilson in the business department, who will manage for me in my name."

This arrangement still exists. I have known persons in my time who made fortunes and preserved a character for veracity by attending to their own business, and letting other people's alone. This is a good rule. I have uniformily been governed by it; and I avail myself of this occasion most respectfully to comment it to others for their consideration and adoption.

W. W. Holden

Raleigh, May 17, 1860

Holden to Th. Goode Tucker, Esq. Chi:Douglas

Raleigh, May 19, 1860

My dear Sir: Your esteemed favor of the 16th has been received. I received your communication but a short time before leaving for Charleston, and I was compelled to postpone it until my return, on account of the difficulty which I knew the compositors would encounter in reading your handwriting. I promised in the last weekly Standard to give it in the next. It is already in type, and under the circumstances is it not best to publish it?[1] You can follow it up with other numbers, which I would be glad to have; for though I may not agree with you in some of your views, still it will always afford me pleasure to give you a hearing through the Standard. But please write as plainly as you can.

I am gratified to hear that the Democratic cause is prospering in your part of the State. I receive equally cheering intelligence from other portions of the State. If we should have a fortunate issue at Baltimore, we will carry both the Legislature and the Governor by handsome majorities. I voted 57 times at Charleston against Douglas.[2] I expect to vote *for* him at Baltimore. The choice is now between Douglas and defeat and vertual disolution. I am not *now* prepared for disolution. God forbid that the madness of the North, and our own blindness, prejudice and folly should ever compel us thus to prepare! From what I saw and heard at Charleston I am convinced that the leaders of the seceders, especially, Yancey[3] and Meek[4] are disunionists *per se*. We must check this movement. I look to Baltimore with mingled hope and fear. The nomination of Lincoln by the blacks, will strengthen Douglas. Without him we may lose Illinois and all the Northwest, while Lincoln will be easier to beat in New York than Seward.

I would be glad to hear from you often, and nothing would give me more pleasure than to see you in Raleigh. Mrs. H. would be happy to visit you, and may do so sometimes this summer. She desires to be kindly remembered.

Very Truly Yours,
W. W. Holden

Th. Goode Tucker, Esq.[5]

[1] An article on ad valorem taxation and entitled "No. 1" was printed in the *Standard* on May 26, 1860, and signed "Northampton."

[2] Stephen Arnold Douglas.

[3] William Lowndes Yancey, Alabama.

[4] Alexander Beaufort Meek, editor and legislator; associate editor, Mobile *Daily Register*; pioneer worker in Alabama history; leader in founding of Alabama public school system; member, Alabama House of Representatives, 1853, 1859; speaker, 1859; delegate to Charleston Convention. *Dictionary of American Biography*, s.v. "Meek, Alexander Beaufort."

[5] Thomas Goode Tucker, Northampton County; wealthy farmer. 1860 U.S. Census Population Schedule, North Carolina: Northampton, 110 (microfilm). Tucker forwarded this letter from Holden to Senator Douglas, with the admonition "Read it & destroy it." He also commented to Douglas: "The excitement against you in this section does not seem to be so great as immediately after the adjournment of the Convention at Charleston." Thos. Goode Tucker to Hon. S. A. Douglas, May 30, 1860, Stephen A. Douglas Papers, Special Collections Department, University of Chicago Library, Chicago, Illinois.

Holden to Hon. S. A. Douglas Chi:Douglas

Raleigh, N. C. June 1, 1860

My Dear sir: I take the liberty of enclosing to you a copy of my Wake County resolutions, as they appeared in the Standard.[1] They are not entirely correct as they were printed in the States. These resolutions were passed unanimously and enthusiastically in one of the largest meetings ever held in the County. My opinion is that our State will give you on the first ballot at Baltimore at least six votes, and it may be that we will be able to cast the entire vote of the State for you on the first ballot. The feeble support I am now giving you is prompted solely by a desire to do justice to a faithful public servant,[2] and to save the party and the country. I have always esteemed you personally, and regretted to have to pursue the course I did towards you on Lecompton.

I am sorry to learn that your health has been affected by your recent effort in the Senate. Trusting that you may soon be restored to your accustomed health, and that you may triumph over all your enemies at Baltimore.

I am Truly Yours,
W. W. Holden

Hon. S. A. Douglas

[1] The Wake County Democratic Convention was held May 21, 1860, and a complete account appeared in the *Standard*, May 26, 1860.
[2] Robert Mercer Taliaferro Hunter, governor of Virginia.

The Presidency *Standard*
July 18, 1860

Unfortunately for the country the present contest for the Presidency is more or less sectional, in whatever aspect it may be viewed. Every one admits that the Lincoln and Hamlin ticket is a sectional one. The Convention which nominated Bell and Everett was not composed of all the States. The delegates were for the most part appointed by small bodies of people. The ticket has excited no enthusiasm. It has no strength in the North, and the strength only of a respectable minority in the South. It is, therefore, a sectional ticket. The convention which nominated Breckinridge and Lane contained representatives from twenty States out of thirty-three. Only forty-two of these representatives were from the North; those from the South numbering one hundred and eighty-eight, making in all two hundred and thirty. The Douglas Convention contained representatives from twenty-five States, a large majority of whom were from the North. The whole number was about three hundred and seventy-six, of whom about seventy were from the south. The strength of Douglas is, therefore, mainly in the North; and the strength of Breckinridge is, therefore, mainly in the South. Both tickets are more or less sectional; but whatever of regularity exists belongs to the Douglas convention.

A public man must deal with things as they are, and not as he would have them. We regret the disruption at Baltimore, but regrets are vain for what is past. We endeavored so to act at Baltimore as to be able to harmonize with our Democratic friends at home. If we had voted for Mr. Douglas we should have felt bound in honor to raise his name and advocate his election; but we did not vote for him, though we remained in the old or regular Convention, and as we took no part in the new or Breckinridge Convention, we are free as a party man to support either or neither of them. Nearly all the delegates from this State in Baltimore are in favor of Breckinridge—all the Electors but one are for him—nearly all the members of the Democratic State Committee are for him—and all the Democratic papers of the state, with the exception of two, have raised his name and are advocating his election.—Every Democratic County meeting held since the nominations were made at Baltimore, has declared for Breckinridge and Lane; and the Democratic candidate for Governor has taken ground for them on the stump. We believe that a large majority of the Democratic people of the State, whatever their preferences and feelings may have been heretofore, and whatever they might have been under other circumstances, are now in favor of Breckinridge and Lane. *The Democratic people, whose voice is above all committees, conventions, and caucuses, have commanded us to raise the names of Breckinridge and Lane, and we obey*. We go, in the last resort, with our State, as the illustrious statesman of the Northwest himself went with his State when he differed and opposed the administration on Lecompton. Breckinridge and Lane in the South, and Douglas and Johnson in the North will make common cause against Lincoln. While Douglas battles with black Republicanism in its strongholds in the North, let us endeavor to save the Southern vote, so as to render available *all* the Democratic strength in the hour of need.

Whatever we may think of the manner of their nomination, or of some of the company in which they find themselves, we believe that John C. Breckinridge and Gen. Jo Lane are faithful to the rights of the States and a Constitutional Union. The former is a brilliant and able statesman, and the latter is an honest man. Believing this, in obedience to the wish of a large majority of our Democratic friends, we raise their names at our masthead. But while we do this we are not unmindful of the patriotism and lofty integrity of Judge Douglas, or of the fidelity with which the great body of his friends in the non-slaveholding States have stood by the rights of the South. Never shall one word be uttered in these columns against him or them. We look forward to a re-union with the twelve hundred thousand Democrats in the free States who are this day marching under the Douglas banner. With some few exceptions they are the only friends the South has in that region of the Union.

And now let us have unity and harmony in North-Carolina. Let us determine first to elect Ellis and carry the Legislature, and then enter as a band of brothers on the Presidential campaign. We *can* carry, and we *must* carry the State in August and November.

In this connection we invite the attention of our readers in the letters of acceptance in our paper to-day of Mr. Breckinridge and Gen. Lane. We also call attention to the conditions, stated under our editorial head, on which we propose that the entire party vote for the same Electoral ticket. These conditions, we presume, will meet the approval of every Democrat in the State.

W. L. Saunders to Holden *Standard*
July 21, 186

Raleigh, July 18th, 1860

Mr. W. W. Holden

Sir: In your paper of the 14th inst. there is an article containing expressions it seems to me, unwarranted by anything I have said of you.[1] It is true that, at the ratification meeting in Salisbury, on the 7th inst, I spoke in terms of condemnation of the course of your paper towards Breckinridge and Lane, and their supporters.

I do not desire to seek a difficulty with you, and in order to prevent the occurrence of such a thing, I think it better to state what I did say. I made a proposition to form a Breckinridge and Lane club; said it was necessary to be organized, as we would have to fight both the regular opposition and an irregular one. I was glad to say, however, that the latter was small in numbers. I was sorry to see that the nomination of Breckinridge and Lane had been denounced as sectional and irregular. I thought any one who denounced as sectional and irregular a nomination that had received the cordial approbation of a large majority of the delegates, not only of the States, but of the country, ought himself to be denounced as sectional and irregular. I could not approve of the course of that paper which had for so many years been the organ of the party at Raleigh; that it was such as ought to be denounced by every Democrat in North Carolina. This is the substance of what I said, and as nearly the words as I can recollect. I said nothing, whatever, about you personally. My denounciation was entirely political, and my reason for it was that I saw your paper would have to be repudiated as our organ or we would be compelled to sacrifice Breckinridge and Lane, as I knew that your article of the 7th inst., would be used by the Opposition to show that the nomination of Breckinridge and Lane was a disunion movement.

In your paper of the 14th, you indulge in remarks about me, that seem intended to be purely of a personal nature. It seems that you desire to change the issue from one entirely political to one entirely personal. Personal newspaper warfare is wholly repugnant to my disposition, and I shall never consent to engage in such a controversy with any one. My object, therefore, in writing is to ask if I am correct in supposing you intended in your article of the 14th inst., to derogate in any respect from my character and honor as a gentleman.

I have been unavoidably absent from home, or I would have attended to the matter sooner.

Respectfully,
W. L. Saunders[2]

[1] On July 14, 1860, Holden had written "Mr. William L. Saunders took occasion to denounce the *North Carolina Standard* as faithless to the Democratic party, and to express the opinion that it ought to be denounced by every Democrat in the State."

[2] William Lawrence Saunders, lawyer, editor, state official; A.B., U.N.C., 1854; colonel commanding the Forty-Sixth Regiment North Carolina Troops; chief clerk, state Senate,

1870-1874; with Peter M. Hale, established Raleigh *Observer*, 1876; secretary of state, 1879-1891; alleged to be head of the Ku Klux Klan in North Carolina; edited and published *Colonial Records of North Carolina. Dictionary of North Carolina Biography*, s.v. "Saunders, William Lawrence."

Holden to Mr. W. L. Saunders *Standard*
July 25, 1860

Raleigh, July 19, 1860

Mr. W. L. Saunders—

Sir: The article in the *Standard* of the 14th, to which you refer, was political in its nature. It was written under the impression I had received from what I considered good authority, that you had gone out of your way to speak in harsh and denunciatory terms of the *Standard* and its Editor. I knew you could have no good reason to do that, and hence my notice of your remarks. Ridicule and sarcasm are legitimate weapons in political warfare. I resorted to them, and used them freely, but certainly with no intention and no wish to injure you as a man. On the basis of your letter to me, and as a simple matter of justice, I have no hesitation in saying, and I take pleasure in saying that it was not my purpose in the article referred to, which I considered entirely political in its nature, to derogate in any respect from your character as a gentleman.

It is not necessary that I should reply to your remarks, as set forth in your letter, in relation to the *Standard*. I am prepared to abide the consequences of my course in relation to the Presidential nominations, and to leave it to time and events to vindicate that course both at Charleston and Baltimore, and since my return home.

Respectfully,
W. W. Holden

T. L. Clingman to Holden *Standard*
July 28, 1860

Asheville, July 22, 1860

Dear sir: I am much gratified to see the position you have taken in the *Standard* of the 18th inst.[1] I have myself uniformly advised our political friends, without regard to their individual preferences, to sustain the Democratic electoral ticket already in the field. Any other course, by dividing our strength, might defeat the object which every Democrat has at heart. No one acquainted with our electors can doubt but that if elected they will do whatever intelligence and patriotism may indicate as best calculated to advance the interest of the Democratic party, and promote the welfare of the country.

From all I have seen since I came into the State, we shall have a decisive victory in August, and unity of action will ensure the same result in November.

You are at liberty to publish this note, should there be any doubt as to my opinion in your section of the State.

Very truly yours, &c.
T. L. Clingman[2]

Wm. W. Holden, Esq.

[1] Holden originally took the position that the state should support either the Breckinridge-Lane or the Douglas-Johnson ticket, whichever were stronger, in order to defeat Lincoln or to throw the election into the House of Representatives. On July 18, 1860, however, Holden editorially endorsed the Breckinridge-Lane ticket.

[2] Thomas Lanier Clingman.

Holden to Louisa Holden DU:Holden

Raleigh, Aug. 30, 1860

My dear Wife:

I reached home in quite a feeble condition, but I am now much better. Lotty's[1] baby is also much improved, and is of course out of danger.

I found the children and all well. The household affairs seem to be well managed. Poor little Bell is still sick. I think it doubtful whether she will recover.

This is the day for the Douglas Convention. A considerable number of Douglas Democrats are here, and Douglas[2] himself arrived last evening. I suppose, from appearances, there is no chance of reconciling the difference between the Douglas and Breckinridge men.

T. G. Tucker[3] is here, and called to see me this morning. He is for Douglas. He inquired for you.

I sincerely hope that your neuralgia has left you by this time. I do not know what day I will return, but I will write you again to-morrow. I would write more now but for the crowds around me. My love to Mary and Charley.[4] As for yourself you know you have all my heart.

Good-bye!
W. W. Holden

(If comfortable and pleasant, do not come home, but stay your month out.)

[1] One of the Holden servants.

[2] Stephen Arnold Douglas.

[3] Thomas Goode Tucker.

[4] Holden children: Mary Eldridge and Charles C.

Holden to Louisa Holden DU:Holden

Raleigh, Sept. 1, 1860

My dear Lulu:[1]

I write again to-day, though you will perceive I am a little nervous from taking morphine and quinine. I think now that I am well. My tongue is all right, and appetite pretty good. Do not be alarmed. If at all sick I will write or send for you.

My room has been so crowded that I have but a few moments left to write. We are all very well, and household affairs well managed. I do not know what day I shall go to Beaufort. I have just seen Mr. Scott,[2] of Jones, who told me you were well. I will write you again to-morrow. Between the Douglas and Breckinridge men my position is a critical one, and this may detain me a few days longer than I expected.

Love to Mary and Charley,[3] and respects to all friends. I think of you a great deal. The house seems a blank without you. Adieu my dearest Wife!

W. W. Holden

[1] Nickname by which Mrs. Holden was commonly addressed.
[2] Not identified.
[3] Holden children.

Holden to Hon. D. M. Barringer SHC:Barringer

Raleigh, Sept. 2, 1860

My dear Sir: Under the advice of my physician, which I am not at liberty to disregard, I will leave in the morning for Beaufort, and will be absent eight or ten days. I write to urge you as a friend to induce the Committee if possible to make some tender of compromise to the Douglas men. If rejected, as it probably will be, it will place them in the wrong and save us many votes. I regret that I cannot be here at the Barbecue, but my best wishes will be with you[1].

I would be greatly obliged to you if you would do two things: First, write me at Beaufort as soon as final action is had by the Committee, and second, prepare an Editorial for the Standard of Tuesday week next, on Friday, if you can that soon, on the state of the country. We agree so well that I have no doubt you will utter my sentiments.

I am too feeble to write more, and this is broken by the morphine and quinine I have taken.

Your friend,
W. W. Holden

Hon. D. M. Barringer[2]

[1] A Douglas rally was held in Raleigh on August 30, at which time Senator Douglas spoke. Holden was trying to get the state Democratic committee to seek an arrangement between Douglas and Breckinridge to prevent the election of Lincoln. When the Douglas supporters committed themselves to a campaign to carry the election to the House of Representatives, Holden endorsed the Breckinridge ticket. *Standard*, September 22, 1860.

[2] Daniel Moreau Barringer.

Marcus Erwin to Holden *Standard*
January 12, 1861

Raleigh, Jan. 11, 1861

To the Editor of the Standard:

Dear Sir: In the *Standard* of the 10st inst., I find the following paragraph in your editoral account of the debate wich accurred in the Senate on the 9th:

"Mr. Person[1] and Mr. Avery,[2] it seems, want a Convention to take the State at once out of the Union; but judging from Mr. Erwin's remarks in the Senate, he looks to a Convention to take the State out of the Union, and in addition to make changes in the Constitution with reference to *ad valorem* and free persons of color."

If you understood me to say, and therefore intended to make the impression upon your readers, that I did say that I desired a Convention to be called now for the purpose of adopting *ad valorem* taxation, you certainly were mistaken, and have unintentionally no doubt done me injustice. I only alluded to *ad valorem* taxation as a present existing element of domestic discord and strife, which had better be disposed of in some way; and only suggested that the substittute offered by Mr. Avery to the Convention bill, would enable the people, *if they wished to do so*, to settle this question as well as to determine the future status of the free colored population of the State. I do not urge the call of a Convention in order to have *any* change in the present Constitution of the State. I want a Convention called to announce, as I have no doubt it will, the final determination of the people of North-Carolina to abandon a Union in which they can no longer remain without dishonor and disgrace.

Very respectfully and truly yours,
Marcus Erwin

[1] Samuel Jones Person.

[2] William Waightstill Avery.

Union Men to the Polls! *Standard*
February 27, 1861

We have no time—engaged as we are in the campaign—to write for this issue of the *Standard*, but we snatch a few minutes to appeal to every Union man who may see this, *to be certain to go the polls and work for the cause on the day of election*. Rain or shine, turn out and vote. Let nothing prevent you from discharging this great duty to yourselves, to your families, and to your country. Appeal to your neighbors to go to the election, and if any of them are infirm or aged, provide the means for conveying them to the polls.

Remember that the issue is UNION or DISUNION. Remember, people of Wake County, that if you vote for Messrs. Rand,[1] Wilder,[2] and Lewis[3] *you vote for disunion*. Are you prepared for disunion? These gentlemen stand on a a platform which binds them at once to cut the State loose, for their platform declares that North-Carolina is not safe in the existing Union; and if not safe, what remains but to leave the Union.

We have recently visited various portions of the County, and we believe seven-eighths of the people are for the Union. Maj. Wilder believes so too, for *he* professes to be a most devoted Union man; yet the Major is not willing, when pressed, to give the time necessary to preserve the Union.

Let the Union men of the County *turn out and work*, and they will achieve a signal victory. Beware of false reports and "sensation" dispatches on the day of election. The disunion clique in this City, who imagine they have Wake County in a swing and can sweep her in any direction, will not be very scrupulous as to the means employed to influence votes.

Union men, your minds are already made up— vote accordingly. Vote for no man who will not pledge himself to work hopefully and zealously for the Union. That is the touchstone, after all. He who says there is no hope is a disunionist. He who will not work to save the Union is an enemy to the Union, no matter what he may say to the contrary.

[1] Nathaniel G. Rand, Wake County; member, House of Commons, 1825-1827, 1830-1834, 1835-1843, 1854-1857. Cheney, *North Carolina Government, 1585-1979*, 1296.

[2] Gaston Hillary Wilder.

[3] Augustus Marion Lewis.

Standard
March 2, 1861

The Result in this State

The people of this State voted on Thursday last for one hundred and twenty delegates to a convention and also for or against a convention. The results received up to the time of going to press indicate that the Unionists have triumphed by a large majority.

In speaking of the successful party as unionists, we must not be understood as saying that they will submit to the administration of the government on sectional or black Republican principles, but that they are anxious to preserve the Union on a constitutional basis, and to obtain such guarantees as will lead to a permanent re-construction of the Union. The Unionists entertain hopes, and nearly all of them strong hopes that the Union can and will be preserved, and they are willing to show their faith in this respect by their works. They are opposed to disunion at this time, and would regard it an any time as fraught with numerous and great calamities; and they are opposed to the attempts that are being made to *Mexicanize* this Republic by breaking it up and incurring the hazards of revolution simply on account of the election of Mr. Lincoln to the Presidency.

We are not sure that the people have voted for a Convention. In some of the Counties heard from the vote for it is large, and in others the vote against it is large. The vote on Convention will be close, but we incline to think that a small majority has been cast in favor of it.

Holden to the Voters of Wake County *Standard*
May 4, 1861

Fellow-Citizens: I am a candidate for a seat in the approaching State Convention.

My opinions are so well known to the people of Wake County that I so not deem it necessary to set them forth at length. The old federal Union is dissolved. The President of the late United States is attempting to coerce and subjugate the people of the South. I need only say that I am with North-Carolina and the South, and for resisting to the last extremity the usurpations and aggressions of the federal government.

W. W. Holden

May 2, 1861

Holden to the People of Wake County *Standard*
May 8, 1861

Fellow Citizens: In the *Register* and *Standard* of Saturday last I briefly announced myself a candidate for the State Convention. I did so at the solicitation of friends, and because of the flattering vote by which I was elected in February last. My business engagements are such as to prevent me from appearing before you in person; besides, the time between this and Monday next, the day of the election, is too short to admit of any thing like a thorough canvass of the County. In addition to this I will add that I have already recently canvassed the County, and that my views and opinions, as set forth twice a week in the *Standard*, are well known to the people. I have the fullest confidence in the intelligence of the people of Wake.

I believe they know their own minds, and will vote quite as understandingly without speeches from me. Besides, a canvass by me at this time, while it could do no good, would inevitably force me in self-defence to discuss the past course of parties. This would revive and embitter old party feeling, and impair that fortunate unity of sentiment which now prevails. I would rather bear misrepresentations, and trust to the people to correct them and to do me justice, than, by replying to them, and assailing others in turn, divide and injure my State. It shall never be said of me that I made party capital out of the misfortunes of my country.

Fellow-citizens, we are in the midst of war. The time which we all feared, and which many of us labored to avert, has arrived. I told you in February that I would resist all attempts by the federal government, "under any pretence whatever," to maintain the Union by force. The proclamation of Mr. Lincoln, calling for troops to make war on Southern States, dissolved the Union so far as we are concerned, and summomed every true Southern man to arms. It is idle now to speculate upon the past. The proclamation referred to, as by a stroke of lightning, made the North wholly North and the South wholly South. There is no issue before us for discussion. We are now a unit in defence of our rights and liberties. I am for a union of the South for the sake of the South, and for all of Constitutional liberty that yet remains. If elected to the Convention I will vote to disconnect North-Carolina from the old federal Union; and I will also vote to make North-Carolina a member of the Confederate States. As I told you in February last, I will go with Virginia and Tennessee. Virginia has already cast her fortunes with the Confederate States, and even if any could wish to do otherwise, a stern necessity impels us in the same direction.—But I am willing to vote, and I prefer to vote, to submit the ordinance preposing to connect this State with the Confederate Satates to the people at the polls, for their approval or rejection. I repeat, I have all confidence in the intelligence of the people and in their capacity for self-government.

Thanking you for former expressions of your confidence in me, I am your fellow-citizen.

W. W. Holden

May 6, 1861

Holden to Louisa Holden DU:Holden

Camp Bragg [Virginia], July 8, 1861

My dear Wife: I am now near Suffolk, at Camp Bragg. I expect to leave this evening for Norfolk, and shall return here Wednesday, and on Thursday evening I expect to be at home. I would go to Richmond and Yorktown, but it would take too much time.

I spent the most of Sunday in camp here, and took dinner with Capt. Harrison,[1] Rogers[2] and others. Their duties are laborious, but they are cheerful and hearty. This is so of all the troops. Just before I left the 3d Volunteer regiment left for Smithfield on the James River, about twenty miles from this place. It is probable that this, the 4th regiment, will be here for some three or four weeks. I have had several conversations with Col. Daniel,[3] the commander here, who appears to be excellently qualified for his position. He spoke to me privately in the highest terms of Capt. Harrison, Sion H. Rogers, Seaton Gales, Dick Badger,[4] George Hood[5] and others of the Rifles and Guards. Henson[6] is to be made flag-bearer of the Regiment—an honorable position.

I am stopping at the Washington Hotel. Mr. Busbee[7] is there, and is looking remarkably well. Mrs. Col. Daniel is also at this Hotel, and Mrs. Capt. Hargrave[8], of Davidson, formerly Miss Cowan, of Wilmington—a very handsome woman; but I have seen no one as lovely as my own dear little wife, especially when she is in good health and cheerful. I have discovered the remedy for both you and myself, and this is, early rising and active exercise, like the soldiers. That would make us brand-new in less than a month.

I hope you are all very well. I have thought of you a great deal since I left. I never felt better than I do now.

At Weldon I found some fine peaches, *from Georgia*, at 5 cents apiece. If there are any there I will bring you some when I return.

Capt. Harrison is very well. So is Mr. NcNair,[9] whom I have just seen. Tell Molly so if you see her. Good-bye! God bless you.

Your Afffectionate husband,
W. W. Holden

[1] William H. Harrison, former mayor of Raleigh; elected captain, company K, 14th Regiment, North Carolina Troops, 1861-1862. Louis H. Manarin and Weymouth T. Jordan, Jr., comps, *North Carolina Troops, 1861-1865: A Roster*, 14 vols. to date (Raleigh: Division of Archives and History, Department of Cultural Resources, 1966-), 5:482.

[2] Sion Hart Rogers, lawyer and attorney general; A.B., U.N.C., 1846; A.M., 1849; member, U.S. House of Representatives, 1853-1855; first lieutenant, Fourteenth Regiment, North Carolina Troops; later colonel, Forty-seventh Regiment; attorney general, 1863-1868. *Dictionary of North Carolina Biography*, s.v. "Rogers, Sion Hart."

[3] Junius Daniel, graduate of U. S. Military Academy, West Point, 1851; resigned commission, 1857; colonel, Fourth (later Fourteenth) Regiment N.C. Troops; commanded Forty-fifth Regiment; brigadier general, 1862; led brigade at Gettysburg. *Dictionary of North Carolina Biography*, s.v. "Daniel, Junius."

[4] Richard Cogsdell Badger, lawyer; A.B., U.N.C., 1859; third sergeant, Fourth Regiment, N.C. Troops; U.S. district attorney, 1873-1877; member, General Assembly, 1872. Grant, *Alumni History*, 26; Murray, *Wake, Capital County of North Carolina*, I:472.

[5] George A. Hood, former apprentice in office of the *Standard*; volunteered before he was eighteen; killed at Winchester, October, 1864. Murray, *Wake, Capital County of North Carolina*, 1:479.

[6] Probably Jefferson M. Henson, Wake County printer; enlisted 1861; promoted to corporal and sergeant; commissioned 2nd Lieutenant, 1862; promoted to 1st Lieutenant, 1862; promoted to Captain, 1864; served in Company E, 14th Regiment, N.C. Troops. Manarin and Jordan, comps., *North Carolina Troops, 1861-1865: A Roster*, 5:435

[7] Quentin Durward Busbee.

[8] Wife of Capt. Jesse Hargrave, lawyer from Davidson County, captain of Company I, 14th Regiment, North Carolina Troops, 1861-1862. Manarin and Jordan, comps., *North Carolina Troops, 1861-1865: A Roster*, 5:473.

[9] Malcom NcNair, Robeson County farmer. 1860 U.S. Census Population Schedule, North Carolina: Robeson, 945 (Microfilm).

Holden to Mrs. L. H. Holden *DU:Holden*

Kittrell's, Sept. 22, 1861

My dear Wife:

I arrived here yesterday about ten o'clock. I have a good room and all the attention I could desire. This is certainly excellent water. I feel already much improved from the use of it. There are about seventy-five persons here, for the most part ladies and children. I have not seen any of the Peace's.[1] But few persons were here yesterday from the neighborhood. We had a very heavy rain here last night. To-day the weather is clear and pleasant.

The arrangements here are on a considerable scale, and quite comfortable. They have music and dancing every night. I regret that you could not come, as I am satisfied the water would have benefitted Charley, and Mary, [2] and yourself.

I may return home on Wednesday, and certainly on Thursday evening. By that time I trust I shall be as well as ever. I have no cough now. I drink large quantities of the water, which has a fine effect upon me.

Give my love to all, and believe me, as ever.

Your affectionate and devoted
Husband,
W. W. Holden

Mrs. L. H. Holden

[1] Holden's first wife, Ann Augusta Young, was a niece of William Peace, Raleigh merchant and founder of Peace College, who continued to live in the Holden household after her death. The Peace family came originally from Granville county and family members lived nearby.

[2] Holden children.

Holden to the Public *Standard*
December 7, 1861

On Wednesday, the 27th of last month, I attacked Mr. William Robinson[1] on the pavement in Raleigh, near Mr. Turner's Bookstore, and caned him, and otherwise punished him. We both subsequently appeared before the Mayor, [2] and gave bond to appear at the February term of Wake County Court. I have no taste for statements or disputes about such matters, and I was consequently disposed to make no public allusion to the rencontre; but as the nominal senior Editor[3] of the *State Journal* has given a totally false account of the affair in the last number of that paper, justice to myself requires that I should state the facts, as they appeared in evidence before the Mayor, and as they will appear more fully before the Court. The *State Journal* says:

"On Wednesday last, while our Assistant Editor, Mr. Robinson, was standing on Fayetteville street, examining a paper in the hands of Hon. D.M. Barringer,[4] Holden, of the *Standard*, advanced upon him nearly from behind, and wholly unobserved, and struck him over the head with a heavy loaded gold headed cane—remarking as he struck, 'you call me a poltroon, do you?' A second blow was received upon a sword-cane held by Mr. Robinson, and then the beligerents closed. After a struggle of some minutes, during which Mr. Robinson drew the sword from his cane and made an effort to use it on his assailant, they both fell together. They were immediately pulled apart. As soon as Mr. Robinson regained his feet, he tore loose from the persons holding him and brought his cane down with a vim upon Holden's head, making him bleed profusely."

Now, it is not true that I approached Mr. Robinson "nearly from behind, and wholly unobbserved." He was conversing with Mr. Barringer, and both of them were standing with their backs to the south, with their faces slightly turned towards each other, while I approached them from the north. As I approached, and when within ten feet of Mr. Robinson, I gave him warning, by the expression repeated above by the *Journal*. Those who were present at the examination of the witnesses before the Mayor, will recollect that Mr. Robinson endeavored, after the examination was closed, to produce the impression that I had approached him and struck him as stated in the *Journal*; and they will also recollect that I at once rose and stated I had approached and struck him boldly, fairly, and squarely, and that *my statement was not to be disputed*. Neither Mr. Robinson nor his counsel made any reply.

Nor is it true that I struck him with "a heavy loaded gold-headed cane." The cane, it is true, has a golden head, but it is not loaded. Nor is it as heavy as many canes which are worn. The nominal senior Editor speaks *feelingly* on the subject, and imagines that the stick is much heavier than it really is. It is the same with which I often chastised him through all the meanderings around the pillars in front of the Yarborough House, in this City.

Nor is it true that the struggle lasted "some minutes." Mr. Robinson made effort after effort to stab me with the sword-cane, but failed. I held his sword arm with one hand, and punished him with the other; and I would have thrown him instantly, but for the apprehension that, in falling on him, the point of the sword cane might be turned upwards and run through me.

Nor is it true that we "fell together." He fell before I did, for I was on top of him.

Nor is it true that "as soon as Mr. Robinson regained his feet, he tore loose from the persons holding him," and struck me with his cane. Mr. Barringer testified before the Mayor that two minutes elasped between the time we were sepatated and the time he struck me with his cane; and another witness testified that when he struck me I was held by at least two persons. My belief is that one had me by the left arm, another by the right arm, and another by the shoulders,—and I think the evidence, when fully brought out and sifted, will show this, though it is far from my purpose to reflect in the slightest degree on the witnesses who were examined. He advanced ten feet, and struck me when I was powerless, I looking him in the eye. The friends who held me no doubt meant well, but it was hard to be struck in a manner so cowardly, when I could not wield a finger in self-defense. The blow, it is true, was a slight one. It occasioned no jar, but only broke the skin; and the nature of the wound, so greatly magnified by the senior nominal Editor, may be judged of by the fact that it did not need to be dressed, and occasioned one no inconvenience.

I have thus shown that there are at least five palpable falsehoods in the above brief extract from the *Journal*. The writer knows them to be false when he penned them, for he was present at the examination and heard all the evidence. But I am not at all surprised at the account which the *Journal* has given of the rencontre. I expected, if it noticed it at all, that it would misrepresent the whole affair deliberately and wilfully; and the result has shown that I was not mistaken. My observation has convinced me that that paper will never tell the truth when a falsehood will suit its purpose better.

The intimation by the nominal senior Editor that I am not under bond to keep the peace towards *him*, and that *he* is ready to fight me, is unworthy of notice, especially after what occurred in front of the Yarborough House, some time since.

In conclusion, I beg leave to say that no man is more averse than I am to personal broils and conflicts. I have resided for the last twenty-five years in Raleigh, during all of which time I have conducted myself and been regarded as a peaceable citizen. But I have been pursued for months by certain politicians with the utmost malignity; and the nominal Editors of the the *State Journal* have been instruments, and are now instruments in the hands of these politicians in their warfare against me. For months that paper has teemed with the most bitter personal abuse of my friends and myself. We have been assailed as untrue to the South, and as unworthy to be trusted in the present crisis. The people have been called upon to put a "hideous mark upon our brow," as persons whose "wicked counsels" have brought the "present sufferings" upon the South! Indeed, this abuse has been so vile, and has been indulged in to such an extent by the *State Journal*, that Mayor Root, on the occasion of the examination referred to, distinctly intimated to Mr. Robinson that the course of that paper had tended to discord and breaches of the peace in this community, and that, as a Magistrate, even if he were not guilty in law of an affray, it would be his duty, on account alone of the character of the paper with which he is connected as associate Editor, to bind him to the peace. Mr. Spelman was present, and heard this warning given by the Mayor. I have paid but little attention to this abuse, and, so far as Mr. Robinson is concerned, I have never even alluded to him. I know that I can gain no credit by personal collisions, especially with such persons as Mr. Spelman and Mr. Robinson, but I trust my friends will pardon the sudden impulse under which I acted in chastising them. I intend to maintain my position firmly and fearlessly, and to tear this mask from the faces of those who own and control the State *Journal*, and who, if not checked in their partisan conduct by the people themselves, will inflict great injury upon the character of the State, and divide and paralyze the public councils at a time when a common front should be presented to our enemies.

W. W. Holden

Raleigh, Dec. 6, 1861

[1] William Robinson, assistant editor of the (Raleigh) *State Journal*. An account of the episode is in the *State Journal*, December 4, 1861, in which Robinson is identified.

[2] Charles B. Root, acting mayor; Raleigh jeweler. Murray, *Wake, Capital County of North Carolina*, 1:472.

[3] John Spelman, printer and newspaper editor; reporter for the *Standard*; editor of the Salisbury *Banner*, 1859-1860; editor and proprietor of *State Journal* in Raleigh, 1860-1882. *Dictionary of North Carolina Biography*, s.v. "Spelman, John."

[4] Daniel Moreau Barringer.

Holden to Hon. W. A. Graham A&H:Graham

Raleigh, Jan. 1st, 1862

My dear sir: I trust you will prepare your remarks on the "Test Oath" Ordinance for the press.[1] They will not only fully vindicate the course of the conservatives of the State on the question, but they will do good among the reflecting masses of the people. With your permission, I propose to print an edition of some five thousand copies in pamphlet form, and I make no doubt our friends in Convention and others will subscribe for enough copies to save the printer at cost. I am anxious that the speech should be widely circulated.

I see by the last Observer, that Mr. Winslow[2] has resigned and that Mr. McKay[3] will probably succeed him.[4] The latter I know to be true and sound. He is a Union

Democrat, and will set his face against the faction which now misgoverns the State. I have strong hopes, also, that we shall make a gain in Forsyth.

Should you conclude to write out your remarks, and favor me with them, I promise to read the proof very carefully, so as to ensure correctness in the publication; or I will send the proof to you, if you desire it.

Very truly yours,
W. W. Holden

Hon. W. A. Graham

Just a I had finished the foregoing Mr. Battle[5] called with the manuscript of your speech, for which I am much obliged. It will appear in the weekly and semi-weekly issue of Wednesday next. I will also publish it in pamphlet form.

W. W. H.

[1] Graham's speech to the Convention on December 7, 1861, is reproduced in J. G. de Roulhac Hamilton, Max R. Williams, and Mary Reynolds Peacock, eds., *The Papers of William Alexander Graham*, 8 vols. (Raleigh: Division of Archives and History, 1957-1992), 5:311-340.

[2] Warren Winslow, lawyer and governor; A.B., U.N.C., 1827; Member, state Senate, 1854-1855; speaker, 1854; succeeded to governorship when David S. Reid resigned to take seat in the U.S. Senate; member, U. S. House of Representatives, 1857-1861. *Dictionary of North Carolina Biography*, s.v. "Winslow, Warren."

[3] Probably William McL. McKay, Cumberland County; member, House of Commons, 1858-1859, 1866-1867. Cheney, *North Carolina government, 1585-1979*, 1114.

[4] Malcolm James McDuffie, lawyer, replaced Winslow as a member of the 1861 secession convention; A.B., U.N.C., 1851; member, House of Commons, 1854. Grant, *Alumni History*, 388.

[5] Kemp Plummer Battle, lawyer and educator; A.B., U.N.C., 1849; delegate from Wake County to 1861 secession convention; president, Chatham Railroad; state treasurer, 1866-1868; president, University of North Carolina, 1876-1891; professor of history, 1891-1907. *Dictionary of North Carolina Biography*, s.v. "Battle, Kemp Plummer."

C. H. C. *to Editor of the Standard* *Standard*
March 15, 1862

Harnett Co., N.C., Feb. 6, 1862

Editor of the Standard:

Sir: I have not seen you since the fall of Roanoke Island. I should have written to you before now, but I have been confined to my room ever since I reached home. I understand the Virginia papers charge the North Carolinians with cowardice. This is unjust and mean. The first account of the battle was given by men who ran from the Island before the battle was ended, and I think they knew nothing about the matter, except that they ran with all their might. I was placed about 250 yards in the rear of the fortification, where I could see everything going on on our side. There was a portion of Wise's Legion[1] sent to the left flank to watch the movements of the enemy in that direction. Soon I saw six men coming from that direction. Whey they came up to us, I hailed them.—They said they belonged to Wise's Legion. This was about an hour before we abandoned the breastworks. These men went towards Nag's Head, and I suppose they reached the place in time to join Gen. Wise and his Legion, on their rapid march to the Canal Bridge, which they reached, making about four miles per hour, notwithstanding the General was said to be very ill. The march appears to have been good medicine for the General, for when the picket guard reached the Canal bridge he was able to curse them until he was almost blue. Now did the pickets act cowardily? I answer, no. The picket was taken from Co. I, 31st regiment of Cape Fear boys, and sent to the lower end of the Island, where they remained until the enemy had landed and cut them entirely off from the main army. They had to come up and surrender as prisioners, or take a boat and go to Nag's Head.—This they did, and made their way to the Canal bridge, where Gen. Wise took their guns from them, and cursed them for every thing mean.—Now, if these men are to be branded as cowards for leaving, where will Gen. Wise stand? I heard while in Raleigh that the guns intended for the 31st Regt. were in Raleigh, and had been for some time. I suppose this is not true—for I was sent to Raleigh twice by the Colonel for the regiment, and applied for the guns, and failed to get them.

C.H.C.[2]

[1] Henry Alexander Wise.

[2] Probably Cornelius H. Coffield, 1st Lieutenant, Company I, 31st Regiment North Carolina Troops; from Harnett County; commissioned 1st Lieutenant, October 30, 1861; resigned September 15, 1862. Manarin and Jordan, comps., *North Carolina Troops, 1861-1865: A Roster*, 6:497.

Wm. H. Thomas to Holden *Standard*
June 4, 1862

Strawberry Plains,
Camp Junaluske,
May 10, 1862

W. W. Holden, Esq:

Dear sir: From information received from Raleigh, I presume that the convention remained in session but a few days. I am at present with the 1st and 2d companies of the "North Carolina Cherokeee Battalion," stationed at this place to guard a

Railroad bridge, which the tories around it are so anxious to destroy. The troops that had been stationed here having been armed and equipped, have been sent to the Cumberland mountain, where a battle will be fought soon, of vast importance in its results. If overpowered at the Cumberland, our troops will very probably have to fall back on the Iron or Smoky mountains. So far, the Indian companies have set an example worthy of initation by the whites, in sobriety, morality, and submission to the duties required of soldiers. They bid fair at no distant day, in Tennessee, at least, to prove themselves better friends to the South and the Southern cause, in this our day of trial, than some persons who claim to be of pure white origin—who have no merit of their own, besides, except to stay at home, and speculate on the necessities of the families of the soldiers who are fighting the battles of their country, for the purpose of adhieving our liberty and independence.

I have no fears of the final result, but I have no doubt that many important battles will be fought during next summer. In my opinion, our forces ought to be strengthened in East Tennesseee during next summer, and, if necessary, a portion of our forces could be removed to Eastern North Carolina upon the coming of frost.

Yours truly,
Wm. H. Thomas[1]

[1] William Holland Thomas

Candidate for Governor *Standard*
June 4, 1862

In obedience to what we believe to be the wish of a large majority of the people of the State, we hoist to-day the name of the patriot, soldier, and statesman, Col. Z. B. VANCE,[1] for Governor.

We not authorized to speak for Col. Vance on this subject; but, while he has not sought the office, and while he would much prefer to remain with his regiment or legion until the war shall have ended, yet we believe that he will not refuse to serve the people, it is should be their wish to make him Governor, and at the same time *Commander-in-chief* in this State. We need just such a man in the office at this time. He has had experience both as a statesman and soldier; and he has not only the disposition, but the ability and the will to do right.

Col. Vance has seen service both in the Legislature of the State and in the old federal Congress.—He is a man of sound judgment, and energy and decision of character. No public man of his age in the State has more judgment or forethought; and while genial and generous in his disposition, there is no one who possesses more positiveness of character than he does. He is most popular where he is best known. In the mountain country, and in the army, among his fellow-soldiers, the mere mention of his name for this or any other position will call forth the highest enthusiasm.

Col. Vance, in common with a large majority of our people, labored to save the old government as long as it was honorable to do so; but when the proclamation of Mr. Lincoln was issued, in April, 1861, requiring the people of this State either to separate from the non-slaveholding States or to become the executioners of their own brethren, Col. Vance volunteered as a private, was elected Captain of a Buncombe company, and served for some time in this capacity in the 4th or 14th volunteer regiment.—He was subsequently elected Colonel of the 26th regiment, and at the head of that gallant body of men, participated actively in the battle of Newbern. We learn that his regiment was ordered to leave Goldsborough on Monday morning last for Richmond, and he may be now in the thickest of the conflict fighting for his country. We may be sure that he will do his whole duty, and that the cause will suffer no detriment in his hands.

If Col. Vance should consent to be a candidate for Governor, as we believe he will, he will remain in the field at the head of his regiment or legion, until September next,—the time fixed for his inauguration—when he will appear in Raleigh, take the oath of office, and enter upon his duties as Governor.

Let the watchword of the conservatives of the State, and of those who desire reform in the government, and better and abler men in office, and who would honor a gallant soldier and an honest man, be henceforth VANCE and VICTORY! Under that sign we will conquer, and partyism, favoritism, and inefficiency in office will give place to wiser, better, and more patriotic rule.

In this connection we invite attention to the proceedings of meetings in Rutherford and Wake Counties, in our paper to-day. The proceedings of meetings in Polk and Wilkes, nominating Colonel Vance for Governor, shall appear in our next.

[1] Zebulon Baird Vance, soldier, governor, congressman; member, House of Commons 1854; member, U.S. House of Representatives, 1857-1861; captain, Company F, Fourteenth Regiment North Carolina Troops; colonel, Twenty-sixth Regiment North Carolina Troops; elected governor, 1862; broke with Holden over peace movement; reelected governor, 1864; imprisoned, 1865; elected governor on Democratic ticket, 1876; elected U.S. Senator, 1878, and served until 1894. *Dictionary of North Carolina Biography*, s.v. "Vance, Zebulon Baird."

TELEGRAM *Holden to Col. Z. B. Vance* A&H:Vance

Aug. 10, 1862

From: Raleigh To Col. Z. B. Vance

Majorities for Vance franklin 147 Northampton 90 Greene 180 Granville 475 Harnett 186 Roberson 600, Monroe 125, Chatham 1300, Eilkes 1401, Yadkin 1110, Caswell 263. Majorities for Johnson Duplin 850, Vance's majorities in 25 Counties seventeen thousand 17,000 legislature largely conservative Your friends think you ought to resign next Thursday the 8th of September You will take the oath as Governor Entitled to some rest & time to get ready to remove to Raleigh

W. W. Holden

Holden to Gen J. Johnston Pettigrew A&H:Pettigrew

Raleigh, Oct. 28, 1862

My dear sir: Your favor of a recent date, offering to my son, Lt. Holden,[1] The position of Volunteer Aid, has been received. My son and myself highly appreciate this evidence of esteem and confidence, and feel greatly obliged to you for it. He could not fail to learn much in his intercourse with you, and in your military family; and I regret that his determination, formed some two or three weeks since, to enter the State service, puts it out of his power to accept your kind offer. I think it almost certain that Gov. Vance will recommend to the Legislature, which will assemble on the 17th of next month, the raising of five to eight or ten regiments for the defense of our coast; and I think it equally certain that the Legislature will concur in the recommendation, unless the government at Richmond should show a proper determination to defend our coast. My son is looking to this, and will no doubt go into State service, should the recommendation referred to be made and carried out.

We feel, Sir, that we have been neglected. The whole of the Eastern portion of the State is at the mercy of the enemy. If the Governor cannot beat back the Yankee forces, he hopes at least to be able to aid our Eastern fellow-citizens in removing their slaves, and with them enough meat and bread to subsist them in the interior until another crop is made. We want a Confederate General in whom our people have confidence, and he must have troops for defence, or the enemy will in all probability overrun the State as far West as the Wilmington and Weldon Road.

Again thanking you for your kind offer to my son,

I am Very Truly Yours,
W. W. Holden

Gen J. Johnston Pettigrew[2]

[1] Joseph William Holden, elder son of William W. Holden; in state troops, but captured by Union forces at Roanoke Island and imprisoned for a year; staff of *Standard*, 1863-1868; member, House of Commons, 1868-1870; Speaker, 1868-1870; managing editor, Leavenworth, Kansas, *Times*, 1872-1873; mayor of Raleigh, 1874-1875. *Dictionary of North Carolina Biography*, s.v. "Holden, Joseph William."

[2] James Johnston Pettigrew, lawyer and Confederate general; A.B., U.N.C., 1847; member, South Carolina House of Representatives, 1856-1857; colonel, Twenty-second North Carolina Regiment, 1861-1862; brigadier general, 1862, commanding brigade in eastern North Carolina; participated in Pickett's Charge at Gettysburg; killed in action in retreat from Pennsylvania. *Dictionary of North Carolina Biography*, s.v. "Pettigrew, James Johnston."

P. F. Pescud to Holden *Standard*
October 31, 1862

Mr. Holden:—The Citizens of this City have responded with their accustomed liberality for the relief of the sick and suffering at Wilmington. Besides the contributions of bacon, flour, meal, potatoes, vegetables and dried fruit, we have received in cash up to this date ($2,388.15) two thousand three hundred and eighty-eight dollars and fifteen cents. $989.10 has been forwarded to John Dawson,[1] Mayor of Wilmington; $685.05 has been expended in bacon, chickens, &c., and forwarded; a trusty messenger, with $300, is now absent in the country buying chickens, and I have on hand $400, subject to the order of the Mayor of Wilmington, or to be expended in such provisions as he needs most. He has kept the committee advised every day of his wants, which we have supplied to the extent of our ability.

A list of contributors and disbursements may be seen at my drug store, the committee deeming it prudent not to publish them,

P. F. Pescud[2]
Chm'n R. Relief Com.

Oct. 28, 1862

[1] John Dawson, wealthy merchant who served as mayor of Wilmington during the yellow fever epidemic of 1862. 1860 U.S. Census Population Schedule, North Carolina: New Hanover, 793 (microfilm); Lower Cape Fear Historical Society, Inc., *Bulletin*, Vol. XI, No. 1 (November, 1967), "The Prevailing Epidemic-1862," by Leora H. McEachern and Isabel M. Williams.

[2] Peter Francisco Pescud, Raleigh civic leader and proprietor of Pescud's Drug Store. Murray, *Wake, Capital County of North Carolina*, 1:442.

Holden to Hon. Robert B. Gilliam *Standard*
November 21, 1862

Raleigh, Nov. 19, 1862

To the Hon. Robert B. Gilliam[1]
Speaker House of Commons

Sir:—I beg leave to say that I accept the office of State Printer to which I was elected by the joint vote of the two Houses of the General Assembly.[2] It is, perhaps, proper that I should add that I did not desire the office, and that I had asked no one to support me, not even to put me in nomination for it. My ordinary business as a printer and publisher requires all my time and attention, and is more agreeable and profitable to me than the office of State Printer. Indeed, on learning the I had been elected, I determined to decline, and such was my purpose formed several months since. But inasmuch as I have been elected, and as the public business may be delayed if I should decline to accept, and as I am always disposed to serve my friends and the State when called upon to do, so, I accept the office and will endeavor to discharge its duties, as I trust I have heretofore done, with fidelity and dispatch.

It has been suggested, on the score of enconomy [*sic*], that it is advisable that the Legislature should take the necessary steps to have the public printing executed at the asylum for the Deaf and Dumb and Blind, in this City. No citizen of the State is more anxious than I am to save the public money and to lighten the burdens of the people, and no one is less disposed than I am to realize profits, in a crisis like the present, out of the State Treasury; and without expressing an opinion as to the propriety of establishing a State printing office, I beg leave to say, that if the Legislature should see proper to put the Asylum printing office in a condition to do the public work, I will at once and with pleasure retire from the office of State Printer, and shall be gratified if the plan suggested should operate in such a way as to promote the public interests.

Permit me to add in conclusion, that I am profoundly grateful to those who voted for me for State Printer, and that I shall spare neither pains nor expense to execute the work promptly and faithfully.

I have the honor to be, sir,
with much respect,
Your ob't ser'vt.
W. W. Holden

[1] Robert Ballard Gilliam, Granville County; lawyer, A.B., U.N.C., 1823; A.M., 1826; member, House of Commons, 1836-1840, 1846-1848, 1862; speaker, 1848, 1862; member, convention of 1835; superior court judge, 1863-1865, 1867-1868. Grant, *Alumni History*, 220.

[2] The vote was 80 for Holden and 60 for Willie J. Palmer. The Senate vote was 27 for Holden, 9 for Palmer; the House of commons vote was 53 for Holden, 42 for Palmer. *Journal of the House of Commons of North-Carolina at its Session, 1862– '63* (Raleigh: W. W. Holden, Printer to the State, 1862), 12; *Journal of the Senate of the General Assembly of the State of North-Carolina at its First Session, 1862* (Raleigh: W. W. Holden, Printer to the State, 1862), 9.

The Duty of the Conservatives

Standard
November 21, 1862

When the present unhappy war was begun, though our people had been thoroughly and even bitterly divided as to the causes that led to it, the Conservatives of the State came forward as one man and laid their prejudices and dislikes on the altar of the country and proposed to the Destructives to forget the past and labor together against the common enemy. The proposition appeared for the moment to have been accepted, and for a brief space union and harmony prevailed among us. But the Destructives were then in power, and their love of office was stronger than their love of country.–Though the Conservatives sent more men to the field than they did, and expended more money than they in equipping and furnishing the troops, yet as a general rule they were proscribed from all positions of honor and trust, and at last plainly told, that as they did not originate the revolution it was their business to fight it on foot, and that the originators of the movement were alone entitled to lead it and conduct it. The members of the Military Board, Colonels, Lieutenant Colonels, Majors, Captains, Lieutenants, Drillmasters, Judges, Railroad Directors and officers of all kinds, even Chaplains in the army, were appointed, not for their merits or on account of their peculiar fitness for their places, *but because they had been original secessionists*. This was bad enough; but bad as it was, it might have been endured, if our opponents had not gone further and endeavored to place upon us a "*hideous mark*" as traitors to our country. But forbearance on the part of the people at length ceased to be a virtue.–They rose, in *self-defence*, and hurled the secessionists from power. They did this in defence of themselves and their country. The election of Governor Vance and a Conservative Legislature was not only a rebuke to the Destructives, *but it was the expression of a wish on the part of the people that thenceforth Conservative men should be placed in office, and conservative principles and counsels should direct the ship of State*. Who so blind as not to perceive this?—and who, perceiving it, so bold as to set up his judgment against the people's judgment?

Gov. Vance will meet, and more than meet the expectations of the people, if he is only surrounded by the Legislature with Conservative men like himself. To refuse to surround him with such men, but, on the contrary, to place about him those who voted against him, and sought to defeat him, and joined in the effort, whether actively or passively, to put the "hideous mark" on him and his friends, would be in fact to abandon Conservative principles, and to declare to the world that the recent struggle by the people to oust the Destructives and to reform the government, was not only unnecessary, but a mockery of popular elections. Those who opposed his election, and maligned him and his friends, would rejoice in the failure of his administration, and, if placed in office around him, would lose no opportunity to embarrass him. Especially do recent events admonish the Conservatives to be on their guard–to give but little if any heed to suggestions which come from their opponents, and to *organize themselves thoroughly*. If there be those among us who are too tender-footed to tread boldly in the path of duty, let them take some other path, and answer for it to the people. The time has arrived, in our humble opinion, when the Conservatives must organize and assume the control of public affairs in every department, or *disband*! To hesitate or temporize is to disband. There is but *one* course, and that is, to vote out every man who is not *known* to be true, and to vote in Conservatives. Let this be done, and our word for it all people will say, amen!

The Conservative party is composed of the cream of the two old parties, and that which is outside of it is skimmed milk, and very blue at that. We take it for granted that justice will be done among Conservatives to old line Democrats as well as old time Whigs. So far as we are concerned, we desire no office, and we have no favorites to press for office. We are in an condition, therefore, to speak plainly. Justice and equality constitute, in this respect, the surest guarantee for future harmony. Those Conservatives who were once Democrats, were proscribed by their former associates because they were true men, and opposed to disunion and civil war.–Old Whigs who are now Conservatives were proscribed by their associates for the same cause; and the two are now *one* in sentiment and action. We believe they will continue to be *one*, and that, forgetting past party differences and party strifes, they will do justice to each other in *all* things.

Holden to Edward J. Hale, Esq. A&H:Hale

Raleigh, Nov. 21, 1862

Edward J. Hale, Esq.[1]

My dear Sir: I have been endeavoring for several days to make an opportunity to reply to yours of a recent date, but have been prevented by the pressure of business and the calls of friends.

I sent you by the mail, night before last, a couple of copies of the message,[2] the earliest moment at which I could send them. I regret that it was not possible to furnish you with a copy sooner. I see that, by an extraordinary effort, you have it in the last Observer.

I was elected State Printer on Tuesday, and, under the circumstances, determined at first to decline it. Some of our friends are misled in their votes by misrepresentations from the secession side of the House. It was well known that Mr. Palmer[3] could not do the work. His Foreman was in the House at the time, remonstrating at his request against the effort to elect him. As I did not desire it, and had not asked for it, I for awhile refused it, but at the urgent appeals of many friends, including Mr. Badger[4] and Gov. Vance, I concluded to accept, and sent in the letter you will find in the Standard.

The telegraphic dispatches cost $25 per week. I have not concluded to take them, and hardly think I shall. It is my intention, at the close of the war, if my life and health should be spared, to established a permament Daily. If I can serve you here in any way, let me know it.

Very Truly Yours,
W. W. Holden

[1] Edward Jones Hale, editor and publisher; editor and publisher of the *Fayetteville Observer*, 1825-1865; one of organizers of Whig Party in North Carolina; *Fayetteville Observer* destroyed, 1865, on orders from General William T. Sherman; formed E. J. Hale

and sons, publishers, in New York City. *Dictionary of North Carolina Biography*, s.v. "Hale, Edward Jones."

[2] Governor Zebulon Vance's first message to the General Assembly, November 17, 1862, and printed in the *Standard* November 21, 1862.

[3] Willie J. Palmer, principal of the North Carolina Institution for the deaf and Dumb and Blind. Document 4, *Legislative Documents, Session 1865-'66.*

[4] George Edmund Badger.

C. W. Wooley and E. G. L. Barringer to Holden *Standard*
January 27, 1863

Raleigh, N.C., Jan. 22, 1863

W. W. Holden:—Sir:—We see in the papers of this City, an extract from an article in the Wadesboro' *Argus*, stating that it was rumored that certain persons in Montgomery County were in favor of a reconstruction of the Union, and that certain persons were expected to address them in public meeting.

We feel authorized to state that said rumor is entirely false and slanderous as to the citizens of Montgomery County, and excepting a mere squad, not enough to form a corporal's guard, there are no people more loyal and patriotic than the citizens of Montgomery; and they are the very last people who would be in favor of a reconstruction of the Union, under any circumstances whatever.

Montgomery County, out of a voting population of between nine hundred and a thousand, has sent about 800 able bodied soldiers to the army, and has lost many of her best sons on the bloody field in the defence of our country.

Yours truly,
C. W. Wooley[1]
E. G. L. Barringer[2]

[1] Calvin W. Wooley, Montgomery County; member, state Senate, 1862-1864. Cheney, *North Carolina Government, 1585-1979*, 329.

[2] Edmund G. L. Barringer, Montgomery County; member, House of Commons, 1860-1864. Cheney, *North Carolina Government, 1585-1979*, 328, 330.

Peace–When shall we have Peace? *Standard*
July 17, 1863

We copy the following from the Raleigh Daily *Progress* of the 15th instant:

"We favor peace because we believe that peace now would save slavery, while we very much fear that a prolongation of the war will obliterate the last vestige of it. We are for peace because there has been enough of blood and carnage, enough of widows and orphans, heartbroken mothers and sorrowing fathers. We are for peace, because, with an implicit faith in Divine teaching, we believe that the sins of nations as of individuals will overtake them, and that God will avenge himself on this American people, if this unnatural, fratricidal butchery is suffered to go on. We have nothing to advise, nothing to suggest, but we know we but express the truth when we declare that the earnest prayer of all right thinking men, everywhere, is for peace, and that our people, here, in North Carolina, now as several months ago, are in favor of any peace that does not enslave and degrade them–any peace that is honorable and that respects our rights.

"We earnestly hope that the peace element at the North will revolt at the great struggle at Gettysburg, and compel the despotism that is consuming them to agree, to a settlement of the whole matter, upon terms that we can accept. They have to choose between giving us peace upon our own terms, and fighting on, for we have three or four hundred thousand men in the field and can fight for years yet.

"The horizon is dark and gloomy, people are thoughtful and anxious, and men are eagerly asking what is to come. We have no comfort for any one, for our perils are great and our future is gloomy.–Let every man put himself on a war footing and nerve his arm and steel his heart for the trying scenes through which he is to pass."

We agree with our cotemporary [*sic*] in much of the above. But we have no idea that we can obtain "peace upon our own terms." The most powerful nations seldom succeed in doing that. What the great mass of our people desire is a cessation of hostilities, and negotiations. If they could reach that point they would feel that the conflict of arms would not be renewed, and that *some* settlement would be effected which would leave them in the future in the enjoyment of "life, liberty, and happiness."

It is a great crime, especially at a time like this, to conceal the truth from the people. We intend to tell them the truth as far as we know it, let the consequences be what they may.

From the beginning of the war to the present the enemy has slowly but surely gained upon us; and but for the extraordinary endurance and courage of our troops, his flag would now be floating at the capital of every State. We have lost Missouri, Maryland, Kentucky, Tennessee, the Mississippi valley, Texas, Louisiana, Arkansas, and considerable portions of other States. Vicksburg has fallen, as we feared many months ago it would. Port Hudson has fallen. Charleston, Mobile, and Savannah will probably go next. Gen. Lee is attempting to retire from Maryland with his spoils, but no substantial victory has crowned his arms. We are weaker to-day than when he crossed the Potomac into Maryland. Our recruits in the way of conscripts will scarcely keep our regiments full, and we cannot hope to add materially to our forces. Our fighting population is pretty well exhausted. Everybody knows this.–The North knows it, and so does Europe. On the contrary, our enemies, flushed with triumph, have a large army in the field, and their President has just called for three hundred thousand more. He will get them. The movement on Pennsylvania by Gen.Lee, and the fall of Vicksburg and Port Hudson, have hushed all clamors for peace in the North, and have banded the people there as one man for the prosecution of the war. We have nothing to hope for from foreign nations, and, just as our cause is, we see no indications that Providence is about to interpose on our behalf. The war, then, will go on. One side or the other must *conquer*. Will five millions of whites conquer twenty millions of the same race? Will they conquer a peace on the very soil of these twenty millions? Not, in any event, if these twenty millions possess ordinary manhood and will fight. They fought at Sharpsburg and at Gettysburg, and they worsted us at the latter place.–Northern troops are not cowards,–they fight nearly as well as Southern troops. We cannot achieve signal victories over them on their own soil.

What then? If the worst is destined to overtake us, would it not be wise and prudent to take less than the worst, provided we could do so compatibly with honor?

The Richmond *Enquirer* recently declared that there were but two roads before the South—one, to invade the North and conquer a peace, and the other, to restore or reconstruct the old government.—That paper was either indulging vain speculations as to the future, or it will be prepared to abandon the contest if Gen. Lee should fail in his efforts to conquer a peace by invading the North. To abandon the contest, or to attempt to endure the presence of Northern armies on our soil, and resist them only by guerrilla warfare, is most probably to be conquered. It does not follow that a nation is not conquered because all its troops, or a considerable portion of them are not whipped or captured. *Whipped* we have never been, and never will be, but we may be overcome by mere physical force. Such was the fate of Poland, Hungary, and Ireland. It is no disgrace to a people to be over-powered by mere brute force, if they resist manfully and desperately. No troops since civilization commenced have fought with more courage, or constancy, or ardor than Southern troops. Their future, and the future of the country for which they are still contending, can never be, in any event, otherwise then respectable and honorable among nations. We grope in the dark like children looking for the designs, and endeavoring to interpret the workings of Providence in the affairs of nations. The birth of a nation on this planet is a great event. The decay and death of a nation is a great event. If it should please Him to build up and perpetuate this new nation of Confederate States, He will do it; if not, He will not do it.—That is all we know about it.

It is time to consult reason and common sense, and to discard prejudice and passion. Our people must look at and act upon things as they are, and not as they would have them. They must remember *that they are sovereign*—that they are the masters of those who administer the government –that the government was established by *them*, for *their* benefit, and they must not be afraid to utter their opinions freely and boldly. If they want continued, wasting, bloody war, let them say so; if they want peace, let them say so, and let them state the terms on which they would have it. That peace cannot be attained by fighting merely is now apparent to all. In the language of a highly intelligent friend who writes us from a County bordering on the South Carolina line, (from whom we should like to hear at some length,) "the people are tired of this awful war. It must end at some time, and there must be a starting point to an end. Let our next Congressional elections turn on the proposition that Congress shall appoint commissioners to meet others on the part of Lincoln, to make an honest effort to stay the effusion of blood by an honorable adjustment. Let what these commissioners may do be submitted to the people. If they approve it, peace will be the result; if they reject it, the war will be renewed and continued indefinitely." If an honorable peace were tendered by the South and rejected by the North, desperation would then nerve every Southern arm, and our people would share a common fate and fill a common grave. But this awful result, it seems to us, may be averted. It may do much good, and do no harm to talk–to negotiate, or to pave the way to negotiations while we fight.

We spoke just now of the worst befalling our people as the result of this war. What *is* the worst? It would be the condition of provincial dependence on the federal government, each State being ruled by a military Governor as Tennessee is, and the emancipation and arming of our slaves in our midst. That would be the worst. It the war continues is it not likely that this will happen?–Judging the future by the past–and we have no other means of judging–we fear it will. What then? Must we rush on to our doom? Must the sword still wave, and the strong arm of physical force still exert itself, and no effort be made by mental and moral means to close the war? Why, North-American savages sometimes bury the tomahawk and meet together to smoke the pipe of peace. Are we of the North and South–Christians as we profess to be–more savage than the savages?

These are sad truths, but we feel it to be our duty to lay them, before our readers. We do not censure others for entertaining their own opinions, and we have a right to express ours without censure from friend or foe. But censure, and even the grossest abuse we feel sure we shall incur; yet "none of these things move us," when we know we are speaking the truth, for the sake of humanity and liberty, in the name of the people themselves, who ought to be, if they are not practically, the masters of us all.

For the Standard

Standard
August 18, 1863

W. W. Holden

Dear Sir—In your issue of the 22d inst, there is copied an article from the Raleigh Daily Progress, and your editorial remarks of concurrence on the subject of *peace*. I desire to express not only my own, but I think, at least nine-tenths of the people of this county's entire approval of these sentiments. You are correct in saying the people desire a cessation of hostilities, and peace, and Mr. Editor, I believe they intend to have it at no distant day. You are also correct, and the people will sustain you, in the opinion that an honorable compromise now is preferable to a continuance of this bloody and desolating war; and the risk of a total subversion of the institution of slavery—nay, of civil liberty itself, for I am fully persuaded that both are in imminent jeopardy, by and on account of this war.

But how are the people to be heard and their wishes accomplished? Most clearly in the manners pointed out in your useful and widely circulated paper. Let the people assemble at their respective county towns or other places of business, and in calm deliberate convention, give expression, by resolutions, to their feelings. I do believe Mr. Editor, that nine-tenths of the men in this county (as well as a large majority of other counties,) will eagerly quit the most pressing business engagements on such a call and fly to the place of meeting, cheered on by mothers, wives, and daughters in so righteous and humane purposes.

It is true, Mr. Editor, there are some who will stand aloof with folded arms, and denounce you, and all others like you, as traitors, They are the men who were mainly instrumental in bringing on this unhappy war. They are generally those who have some lucrative business or trade that war stimulates and renders profitable, or who hold some office under the Jefferson Davis dynasty; men whose eyes can gaze on blood and carnage and the dead bodies of the humble poor, so their coffers are made to run over with filthy lucre. To all such men you may say "cease viper-you bite a file". I agree with you in another suggestion in a later paper, it is, that the people make the issue broad and clear in the approaching congressional election, and require our members, when elected, to advocate an armistice of hostilities and enter into negotiations with the federal government for a peaceable settlement of our disputes on the best terms not involving dishonor.

I also trust and hope the people of North-Carolina will vote for no one for Congress who is not pledged to vote for the repeal of the odious tithe law, that vestige of feudal ages, which serfs only willingly submit to. A law that in fact makes every farmer in the land, however opulent or humble he may be, a tenant of Jefferson Davis and his creatures in power. A law designed to flood the States with police spies and government stipendiaries. Already are we having imported into our States for the execution of this destable law, perhaps some broken down politicians or impoverised F. F. V. Will North-Carolina submit to such indignity much longer? I trust not.

Freedom of Speech and Press

Lenoir, Caldwell Co, July 28, 1863.

S. H. Christian for the Standard *Standard*
August 21, 1863

Mr. Holden:—The last *Observer* contains an account of the recent discussion at Albemarle, Stanly County, between Mr. Ashe[1] and myself, the latter part of which is not correct.

I stated then, as I state now, as there is a disposition in some portions of the district to misrepresent me, that I am for a Peace convention of all the Southern States, to assemble at some point in the South. Then, first, an armistice; secondly, to enter upon negotiations for conditions of peace honorable to both sections. If the North should respect the offer, the next Congress which will assemble at Washington may be opposed to Lincoln, and the proposed Convention may negotiate with it. If we are finally refused a hearing, then our people to unite to a man to resist, as they did immediately when the proclamation of Lincoln calling for troops in April, 1861. Then we can call upon the peace party at the North to put Lincoln out of power, and place men in power who will make an honorable peace with us. All wars must have an end, and no war can be closed but by negotiation. The enemy now hold more than half our territory, and nearly all our ports and rivers. Can we drive the enemy off this territory, and possess ourselves again of our parts? This whole matter must be closed in the end by negotiations; and why not commence now? The people of the North and South are clamorous for peace, and if they had a chance they would make it. I am for holding the sword in one hand and the olive branch in the other. My sentiments in relation to the origin of our troubles, and as to our present condition, may be found in a communication recently published in the *Standard* over the signature of "Davidson."

I am in favor of the repeal of the odious Jew law of Congress, two thousand years old, taking one-tenth of all the produce raised by the people, and if elected I shall vote to repeal the law.

S. H. Christian[2]

August 19, 1863

[1] Thomas S. Ashe, Anson County; member, state Senate, 1854-1855; member, Confederate House of Representatives, 1862-1864; member, Council of State, 1866; member, U.S. House of Representatives, 1875-1877; associate justice, North Carolina Supreme Court, 1879-1887. Cheney, *North Carolina Government*, 1585-1979, 322, 388, 180, 697, 575.

[2] Samuel H. Christian, Montgomery County; member, state Senate, 1854-1857; member, secession convention, 1861-1862; member, Confederate House of Representatives, 1864-1865. Cheney, *North Carolina Government*, 1585-1979, 322, 324, 389, 386.

E. M. Seago to Holden *Standard*
October 27, 1863

Raleigh, Sept. 9, 1863

Mr Holden Sir:—

One of the soldiers of this regiment brought into camp this package of paper, and offered it for sale. I do not think the object of the party was to make money out of the attack on your office. Therefore I return it to you.

From what I learn, considerable injury has been done your office. I hope it will be a warning to you and all others not to pursue a course calculated to encourage the enemy either by words or acts. The motive of this party were patriotic. They believe you to be opposed to our cause, and desire to betray us into the hands of the enemeies of our peace, our property, and our independence.

I am, very respectfully,
E. M. Seago[1]
Lt. Col. 20th Geo. Reg.

[1] Eli M. Seago, promoted to Lieutenant Colonel, July, 1863, Company F, 20th Regiment, Georgia Volunteer Infantry. Lillian Henderson, comp., *Roster of the Confederate Soldiers of Georgia* (Atlanta: Department of Confederate Pensions and Records, 1967), 2:804.

Holden to [E. J. Hale] A&H:Hale

Near Raleigh, Sept. 14, 1863

My dear Sir:[1] Your late kind favor was received, and perused with much interest. I regret that I am so situated as to be unable to reply to it at length at this time. I sincerely appreciate your views and your friendship, and if I may not be able to agree with you in all of the former, I trust I shall not forfeit the latter.

Troops are still passing through, and my family and friends are so concerned for my personal safety that I have not deemed it prudent to remain in Raleigh so as to spare the Standard. Indeed, the type have all been pied, and it will require five or six days' constant work to apart and distribute them. On Friday evening last another demonstration was made by the 4th Alabama, or a portion of it, and but for the prompt appearance of Gov. Vance and a guard from Camp Gilmer, the office would have been sacked again. I was in the country, and this second demonstration so excited my friends that, with the approval of Gov. Vance, they closed the office. In defiance of every effort at the depot to prevent it, squads are constantly passing threatening violence; and it was thought that if the office remained open this feeling would be aggravated. I hope to be able to issue a paper on Monday next. Please do me the kindness to state in the Observer that the Standard will appear again soon. I would publish a Card in the Progress, but as that paper has also been threatened, I do not wish to add to the danger by which the editor is surrounded.

All mob law is wrong, and thinking so, it cannot be too soon arrested. I regret the destruction of the Journal's materials. I knew nothing of it until the work was accomplished. But for the presence of Gov. Vance, Mayor Harrison,[2] and myself, the Register office would certainly have gone next.

I mourn over the distractions and dissention of our beloved State. I shall endeavor so to act as not to add to those dissentions. Three weeks ago, at the instance of Gov. Vance, I cheerfully agreed to forget or sink all party differences, if the Register and State Journal would do the same, and cease to assail me and my friends. Gov. Bragg[3] approached them with this proposition, at the request of Gov. Vance, and they refused to accede to it. What was I to do? The next thing was the sacking of my office as the result of the inflamatory teachings of these papers and the Rich. Enquirer.

Your friend,
W. W. Holden

[1] This letter, from the Edward Jones Hale Papers in the Private Collections, North Carolina State Archives, does not indicate to whom it was addressed. From references in the letter, there is no doubt that it was addressed to Hale.
[2] William H. Harrison.
[3] Thomas Bragg.

Holden to the Public *Standard*
October 2, 1863

On Wednesday night the 9th of September, 1863, my printing office was mobbed by a portion of Gen. Benning's Georgia brigade,[1] with arms in their hands. It is believed that the officers and men who composed this mob belonged to the 2d and 29th Georgia regiments. I owe it to the public as well as to my-self to give the facts connected with this outrage on my Constitutional rights.

Troops were known to be passing through Raleigh at the time on their way to the South, but, though threats had been made against me, I entertained no serious apprehension that they would be executed. On the evening referred to, about dusk, an officer accompanied by a soldier called at my house and enquired for the printing offices in town. I told him what offices there were, and where, and handed him a copy of the *Standard*. I also invited them to come in the house and be seated, which the officer politely declined. About eight o'clock a couple of friends called to see me, and we conversed until about half past nine, when one of them left. Soon after, my door bell was rung, when I went to the door and met, I think, the same officer and soldier who had previously called. I invited them in the house, which the officer declined, saying he desired to see the Editor of the *Standard* in his office. (My office is on the lot with my house, some twenty yards from the latter.) I told him it was late—that my office was closed for the night, and again invited him in. He replied that a number of gentlemen desired to see the Editor of the *Standard* in his office. I again told him it was too late to go the office, but that I would be glad to see him and his friends in my house. He bowed and retired. I had no other thought than that they were some North-Carolinians who were friends, on their way South, who desired to call upon me. In the course of five or ten minutes a body of armed men filed by on the pavement opposite my house, on the way towards the office. My friend and myself were looking out through the window at them, when one of three or four officers in the rear exclaimed, "only the provost guard, gentlemen." Even then I did not suspect their purpose, but thought they had been sent out from the depot as a guard to pick up stragglers. They halted, however, at the office, and I soon became aware that their object was unfriendly. I immediately retired from my house, feeling that I was not safe on the premises. Meanwhile some friends, who had earlier intimation than I of the purpose of this armed band, repaired in haste to the Executive mansion and informed Gov. Vance[2] of the movement. He instantly hastened up Fayetteville street, accompanied by a member of his staff who happened to be with him, and met the Mayor of the City[3] just before he reached the office. He then looked for Gen. Benning, but, being unable to find him, he met Col. Harris,[4] of one of the Georgia regiments, to whom he appealed to aid him in arresting the movement, then fully under way. Col. H promptly responded, and they hastened to the office. When they arrived the men were engaged, evidently under orders, in pouring the type in the street, and some of them were trying to to pull down the power press. A Maj. Shephard[5] was called for—it is said he apppeared, and telling the men that the Governor of the State was present and desired to address them, he ordered them to leave the office and fall into line. This they did quietly and at once. Gov. Vance, we learn, reproved them in the strongest and most pointed terms for their conduct, whereupon they cheered him, and one of the officers replied, "Governor, we have done what we came to do, and will now retire."

It is not true, as stated some of the Georgia papers, that there were North Carolinians in this mob. They were all Georgians, with arms in their hands, led and directed by officers. The men were no doubt picked out for this work from the 2d and 20th Georgia, and officers from both these regiments were no doubt in the mob. I learn that Gov. Vance immediately wrote to President Davis, characterizing the outrage as it deserved, and demanding the trial and punishment of the officers and men engaged in this disgraceful business; and that the President replied, informing the Governor that he had given directions to the commanding General of the department to investigate the matter. I take it for granted that the investigation will take place, and just punishment will be influcted. To suppose otherwise would be to conclude that our government was *Mexicanized* and that the President was deliberately faithless to the Constitution which he has sworn to support. But even if this were possible, such is my confidence in Gov. Vance that I believe he will see to it at all hazzards that this outrage is properly atoned for.

The extent of the injury to my office is not so great as it first supposed. Nearly all the types were poured out of the cases, several forms of type, including a form of the State laws, knocked into pi, and some paper damaged; but the presses were not injured, nor was the house itself seriously damaged. But several gold and steel pens, postage stamps, small change, inkstands, four large bottles of ink, some books, and other articles mysteriously disappeared; and I learn that some of the mob were engaged next day in showing some old federal postage stamps which I had before the war, as evidence that I was a traitor and in correspondence with the enemy!

Early on the next morning after this occurrance, a number of the citizens of Raleigh, and others who happened to be present, attacked the office of the State *Journal*, threw the type into pi, broke the press, &c, inflicting serious injury on the establishment. This was done by my friends, by way of retaliation for the injury inflicted on me the night last. I knew nothing about it, and had nothing to do with it. I arrived at the spot after the work of destruction was over, but, with Gov. Vance, the Mayor of the City, and others, I aided in preventing the destruction of the *Register* office, which would otherwise in all probability have followed.

All mob law is wrong, and cannot be too soon arrestd. I have reason to believe that the attack on my office was premeditated, and that Destructives in this City and elsewhere knew it would be made. It is stated that the Georgia soldiers, while on their way, were urged at Weldon, Henderson, and Franklinton to destroy the *Standard* office; and that they had been so deceived as to the character of the paper and its Editor, that they enquired at Pacific depot, a few miles this side of Franklinton, if it was true that the federal flag was flying over the *Standard* office!

On the subsequent Friday evening another attempt was made to mob my office by a portion of the 4th Alabama, which was prevented by the presence of Gov. Vance and an armed force from Camp Holmes. And I learn also that a night or two afterwards, some twenty-five South-Carolinians, with arms in their hands, were met on Hillsborough street looking for the *Standard* office, with the intention of completing what the Georgians had begun. They were told that if they attempted it they would be fired upon by the provost guard, and resisted by the citizens, whereupon they returned to their camp.

I trace this mob spirit to the course pursued by the Richmond *Enquirer*, the Raleigh *Register*, the State *Journal*, and Charlotte *Bulletin*; and also to the so-called "Army Convention." All the papers named had repeatedly called for mob law against the *Standard*. Some of them had urged the government, the people and the soldiers to suppress the paper by force; and the so-called "Army Convention," whose proceedings were first given to the public in the *religious* press, advised a course in relation to the *Standard* which the members of the Convention knew the government could not adopt, if it would, and which inevitably tended to and encouraged mob law, as is clearly shown by the communication from the *Progress* copied in the *Standard* of today. The fruits of these appeals were seen in the mob of troops from another State which assailed my office, and in the destruction of the establishment of the State *Journal*. My readers will bear witness that I have at all times opposed mob law. Nothing will justify a resort to it.

And now, what have I done, or omitted to do, to justify or palliate such an outrage? If I had committed treason, it was the duty of Gov. Vance to arrest me; and even if he had believed that I was at heart opposed to the Confederate cause, it would have been his duty to have withheld his official papers from my columns, and to have discountenanced me personally as a disloyal man. I was assailed in a cowardly manner, my property injured, and my Constitutional rights trampled down, *on account of my opinions*. It was done because I had boldly and uniformly defended the rights and the honor of my native State—and had labored to reform the administration at Richmond, so as to save the cause—and had vindicated the rights of the soldiers against oppression in the army, and their families against the injustice and cold charity of certain characters at home—and had exerted myself to maintain civil law against military power—and had insisted that whilst the war should be pressed with the utmost vigor, and desertion and resistance to law discountenanced and repressed, statesmen and people at home should cast about anxiously for some means to initiate negotiations that might end in an honorable peace. "My offence hath this extent—no more."

With a vast majority of the people of this State I was a Union man up to Mr. Lincoln's proclamation, calling for troops to make war on Georgia and other seceded States. I then ceased to be a Union man. I advocated, as I advocate now, resistance to Mr. Lincoln. As one of the 120 delegates to the State Convention I signed the ordinance of separation, and voted to make North Carolina a Confederate State. I did this sadly but firmly. While a member of the Convention I voted for every measure which I thought would advance the Confederate cause, and sustained every measure of the kind in the *Standard*. I have contributed as much in proportion to my means to the Confederate cause as any man in the State. It was my earnest wish from the first that party feeling should be buried, and that our whole people as a band of brothers should make common cause against the common foe. But this was not permitted by those who controlled the Confederate government and the government of this State. The most rigid partyism was inaugurated at Montgomery and Raleigh, and subsequently carried out at Richmond. Every citizen of this State who had labored to preserve the Union up to Mr. Lincoln's proclamation, and who would not, for personal or pecuniary advantage, admit that his opponents were right in urging secession before the appearaance of that document, and right in preferring to break up the old government, was marked as unfit for civil or military office. Mr. Davis filled his Cabinet and appointed his foreign ministers from his partizan friends. His example was followed in this State. Mr. Davis appointed nearly all his Brigadiers and Major-Generals from his partizan supporters; and his example was followed in this respect by Governors Ellis and Clark, in their appointments in the ten State regiments. When the old Union men, but now true Confederates, remonstrated against this injustice, and reminded their opponents that they were sending two men to the field to their one to fight the battles, they were insultingly told that it was *their* duty to serve—that "those who made the revolution were alone entitled to conduct it"—and that the old Union men, but now true Confederates, unless they submitted quietly to such treatment, and behaved themselves, would have a "hideous mark" put on their foreheads, by which they and their children after them would be known as traitors. This led to the formation of the Conservative party of this State, composed of persons who had belonged to the Whig and Democratic parties. Those who formed this party did so reluctantly, in self-defense. At the next election they carried their nominee (Gov. Vance) by thirty-five thousand majority, and both branches of the Legislature. My opinions are now what they were then, and if I am a traitor, then are two-thirds of our poeple also traitors.

Meanwhile the proscriptive partizan policy of the administration at Richmond was filling the army and the civil offices with original secession partizans, and such as had abandoned their former views for place, to the almost total exclusion of the old Union men, but now true Confederates. Every Confederate office in this State, I believe, was occupied by these partizans; and of the eighteen Brigadiers appointed by Mr. Davis from this State, but two were Conservatives. Persons from Virginia, South-Carolina, Mississippi, and even the *foreign* State of Maryland, were appointed to offices in our midst over the heads of our people. The fifth medical director for the State, for example, had been appointed from Virginia or Maryland; and on the back of this came the appointment of a Virginian as Chief Tithingman.[6] This was more than our people could bear. Those of them who had been Union men felt that the "hideous mark" was indeed upon them, and that persons from other States had been chosen to fix it on their foreheads. The people of Greene County held a meeting in which they complained in strong terms of the injustice done this State, and demanded the removal of the Tithingman. Their proceedings were instantly caught up, and some seventy meetings were held, in all of which the partyism of the administration at Richmond was rebuked, and justice demanded for North-Carolina. This was the origin of the so-called "Union" or "peace meetings" in this State. Not one of them would have been held but for the course of the administration at Richmond towards North-Carolina. If it be true that causes will produce effects, then is the administration responsible for these meetings. But it is answered, some of these meetings called for peace on any terms, and some of them proposed a reconstruction of the Union.—It is true, a few of them called for peace on the best terms that could be obtained, and a few of them proposed reconstruction. I published the proceedings, but my whole course both as a man and an Editor was against reconstruction, and against unconditional submission to the federal government. I published the proceedings of these meetings because a portion of the people had held them—not because I approved them. At least sixty out of the seventy meetings breathed a spirit of devotion to the cause, and the proceedings of many of these meetings met my approval, especially those of the people of Johnston County. Forty old Counties in Virginia go about to reconstruct the old Union, and actually do reconstruct it as far as they can, and no denunciation are heaped on them; yet, when the people in a few precincts in North-Carolina, worn and wasted by war, express a desire for peace, and favor a return to the old government, not as a matter of choice, but, as they think, of stern necessity, a great outcry is raised—the State itself is charged with disloyality, and my office is mobbed for publishing the proceedings, though every intelligent person in the State who reads the *Standard*, know I did not approve them.

But, it is said that to talk for peace at home while our troops are fighting for it in the field, operates against the cause. I do not believe it. What sort of peace? A return to the old government? No. Submission to Mr. Lincoln? No. What then? *A peace based on the separation of a portion of the Southern States from the other States, and two or three independent governments*. That is what I would call "an honorable peace." How is this to be effected? By invading Maryland and Pennsylvania, and by claimiug Maryland, Missouri, Kentucky, and Western Virginia as Confederate States? I think not. Who knows but the Northern Congress would consent to let us go, if we would give up those States, a majority of whose people are against us? Why not say to the North, take those States–take public lands—take the navy and all the public property within your borders – *only let us go, and let us alone*. Why not say to the North, we were once friends–we are now enemies–we may be friends again under different governments; let us reason together, and make a treaty offensive and defensive on the subject of the Chesapeake and the Mississippi, and against the encroachment of European powers? That is what I call talking for peace. Is there any treason in it? I admire the zeal which says, conquer a peace—drive the enemy out of Kentucky, Missouri, Maryland, and Western Virginia—demand, insist upon, and have at all hazards, a fair share of the public property, with indemnity for all that has been destroyed; but my judgment tells me this is hardly possible.—As the French say, whose breath is that of revolution, I "accept the situation, and make the most I can of it." If it be treason to think thus and reason thus, then is free speech dead in North-Carolina, and we are committed to a whirlwind of passion which may destroy every interest. But it may be said that it would be submission on our part to offer such terms to the North, and a concession of what justly belongs to us. What, submission to obtain *independence*? If they should let us go on these terms, or on any terms, *we would be independent*. That is the answer. We would start the world anew, as the young man of twenty-one leaves his father's house to make a name and a fortune.—We would not be poor long. If we could only remain united with a government of eight or ten States, we would soon be in a condition to command the respect of the world.

But suppose these terms, or some terms should be offered to the North and rejected, and the answer should be, lay down your arms, ye rebels—submit to a territorial condition, or return to the old government deprived of your slave property, with your slaves set loose in your midst, with the loss of all your currency and your bonds, to be saddled with the payment of the federal war debt, and yourselves the inferiors of the Northern States in the federal government. What would be the effect of this? It would *re-unite* our people as one man, and boy and grandsire would fight to the bitter end side by side with our veteran soldiers. Is there any treason in that?

But I am told if I talk for peace while our brave soldiers are fighting for it, I am aiding and comforting the enemy. If this be so, when will the time come to talk for it? Next year, or the next? We shall see. But what meant that mission of vice President Stephens[7] to Fortress Monroe and Washington City? Surely the second officer of this great government was not deputed merely to make arrangements about the exchange of prisoners. No, that mission meant a peace proposition of some sort from President Davis to President Lincoln. Was it rejected? Mr. Stephens was not heard, but who can say his proposition would not have been entertained if he had announced the real character of his mission? If he went to talk about peace, those who sent him did not adopt a direct and manly course in their instructions to him, for he was told to present himself in one character and then act in another.

Every battle is an argument for peace, and every improvement by statesmen and people at home of the results of battle, is an argument for peace.—Negotiations, to have an end, must certainly have a beginning. The battle of New Orleans was fought after the treaty of peace had been signed by our Commissioners at Ghent. The statesmen of that day did not think they were lowering the character of their country, or injuring the cause, or giving aid and comfort to the British, by sending Commissioners to Europe to urge on their enemies an honorable peace. If those officers in the army, and those office-holders in our midst, some of whom are making fortunes out of the war, whose bitter and unjust denounciations of me were partly instrumental in causing the late mob, will only change places for three months with the privates in the ranks, and with the great mass of our laboring people at home who are feeling the pinch of the war, and then say that they are opposed to negotiations for peace, and that any suggestion of the kind would be injurious to the cause, then for one I will never utter the word *peace* agains as long as I live.

It has been charged that the course of the *Standard* has caused desertions from the army. Soldiers will look in vain for any thing in the *Standard* which justifies desertion. I have called on our soldiers as frequently as any Editor in the State to remain true to their colors, and I have sustained every measure designed to improve the condition of the soldier and render him satisfied with his condition. I voted in the Convention for the fifty dollar bounty to all our soldiers, conscripts included. I drew up and voted for the ordinance securing to our soldiers the right to vote in camp. And I have written hundreds of articles appealing to the government, and to the people at home to do justice to the soldiers and their families. What for? To make the soldier satisfied with his condition, and to nerve his arm in the day of battle. The soldiers know this, and they like me for it—and hence one of my crimes is that I am "too popular with the soldiers." Some months since the Columbia (S.C.) papers contained an official notice of *six hundred* deserters from Gen. Evan's brigade;[8] and I have been informed that while this brigade and the regiment of Col. Colquitt,[9] of Georgia, were on their way to reinforce Gen. Johnston,[10] some fifteen hundred of these South Carolinians and Georgians "stepped aside" (that is the expression used in relation to desertions in other States,) to their homes. Mississippians and Virginians have also deserted by hundreds, if not thousands. Did *I* do all that? Again, for at least six weeks before my office was mobbed the circulation of the *Standard* was prohibited in the army of Virginia. Men were "bucked" because they wrote to me approving my course, and some were punished for reading the *Standard*, which they obtained now and then from friends visiting the camps. Did desertion cease, or did it increase during these six weeks? The truth is, North-Carolina is to be the scapegoat to bear the sins of my enemies into the wilderness. But truth, reason, and justice will yet prevail. I have an abiding faith in the people of my native State; and because I have this faith in them, and hold to their right to govern themselves, I am assailed and persecuted.

It has also been charged that I got up the public meetings in this State in order to detach Gov. Vance from his Conservative friends, and defeat his re-election for a second term. This is utterly untrue. I do not desire the place occupied by that gentleman. My only wish in regard to Gov. Vance is that he may retire after his *second* term with the confidence of his friends and the plaudits of his country. As long as he is true to the principles on which he was elected, and as long as he demands and obtains justice for his State, and sees to it that military despotism does not override the civil law, I will give to his administration a steady, straight forward, manly support. A cringing support I would not give to any man. I now tell the people that I have confidence in Gov. Vance. I believe he is doing the best he can under the circumstances. I think he has a heart for his friends and for his country, and that his heart is in the right place; but if, in the vicissitudes still before us in this revolution, or after it, I should find myself mistaken, I shall not hesitate to say so. If his enemies praise him, he cannot help it; and as long as his friends are satisfied with him, they should regard this praise as the moralist regards hypocrisy, as "the tribute which vice pays to virtue."

I am the same Conservative I was in 1861, in 1862, and when my office was mobbed. My enemies may destroy my property, and even take my life, but they cannot break my spirit. If *my friends* think I have acted indiscreetly, or that , in my deep resentment for the wrongs heaped on the State, I have assailed the administration with too much heat, I will heed their advice, and endeavor to moderate my tone; but to my enemies I concede nothing and promise nothing. I have strong friends and bitter enemies. I am proud of it it. The former I will never desert, and the latter I defy.

I now declare, as I have frequently done, that I am a sincere and steadfast friend of the Confederate government; and that, whatever may be the result of the terrible ordeal through which it is passing, I will be among the last to desert it.—I have striven in my feeble way to reform its administration, so as to give more efficiency to it, and thus ensure its success. If it should succeed, I will rejoice; but if it should perish, the fault will not be mine.

I shall issue the *Standard* regularly hereafter, and I think I have a right, as a law-abiding and tax-paying citizen of the Confederate States, to expect of Gen. Lee that he will allow the *Standard* to be read by the privates in the army.

W. W. Holden

Raleigh, Oct. 1, 1863

[1] Henry Lewis Benning, judge of the Georgia Supreme Court, 1853-1859; colonel, Seventeenth Georgia Regiment, 1861; brigadier general, 1863. Jon L. Wakelyn, *Biographical Dictionary of the Confederacy* (Westport, Connecticut: Greenwood Press, 1977), s.v. "Benning, Henry Lewis."

[2] Zebulon Baird Vance.

[3] William H. Harrison.

[4] Not identified.

[5] William S. Sheperd, lieutenant colonel, Second Georgia Infantry. Janet B. Hewett, ed., *Roster of Confederate Soldiers* (Wilmington, N.C., Broadfoot Publishing Company, 1996), 14:53.

[6] Edmund Bradford, a native of Pennsylvania who moved to Virginia after graduation from West Point and service in the U.S. Army, was appointed North Carolina collector of the tax in kind levied against all Confederate farmers. Glenn Tucker, *Zeb Vance: Champion of Personal Freedom* (Indianapolis: Bobbs-Merrill Co., 1965), 250-251. See also Johnston and Mobley, *The Papers of Zebulon Baird Vance*, 2:206.

[7] Alexander Hamilton Stephens, Georgia; member, U.S. House of Representatives, 1843-1859, 1873-1882; member, Georgia secession convention, 1861; vice-president, Confederate States, 1861-1865; governor of Georgia, 1882-1883. *Dictionary of American Biography*, s.v. "Stephens, Alexander Hamilton."

[8] Clement Anselm Evans, major, 31st Georgia Regiment, 1861;colonel, 1862; brigadier general, 1863; acting major general in Gordon's Corps, 1864. Wakelyn, *Biographical Dictionary of the Confederacy*, s.v. "Evans, Clement Anselm."

[9] Alfred Holt Colquitt, colonel, 6th Georgia Infantry Regiment, 1863; governor of Georgia, 1876-1882; member, U.S. Senate, 1882-1894. Wakelyn, *Biographical Dictionary of the Confederacy*, s.v. "Colquitt, Alfred Holt."

[10] Joseph Eggleston Johnston; graduate of West Point, 1829; quartermaster general of the U.S. Army, 1860; organized Virginia volunteers, 1861; full general Confederate States Army, 1861; commanded Army of Tennessee, 1862-1864; surrendered to Major General Sherman, April 26, 1865. Wakelyn, *Biographical Dictionary of the Confederacy*, s.v. "Johnston, Joseph Eggleston."

Holden to E. J. Hale, Esq. A&H:Hale

Raleigh, Oct. 7, 1863

My dear Sir: I regret that I have been unable, owing to the pressure of much business, to reply sooner to yours of the 8th September, and the letter of E. J. Hale & Son of the 22d. Your first letter was received about the time the mob occurred. I replied to it briefly, but being in the country, and somewhat troubled at the restriction in which I was placed, I could not reply at any length. I beg you to be assured that I regarded your letter as altogether kind and friendly, and the views it contained worthy of consideration. The conversation I had with Dr. Smith[1] was very agreeable in all respects, though I thought him in error in some of his views. If all the "originals" would act and talk with the same reason and toleration which seems to govern his course, the bitterness unfortunately prevailing would soon cease, and we should have unity and harmony among ourselves.

But the mob came right on the heels of your letter, and left me in no condition to consider calmly the views you presented, nor to change my course, even if disposed to do so. I could not change or modify materially in the face of mob violence, and of threats almost constantly made since. My position is clearly and thoroughly set forth in my Card. I shall not deviate from it. I am for independence, as I have been from the first, but I am opposed to fighting indefinitely for West Virginia, Missouri, Kentucky, and Maryland.

I was pained to perceive that the Observer did not do me justice in relation to the mob. I was placed on the same footing with Spelman,[2] who had called for more than a year for mob violence against me. It is true that in private conversations I used the language to which you refer, for I was smarting under my misfortune, and mortified, not angered, at the course of the Observer towards me. Depend upon it, if you had been in my place, I should have pursued a very different course. I should have denounced the men and the officers who had mobbed you, and should have traced the mob itself to its true source. I have the strongest evidence that President Davis has been anxious for months past to suppress the Standard. This is strictly confidential. The day will come when I can give you my authority for this.

I had nothing in the world to do with the communication I copied from the Progress. I copied it, because it was a truthful statement, as far as it went, of the origin and character of the mob. If any part of it does you injustice, I do not endorse that part.

I shall feel obliged in my next to refer to the Observer, but I shall do so in no spirit of injustice or unkindness. You have advised me very freely, and I thank you for it; but allow me to say that I do not propose to pursue such a course as to meet the political approval of Judge Ruffin,[3] John M. Morehead,[4] William K. Lane,[5] David S. Reid, John Kerr, Walter L. Steele,[6] and the like. To please them in every thing politically is to abandon the Conservative party. I trace nearly all our calamities to this order of politicans. They must either rule or ruin, I fear they may do both. Mr. Davis is their model of a statesman. I have no confidence in him. This may be wrong, but I cannot help it. There are no statesmen among them. Some of them might be, but for their partisan and intense selfishness.

In conclusion, I beg you to believe that I am still your friend. I should deeply regret any break between us. There is no good reason why there should be any. But I must defend and take care of myself as far as I can, and I am sure you will not fall out with me for that.

I do not envy the character of the person who caught up a portion of my private conversation and retailed to you. Such persons are not "peacemakers."

Very Truly Your Friend
W. W. Holden

E. J. Hale, Esq.

[1] Probably William Nathan Harrell Smith, congressman and judge; member, House of Commons, 1840, 1858, 1865; member, state Senate, 1848; member, U.S. House of Representatives, 1859-1861; member, Confederate House of Representatives, 1861-1865; chief justice, North Carolina Supreme Court, 1878-1889. *Dictionary of North Carolina Biography*, s.v. "Smith, William Nathan Harrell."

[2] John Spelman.

[3] Thomas Ruffin.

[4] John Motley Morehead, governor and railroad promoter; member, House of Commons, 1821, 1826-1828, 1858-1859; member, state Senate, 1860-1861; governor, 1840-1844; president, North Carolina Railroad; delegate to 1861 peace conference. *Dictionary of North Carolina Biography*, s.v. "Morehead, John Motley."

[5] William K. Lane, Wayne County; member, state Senate, 1858-1863; member, council of state, 1850-1854; president, 1850-1851. Cheney, *North Carolina Government, 1585-1979*, 178, 1037.

[6] Walter Leak Steele, lawyer; A.B., U.N.C., 1844; A.M., 1847; member, House of Commons, 1846-1850, 1854-1856; member, state Senate, 1852, 1858; member, secession convention, 1861; member, U.S. House of Representatives, 1877-1881. Grant, *Alumni History*, 590

Holden to Thomas Settle, Jr. SHC:Settle, Jr.

Raleigh, Dec. 22, 1863

My dear Settle: I have just heard incidentally that when you were here, soon after the mob, and when you delivered my note, which I handed you at Mr. Mitchin's,[1] to Gov. Vance, he made some remarks highly derogatory to my character in connection with the mob. Please do me the kindness as a personal and political friend, to inform me what he did say, and what his manner was on the occassion.

The future darkens, and I can see no ray of hope. It is now apparent that North-Carolina must soon look to herself. The power that made the war can alone close it—The power of the sovereign States. Our next election will turn on the question of a State Convention. You will know where to find me on such a question.

Please let me hear from you soon, and believe me

Very Truly yours,
W. W. Holden

[1] Not identified.

Standard
March 3, 1864

HOLDEN TO THE PEOPLE OF NORTH-CAROLINA

In compliance with the wishes of many friends, I announce myself a candidate for the office of Governor of North Carolina, at the election to be held on the first Thursday in August next.

My principals and views, as a Conservative "after the straitest sect," are well known to the people of the State. These principles and views are what they have been. They will not be changed.

I am not disposed, at a time like this, to invite the people from their employments, and add to the excitement which prevails in the public mind, by haranguing them for their votes. We need all our energies to meet the common enemy, and to provide means of subsistence for our troops in the field and the people at home. Let the people go calmly and firmly to the polls and vote for the men of their choice. I will cheerfully abide their decision, whatever it may be.

If elected I will do everything in my power to promote the interests, the honor and the glory of North Carolina, and to secure an honorable peace.

W. W. Holden

March 2, 1864

Holden to C. J. Cowles, Esq. A&H:Holden

Raleigh, March 18, 1864

My dear Sir:[1] Your esteemed favor of the 10th has been received. It was not my wish to run for Governor, and I was led to announce my name by two reasons; First, the *knowledge* that Gov. Vance was gone from us, and secondly, the urgent appeals of numerous friends. It is my opinion that Gov. Vance had made up his mind deliberately to go with Davis and the Destructives since his visit to Richmond last August. Soon after his return from Richmond he wrote a letter of ..[illegible], addressed to J. H. Haughton,[2] of Chatham, of the most ultra Jeff Davis war character, and he would have published it but for my earnest remonstrance. I told him it would destroy him at once with his friends, and he consented at last to consult Gov. Graham on the subject. At my instance he sent the letter to Gov. G.,[3] who read it and returned it, advising against any publication, but suggesting, if he would publish, to strike out about one-half, including of course the Jeff. Davis views.[4] So I saved him then by good advice, which Gov. G. endorsed. I labored for months in the same way, but in vain. I have no doubt that he approved, if he did not suggest the course of the Observer last summer. His appointments for the last six or eight months have been nearly all Destructive. He has promised repeatedly to stand by the civil law, but there is no marked instance in which he had done so in opposition to the aggressions of the administration. It was well understood here that his Wilkesborough speech was to be aimed at the bulk of his old friends, and consequently the Confederate heralded his speech, and bestowed upon it, both before and after it was delivered, the warmest encomiums. That paper is now out for him for re-election; and it is well understood here that Gov. Bragg,[5] Col. Barringer,[6] N. W. Woodfin[7] and other Destructive leaders now look to him as the only instrument by which they hope to prostrate the Conservative party.

The latter gentleman has been here for several days past, at the request as is said of Gov. Vance, arranging with the Destructive leaders to support him. I understand he says that Holden is dangerously strong in the West, and that the only hope to defeat him is by Gov. Vance's joining . . . [illegible].

If Gov. Vance had been permitted to walk over the course without opposition he would have demoralized and destroyed the Conservative party, just as John Tyler would have destroyed the Whig party in 1841, if Mr. Clay had not exposed him.

You are right in supposing that Gov. Vance's speech was framed by the reporter under the eye of Gov. V. The reporter stopped at his house, and was engaged several days in the work.

I am receiving the most encouraging reports from all parts of the State. Col. Harris, [8] the Senator from Rutherford and Polk, writes me that I will receive a larger vote in those Counties than Gov. Vance received in 1862. And the Sheriff of Jackson County writes, "The Western Counties almost to a man will go for you." I give these as specimens. I learn also that the army is for me four or five to one.

I suspended the Standard on account of the suspension of habeas corpus, abolishing civil law. I felt that if I could not continue to print as a free man I would not print at all, and I could not bear the idea of lowering or changing my tone. Thank God, the Governor of Georgia[9] has spoken out like a man, in a spirit worthy of American manhood and American liberty. I indulge the hope that the Congress when it meets in May, will repeal the obnoxious law, and then I can print again.

If you and other friends in Wilkes concur with me you will perceive that we will have to oppose Gov. Vance boldly, and defeat him. He is, to all intents and purposes, the Destructive candidate. It is important, therefore, that the Conservatives should move promptly . . .[illegible] to run through. This being the case, I respectfully submit if it would not be good policy to hold meetings at once and take position. The Progress, the Salem Press and Henderson Times will publish proceedings.

Please show this, if you choose, to discreet friends. Should be glad to hear from you soon.

Very Truly Yours,
W. W. Holden

C. J. Cowles, Esq.[10]

[1] The letter is torn and damaged and some words are missing or illegible.

[2] John Hooker Haughton, Chatham County; lawyer; member, House of Commons, 1844-1845; member, state Senate, 1850-1851, 1854-1855; firm defender of slavery. *Dictionary of North Carolina Biography*, s.v. "Haughton John Hooker."

[3] William Alexander Graham.

[4] The letter is printed in full in Johnston and Mobley, *The Papers of Zebulon Baird Vance*, 2:242-247.

[5] Thomas Bragg.

[6] Daniel Moreau Barringer.

[7] Nicholas Washington Woodfin, Buncombe County lawyer and planter; member, state Senate, 1844-1852; member, secession convention, 1861. *Dictionary of North Carolina Biography*, s.v. "Woodfin, Nicholas Washington."

[8] Ceburn L. Harris. Rutherford County; member, state Senate, 1863-1864, 1865-1867; represented Rutherford and Polk counties at 1865 constitutional convention. Cheney, *North Carolina Government*, 1585-1979, 833, 1264.

[9] Joseph E. Brown, governor of Georgia, 1857-1865. *World Book Encyclopedia*, 8:180.

[10] Calvin Josiah Cowles, merchant and real estate owner; operated trade in Elkville and later in Wilkesboro; interested in mining; originally a Whig, became a Republican during Reconstruction; delegate to 1868 constitutional; superintendent of Charlotte mint, 1869-1885. *Dictionary of North Carolina Biography*, s.v. "Cowles, Calvin Josiah."

Holden to the Public *Standard*
April 20, 1864

I have received several invitations to address the people as a candidate for Governor. Under the circumstances, I most respectfully decline to canvass the State. This determination was made known in my card announcing myself a candidate, of date March 5th, 1864. I am not afraid to meet Gov. Vance, or any other candidate who may be supported by the Destructives or partizans of the Confederate administration; but I am not vain enough to hope that I could change or control the opinions of the people by a canvass, and I am not disposed to add to the excitement which prevails, in the public mind, by haranguing the people for their votes. Let them go calmly and firmly to the polls and vote for the man of their choice. I will cheerfully abide their decision, whatever it may be

There was no canvass in the State in 1862, for Governor, and no canvass in Virginia, Alabama and Georgia by the candidates for Governor at their late elections.

I trust that those of my fellow citizens who have done me the honor to address me on the subject will receive this an an answer to their invitations.

W. W. Holden

April 18, 1864

Jonathan Worth to Holden A&H:Worth

Raleigh Apl. 23rd, 1864

W. W. Holden, Esqr.

Dear Sir: The kind personal relation existing between Govr. Vance and myself and between you and myself and a firm conviction that a breach between you would be detrimental to the Public good made me hope such collision would be avoided, until Gov. Vance's Wilkesboro Speech was published[1] and you became a candidate; and I have still hoped that some means of reconciliation might be found, and hence have avoided taking any part in the Contest. I presume the immediate cause of your declaring yourself a Candidate was the changed tone of the Govr. In that speech on the suspension of the Habeas Corpus and the general drift of the speech imparting to the Conservative party the purpose of seceding from the Confederacy & re-constructing. This imputation, so far as it applied to you, or any considerable number of your friends, was not warranted by any thing you had said, so far as I know. You had a thousand times affirmed the reverse. A very small number, until lately, hoped for re-construction. You have all the time opposed it.—None can now entertain this. It is probable you may have felt that Gov. V. has not extended to you the protection you had a right to expect. If your information that Hoke's Brigade was about to be stationed here with Gov. Vance's approval, just before you suspended your paper, the presumption was a probable one that it sprung from hostility to you.

I perceive you publish Stephen's[2] Speech with approval. I regard it as the most Statesman-like & conclusive argument on all the points he touches, which has appeared since the war began. I perceive by the editorial of the Governor's paper & what I hear from other sources, that the Governor fully & heartily endorses it, and says his softened tone in his Wilkesboro speech was intended to soothe an excited community. From what I hear I presume he will put himself right on the peace and Habeas Corpus questions by the publication of his correspondence with the President & his next message to the Genl Assembly. If he should do so—the difference between you on the questions of public interest will be narrowed down to the Convention question, an issue at present, not warranting a contest; and as to any personal alienation, I trust the Governor and you might, by mutual explanations, be restored to your former relations.

Now I submit to you whether the adoption by the Govr. of Stephen's speech—and his explanation of his softened tone on Habeas Corpus in his Wilkesboro Speech, especially if accompanied by the publication of a manly remonstrance against the Habeas Corpus *act*, made to the president in anticipation of the passage of the Act, would not warrant you in withdrawing your name on the ground of his rectified position,—I have the highest possible respect for your judgment—and especially for your knowledge of public opinion in N.C.—It appears to me, especially with proper explanations of my personal grounds of opinion, if there be any, that there is an opportunity for you to place yourself on higher grounds of personal popularity than you ever occupied, at the same time cementing the Conservative party and inflicting on your enemies a most fatal blow. The Destructives have disapproved Stephen's speech—have justified the suspension of Habeas Corpus—and if you and the Govr. were reconciled, would fall the flattest that ever party did fall—and your generosity would give you a popularity insuring to you any position you may desire—I think you might be elected our next Govr, almost by acclamation.—At present I regard the result of the election as dependent on the opening military campaign.

I have had no conference on these views with the Govr. or any body else, save a few words with our friend B. F. Moore[3] I beg you to consider them and if there be any thing in them meeting your approval: or you can suggest any other mode of avoiding a contest which I am persuaded is as unpleasant to you, as it is likely to be damaging to the success of our great and patriotic party, I shall be glad to give my aid in carrying it out—but if there be no mode of avoiding the contest, I shall feel unwilling, on personal and political considerations, to take a decided part in this most unfortunate division.[4]

Yours very truly & respectfully
Jonathan Worth[5]

I have not made known to any person whatsoever that I had it in contemplation to write this letter or in other way to communicate with you on the subject.

[1] Governor Vance's Wilkesboro speech in which he called for no separate state action towards peace and for support of the Confederate government was published in the *Standard*, April 20, 1864.

[2] The speech of Vice-President Alexander H. Stephens before the Georgia legislature was printed in the *Standard*, April 20, 1864.

[3] Bartholomew Figures Moore, lawyer; A.B., U.N.C., 1820; trustee, U.N.C., 1840-1868, 1871-1878; member, House of Commons, 1836-1837, 1840-1845; attorney general, 1848-1851; opposed to secession; considered Andrew Johnson's plan for presidential reconstruction unconstitutional. *Dictionary of North Carolina Biography*, s.v. "Moore, Bartholomew Figures."

[4] Holden's response is contained in his statement "To the Conservative Party Voters" published in the *Standard*, May 20, 1864.

[5] Jonathan Worth, lawyer and planter; member, House of Commons, 1830, 1831; member, state Senate, 1840, 1858; state treasurer, 1862-1865; elected governor 1865 and 1866; opposed radical reconstruction. *Dictionary of North Carolina Biography*, s.v. "Worth, Jonathan."

Holden to the Conservatives of North Carolina *Standard*
May 20, 1864

Fellow Citizens: I understand a plan in on foot to induce or require me to withdraw from the contest for Governor, and this fact will furnish my apology for addressing you in this mode and on this occasion. I shall speak plainly, and deal with propositions, facts, and events as I understand them to exist; and while I shall not assail the motives of those (outside the circle of Executive influence,) who have suggested this plan, I shall nevertheless defend my own motives and views, and shall show that any attempt to rally the Conservative party on Gov. Vance would fail; and that, even if it could succeed, it would prostrate the party at the feet of the Destructive leaders, and thus sink its principles and destroy its usefulness.

In July, 1863, perceiving that fighting merely would not end the war, and believing that the Southern States could obtain better terms *then* than they could when they should be still further exhausted, I took grounds in favor of negotiations for peace. I was not mistaken as to public sentiment in the State. The great mass of the Conservative party entertained the same views as I did, and they spoke out in numerous meetings for negotiations. My competitor, Gov. Vance, was opposed to these meetings, and did all he could by letter and otherwise to discountenance and put them down.—At his special personal request I stated in the *Standard*, at the time, that he was opposed to these meetings and to negotiations for peace. Having taken my position, and the people sustaining me in it, I maintained it. Soon after, the Fayetteville *Observer*, a paper avowedly neither Conservative nor Destructive, moved no doubt by Gov. Vance or one of his Aids, Col. George Little, assailed my peace views at first moderately and by argument, but at length passionately, and by misrepresentation, invectives and abuse. The *Observer* was sustained by the State *Journal*, the Richmond *Enquirer*, and other Destructive journals; and then we had the so-called "army Convention," which I have reason to believe Gov. Vance encouraged and approved. Then came the mobbing of my office by certain Georgia troops, acting under orders. Gov. Vance said to this mob, among other things, that he and I differed politically, of course on the subject of peace; and he also said I had not *yet* committed treason, but that if I did he would have me arrested and punished. In a conversation I had with him on the 22d of September, thirteen days after the mob, of a public official character, he declared to me, after having labored in vain to induce me to change my course, so fixed and bitter was his repugnance to the peace movement, that if I persisted in publishing the peace meetings and encouraging the peace movement in the South, my property would be laid in ashes by an armed mob, and I would meet a violent death. Meanwhile the *Observer*, known in this city as the organ of Gov. Vance, (an effort having been made by persons near the Governor to induce the Editors of that journal to remove to Raleigh,) continued its assaults on me, declaring that Gov. Vance had no more personal sympathy with me than he had with John Spelman[1]—that the mobbing of my office, though it was wrong in itself, would turn out a good thing in its results if it would only induce me to change my course—that the peace meetings were unpatriotic and dangerous, and that the proposition to hold a State Convention to pave the way to peace, was paralleled in infamy only by the Hartford Convention. In December, 1863, or January, 1864, Gov. Vance was invited to deliver a speech in Wilkesborough on the 23d of February. It is my opinion, from information in my possession, that Destructives first suggested or got up the invitation to the Governor, if he did not suggest it himself; and that Conservatives acquiesed in the invitation as a matter of courtesy to the Governor of the State. Previously to this, however, he had written letters to all portions of the State against the peace movement and had boasted especially that he would "nip the Convention proposition in the bud," and in the election of members of Congress in November he took an active part, throwing his influence in the case against Messrs. Logan,[2] Christian,[3] and Rev. Mr. Smith,[4] and sympathising but little, if to any extent, with Dr. Leach[5] against Col. McRae.[6] He seemed to prefer Dr. Ramsay,[7] peace candidate, to Mr. Lander,[8] and Mr. Turner,[9] peace candidate, to Mr. Arrington,[10] on account of some particular antipathy to Messrs. Lander and Arrington, and although Mr. W. N. H. Smith[11] agreed with him in his views on the subject of peace, and Dr. Warren[12] differed somewhat with him and agreed substantially with Messrs. Logan, Christian, Turner, and others, yet he seemed to prefer Dr. Warren, probably because he was a member of his Staff. But he went to Wilkesborough and made his speech. It was a war speech of the most ultra character. The friends of peace were falsely charged with a design to call a Convention to secede from the Confederacy, and the State was threatened, if such an event should occur, with coercion by Confederate troops. The act of Congress suspending the writ of *habeas corpus* was substantially endorsed, and the people were exhorted to "stand up to it" as a constitutional measure. And so far from advising negotiation with a view to peace, the Governor said we "must fight it out"—and he pointed to the examples of the Hollanders, the Prussians, and the Scotch to encourage the people to fight indifinitely. His next speeches were delivered to the army, and were also of the most ultra war character. But in his Fayetteville speech, he changed its tone, claiming the credit of the Georgia movement in favor of peace; and in his recent message to the Legislature he takes strong ground in favor of peace. He also takes ground in his message in favor of the repeal of the act suspending the writ of *habeas corpus*. And generally, he makes an effort to place himself fairly and squarely on the Conservative platform.

This is the peace man, fellow citizens, who pants for negiotations and also endeavors to show that he is the author of the peace movement! What assurance!

Gov. Vance, as I have shown, commenced to disorganize the Conservative party in July last; and he continued in this course, opposing the peace movement and sympathazing with the Destructives, appointed Destructives to office and favoring the election of members to Congress who were supported by Destructives, and prostrating himself at the footstool of Executive power in Richmond, and at the footstool of Confederate military power here at home, until at length he was abandoned by the great body of those who elected him, and found himself the choice for Governor of the Destructive leaders. I did not announce myself for Governor until I perceived, that unless some true Conservative announced himself Gov. Vance would *Tylerize* and destroy the party. I am in the field at the earnest soliciations of many citizens and soldiers and I will not withdraw. *My* Conservetism is above suspicion. This is no cause why *I* should "repent and do my first works over." *I* am not put to the necessity of *obtaining* or *re-obtaining* the confidence of the Conservative party, for I have it already.

I am opposed to caucuses and conventions. The people alone have the right to rule through mass meetings and through the ballot box. Caucuses and conventions were more or less instrumental in destroying the old government, and they should be avoided by the new. I have no right to agree to any compromise which withdraws this man and puts up that man, and assigns one office to one man and another office to another. These things belong to the people at the ballot box. The Conservative party cannot succeed under an effort to commit it to Gov. Vance, who has departed from its principles, and made war upon the great body of the party; and even if it could, its success would enure substantially to our political enemies who now constitute the bulk of his supporters,—and such success, if it can be called so, would necessarily entail upon the party endless feuds, heart burnings, and divisions. There is no ground for hope except in "the straightest sect." Nor does it follow, because Gov. Vance despairs of his election and is prepared to withdraw from the contest, that I should withdraw also. On the contrary, it furnished the strongest reason why I should remain in the field, for it is a virtual admission that I will be elected, and that the people desire that I should be.

Gov. Vance has no claims on me personally or politically. He endeavored, in his Fayetteville speech, in his allusion to the mob, to degrade me personally and destroy my good name, and that by a willifully false statement as to what occurred at his own house. He said, in his recent speech in Raleigh, that I "ran like a scared dog" to his house the night of the mob. He also said, that if I was not a tory all the tories and deserters in the State were my friends—the same charge which was made against him by the Destructives in 1862, and against which I defended him; and he repeated the cast off calumny of Spelman's press, that the Yankee prisoners taken at Plymouth cheered for me on the Railroad. I have no more sympathy with the invaders of my country than he has; and if such a thing happened, which I do not be-lieve, the prisoners referred to were bribed to do it by some unscrupulous Destructive. He encourages the *Confederate*, of this City, in its defamatory attacks on me; and he has procured to be established by his official influence another journal, the *Conservative*, which is devoted to indiscriminate abuse of me and indiscriminate praise of himself. One of his Aids, Col. Little, who enjoys the special privilege of sending off his cotton on the Advance, and getting in exchange for it the luxuries of the Yankee and English markets, is known to be an active manager of the *Conservative* establishment, and devotes much of his time in the Executive office and on the street to electioneering against me. He is using the patronage of his office without stint to build up a Vance party to reelect himself, and to prostrate the Conservative party; and even if I were to withdraw, and thus abandon the principles of the party to his tender mercies and those of Spelman, Little, McRae, Ezekiel Jones,[13] and Jim Morris,[14] he and his minions would still pursue me with a malice which would have no bounds. And yet he says he is *friendly* with me, and wants a *compromise*! Yes, such a compromise as the wolf gives to the lamb or the kite to the dove. I verily believe that he, and many of those who are about him and do his work for him, dislike me so much because I am true to the people and the soldiers, and have the confidence, and am an honest man, that if they had me in their power, and could do it without fear of punishment, they would not only render me infamous personally, but they would confiscate my property and then "break me on the wheel" But my trust is in the Conservative people of the State. I am an humble newspaper Editor, possessed of no patronage, and surrounded by no troops of favorites to urge my claims; but even if I possessed all these things, I would scorn to use them to deceive and mislead the people and secure my election. Thank God, I can say with Mr. Burke, "I have no arts but honest arts." Strong in the consciousness of right, panoplied with truth and justice, and standing on *principle*, I can defy alike the stratagems and threats of my enemies. I appeal to my friends, the true Conservatives in all parts of the State, to stand firm. My election is certain, if my friends will but stand by their principles and go to the polls. The Conservative party will thus be saved from the disorganization which threatens it through the treachery of Gov. Vance; the party will be purified, its great principles will be maintained, civil liberty will be preserved, and the cause of blessed peace will be promoted, and finally established on lasting foundations.

W. W. Holden

May 19, 1864

[1] John Spelman, editor of the *State Journal*.

[2] George Washington Logan, Unionist; member, Confederate House of Representatives as a peace candidate, 1863-1865; member, House of Commons, 1866-1867; superior court judge, 1868-1874; opposed Ku Klux Klan. *Dictionary of North Carolina Biography*, s.v. "Logan, George Washington."

[3] Samuel H. Christian.

[4] Samuel P. Smith, Wilkes County; farmer and Baptist minister; unsuccessful candidate for Confederate House of Representatives, 1863; member, state Senate, 1868-1870. Cheney, *North Carolina State Government*, 1585-1979, 393, 1311; 1860 U.S. Census Population Schedule, North Carolina: Wilkes, 140 (microfilm)

[5] James Thomas Leach, lawyer and physician; member, state Senate, 1858; opposed secession; member, Confederate House of Representatives, 1863-1865; advocated peace negotiations. *Dictionary of North Carolina Biography*, s.v. "Leach, James Thomas."

[6] Duncan Kirkland McRae.

[7] James Graham Ramsay, physician; A.B., Davidson College, 1841; M. D., Jefferson Medical College, 1848; member, state Senate, 1856-1864; member, Confederate House of Representatives, 1863-1865; advocated peace terms; advocated convention to return North Carolina to the Union, 1865. *Dictionary of North Carolina Biography*, s.v. "Ramsay, James Graham."

[8] William Lander.

[9] Josiah Turner, Jr.

[10] Archibald H. Arrington, Nash County; member, U.S. House of Representatives, 1841-1845; member, Confederate House of Representatives, 1861-1863. *Dictionary of North Carolina Biography*, s.v. "Arrington, Archibald Hunter."

[12] William Nathan Harrell Smith.

[12] Edward Jenner Warren, Beaufort County; lawyer and legislator; member, secession convention, 1861; member, state Senate, 1862-1866, where he consistently voted to

support Governor Vance; member, state Senate 1870-1872. *Dictionary of North Carolina Biography*, s.v. "Warren, Edward Jenner."

[13] Not identified

[14] Not identified.

Holden to C. J. Cowles, Esqr. A&H:Holden

Raleigh, July 19, 1864

My dear Sir: Your esteemed favors have been received, and the subscribers duly entered.

I have sent out a vast number of tickets for Governor. I trust your County will be supplied. I hope you will do me the favor to speak to as many as you can to attend at the various precincts in your County, to see that tickets are supplied and fair play observed.

The intelligence I receive continues to be of the most cheering character. I feel sure of a decided majority in the army. The minds of the people and soldiers are made up, and nothing will change them.

Very truly yours,
W. W. Holden

C. J. Cowles, Esqr.[1]

[1] Calvin Josiah Cowles.

Holden to [Calvin J. Cowles] A&H:Holden

Raleigh, July 29, 1864

Dear Sir.[1]

Yours of the 26th purporting to contain an advertisement that never came to hand, has been received.

The advertisement must have been omitted by accident.

You have no doubt seen or heard ere this letter reaches you of the wonderful successes of Gov. Vance in the Army. My heart sickens at the memory of what occurred yesterday. Never before in the annals of American history did such voting take place. The Provost Guard of this place was marched up and voted under orders, and beneath the supervision of Confederate officials. All Holden's men were summarily disposed of, in guarding the bridges in the vicinity and those who did vote have been sent forward to the Army in many instances. The Hospitals were filled with Secesh women who, in some instances, "maligned" the soldiers bitterly, snatching the tickets from their hands, tearing them up and stamping upon the remnants. They then gave them Vance tickets. The Surgeons also browbeat and abused the privates. There was no withstanding such purpose. So the Holden men generally refused to vote, and some timid ones were forced to vote the other way. Col. Geo. Little of Vance's Staff engineered the whole matter. We have the proof.

The returns published by the Conservatives are picked. Up to this writing none others have been recd. How has the balance of the Army gone? If they have voted freely, we have no fears, If tyranny has been put upon them also, God only knows. We have no dispatches and no one else seems to have.

It is fraud and despotism. Where are our liberties?

But we are cheerful. Our people are much aroused and seemed determined to vote at all hazards.

It rests with them now. We issue an extra Standard to-day. Will send you one. Keep a bold stand and much may get be accomplished.

Truly,
W. W. Holden

Per J.W.H.[2]

[1] The addressee of this letter is not indicated, but from internal evidence it appears to have been sent to Cowles.

[2] The letter was signed by Joseph W. Holden.

The North-Carolina Standard *Standard*
August 12, 1864

I am neither dismayed nor depressed by the result of the recent elections in this State. I am the same sound and true Conservative I was when the party was formed in 1860; and I believe the existence of the party will be more necessary in the future than in the past. Principle, and not expediency, has been my guide heretofore, as it will be hereafter; and when I follow principle, I have no regrets to express at defeat so far as I am personally concerned, as I would not have exulted over any one if I had been successful. I will never, in any event, humiliate myself at the footstool of the Destructive party, or fuse with that party. Nothing shall separate me from Conservative principles or from the Conservative party, for it is my firm belief that it is the only party that can heal the bleeding wounds of the Constitution, protect and preserve the liberty of the citizen, and secure to the country an honorable and lasting peace. I hold "the sword in one hand and the olive branch in the other,"—the sword for the Destructives, and the olive branch for all good and true Conservatives. It would be the height of vanity and arrogance in me to assume that citizens professing to be Conservatives who did not vote for me are not good Conservatives, however much I may regret the recent union at the ballot-box of the Destructives and of many tried Conservatives. *It shall not be my fault if this union is continued and perpetuated.* If it should be, the conservative party will be swallowed up and lost; but if every true Conservative, forgetting the past, and impressed alone with the importance of maintaining his principles in their purity, will dissolve this union, and resolve to have no political affiliation or correspondence of any kind with the Destructives, and will so act on all occasions, whether as a representative of the people or as a citizen, as to put the Destructives outside the pale of his associations, the great Conservative party will be restored to its former integrity and strength, and will be enabled hereafter, as heretofore, to confer upon the country all those benefits and blessings which it was hoped would flow from it when it was formed and organized.

I am a friend to both the Confederate and State governments, and because I am, I am anxious to see them ably and honestly administered. The best friend to the Confederate government is he who submits to its authority, and labors to confine it to its constitutional limitations; and the worst enemy to the government, to the South, and to the cause of liberty, is he who seeks to exalt that government above the States, to enlarge its powers, and to render the judiciary, the freedom of the press, and the freedom and purity of the ballot box dependent on the mere will of those who have been called to administer its affairs. No personal antipathy to those who may conduct the governments will influence my judgment as to the measures they may suggest or adopt. I shall judge all measures on their merits, without regard to those who may recommend or advocate them. I have already given proof, by my advocacy of Mr. Badger's[1] nomination for the Convention in Wake County, in February, 1861, and by my vote for Mr. Graham[2] for President of that body in May, 1861, when there had been no personal intercourse between us for the space of eighteen years, that I am not to be influenced in my course as a public man by private, or selfish, or personal considerations.

With regard to the prosecution of the war and negotiations for peace, my views have undergone no change. It is not true that I have counseled the withdrawal of North Carolina from the Confederacy, or the submission of the State to federal authority, or the reconstruction of the federal Union. On the contrary, I have uniformly maintained, as I do now, that the war must be prosecuted in self-defence, but that at the same time the President, the Congress, the Governors of the States, and the States themselves should resort to every means in their power to obtain an armistice, so as to transfer the great questions in dispute between the two sections from the smoke of the battle-field to the calm, clear atmosphere of reason and diplomacy in the civil councils, where alone, in the end, these questions must be settled. My views are embodied in the following resolutions introduced in the House of Representatives at the last session, by the Hon. J. T. Leach,[3] of this State, and laid on the table by that body:

> "*Resolved by the Congress of the Confederate States*, That the delegations from each State, acting in its sovereign and independent character, for the purpose of adding moral to

our physical force, and placing ourselves properly before the civilized world, do most earnestly appeal to the President, by and with the advice and consent of the Senate, to appoint commissioners whose duty it shall be to propose an armistice of ninety days to the proper authorities of the federal government, preliminary to negotiations for peace upon State sovereignity and independence, and that said commissioners shall report in writing to the President the answer received from the federal government upon the subject.

Resolved, That should the peace making power of the federal government accede to the proposition for an armistice of ninety days, the President be requested to convene the Congress of the Confederate States for the purpose of appointing commissioners, by and with the advice and consent of the Senate; and that he also be requested to notify the Executives of the several States of the fact, and ask their cooperation by appointing commissioners, either by the Legislature or Convention, to co-operate with the commissioners appointed by the President to negotiate with commissioners appinted by the federal government upon such terms of peace as will be consistent with the honor, dignity and independence of the States, and compatible with the safety of our social and political rights.

Resolved, That in maintaining the rights guaranteed to us by the blood and treasure of our Revolutionary fathers, and dearest at all times to free men, we desire to be let alone—we ask no man's property—we fight not for conquest, but for our rights; the independence of the States, our equality, our civil and religious liberties.

Resolved, That such terms of peace as are agreed to by the commissioners ought to be endorsed by the President and Senate, and submitted to the people for ratification or rejection."

It is my firm conviction that if the views which I advanced in the *Standard* in July, 1863, on the subject of peace, had been adopted and carried out, an armistice would have been obtained, and commissioners from the two sections would have been in council when the Congress last assembled in Richmond; and it is my firm conviction that if the foregoing resolutions had been adopted by the Congress at its last session, measures would at this time have been in progress tending to a final and satisfactory settlement of the questions at issue between the North and South. But if those efforts had been made and had failed, we should have been no weaker either in moral or in physical resources at home, while abroad, among the people of Europe and of the North, we should have gained great moral power by the exhibition on our part of an earnest disposition to stay the effusion of blood, and to terminate this awful conflict in accordance with those principles of reason and justice which reflect lustre on civilized, Christian nations. We might then have hoped that the people of the North, giving heed to this appeal, and anxious as they must be for peace, would have risen up at the polls and defeated Mr. Lincoln's re-election in November next, and thus have paved the way for a settlement of our difficulties by the conservative men of the two sections. As it is, with the temper which seems to govern the rulers of the two sections, I can perceive no reasonable ground for hoping that Mr. Lincoln will be defeated, or that the war will cease until the South shall have been conquered by the North, or the North the South. We are not fighting for conquest, and we should not incur the risk of being conquered by the North without putting forth every effort meanwhile to terminate the stuggle by negotiatons.

The *Standard* will continue to be devoted to the rights of the people and to the independence and sovereignty of the States. It will maintain the integrity and independence of the judiciary, the freedom of the press and of speech, and the freedom and purity of the ballot-box, without which our present struggles will be in vain, and our free forms of government an empty mockery. It will insist on a strict construction of the Confederate constitution, and on a searching but not ungenerous scrunity of the acts of our rulers. It will inflexibly oppose any and every attempt to render the civil authority subordinate to the miliary power. And it will oppose, at all times and everywhere, with the utmost earnestness to the last moment, all attempts to subvert our present form of government and to establish a dictatorship or monarchy on its ruins.

As the elections are now over, and as the *Standard* will be relieved for some time to come of the pressure of matter purely political in its character, I will endeavor to render it a more welcome and entertaining vehicle of news, literature, and science. I trust my friends will exert themselves somewhat to increase the circulation of the paper.

With many, many heartfelt thanks to my friends and patrons, I am

Very Respectfully,
W. W. Holden

[1] George Edmund Badger.
[2] William Alexander Graham.
[3] James Thomas Leach.

Robt P. Dick to Holden DU:Holden

Greensboro
August 20th, 1864

My dear Holden.

I was so perfectly astounded by the result of the recent elections that I have not yet recovered from the shock. I can not account for so universal and so sudden revulsion in public sentiment. In this county the old spirit of Whiggery was in some degree resurrected. It is possible that N.C. has declared for Jeff Davis, for war and utter ruin and desolation! What has become of the reason, the patriotism, and the Christianity of our people!

I am not as much elated by my election as I expected to be.[1] So many of my friends are beaten that I feel lonesome and dejected. I bore with great fortitude the falsehoods and villainies of the canvass but I am exceptionaly annoyed by a rumor started by the Destructives: to the effect that I had "changed my bow." I am now more firmly fixed and determined in my political opinions than I ever was in my life. I feel satisfied that my views cannot now be carried out, but with the most fearless confidence I am content to "watch and wait." I feel sure that the future will show the wisdom of our course. Our views must prevail or the country will be sunk in the abyss of subjugation and other ruin.

How many friends will we have in the Legislature? I want only to know those who can be relied on implicity, & who can stand the fire? I want to think over carefully some plan for inaugurating some peace movement in the legislature. I will try to have my views mustered. We must do something although the State has declared against us. I am for holding on the ship amidst all the storms and peril. We are overthrown but still I am not conquered. I want to see you very much and have a full talk. I think I will visit Raleigh before the meeting of the legislature. I want you to write to me and give yr views of matters generally. We have stood together in trying and dark times before—and I still call out to you with confidence—"Watchman what of the night?"—I know full well that the morn is not yet breaking. Write soon.

Your friend,
Robt. P. Dick

[1] Dick was elected to the state Senate in 1864. Cheney, *North Carolina Government, 1585-1979*, 331.

Robt P Dick to Holden *DU:Holden*

Greensboro
Feby. 24, 1865

My Dear Holden.

I have just seen the *Standard* and read my Remarks[1] They are very accurately printed, and I thank you for the care you took in the proof &c. I was very anxious for you to have written the *last scene in the Senate*, as you could have made a good & effective article out of it. I know that you will have my speech well printed. I send you $5 for some extra copies which you can send by mail.

Our people are very quiet, but anxious about the future. We have had no *war meeting* yet. and I do not think any effort will be made to have one. J. T. Morehead[2] and J. R. McLean[3] made some war speeches on questions before the Court, and I replied to them, and public feeling was evidently on my side. I carried the *questions*.

I am well satisfied that Gen Sherman's[4] objective point is Greensboro. I feel very uneasy but I will endeavor to act right and risk consequences. I will remain at home with my family. The crisis is nearly upon us, and the war will be virtually ended in ninety days. I want the end to come, no matter what be the consequences.

My best wishes for you, your family and friends. In haste.

Most truly
Your friend
Robt P Dick

[1] Dick was referring to a speech he had made in the state Senate on January 23, 1865, regarding arming and using slaves in the Confederate army. The speech was printed in the *Standard* on February 28, 1865.

[2] James Turner Morehead, lawyer; A.B., U.N.C., 1819; member, state Senate, 1835-1842; member, U.S. House of Representatives as Whig, 1851-1853. *Dictionary of North Carolina Biography*, s.v. "Morehead, James Turner."

[3] James Robert McLean, lawyer; member, House of Commons, 1850-1851; active secessionist; member, Confederate House of Representatives, 1861-1863; major, North Carolina Seventy-seventh Regiment. *Dictionary of North Carolina Biography*, s.v. "McLean, James Robert."

[4] William Tecumseh Sherman, major general, U.S. Army; commanded Union Army of the Tennessee and military division of the Mississippi; from Chatanooga, began engagement through Georgia, South Carolina, and North Carolina ending with surrender of confederate General Joseph E. Johnston at Durham Station, Orange County, North Carolina. *Dictionary of American Biography*, s.v. "Sherman, William Tecumseh."

G .W. Blount and Others to Holden *Standard*
May 3, 1865

Wilson, N.C., April 29, 1865

W. W. Holden, Esq.

Dear Sir: We have in contemplation a large Union Meeting in this town, to come off next Thursday, the 4th of May. Several Counties will be represented, and a number of distinguished men have been invited and are expected to be present. We therefore respectfully and urgently invite you to make one of our number. You, to whom so many of us have looked for counsel and advice, now in the hour of our return to the glorious flag of our fathers, should be a participant in our rejoicings.

Respectfully,
Your ob't. servants,
G. W. Blount[1]
Willie Daniel[2]
J. J. Lawrence, M.D.[3]
C. J. Rountree[4]
W. J. Bullick, M. D.[5]

[1] George W. Blount, lawyer. 1870 U.S. Census Population Schedule, North Carolina: Wilson, 605 (microfilm).

[2] Willie Daniel, farmer. 1870 U.S. Census Population Schedule, North Carolina: Wilson, 612 (microfilm).

[3] J. J. Lawrence, physician and editor. 1860 U.S. Census Population Schedule, North Carolina: Wilson, 410 (microfilm).

[4] Charles J. Rountree, druggist. 1870 U.S. Census Population Schedule, North Carolina: Wilson, 604 (microfilm).

[5] William J. Bulluck, physician. 1860 U.S. Census Population Schedule, North Carolina: Wilson, 396 (microfilm).

Holden to Messrs. G. W. Blount, W. Daniel, and Others *Standard*
May 3, 1865

Raleigh, May 2nd, 1865

Gentlemen:—Yours of April 29th has been received at the hands of my friend, Mr. Short.[1] I regret that it is not in my power to be present at the meeting on the 4th, but I will be with you in sentiment and spirit.

Gentlemen, we are once more *Americans all.*—We told the authors of the rebellion in 1860, that disunion would be civil war, murder, arson, pillage, robbery, and fire and blood through long and cruel years. We told them it would unsettle all business, dimish the value of all property, put the lives of both sexes and all ages in peril, and launch the States on a sea of scenes which no eye had scanned, and no navigator sounded. We told them it would bring debt, and misrule, and oppressive taxes, to be followed, perhaps, by the military rule of titled tyrants. We told them the instead of preserving States rights, it would destroy them; and that slavery itself, the great object for which disunion was urged, would perish in the vortex of revolution.—We appealed to them in the most earnest terms to submit to federal authority, and to give to the administration of Mr. Lincoln a fair trial. We felt, as they could have seen, if their could have seen, if their vision had not been infected with the insanity of secession, that even if Mr. Lincoln was disposed, as he was not, to assail our Constitutional rights, we had the amplest guarantees of protection in the Congress and the Supreme Court; and that if our rights were denied us, as law abiding citizens of the United States, our best, and indeed our only hope to vindicate and maintain them would be in the Union and under the old flag.

But the instigators of the rebellion were fatally bent on mischief, and therefore heeded no warnings. They would have it so, and behold the result! They went to war for slavery in the Territories, and they have lost it in the States. They attempted to dissolve the Union to preserve State rights; and the result was long before the pillars of their badly constructed edifice were shivered and prostrated, they had reduced the States to the condition of petty provinces. Our own noble old State especially, on account of her Union sentiemts and her fearless assertion at all times of the great principles of civil liberty, became

"An appanage to those
Who did dispise her."

They promised us liberty, but they gave us conscription laws, and tithing laws, and impressment laws, until the spirit of our people fainted under the infliction, and the manhood of the country was compelled to utter itself in whispers or be hurried to "the front" in ropes or handcuffs. They promised us freedom of speech and of the press, but they silenced both through the suspension of *habeas corpus*, by the strong hand of power. And at last, after they had dragged an unwilling people through seas of horror, at the end of four years, and just as the old flag of Washington was about to be unfurled at Richmond and Raleigh, the guilty authors and abettors of all this crime fled with precipitation before the armies of the Union, abandoned their capitals and those who had confided in them, some of them clutching and taking with them the treasures which, by unjust laws and by speculation and peculation, they had wrung from the blood and fears of our people.

But "Babylon is fallen, is fallen," and thank God for it. We are once more free. The flag of the United States, which, previously to the rebellion, had never waved but as a symbol of protection and security to us all, is again unfurled in every State. We shall again enjoy the protection of a strong and just government, under the benign influence of virtuous rulers and wise laws. Let us rejoice, gentlemen, that we behold this day. Let us "rally to the flag," and give a cheerful and active support to those in whose hands it has been placed.—I deplore as you do, and as all good citizens must, the untimely death of Abraham Lincoln. I remember with pride and pleasure that I endorsed his first Inaugural Speech in my newspaper, and begged our people to submit to his authority and extend to him a generous confidence. The people of the South abhor the foul deed which bereft him of life. With their Northern brethern they mourn his fall, and, with them, they will cherish the remembrance of his noble qualities. Washington, and Clay, and Jackson, and Webster, and Douglas, and Everett, were already "in the upper sky," and the lustre of their abode was heightened when the star of the martyred Lincoln took its place in the cluster. One and all, they lived, and labored, and died in the cause of the Union. "Their bodies are buried in peace, but their name liveth evermore." They are safe from the accidents of time. Our children, and our children's children, for a thousand generations, will learn and recount their virtues and walk in the light of their example; and Liberty itself, when erecting its altars in other lands, will kindle the fires from the great fountain of light which shines in their actions and recorded words.

But, Gentlemen, while we deplore the untimely death of Mr. Lincoln, we are consoled by the reflection that the Constitution has put in his place a native of our State—a man who has always been true to the people and to the Union of the States. I believe that Andrew Johnson will acquit himself well in the great office which had devolved upon him. I have full confidence in his judgment, his integrity, and his patriotism. If it be true our Northern brethern entertain a peculiar regard for North Carolina, how much more must it be true of this son of hers, thus elevated to power? I believe that while he will be just, and even generous to the great masses of all the people in the insurgent States, and while he will visit the wicked leaders of the rebellion with condign punishment, he will incline his ear especially to the State which gave him birth, and extend to her every aid in her present distressed condition that may be compatible with his duties to the country generally. Let us, then, gentlemen, go to work to reorganize our State government and to lay anew the foundations of prosperity and happiness. Let us regard the instiution of slavery as already disposed of, and thus avoid the ill feelings which a discussion of it would excite. That it will be abolished by the States themselves, in accordance with the federal Constitution, by their ratification of the act of Congress on the subject, there can be no doubt; and it will then remain for the Congress, or for the States themselves with the consent of that body, to declare and define the *status* of the colored race. I have no serious apprehension on this subject. I believe the whole question can be settled in such a manner as to secure the greatest good which is possible under the circumstances, to both races. Let us, them, avoiding a premature discussion of this question, address ourselves to the noble work of restoring order, of fostering industry of all kinds, of laying the foundations for schools and colleges, and of inviting labor and capital from other regions to aid in developing our vast physical resources.—"Peace hath her victories no less than war." Our population is now increasing by the return of thousand of our soldiers from the war. They are welcome to our homes and our firesides. They have not only our respect, but the respect of those who were recently their enemies. We have room not only for our own people, but for thousands—yea, millions more. Let our brethern of the North, and East, and West, come and settle among us. Let those who have met as enemies on bloody fields, under the lurid star of War, now meet as brethern, under the eye of Peace, and emulate each other in the race for prosperity and distinction. God bless old North Carolina, and give to her in the future, with restored brotherhood, a fullness of prosperity, of happiness, and glory which was not realized even in former days!

Allow me to repeat my regret, gentlemen, that I cannot be present at your meeting. With thanks for the honor you have done me by your invitation, and with a grateful sense of obligation to friends in your portion of the State, who have stoody by me so unflinchingly through all the dangers and trials of this revolution, I am, gentlemen,

Your obedient servant,
W. W. Holden

To Messrs. G. W. Blount, W. Daniel, and others.

[1] Probably Richard Short, Pitt County; member, House of Commons, 1868-1869. Cheney, *North Carolina Government, 1585-1979*, 448.

TELEGRAM Andrew Johnson to Holden LC:Johnson

Executive office,
Washington May 9, 1865

W. W. Holden, Esq.
Editor of Raleigh Standard

Can you come to Washington immediately? I wish to confer with you in reference to North Carolina affairs. The Military authorities will pass W. W. Holden and such other persons as he may indicate to Washington and return on Government transports and over military Rail Roads, and furnish transportation and subsistance.

General Schofield[1] will please afford every facility to Mr. Holden for said visit.

Andrew Johnson[2]
President U.S.

[1] John McAlister Schofield, commanding general, Department of North Carolina; graduate of West Point, 1853; November, 1861, brigadier general of volunteers; major general, May, 1863; command of XXIII Corps and Army of the Ohio, February, 1864; March 1865, command of Department of North Carolina until June, 1865. *Dictionary of American Biography*, s.v. "Schofield, John McAlister."

[2] Andrew Johnson, Tennessee; military governor of Tennessee, 1862-1865; vice-president of United States, 1865; succeeding to the presidency as seventeenth president of the United States upon the assassination of President Lincoln. *Dictionary of North Carolina Biography*, s.v. "Johnson, Andrew."

Speech to Union Mass Meeting in Raleigh[1] *Standard*
May 12, 1865

Fellow Citizens of the County of Wake—Fellow Citizens of the State of North Carolina—Fellow Citizens of the United States of America: Let us rejoice that we behold this day. We see the same old flag clustering around us. We hear the same national songs—we meet and greet around our firesides, and in the streets our brethern from the head waters of the Mississippi, from the Hudson, and from New England; and we feel in our limbs a renewed and invigorating sense of the freedom we formerly enjoyed. The sweetest and most touching anthem that ever descended from heaven to the ears of man, was that chanted by the angels above the plains of Bethelehem when they announced the birth of the Redeemer. "Glory to God in the highest; on earth Peace, good will toward men."

That Peace to day is all around and about us—it pervades all our walks and nestles with our children by our firesides. This Peace we owe to the Conservative people of the South and the millions of the Conservative men of the North.

The prospects of our people are not unmixed with gloom. The plough-share of war for four years has scarred and furrowed the land from the St. Lawrence to the Rio Bravo. Who, he asked, were responsible for this severance of a happy brotherhood? Bad men—designing men—small men—ambitious men desirous of rule. These had commenced agitation with a view to the disruption of the government, and in and out of Congress—inside National Conventions and outside National Conventions. Five years ago our people were contented, prosperous and happy. The National flag was respected everywhere—the disruption of the Union was the handiwork of vile agitators and secessionists. . . .

He then characterized the "so called Confederate government" as utterly false to the promises by which its architects had deluded the people. They had promised States' Rights but they had given us an oppressive consolidation. They had promised us free speech, but suspended the writ of *habeas corpus*. They had promised not only the preservation of slavery in the States, but its further territorial expansion and protection. The results of secession is its final extinction in the States.

They promised that no partizan feeling should be exhibited in the administration of the government; and yet they marked and prescribed all who had been Union men and—especially in North Carolina—denied us participation in the honors and offices. They enforced a rigorous and brutal conscription, *skulking themselves* into shade offices and shunning the fight of their own creation. "Were not these," asked the speaker, "the most infamous pretenders and hypocrites?"

Of Jefferson Davis, Mr. Holden spoke in terms of severest reprehension. Adverting to his advocacy of repudiation in early life, he remarked, "that Davis had been a repudiator of all honesty and all integrity from that day to this," and asked, "what has he not done to gratify his wicked—not insane—ambition?" He has turned a deaf ear to every appeal for peace, and at the time of the conference in Hampton Roads, when he knew—none better than he—that further resistance was worse than futile, he remained inexorable.

He waited for the very last mite in the way of trinkets and gold and silver, that he could wring from the enthusiatic, though misguided devotion of men and women in these Southern States. He had been first, a repudiator, secondly, a formenter of bad feeling between the States, thirdly a secessionist and traitor, fourthly, a flying robber, and lastly an alleged accomplice in the assassination of President Lincoln.

Around him as a common centre the lesser systems and smaller satelites revolved.

"I entertain," said the speaker, "no personal malice towards any one—but I do and shall always entertain the strongest possible political repugnance to those who wrought the desolation and destruction of our dearest interests." While Invoking leniency—generosity to the masses, justice demands the punishment of the leaders.

Prevention of secession was absolutely impossible in this State. He with others, signed the ordinance of secession under the force of unavoidable circumstances. Union men, bowed down and stricken in spirit, silently acquiesced, while secessionists greeted the act with hats off and hurrahs, the firing of cannon and the ringing of bells.

The war has resulted in the utter extinction of African Slavery. This was an accomplished fact. There could and would be no question about it. It remained for the people of this State, in Convention and by legislative action, to define the status of the emancipated race. He, for one, had no fear in this regard. He was willing to see the alphabet, the Bible and the school book placed in their hands, and to recognize among them the marriage relations, heretofore so culpably disregarded. The extent of their further elevation belonged legitimately to the governing race.

"In my opinion," he said, "this emancipated race must have, to a large extent, the sympathy, the aid and support of the white race, without which they would soon be extinct." Alluding to the emancipation views of Clay, Frelinghuysen, Gales of the *National Intelligencer* and others, Mr. Holden regretted that their efforts to this end had been unavailing.

He next depicted a glowing and glorious future—the development and prospective empire of the Anglo-Saxon race, whom he happily styled "the governing and self-governing race." He then adverted to the condition of North Carolina in this crisis, which he deemed peculiarly unfortunate. We were financially ruined. The bonded debt of the State prior to the secession, was $7,000,000, and this had been since increased by an indebtedness of at least $40,000,000 incurred by the State and counties during the war. Of the Banks some were probably bankrupt while others were materially crippled. If we add to this the loss of fifty thousand men who had been slain in battle or had died in hospitals, and the devastation of a large portion of the State by both armies, no little nerve is required to meet the future. He believed, however, that the old government—

the parental government, will be kind. "It would devolve," he said "on the Assembly to maintain the integrity of the State and to encourage the people to resume their wonted pursuits."

And now, fellow citizens, said he, what remains but to address ourselves to our duties as loyal citizens and to improve and build up our native State? At the formation of the federal Constitution, North Carolina had, as she has now, the same area of territory, 50,000 square miles, with the State of New York, and the same representation in Congress, 15. In 1860, New York had 36 members of Congress, and North Carolina 8. To what was this difference to be attributed but to the retarding, dwarfing influence of slavery? With this incubus removed let us start anew in the career of prosperity. Our latitude is the best on the globe, and we have a climate capable of producing nearly every article produced in any other state. We have a long sweep of seacoast, and one of the best harbors on the Atlantic front, and from Nash County to the Tennessee line our water power is inexhaustible. We grow all the the cereals, besides cotton and tobacco; and the bowels of the earth are stored with iron, coal, marl, copper, marble, gold, silver, and precious stones. We have vast forests of the most valuable timber, and large resources of naval stores. In a word, though greatly impoverished by the war, we have all the resources and all the elements of a great State. Let us go to work to develop these resources. We need capital and labor. To our brethern of the North, and East, and West we say, come over and help us. Bring your capital, your muscle, your intelligence, your industry, your ingenuity, and settle among us. The way is now open, and with us and our children you can purchase and build, and plant and reap, and repose and labor, and live and die, leaving your possessions an assured inheritance to your children; for I tell you, said he, that the stars in that banner will never go out, and the sun of American liberty will never go down. Our banner staff is at last so firmly planted that no convulsion which did not split the earth could upheave it from its place.

"Moored in the rifted rock,
Proof to the tempests' shock,
The harder the storm beats the firmer it grows."

May our children and our children's children, said he, for a thousand generations, walk and be happy in the light of that glorious ensign; and may they, as we do now, on the distant shores of all coming time, by the waters of the two great oceans, by the lakes of the North, and amid the central portions of the continent, and far towards the sun, "where tropic groves perfume the breath of morn," repeat with the same heartfelt, impassioned, holy zeal, those thrilling words of Mr. Webster.

"When my eyes shall be turned to behold for the last time the sun in heaven may they not see him shining on the broken and dishonored fragments of a once glorious Union; on States disserved, discordant, belligerent; on a land rent by civil feuds, and drenched, it may be, in fraternal blood. Rather let my last glance, go out on that gorgeous ensign of the republic, now known and honored throughout the earth, still full and high advanced; its arms and trophies streaming in all their original lustre, not a stripe erased or polluted, nor one single star obscured; bearing for its motto no such miserable interrogatory as What is all this worth?—nor those other words of delusion and folly, liberty first, and Union afterwards;—but every where spread all over in characters of living light, blazing on all its ample folds, as they float over the land, and over the sea, and in every wind under the whole heaven, that other sentiment, dear to every true American heart, Liberty and Union, now and forever, one and inseparable."

[1] The speech was delivered May 11, 1865. This version has been taken from the report of the mass meeting in the *Standard*. A slightly different version appears in Holden's *Memoirs*, 52-55.

TELEGRAM *Holden to Andrew Johnson* LC:Johnson

Raleigh
May 12, 1865

His Excellency
Andrew Johnson—

Your dispatch has been received I will visit Washington at once.

W. W. Holden

TELEGRAM *Holden to President Johnson* LC:Johnson

Raleigh, N.C. May 13, 1865

His Excy
President Johnson

I have been unavoidably detained but will reach Washington by Thursday evening next.[1] The condition of affairs in this state is cheering. A large majority of the people are delighted on immediate emancipation and are ready for civil Government as soon as it can be conveniently established. Gen. Schofield, the Dept Commander, is acting with wisdom and firmness and giving satisfaction to the true men.[2] With high respects

W. W. Holden

[1] Holden remained in Raleigh to address the Union Mass Meeting on May 11, 1865.

[2] On May 13, General Schofield sent a telegram to President Johnson advising him "Ex gov Swayne [*sic*] Mr D [B] F Moore and Mr Wm Eaton of North Carolina desire permission to visit you on business connected with the future of the state they are men of unquestionable loyalty and of great influence I suppose they represent some shade of political opinion different from that of Mr Holden and his friends who are going to Washington but I understand they all agree on the main question of union and freedom" J M Schofield to President Johnson, May 13, 1865,Andrew Johnson Papers, Library of Congress. Schofield had reference to David L. Swain, Bartholomew F. Moore, and William Eaton, Jr.

Standard
May 15, 1865

We shall be absent for some ten days on important business, but we have left the *Standard* in the hands of friends who will conduct it prudently, and continue to render it an acceptable vehicle of general news.

We have time only to say that the great want of North Carolina now is *civil government*. We believe a large majority of her people are prepared to organize a new State government—one that will recognize and carry out the emancipation views of the national administration, and in other respects evince a feeling of undoubted loyalty to the old government and to old flag. The question of emancipation is already settled. The Africans are already "freed" men and "freed" women; but it will remain for future action to give full effect to their freedom, and to declare and define the condition of the emancipated race. We have confidence in the great majority of our people, and in the national administration on this subject.

There are other matters of a grave character which must be considered and disposed of by the people's representatives during the present year. The State is not extinct—its "life-breath" has only "been suspended." We trust the day is not distant when North Carolina will enjoy the same privileges and benefits that are enjoyed by the other States of the Union.

Let differences among our people be only *political* and not personal or social. Surely we have suffered enough, and been sufficiently scourged to be ready to sink or forget personal animosities. For our part, we shall neither indulge for ourselves nor seek to injure others; but if there be among us those who hate the old government, or who would contrive any measure designed to impede the progress of reconstruction, we desire it to be distinctly understood that we have no sympathy with such, but we regard them as traitors and enemies to the people of the State. We warn the people to be on their guard against such men, no matter what their professions or conduct may have been heretofore.—The slaveocracy dies hard; the heads of the hydra will inflict wounds even after they have been severed from the body. Crush them as they are cut off. The honest, hardworking *people* of the State are at length in a situation to obtain the control of their own affairs. If they should let this opportunity slip, and if the old fogies who are wedded to certain interests and certain families should obtain power, free government in their hands will be virtually ignored, and the success of the Union armies will have been in vain. The *war* Conservatives who supported Vance are as objectionable as the original secessionists; and those professed Union men apparently in good standing, who are acting with or for these *war* conservatives, will bear watching. Forewarned, forearmed. Let the people be on their guard.

Robert P Dick and Others to Andrew Johnson LC:Johnson

Washington City
May 26th, 1865

His Excellency
Andrew Johnson,
President of the United States.

We the undersigned citizens of North Carolina, most cordially approving of your Excellency's plan for establishing civil authority in our State, and restoring her to her proper relations with the government of the United States, would most respectfully recommend our fellow citizen William W. Holden Esqr as a Suitable person for the office of Provisional Governor, as we have the highest confidence in his firmness, integrity, and ability, and his devoted loyalty to the Constitution and Union of the States; and we feel assured that he will be very acceptable to our people.

Robt. P. Dick
J. P. H. Russ[1]
W. R. Richardson[2]
W. S. Mason[3]
Jno. G. Williams[4]
R. J. Powell[5]
E. W. Jones[6]

[1] John P. H. Russ, Wake County farmer. 1860 U.S. Census Population Schedule, North Carolina: Wake, 179 (microfilm).

[2] W. R. Richardson, clerk in the Raleigh city treasury; later Governor Holden's secretary. 1860 U.S. Census Population Schedule, North Carolina: Wake, 297(microfilm); 1870 U.S. Census Population Schedule, North Carolina: Wake, 284 (microfilm).

[3] William S. Mason, Wake County lawyer. 1860 U.S. Census Population Schedule, North Carolina: Wake, 291 (microfilm).

[4] John G. Williams, Wake County broker. 1860 U.S. Census Population Schedule, North Carolina: Wake, 277 (microfilm)

[5] Robert James Powell, Wake County planter and civil engineer; member, state House of Representatives, 1870-1872; member, state Senate, 1872-1874. Cheney, *North Carolina Government, 1585-1979*, 451, 453.

[6] Edmund W. Jones, lawyer; member, state Senate, 1868; member, state House of Representatives, 1870-1874; member, convention of 1875; judge superior court, 1868-1871. Cheney, *North Carolina Government, 1585-1979*, 1079, 874, 578.

William H. Seward to Holden LC:Johnson

Department of State
Washington 29 May, 1865

To William W. Holden, Esquire,

Sir:

I enclose a copy of the President's Proclamation of this date appointing you Provisional Governor of the State of North Carolina. The reasons for the appointment are fully set forth in the preamble to the instrument. You will hold this office during the pleasure of the President. Your compensaton will be at the rate of three thousand dollars a year from this date. For this you may draw monthly or quarterly. Send your drafts to this Department.

I am, Sir,
Your obedient servant,
William H. Seward

BY THE PRESIDENT OF THE UNITED STATES OF AMERICA;
A PROCLAMATION[1]

Whereas the fourth section of the fourth article of the Constitution of the United States declares that the United States shall guarantee to every state in the Union a republican form of government, and shall protect each of them against invasion and domestic violence; and whereas the President of the United States is, by the constitution, made commander-in-chief of the army and navy, as well as chief civil executive officer of the United States, and is bound by solemn oath faithfully to execute the office of President of the United States, and to take care that the laws be faithfully executed; and whereas the rebellion, which has been waged by a portion of the people of the United States against the properly constituted authorities of the government thereof, in the most violent and revolting form, but whose organized and armed forces have now been almost entirely overcome, has, in its revolutionary progress, deprived the people of the State of North Carolina of all civil government; and whereas it becomes necessary and proper to carry out and enforce the obligations of the United States to the people of North Carolina, in securing them in the enjoyment of a republican form of government:

Now, therefore, in obedience to the high and solemn duties imposed upon me by the Constitution of the United States, and for the purpose of enabling the loyal people of said state to organize a state government, whereby justice may be established, domestic tranquillity insured, and loyal citizens protected in all their rights of life, liberty, and property, I, Andrew Johnson, President of the United States, and commander-in-chief of the army and navy of the United States, do hereby appoint William W. Holden provisional governor of the State of North Carolina, whose duty it shall be, at the earliest practicable period, to prescribe such rules and regulations as may be necessary and proper for convening a convention, composed of delegates to be chosen by that portion of the people of said state who are loyal to the United States, and no others, for the purpose of altering and amending the constitution thereof; and with authority to exercise, within the limits of said state, all the powers necessary and proper to enable such loyal people of the State of North Carolina to restore said state to its constitutional relations to the federal government, and to present such a republican form of state government as will entitle the state to the guarantee of the United States therefore, and its people to protection by the United States against invasion, insurrection, and domestic violence; *Provided* that, in any election that may be hereafter held for choosing delegates to any state convention as aforesaid, no person shall be qualified as an elector, or shall be eligible as a member of such convention, unless he shall have previously taken and subscribed the oath of amnesty, as set forth in the President's Proclamation of May 29, A.D. 1865, and is a voter qualified as prescribed by the constitution and laws of the State of North Carolina in force immediately before the 20th day of May, A.D. 1861, the date of the so-called ordinance of secession; and the said convention, when convened, or the legislature that may thereafter be assembled, will prescribe the qualification of electors, and the eligibility of persons to hold office under the constitution and laws of the state,– a power the people of the several states composing the Federal Union have rightfully exercised from the origin of the government to the present time.

And I do hereby direct–

First. That the military commander of the department, and all officers and persons in the military and naval service, aid and assist the said provisional governor in carrying into effect this Proclamation, and they are enjoined to abstain from, in any way, hindering, impeding, or discouraging the loyal people from the organization of a state government as herein authorized.

Second. That the Secretary of State proceed to put in force all laws of the United States, the administration whereof belongs to the State Department, applicable to the geographical limits aforesaid.

Third. That the Secretary of the Treasury proceed to nominate for appointment assessors of taxes, and collectors of customs and internal revenue, and such other officers of the Treasury Department as are authorized by law, and put in execution the revenue laws of the United States within the geographical limits aforesaid. In making appointments, the preference shall be given to qualified loyal persons residing within the districts where their respective duties are to be performed. But if suitable residents of the districts shall not be found, then persons residing in other states or districts shall be appointed.

Fourth. That the Postmaster-General proceed to establish post-offices and post-routes, and put into execution the postal laws of the United States within the said state, giving to loyal residents the preference of appointment; but if suitable residents are not found, then to appoint agents, &c., from other states.

Fifth. That the district judge for the judicial district in which North Carolina is included proceed to hold courts within said state, in accordance with the provisions of the act of congress. The Attorney-General will instruct the proper officers to libel, and bring to judgment, confiscation, and sale, property subject to confiscation, and enforce the administration of justice within said state in all matters within the cognizance and jurisdiction of the federal courts.

Sixth. That the Secretary of the Navy take possession of all public property belonging to the Navy Department within said geographical limits, and put in operation all acts of congress in relation to navy affairs having application to the said state.

Seventh. That the Secretary of the Interior put in force the laws relating to the Interior Department applicable to the geographical limits aforesaid.

In testimony whereof, I have hereunto set my hand, and caused the seal of the United States to be affixed.

Done at the city of Washington, this twenty-ninth day of May, in the year of our Lord one thousand eight hundred and sixty-five, and of the Independence of the United States the eighty-ninth

ANDREW JOHNSON

By the President:
William H. Seward, *Secretary of State*

[1] *United States Statutes at Large*, 13:1866, 760-761.

R. L. Patterson to Holden A&H:GP(Prov)

Salem, June 8th, 1865

His Excellency
Gov. W. W. Holden.

Dear Sir. I wrote you in behalf of the people of Wilkes, Caldwell, Ashe & Watauga. I learn from there that they are entirely uninformed as to the present status of affairs, & the loyal men greatly neglected. I am going to my home in Caldwell in a few days, & should like very much if you could send the true men such information as would prevent hasty action & prepare their minds for the new regulations which you will shortly direct to be observed. I mention this because my information leads me to believe that many original secessionists & later day fireeaters are working themselves into meetings & are preparing to climb into the first offices that present themselves, provided they are allowed to do so. As I shall pass directly into Yadkin, Wilkes, & Caldwell, & will have communication with Ashe & Watauga in a few days, I shall take great pleasure in spreading any information you may see proper to entrust me with.

If, in addition, you could order 100 picked cavalrymen to Caldwell & adjoining counties I think it would be of great service in putting down bushwackers, robbers &c. The Lt. Col of the 10th Ohio Cavalry now stationed at this place, expresses a desire to go in that direction—& he would be an excellent man for the purpose of quieting the country.

I make these suggestions out of a desire to aid my section. I am not & do not desire to be a candidate for any office, but so far as my humble efforts can accomplish anything I entend to aid you in building up a new & on a more lasting foundation, the prosperity, peace & happiness of our people.

Having always, from the date of the Charlotte Convention been your strong personal friend, & agreeing in your Union views, it will be a labor of love to assist you in whatever way I can.

Very Truly,
R. L. Patterson

[*Endorsed*] Write him to Salem, thanks for his offer; and ask him to furnish lists of loyal Magistrates for Wilkes, Caldwell, Ashe & Watauga.

W. H. Eddins to Holden A&H:GP(Prov)

Head Quarters 1st Regiment N.C. Vols.
Camp Chattanooga, Near New Berne N.C.
June 10, 1865

To
His Excellency, W. W. Holden
Provisional Governor of N.C. Governor:

Pardon this intrusion on your valuable time. I will be brief.

The Commanding officer[1] of this regiment forwards two applications this day to Department Headquarters—one for certain promotions, the other for the men, on being mustered out of service, to be allowed to take their arms with them to their respective homes, and those of Co. "L" serving as Cavalry to be allowed to retain their horses as private property.

Among the promotions recommended are the names of six North Carolinians (My own among the rest). Will you not do us the Kindness to intercede and throw the weight of your influence in our behalf in both applications.

I have the honor to be Governor,
Your obdt servant,
W. H. Eddins,[2]
Sergt. Maj.

[*Endorsed*] Write Eddings and Atwell that Govr has taken great pleasure in urging their requests in the strongest terms he could—Hopes they will be favorably considered. Write to Gen Schofield, requesting him to promote these North Carolinians, especially Mr. Eddings, who is a worthy young man. Also, request Gen. Schofield to release the 1st Union Volunteers in service to garrison Eastern North Carolina—that is, those whose time has not expired. Preferred to this to colored troops. This is the wish of many loyal men of character in Eastern Carolina. See dispatch. Write to Maj. Atwell that his dispatch received, and I concur with him in opinion.

[1] James W. Atwell, Major, First North Carolina Infantry. Compiled Service Records, U.S. National Archives, First Infantry (microfilm copy in North Carolina State Archives).

[2] William Henry Eddins, volunteered at Beaufort, North Carolina, December 24, 1863; promoted to Sergeant Major, February 20, 1865. Compiled Service Records, U.S. National Archives, First Infantry (microfilm copy in North Carolina State Archives.)

R. W. King to Holden A&H:GP(Prov)

Kinston June 10 1865

His Excellency W. W. Holden

Dear Sir

I have enclosed you the list of names to be appointed magestrates & names for the board &c—quite a number of loyal men met at my Country home on this day & agreed upon this list which is perhaps as good as can be done. some of them did not vote as they ought to last August, but under the circumstances I suppose they might be excused. Doct Heartfield[1] name is on the list, he was magistrate before. I believe he is getting to be a right good friend both of you and myself—he says he misunderstood me, at our meeting &c. I think they will be right hereafter—the only new name is that of Wm A. Croom,[2] who is a true & loyal man, in his district all the former magistrates was considered as disloyal, & Mr. Croom was added for that district. Mr. Sylvester B. Turnage[3] also petitions to be appointed a magistrate there is no doubt about the Loyalty of Mr. Turnage & he is also competent—I have enclosed you petitions for persons that has held civel offices or appointment under the Confederacy–they wish to be pardoned so they can vote &c. Mr. William Walsh, a methodist minister, wishes me to ask you to have his son Wm. A. Walsh[4] a private 10 Redgment Heavy Artillery N. Ca. State troops, now a prisoner of War at Hearts Island New York, released from prison–he says he has written to his son to take the oath of allegiance & that he cannot hear from him he thinks he is willing to take the oath—the father stated that he himself had taken the oath.

I have not yet ascertained about the names of a sufficeint number of loyal men for directors upon the Atlantic & North Carolina Rail Road—the meeting of the Stock Holders is the last of June (Instant) at Kinston, I think I will come up to Raleigh before that time & see you–If I should not come up I will write you again–Mr. Lewis McCullers[5] is going up to day with his petition for Rout agent upon the Atlantic & No. Carolina Rail Road—Mr. McCullers is a loyal man & competent for the position–he is also a poor man.

I remain your friend & obdt. Svt.
R. W. King[6]

[1] Jacob A. Hartsfield, Lenoir County physician and farmer. 1860 U.S. Census Population Schedule, North Carolina: Lenoir, 111 (microfilm).

[2] William A. Croom, Lenoir County farmer 1860 U. S. Census Population Schedule, North Carolina: Lenoir, 045 (microfilm).

[3] Not identified.

[4] William A. Walsh, Lenoir County; private, Company F, Tenth Regiment North Carolina troops; captured at Goldsboro, March 19, 1865; confined Hart's Island, New York; released when took oath of allegiance, June 6, 1865. Manarin and Jordan, comps., *North Carolina Troops, 1861-1865: A Roster*, 1:112.

[5] Not identified.

[6] Richard W. King, Lenoir County farmer; member, state Senate, 1870-1872; member, conventions 1865, 1868, 1875. Cheney, *North Carolina Government, 1585-1979*, 451, 832, 845, 874.

D. H. Hill to Holden A&H:GP(Prov)

Davidson College N.C.
June 11th 1865

His Excellency W. W. Holden
Governor of North Carolina

The Amnesty Proclamation of the President requires the excepted classes to make special application for pardon. The form of the application and the conditions connected with it are not prescribed. It has occurred to me that it would be proper to refer the whole matter to you and that no more suitable channel could be found for the exercise of the Executive clemency in my case than the Chief Magistrate of the State. Your intercession in my behalf would be a graceful act in that capacity, would be gratefully appreciated by myself & friends & I flatter myself, would be gratifying to the N.C. soldiers lately in the Confederate Service.

Your oft-expressed feelings of personal kindness towards me must be my excuse for obtruding private matters upon you in the midst of your onerous and important duties

With great respect
Your obt Servant
D. H. Hill[1]

[*Endorsed*] Reply to him to address the President setting forth the facts. It will be sent to me and then to the President. I do not state in any case what endorsement I make. Reciprocate his kind personal feelings.

[1] Daniel Harvey Hill, soldier; graduate of West Point, 1842; colonel, First North Carolina Regiment; brigadier general, September, 1861; major general, March, 1862; 1863 assumed command in eastern North Carolina; commanded division at Bentonville, N.C. *Dictionary of North Carolina Biography*, s.v. "Hill, Daniel Harvey."

C.H. *Wiley to Holden* SHC:Wiley

Greensboro, N. C.
June 12, 1865

To
His Excellency,
W. W. Holden,
Provisional governor of N. Carolina

Sir: I need hardly suggest to you that in the re-organization of our State the interests of the Common School System should claim special attention. You have, heretofore, manifested a deep interest in this beneficent institution, & I cannot doubt but that you will wish to see it continued, & established on a permanent basis.

As I was for a long time officially connected with it, & watched over it with a father's care during all the night of darkness & tempest which has just passed away, I feel it to be my duty to offer you any aid which my intimate knowledge of the history and condition of the system may enable me to bring to your assistance; & allow me to say that I do this with a pure desire to enhance the usefulness of your most responsible position, to discharge my own conscience, & to do good, without any reference whatever to my future personal promotion.

By the blessing of god I was instrumental in preventing the spoliation of the School funds at a time when madness seemed to rule the hour; & I am of opinion that a large amount can yet be realized from the assets, real & personal, of the system.

Several plans for this purpose have suggested themselves to my mind, & which I would like to have considered by better financiers & sounder judgment; & if I can be of any service to you in these matters, you can command me freely, while I hope you will distinctly bear in mind that I am aiming at nothing for myself, & do not wish to embarrass you by any individual pretentions.

Very respectfully & truly yours,
C. H. Wiley
Former Supt. Com. Schools of N.C.

P. S. I suppose that the banks will have to wind up, but I trust that the interest of the Literary Fund can be saved.

PROCLAMATION A&H:Holden

BY WILLIAM W. HOLDEN, PROVISIONAL GOVERNOR, TO THE PEOPLE OF NORTH CAROLINA

Whereas, by the Proclamation of Andrew Johnson, President of the United States of America, dated May 29th, 1865, I have been appointed Provisional Governor of the State of North Carolina, with instructions to "prescribe, at the earliest practicable period, such rules and regulations as may be necessary and proper for convening a Convention, composed of delegates to and chosen by that portion of the people of said State who are loyal to the United States, and no others, for the purpose of altering or amending the Constitution thereof; and with authority to exercise within the limits of said State all the power necessary and proper to enable such loyal people of the State of North-Carolina to restore said State to its Constitutional relations to the Federal Government, and to present such a Republican form of State Government as will entitle the State to the guarantee of the United States therefor, and its people to protection by the United States against invasion, insurrection, and domestic violence":—

And, Whereas, It is proper that the people of the State should be informed as far as may be, at this time, of the measures that will be necessary to attain this end, so that they may be ready to offer as intelligent and willing co-operation in the same:—

And Whereas, It is also proper that the purposes of the Federal Government in relation to the people of the State should be made known, so that the loyal may receive assurances of protection and encouragement, and the disloyal, if any there be, may know that the eye of authority is upon them, and that they will not be permitted with impunity to resist the laws or to disturb the peace of society:—

Now, Therefore, I, William W. Holden, Provisional Governor as aforesaid, do proclaim and declare:—

1st. That a convention of the people of North-Carolina will be held, at as early a period as practicable, to be composed of the number of members to which the Counties are spectively entitled in the House of Commons of the State Legislature.

No person will be a candidate for the convention, and no person will vote for members to compose it, who shall not previously thereto have taken and subscribed the following oath, prescribed in the Proclamation of the President of the United States, dated May 29th, 1865:

"I,__________, do solemnly swear or affirm, in presence of Almighty God, that I will henceforth faithfully support, protect, and defend the constitution of the United States, and the Union of the States thereunder; and that I will in like manner abide by and faithfully support all laws and proclamations which have been made during the existing rebellion with reference to the emancipation of slaves. So help me God."

And no person not well affected towards the Federal Government, and not loyal thereto, will be permitted to take said oath, or to vote in said election.

Measures will be perfected as early as practicable for administering the above oath to such persons as may be entitled to take it, and for providing them with certificates of the same as evidence of their loyalty. The said oath is regarded as a part of the benefits of the Proclamation referred to, and will not be administered to any of the classes excluded by said Proclamation, save on the exhibition by them of a full pardon from the President of the offence they may have committed against the United States.

2d. The Convention thus to be called will alter or amend the Constitution of the State, and will submit said Constitution thus altered or amended, to the voters of the State at the ballot box for their acceptance or rejection.

3d. The convention will provide for the election by the people of a Governor and members of the Legislature; and the Legislature will elect two Senators to represent the State in the Congress of the United States.

4th. An election will also be held, in due time, for members of the House of Representatives from the State in the Congress of the United States.

Inasmuch as there are no civil magistrates in this State, nor State officers of any kind, the Provisional Governor, by virtue of authority in him vested by the President of the United States, will proceed:

1st. To appoint Justices of the Peace for the various Counties, loyal men, by whom the above oath will be administered, and who will also conduct the elections, through subordinates, for members of a convention, in accordance with instructions from this office, and agreeably to the laws of this State in force previously to the 20th day of May, 1861.

2d. Superior Courts of Oyer and Terminer will be held, when necessary, by Judges specially appointed and commissioned, to dispose of criminal cases.

3d. That Justices of the Peace, appointed as aforesaid, will be authorized to hold courts for the transaction of all such business as may not be of the class of cases triable by a jury. The Justices, by a majority of their whole number, will also be authorized to appoint their Sheriffs and their Clerks for the time being, and such other officers as may be indispensable to a proper transaction of business. And they will also be vigilant and will exert themselves to maintain the laws and to promote the peace of society in their respective Counties; and especially to arrest and commit for trial, when the Courts may be held, all offenders against any law of the State in force previous to the 20th of May, 1861; and to allow bail where the case is bailable, according to the usage of the State.

4th. The Provisional Governor will appoint the State Directors and State proxies in the various corporations in which the State is interested, as the exercise of such power by him cannot be avoided. But the control of the Railroads, the Asylums, and other corporations in which the State is interested, thus unavoidably to this extent committed to him, will be relinquished for the action of the Convention when that body shall have assembled.

Such in brief is an outline of the policy deemed necessary to reconstruct the government of North Carolina, and to restore the State to its Constitutional relations to the Federal Government.

And now, as Provisional Governor of the State, I invite the loyal people thereof to resume with cheerfulness, and with confidence in the future, their accustomed pursuits; and I invite those who have been driven from the State by despotic power, to return; assuring all loyal citizens of the State that they will be protected in their persons and property, and encouraged in their exertions to improve their condition. I also exhort them not to cease to take an interest in public affairs, but to unite with me in the purpose to reconstruct the State Government through the aid of loyal citizens; and to be vigilant and active in discouraging disloyal sentiments, and in ensuring the election of known friends of the Federal Government to every office. Your experiences, fellow-citizens, during the rebellion, should attach you by the strongest ties to the government of the United States. You have just been delivered by the armies of the Union from one of the most corrupt and rigorous despotisms that ever existed in the world. Many of you have been forced, for opinion's sake, and because of your love for the flag of your fathers, to fly from the land of your birth or of your adoption, and seek a refuge among strangers, to escape the hand of arbitrary power. Many of you have been torn from your homes, or hunted down like wild beasts in the forest, and forced into the rebel armies as conscripts, to fight for the continued enslavement of the colored race, and also for a state of slavery for yourselves and your children. Some of you have been subjected to imprisonment and tortures on account of your opinions; and all of you have been deprived for years, up to a recent period, of freedom of speech and of the press, and of every essential guarantee of liberty and of protection to person and property, which is contained in the Constitution of the United States. You are once more free citizens of the United States. By your sufferings in the past and by your hopes for the future, I adjure you to guard well your freedom. Remember that all that you have, and all you can hope to be, and all of good that is in reserve for your children, are indissolubly bound up with the American Union. The "unity of government which constitutes us one people," should be more dear to us than ever, on account of the sufferings through which we have passed. In the language of Washington, "it is of infinite moment that you should properly estimate the immense value of your national Union to your collective and individual happiness; that you should cherish a cordial, habitual, and immovable attachment to it, accustoming yourselves to think and to speak of it as the palladium of your political safety and prosperity; watching for its preservation with jealous anxiety; discountenancing whatever may suggest even a suspicion that it can in any event be abandoned; and indignantly frowning upon the first dawning of every attempt to allienate one portion of our country from the rest or to enfeeble to sacred ties which now link together the various parts."

To the colored people of the State I would say, you are now free. Providence has willed that the very means adopted to render your servitude perpetual, should be His instruments for releasing you from bondage. It now remains for you, aided as you will be by the superior intelligence of the white race, and cheered by the sympathies of all good people, to decide whether the freedom thus suddenly bestowed upon you, will be a blessing to you or a source of injury. Your race has been depressed by your condition of slavery, and by the legislation of your former masters, for two hundred years. It is not to be expected that you can comprehend and appreciate as they should be comprehended and appreciated by a self-governing people, the wise provisions and limitations of Constitutions and laws; or that you can now have that knowledge of public affairs which is necessary to qualify you to discharge all the duties of the citizen. No people has ever yet bounded at once into the full enjoyment of the right of self government. But you are free, in common with all our people, and you have the same right, regulated by law, that others have, to enter upon the pursuit of prosperity and happiness. You should henceforth sacredly observe the marriage relation, and you should provide for your offspring. You can now not only learn to read yourselves, as some of you have been able to do do heretofore, but you can instruct others, and procure instruction from others for yourselves and your children, without fear of punishment. But to be prosperous and happy you must labor, not merely when you feel like it, or for a scanty support, but industriously and steadily, with a view to making and laying up something for yourselves and your families. If you are idle you will become vicious and worthless; if vicious and worthless you will have no friends, and will at last perish. "In the sweat of thy face shalt thou eat bread all the days of thy life." The same Providence that has bestowed freedom upon you, has told you that dilgence in business is required of all his creatures; and you cannot expect that your race will escape ultimate extinction, if you wilfully violate or disregard this, one of His great commands. Freedom does not mean that one may do as he pleases, but that every one may, by industry, frugality, and temperance, improve his condition and enjoy the fruits of his own labors, so long as he obeys the laws. I have no prejudice against you. On the contrary, while I am a white man, and while my lot is with my own color, yet I sympathize with you as the weaker race; and I cannot forget that during the rebellion many of you fought for the preservation of the Union, and that those of you who remained at home in the then slaveholding States, were, for the most part, docile and faithful, and made no attempt by force of arms to gain even their own freedom. I will see to it, as far as I can, that you have your liberty; that you are protected in your property and persons; and that you are paid your wages. But, on the other hand, I will set my face against those of you who are idle and dissipated, and prompt punishment will be inflicted for any breach of the peace or violation of law. In fine, I will be your friend as long as you are true to yourselves, and obedient to the laws, and as long as you shall labor, no matter how feebly, if honestly and earnestly, to improve your condition. It is my duty, as far as I may, to render the government "a terror to evil doers, and a praise to them that do well;"—and thus I will endeavor to do in relation to the whole people of the State of North Carolina, "without fear, favor, or affection, reward, or the hope of reward."

And now, "with charity for all, with malice towards none," I enter upon the discharge of the duties assigned me by the President, earnestly and solemnly, invoking the good people of the State to aid me in the work of reconstructing the government, and in restoring the State to the protection, benefits, and blessings of the Union.

Done at our City of Raleigh, the 12th day of June, in the year of our Lord one thousand eight hundred and sixty five, and in the 89th year of American independence.

William W. Holden
Provisional Governor.

By the Governor:
Jos. W. Holden. Private Secretary

TELEGRAM *Holden to A Johnson* LC:Johnson

Raleigh, June 13th 1865

His Excellency A Johnson

Col D Heaton, treasury Agent,[1] is about removing a lot of Cotton belonging to this state at Graham Depot NC This Cotton was not captured prior to the surrender of Genl Johnston Genl Schofield favors its restoration to the State but does not feel empowered so to order. I earnestly hope that none of the property belonging to the State will be claimed as forfeitted to the United States. Enough of payments can be collected to pay the Expenses of the Provisional Government including the Convention & first meeting of the General Assembly. In view of the distitute condition of our people I beg you not to enforce confiscation of State property

Very Respy
W. W. Holden
Prov. Gov.

[1] David Heaton, former state senator of Ohio and Minnesota, was appointed special agent of the Treasury Department and U.S. Depository in New Bern, N.C.; member, U.S. House of Representatives, 1868-1870. *Dictionary of North Carolina Biography*, s.v. "Heaton, David."

Holden to Major General Schofield A&H:GP(Prov)

State of North Carolina
Executive Department
Raleigh June 16th 1865

Major General Schofield

General:

I desire to request your favorable consideration and kind action in relation the First Regiment North Carolina Volunteers. Most of them are men of very small means and volenteered to Stand by the Government, when a failure of the national cause would have cost them their lives and their property and when the men by whom they had usually been controlled were doing every act in their power against the National Government.

First, that you will continue them in the United States Service, especially those of them whose time has not expired, because it is now too late in the season for them to raise a crop, if they return home.

Second, that they be retained in the Service to garrison Carolina because most of them belong in that portion of the State, and because the citizens of that section urgently request it, prefering them to colored troops. This is the general wish of the loyal men of that portion of the State.

Third, that you will favorably consider the application and recommendations for their promotion lately forwarded to you, especially the claims of W. H. Eddins, Sergt. Major.

Fourth, that those of them who may be mustered out of the Service, may be allowed to retain their arms and those having horses be allowed to take them home with them.

I have the honor to be
Your Obdt Servant
W. W. Holden

Jonathan Worth to Holden A&H:GP(Prov)

Treasury Dept of N.C.
Raleigh, June 16th 1865

Govr. Holden

Dear Sir

I desire to execute the duties of the appointment I hold under you to promote the real interests of the State, and consequently the success of your administration. By the terms of my appointment and the laws in force prior to the Rebellion, I am Ex-Officio, a Director of the Bank of North Carolina. I have not now & never had any stock in any Bank and hence can make any suggestions which seem to me proper without any fear that my personal interests may unconsciously warp my judgment.

I feel it my duty to you and to the State to submit to you in writing my views, knowing you will give them due consideration. I do it in writing because your multifarious duties continually keep around you so much Company that I am reluctant to interrupt you. I do not expect a written answer, but when you have considered my remarks, would like at your earliest convenience to have an interview with you.

I understand by your proclamation, that you have decided to appoint Directors for the Rail Roads, Asylums & Banks in which the State has an interest, but I hear that you incline to disallow the Banks to do any Banking business until the Convention shall so order.

It seems to me that the preliminary duties imposed on you by the Proclamation of the President will require months; and as I understand that Proclamation that convention is called for the sole purpose of amending or altering the Constitution and I presume it will not attempt to legislate on any other subject. It must be a long time after the meeting of the Convention before its adjournment, the ratification of its action by the people, the election of a Genl. Assembly and the passage of needful laws pertaining to the Banks. How will this delay affect the Banks and the State's interest therein?

The University holds $200,000 of Stock in the Bk of N.C. and the Literary Board holds $500,000 of stock in the same Bank and a like sum in the Bank of Cape Fear.

By investing Confederate & State currency and the bonds of the Confederacy & of the State, issued to raise funds to carry on the war, these Banks have certainly sunk so much of their resources that their corporate means will not pay in specie their liabilities. Since this State of things they have adopted a species of voluntary Bankruptcy by which they pay to such of the holders of their bills as will accept it, one dollar in specie for four of their currency or other agreed rate. If these banks could pay the whole of their currency, this course would be reprehensible—but I perceive nothing in their charters forbidding them to compound with a creditor on any terms to which he may assent; and this course is especially beneficial to the holders of a small amount of their bills, because only those will resort to legal coercion who hold a large sum, and the first judgments would consume the assets, leaving all others to lose the amount due to them. The act of the 24 Nov 1860, suspended, during the pleasure of the Genl Assembly, the laws imposing penalties on the Banks in case of failure to redeem their notes in specie—and this act being passed prior to the Rebellion, is still in force.

I do not perceive why Directors for the Banks shall be appointed, if they may not proceed to carry on their business, not inconsistent with their charters and the laws of the United States. I learn that no inconsiderable part of the available means of the Banks, consists of debts contracted before the war. Some of these are ready to pay,—and others who contracted debts since the war would probably compound with the Banks. They received some value and will generally be willing to pay something.

I think it will, in divers ways, be very detrimental to the Banks if their operations be suspended entirely—and consequently injurious to the State. The University owes the Bank of N.C. about $90,000. If, in addition to losing her stock, she has to pay this debt, it will take the whole corporate property of the Institution—and if the $1,000,000 held by the Literary Board in the Banks of N.C. & C.F. be lost, both the University & our system of Common Schools must go down.

I am informed, if any of the present officers of either of these Banks should not be allowed to take the oath of amnesty prescribed in the President's proclamation, they will at once resign their positions to the end that qualfied persons may be appointed and the operations of the Banks resumed, so far as they can resume, consistent with their charters and the laws of the United States.

I am decidedly of opinion that the interests of the State will be promoted by appointing Directors for the State, allowing a general meeting of the Stockholders, and the corporations to continue their operations in obedience to their charters and the laws in force applicable to them, with no other limitation upon their action, provided that no Stockholder or Director or other officer should be allowed to act or vote, until qualified by being allowed to to take the aforesaid oath, or receiving the pardon of the President. In adopting this course I can conceive of no detriment which can arise out of it to the public; & believe the Bank, and consequently the State, would be greatly benefitted.

Very respectfully
Your obt. servt.
Jonathan Worth Pub Tr.

Holden to R. L. Patterson, Esqr. A&H:Patterson

State of North Carolina
Executive Department
Raleigh, N.C., June 18th, 1865

R. L. Patterson, Esqr.

Dear Sir:

I was very glad to receive your letter[1] containing renewed assurances of kind feelings, and desiring to contribute to the permanent establishment of good government for our state.

You will confer a great favor if you will forward a list of good and loyal men for justices in the Counties of Wilkes, Caldwell, Ashe and Watauga. Also the names of suitable person for Mayor and commissioners of any town in either County, that may wish it.

An efficient Military organization will soon be established in every county, for the purpose of suppressing Bushwhackers, keeping the peace and promoting prosperity.

I shall greatly call upon you for assistance in the course of my administration, and shall expect you to advise and suggest such acts and such policy as you may think best, at all times, without being called upon.

I inclose some copies of my proclamation which you will please distribute.

I shall be glad to see you in Raleigh whenever you can come.

Very truly yours,
W. W. Holden

[1] Letter of June 8, 1865, in this volume.

Z. B. Vance to Holden A&H:GP(Prov)

Old Capitol Prison
Washington, June 18th '65

His Excellency
W. W. Holden
Raleigh, N.C.

Sir:

Seeing that you are making disposition of the State property for the purpose of meeting the interest of the public debt, I deem it my duty to inform you that there is a considerable sum to the credit of the State in England. An approximate estimate of this amount can be obtained from Maj. J. Devereux,[1] or the precise amount can be obtained from Mr. John White[2] State Agent, if he has returned from Europe.

If this money, has been so deposited by my agent as to require the use of my signature in order to draw it, I am ready at any time to give it when legally authorized so to do. Of this I presume Mr. White can also inform you.

There is also a small lot of furniture, belonging to the Executive Mansion, now in the possession of Mrs. Vance at Statesville, which I ordered to be returned as soon as a successor to myself had been appointed. I can not hear from home but hope the order has ere this been complied with.

I am Sir, &c. &c.
Z. B. Vance[3]

[1] John Devereux, Jr., planter; assistant commissary of subsistence with rank of captain, May, 1861; promoted to chief quartermaster with rank of major, September, 1861. Dictionary of *North Carolina Biography*, s.v. "Devereux, John, Jr."

[2] John White, merchant; commissioner for North Carolina in England during the Civil War, 1862-1864; borrowed money and secured credit on state warrants payable in cotton and rosin; purchased steamer and converted it to blockade runner *Advance*. *Dictionary of North Carolina Biography*, s.v. "White, John."

[3] Vance was imprisoned in the Old Capitol Prison from May 13 to July 6, 1865. This letter was sent to Governor Holden through Edwin M. Stanton, Secretary of War.

A. M. Waddell to Holden A&H:GP(Prov)

Wilmington N.C. June 18th 1865

His Excellency
Wm W. Holden
Provisional Governor &c.

Sir:

I address this communication to you at the request of a number of the most intelligent and respectable citizens of Wilmington, and urgently request that you will take such prompt action upon it as may seem best. A memorial signed by the citizens generally would be substituted for this letter, but for the delay which would necessarily accompany it.

Wilmington is garrisoned by negro troops, and, although our people behave with remarkable propriety, the frequent and indeed daily outrages perpetrated by them, or by other negroes instigated by them, have excited serious and well-grounded fears for the safety of our unarmed and defenceless people. This is not the result of panic, nor is it the utterance of passion or prejudice, but I do assure you that our people of all classes are alarmed, and justly so, at the very threatening aspect of affairs here.

The military authorities have generally protected the citizens and punished evil-doers, but it is impossible to deny the fact that greater latitude is allowed to the negro soldiers than was allowed to the white, and that there is less disposition to investigate and punish offences committed by them.

The effect of this state of things upon the negro inhabitants is growing worse every day, and unless there is a change for the better, it will inevitably result in *massacre*. The negroes firmly believe that all the property is theirs of right and that every day of delay in the assertion of their rights is rendering their claims weaker; and they are strengthened in this belief by their teachers and preachers. They believe that the Govt. will wink at the attempt to assert, even by force of arms, these ideas, and will maintain them in their claim of equality. If they read an official denial of such intention on the part of the Govt, of (as in two cases of which I am personally cognizant) even if told by the "Freedman's Agent" of their mistake, they are utterly incredulous, and become impatient until their faith is bolstered by assurances from the negro soldiers or others of like ideas.

These, governor, are facts, not inferences. You may form some idea of the *animus* with which these negro soldiers regard our citizens when I tell you that the Brig. Gen. Comdg. here,[1] stated in my office a day or two since that he heard an orderly sergeant in charge of the guard in the centre of the town direct a negro soldier to arrest a citizen who though intoxicated was violating no order and committing no breach of the peace, and further tell him that if the citizen said or did anything to run his bayonet through him!! The General *reprimanded* the Sergeant.

These soldiers insult and curse the most respectable ladies in Wilmington in the presence of the so-called negro citizens, and if they find one of the latter engaged in a quarrel with, or abusing a white person they invariably "back up" the negro. They continually arrest, in violation of orders, unoffending citizens even when walking the streets with ladies and now complaints are not made by many persons because, they say, there is little or no redress to be had.

It is proper for me to say that personally, or on behalf of my family I have no cause of complaint about these matters, but my exemption from such outrages is simply accidental. Even the clergymen of the city are subjected to them. I think it is our duty to inform you of them, and I feel well assured that you will do all in your power to alleviate the condition of any portion of the people of North Carolina who may be in danger or distress.

All that the loyal people here ask is *protection* and the enjoyment of such rights as have been promised to them by the President's Proclamation. There is no disposition to interfere with the negroes in any way, but there is a very strong indisposition to be placed at their mercy.

I am requested to state that, if you would prefer a delegation of citizens to wait on you in regard to these matters, or will designate any one person whom you would wish to advise with on the subject the citizens would be glad to comply immediately. We desire a whole garrison if possible.

I respectfully tender you my congratulations Sir, and subscribe myself

Your friend and fellow citizen
A. M. Waddell[2]

[1] Joseph Roswell Hawley, lawyer and newspaper editor; commanded Seventh Connecticut Regiment; 1864 promoted to brevet brigadier general; placed in command of eastern North Carolina. *Dictionary of North Carolina Biography*, s.v. "Hawley, Joseph Roswell."

[2] Alfred Moore Waddell, lawyer and newspaper editor; opposed secession; bought and edited *Wilmington Herald*, 1860-1861; lieutenant colonel, Forty-first North Carolina Regiment; member, U.S. House of Representatives, 1871-1879. *Dictionary of North Carolina Biography*, s.v. "Waddell, Alfred Moore."

Holden to R. M. Henry A&H:GP(Prov)

State of North Carolina,
Executive Department,
Raleigh, N.C. June 19, 1865

To R. M. Henry, Esq.[1]
Macon, Franklin

Dear Sir: In reorganizing the State government it is necessary that I should appoint Justices of the Peace in all the Counties; and I respectfully request that you will aid me in so doing. Please examine the present list of Magistrates in your County, and select from it all the truly loyal men; if you think the number thus selected not sufficient for the County, add the necessary number of persons not now on the list of Magistrates. And then, of the list thus prepared, designate three of the most intelligent, men of firmness and discretion to act as a Board or Boards for administering the amnesty oath to such as may be entitled to take it.

It is very important that you or some other loyal man should visit Raleigh with the above list, so as to take the oath, and thus be qualified to administer it to the Magistrates of the County.

Your *immediate* attention is earnestly invited to this matter, as the work of the reconstruction cannot be commenced until the Magistrates in the various Counties shall have been appointed and qualified.

Very Respectfully,
W. W. Holden, Prov. Gov.

[1] Robert M. Henry, Macon County; member, 1865 constitutional convention. Cheney, *North Carolina Government*, 1585-1979, 832. This was a printed form letter that was widely distributed throughout North Carolina.

James Speed to Holden A&H:GP(Prov)

Attorney General's Office
Washington, June 19th, 1865

W. W. Holden
Provisional Governor
Raleigh N. Carolina

Sir.

The President has referred to me so much of your letter of the 13th inst. as refers to the 12th Exception in the proclamation of 29th May 1865.

I am instructed to say that the parolled Rebel soldiers, who are not excluded because of some other exception in the proclamation, should be allowed to take the benefit of the Amnesty and vote.

I am Sir, most respectfully
Your Ob'dt Servant
James Speed[1]
Attorney General

[1] James Speed, Kentucky; opposed to slavery; 1861 elected to Kentucky state Senate as a union supporter; 1864, appointed attorney general; resigned July, 1866. *Dictionary of American Biography*, s.v. "Speed, James."

Holden to Wm. H. Seward A&H:GLB(Prov)

June 19th 1865

Hon. Wm. H. Seward
Secretary of State

Sir:

I shall soon have to give directions to County Boards, making provisions for the enrollment of Voters.

I respectfully request to be instructed, whether Parolled soldiers will be allowed to vote for Delegates to the Convention, upon taking the oath of Amnesty, or will each soldier have to procure the President's Pardon.

I am Most Respectfully
Your Obedient Servant
W. W. Holden

James Speed to Holden A&H:GLB(Prov)

Attorney General's Office
Washington June 21st 1865

Hon. W. W. Holden
Provisional Governor of N. Carolina
Raleigh, N.C.

Sir:

We are very anxious to appoint a Judge, Attorney and Marshall for North Carolina.[1] It is very important that the Court should be open. We want natives or residents of your state and fit men. It is greatly to be regretted that the gentlemen appointed cannot take the oath prescribed. Such men should be in the service of the Government.

This disappointment must not stay our efforts—through you and your efforts we hope that proper men may be found who can qualify. Will you be good enough to look around, and see whether the places cannot be filled? I earnestly invoke your prompt attention to this matter.

I am Sir, Very Respectfully
Your Obedient Servant
James Speed
Attorney General

[1] Holden had recommended Robert Paine Dick for appointment as U.S. District Court judge, William S. Mason as U.S. attorney, and William R. Richardson as U.S. marshall

(Holden to the President, May 26, 1865, Andrew Johnson Papers, Library of Congress). None of the three could qualify, however, because of the required oath.

Holden to Major General J. D. Cox A&H:GP(Prov)

Executive Department
Raleigh, N.C., June 22nd, 1865

Major General J. D. Cox.[1]

General.

I forward for your perusal, a letter from A. M. Waddell Esqr[2] of Wilmington, and one from John Pool Esqr[3] of Windsor. These gentlemen are true and loyal, and very reliable and influential citizens.

Similar complaints have been made to me by many worthy citizens of Wilmington, of Newbern and the adjoining counties.

I earnestly commend these matters to your favorable consideration, and ask that you take such action as in your judgment will relieve the citizens.

Very respectfully
Your Obdt servt
W. W. Holden

[1] Jacob Dolson Cox, brigadier general of volunteers, 1861; appointed major general, December, 1864; joined Sherman at Goldsboro; commanded Department of North Carolina; governor of Ohio, 1866-1868; secretary of the interior, 1869-1870. *Dictionary of American Biography*, s.v. "Cox, Jacob Dolson."

[2] See A. M. Waddell to Holden, June 18, 1865, in this volume.

[3] The letter of John Pool is no longer extant.

J. D. Cox to Holden A&H:GP(Prov)

Dept. of North Carolina
Headquarters, Army of the Ohio.
Raleigh, N.C., June 23d 1865

His Excellency
W. W. Holden
Provisonal Governor of N. C.

Sir

I have the honor to acknowledge the receipt of your communication of the 22nd inst. in reference to complaints made by the citizens of Windsor and Wilmington of misbehavior of the troops stationed in those vicinities, and to state, in reply,

David S. Reid served as governor, 1850-1854, and as U.S. senator, 1854-1858. Holden promoted Reid's candidacy for governor and competed against him for election as senator in 1858. Photograph of Reid from State Archives, N.C. Division of Archives and History, Raleigh.

John W. Ellis received the nomination for governor at the Democratic Party convention in 1858. At that same convention, Holden was the unsuccessful candidate. Ellis served as governor, 1858-1861. Photograph of engraving of Ellis from State Archives.

When the Democratic Party split over the sectional controversy during the presidential election of 1860, Stephen A. Douglas became the party's moderate candidate. Holden ultimately opposed Douglas's candidacy. Photograph of Douglas from *Dictionary of American Portraits* (New York: Dover Publications, 1967), 170.

John C. Breckinridge became the secession candidate of the divided Democratic Party in the presidential race of 1860. Holden supported Breckinridge in the columns of the *Standard*. Photograph of engraving of Breckinridge from *Dictionary of American Portraits*, 74.

Zebulon B. Vance served as governor, 1862-1865. Holden and the *Standard* proposed Vance's candidacy. The two men, however, eventually clashed over the peace movement, and Holden ran unsuccessfully against Vance in the 1864 gubernatorial compaign. Photograph of portrait of Vance from State Archives.

In accordance with his plan for Presidential Reconstruction, President Andrew Johnson appointed Holden provisional governor of North Carolina in May 1865. Photograph of engraving of Johnson from State Archives.

In the election of November 1865, Jonathan Worth, state treasurer, defeated Holden for the office of governor. Worth was reelected in 1866 but was removed from office in July 1868 by the federal district military commander. Holden then assumed the governor's office again to lead North Carolina under the plan of Congressional Reconstruction. Photograph of portrait of Worth from State Archives.

William A. Graham—a former governor, U.S and Confederate senator, and U.S. secretary of the navy— became an outspoken advocate of North Carolina's Conservative Party in its support for white supremacy and opposition to Congressional Reconstruction. Photograph of engraving from State Archives.

Joseph W. Holden, the elder of two sons of William W. Holden. He was elected to the General Assembly in 1868 and served as speaker of the House of Representatives. He was mayor of Raleigh at the time of his death in 1875. Photograph of portrait from State Archives.

Louisa Virginia Harrison Holden was William W. Holden's second wife and the mother of four of his eight children. Photograph of portrait from State Archives.

that I have given stringent orders to the Commanding Generals of the Districts of Beaufort and Wilmington in regard thereto, and which I sincerely hope will prevent any like outrages in the future.

I am Sir,
Very Respectfully
Your Obedient Servant
J. D. Cox
Maj. General Comd'g

I. Hubley Ashton to Holden A&H:GP(Prov)

Attorney General's Office
Washington, June 23, 1865

Sir:

After consultation with the President, I desire to call your attention to, and ask your cooperation in, cases arising under the Proclamation of Amnesty and Pardon of May 29, 1865. While the Administration desire to make the operation of that Instrument as general as possible, it is obvious that great dangers are to be apprehended from a loose or indiscriminate exercise of Executive clemency.

In order, therefore, to protect your State and the General Government from the evils resulting from such use of the President's pardoning power, I desire to refer you hereafter the applications for pardon made, in pursuance of that Proclamation, by citizens of your State, in relation to which this Department lacks information; and to ask from you a report in each case as to the propriety of granting the clemency invoked.

The especial points on which information is desired, are—

1st. Is the petitioner (from such information as you can obtain) likely to be a useful and peaceable citizen in the future?

2d. Have any proceedings been instituted against his property under the Confiscation Acts?

3d. Is any property belonging to him now in possession of the U.S. authorities as "abandoned property," or otherwise?

In cases where reference is made to you, all the papers on file in this Office will be sent to you for your information, and it is earnestly desired that you will give them a prompt and careful attention, and *return* them, with your report.

The President desires these cases to be referred to you for two objects; 1st, to do away, as far as may be possible, with any risk of granting pardons to disloyal or otherwise improper persons, and especially to such persons as, from previous conduct and character, are not to be trusted with the control of that class which has been happily converted, by rebellion and war, from slavery to freedom, and to which the General Government looks, in the not far distant future, for support, as from intelligent and loyal citizens. 2d. The President desires to strengthen your hands in the reorganization of society in your State by every means Constitutionally belonging to him. To you, primarily, he looks for the support of law and order in your State, and for the initiation of such measures as will, at the earliest day possible, place her in proper relations with the Federal Union, and thus restore her to all the blessings of a Government which we proudly think to be as strong as it is merciful.

The U.S. District Attorney, as soon as one shall be appointed in your State, will be ordered to render you any assistance you may need in these matters.

I enclose you herewith a printed form, which will indicate the conditions which have been substantially determined on by the President as essential before granting a pardon.

Very respectfully,
Your obedient servant,
I. Hubley Ashton
Asst. Attorney General.
for the Attorney General

W. W. Holden.
Provisional Governor of N.C.

W. Hunter to Holden A&H:GP(Prov)

Department of State
Washington, June 24th 1865

To His Excellency
W. W. Holden.
Provisional Governor of North Carolina.

Sir;

I have received you letter of the 19th instant,[1] asking whether it will be necessary for paroled soldiers to obtain a special pardon from the President or whether the taking of the amnesty only will entitle them to vote at the election to which you refer. In reply, I have the honor to enclose a copy of the Circular of this Department of the 29th Ultimo, and if the accompanying proclamations of the President, from which it will be seen that a special pardon is not necessary for any military men below the rank[2] specified in the Proclamation of that date.

I am your Excellency's
Very Obedient Servant
W. Hunter
Acting Secretary

[1] In this volume.
[2] Rank of captain.

Holden to R. M. Henry A&H:GP(Prov)

State of North Carolina,
Executive Department,
Raleigh, N.C., June 26, 1865

DIRECTIONS FOR QUALIFYING MAGISTRATES AND ORGANIZING THE COUNTY COURTS.

To R. M. Henry,[1] Commissioner:

If necessary, you will call on the officers of the Local Police to notify the Justices to meet at the Courthouse, on a day to be appointed by you. And said officers are hereby commanded to aid you in notifying the Justices to attend.

When the Justices shall have assembled you will administer to them, first, the oath of amnesty; secondly, the oath to be found in the Revised Code, chapter 76, page 434, to maintain the Constitution of the State not inconsistent with the Constitution of the United States; thirdly, the oath of office, to be found in Revised Code, chapter 76, page 441.

Two copies of the amnesty oath for each Justice have been handed or sent to you. One of these, when properly filled out, will be signed by the Justice, and this copy you will send to this office; and the other you will deliver to the Justice, having first written on the back of it and signed it as follows: "A True Copy. R. M. Henry, Commissioner." When the Enrolling Board of the County shall have been established the Justice will by this copy or duplicate before the Board, and the Board will take it up, enter his name on the books, and give him a voting certificate, or certificate of loyalty.

No Justice or other officer who is included in any of the fourteen excluded classes of the President's amnesty proclamation, will be permitted to take the oaths prescribed, or enter on the performance of duty, until a pardon shall have been received by him from the President. And the oath of amnesty is not to be administered to any one who is not disposed to take it willingly and cheerfully. If any Justice named in the commission hesitates to take the oath, it will be your duty to withhold it from him.

The Justices, after being qualified as above, will proceed to elect a Sheriff, a Clerk, a County Attorney, and such other officers for the time being as they may deem necessary to the transaction of business. For the powers of the Justices in this and other respects, see the proclamation of the Provisional Governor, dated June 12th, 1865.

The Clerk will make a full and complete record on his books of the proceedings of the Justices, a copy of which you will at once transmit to this office.

W. W. Holden, Prov. Gov.

By the Governor:
R. C. Badger, Private Secretary

[1] R. M. Henry, Macon County; member, constitutional convention of 1865. Cheney, *North Carolina Government, 1585-1979*, 832. This letter was a printed form sent to a principal commissioner in each of the counties.

Holden to Major General J. D. Cox A&H:GLB(Prov)

State of North Carolina
Executive Department
Raleigh, N.C., June 26th 1865

Major General J. D. Cox.

General:

A county police has been appointed in Halifax and Northampton Counties, they are armed with muskets but they have not been furnished with ammunition.

There is a large class of idle population in those counties and I respectfully request that you furnish the police with ammunition as speedily as you can.

I am most respectfully
Your Obedient Servant
W. W. Holden

Holden to the President of the United States LC:Johnson

State of North Carolina
Executive Department
Raleigh, N.C., June 27th, 1865

His Excellency
President of the United States

Sir:

Allow me most respectfully to ask your favorable consideration of the accompaning petition. This Religious Sect in North Carolina, have been true and faithful union men during the rebellion.

The oath of Amnesty is "faithfully to support, protect and *defend*" the Constitution. They fear this may mean to defend by arms, therefore they desire,

First to be excused from having to take this oath. Second, if any oath of allegiance be required of them that it may be the one proscribed by North Carolina Statutes, namely. "I do solemnly and sincerely declare and affirm that I will truly and faithfully demean myself as a peaceable citizen of North Carolina: that I will be subject to the powers and authorities, that are or may be established for the good government thereof, not inconsistant with the constitution of the said State and the constitution of the United States, either by yielding an active or passive obedience thereto, and that I will not abet or join the enemies of this State, by any means, in any conspiracy whatsoever, against the said State, that I will disclose and make known to the legislative, executive or judicial powers of the said State, all treasonable conspiracies, which I shall know to be made, or intended against the said State."

Third: If neither of these requests can be granted, that it may be stated by authority in the Newspapers that when Quakers take the Oath of Amnesty it is not expected that they bind themselves to defend the Government with arms.

I am Most Respectfully
Your Obedient Servant,
W. W. Holden

[*Enclosure*]

Petition

To Andrew Johnson, President of the United States

From the Meeting for Sufferings of North Carolina yearly meeting of Friends, held 19th of 6 mo 1865

We respectfully petition that members of the religious society of Friends be excused from taking the oath or affirmation prescribed for all citizens of those states which have been in rebellion against the United States Government.

Our reasons are, first, that we believe said obligation, as to us, to be unnecessary, from the fact that our religion prevents us from ever placing ourselves in rebellion against the government under which we live, or from ever offering violent opposition to the execution of its laws. And accordingly, we do not know a single instance among the members of our Society, of any who were in favor of a rupture of the U.S. Government, or who were in favor of the war which was waged against it. On the contrary, we were much opposed thereto, and many of use suffered both in property and person rather than give any aid therein. Some were imprisoned for months, some were whipped on the bare back, suspended for hours by the thumbs and suffered other personal indignities and abuse; Some were kept for days (in two instance for five days and nights) without a particle of food or a drop of water—for refusing to take up arms. Their firmness and constancy, in this respect, were and are heartily approved by the whole body of the Society.—Hence for us, we believe said obligation to be unnecessary.

Secondly, we have felt a scrupulous tenderness as to taking affirmations "to defend" any government lest it may be construed that we could bear arms in its behalf—a practice in direct violation of one of our primary principles; and a principle which has characterized us for our Society from its very origin, now more than 200 years ago.

If it should not meet the approbation of the President to release us entirely from said affirmation we ask that it may be so modified as not to violate our conscientious scruples.

Signed by direction and on behalf of the meeting aforesaid.

Nereus Mendenhall,[1] Clk.

[1] Nereus Mendenhall, clerk of the yearly meeting, 1860-1872; member, state House of Representatives, 1874-1875. *Dictionary of North Carolina Biography*, s.v. "Mendenhall, Nereus."

Holden to the President LC:Johnson

State of North Carolina
Executive Department
Raleigh, N.C., June 29, 1865

To His Excellency the President:

Sir: You will find herewith a letter from Judge Dick[1] in relation to the oath he is required to take to qualify him for his office. Allow me to invite your careful attention to his letter. Mr. Mason,[2] the District attorney, is in a similar situation. If it be at all possible I would be greatly gratified to see it so arranged the these gentlemen could fill these places. The oaths required is, it is true, the law of the land, but it seems to have been framed for a state of war, and not of peace. This State is now *at peace* with the federal Union and with all the world. If such men are to be deprived of the right to hold office, it will be difficult to fill the federal offices in this Sate with any but strangers.

I need not add more. Judge Dick and Mr. Mason are warmly attached to the administration and to you personally, and they are anxious to accept positions in which they can most effectually serve the administration and the country.

Very Respectfully,
W. W. Holden

[1] Robert Paine Dick

[2] William S. Mason.

[*Enclosure*]

Raleigh NC
June 29th 1865

His Excellency, Andrew Johnson.
President of the United States.

Sir.

Gov Holden has just informed me that the difficulty in relation to my qualifying as Judge of the U.S. district court, —has not, —and in the opinion of the cabinet, cannot be removed. I greatly desired the position, as it would be an endorsement by you of my fidelity to the Government of the United States. If the appointment in any way embarrasses you in the discharge of your official duties, let it be withdrawn as I am willing to make any sacrifice for the public good.

I deeply regret the difficulty as my removal from office will seriously injure me in public opinion, as it will be regarded as a disapproval of my past political course by your administration. My appointment is generally known throughout the State and universally approved of by loyal men. I have been opposed to secession all my life. I took an active and prominent position against the rebellion. I have never for a moment either expected or desired the success of the Confederate Government. I held office under the State government, but not for the purpose of aiding the rebellion, but to try and assist in extricating my state from the impending ruin of treason. I have always loved the Union, and ever desired to see it restored, and I have constantly labored (indirectly) to that end. I could not throw myself in *direct* opposition to the overwhelming torrent of rebellion without losing my life. For four years I have endured proscription and persecution, in church, society, and state, and I have ever fought as good a fight against treason as was possible for any one to do *and live*. If I cannot hold office in North Carolina no one else can, who remained at home in the midst of the storm. Those who left may have shown *loyalty*, but they showed little true courage. If I cannot hold office, then every federal appointment must be made from the Northern States. Nine tenths of our people are earnestly desirous of returning to the Union with their whole soul, but foreign tax gatherers and northern Judicial officers will necessarily greatly try their patience and retard the restoration of genuine fraternal feeling

There is no northern man,—who has not entered the army,—who has endured more for the union than I have—or who has *loved* it with a deeper and prouder affection

My *loyal people* know this and they are rejoiced when they heard that I had received the endorsement and approval of the President of the United States.

There are many difficulties yet ahead. I have given up a hundred slaves— *my whole estate*—cheerfully and cordially because the peace and quietude of the country demanded it. I have entered the field for immediate and complete emancipation. I shall sustain with my whole strength your policy for I am satisfied that it is the wisest and best course that can be adopted. I want to elevate the negro as rapidly as possible by education and christian influences, and I want to see him kindly and generously treated. I fully approve of your position on the question of negro suffrage.

As Judge of this district I could exert a wholesome influence upon our people, which cannot be done by a foreigner.

I do sincerely trust that some way can be derived by which genuine North Carolina men can hold the federal offices in this state. Suspicion and rebellion have destroyed nearly all of the property of a people who, at least, have ever been loyal to the Union of their fathers,—and I do hope that a great and magnanimous government will not *long make* them feel the humiliation of subjugation in seeing foreign *tax gatherers* "sitting at the receipt of customs," and strange judges administering *law and equity*.

But let this matter end as it may, be assured that I am the firm and steadfast friend of your administration, as I honestly believe that you will do all you can for our *loved* and common country.

Your kindness to me while in Washington will ever be remembered as one of the most pleasant recollections of my life. With the best wishes for you and yours—I am with high regard

Your true friend & servant
Robert P. Dick

TELEGRAM *Holden to the President* A&H:GLB(Prov)

State of North Carolina
Executive Department
Raleigh N.C. July 4th 1865.

To the President of the United States.
Washington

Sir:

I am informed that Mrs. Vance, the wife of Z. B. Vance, is dangerously ill at Statesville in this State. I respectfully ask that he may be permitted to visit his family on his parole of honor.[1]

Very Respectfully
W. W. Holden

[1] In his memoirs, Governor Holden said that his appeal to President Johnson resulted in the release of Governor Vance to visit his wife. *Memoirs of W. W. Holden*, 49.

Jos. S. Cannon to S. D. Wallace, Esqr. A&H:GP(Prov)

July 4th, 1865

S. D. Wallace Esqr.[1]

Sir.

I am requested by the Governor to say that the Quarter Master, Col. Boyd,[2] has informed him, that the Rail Road from Wilmington to Goldsboro, will be turned over to the Corporation officers in a short time.

He wishes you to appoint a Meeting, at an early day, for the purpose of reorganizing the officers of the Road. Please make your notice correspond with Mr. Webbs[3] and Mr. Whitfords[4] in reference to excepted classes and the necessity of having taken the oath of Amnesty.

Very Respectfully Yours,
Jos. S. Cannon,
Aid de Camp

[1] Stephen D. Wallace, Wilmington wholesale commission merchant. 1870 U.S. Census Population Schedule, North Carolina: New Hanover, 416 (microfilm).

[2] Andrew Jackson Boyd, state quartermaster, lieutenant colonel, Forty-fifth Regiment North Carolina troops; member House of Commons, 1864-1865. Samuel A. Ashe, Stephen B. Weeks, and Charles L. Van Noppen, eds., *Biographical History of North Carolina*, 8 vols. (Greensboro: Charles L. Van Noppen, 1905-1917) 7:49-51.

[3] Thomas Webb, lawyer; A. B., U.N.C., 1847; M.A., 1851; president, North Carolina Railroad Company. Grant, *Alumni History*, 653.

[4] John Dalton Whitford, president, Atlantic and North Carolina Railroad Company. 1860 U.S. Census Population Schedule, North Carolina: Craven, 085 (microfilm).

Robt. P. Dick to Holden A&H:GP(Prov)

Greensboro
July 6th 1865

Gov. Holden

My Dear Friend

I send you an application to the President in behalf of Cantwell.[1]—He was a terrible sinner, but I hope you will take pity on his poor wife and children and endorse my letter and send it in soon.—

Cantwell wrote me a letter full of penetence and I hope he will do better in future. *He can hurt no one*. Let him go!

Your friend
Robt P Dick

[1] Edward Cantwell, lawyer; lieutenent colonel, Twelfth Regiment North Carolina troops, 1861; aide to Brigadier General Thomas Lanier Clingman; lieutenent colonel, Fifty-ninth Regiment North Carolina troops, 1862-1865. Manarin and Jordan, comps., *North Carolina Troops, 1861-1865: A Roster*, 5:114.

William H. Seward to Holden A&H:GP(Prov)

Department of State
Washington 8th July 1865

To His Excellency
W. W. Holden
Provisional Governor
of North Carolina, Raleigh

Sir;

Your letter to the President of the 26 ultimo was delivered by Mr North.[1] The President is gratified with the opinion expressed favorable to the prospect of State organization in North Carolina. Your remarks in regard to collisions between colored troops and white persons have been referred to the War Department. Mr North will make an estimate of the expenses which may attend the special trust conferred upon you, namely, the organization of the State of North Carolina. The amount thus reasonably estimated will be paid at the War Department as an expense incident to the suppression of the rebellion. The estimate, however, will carefully exclude all expenses which may arise from the administration of the civil government of the State, including the charities thereof. It is understood here, that, besides cotton which has been taken by the Secretary of the Treasury, under Act of Congress, there were quantities of rosin and other articles as well as funds lying about in different places in the State and elsewhere not reduced into possession by United States officers as insurgent property. The President is of opinion that you can appropriate these for the inevitable and indispensable expenses of the civil government of the State during the continuance of the provisional government. He is also of the opinion that you can levy taxes or assessment for the same inevitable and indispensable provisional expenses and enforce their collection.

Should you adopt this course and find yourself impeded or embarrassed in the execution of the measure, you will then report to this Department, and orders will be given by the War Department to the military authorities to take charge of the matter.

I am Sir
Your obedient servant
William H. Seward

[1] Should have read Jonathan Worth, state treasurer, who had been sent to Washington to arrange financing for the provisional government.

William H. Seward to Holden A&H:GP(Prov)

Department of State
Washington, July 10, 1865

William W. Holden
Governor &c., Raleigh, N.C.

Sir:

This Department has information from its consular officers, and particularly from the U.S. Consul at Liverpool, that Powers of Attorney and other papers, addressed to parties in this country by enemies of the United States residing abroad, empowering them to collect debts and demands against other parties residing here, have been presented to such officers for verification by them.

As an instance of this proceeding, you are informed that Edward Lawrence Esqr., the Mayor of Liverpool, on the 22d of June ultimo, presented for verification to the Consul at Liverpool a Power of Attorney addressed to Edward Kielder [Kidder}[1] of Wilmington, N.C., empowering him to collect a certain debt of six thousand pounds sterling from Thomas Barrat Power,[2] late of Wilmington, given to secure said debt.

The Consul at Liverpool has been instructed to refuse his verification of such documents, and you are hereby respectfully requested to arrest all proceedings of this kind in North Carolina, and prevent as far as possible the payment of all demands whatever to traitors, blockade runners, spies, aiders or abettors of the insurrection or in any other form or character enemies of the United States.

I have the honor to be Sir
Very Respectfully
Your Obedient Servant
William H. Seward

[1] Edward Kidder, Wilmington wholesale lumber dealer. 1870 U.S. Census Population Schedule, North Carolina: New Hanover, 445.

[2] Not identified.

J. A. McMannin to Holden A&H:GP(Prov)

South Lowell N.C. 10th July 1865

Gov. Holden,

My Dear sir I sind you by my son Dr. Charles T. McMannin[1] my application to the Prest. for the rimission of my Political sins, I prey you to act as Mediator between us, & if mercy can be found & pardon obtained please see that it is done, and that I may as soon as possible have the bennefit, thereof I also send the application of Capt. Mangum[2] The Papers we sent from Hillsboro is still in your office as I did not get them, pleas have the oath to which I was sworn attatched to this, you will find it in My first application. I wish to see you on important matters. Would you prefer to be the next Gov, or go to the Senate. We think either is in your reach and we wish to know which you prefer. We will have a Large Gathering at Mangums the second Sat in Augst at which time Orange will speak out for *you* as she has never spoken before. You can communicate freely with me and confidentially. I have but one object in view which is to see you Go Up, (not up the spout) Nothing short of the presidency now, I shall then Expect an appointment of bearror of dispatches to some foreign country. If you have time pleas write me by the Dr.

Yours truly
J. A. McMannin[3]

P.S. Pleas attach the oath to Capt Mangums application. You will find it in the papers sent from Hillsboro.

[1] Charles T. McMannin, Orange County; physician and farmer. 1860 U.S. Census Population Schedule, North Carolina: Orange, 454 (microfilm).

[2] Addison Mangum, Orange County farmer. 1870 U.S. Census Population Schedule, North Carolina: Orange, 284 (microfilm).

[3] John A. McMannin, Orange County Methodist minister and farmer. 1870 U.S. Census Population Schedule, North Carolina: Orange, 204 (microfilm.)

Mayor and Commissioners of the Town of Wilmington to Holden A&H:GP(Prov)

Mayors Office
Wilmington N.C.
12th July 1865

To His Excellency W. W. Holden
Prov. Gov of No. Carolina

Sir

The undersigned, Mayor and Commissioners of the Town of Wilmington, respectfully represent to your Excellency, that it is very generally believed in this

Community that some insurrectionary movement is contemplated by the Colored Citizens of this Town and vicinity, aided and abetted by United Colored Troops, and further encouraged by their Preachers and Teachers, who are generally denizens of the North; and we, representatives of the wishes of the citizens, would recommend some speedy action through your Excellency, or we fear that the purposes of these persons may be so far consummated, as to be not so easily checked, as the object of this communication is to prevent so sad an occurance.

Our own Colored population are assuming a somewhat dictatorial spirit, and insolent, and claiming through a written petition to our Board by "The Union League" composed of colored persons, or rather by a committee from said "Union League" a participation in the offices and appointments of this Board, say Policemen, and Inspectors of fuel for the Town. Their Petition has been answered that this Board has no legal authority, if they were so inclined, to appoint them to any office within their gift.

The proclamation of Your Excellency has been read to them, and they still insist that they are entitled to all the social and political rights of white citizens, and they have made objections to this Board, through our Mayor, to some of the Justices appointed by Your Excellency, and further insist that they should have been consulted.

And we would further represent, that notwithstanding the stringent orders of the Commanding General, our streets are continually thronged with Black Troops, many frequently in a state of intoxication, which in the present excited state of the different classes, liable at any moment to create a riot, or even something worse; besides frequent occurrences have taken place, bringing the Colored Troops and citizens in contact with the whites, resulting in the indication of smothered revenge towards the whites. These things, together with conversations frequently heard, & which they are not very careful to conceal, as the conversations were in a loud tone, and savoring an insurrectionary spirit.

Now, in view of these facts and the painful apprehension pervading our community, we feel it to be our duty to make known to you the situation, and circumstances by which we are surrounded, and would respectfully suggest to Your Excellency that you will urge upon the Military authorities the propriety as well as the necessity of removal of the colored Troops, as we think that, would in a large measure remove the present apprehensions, and do away with the evil influence exerted upon our colored citizens.

And we would further represent that we are somewhat apprehensive that when the Municipal Government is organized and an attempt is made to assume and exercise authority not in accordance with the views of this particular class, resistance will be made, and we feel ourselves powerless, in the absence of a sufficient number of white troops to enforce our authority; as we verily believe, the colored Troops could not be controlled by their officers, and would take sides with the colored citizens.

We would assure Your Excellency that the suggestion of the removal of the colored Troops is not done from prejudice against this particular class of Troops, but for the reasons set forth in this our appeal, and our anxiety to restore civil authority in our Town.

Since the forgoing was written a Document, copy of which is herewith sent (was handed to the Mayor). You will observe it is dated 3d June ulto. & the reason assigned for the delay in handing it to the Mayor, is that the writer wished to leave the place before its delivery. He left this place for home a short time since.

John Dawson Mayor
S. D. Wallace[1]
Alfred Martin[2]
John G. Bauman[3]
Wm. S. Anderson[4]
J Shackelford[5]

[*Enclosure*]

Notice this!

Cezer Daniels of colored Hospital, this 3rd day of June 1865, informed me of a conspiracy among the colored race to murder all the white race, the old slave-owners, to get their lands and houses (they say they made themselves) as soon as our Soldiers leave, He himself is not in league with them. I told him to learn their secret and report to me at this Hospital (citizens) says he will. I told him to discountenance any such thing. I told him they would all be exterminated if they commenced any such wicked thing. He says he is confident they, the colored, are holding secret meetings now in this city. Their Preachers (colored) are talking these things to their people.

I expect to go home in a few days, and so leave this note behind me.

Signed C. C. Emerson
A Steward of Citizens Hospital
Wilmington, N.C.
Place of residence,
Kohomo, Ind.

[*Enclosure*] Send a copy of this at once to Gen. Ruger, and earnestly appeal to him to take steps to prevent the apprehended result. Suggest the importance of arming the Police Guard of New Hanover, and of placing arms at the disposal of the City authorities.

Write the Mayor and Alderman what has been done. Say to them they have acted correctly in not appointing any of the colored population to office — That the right to hold office depends upon the right of suffrage, which is to be settled hereafter by the State as provided for in the President's proclamation. That any attempt by armed force by the colored population to obtain control of public affairs, or to avenge any supposed wrongs or grievances at the hands of the whites, will be visited with swift and condign punishment. That the colored people now free will be protected and respected as long as they are obedient to the laws, but if they resist the laws and shed blood they must abide the consequences.

[1] Stephen D. Wallace

[2] Alfred Martin, Wilmington wholesale commission merchant. 1870 U.S. Census Population Schedule, North Carolina: New Hanover, 442 (microfilm).

[3] John Gerhardt Bauman, Wilmington grocer; officer of the German Volunteers prior to the Civil War. Bill Reaves Collection, New Hanover County Public Library, Wilmington, N.C.

[4] William S. Anderson, Wilmington jeweler. 1860 U.S. Census Population Schedule, North Carolina: New Hanover, 786 (microfilm).

[5] James Shackelford, Wilmington business man; former member of board of aldermen; acting mayor who surrendered the city to Union forces. Bill Reaves Collection, New Hanover County Public Library, Wilmington, N.C.

St. John E. S. Skinner to Holden A&H:GP(Prov)

Post Office Department,
Appointment Office
Washington, July 14th, 1865

Sir:

Mr. William W. Poisson,[1] who was recently appointed Postmaster at Wilmington on your recommendation; in a letter to the Department of the 6th instant, states that he cannot take the oath prescribed by Act of Congress of July 2, 1862, and March 3, 1863. He says, "when a convention was called in my state, I voted for the Union candidate, and was always opposed to the war. After a while the conscription act was passed, and to prevent having to enter the Confederate Army and to fight against the old "Stars and Stripes," I took a position as Clerk, and Government Agent in the Commissary Department. This position I only held until I could secure a position on the Wilmington and Weldon Rail Road which would exempt me from service in the Confederate Army. I have taken President Lincoln's amnesty oath and can prove my union sentiments throughout the war &c." He adds "if the oath can be modified I would be pleased with the appointment and would forward bond immediately."

The Postmaster General has no power to modify or change the oath. This can only be done by Act of Congress; and I am directed by him to express his regret that Mr. Poisson cannot qualify; and to say, that the law will not authorize the appointment of any one as postmaster, who cannot take and subscribe the oath, which the law requires; and to request that you will at your earliest convenience recommend some one for appointment who can qualify according to law.

Very Respectfully
Your Obedient Servant
St. John B. S. Skinner
Acting First Asst. P.M. General

Hon. W. W. Holden
Governor &c.
Raleigh, N.C.

[1] William W. Poisson, Wilmington railroad ticket agent. 1870 U.S. Census Population Schedule, North Carolina: New Hanover, 417 (microfilm)

Holden to the Mayor and Commissioners of the Town of Wilmington A&H:GLB(Prov)

State of North Carolina
Executive Department
Raleigh, N.C., July 15, 1865

To the Mayor and Commissioners of the Town of Wilmington.

Gentlemen,

Your communication of the 12th inst. concerning the conduct of colored people of your Town, and your apprehensions of an insurrection, has been received, and forwarded to Maj. Gen. Ruger,[1] Comdg the Department of North Carolina, with an earnest appeal to him to take the matter immediately into his consideration, and with a request that he arm the Police Guard of New Hanover, and also furnish you with arms and ammunition.

You acted rightly in not appointing any of the colored people to office—That the right to hold office depends upon the right of suffrage is plain—and this is to be settled hereafter by the States, as provided for by the Proclamation of the President.

If the colored people attempt by armed force to obtain control of public affairs, or to avenge any supposed wrongs or grievances at the hands of the whites, they will be visited with swift and condign punichment.

The colored people are now free, and will be protected and respected as long as they are obedient to the laws, but if they resist the laws and shed blood they must abide by the consequences.

Very Respectfully,
Your obedt. serv't
W. W. Holden
Prov. Governor

[1] Thomas Howard Ruger, graduate of West Point, 1854; lieutenant colonel and colonel, Third Wisconsin Infantry; major general of volunteers, 1864; commander, Department of North Carolina, 1865-1866. *Dictionary of American Biography*, s.v. "Ruger, Thomas Howard."

Holden to Major General Ruger A&H:GLB(Prov)

Raleigh, July 15 1868

Major General Ruger
Commanding Dept of N.C.

General:

I have the honor to forward to you a copy of a communication from the mayor and commissioners of Wilmington, to which I call your attention.

I earnestly appeal to you to take such steps as may seem proper to you, to prevent the apprehended result, and would suggest that it would be of great advantage to arm the Police Guard of New Hanover County, and also to place at the disposal of the City authorities arms and ammunition.

With confidence that you will do all that is necessary and proper

I am General Very Respectfully
Your Obedient Servant
W. W. Holden
Prov. Gov.

TELEGRAM *Holden to the President* A&H:GP(Prov)

State of North Carolina
Executive Department
Raleigh, N.C., July 17th 1865

To the President of the United States

Sir: I have appointed about three thousand Magistrates and Mayors and Commissioners for all the towns. County Courts have been organized, and I am now prepared to issue a proclamation for a Convention.

I will write you at length by a special messenger in the course of a few days. I desire your approval of a plan for administering the Amnesty oath to the people of the State, and also your approval of my proclamation. I send these with my letter.

I think a convention may be assembled on the tenth day of October. It could be called sooner, but in so important a matter I think I ought to proceed deliberately and carefully.

Please answer so that I may know this has been received.

W. W. Holden
Provisional Governor

Holden to R. Swann, Esq. A&H:GP(Prov)

State of North Carolina
Executive Department
Raleigh, N.C., 19th July, 1865

R. Swann Esq.[1]
Commissioner &c.

Sir. Satisfactory information having been furnished to me as Provisional Governor of North Carolina, that in the organization of the County Court of Cleaveland County & also of the County officers a due regard has not been manifested to the present and past loyalty of the appointees to office, I therefore for sufficient reasons, and having due regard for the interests of the State and particularily for the County of Cleaveland do hereby declare the action of the magistrates heretofore appointed by me to be null and void and of no binding force whatever. And I do further order and direct that after the qualification of certain Justices of the Peace by me this day appointed for said County of Cleaveland, they together with those heretofore appointed, shall at such time as they may select meet at the Court House in the town of Shelby and proceed to a reorganization of the County Court & such county officers as they may deem necessary for the time being.

I deem it proper also to say to the commissioner that no one, even though he may have been appointed & commissioned as Justice of the Peace, can be qualified if he falls within the exceptions of President's amnesty proclamation of the 29th May 1865, until he shall have petitioned for & received a pardon of his offences.

Given under my hand at the City of Raleigh on this the 19th day of July A.D. 1865 & in the 89th year of American Independence.

W. W. Holden

[1] Reubin Swann, Cleveland County ironmaster; delegate, 1865 constitutional convention. 1860 U.S. Census Population Schedule, North Carolina: Cleveland, 874 (microfilm); Cheney, *North Carolina Government, 1585-1979*, 832.

Holden to Dr. E. A. Crudup A&H:GP(Prov)

State of North Carolina
Executive Office
Raleigh N. C. July 20 1865

To Dr E A Crudup[1] State Proxy

Sir

In the meeting of the Stockholders of the Raleigh and Gaston Railroad Company to be held this day, you are instructed to state that no stock will be represented but such as is owned and held by persons who are excepted from the fourteen excluded classes, of the President's Amnesty Proclamation of May 29th 1865; and further, if a sufficient amount of stock, now owned and held by excluded classes, is not represented to justify action in accordance with the charter of the company, then and in that case, the State will take charge of the Road and conduct its operations for the present—Of course, Stockholders who have been pardoned by the President will be entitled to be represented.

Very Respy
W W Holden

[1] Edward A. Crudup, Franklin County physician and planter. 1870 U.S. Census Population Schedule, North Carolina: Franklin, 498 (microfilm).

TELEGRAM *Holden to Attorney General* A&H:GP(Prov)

State of North Carolina
Executive Department
Raleigh, N.C., July 22d 1865

To the Attorney General[1] U. States Washington

Sir: The appointment of G. W. Brooks Esqr[2] of Pasquotank County to the office of District Judge would be very acceptable to our people. If Mr. Dick[3] cannot hold the office I should be very glad to see Mr. Brooks appointed.

Very Respectfully
W. W. Holden

I also recommend Jefferson Fisher[4] for the office of Marshall. He can take the oath and is very well qualified.

[1] James Speed.

[2] George Washington Brooks, lawyer and judge; member, House of Commons, 1852; superior court judge, 1865; U.S. district court judge, 1865-1882. *Dictionary of North Carolina Biography*, s.v. "Brooks, George Washington."

[3] Robert Paine Dick.

[4] Jefferson Fisher, Wake County farmer. 1870 U.S. Census Population Schedule, North Carolina: Wake, 286 (microfilm).

Holden to the President LC:Johnson

EXECUTIVE DEPARTMENT
Raleigh, N.C., July 24, 1865

To the President.

Sir: I send herewith a proof sheet of the Proclamation I propose to issue for a Convention. I could have prepared it ten days ago but for indisposition, which continues, and which has somewhat unavoidably retarded public business. Please examine the proof-sheet, make such corrections as you may deem necessary, and hand or send to Mr. Mason[1] or Dr. Powell,[2] to be returned to me. I had thought of several plans for administering the amnesty oath to the people, and the plan adopted in the Proclamation seems to be the best. It would not be safe to confide this power to all the Justices, though I believe they are all loyal, yet there are weak men among them, and persons would be qualified to vote who ought not to be.

If the Convention should assemble on the 2d of October the Constitution could be altered and submitted to the people by the 20th November; and then, in anticipation of the ratification of the Constitution by the people, the Convention could provide for the election of Governor and members on the 15th or 20th December, so that the new or regular government could be inaugurated on the 1st January, 1866.

I have thought it best to begin at the foundation and build upwards. We now have 3,500 Magistrates, Mayors and Commissioners in all the towns, with police, with Sheriffs and Constables in all the Counties. The civil power is now felt in every neighborhood in the State; and the result is, as a general rule, that the people are submissive and quiet, and looking anxiously to the time when the State will be restored to her relations with the government. In addition to this heavy labor, (for the antecedents and present disposition of every man appointed had to be ascertained,) I have had to see to the reorganization of the Banks and the Railroads. This latter work is well nigh accomplished, and those corporations will pass from the hands of traitors into the hands of the loyal men.

Many of the oligarchs are still unsubdued. I think it a good plan to hold their pardon in suspense, and whether their estates are to be confiscated or not, they ought not to be allowed to vote for twelve months to come. But I find, what is a little singular, that the ultra original secessionists who profess to have repented, appear to be really more penitent than the ultra partisans of Vance who were Union men. By the way, it would not be a good policy to extend a pardon to Vance for some time to come. Your administration is very popular in North Carolina, but there are indications on the part of some of the oligarchs and the old Whig leaders to concoct opposition. A firm, discreet use of the pardoning power and the patronage of the government will contribute greatly to keep them down, and thus preserve tranquility and order in the State.

The amount, $7,000, brought by Mr. Treasurer Worth[3] will probably be enough to defray the expenses of my office until the regular government is established. We shall be able, I think, to realize several hundred thousand dollars from the cotton and rosin you were kind enough to allow us.

My health is very feeble, and I have written this while suffering pain.

I am rejoiced to learn that your health has been restored. May your valuable life long be spared to your friends and your country.

With high respect,
W. W. Holden

[1] William S. Mason.
[2] Robert J. Powell.
[3] Jonathan Worth.

Holden to Maj. Gen. Ruger A&H:GP(Prov)

State of North Carolina
Executive Department
Raleigh, N.C., July 27th, 1865

Brevet Maj. Gen. Ruger,
Commanding Post at Raleigh:

Sir:

Information has reached this department that three citizens of the County of Person State of North Carolina have been arrested and sent to this post for trial by a military court upon the charge of an assault mad by them upon the body of a freedman named Currie.[1]

I beg to call your attention to the fact that civil law has been organized in the County of Person and an eminent and upright Judge[2] appointed to hold a court of oyer & terminer in said County, and that said appointment was made prior to the commission of the alleged offence.

This is a matter in which I conceive the civil courts have sole and exclusive jurisdiction and I have every confidence that strict and impartial justice will be administered and therefore respectfully suggest that the parties be remanded to the county of Person for trial by the civil tribunal of the state. This course in my judgment will avoid any unpleasant conflict between the civil and military authorities and at the same time insure impartial justice in the matter.

The parties under arrest are T. A. Woody[3], H. Carver[4] and S. C. Barnett.[5]

I am, Gen'l, very respectfully,
Your obdt. servant,
W. W. Holden

[1] Not identified.

[2] Edwin Godwin Reade, Person County: member, U.S. House of Representatives, 1855-1857; member, Confederate Senate, 1864; superior court judge, 1864-1865; associate justice, North Carolina Supreme Court, 1865-1879. *Dictionary of North Carolina Biography*, s.v. "Reade, Edwin Godwin."

[3] Tinsley A. Woody, Person County farmer. 1870 U.S. Census Population Schedule, North Carolina: Person, 677 (microfilm).

[4] Henry Carver, Person County farm laborer. 1870 U.S. Census Population Schedule, North Carolina: Person 626 (microfilm).

[5] Sam C. Barnett, Person County lawyer; member, House of commons, 1865-1866, 1868-1870, 1874-1875; member, state Senate, 1870-1872. Cheney, *North Carolina Government, 1585-1979*, 1241-1242.

Thos. H. Ruger to Holden A&H:GP(Prov)

Head Qrs Department of North Carolina
Raleigh Aug 1st 1865

His Excellency
Hon W. W. Holden
Governor of N.C.

Sir

I have the honor to acknowledge the receipt of your communication of the 27th of July, requesting that three citizens of the County of Person, State of North Carolina, now held for trial before a military commission, under charge of an assault made by them upon the person of a freedman named Currie "be remanded to the County of Person for trial by the Civil tribunal of the State." I regret that after full consideration of the matter, it appears to me inexpedient to comply with your request.

The reasons influencing me are briefly as follows:

In your communication occurs the following: "This is a matter in which I conceive the Civil Courts have sole and exclusive jurisdiction." Without considering the question as to whether civil law is so far operative as to give civil courts jurisdiction of the case in question, it seems clear to me that without doubt, military tribunals have jurisdiction in all that relates to the preservation of order, including the trial and punishment of those guilty of acts of violence. One of the important duties of the Military Authorities during the interim prior to the complete restoration and full operation of civil law, I understand to be the maintainance of good order and protection of society from acts of violence, and this duty must necessarily carry with it, the power of its fulfillment. It would not under existing circumstances, as I believe, be the duty of the military authorities to await, in case of the disturbance of the peace, or not amounting to hostile act to the government, the call of the civil authorities before interposing for the preservation of order, but that they would be in duty bound, to summarily quell such disturbance and bring the guilty to punishment. —Neither do I believe that the military authorities would be bound to obey writs of Habeas Corpus issued by the State Courts. At the time of the arrest of the citizens, before referred to, no civil court had taken cognizance of the matter.

Magistrates were some time since appointed by your Excellency, and have been acting in the various counties of the State, yet in no instance have I heard or known of official notice having been taken by any of them of acts of unlawful violence towards freedmen although such acts have been by no means infrequent in the different secions of the State.

Of late several cases of homicide of freedmen by whites have been brought to my knowledge but in no case so far as I have learned was any arrests made by the magistrates or civil officers, and no attempt had for investigation. From my own observation, and information obtained from the commissioner of Freedmen, I am of the opinion that acts of unlawful violence toward the freedmen are becoming more frequent. The first effect on the mind of the people of the dispersion of the rebel forces and the occupation of the country by our troops, is, in a measure wearing off, and the apparent apathy and stuper resulting from the changed condition of things, is replaced in the minds of those who give up Slavery with reluctance, by feelings of hostility to the freedmen. Under all the circumstances, I think that the restraining influence of prompt trial and punishment of offenders, particularly those guilty of homicide, by military Commissions is the only adequate remedy for the existing evil. The action of Grand Juries would not I fear, under the condition of things now existing in the State, correct the evil.

There are at present several citizens charged with homicide held for trial by military Commission, at different places in the State. In all cases of importance the proceedings will be forwarded to Washington for final review and orders. If it shall appear expedient to you to refer this matter to his Excellency the President, I respectfully request that a copy of your communication, to which this is an answer; and also this my reply may be sent, that my motives, and the reason of my action in the matter may clearly appear. I regret that we entertain different views of the subject.

Very Resty
Your obedt Servt
Thos. H Ruger
Brevt Major General U.S. Vols Comdg

Mayor and Commissioners of Wilmington to Holden A&H:GP(Prov)

Wilmington N.C. August 3rd 1865
Mayors Office

To His Excellency
W. W. Holden

Sir:

The Commissioners of the town of Wilmington are again impelled from a sense of duty to address your Excellency in relation to the position of affairs in this community; they regret the necessity of trespassing on your time and attention, occupied as you must be with important State interests, and they would desist therefrom, but from the responsibilies of official obligations.

Events, startling & alarming, crowd each other, and the progression has assumed a character which unless checked will end in the subversion of order, and the disruption of civil authority.

Open violations of law are of frequent recurrence, the authority of the Municipality defiantly challenged, the ordinances of the town disregarded, the police insulted & assaulted, and life itself is held by very uncertain tenure.

For several days past a spirit of rebellion has been manifest & many violations of law have been brought to the notice of the Commissioners. On yesterday the most aggravating demonstrations were witnessed, and great excitment prevails in the community. This portraiture though highly wrought is truthful & facts will sustain it allegations. The Commissioners are witnesses to many occurrences that have transpired & they have no hesitancey in alledging that the United States Colored troops are the source & cause of these outrages, and although the attention of the Military Commandants have been directed to these grievances they continue to be repeated. It is just to say that the officers in command profess to regret the existence of these difficulties & assure us of their determination to put them down & maintain order, yet it is evident that proper discipline does not exist among the troops, or that subofficers are not disposed to execute the orders of superior officers. The Commissioners see no remedy but the removal of the Colored troops & the substitution of White troops, or the absence of a Military force entirely. We candidly believe that the colored population of this town would not be disorderly & could be controlled if they were not incited by the presence & acts of the Military & we regret to state that the disorder is confined chiefly to that class.

Many cases of recent origin might be instanced, but we call to your attention especially to the enclosed article from the "Wilmn Herald" which is strictly correct, and to the report of Mr. Harmon, Capt. of Police which is alike truthful. On account of these occurrences, the entire police force have resigned, regarding their lives to be in constant peril, and the commissioners have to rely upon a Military guard to enable them to execute the town ordinances, until they can reorganize their police. The written instructions furnished the police by the order of the Commissioners were of a temperate character & well guarded, so as to prevent abuses, & were approved by the Military Commandant & we believe they have been executed in the spirit with which they were dictated.

In conclusion the Commissioners request your Excellency to aid them in procuring one hundred "Spencer" Rifles or Navy Revolvers with which to arm the police & other citizens, so that we may not be entirely defenceless in the case of an emergency.

With sentiments of esteem

We are Your Excellency's
Most obt. Servts.
John Dawson Mayor
Alfred Martin
S. D. Wallace
Wm. S. Anderson
John G. Bauman
E. Murray[1]
J. Shackelford

[*Enclosure*]

Statement of L. W. Harmon, Captain of the police from the Town of Wilmington, on night servide:

On my rounds, I found about 8'o'clock, a crowd of soldiers and other colored persons assembled at the corner of Market and Master streets, indulging in vehement abuse of the police force generally, and particularly the police on that beat, threatening to kill them, &c. The police had left their post in consequence of the above demonstration. I ordered them back, with instructions to discharge their duties by keeping order if possible, but not to engage with colored persons in conversation and not to enter into any conflict with them by resort to weapons. On their return they were attaacked by said parties and halted, pistols and bayonets were presented and they were told if they attempted to exercise by their presence or otherwise, their duties that night, they would be killed.

On the S. E. corner of Market & French Streets, I saw what I supposed to be a military patrol. I saw the officer in charge, either a corporal or sergt., and asked him to dispense that crowd, giving him the information I had. He replied, the blacks were perfectly right, they might kill the last policeman there was, that he himself had a pill in his gun he intended to give me before morning, and walked his guard up French Street. About 10 o'clock, a report was made to me by one of my men that a policeman had been shot near Mr. Gile's Residence, which has since been confirmed by a policeman sent to learn the facts. The wounded man was taken home and the doctor sent the police over to the railroad to get bandages &c., and in their return they report being fired upon four times. Also they were halted and abused by the colored guard over entrance at the Railroad.

(Signed) L. W. Harmon

[1] Eli Murray, Wilmington wholesale grocer and commission merchant. *Wilmington Directory*, 1865, 58.

Jos. S. Cannon to R. R. Bridgers A&H:GP(Prov)

State of North Carolina
Executive Department
Raleigh, N.C., Aug.4th, 1865

Hon. R. R. Bridgers,[1] President Wilmington and Weldon Rail Road

Sir.

I am instructed by the governor to say to you that the Post Master Genl has notified him that he is ready to contract with you for carrying the mails, on the Wilmington and Weldon Rail Road as soon as he is notified that you are in a condition to convey them safely.

The compensation offered is one hundred dollars per mile per annum.

Pleass address the governor an answer stating the condition and length of your road and your willingness or unwillingness to convey the mails for the compensation proposed.

Very Respectfully yours,
Jos. S. Cannon
aid de camp

[1] Robert Rufus Bridgers.

Lewis Hanes to Major General Ruger A&H:GP(Prov)

State of North Carolina
Executive Department
Raleigh, August the 4th 1865

Major General Ruger,

Sir:

The great Seal of the State of North Carolina is missing from this office, and from information which I have received from A. M. McPheeters, Esqr, late Secretary of the late rebel Governor Vance, and also from Jonathan Worth, Esqr, Treasurer of the State, I have reason to believe that the great Seal, together with the letter book of the rebel Governor Vance, was captured by the United States troops at Greensboro.

Mr. McPheeters states that the Great Seal of the State, and the rebel Governor's letter book were packed up in the same box, and the box containing them was captured; and Mr Worth says that Gen Cox[1] told him that he had captured, and had in his possession the letter book.

My object in writing to you is to inquire whether there is any chance of recovering the Seal, as it is difficult for the Executive office to get along without it.

I have the honor to be, Very
Respectfully,
Your Obt. Servant
Lewis Hanes[2]
Private Secretary to the Governor

[1] Jacob Dolson Cox.

[2] Lewis Hanes, newspaper editor; private secretary to Governor Holden, 1865. *Dictionary of North Carolina Biography*, s.v. "Hanes, Lewis."

TELEGRAM *Andrew Johnson to Holden* LC:Johnson

Washington Aug 7, 1865

Governor W. W. Holden

Raleigh N.C.

Your proclamation has just been read and is fully approved. It would have received earlier attention but for my indisposition. I would suggest the importance of organizing at the earliest practicable date,

Andrew Johnson
President U.S.

SHC:Holden

A PROCLAMATION, BY WILLIAM W. HOLDEN PROVISIONAL GOVERNOR TO THE PEOPLE OF NORTH CAROLINA

In pursuance of power vested in me by Andrew Johnson, President of the United States, by his Proclamation of May 29, 1865, appointing a Provisional Governor of North Carolina, under the fourth article of the Constitution of the United States, which guarantees to every State in the Union a republican form of government: and in order to enable the loyal people of said State to organize a State Government, whereby justice may be established, domestic tranquility restored, and loyal citizens protected in all their rights of life, liberty, and property; and in order, also, that said State may be restored to its constitutional relations to the Federal Government, by presenting such a republican form of government as will entitle the State to the guarantee of the United States therefor, and its people to protection by the United States against invasion, insurrection, and domestic violence, I, William W. Holden, Provisional Governor as aforesaid, do hereby proclaim that an election will be held in said State, on Thursday, the 21st day of September, 1865, for a Convention, to be composed of one hundred and twenty delegates, to be chosen as follows:

[There follows a listing of counties and the number of delegates allocated to each or in combination with another county.]

The Clerks and Sheriffs of the respective counties will proceed at once to assemble the Justices of the Peace, a majority of whom will select from their number not less than six nor more than eighteen Justices, men of intelligence, discretion, firmness, and approved loyality, whose duty it shall be to administer to those who may be entitled to receive it, the oath contained in the President's Amnesty Proclamation of May 29th, 1865, under such instructions as may be prescribed in this Proclamation. The Justices shall, at the same time, appoint Inspectors of the elections at the various precincts in their respective Counties, in accordance with the law in relation thereto, Chapter 52, Revised Code of North-Carolina. The elections for members of the Convention shall be conducted in the same manner as elections for members of the House of Commons, in accordance with the provisions of chapter 52, Revised Code, so far as said provisions may be applicable; and the officers appointed to hold said elections, and to make returns thereof, shall be liable to the same penalities for failure to act, or for neglect of duty, as are prescribed in chapter 52, Revised Code.

No person will be allowed to vote who is not a voter qualified as prescribed by the Constitution and laws of the State, in force immediately before the 20th day of May, 1861; except that the payment of a poll tax shall not be required.

All paroled soldiers of the army and navy of the pretended Confederates States, or of this State, and all paroled others of the army and navy of the pretended Confederate States, or of this State, under and including the rank of Colonel, if of the army, and under and including the rank of Lieutenant, if of the navy, will be allowed to vote, provided they are not included in any of the fourteen excluded classes of the President's Amnesty Proclamation: and, provided further, that they are citizens of the State in accordance with the terms prescribed in the preceding paragraph.

No person will be allowed to vote who does not exhibit to the Inspectors a copy of the Amnesty Oath, as contained in the President's Proclamation of May 29th, 1865, signed by himself and certified by at least two Justices of the Peace.

Printed copies of the Amnesty Oath will be furnished to the Clerks, who will distribute them to the Justices appointed to administer the oaths. The Justices will deliver the certified copy to the person taking the oath, and retain the original to be transmitted to this office.

Justices of the Peace are authorized to administer the Amnesty Oath to persons who may desire to apply to the President for a pardon.

The Sheriffs of the respective Counties shall furnish, as soon as practicable, certificates of election to those persons who may have received the highest number of votes as members of the Convention: and the sheriffs shall also immediately send to the office of the Secretary of State, Raleigh, a statement of the vote in their respective Counties for the members aforesaid, and also a statement of the said vote, sealed up, directed to the President of the Convention, Raleigh, to be laid before the Convention.

The members of the Convention thus chosen, will assemble in the city of Raleigh, on Monday, the second day of October, 1865.

The attention of Justices appointed to administer the Amnesty Oath, is especially directed to the following fourteen excluded classes of the President's Amnesty Proclamation of May 29th, 1865:

"First—All who are, or shall have been, pretended civil or diplomatic officers, or otherwise, domestic or foreign agents of the pretended Confederate government.

Second—All who left judicial stations under the United States to aid the rebellion.

Third—All who shall have been military or naval officers of said pretended Confederate Government, above the rank of Colonel in the army or Lieutenant in the navy.

Fourth—All who left seats in the Congress of the United States to aid the rebellion.

Fifth—All who resigned or tendered resignations of their commissions in the army or navy of the United States to evade duty in resisting the rebellion.

Sixth—All who have engaged in any way in the treating otherwise than lawfully as prisoners, war persons found in the United States service, officers, soldiers, seamen, or in other capacity.

Seventh—All persons who have been or are deserters from the United States for the purpose of aiding the rebellion.

Eight—All military and naval officers in the rebel service who were educated by government in the Military Academy at West Point, or the United States Naval Academy.

Ninth—All persons who held the pretended offices of Governors of States in insurrection against the United States.

Tenth—All persons who left their homes within the jurisdiction and protection of the United States, and passed beyond the federal military line into the so-called Confederate States for the purpose of aiding the rebellion.

Eleventh—All persons who have been engaged in the destruction of the commerce of the United States upon the high seas, and persons who have made raids into the United States from Canada, or been engaged in destroying the commerce of the United States upon the lakes and rivers that separate the British provinces from the United States

Twelth—All persons who, at the time when they seek to obtain the benefits thereof by taking the oaths herein prescribed, are in military, navy, or civil confinement or custody, or under bond of the civil, military or naval authorities or agent of the United States, as prisoners of war, or persons detained for offences of any kind either before or after conviction.

Thirteenth—All persons who have voluntarily participated in said rebellion, and the estimated value of whose taxable property is over twenty thousand dollars.

Fourteenth—All persons who have taken the oath of amnesty as prescribed in the President's proclamation of December eighth, A.D., one thousand eight hundred and sixty three, or an oath of allegiance to the government of the United States since the date of said proclamation, and who have not henceforward kept and maintained the same inviolate: Provided, That special application may be made to the President for pardon by any person belonging to the excepted classes, and such clemency will be liberally extended as may be consistent with the facts of the case and the peace and dignity of the United States.

Under the first exception are included all persons who have been civil or diplomatic officers or agents of the pretended Confederate Government, either within or without the territorial limits of the United States.

Under the seventh exception are included all officers, agents, or private citizens who have been absent from the United States for the purpose of aiding the rebellion.

Under the thirteenth exception are included all who, during the rebellion, have held any office or agency under the State or pretended Confederate government: or have in any way voluntarily joined in the rebellion, as, for examble, by entering or marching with armed forces hostile to the United States: by sending or furnishing money, provisions, or arms to persons engaged in the rebellion, save in cases where money or provisions were furnished from the promptings of charity or humanity: by acting with assemblages of persons, whether organized or unorganized, hostile to the United States: or in any other way giving voluntary aid, assistance of encouragement to the rebellion: and whose taxable property on the 29th day of May, 1865, exceeded in value the sum of twenty thousand dollars.

The other exceptions are so plain as not to require explanation.

No certificate will be presented by the Justices to any person who is included within any of the fourteen excluded classes, unless on exhibition by the party of his pardon for his offence from the President.

The Justices appointed to administer the Amnesty Oath, and to furnish certificates of the same which shall be evidence of loyalty, are especially instructed to be vigilant and faithful. While it will not be their duty to attempt to pry into the hearts and consciences of men, they will nevertheless admonish those who may apply to take the oath, that it must be taken and subscribed in good faith, with an honest intention on their part to keep it without secret purpose or mental reservation upon any occassion or at any time to commit any act in violation of said oath: and they will warn them that if the oath is not thus taken and kept, the pardon offered them by the President will be void, and they will remain subject to trial under the law for perjury and treason.

The Justices, Clerks and Sheriffs, whose duty it is to provide for administering the oath and to conduct the elections, are enjoined to use every practicable means to enable every citizen to take the oath who may desire and be entitled to do so. And the Inspectors are enjoined to inspect and examine fairly and truly, to decide in every case in accordance with the law, and with the instructions they have received from this office; and to make prompt and correct returns of the number of votes and for whom cast, at their respective precincts.

Done at our city of Raleigh, the eighth day of August, one thousand eight hundred and sixty-five, and in the year of the independence of the United States the Ninetieth.

William W. Holden
Provisional Governor

By the Governor
Lewis Hanes, Private Secretary

Holden to the President LC:Johnson

State of North Carolina,
Executive Department
Raleigh, N.C., August 10th, 1865.

His Excellency
The President of the United States

Sir

I most respectfully forward for your consideration, the Petition of the Mayor and other citizens of the town of Wilmington.

I am well acquainted with the signers, and know them to be reliable and influential men, and among the best citizens of the state. I know that any statement made by them, can be fully relied on, and from abundant information derived from other sources, I am sure that their troubles are not too strongly stated.

I am glad to be able to add, that, though the Citizens of Wilmington, were once furious secessionists, are now quiet and orderly citizens. I believe they are truly loyal to the National Governmnet, and may confidently be relied on as such.

I know no difference between National Troops, whether white or black, but existing facts compel me to state, that the presence of Colored Troops, in Wilmington and other places, has greatly increased the jealousy and unkind feeling between the white and colored citizens.

If these troops could be removed to the forts, or kept entirely away from the towns, it would greatly add to the quiet and content of both the white and black inhabitants.

I most respectfully desire your Excellency's kind consideration of this matter, and sincerely desire that such relief may be given the Petitioners as your judgment approves.

I am most Respectfully
Your Obedient Servant
W. W. Holden

Tod R. Caldwell to Andrew Johnson LC:Johnson

State of North Carolina
Executive Department
Raleigh, N.C. August 18th 1865

To Andrew Johnson
President of the United States

Sir:

I am directed by His Excellency, Gov. Holden to transmit to you the accompanying correspondence between himself and Brev. Maj Gen'l Ruger,[1] commanding Dept. of North Carolina.

The governor begs you to give the subject matter a careful examination, and if you concur with him in opinion, to cause the administration of justice in North Carolina to be turned over exclusively to the civil authorities of the State.

I have the honor to be, sir,

Your Obt. Servt.
Tod R. Caldwell[2]
Aid to Gov. Holden

[1] See Holden to Maj. Gen. Ruger, July 27, 1865, and Thos. H. Ruger to Holden, August 1, 1865, both in this volume.

[2] Tod Robinson Caldwell, lieutenant governor and governor; member, House of Commons from Burke County, 1842-1845, 1848-1849; 1858-1859; member, state Senate, 1850-1851; elected lieutenant governor, 1868, succeeding to governorship with Holden's impeachment; elected governor, 1872. *Dictionary of North Carolina Biography*, s.v. "Caldwell, Tod Robinson."

TELEGRAM *Andrew Johnson to Holden* A&H:GP(Prov)

August 22d, 1865
Washington D.C.

Gov. Wm. W Holden
Raleigh

Information[1] comes to me that reports are freely circulated in influential quarters and where without contradiction they are calculated to do harm to the effect that in appointments to Office and in the recommendations for appointments the true Union men are totally ignored and the Provisional Governors are giving a decided preference to those who have participated in the Rebellion.–The object of such representations is to embarrass the Government in its reconstruction Policy & while I place no reliance in such statements I feel it due to you to advise you of the extended circulation they have gained and to impress upon you the importance of encouraging & strengthening to the fullest extent the men of your State who have never faltered in their allegiance to the Government,– Every opportunity should be made available to have this known & understood as your Policy & determination—

Acknowledge receipt of this Telegram

Andrew Johnson
President U.S.

[1] The Raleigh *Daily Sentinel* of August 10, 1865, quoted the New York *Tribune* as follows: "The pardoned rebels of North Carolina are more defiant and disloyal than before. The negroes and Union men are special objects of their hatred, whose protection depends entirely upon the enforcement of the Confiscation law, which disarms only the disloyal, who will be beyond the reach of the Federal authorities as soon as the new State Government is inaugurated. It is understood that this element, who hold State securities for upwards of $40,000,000, contracted since the Rebellion for war purposes, will make a strong effort to have the same assumed, by not providing against it in the new Constitution, but leaving it to further legislation."

J. Mc.Davis to Holden LC:Johnson

Mayor's Office
New Bern, N.C., August 25, 1865

Hon. W. W. Holden
Provisional Governor State of N.C.

Sir:

I have the honor to inform you that a petition, to the Secretary of War, is being secretly circulated here among the secessionists and those disunionists from the North who oppose the reconstruction of the State and the restoration of civil government stating that the Provisional government here is a failure and asking that Martial law be once more established here and the Provisional government abolished.

I deem it my duty to inform you of this fact as it forms a part of the deliberate plot of these disunionists to prevent the People of the State of North Carolina from assisting you to bring about the speedy restoration of civil government in the state and her representation in the Congress of the United States.

Very Resp.
Your obedt. Servt
J. Mc.Davis[1]
Acting Mayor Town of New Bern

Raleigh, North Carolina
August 28th 1865
Executive Office

[*Endorsed*] Respectfully forwarded to the President of the United States for his information.

Much of this sort of management is going on in Newbern and in Beaufort. A brother of B. S. Hedrick[2] a clerk in the Patent Office Building, is Collector at Beaufort.

[1] Dr. John M. Davis, appointed a commissioner of the town of New Bern by Governor Holden, June 22, 1865. Alan D. Watson, *A History of New Bern and Craven County* (New Bern: Tryon Palace Commission, 1987), 438.

[2] Benjamin Sherwood Hedrick. See 249n.

TELEGRAM *Holden to the President* LC:Johnson

Raleigh, N.C. Aug. 26, 1865

The President

Sir: In reply to your dispatch of the 22d August I have the honor to state that in no instance in making appointments to office or in recommending for appointment have I shown any preference for persons who have participated in the Rebellion. On the contrary I have been very careful to prefer and to appoint persons who were originally union men & persons who were in favor of restoring the authority of the Federal Govt. Doubtless in many appointments (some four thousand) some have been appointed who ought not to have been & in some cases even friends have misled to some slight extent by their recommendations But upon the whole, only loyal Union men have been appointed & recommended at Washington It is my purpose & wish to encourage & strengthen those who have never at heart faltered in their allegiance to the federal Govt. I have proceeded deliberately and carefully in the work of reorganizing, & thus far I am sure there are no grounds for apprehending that North Carolina will not present an acceptable Constitution. The great body of her people are loyal & submissive to National Authority. I know there are malcontents, radicals, & not good men, who are engaged in misrepresenting facts & formenting strive for certain purposes; but none of these things move me in the performance of duty.

Thanking you heartily for the confidence you have heretofore reposed in me, and for the honor you have done me in making me Provl Gov of this noble State.

I am, Sir, &c.
W. W. Holden, Prov. Gov.

Holden to Hon. Wm. Dennison A&H:GP(Prov)

State of North Carolina
Executive Department
Raleigh, August 28th 1865

Hon. Wm. Dennison,[1] Post Master General.

Sir:

Hon. R. R. Bridgers, President of the Wilmington and Weldon Rail Road, has this moment notified me that he is ready to convey the United States mails on that road, at the price you propose, namely: one hundred dollars per mile.

I am very Respectfully
Your Obedient Servant
W. W. Holden
Prov. Gov.

[1] William Dennison, Ohio; governor of Ohio, 1859-1861; postmaster general, 1864-1866. *Dictionary of American Biography*, s.v. "Dennison, William."

Geo. W. McLelland to Holden A&H:GP(Prov)

Post Office Department,
Contract Office,
Washington, August 30, 1865

Sir:

I have the honor to acknowledge your telegram of the 28th instant, and to state that the Postmaster General has issued an order to accept the offer of R. R. Bridgers, President of the Wilmington and Weldon Rail Road Company to convey the mails between Weldon and Wilmington daily, or as much oftener as trains may run, if required, at One Hundred Dollars per mile per annum; and the parties concerned are notified accordingly, by letters of this date—that to R. R. Bridgers being directed to Wilmington

Very Respectfully, &c.,
Geo. W. McLelland
Second Asst P. M. General

Hon W. W. Holden,
Provisional Governor of North Carolina
Raleigh, N.C.

TELEGRAM *Andrew Johnson to Holden* A&H:GP(Prov)

Aug 30. 1865 Washington

Gov. W. W. Holden

Maj Gen Meade[1] has been sent south for the purpose of inspecting all the troops with power to assign them as the interests of the country seem to demand I hope you will see Gen. Meade & confer with him freely as to the disposal of the forces in N.C. I have no doubt all will be arranged satisfactorily to the people. I hope all is going on right.

Andrew Johnson
President

[1] George Gordon Meade, graduate of West Point, 1835; brigadier general of volunteers, 1861; major general of volunteers, 1862; commander, Army of the Potomac, 1863; major general, regular army, 1864. *Dictionary of American Biography*, s.v. "Meade, George Gordon."

Holden to Maj. General Thomas H. Ruger A&H:GLB(Prov)

State of North Carolina
Executive Department
Raleigh, N.C. Aug. 30 1865

Maj. General Thomas H. Ruger

General:

I have issued a Proclamation, to call a Convention, the Delegates to which are expected to meet in Raleigh on the 2nd day of next October.

I have most respectfully to request that you will give me the control of the Capitol, as early as convenient, that it may be put in order for the use of the Convention, and that you will give such orders as will cause the furniture, temporarily removed therefrom, to be returned.

I am Most Respectfully
Your Obedient Servant
W. W. Holden

Holden to W. R. Albright, Esqr. A&H:GP(Prov)

State of North-Carolina
Executive Department
Raleigh, N.C., August 31st 1865

To W. R. Albright, Esqr.[1]
Clerk County Court, Alamance.

Sir

Complaints has been made to me by one hundred and forty citizens of the County of Alamance, that Justices have been appointed to administer the amnesty oath and persons have been appointed Inspectors of the election, Who are very objectionable to the loyal citizens, and they have appealed to me, to remove Jesse Gant, Esq[2] the chairman of the court and to revoke the commissions of several Justices who as they declare, have been active in making the above appointments. They also represent that unless a change is made in this respect, and unless a preference is given in these matters to the original union men, many of the loyal men will not take the oath before some of the Justices who have been appointed to administer it, and the cause of the Government will thereby suffer. At the request of these one hundred and forty citizens who have made this complaint, I have appointed Seventeen more Justices for the County, so as to give the absolute control to the original Union men. Let these Justices thus appointed be qualified whenever they may appear before you.

Permit me to call your Special attention and that of the Sheriff[3] to the complaint referred to. Justices ought not to be appointed to administer the oath, nor should Inspectors be appointed who are regarded with distrust or aversion from whatever cause by any considerable portion of the original loyal men of the County. It is very far from my purpose to reflect upon those original Secessionists and ultra war men who have sincerely and honestly, acknowledged their error and who are submitting in good faith to the National Authority. I would not proscribe them or persecute them, but on the contrary, I am glad to see them ranging themselves on the side of the Union, and doing what they can to restore the State to its true position. Yet these gentlemen cannot expect to be leaders in this crisis. It must be left to the original Union men, as a general rule to lead while they cooperate with them in the good work of restoring the National authority.

All that I require is that these general views should be carried out. I should regret to hear of Strife or divisions among the people of Alamance. Let them by all means be as united as possible and send to the Convention loyal delegates who will concur in those measures which are indispensable to resotre the State to the Union. I look to yourself and the Sheriff to take such steps as will prevent discord in Alamance, by removing all just grounds of complaint on the part of Loyal Citizens.

Very Respectfully
W. W. Holden.

[1] William R. Albright, Alamance County clerk of superior court. 1870 U.S. Census Population Schedule, North Carolina: Alamance, 53 (microfilm).

[2] Jesse Gant, Alamance County farmer. 1870 U.S. Census Population Schedule, North Carolina: Alamance, 49 (microfilm).

[3] Albert Murray, Alamance County sheriff. 1870 U.S. Census Population Schedule, North Carolina: Alamance, 50 (microfilm).

Holden to the Justices of the Peace of the County of Yadkin A&H:GP(Prov)

State of North Carolina
Executive Department
Raleigh Sept 13 1865

To the Justices of the Peace of the County of Yadkin.

Gentlemen:–Complaints have been made to me that there is a disposition on the part of a portion of the people of Yadkin to take the law into their own hands– and to inflict punishment on certain persons for real or supposed past injuries. The

War is over and the most desirable of all things now is peace. The peace of society must be preserved at all hazards. No man has the right to right his own wrongs by the strong hand. The law of force must give way to the law of the Statute book. While my sympathies are with the ultra union men, and while I feel that they were unjustly, and in some cases harshly treated during the late rebellion—yet the President himself has proclaimed a general amnesty and pardon to the great body of our people—and has left no room for the hand of violence among neighbors. The civil law will soon be established, I trust, in its full force in this State and then and not before will juries of the counties be called together to decide in criminal cases and to award damages to injured parties.

Meanwhile during the existence of the Provisional Government, I earnestly appeal to you to discountenance and refuse all breaches of the peace—and to protect all loyal and peaceable people. The law must be maintained and the peace of society preserved. One act of retaliation would lead to another and the end would be neighborhood feuds, bloodshed, civil strife, and the total destruction of the peace of society. Let me urge you in the most earnest terms to guard against the first approaches towards such a state of things in your county.

With much respect your
Obedt Servt
W. W. Holden

C. H. Wiley to Holden A&H:GP(Prov)

Greensboro N.C.
Septr 14th 1865

To His Excellency,
W. W. Holden

Dear Sir:

I feel it to be my duty to offer to you, & thro' you to the Convention which is soon to meet, a Statement (not an official report) of my general action in connection with our Common Schools, during the late civil war. Such a paper is herewith enclosed; & I send to the public Treasurer some suggestions in regard to a part of the resources of the Literary Fund.

I regret that I have been unable to see you before preparing my statement—for if I could do so without having my motives misconstrued by the world, I would risk the chances of a cold reception (on personal grounds, or at least on grounds not connected with the schools,) to indicate my sincere desire to aid the usefulness & promote the honor of your administration in reviving the cause of popular instruction. We have differed in opinions of political matters, at different times; but for a long period, dating back beyond the excitements of the present, I have daily prayed that your influence might be directed to the glory of God in the good of the State. I will not say more of my inner life than this, *to wit*, that thro' all the passional trials of past years, the names of certain men, of different parties, have invariably mingled with my private petitions to the Almighty Ruler. I say this not for my sake, for as far as your power is concerned, I am in your hands to do as you like; but I say it that the knowledge of the fact may have its influence in shaping your course as far as it concerns your own spiritual interests, & the welfare of a bleeding people. May I ask that my statement be presented to the Convention?

Very Respectfully,
& truly yours,
C. H. Wiley

Holden to Major General T. H. Ruger *Standard*
September 20, 1865

Executive Office
Raleigh, Sept. 14, 1865

To Major General T. H. Ruger, Commanding Department of North Carolina:

Sir:–I have appointed Judge Anderson Mitchell to hold courts of Oyer and Terminer in several of the Counties west of the Blue Ridge, and have given him the following directions with regard to his jurisdiction, a copy of which is forwarded to you for your information:

"You will not take jurisdiction of cases of wrongs committed by freedmen or free persons of color, or wrongs committed against them by white persons or freedmen or free persons of color. The laws of North Carolina do not admit the testimony of freedmen or free persons of color in cases wherein white persons are concerned; and the military authorities will not allow them to be tried in courts which do not admit their testimony. All such cases will therefore, be left to be tried by the military courts. Your jurisdiction will extend to all breaches of the criminal law of North-Carolina by white persons against white persons."

I would suggest that it might serve a good purpose for the protection of the freedmen and free persons of color, if this jurisdiction were extended to allow the Judge to arrest and have bound over to keep the peace *all* persons whether white or of color—to require bail when the case is bailable at common law, and where not, to lodge the offender in the County jail, subject to the orders of the military commanders of the district. Otherwise the persons of color will be and will feel themselves in a very helpless condition in those Counties out of the reach of the direct authority of the military.

Should you concur with me, I will send such directions as will extend the Judge's jurisdiction in this latter respect.

Very respectfully,
W. W. Holden
Provisional Governor

Thos. H. Ruger to Holden A&H:GP(Prov)

Headquarters Department of North Carolina
Raleigh, N.C., Sept 14, 1865

His Excellency,
W. W. Holden,

Sir.
I concur with you that the interests of the State would be promoted by the action of the Courts to be held west of the mountains, as stated in your letter of this date.

Such persons as would be bound over, and not of the class specified in your letter to be tried by the Civil Courts, would of course be subject to trial by military tribunals, as well as those committed for offenses not bailable.

Very respectfully,
Your obt. servt.
Thos. H. Ruger
Bvt. Maj Genl Vol.

R. C. Badger to Judge Anderson Mitchell A&H:GP(Prov)

Executive Department
Raleigh N.C. Sept. 14th 1865

To His Honor
Judge Anderson Mitchell[1]

Sir:
I enclosed a Special Commission to you to hold Courts of Oyer and Terminer in the Counties of Wilkes—4th Monday in September; Buncombe— 2d Monday in October; Henderson—3d Monday in October; Transylvania—4th Monday in

October; Madison—5th Monday in October; Cherokee—the 1st Monday in November; Clay—the 2d Monday in November.

Writs have been issued to the Sherriffs of the Various Counties notifying them of your appointment and ordering them to have proper juries summoned at the appointed days.

The Solicitors have been notified to attend the Courts. The Gov directs me to say to you that you will not take jurisdiction of cases of wrongs committed by freedmen *or* free persons of color or of wrongs committed against them by white persons or freedmen or freed persons of color. The laws of North Carolina do not admit the testimony of freedmen or freed persons of color in cases wherein white persons are concerned, and the Military Authorities will not allow them to be tried by courts that do not admit their testimony. All such cases will therefore to be left to be tried by the Military courts.

Your Jurisdiction will extend to all cases of breach of the criminal law of North Carolina by white persons against white persons.

I am Sir
Very respectfully
Your Obdt Svt
R. C. Badger[2]
Asst Sec

P.S. In all cases of breaches of the peace where freedmen or free persons of color are concerned, which may be reported in the Counties in which you hold courts, have the offenders arrested, and bailed or lodged in jail, according to the nature of the offense, and the security offered, to be tried by the military courts when they shall be held. Order the clerks to send statements of such cases to the commander of the military district in which the County lies.

Respectfully,
R. C. Badger

[1] Anderson Mitchell, lawyer and judge; A.B., U.N.C., 1821; A.M., 1824; member, House of Commons, 1827-1828, 1854-1856; member, state Senate, 1829, 1840, 1860; member, U.S. House of Representatives, 1842; member, secession convention, 1861, but voted against secession; appointed judge of superior court, 1866, serving until his death in 1876. *Dictionary of North Carolina Biography*, s.v. "Mitchell, Anderson"

[2] Richard Cogsdell Badger.

H. McCulloch to Holden A&H:GP(Prov)

Treasury Department
September 16, 1865

Sir:

In reply to your communication of the 2nd inst., in regard to raising a steam ram which lies sunk in the Neuse River, I have to state that the matter has been referred to Supervising Special Agent Heaton,[1] for such action as he may consider necessary and proper under the regulations of this Department concerning captured and abandoned property.

You will please confer with Mr. Heaton on the subject.

Very Respectfully,
H. McCulloch[2]
Secretary of the Treasury

Hon. W. W. Holden
Prov. Governor &c
Raleigh, N. C.

[1] David Heaton.

[2] Hugh McCulloch, manager, state bank of Indiana; 1863, comptroller of the currency; secretary of the treasury, 1865-1869. *Dictionary of American Biography*, s.v. "McCulloch, Hugh."

Holden to Revd. C. H. Wiley A&H:GP(Prov)

State of North Carolina
Executive Department
Raleigh, N.C. Sept. 18th 1865

Revd. C. H. Wiley.

Dear Sir.

Your communication has just been received, inclosing your statement or report, as Superintendent of Common Schools, for the use of the Convention.

It has been decided by the President and Cabinet, that all the officers of the late state government had lost their positions, on account of the Rebellion of the state. You stand on the same ground as Judges of the Courts, and all other state officers. Hence it is, that you are not the Superintendent of Common Schools, and can, as such, make no report to me or to the Convention. There can be no objection to the publication of the paper you inclose or any other you wish, in the newspapers. Your report or statement is here and you can make such disposition of it as you think best.

I am sorry that you think I would treat you coolly or discourteously. I am not in the habit of treating persons in this manner who call on me. I certainly have no unkind feelings towards you and I hope I am prepared to do you full justice on all occasion.

Very respectfully yours,
W. W. Holden

TELEGRAM *Holden to the President* A&H:GP(Prov)

State of North Carolina
Executive Department
Raleigh, Sept. 21st, 1865

To the President.

Sir.

I have decided that as persons who belong to the excluded classes cannot vote, so they cannot sit in the Convention unless they exhibit their pardon. Ex-Governor Graham[1] of Orange, in a letter published in the newspapers, holds that unpardoned persons can sit in the Convention. He declines being a candidate, but urges this view.

Am I right or wrong?

The letter addressed to Ex-Governor Graham, to which he replies taking this view, does not show a good spirit.

The election here is progressing quietly. A large vote will be polled in the State. I will telegraph you as the returns come in.

Very Respectfully,
W. W. Holden

[1] William Alexander Graham. The letter was originally published in the *Raleigh Sentinel*, September 21, 1865, and is reproduced in Hamilton, Williams, and Peacock,eds., *The Papers of William Alexander Graham*, 6:353-357.

TELEGRAM *Andrew Johnson to Holden* LC:Johnson

Sept. 21 1865

Gov W. W. Holden:—
Raleigh, N.C.

Your decision is correct that under the proclamation they cannot vote for members or sit in convention as members without first being pardoned on taking the Amnesty Oath. If the party comes within any of the exceptions they must obtain a pardon before voting or sitting as a member. All those who are aspirants to seats in the Convention and are elected will be pardoned on your recommendation and a submission of their names by telegraph.

Andrew Johnson
President US

Geo. G. Meade to Holden A&H:GLB(Prov)

Head-Quarters Military Division of the Atlantic,
Philadelphia, Pa. Sept. 22d, 1865.

To His Excellency
W. W. Holden
Prov. Governor
Raleigh, N.C.

Dear sir:

I have acknowledge the receipt of your letter of the 12th inst., I think the arrangement you report in reference to the jurisdiction of the military courts, is the best that, under existing circumstances, can be made. When ever the laws of the state and the practice of the courts are such as to leave no doubt the freedman will have justice done him there will be no occasion for the use of military courts, except for purely military offences.

I am glad to hear the favorable account you give of the condition of the State. You may rest assured you will receive every co-operation from Maj. Genl. Ruger[1] and the military under his command, in your efforts to preserve order and do justice to all parties.

Major General Ruger was instructed when I was in Raleigh, to promptly check and correct the disorderly spirit, which was showing itself in the western part of the State, and he reported he had already sent a cavalry regiment on this duty. I trust the good feeling existing between General Ruger and yourself will continue.

I hope you will impress on your people that the military are in the state for their security, and not for their oppression. It will take time, both for the land owners and laborers, to appreciate and realize the great change that has taken place in their relative positions. During this transition period, the presence of the Military power will serve as a check on both races, to prevent maltreatment and oppression of the one part, and to correct idleness, vagrancy and insubordination on the other. Whenever it is evident their presence for these purposes is unnecessary, you may rest assured they will be withdrawn. In the hopes this time is near at hand, and reciprocating most cordially your wish that your good state may soon be restored to her place in the Union.

I remain
With great Respect
Your Obt. Servt.
Geo G. Meade
Maj. Genl U.S.A.

[1] Thomas Howard Ruger.

TELEGRAM *Holden to the President* A&H:GLB(Prov)

State of North Carolina
Executive Department
Raleigh, Sept. 25th 1865

To the President of the United States

Sir:

Please include in the list of pardons of members elect to the Convention, A. A. McKay[1] of the County of Sampson. His application is filed, marked suspended. But he is now thoroughly sound.

I am sorry to state that Judge R. M. Pearson[2] has been defeated.

The returns generally are very satisfactory. Quite a large vote has been polled.[3] You would greatly oblige me by having all the pardons for this State made out and forwarded.

Very Respectfully
W. W. Holden, P. Gov.

[1] Allmand A. McKay, Sampson County; member, Council of State, 1856-1857; member, state Senate, 1858-1859; member, constitutional convention, 1865; superior court judge, 1874-1885. Cheney, *North Carolina Government*, 1585-1979, 179, 325, 833, 578.

[2] Richmond Mumford Pearson, jurist; A.B., U.N.C., 1823; member, House of Commons, 1829-1832; superior court judge, 1836-1848; associate justice and chief justice, 1849-1878.

Dictionary of North Carolina Biography, s.v. "Pearson, Richmond Mumford."

[3] On September 23, Holden had notified President Johnson of preliminary results of the election, which he called "very gratifying." He requested pardons for several persons who had been elected but not yet pardoned, and assured the president that "ultra Union" men would control the convention. Holden to the President, September 23, 1865, Archives and History: Governor's Papers (Provisional).

TELEGRAM *Holden to the President* LC:Johnson

Raleigh N.C. Oct 2d 1865

The President of the U.S.

Sir,

The convention has just organized by the election of Hon Edwin G. Reade of Person as President the attendance is quite full the best feeling prevails.

Very Resp'y
W. W. Holden

Holden to Dr. R. J. Powell LC:Johnson

State of North Carolina
Executive Department
Raleigh Oct. 5th 1865

My dear Sir

Your long and very interesting letter, in which you furnish an account of your conversation with members of the Cabinet, has been received.[1] Also, your last letter by the hands of Mr. Wooten.[2]

I wish the President to see this letter, or to hear it read. Please say to him that the exercise of the pardoning power has been of material benefit in encouraging this State. I trust that no general amnesty will be proclaimed until all the popular elections have been held in this State. Next to the real union men the most submissive among us are the well whipped original secessionists; and the most rebellious among us are the Vance Destructives. The reason is, the former commenced early and are thoroughly subdued; whereas the latter, the Vance war men, had not quite fought it out. To pardon such men as Vance,[3] Graham[4] and Turner[5] now, and those who agree with them, would be to open in this State bitter discussion and would strengthen the faction now being secretly organized against the administration. There is no harm in Gilmer[6], and none in Arrington[7]. The latter was active in securing the election of Mr. Baines,[8] the Union delegate from Nash and before I would promise to endorse him for pardon to the President I required him to pledge himself that he would make Nash a unit as far as he could for the administration. He has redeemed his pledge.

There are some six or seven hundred endorsed for pardon from this State. Nearly all of these are friends of ours. I wish the President could find time to sign their pardons. We may need their votes and influence in the coming elections. So far as to those who are suspended are concerned, I have done my duty, and I do not fear their opposition hereafter. Mr. Turner, I learn, has been in Washington denouncing me. His unionism consists in hatred of the old Democratic party. He supported Vance for Governor because he had been a Whig, though Vance was and is as bad as Davis, and is at heart at this time as rebellious as Davis is. Mr. Turner waited on me and demanded to know, before he went to Washington, how I had endorsed his petition. I declined to tell him. But I told him the so-called Union leaders of Orange county had held two meetings, in both of which they had declined to endorse President Johnson, because he had not pardoned Gov. Graham and that the clemency of the President would "be measured by the confidence reposed in him in his efforts to restore the Union."

I have conclusive proof that Mr. Hedrick [9] is constantly engaged in the various departments interfering with North Carolina appointments. A friend has shown me a letter from Hedrick in which he makes insulting allusions to me in connection with the Internal Revenue Districts. He falsely charges among other things, that the person recommended by me for some of the Districts are secessionists. He has poisoned the mind of Mr. Starbuck,[10] the new District Attorney, against me on the subject of the State debt; and he is writing all over the State stirring up discord. It would be a great relief to me if the President would direct the federal appointments for our State to be made through some other channel than myself. I am willing to serve him in every way I can, and I feel the deepest solicitude for him personally and officially; but I cannot do justice to him or myself when thus thwarted and embarrassed.

Ordinances have been reported in the convention abolishing slavery and declaring the federal Constitution as always of binding force, of right, in the State, and therefore the so-called Ordinance of secession null and void. I feel sure the Convention will do what is right and what is expected, though there are some malcontents in the body. The great bulk of the members, however, are ultra Union in their views. I have shown your letter to our leading reliable friends, and I find that your views are generally approved.

Very Truly Your friend
W. W. Holden

To Dr. R. J. Powell

[1] Not extant.

[2] Council Wooten, Lenoir County farmer. 1870 U.S. Census Population Schedule, North Carolina: Lenoir, 94.

[3] Zebulon Baird Vance.

[4] William Alexander Graham.

[5] Josiah Turner, Jr.

[6] John Adams Gilmer, lawyer; member, state Senate, 1846-1856; member, U.S. House of Representatives, 1857-1861; member, Confederate House of Representatives, 1864-1865. *Dictionary of North Carolina Biography*, s.v. "Gilmer, John Adams."

[7] Archibald Hunter Arrington.

[8] A. B. Baines, Nash County farmer and delegate to the 1865 constitutional convention. 1870 U.S. Census Population Schedule, North Carolina: Nash, 98; Cheney, *North Carolina Government, 1585-1979*, 832

[9] Benjamin Sherwood Hedrick, educator and antislavery leader; A. B., U.N.C., 1851; appointed to U.N.C. faculty in 1854; dismissed October, 1856, because of his antislavery views. *Dictionary of North Carolina biography*, s.v. "Hedrick, Benjamin Sherwood."

[10] Darius H. Starbuck, Forsyth County; member, secession convention, 1861; member, constitutional convention, 1865-1866. Cheney, *North Carolina Government, 1585-1979*, 386, 832.

TELEGRAM *Holden to the President* LC:Johnson

Raleigh Oct 5 1865

The President US

Sir

Josiah Turner Jr ought not to be pardoned at this time I have written to Dr Powell[1] on this & other matters & he will show you the letter a General amnesty at this time would operate injuriously in the state Hope to be able to telegraph some definite action by the convention tomorrow all right

Very Respy
W. W. Holden

[1] Robert James Powell.

TELEGRAM *Holden to the President* LC:Johnson

Raleigh Oct 6 1865

The President of the U States

Sir,

The convention has just passed the following by an unanimous vote. That the ordinance of the convention of the state of North Carolina ratified on the twenty-first day of November seventeen eighty nine which adopted & ratified the constitution of the united States & also all acts & parts of acts of the general assembly ratifying & adopting amendments to the said constitution are now & at all times since the adoption and ratification thereof have been in full force & effect notwithstanding the supposed ordinance of the twentieth of may eighteen sixty one declaring the same to be repealed rescinded & abrogated & the said supposed ordinance is now & at all times hath been null & void.

The Convention will dispose of the slavery question tomorrow

The State elections will be fixed on the first Thursday of November

Very Respectfully
W. W. Holden
Prov Gov

TELEGRAM *Holden to the President* LC:Johnson

Raleigh NC Oct 7 1865

The President of the U.S.

Sir

The Convention has just passed unanimously the following ordinance. That Slavery & involuntary servitude other wise than from crime whereof the party shall have been duly convicted, shall & is hereby forever prohibited within the state the convention will in all probability ignore the rebel state debt.

Very Respy.
W. W. Holden
Prov Gov

TELEGRAM *R. J. Powell to Holden* *Daily Sentinel*
October 10, 1865

Washington, Oct. 7th 1865

The President is very much gratified with the action of the Convention.[1] I write this in his office, and he tells me to say the Convention had done what is right, and that such action adds greatly to our strength here.

R. J. Powell

[1] The president referred to the action of the convention abrogating the May 21, 1861, secession ordinance and in recognizing the abolition of slavery. Holden reported the telegram to Edwin G. Reade, president of the convention, and the report, with the telegram, was printed only in the *Daily Sentinel.* The original telegram is not in the governor's papers, nor is it recorded in the governor's letter book; it is not in Holden's private papers in the Special Collections Library, Duke University, or in the North Carolina State Archives.

TELEGRAM *Holden to Prest of the U.S.* LC:Johnson

Raleigh Oct 7 1865

Prest of the U.S.

Sir

The Convention has passed an ordinance providing for the election of Governor Members of the legislature & seven Members of Congress on the ninth (9) of November the legislature to meet on the 19th November.

Very Respy
W. W. Holden
Prov Gov

Convention Delegates to Holden *Standard*
October 18, 1865

Raleigh, N.C. Oct. 14th. 1865.

Hon. W. W. Holden—

Sir: The undersigned members of the State Convention of North-Carolina, fully appreciating your earnest and effective efforts towards restoring our State to her constitutional relations with the Federal Government, and being desirous that restoration should be completed by one under whose guidance it has been so auspiciously begun, respectfully request that you will allow your name to be placed before the people of North-Carolina for the office of Governor, at the ensuing election.

Very respectfully yours[1]

[1] This petition was signed by fifty-one delegates to the convention.

TELEGRAM *Holden to the President* LC:Johnson

Raleigh, Oct 17, 1865.

His Ecy the President of the United States:

Sir Contrary to my expectations, the convention has involved itself in a bitter discussion of the State debt made in aid of the Rebellion. A continuance of this discussion will greatly excite the people and retard the work of reconstruction Our people are believed to be against assuming this debt by a large Majority. Is it not advisable that our convention, like that of Alabama should positively ignore this debt now and forever Please answer at once.

W. W. Holden
Prov Gov

Holden to Convention Delegates *Standard*
October 18, 1865

Raleigh, Oct. 17, 1865

Gentlemen: Your letter of the 14th instant., requesting me to be a candidate for Governor at the election to be held on the 9th of next month, has been received. I beg to assure you that I am very grateful for this proof of your esteem and confidence.

I did not seek the place I now occupy, nor have I sought a nomination for election by the people. I have been content to do my duty to the best of my ability under the instructions of the President, and to leave my conduct to be judged by an intelligent and indulgent people. I do not fear that judgment.

My duty has been, in many respects, new unusual, and very onerous. I had no lights to guide me in the work of reorganizing and reconstructing an American State, save the instructions received from time to time from the President; and necessarily, those instructions have been only of a general character. My paramount concern has been, so to do that part of the work assigned to me as to secure the restoration of the State to the Union at the earliest practicable period. To what extent I have succeeded in this respect it is for the people to say. I can only declare, as I most solomnly do, that I have labored with an eye single to the good and glory of North-Carolina; and that, whatever may be the decision of the people on the ninth of November, I shall always possess the consciousness that I am a faithful and devoted son of our dear old State, and that I have labored with zeal, and with what success my poor faculties could command, to improve the condition of her people, and to restore her to her appropriate and natural position in the Union.

Gentlemen, it is not agreeable to my feelings in a crisis like the present, when everything dear to us depends upon union and harmony among ourselves, to speak of parties. I deprecate faction and bitter party spirit as the bane of the Republic. The evils we are now suffering, with all the calamities that have befallen us, may be traced to this source.. As Provisional Governor of the State, in all I have said and done, I have known no party but the sincere friends of the Union. I am neither a Democrat nor a Whig. Both these parties were buried in the grave of the rebellion. All I can say is, I am a North Carolinian, heart and soul–"*I am an American*," the proudest expression that can issue from human lips; and while I hold with Andrew Jackson and Henry Clay, that the *people* are the source of all power in this country, and alone entitled to rule, I declare that the only party to which I belong is the *National Union party*, composed of the best elements of the old parties, of which Andrew Johnson is the head.

If elected Governor by the people, I will do every thing I can to promote the prosperity and the happiness of North Carolina, and to secure her return at the earliest possible moment to her place in the federal Union.

With many thanks, gentlemen, for the confidence you have reposed in me, and for the flattering manner in which you have been pleased to allude to me in your letter, I have the honor to be

Your most obedient servant,
W. W. Holden

TELEGRAM *Andrew Johnson to Holden* A&H:GP(Prov)

Washington, October 18, 1865

W. W. Holden, Pro. Gov

Every dollar of the debt created to aid the Rebellion against the United States should be repudiated finally and forever. The great mass of the people should not be taxed to pay a debt to aid in carrying on a rebellion which they in fact if left to themselves were opposed to. Let those who have given their means for the obligations of the State look to that power they tried to establish in violation of law Constitution, and the will of the people. They must meet their fate. It is their misfortune and cannot be recognized by the people of any State professing themselves loyal to the Government of the United States and in the Union. I repeat that the loyal people of North Carolina should be exonerated from the payment of every dollar of indebtedness created in aid in carrying on the rebellion.

I trust and hope that the people of North Carolina will wash their hands of everything that partakes in the slightest degree of the rebellion which has been so recently crushed by the strong arm of the Govt in carrying out the obligations imposed by the Constitution of the Union.

Andrew Johnson
President

Holden to Hon. Edwin G. Reade A&H:GLB(Prov)

State of North Carolina
Executive Department
Raleigh, Oct. 18th 1865

To the Hon Edwin G. Reade
President of the Convention

Sir:

I have just received the following telegraphic dispatch from the President of the United States, and respectfully request that you will lay it before the Convention. I have the honor to be with high respect your obedient servt.

W. W. Holden
Pro. Gov.

Jonathan Worth to Holden A&H:Worth

Raleigh, Oct. 18th 1865

Govr Holden

Dear Sir

I decided two days ago to allow my friends to run my name as a Candidate for civil Governor of the State. As you are a Candidate for the same position, and I hold the office of Public Treasurer under your appointment, it occurs to me as possible that it may not be agreeable to you for me to continue in my present position. I therefore tender to you my resignation to take effect whenever you shall appoint my successor, assuring you however that in the mean time I will diligently attend to all the duties of the office.[1] I do not propose to make any canvass or otherwise withdraw my attention from my responsible official duties. I am determined that on my part nothing shall be done which shall furnish any just cause for any personal estrangement between us: and I am willing, if it be done, so long as it may be agreeable with you.

I desire that the personal rivalry between us for a highly honorable position, may be generous, furnishing no just occasion for marring the friendly, personal and official relations which have hitherto existed between us.

Jonathan Worth

[1] Governor Holden did not accept Worth's resignation as public treasurer until later.

TELEGRAM *Holden to the President* LC:Johnson

Raleigh Oct 20, 1865

The President US

Sir: The convention has adjourned It has promptly repudiated every dollar of the rebel debt & bound all future legislatures not to pay any of it. Your telegram had a most happy effect. The Worth faction is working hard but will be defeated by a large majority. Turner[1] and other Contumacious leaders ought to be handled at the proper time. Please pardon no leading man unless you hear from me.

Very Respy
W. W. Holden

[1] Josiah Turner, Jr.

TELEGRAM *Holden to the President* LC:Johnson

Raleigh, N.C., Nov. 4th, 1865

The Pres't of the United States

Sir.

Dr Powell[1] telegraphs me you were kind enough to authorize him to frame a telegram from you in relation to the election in this state if such a telegram should be published. I prefer it directly from you. I am morally certain of my election but I cannot tell what will happen all the rebel debt interest of the state is against me. the money power is making a last desperate effort to commit the state to the treason of assuming the state rebel debt after the state gets back a powerful effort is making to rally the old whig party against me and this is succeeding to some extent. Traitors & malcontents have grown bold & insolent because the hand of power has not been placed upon them. If I am beaten a powerful party will at once exist against your administration and what is also to be deplored confiscations arrests &

imprisonments would necessarily follow. Vance[2] & Davis[3] & Graham[4] would be the big men of those in power here. few lines from you would place it beyond all doubt but dont send them if you think it in any respect improper. I would as soon the triumph should be considered Andrew Johnsons as my own if Mr. Badger[5] has arrived he has a letter from me to you giving a detailed account of affairs in this state.

Very Respy.
W. W. Holden

[1] Robert James Powell.
[2] Zebulon Baird Vance.
[3] Jefferson Davis.
[4] William Alexander Graham.
[5] Richard Cogsdell Badger.

TELEGRAM *Andrew Johnson to Holden* LC:Johnson

Washington Nov 5th 1865

W. W. Holden
Provisional Governor
Raleigh
North Carolina

Your dispatch has been received. I thank you most sincerely for the deep interest you take and manifest in the administration of the Government. From your dispatch, and information derived from other sources I feel well assured that your election is certain. It is doubtful whether further interference would be sound policy. I hope all will come out right.

Andrew Johnson
President US

TELEGRAM *Holden to the President* LC:Johnson

Raleigh NC Nov 6 1865

The President US

Sir

Your dispatch received. Your are right. Friends were alarmed & I yielded to their importunities but reserved to myself the determination to publish or not I am more than ever convinced of my election by a large Majority. Will write you at length after election. Have you seen Mr Badger[1] He can give you valuable information

Very Respy
W. W. Holden
Gov

[1] Richard Cogsdell Badger.

E. G. Reade to Holden *Standard*
November 28, 1865

Washington City, Nov. 11th, 1865

His Excellency, W. W. Holden,
Provisional Governor of North Carolina:

On the 10th instant I had an interview with His Excellency, the President, for the purpose of presenting to him such of the proceedings of our State Convention as the Convention directed me to present to him. I addressed him as follows:

Mr. President:–In behalf of the Convention of North Carolina, lately in session, over which I had the honor to preside, I present for your favorable consideration certain of its proceedings.

In the late war there were two issues:

First, the existence of the Union and second, the existence of slavery. The result was favorable to the Union; and adverse to slavery.

North-Carolina submits not in degradation, but in the moral gradeur of resignation to rightful authority.

The first thing done by the Convention was to declare her uninterrupted connection with the Union; and that the ordinance of May, 1861, by which she was attempted to be severed, was null and void. This was done by a vote very nearly approaching unanimity—and thus the first issue was yielded.

The next thing done was to prohibit slavery; and this was done by a unanimous vote. And a committee of able lawyers was provided to prepare wholesome laws for the consideration of the Legislature, and thus the second issue was yielded.

The excellent temper and disposition of our people induced the Convention to ask your Excellency for a universal pardon for them. This was done, not in any spirit of complaint, for we concede that the action of your Excellency, has been prudent, and was designed to be magnanimous and conciliating; but our people are so well affected to the Government and are so little sensible of any sentiment of alienation, that they feel some mortification at being kept in a condition, implying that they are not—what they so well know themselves to be—entirely reconciled to the Union.

The Convention having yielded what was involved in the war and being of the opinion that the State was, and always had been in the Union, and that our relations had only been disturbed and not destroyed, respectfully asks your Excellency to declare on the part of the authorities of the United States, as the State has done on her part, that our governmental relations have been reconciled.

Not only are our people well disposed towards the United States, but their appreciation of the administration of the Government by your Excellency has been so marked and universal, that the Convention thought it due to their constituency, and eminently due to your Excellency to vote a resolution of thanks for the ability and impartiality with which you have discharged your duties to every portion of the country.

We have heard that notwithstanding the State might yield, and, as she understands it, has yielded all that was involved in the war; and notwithstanding our people are submissive well disposed and anxious for fraternal relations, her delegates to Congress would not be admitted unless they had qualifications not prescribed by the Constitution, that they would be required to take an oath, which few men in the State can take, affirming not merely that they are right now, but that they have never been wrong. The exclusion of her delegates upon any such test as is suggested would be felt by our people universally as such a deep wrong that it would put their strong devotion to the Government and their lively hope of perfect reconstruction to the severest trial. They can understand the bitterness of strife and the aversion to treason. But they will be confounded at the repulsion of offered friendship and aroused loyality. The Convention therefore respectfully asks Congress to repeal the "Test Oath." I have thought it respectful both to you and to Congress—that this request of the Convention should pass through your hands with the hope that your Excellency's magnanimity would add to it some reflection which would avail with that body.

The Convention instructed the Legislature to provide for the payment of the debts of the State, and declared all debts contracted in aid of the rebellion to be illegal and prohibited the payment of the same.

So what has been done by the Convention I can add nothing of my own except to assure your Excellency that my own sentiments are in accordance with the best deeds of the convention, and with the best sentiments of our people.

I have the honor to lay before your Excellency a copy of our Constitution, with the amendment, and the ordinances of the Convention.

The President replied as follows:

"Hon. Mr. Reade:—I received from you with pleasure, a copy of the proceedings of the Convention of North-Carolina. I reciprocate cordially the conciliatory spirit in which you have addressed me.

The Convention of North-Carolina has done much and well toward restoring the State to her proper natural relations, but something yet remains to be done to render her restoration immediately practicable. An acceptation of the

Constitutional amendment abolishing slavery throughout the United States by the Legislature of North-Carolina, is in my judgment practically important to the successful restoration which is so much desired by all.

Without answering specifically the questions you have proposed to me, it will be sufficient to say that my action must depend upon events, and that Mr. Holden will be again instructed to continue the exercise of his functions as Provisional Governor until he shall have been expressly relieved by orders to that effect."

The President was frank and cordial, as was also Mr. Seward,[1] who was present.

My mission was limited to the business indicated and I had no further interview.

I am sir, very truly,
Your obedient servant,
E. G. Reade[2]

[1] William Henry Seward.
[2] Edwin Godwin Reade, chairman of the 1865 convention.

TELEGRAM *Wm. H. Seward to Holden* *Standard* November 13, 1865

Washington, Nov. 11th, 1865

His Excellency, W. W. Holden:–The President directs me to say that he expects you to continue in the exercise of the functions of Provisional Governor of North Carolina until you shall have been relieved by directions from him.

Wm. H. Seward.

Jos. S. Cannon to the President LC:Johnson

State of North-Carolina
Executive Department
Novr. 13, 1865

His Excellency
The President, United States

Sir.

Governor Holden is confined to his bed from illness, and directs me to write you a few lines.

Only thirty three counties have been heard from, the returns of which leave the election of Governor uncertain. Governor Holden does not dispair of his election.

Hon. William A. Graham has beeen elected to the State Senate from Orange County. Josiah Turner is elected to Congress from this district, and Rufus Y. McAden[1] to the House of Commons from Alamance County.

They are unpardoned and have been recommended for Suspension by the Governor.

It is believed they will soon apply in person to Your Excellency for Pardon.

Governor Graham is the originator and leader of all the disaffection in North Carolina. His great desire is to unite enough of the old whigs to the Secessionists, the advocates of the payment of the Rebel Debt, and disaffected men, to break down the National Union Party. His opposition to you is as strong as it is to Governor Holden. Jonathan Worth, Josiah Turner and Rufus Y. McAden were put forward at his instance, against the repeated remonstrances of all the leading union men in this State.

Josiah Turner convassed the district greatly exciting and increasing the disaffection. The body of his speeches consisted of ridicule and slander of the democratic party. He declared "he would not vote for you to save your life." McAden has done all he could for the same purpose.

The Union men of the State believe that if your Excellency will refuse to Pardon these men, disaffection will be struck a death blow in North Carolina, and will not again be able to rise. The Governor greatly desires that these men may not be Pardoned, but may receive a merited rebuke at the hands of Your Excellency.

I am Most Respectfully
Your Obdt. Servt.
Jos. S. Cannon
Aid de Camp

[1] Rufus Yancey McAden, Caswell County; legislator and financier; A.B., Wake Forest College, 1853; member, House of Commons, 1861-1867; speaker, 1866; president, First National Bank, Charlotte; president, Spartanburg and Asheville Railroad. *Dictionary of North Carolina Biography*, s.v. "McAden, Rufus Yancey."

William A. Graham to Holden SHC:Graham

Hillsboro', November 14th., 1865,

His Excell. W. W. Holden
Provisal. Govr. &c

Sir

Having been elected a senator from the district of Orange in the ensuing General Assembly of N. C., I have the honor herewith to enclose a copy of the Sheriff's certificate of the fact, and respectfully to request, that the information may be communicated to the President of the United States, to the end that his determination in regard to my Petition for pardon under his Proclamation of the 29th. of May last, may be obtained, as early as his convenience may allow.

Very Respectfully,
Your Obed't Serv't,
William A. Graham

Jos. S. Cannon to Jonathan Worth A&H:GP(Prov)

State of North Carolina
Executive Department
Raleigh, Nov. 15th, 1865

Jonathan Worth Esqr.
Public Treasurer and Property Agent of North Carolina

Sir.

I am directed by the Governor to inform you that your resignation is accepted, to take effect from today and to request you to turn over the records and effects of the office to Dr William Sloan[1] your successor.

I am very respectfully
Your Obdt Servt
Jos S. Cannon
Aid de Camp

[1] William Sloan, state treasurer, November 16, 1865, to January 1, 1866; delegate 1865 convention; later president of the Wilmington, Charlotte and Rutherfordton Railroad. Harlan E. Boyles, *Keeper of the Public Purse* (Boone: Appalachian State University, c. 1994), 47.

William H. Seward to Holden A&H:GP(Prov)

Department of State,
Washington Nov 18th, 1865

To His Excellency
The Governor of North Carolina,
Raleigh, N.C.

Sir.

Congress in February last, by the requisite vote of two-thirds of both houses, passed a resolution, proposing an amendment to the Constitution of the United States, which declares that neither slavery nor involuntary servitude, except as a punishment for crime, whereof the party shall have been duly convicted, shall exist within the United States, or any place subject to their jurisdiction, and that Congress shall have power to enforce this article by appropriate legislation. A certified copy of this resolution was promptly transmitted by mail to each of the Governors of all the States. When the proposed amendment shall have been adopted by being ratified by the legislatures of three fourths of the States, the law makes it the duty of the Secretary of State, after official notice thereof has been received at the Department of State, forthwith to cause the said amendment to be published in the newspapers authorized to promulgate the laws, with his certificate, specifying the States by which the same may have been adopted, and that the same has become valid, to all intents and purposes, as a part of the Constitution of the United States.

Up to the present time, official notice of the ratification of said amendment by the Legislatures of eighteen States has been received; but there is reason to believe that the Legislatures of other States have ratified the said amendment. It is also supposed to be probable, that the Legislatures of still other States will shortly ratify it. In that case and upon receiving the proper notices, it will become necessary for this Department to fulfill the duty of publication and certification, already referred to.

With a view, therefore, of being prepared for the prompt performance of the important duty thus enjoined by law, I have to request that Your Excellency will be pleased to give to this Department, as soon as convenient, the official notice contemplated, whenever the Legislature of the State of North Carolina shall have duly ratified the amendment in question.[1]

I have the honor to be
Your Excellency's
Most Obedient Servant,
William H. Seward

[1] North Carolina ratified the Thirteenth Amendment on December 4, 1865. Cheney, *North Carolina Government, 1585-1979*, 783.

Wil. H. Seward to Holden *Standard*
November 27, 1865

Department of State,
Washington, November 21, 1865

To His Excellency
W. W. Holden, Provisional Governor of State of North Carolina, Raleigh

The President sincerely trusts that North-Carolina will, by her legislature, promptly accept the Congressional amendment of the Constitution of the United States abolishing slavery.

He relies upon you to exercise all your functions as heretofore, with the same wisdom and in the same spirit of loyality and devotion to the Union that have marked your administration hitherto.

The President desires you to feel entirely assured that your efforts to sustain the administration of the government and give effect to its policy are fully appreciated, and that they will, in no case, be forgotten.

I have the honor to be,
Your Excellency's
Obedient Servant,
Wil. H. Seward

TELEGRAM *R. J. Powell to A Johnson, President* LC:Johnson

Raleigh, N.C.
Novr 26. 1865

His Excy
A Johnson
President of U.S.

Dear Sir!

Since my arrival here, I find the rebelous element aided by the aristrocracy much stronger and more bitter than I had supposed before I left Washington and they seem to have full power in their hands—Govr Holden is improving but is still confined to his bed, all profess a desire to carry out your wishes, yet Graham,[1] Vance[2] and other leaders are industriously deceiving the masses as to your views.

Our leading friends are of opinion that is of the greatest importance that your wishes be made known in such manner that they can't be misunderstood by any one. I think that if you can send or telegraph something as follows it will do great good.

"The results of the recent elections in N. Carolina have greatly damaged the prospects of the state in the restoration of it Governmental relations. Should the action and the spirit of the Legislature be in the same direction, it will greatly increase the mischief already done and might be fatal. It is hoped the action and spirit manifested by the Legislature will be so directed as rather to repair than to increase the difficulties under which the state has already placed itself."[3]

Our friends are very confident that such a message from you would do great good, hence I have taken the liberty to suggest it. Please let me hear from you immediately.

Truly yours
R. J. Powell

[1] William Alexander Graham.
[2] Zebulon Baird Vance.
[3] See telegram from President Johnson to Governor Holden, November 27, 1865, in this volume.

TELEGRAM Andrew Johnson to Holden LC:Johnson

Washington Nov 27th 1865

W W Holden
Provisional Governor
Raleigh
North Carolina

Accept my thanks for the noble and efficient manner in which you have discharged your duty as Provisional Governor. You will be sustained by the Government.

The results of the recent elections in North Carolina have greatly damaged the prospects of the State in the restoration of its Governmental relations. Should the action and the spirit of the Legislature be in the same direction, it will greatly increase the mischief already done and might be fatal. It is hoped that action and spirit manifested by the Legislature will be so directed as rather to repair than to increase the difficulties under which the State has already placed itself.

signed Andrew Johnson
Pres't U.S.

TELEGRAM *Holden To The President* LC:Johnson

Executive Department
Raleigh
Nov. 27, 1865

The President of the United States

Sir:

Your dispatch has been received I am very grateful to you for this additional proof of your confidence and friendship My health has much improved hope to be able in a few days to attend actively to my duties I trust your dispatch will have a good effect upon the Legislature but the indications thus far are not satisfactory—

There is a tie in the Senate between Settle[1] Unionist and Ferebee[2] secessionist for the speakership—tomorrow or next day will decide. Mr. Phillips[3] elected

Speaker of Commons, not satisfactory to the Unionists two of the clerks of the Commons Secessionists McAden[4] of Alamance unpardoned rebel has taken his seat and votes.

I will oust him by force if necessary as soon as the Houses are organized. Gov. Graham[5] presented his credentials to the Senate but did not claim his seat. He requested me to inform you that he had been elected to the senate from the County of Orange & he desires to know your determination in regard to his pardon. I do this as a matter of form. I do not advise his pardon.

He ought not to be pardoned at this time. He is the head and front of the present opposition to the administration & his friends are retarding the work of reconstruction. The Worth[6] or Graham faction are said to be alarmed and may offer a compromise–but on the other hand it is the current talk that Graham & Vance[7] are to be the senators.

Rest assured, Sir, I will do all in my power to prevent bad men from running out poor old State.

Very Respectfully,
W W Holden
Prov Gov

[1] Thomas Settle, Jr.

[2] Dennis Dozier Ferebee, Camden County; A.B., U.N.C., 1839; member, House of Commons, 1846-1849, 1856-1861; member, state Senate, 1865-1866; commander, Fifty-ninth Regiment North Carolina troops; member 1865 convention. *Dictionary of North Carolina Biography*, s.v. "Ferebee, Dennis Dozier."

[3] Samuel Field Phillips.

[4] Rufus Yancey McAden.

[5] William Alexander Graham.

[6] Jonathan Worth.

[7] Zebulon Baird Vance.

Governor's Message A&H:GP(Prov)

Executive Department, N.C.,
Raleigh, November 30, 1865

Gentlemen of the Senate and of the House of commons.

I regret that a severe and painful illness, from which I am still suffering, has prevented me from preparing for your consideration a more full and detailed statement of the condition of public affairs, and of the progress which has been made in restoring North-Carolina to her natural position as a member of the Union, under the Federal Constitution. I am gratified to state, however, that my health is improving, and I hope soon to be in a condition to impart to you at length any information in my possession in relation to public affairs which you may desire.

The progress thus far made in the work of restoration has been attended by a great labor; and I have been very anxious to discharge my duties as Provisional Governor, under the instructions of the President, in such a way as to promote the best interests of the State, and to ensure a restoration of our Constitutional relations to the Federal Government at the earliest practicable period.

We can entertain no hope that confidence and activity in business will be revived, or that our people can even begin to renew their former prosperity until the State shall have been fully restored to her place in the Union. The greatest good of the present and of all coming generations, will be embodied in the practical fact that we are once more a part of the freest, proudest and most prosperous government in the world. As long as this fact is unrealized, the State must necessarily languish in all its interests, and springing forward in competition with other States in the career of wealth and prosperity, she will become more and more impoverished.

Let us, then, omit nothing which may be deemed necessary, or even expedient, to attain the great end we have in view, to wit, the complete restoration of the State to all its Constitutional relations to the common government. Let the divisions and differences which exist among us, and which are calculated to obstruct the work of restoration, disappear under the influence of a more intense and a more devoted patriotism. He who does any thing now, whether by word or act, calculated or intended to embarrass the national administration, or to obstruct the work of restoration, incurs a grave responsibility, and can be no friend either to the Federal Union or the North-Carolina.

The Convention of the people of this State, recently in seesion, very wisely ordained,

1st, That the so-called ordinance of secession, adopted the 20th day of May, 1861, "is now, and at all times hath been, null and void," and that "the ordinance of the Convention of the State of North Carolina, ratified on the 21st day of Novbomber, 1789, which adopted and ratified the Constitution of the United States, and also all acts and parts of acts of the General Assembly, ratifying and adopting amendments to the said Constitution, are now, and at all times since the adoption and ratification thereof, have been in full force and effect."

2d. That "slavery and involuntary servitude, otherwise than for crimes, whereof the party shall have been duly convicted, shall be, and is hereby forever prohibited within the State."

3d. That it shall be the duty of the General Assembly to provide for the payment of all debts and obligations created or incurred by the State, otherwise than in aid of the late rebellion. But that "all debts and obligations created or incurred by the

State, in aid of the late rebellion, directly or indirectly, are void, and no General Assembly of this State shall have power to assume or provide for the payment of the same, or any portion thereof."

These are safe and proper steps in the right direction, and such as were expected of the representatives of a loyal people.

But, in order to remove the last obstacle in the way of restoration, it is indispensable that the Legislature shall ratify the amendment to the Constitution of the United States prohibiting the existence of slavery throughout the United States. I herewith transmit to you a communication on this subject, from Hon. William H. Seward, Secretary of State, and also a certified copy of the joint resolution which has passed Congress on the subject, approved February, 1st, 1865.

I beg leave, gentlemen, most respectfully and earnestly to urge on you the propriety of ratifying this amendment unanimously, at the earliest practicable moment. It is the wish of our best friend, the President of the United States, that this shall be done. Such ratification cannot fail to hasten our restoration to the Union, and thus lay anew for us and our children the foundations of permanent prosperity and glory.

Under the provisions of an Ordinance passed by the Convention at its late session, I have appointed the Hon. B. F. Moore, the Hon. Richard S. Donnell,[1] and William S. Mason, Esquire, Commissioners to prepare and report to the Legislature a system of laws upon the subject of freedmen, and to designate such laws and parts of laws, now in force, as should be repealed, in order to conform the statutes of the State to the ordinance of the Convention abolishing the institution of slavery.

In conclusion, permit me to assure you, gentlemen, of my readiness and anxiety to co-operate with you cordially and zealously in every thing which may be calculated to relieve our unfortunate and beloved State from her present depressed and unhappy condition.

With sentiments of high respect, I have the honor to be, &c.,

W. W. Holden, *Provisional Governor*

[1] Richard Spaight Donnell, lawyer; A.B., U.N.C., 1839; member, U.S. House of Representatives, 1847-1849; member, House of Commons, 1860-1864; speaker, 1864; member, conventions of 1861 and 1865. Grant, *Alumni History*, 167.

TELEGRAM *Holden to the President* LC:Johnson

Raleigh Dec 1st 1865

President of U.S.

Sir

The legislature has ratified with but six dissenting votes the congressional amendment abolishing Slavery. five Judges have been elected all good selections. Those of my provisional appointments have been confirmed. Your dispatch has had a good effect but I cannot predict the result as to the senatorships. Senators will be elected on Monday it is believed that Gov Graham[1] will be elected. There appears to be a clear anti-administration or secession majority on Joint ballot. I have not changed my opinion in regard to Gov Graham. He is more subdued however & may take occasion in a day or two to define his position. There are all kinds of combinations here but I still hope for the best.

Very Resp'y
W W Holden
Prov. Gov.

[1] William Alexander Graham.

TELEGRAM *R. J. Powell to the President* LC:Johnson

Raleigh Dec. 1, 1865

The Prest

It affords me great pleasure to inform you that the constitutional amendment was ratified by the House of Commons with but four dissenting voices and by the Senate with but two. This good result is greatly due to your timely Telegram. The struggle for the Senatorship has commenced and it may become necessary to again trouble you in settling the matter

Very Truly Yours
R. J. Powell

TELEGRAM *Holden to the President* LC:Johnson

Raleigh Dec. 4, 1865

The Prest of U S

Sir

William A. Graham has just been elected Senator by the following vote. Graham one hundred Thirty Eight Boyden[1] Seven (7) Dick[2] Six (6) Brown[3] one (1).

Another ballot was had when John Pool of Bertie lacked one vote of an election. Adjourned for the day. Mr Pool would be in all respects acceptable.

If I were a northern member of Congress I doubt whether I would consent to sit with any ex member of the So-Called Confederate Congress. A proposition is pending in the Senate that Thos L Clingman is entitled to the two year term.[4] Of course this will be voted down but it shows the feeling by which some of the members are actuated

Very Resp'y.
W W Holden

[1] Nathaniel Boyden, lawyer and jurist; member, House of Commons, 1838-1842; member, U.S. House of Representatives, 1847-1849, 1868-1869; member, state Senate, 1844-1845; associate justice, North Carolina Supreme Court, 1871-1873. *Dictionary of North Carolina Biography*, s.v. "Boyden, Nathaniel."

[2] Robert Paine Dick.

[3] Bedford Brown.

[4] Thomas L. Clingman was elected to the U.S. Senate in 1860, but withdrew March 28, 1861 subsequently serving as a colonel in the Twenty-fifth Regiment North Carolina Troops. At this time, there were approximately two years remaining of his uncompleted term as a U.S. senator. Cheney, *North Carolina Government, 1585-1979*, 746.

Holden to Andrew Johnson LC:Johnson

State of North-Carolina
Executive Department
Raleigh, N.C, Dec. 6, 1865

Hon. Andrew Johnson, President U. States.

My dear Sir: I received your Message on Tuesday night about ten o'clock, and you may be sure I read it with interest and avidity. As long as I have been in public life I do not remember to have seen any document which I so entirely approve as

I do this; and I venture the assertion that it will command the hearty assent of a vast majority of the American people. The theory of the government, as maintained by the Fathers, and as settled for all time by the result of the late rebellion, is stated with clearness and accuracy. Your plan of restoration, which was the only feasible one under the circumstances, is explained, vindicated and commended to the Congress; yet after all, it is left to that body to say whether the States shall be restored and the work completed by the admission of the members from the insurgent states. The representatives of the insurgent states, having broken away from the Congress to engage in the rebellion, the question is how representatives from these states can again obtain seats, and this is a matter for the Congress itself. You have done your duty in so re-establishing the machinery of self-government in these States in order to render them presentable through their representatives to the common Congress. Whether they shall be admitted or excluded, and the work of restoration commenced *de novo*, your skirts are clear. In a spirit of patriotism, and out of intense love of the Union, you have ventured a great deal; and I regret that in some instances your liberality and self-sacrificing disposition have not been responded to as they should have been.

Allow me also to congratulate you on your foreign policy. We cannot afford to engage in war now, except in a clear case of insult to the national honor. we need at least ten years of profound peace. Believe me, Sir, a foreign war would develop elements in these Southern States little thought of by the superficial observer, and which might seriously embarrass and cloud the national arms.

But I need not dwell on special points in the Message. I repeat, it is what I for the most part expected, and cannot fail to strengthen your hold on the confidence and affection of your countrymen.

Dr. Powell[1] will communicate to you much information in relation to the condition of things in this State; but there are some points to which I wish to call your attention.

The late election in this State was shaped by secession votes and the rebel debt. More than half of those who voted for Mr. Worth[2] are original secessionists and Vance[3] men. Still more or less unsubdued, and who are disposed to return to the Union only under their chosen leaders. Mr. Worth himself was in favor of continuing the rebel State government, and he fled with Vance on the approach of Gen. Sherman.[4] Up to a period somewhat subsequent to the committal of Gov. Graham[5] and other former Union leaders to the Davis policy of "fighting it out," Mr. Worth had been a devoted Union man. I appointed him provisional Treasurer in the liberal spirit which characterized your policy, in the hope that I might therby obliterate lines of difference and make out people at unit. Still I do not think that he would have been a candidate but for the influence of Ex-Governors Vance and Graham. Indeed, it is known that he had agreed to disentangle himself from the secessionists and retire, but another letter from Gov. Graham determined him to be a candidate. These are the facts of which I am well convinced.

I regret to say that there is much of a rebellious spirit still in this State. In this respect I admit I have been deceived. In May and June last these rebellious spirits would not have dared to show their head even for the office of constable; but leniency has emboldened them, and the copperhead now shows his fangs. If these men had supreme power in this State the condition of the real Union men and of the freedmen would be exceedingly disagreeable. They vaunt themselves on their devotion to the Confederacy; they make that a test of fidelity, declaring that as they were true to Davis, so they will be to you. Yet every word that wounds true hearts, and every measure calculated to obstruct the work of restoration, proceeds for them. And strange to say, the true Union men were so oppressed under Confederate rule, and so cowed by the charge incessantly made that they were traitors, that they seem not to have entirely recovered their manhood, and hence it is that these malcontents are not denounced and exposed as they should be.

I communicate these convictions with regret. It may be that the policy of the government has been too lenient; or it may be that I have seriously erred in the discharge of duty, or that I was not the proper person for Provisional Governor. You may recollect that when in Washington I sought an interview with you at your private resident. My purpose then was to ask you to appoint some one else to this position, but I perceived that you were pressed for time, as the moment for the review of troops had arrived, and I told you, in reply to a question, that I had nothing more to say. My friends subsequently urged me in the most earnest terms not to decline the appointment, and I did not, therefore, mention to you what I intended to say on the morning I made the visit referred to. I am ready and willing at any moment to retire from this position; and if you have the shadow of wish that I should do so, I pray you as a friend to let me know it. My chief wish is to be of benefit to my afflicted State, and to see your administration successful.

The election of Mr. Pool[6] to the Senate is highly gratifying to the true Union men of the State. His record is as good as it was possible it could be under the circumstances. He is a gentleman of very high character and marked ability; and he had the cordial confidences of our friends in all parts of the State. In this connection it may not be improper for me to say that I was offered a Senatorship "by authority" with Ex-Governor Graham, but I emphatically declared that I felt I owed it to you to remain where I am, and that in no event could I accept it.

If this Provisional Government is to be continued it will be indispensible that the Courts of the State shall be put in full operation. Thefts, robberies, and murders are increasing, and the strong arms of law is indispensible to preserve life and property. Please give me instructions on this subject. I will have sufficient means to support a Provisional Government, and to put the entire machinery in full operation. A Supreme Court will be necessary as a Court of Appeals, and the Court elected by the Legislature might be appointed a Provisional Court. I am glad to be able to inform you that nearly all my Provisional appointments have been confirmed by the Legislature.

I have thus taxed your patience at much length, but my situation and the importance of the subjects must be my apology. Our friend Dr. Powell who has borne himself here with much discretion, and who has made friends by his visit, can give you all the details.

Very Respectfully Yours,
W. W. Holden

[1] Robert James Powell.
[2] Jonathan Worth.
[3] Zebulon Baird Vance.
[4] William Tecumseh Sherman.
[5] William Alexander Graham.
[6] John Pool, U.S. senator; A.B., U.N.C., 1847; member, state Senate, 1856-1860, 1864-1865; unsuccessful candidate for governor, 1860; opposed secession; participated in peace movement; elected to U. S. Senate, 1865, but denied seat; member, U.S. Senate, 1869-1873. *Dictionary of North Carolina Biography*, s.v. "Pool, John."

Holden to the President A&H:GP(Prov)

State of North-Carolina
Executive Department
Raleigh, N.C. Dec 9th, 1865

To the President of the U.S.

Sir: Both houses of the General assembly have recinded their Joint agreement to administer the oaths of office to Mr. Worth.[1] The votes will only be counted and he will be declared Governor at the close of the Provisional Government.

Very respy
W. W. Holden
Prov. Gov.

[1] Jonathan Worth.

Proclamation A&H:GP(Prov)

By W. W. Holden, Provisional Governor of North Carolina

Whereas it has been represented to me that there is an urgent necessity in many of the counties of this State that funds should be raised by taxation for the support of the poor, now therefore I, W. W. Holden, Provisional Governor of the State of North Carolina by virtue of the power vested in me, do hereby proclaim and declare

That a majority of the Provisional Justices of the Peace in any county in this State are hereby empowered and authorized to impose such a tax as in their judgment may be indispensable to the support of the poor; said tax to be levied, collected, accounted for, and used in accordance with the provisions of Chapter 28 and 86 Revised Code of North Carolina.

Provisional officers whose duty it is to execute the order of the Provisional Justices of the Peace are hereby commanded to be prompt in the performance of their duty under this proclamation.

Done at our City of Raleigh on the 9th day of December, one thousand Eight hundred and sixty-five and in the year of the Independence of the United States, the 90th.

W. W. Holden,
Prov. Gov.

By the Gov.
W. R. Richardson
Priv. Secy.

William H. Seward to Holden A&H:GP(Prov)

Department of State
Washington, 23d Dec 1865

To His Excellency
W W Holden
Provisional Governor of the State of North Carolina

Sir:

The time has arrived when in the judgment of the President of the United States, the care and conduct of the proper affairs of the state of North Carolina may be remitted to the constitutional authorities chosen by the people thereof, without danger to the peace and safety of the United states. By direction of the President, therefore, you are relieved from the trust which was heretofore reposed in you as Provisional Governor of the state of North Carolina.

Whenever the Governor elect shall have accepted and become qualified to discharge the duties of the Executive Office you will transfer the papers and property of the state now in your custody to His Excellency the Governor elect.

It gives me especial pleasure to convey to you the President's acknowledgment of the fidelity, the loyalty and the discretion which have marked your administration

You will please give me a reply specifying the day on which this communication is received

I have the honor to be
Your Excellency's
most obedient servant,
William H. Seward

Holden to William H. Seward *Standard*
December 28, 1865

Executive Office
Raleigh, Dec. 23, 1865

To Hon. William H. Seward, Secretary of State, Washington:

Sir: Your dispatch of this date, relieving me of my duties as Provisional Governor of North Carolina, has been received.

It gives me pleasure to be relieved of the responsibilities and labors of the office. I will at once transfer the Great Seal, the papers, and property of the State, now in my possession, to the Hon. Jonathan Worth, Governor elect.

Be pleased to convey to the President my sincere acknowledgments for the honor he has done me, and the confidence reposed in me, in calling me to this position; with the expression of the hope that his plan for restoring the insurgent States to their natural and appropriate places in the Union, may be crowned with entire success.

I have the honor to be, with high respect, your obedient servant.

W W Holden

Holden to Governor Worth *DU:Holden*

Raleigh, May 21, 1866

His Excellency Gov. Worth.

Sir:

I hereby tender through you, as President Ex-Officio of the Board of Trustees, my resignation as a Trustee of the University of North-Carolina.

I have the honor to be, with high respect, Your obt. servant.

W. W. Holden

Holden to the President LC:Johnson

Ebbit House [Washington, D.C.]
July 11, 1866.

My dear Mr. President.

I have written hurriedly what you will find enclosed.[1] Please read it carefully, and answer accordingly. I will not presume to say what your reply should be, but I trust you will make it as direct and pointed as you can. You can form no idea of the depression among your real friends in our State, or of the exultant, overbearing manner of our enemies and masters.

If you can enable us to carry the State we can help you, and help the Union cause, now in so much peril. Our friends in the Convention postponed the elections until October so as to secure a chance of success. This was all they could do. If you will help us, we will make a united, determined, and successful fight.

I should like much to leave for home to-morrow evening. I would be glad if you could have your reply ready by to-morrow Twelve M. I would like to take the correspondence home, and have it appear first in the Standard, if you have no objection.

Very truly yours.
William W. Holden

[*Enclosure*]

Ebbitt House,
Washington, July 11, 1866

To the President of the United States.

Sir: Your were kind enough to intimate, in the conversation I had the honor to have with you this morning, that if I would reduce the substance of what I had said to writing, you would put your reply in the same shape.

I beg leave to repeat, that under your orders I reorganized the government of North-Carolina on a thoroughly loyal basis, with men in office who had been opposed to the rebellion, who were devoted to the Union, and who were co-operating cheerfully and heartily with you in the work of restoration. At that time loyalty to the national Union was respectable, and treason and disloyalty were odious. I was relieved of office on the 28th December, 1865, and since that period, under the administration of my successor, a marked change has taken place. Loyal men have been turned out of office, and disloyal men put in, for no other reason than that the latter are the special friends and partizans of the present Governor. The original Union men like yourself, and those who were for peace on the basis of the restoration of the Union before the close of the rebellion, are almost entirely excluded from office by my successor, and are thereby deprived of the opportunity and the pleasure of aiding you, as they desire to do, in the work of restoration; while unpardoned rebels are honored, and places of trust and confidence are filled by leading war men and rebels, who have not, in the opinion of our Union people, sincerely or duly repented of their great crime of seeking deliberately and from choice to destroy the national government.

This has been done, Sir, under the lead and direction of the present Governor of the State. The Union men have appealed to him in vain for consideration and protection. They have even offered to forget and forgive his defection from the Union cause last October, and support him for re-election, provided he would cast off the influences by which he was elected, would appoint only true Union men to office, and would co-operate with you in good faith in carrying out the work of restoration. But he has rejected this offer, and is now engaged, as he has been from the first, in undoing the work of restoration in our State, in proscribing Union men, and thus obstructing the return of the State to the Union.

Our Union people look to you for sympathy and succor. They are supporting you in good faith, and they are attached to your administration. They cannot forget your sufferings and sacrifices for the Union, at a time when it required extraordinary moral and physical courage to be a Union man, as you were in Tennessee; and this, joined to the fact that you are a native of our State, disposes our people to look to you with peculiar confidence and affection.

Our Union people believe that loyalty will not be estimated as it should, nor your plan for restoring the States be placed on the high ground it deserves to occupy, until the means and instrumentalities, which you put in operation in 1865 shall have been restored. They feel that in no other way can the State be made to appear in a truly loyal garb, and thus enforce its claims on Congress and the country for admission into the Union, without further changes in the Constitution until all the States are again represented.

Those public men who have control of affairs in our State, insist that you are opposed to the present Congressional test-oath; and that you are in favor of the immediate admission of *all* the members of Congress from the recently insurgent States. When we deny this, and insist that the oath, or some similar oath is necessary, and that the oath is a matter specially with the Congress, they declare it to be unconstitutional; that they do not respect it; and that, if it is to be maintained, it will amount, as recently declared by my successor in his message to the Convention, to the perpetual practical disfranchisement of the State. They thus defiantly set themselves up against one of the laws of the land, and take refuge under your shadow to protect and justify themselves.

The Unionists of our State, so far from desiring to proscribe or persecute their fellow-citizens, are ready to receive into their ranks all who sincerely repent that they deliberately sought to destroy the government, and who give unmistakable proof of their thorough submission to the national authority; but they still think, as they did in 1865, that Justice and sound policy require that such persons should take no active or conspicuous part in the work of restoration, but leave it where it was placed by you in the outset, to wit, in the hands of the loyal Union men.

In conclusion, allow me to say that the cause of restoration is obstructed in our State by those in power; the truly loyal people are depressed and mortified; malcontents and rebels are exultant and defiant; ill feeling is engendered; injustice is perpetrated through the courts by means of disloyal prosecuting officers, and Juries, and some magistrates, though our Judges are loyal yet not always able to withstand the pressure of public opinion; treason and disloyalty are promoted and honored, while loyalty is evinced at the hazard of political, social, and pecuniary proscription.

All we ask is, that the truly loyal of our people shall govern until the State is restored to the Union. This is the best, if not the only assurance we can have of Justice to both races, white and black. And in no other way can good feeling, and harmony, and security to life, liberty, and prosperity be secured, and the State be put upon the clear, open road to the completion of the great work of restoration, so auspiciously commenced by you, Sir, in May, 1865.

I have the honor to be, with very high respect,

Your obt Servant,
W. W. Holden
Late Prov. Gov. N.C.

[*Enclosure*]

(Statement written by Holden for President Johnson)

I have heard with concern of the conditions of Things in North-Carolina.

Your administration as Provisional Governor has my entire approval. I so telegraphed you last November. I regret that you were defeated. It was, and is my wish that the same means and instrumentalities that commenced, should complete the work of restoration. The machinery of restoration has been changed and improved, but it will not work acceptably unless it is managed by the same sort of men whom I at first employed.

I am laboring to restore the Union on the basis of the Constitution. I am doing this, not for section merely, or for a season, but for the whole country and for all time. Those who profess to sustain me should do so practically. They cannot do this by prescribing my friends, or by any policy which tends to make disloyalty respectable, and loyalty odious. Those who stood by the Union ought to be proud of it, and should be respected for it. The flag of the country should command the respect and homage of all.

While I would not persecute any citizens of the country, but will take by the hand and greet cordially all who submit in good faith to the authority of the government, and who show by their acts that they are loyal and well disposed, yet my sympathies are warmly with such Union men as sustained you at the polls; and I deem it highly important that such, and only such should take an active and leading part in the work of restoration. If there be but five thousand loyal men in a State, to them should be entrusted the control of affairs, at least until the State is restored. There are more than five thousand persons in your State.

It is for Congress to say who shall be admitted to seats. The States, in my judgment, are entitled to be represented. But Congress has prescribed a rule, and it is the duty of those seeking admission to comply with it. Unpardoned persons, and persons, who cannot take the prescribed oath, cannot expect to be admitted. This may seem hard to some, but it cannot be objectionable to those whose paramount wish is to see the Union restored.

I would not advise the States to make any more concessions. They are entitled to representation; but in order to secure it, and to retain my plan of restoration, they should send men who can successfully stand any existing Constitutional or legal test.

I ardently trust that the people of my beloved native State will so act as to secure their return to the Union at the earliest possible period; and that the time is not distant when we shall have again a united, contented, prosperous, and happy country.

[1] In a conference with President Johnson, Holden had apparently suggested that he write a letter defending his service as provisional governor, to which the president would respond expressing his approval. The enclosures to this letter were intended to carry out this arrangement. As far as can be determined, President Johnson did not respond to Holden's suggestion.

Holden to the President LC:Johnson

Raleigh, Aug. 1. 1866

My dear Mr. President: Enclosed please find an Editorial of the Standard in relation to a recent letter of Judge Ruffin.[1]

You may remember I told you, when in Washington, that the rebellious leaders in this State held that your whole plan of restoration was a usurpation, and that consequently they denied the validity of the acts of the Convention. Judge Ruffin is the leader of these men, all of whom are high in favor with Gov. Worth.[2]

Our people will vote to-morrow, and next day, and next, for the ratification or rejection of the new Constitution. All things considered, it is an excellent instrument. But these leaders are against it, first, because they deny the authority under which it was made, and secondly, because it abolished the black basis and institutes the white. They also hope that if they can invalidate the Convention they will be able to pay the rebel debt, much of which is owning to them. So far as slavery is concerned, they intend to try that in the Courts, at least for compensation for them, on the ground that they agreed to the amendment abolishing it under duress.

I hear from various parts of the State that there is a concerted movement to defeat the new Constitution. Gov. Worth may vote for it, to hide appearances, but his newspaper organs are doing all they can against it, and the counties that gave him the largest votes last Fall, will give the heavist votes against the Constitution. I hear from the West that Graham[3] is acting with Ruffin, while the whole East is against the Constitution. If adopted at all, which is doubtful, it will be done by the loyal men of the West.

I dislike very much, Sir, to be troublesome. I have been silent and quiet for many months, in the hope that our leaders and rulers here would prove themselves loyal, and would aid in good faith in carrying out your plan. But I have lost all hope in this respect, and hence the trouble I am giving you.

If you would aid us to the extent indicated by me, when in Washington, I am satisfied we could wrest the State from the hands of these men. Indeed if the new Constitution should be rejected, you would be justified in taking the State again into your own hands. Our loyal people would hail such a step on your part with shouts and rejoicings.

With much respect, Your Friend
W. W. Holden

[1] Thomas Ruffin, Sr. The letter attributed to Judge Ruffin was printed in the Raleigh *Sentinel*, July 28, 1866. He not only opposed the white basis of representation but also the authority of the convention. The constitution prepared by the 1865-1866 convention was rejected. Cheney, *North Carolina Government, 1585-1979*, 844.

[2] Jonathan Worth.

[3] William Alexander Graham.

Holden to J. S. Harrington DU:Holden

Raleigh, Sept. 3rd, 1866

To J S Harrington[1]

Dear Sir:

The Loyal Union men of this State, at the suggestion of Loyal men at Newbern and other parts of the State, have determined to hold a convention in Raleigh, on Thursday, the 20th of this month.

The time is short, yet it is hoped there will be a good attendance of Union men. If meetings can not be held in every locality to appoint delegates, it is respectfully urged that Union men come up to Raleigh of their own accord, and thus constitute a Mass Convention.

Please spread this information among Union men as far as possible. Come yourself, and urge others to attend.

Very Respectfully,
W. W. Holden

[1] James S. Harrington, Cumberland County; member, House of Commons, 1858-1861. Cheney, *North Carolina Government, 1585-1979*, 114. This is a printed form letter, individually addressed, copies of which were sent to "Loyal Union" friends throughout the state. An identical copy is in the David Miller Carter Papers, Southern Historical Collection, UNC, Chapel Hill.

"To the People of North Carolina" *Standard*
September 26, 1866

Fellow Citizens:[1]

When the conflict of arms had ceased in the Southern States, the President of the United States appointed Provisional Governors, charged with the duty of organizing new governments for the States. This was indispensable, as the rebellion in its progress had deprived these States of all civil government. The States remained but their governments had ceased to exist. These Governors acted under instructions, sometimes given by the President himself, and sometimes by the Secretary of State for him and in his name, but they were also clothed with large discretionary powers.—They were authorized to call Conventions of the loyal people, and thus enable them to resume the functions of self-government; and as the great body of the people had, by rebellion, forfeited their political privileges, the President issued a proclamation in which all, with certain exceptions were offered pardon, provided they would take an oath to support the Constitution of the United States and the Union of the States thereunder, and also former proclamations emancipating the slaves. This offer of pardon appeared to be generally and cheerfully accepted. The great body of the insurgents, including nearly all of those who were but a short time previously in arms against the national authority, were thus, generously pardoned, and remitted to the exercise of their full privileges as American citizens save that, as a necessary precaution during the formation of the new governments, martial law was maintained, to preserve the peace, and to dispose of such offenses as could not, under the circumstances, be reached by the civil law. After a furious storm there was a great calm. After four years of exhausting war we had peace. Every citizen seemed to submit cheerfully to the new condition of things, and the hope was general that the States would soon be restored to the Union.

In this State, in the space of three months, the Provisional Governor appointed some four thousand officers; the amnesty oath was administered to not less than sixty thousand citizens; an election was held for delegates to a convention which assembled for the purpose of altering and amending the State Constitution, and of presenting "such a republican form of government as would entitle the State to the guarantee of the United States therefor, and her people to protection against invasion, insurrection, and domestic violence." The Convention, after passing such ordinances as were deemed necessary, adjourned. A Governor and a Legislature were then elected. The Provisional Governor was relieved, and the new civil Governor entered on his duties. Senators and representatives to Congress were chosen.—The Convention re-assembled pursuant to adjournment, made further alterations and amendments to the Constitution, and then, divesting themselves of their powers, returned to mingle with the great body of their fellow-citizens.

Here, then, was a State, with a government newly made by the voluntary action of its citizens, and prepared, as many thought, to be admitted to the great family of States. The forms were all there, but the proper spirit was wanting. Five years before, the representatives of this State had deliberately, in their own time and way, walked out of the common Congress to engage in rebellion against the national authority; and it was not to be expected that representatives could return from this State to the Congress on their own terms and in their own way. The President had instructed the Governor, and had told the people of the State, that a spirit of sincere loyalty was the chief requisite in the work of organization. He warned them that those who had been conspicuous as rebels—who had deliberately involved the people in war, or who, being in, had persistently closed their ears to all overtures of peace—should not be prominent in the work of restoration, but must "take back seats" until the work was accomplished. He told them that their members elect to Congress ought to be persons who could comply with any existing constitutional or legal test. He told them that the work performed by the Provisional Governor, in accordance with his instructions, that in all appointments to office "those persons who had never faltered in their allegiance to the government" should be preferred, had his unqualified approval; that treason must be made odious, and loyalty must be encouraged and regarded; that the State could not expect to be restored to the Union until her people had "washed their hands of every thing that partook, in the slightest degree of the rebellion;"—and that any material variation from these views and these instructions would most probably prove "fatal" to the admission of the State.

I undertake to say, and will prove, that the public men of North Carolina who now control her affairs, acting for and in the name of her people, have not even carried out the plan of President Johnson, mild and generous as it is.

The Provisional Governor left some four thousand loyal persons in office. These persons were appointed under the direction of the President and the appointments were approved by him. With few exceptions, all of them that could be reached by the Governor and the Legislature have been ejected from office, and persons less loyal have been appointed in their place. It is not pretended that the public service has been benefitted by the change. Those ejected are in no respect inferior in ability or fitness to those who have succeeded them. We are obliged to conclude, therefore, that these removals were made to regard secession partizans, who are less loyal to the government than the former incumbents. I know they were made in opposition to the President's wishes, if not in contempt of his authority. These appointments constituted a very important part of the work of restoration. It was the wish of the President that his work should be maintained intact until the State was restored. Indeed, it was indispensable, in his judgment, to the restoration of the State, for he has repeatedly declared that the most loyal of our people should alone take part in this work, and that "every opportunity should be made available to encourage and strengthen to the fullest extent those who have never faltered in their allegiance to the government." In the recent appointments in the place of loyal men thus summarily ejected without good cause, a directly opposite rule seems to have been adopted. No opportunity has been lost by the present State Executive to encourage and strengthen those who have not only faltered in their allegiance to the government, but special care has been taken to fill the offices with persons, and among them unpardoned persons, who were conspicous in the rebellion, who have thus far given no substantial evidence that they have repented of their treason, and who, so far as the country is informed, are not disposed to cherish or inculcate national sentiments. It seems to me, that an Executive who was really devoted to the President's plan, and anxious for its success, would have cherished it with care, would have preserved it in all its material and vital parts, and would have touched it only with a view to improve it in accordance with the well-known and oft-repeated views of its author. I can account for the course of our present State Executive in this respect only on two grounds: Either he is opposed to the President's plan, and does not wish it success; or, he is for it, his disposition to reward his partizans who are clamoring for place, is stronger than those convictions of duty which incline him to carry it out.

In addition to this it was considered indispensible that the members elected to Congress should be persons of undoubted loyalty. The President and his Cabinet and the great body of the Northern people had taken it for granted that such persons would be chosen. Every step that had been taken in the work of restoration was with reference to representation in Congress. If the work should fall at this point it would fail entirely. Congress had provided, in 1862, an oath to be taken by all its members. There were worthy and respectable persons in every Congressional District in the State who could have thus claimed their seats. This was well known. But, what was done? In the first district, a person who could have taken the oath was defeated, In the second district, a person who could have taken the oath was defeated. In the third district, a person who could have taken the oath was defeated. In the fourth district, a person who was only technically prevented from taking the oath, and who had already received an important appointment at the hands of the President, was defeated, not by a man equally loyal, but by an "unpardoned rebel" then, as now. In the fifth district, one of the oldest, ablest, and most consistent Unionists of the State, and a particular friend of the President, was defeated by a person who had just apostatized from Unionism and allied himself with the secession party. In the sixth district, a candidate who could have taken the oath was defeated, by a gentleman who had made himself popular outside his County only by the services he had performed as an officer in the Confederate army.—But one district, the seventh, elected a representative who could take the oath, and he has since been an object, on that account, of abuse and ridicule by the secession press. It is true, one of the Senators elected by the Legislature is a loyal man, and is debarred from subscribing the oath only by a technicality; but it is well known that his election was conceded by the majority simply as a matter of policy, and that his colleague, who received nearly all the votes that were cast, had been a conspicous advocate to the rebellion, and was then as he is still, an "unpardoned rebel." Thus was the most vital requisite in the President's policy, deliberately disregarded. The President had said that those only should be appointed or elected to office who had never faltered in their allegiance to the government; but secession leaders said nay,—we will elect whom we please, for we hold that fidelity to the Confederacy is the best evidence of sound Unionism. The President had pointed to the test oath, and had declared that members elected to Congress should be persons who "could comply with any existing constitutional and tyrannical, and we will not degrade ourselves by complying with it." The President had declared that treason must be rendered odious, and that loyalty to the Union and love for the flag should be cherished and honored; but these leaders replied that they had not committed treason, and that supreme loyalty and devotion to the Union constituted no claim either on their votes or on their respect and confidence. The President was thus assaulted and wounded in the house of his own professed friends. Slavery had been formally abolished, for the leaders knew that they had themselves put it to hazard when they involved the States in rebellion, and that, as the result of the war, there was no hope for its perpetuation. It cost nothing, therefore, to proclaim a great fact which the whole world could see. The act of secession was declared null and void. This was equally easy. They hesitated only in relation to the rebel debt, but a sharp rebuke from the President caused them reluctantly to repudiate that. They did what they were told to do on great questions of policy—they conformed, whether reluctantly or cheerfully, to the wishes of the President in relation to measures of the most vital importance, but when the offices were to be filled—when the State was to be clothed in the "wedding garment" to be presented at Washington, they could no longer restrain themselves. The old appetite for office, which had led them to involve the country in war, revived; the President's plan was forgotten, except in so far as they could enjoy offices and honors under it; and for the ignoble party triumphs of the hour they thwarted that plan, and destroyed all hope that the States could be restored to the Union in accordance with its provisions.

These secession partizans are Johnson men only so long as they can enjoy power under his plan of restoration. He may himself be as loyal as he pleases, and may call them rebels and traitors, as he does, and he may denounce secession as a crime, if he will only permit them to hold the offices and to tyrannize over Union men. It is not that they like him, but they love power, and they hate the radicals, so-called, whom he denounces.—They will be very good Johnson men as long as he pursues this course; but if he should turn in this direction, and begin to "fight it out again on this line," he will find so much to reprove and condemn—so many wrongs to right, and so much treason to rebuke and suppress, that praises will be turned into "curses not loud, but deep," and it will be at once proclaimed that President Johnson has proved faithless to his pledges. I tell the President that his plan has been marred and destroyed by malcontents and traitors at this end of the line. I tell him that he has confided where confidence is not deserved; and that, by his clemency, springing from good motives, he has nourished a brood of vipers that will sting liberty, and will sting him, if he should get in their way. I tell him that his line at the end is disorganized. The "captains of fifties and hundreds" whom he appointed, have been cashiered and banished from service, and his enemies, and the enemies of loyal majorities in the United States and of the Union, have assumed and are now exercising supreme control. Devotion to the Union is no longer the passport to office, or even to the respect of those who control our affairs. Regard for the flag, unless it is displayed in such places and in such a way as to suit the fastidious taste of traitors, is no longer commended. Instead of a prompt and cheerful submission to the results of the war and to the legally expressed will of the majority, we hear words of defiance, and hopes expressed that anarchy may intervene, as the result of some vaguely-looked for convulsion at Washington and in the Northern States. Seats are demanded in Congress as a right, even for "unpardoned rebels."—Those who can take the test-oath, instead of being honored for their loyalty, are ridiculed and despised; and such of our people as are most devoted to the Union, and most anxious for its restoration on terms to be prescribed by the majority are characterized as "mean whites," and hold up as odious and infamous. Faithful and capable officers are ejected, for no other reason than that the Unionists, and persons are appointed in their places who sympathize more with the dead Confederacy than with the living Union. In a word, treason has been made respectable, and loyalty is odious. This is not the fault of the President's plan. The beauty and durability of the edifice must depend on the quality of the material used in its construction. "Men do not gather grapes of thorns, or figs of thistles." The President has been deceived. If he had dealt sternly with traitors, and if he had seen to it by special instructions and orders, that the loyal only should conduct the work of restoration, his plan, in my judgment, would have succeeded. We know that in this State there was an abundance of good material for the work of restoration. It was used for a time, and then cast aside. Those politicians who cast this material aside are enemies to the President, and enemies to the Union; and the longer their conduct in this respect is allowed to go unrebuked by him, the more disloyal and defiant these politicians will become.

The Union of the States must be restored at all hazards and on the best terms that can be obtained, and the plan of the President having failed through the treachery and selfishness of politicians, what now remains to be done?

There are but two plans before the country—the Executive plan and that of the Congress or law-making power. The President's plan provides, first, that the States exist as States, though by rebellion they had lost their governments; secondly, that slavery must be formally abolished by an amendment to the federal Constitution; thirdly, that the right of secession must be abandoned; fourthly, that the rebel debt must be repudiated, and, as a matter of course, the national debt must be paid; fifthly, that loyal persons only should reorganize governments for the States, and that no members elect to Congress from the Southern States should be prevented for admission, who cannot take the test-oath.

This is the President's plan. What is the Congressional plan? It is as follows, in the shape of a joint resolution, proposing amendments to the federal Constitution:

Article 14

Section 1. All persons born or naturalized in the United States, and subject to the jurisdiction thereof, are citizens of the United States and of the State wherein they reside. No State shall make or enforce any law which shall abridge the privileges or immunities of citizens of the United States; nor shall any State deprive any person of life, liberty, or property without due process of law, nor deny to any person within its jurisdiction, the equal protection of the laws.

Sec. 2. Representatives shall be apportioned among the several States according to their respective numbers, counting the whole number of persons in each State, excluding Indians not taxed. But when the right to vote at any election for the choice of electors for President and Vice-President of the United States, representatives in Congress, the executive and judicial officers of a State, or the members of the legislature thereof, is denied to any of the male inhabitants of such State, being twenty-one years of age and citizens of the United States, or in any way abridged, except for participation in rebellion or other crime, the basis of representation therin shall be reduced in the proportion which the number of such male citizens shall bear to the whole number of male citizens twenty-one years of age in such State.

Sec. 3. No person shall be a Senator or Representative in Congress, or elector of President and Vice-President, or hold any office, civil or military, under the United States, or under any State, who, having previously taken an oath as a member of Congress, or as an officer of the United States, or as a member of any State legislature, or as as executive or judicial officer of any State, to support the

Constitution of the United States, shall have engaged in insurrection or rebellion against the same, or given aid or comfort to the enemies thereof. But Congress may, by a vote of two-thirds of each House, remove such disability.

Sec. 4. The validity of the public debt of the United States, authorized by law, including debts incurred for payment of pensions and bounties for services in suppressing insurrection or rebellion, shall not be questioned. But neither the United States nor any State shall assume or pay any debt or obligation incurred in aid of insurrection or rebellion against the United States, or any claim for the loss or emancipation of any slave; but all such debts, obligations, and claims shall be held illegal and void.

Sec. 5. The Congress shall have power to enforce, by appropriate legislation, the provisions of this article.

This plan, after recognizing, as the President's plan does, the existence of the States as States, Proposes, first, that a colored man from Massachusetts shall have the same liberty in North Carolina that he possesses in his own State, and that a colored man from North Carolina shall have the same liberty in Massachusetts which he possesses at home. It provides that no State shall abridge the privileges or immunities of a citizen of the United States, or deny to any person life, liberty, or property, or the equal protection of the law. Who objects to that? I am sure President Johnson does not: for the civil rights bill, now in existence as a law; and which will in no event be repealed, makes the same provision for the colored race, and the objection of the President was not to this feature of that law, but to that part of it which as he thought, improperly subordinated the State Courts to the Courts of the United States. If it be said that there is some concealed purpose in this provision hereafter to force negro suffrage on the States, as the only means of securing to colored people the "privileges or immunities" referred to, the answer is that this cannot be so, for the reason that a subsequent section in the amendment leaves the question of suffrage wholly and solely with the States.

The Congressional plan also proposes that representatives in Congress shall be apportioned among the States in proportion to qualified voters. Who can justly object to that? Under the Constitution while slavery existed, not only were the white inhabitants counted in apportioning representatives, but three-fifths of the slaves were added to the whites. This rule has ceased with the extinction of slavery. There are now no such "persons" as those referred to in the Constitution of whom three-fifths must be counted, but the whole population of both whites and blacks must be counted in apportioning representatives. Under this new rule it has been estimated that the Southern States would gain eight members of Congress. Is it to be expected that the free white population of the North will agree to this? As it is, and as it has been from the beginning of the government, five negroes have had as much weight in the Congress of the United States as three white men; for every three white men five negroes have been counted in apportioning representatives. The proposed amendment provides that the Southern States shall be entitled to their present number of members until the period of the next apportionment, in 1872; but after that time representatives must be apportioned according to voters, and not, as now, according to the whole population. Up to 1872 this State will be entitled to seven members, the present number; after that time, she will be entitled for the next ten years to eight members, provided the colored people are allowed to vote, and if they they are not allowed to vote, she will be entitled to five members. The same rule will apply to all the States. If it is said that his rule is unjust, and that the whole population should be counted, I answer, that representation and taxation should go together, and that it is not just to claim representatives on a certain class of population, and then deny to that population the privilege of voting for those representatives. If I am told that the whole population ought to be counted, though one class of it only should be allowed to vote, I answer that the free white men of the North will never consent that the Southern States shall add by the result of their rebellion to their power in the House of Representatives by counting the non-voting negro population; and that, as a citizen of North Carolina, I am unwilling that the Eastern part of the State shall count their manumitted slaves against the free white loyal men of the West. It will be for the people of the State to decide, in 1872, whether they will have eight members of Congress with negro suffrage, or five members without negro suffrage. I have the fullest confidence in the people of the State. I feel sure that their decision on this subject will be a wise one, and for one I expect to go with them and submit cheerfully to the will of the majority.

But we are not without light on this subject from President Johnson himself. In his interview with Mr. Stearns, of Boston, in October last, he said:

"Many years ago, I moved in the Legislature of Tennessee that the apportionment of representatives to Congress from that State would be by qualified voters. The appointment is now fixed until 1872; before that time we might change the basis of representation from population to qualified voters. North as well as South, and in due course of time the States, without regard to color, might extend the elective franchised to all who possessed certain mental, moral, or such other qualifications as might be determined by an enlightened public judgment."

Mr. Johnson is, therefore, not only in favor of this provision of the proposed amendment basing members of Congress on qualified voters, but he looks forward to the period when the States will establish what is called impartial suffrage.

The proposed amendment aslo provides that certain persons who had taken an oath to support the Constitution of the United States, and afterwards engaged in the rebellion, shall not hold any office, civil or military under the United States, or under any State, unless the Congress by a vote of two-thirds shall remove such disability.

What sound objection can there be to this? If it be said that it is harsh and degrading in its nature, I reply that President Johnson has already gone much further in making treason odious than this provision goes. He not only deprived them, at his mere will and pleasure, of the right to hold office, but of the right to vote; and he held them, as he holds some of them today, not only as non-voters, but liable at any moment to the pains and penalties of treason. This proposed amendment deprives no man of his right of suffrage. It simply says to the fomenters and leaders of the rebellion—Your lives and property are spared; you are permitted to vote, as heretofore; you will not be molested in your ordinary rights as citizens; but you will not be permitted just now to occupy the chief places over the heads of those whom your conduct has ruined. You may come into the congregation, and receive the benefit of the exercises, but you cannot be priests or elders at this time. Your hands are still red with the blood of your brethern, whom ye slew while they were struggling to save the Ark of the Covenant, and the fires of resentment and pride are still smoldering in your hearts. But even were this not so, it is not reasonable or seemly that the destroyers of the peace and happiness of the country should at once become the conservators of that peace and the promoters of that happiness. Stand aside for the present. As you have lost position by your bad conduct, so you shall regain it only by your good conduct. We will not judge you harshly, but tenderly and kindly as brethern. We do not punish you. We simply put you on your good behavior for the future; and if you repent and do well, and manifest a sincere purpose to become loyal, Union-loving citizens, it will afford us much pleasure to remove the disability, and allow you to hold office.—What could be more reasonable or generous? But we are told by those who are thus excluded that the object is to punish and degrade them. If this be true, it punished and degrades Union men also. It puts under ban nearly all the leading Union men of the State. Our opponents are candid for once. They admit that they feel "degraded" when they are cast out. These very leaders punished our people for four long years. They tithed them, they impressed them, they conscribed them, forcing even the yearling boys from their weeping mothers into camp, and into the fire of battle, before their bones had hardened,—they hounded down our best citizens as traitors, and shot and hanged them, because they loved the Union and the flag; they plundered, exhausted, impoverished, and ruined this people;—and yet now complain, after having inflicted all these wrongs on their country, that they are about to be punished, because they are not allowed to monopolize for all time all the offices and honors!

I regret this provision as generous and merciful in its character. It seems to me if these politicians thus excluded really loved their country, they would sacrifice themselves temporarily for the good of their country. It they really desired the restoration of the Union, or if they only had becoming modesty and self respect, they would not stand in the way, but would come forward like patriots and men and beg to be overlooked or forgotten until the great work was accomplished. They would say, our country first, our country last, our country all the time. The issue is, the Union of the States with these persons temporarily out of office; or continued disunion, discontent, and probable civil war, with these persons in office. That man is no patriot, but is supremely selfish, who would retain his hold on office, when he knows he is doing so at the expense of the unity, harmony, and prosperity of his country.

The remaining section of the proposed amendment provides that the national debt shall never be questioned, and that the rebel debt shall be held illegal and void. Here also, we have the concurrence and endorsement of the President, repeatedly made known in the most emphatic manner.

The President simply enabled the people of the rebellious States to organize new governments. It was his wish that these governments should be in all respects, unmistakably loyal—that they should have no sectionalism or secessionism about them, but should be living sources of national principles and sentiments. It was his desire, also, as conclusive and crowning evidence of such loyalty and such nationality of sentiment, that the members chosen to Congress should be persons who could take the test oath. I am satisfied that if these States had done what was required of them with alacrity and cheerfulness, and had sent Senators and Representatives who, to a man, could have taken this oath, their claim to be admitted to their seats would have been irresistable. The Union would have been restored last December. We should have had peace and harmony today, and reviving and increasing prosperity, instead of bickerings, and discord, and sectional hate, and threats of revolution, and the locking up, as the result of these things, of all those resources which stimulate and reward enterprise and industry. But such was the destructive and paralyzing influence of the spirit of secession among our people and in our public councils, that the Congress, which is a constitutional co-worker with the President in these things, began to doubt the fitness of the States for admission. That body, without undoing what the President had done, at length required that what the States had agreed to do in their amended Constitutions, or by ordinances of Conventions, or by legislative enactment, should be engrafted in the fundamental law of the nation. That is all. The proposed amendment in relation to representation in Congress, is the legitimate result, as I have already shown, of the extinction of slavery.—There is not a principle in any section of the proposed amendment which has not received, in some form or other, the approval of the President. If, therefore, our people agree with the President, and if they are disposed to carry out in good faith what they have already conceded, (to say nothing of the respect which they owe to the law-making department of the government) I can see no good reason why they should not settle this business finally and forever by placing these guarantees in the national fundamental law. There was no time within sixty days after the surrender of Lee's forces when they would not have accepted such terms gladly. I state the fact, that it was distinctly understood that the whole work of restoration would be subject to the revision, and, consequently, to acceptance or rejection by the Congress. The official record was that Secretary Seward informed Gov. Sharkey in July, 1865, that the government of Mississippi would be "provisional only until the civil authorities shall be restored, with the approval of Congress." And in September, 1865, he also informed Gov. Marvin of Florida, that "it must be distinctly understood that the restoration to which your proclamation refers, will be subject to the decision of Congress." I repeat, the Congress has expressly and intentionally omitted to undo the work of the President. The very able, enlightened and patriotic committee of that body, after the fullest and most anxious deliberation, determined that the present State governments, organized by the President, should stand; but they recommended, as necessary to complete the work of restoration, that the amendments to the Constitution to which I have referred, should be adopted—not, as we have been told, by three-fourths only of such States as are represented in Congress, but by three-fourths of all the States. If it be said that the Southern States, though allowed to vote on these amendments, were excluded from the Congress by which they were proposed, the answer is they had no voice in proposing the most vital of all the amendments, the one which abolished slavery. If it be necessary further to amend the Constitution, as two-thirds of the American people represented in Congress think it is, before the Union can be re-established on a just, solid, and enduring basis, such amendments must be proposed by Congress for the President has no such power under our form of government.

There is, then, no material difference between the President's plan and that of Congress. They are similar in principle, and nearly the same in detail if there be humiliation and degradation for the South in the Congressional plan, there is humiliation and degradation for the South in the President's plan can not be carried into effect without the consent of Congress; and if one man can require so much of the State lately in rebellion, can not the Congress representing so many millions of loyal people, require a little more? We have passed through the wilderness. We have left behind us the horrors which encompassed us, and sat heavy on our hearts, when we wandered in the forbidden fields of rebellion and war. We have at length reached Jordan. The promised land is right before us. Shall we linger and perish on the banks?—or shall we "go up to possess the land?" If a Moses be necessary to divide the waters, Aaron and his sons can alone bear the Ark. The President is a power in this country, but Congress is greater than he. It ought to be, because it is the sole law-making power. The States went out without law; they must go back under the law. The President alone cannot restore to them their forfeited privileges,—This must be done and can only be done by the co-ordinate, co-equal departments of that great and beneficent government against which they revolted and made war. It is idle to despise or reject the authority of the Congress, and then hope that by any means the States can be restored.

But it is asserted that the President will, in the last resort, summon and reorganizie a Congress of his own, including the members from the Southern States. I do not believe the President designs, in any event or for any cause, to plunge the country into civil war, But if such a thing be probable, and the war should be renewed, the end would be the total destruction of government, society, and property in these Southern States. The weaker section would drain the cup of anguish to the very dregs. Those who originate such reports and make such calculations, are slanderers of the President. They are neither friends to him nor friends to the country. The are reckless agitators, who would stand off from the battles which their wicked passions could cause, to plunder the helpless and the dead, or to sate their vengeance by the spectacle of brothers bosoms. There is no

Congress but the Congress recently in session at Washington, which will meet again in December. This congress will increase in numbers as Southern members are admitted to it, but it will not be diminished.

It is also asserted, that the Southern States will vote for President and Vice-President in 1868, though they may not be represented in Congress. It is not to be expected that the majority will permit this. The unrepresented States were not allowed to vote in 1864, and we may be sure a similar law will be passed for 1868. President Johnson will enforce the law. It is his peculiar boast that he is a man of the people, and that he has confidence in the people. He is too sound a republican to oppose the will, in that last resort, to the will of the majority.

There is no hope, therefore, fellow-citizens, but in the prompt restoration of the Union; and this can be effected in no other way, in my judgment, than by accepting the proposed Constitutional amendment. We are admonished by the recent elections that the North will be satisfied with nothing less. It may require more, and I have no doubt it will, if we reject this amendment. During the rebellion, I was for the shortest road to peace. I am now for the shortest and straightest road right back to the Union. I love my State and I want the best terms I can get for her. So strong is this love, and so ardent is my attachment to the Union, that I would be willing to put myself under ban for the remainder of my life to see the State restored. But, because I have told the people the truth, will they censure me? I cannot believe they will. I have been frank with them, it may be to my own injury. I cannot help it, for if I serve them all I must do so with candor and honesty. My interests, my sympathies, my hopes are all indentified with theirs. Passion and prejudice may rule the hour, but a day of reason and reflection will come, and then justice will be done to all. It would have been easy for me to have gone with the current. Like others, I might have made terms with my opponents. I held a position which would have enabled me to do this with some success. I might have grasped honors, and put money in my purse. I could have gone to a party with which I once acted, many of whose members, from former associations, still have my regard and sympathy. But, I could not do it. I could not abandoned the cause of the Union. The path of duty was rugged and thorny, but I continued to walk in it. I am in it still. I will never leave it. I do not fear censure, but I fear to do wrong. Nor am I a slave to party. In 1848 I opposed my party on internal improvements, and I have the gratification to believe that my course then ensured the appropriation for the Central Railroad, which was the great pioneer work of the kind in our State. In 1860 I refused to go with my party in opposing the principle of ad valorem. In 1860 I refused to go with the great mass of my party for disunion. I stand now where I stood then. I am the same loyal man I was when the President appointed me Provisional Governor in May, 1865. I have changed. I do not intend to change. I know this is a dark day for the Union men in the South, but I intend to stand by the Union, in the darkness as in the light, so long as its flag floats or a star glitters in its folds. There is no hope for this people but in the Union. Throughout its whole existence it has been beneficent in its character and operations. It has borne heavily on no State; it has deprived no man of his liberty except from the stern necessity of war; it has laid the hand of correction on its rebellious children more in sorrow than in anger. We attempted recently to "calculate its value" at a time when its flag waved only for our protection, and when its horn of plenty was pouring down every good thing into our midst, and behold how suddenly destruction rushed in upon us like a flood! We then humbled ourselves before God, and promised to submit to lawful authority. Have we so soon forgotten this promise? We have been conquered in battle, because God willed it; let us now show what a great thing it is to conquer ourselves. Let us rule our temper. Let us conquer and subdue our passions and prejudices. The great body of the people of the North are our friends. They wish us well. They do not desire to humble or degrade us. They do not want our lands or our houses. They are not seeking our blood. They are tired of war. They yearn towards us as an elder towards his younger brother, who has been sorely chastised for his first offence. They desire our prosperity, because it is inseparably connected with their own. They do not want to hold us as subject provinces, but they wish to live with us as equals in the Union. That Union stretches out in mighty arms to embrace us . For one, I am anxious to return to it. I regard it, in the language of Washington, as "the primary object of patriotic desire." In it, I know we shall be safe. It will be to us all, as in the past, a copious fountain of innumerable blessings. Out of it, I can see nothing in the future but discord, anarchy, military rule, poverty, ignorance, and wretchedness. I am, therfore, in the fullest and strongest sense, a Union man. Discarding all other platforms. I stand on the platform of Washington. I know we can not err as long as we follow his precepts, and look to his illustrious example for light to guide our footsteps. What would he say, if, appreciating the passions which divide us, he could look down upon us from his blest abode? He would say to the North, "give," and to the South "hold not back." He would tell us that what the sword had settled should be confirmed by the tongue and the pen. He would tell us that the Union, which he toiled and suffered to establish, was the paramount good; that every thing else should be sacrificed, if necessary to its restoration and preservation; that the passions and resentments engendered by the war, should perish with the war; and that nothing should prevent the immediate restoration of the Union and the harmony of its various parts.

Fellow-citizens, there are certain State issues, just now engaging the attention of the people, in relation to which I will submit a few observations.

I regret on several accounts, the rejection of the new State Constitution. It was not all that I desired, but it was in many respects an excellent Constitution, and a decided improvement upon the old one. One of the ablest and most loyal bodies that ever assembled in the State, gave to this instrument the most patient consideration. Among other things, it struck the last fetter from the human conscience, by granting to our Jewish fellow-citizens the right to hold office; it provided for expediting justice, thus maintaining the peace of society; it dealt a deserved blow at the right of secession by substituting an oath to support the Constitution of the State not incompatible with the national Constitution, for the oath of primary allegiance to the State in the old Constitution; it provided for a Lieutenant-Governor by the people, to take the place of the Governor in the event of his death or disability; it abolished, or greatly modified the objectionable landed qualification for members of the Senate and House of Commons: and it established the white basis for the House of Commons. If this constitution was rejected upon the ground that it was too liberal or too radical, I take it for granted, from some knowledge of our people, that the next constitution will be still more liberal and radical. Our people will not be satisfied until the white basis is established for both branches of the Legislature; and it may be that they will require the entire abolition of the property qualification, and the election of many officers by the people now chosen by the Legislature.

The Convention exhibited wise forethought in embodying in separate ordinances its repudiation of secession and the rebel debt, the abolition of slavery, and the provision allowing colored persons to be heard in our courts as witnesses; for, from the spirit manifested at the late voting for and against the Constitution, it is more than probable that these ordinances, if they had been incorporated in the Constitution, would have rendered it much more objectionable than it was to those who voted against it. As it is, these ordinacnces exist for the present. They may be abrogated, however, by any future Convention that may be called.

Our people are impoverished and deeply in debt. Previously to the rebellion the estimated value of all the property of the State was not less than four hundred millions in specie; it is more than probable that the estimated value at present would not reach one hundred millions.—The State debt, with the interest recently added to it, cannot be much less than eighteen millions. It is impracticable, at present, to redeem the principal of this debt. It is impracticable, at present, to discharge old individual debts. The State is not itself, in any sense, in the present condition of things. We shall have not captial from a distance, no emigration, no payment of claims held by our people against the federal government for property taken or destroyed during the war—no adequate or reliable means to stimulate enterprise and industry, and no solid foundation for business of any kind, until the State is restored to the Union. I know it is said the abolition of slavery was a providential act; or, if not, that our slaves were forcibly taken from us, and that, under either view, we have been released from our obligation to pay our debts. I do not concur in this view. Slavery was abolished by the unwise action of the Southern States. That first gun at Fort Sumter, fired by Southern men, who had previously "fired the Southern heart" for rebellion, was the death-knell of slavery. It was our own act, and we cannot take advantage of our own wrong. We should bear in mind, in considering this subject, that if either party is to blame it is not the creditor, but the debtor. The debtor has had, or may now have the benefit of what belonged to another. The events through which we have convulsed, and to a great extent, have, changed society.—They have improverished our people. But they have not, therefore, released us from our lawful obligations. These events constitute good reason for indulgence and forbearance in the collection of debts, but the debts remain, and must be paid. I plead only for indulgence and forbearance. We may honestly say we cannot, but we cannot honestly say we will not pay our debts. An honest bankrupt never loses the respect or the confidence of the wise and good; but an individual or a State that says, "it is my hand and seal, but I will not pay," proclaims for himself and his State that there is no virtue in moral obligation. North Carolina will live always. Centuries hence, her name, and, I trust, her fame will be known among the nations. States prosper and flourish, and are respected, in proportion as they adhere to the eternal principles of justice. Whatsoever we may do now, in this respect, will be known and scrutinized by those who are to come after us; and if our descendants shall be of the noble stamp of our Gaston and Macon, they will blush for their ancestors if they deliberately repudiate their just obligations.

But, we are losing golden moments.—Interest is being added to principal, thus augmenting our own burdens and the burdens of posterity. Our capacity to discharge our obligations, whether public or private is greatly restricted by our exclusion from the Union. The longer we remain out of it, the poorer we shall become and the heavier will be our burdens as a State and as individuals. While every reasonable forbearance should be shown towards tax-payers and debtors, let us at the same time guard the honor of the State, and our credit as individuals, as of more value to us in the long run than everything else.-North Carolina, though now in the dust of poverty, is still rich in resources. She will yet rise and shine among the wealthiest and proudest of her sisters, and will, in the end, redeem all her obligations. I do not despair either of the Republic or of the future prosperity and glory of our State. But one thing is indispensable, and that is, The Restoration of the Union. With it, we shall at once enter on a new career of prosperity. Without it, every interest, will languish, and we shall continue to eat the bread of poverty.

W. W. Holden

Raleigh, Sept. 20, 1866

[1] This was the text of Holden's speech to the Union Convention held in Raleigh, September 20, 1866.

Holden to Mr. James E. O'Hara *Standard*
October 17, 1866

Raleigh, Oct. 3, 1866

To Mr. James E. O'Hara, Secretary.[1]

Dear Sir:

Your letter of yesterday, inviting me to visit the Convention of colored people now in session this City, has been received.

The object of your convention, as I am informed, is to promote education among your race, and thus elevate and improve it mentally and morally. This is a noble work, and one in which every patriot and philanthropist is pleased to see you engaged. I trust the results of your labors may be for good to the colored people; and I feel sure that the country and all its material and moral interests will be benefited in proportion as your race shall be enlightened and elevated in the scale of being.

Be pleased to convey to the Convention my acknowledgments for the invitation thus tendered, and say to them that it will afford me pleasure to visit the Convention before it adjourns.

Very Respectfully,
W. W. Holden

[1] James Edward O'Hara, congressman and educator; secretary of the Freedman's Convention then in session in Raleigh; engrossing clerk for the 1868 convention and for the state House of Representatives, 1868 and 1869; member, U.S. House of Representatives, 1883-1887. *Dictionary of North Carolina Biography*, s.v. "O'Hara, James Edward."

"W. W. Holden's complicity with Thad. Stevens" *Standard*
October 10, 1866

The last *Sentinel* makes an extract from a speech recently delivered at Lancaster, Pa., by the Hon. Thaddeus Stevens,[1] in which it is stated that Gov. Holden, while in Washington last summer, advised Mr. Stevens to introduce a bill to reorganize the Southern States on the basis of white and negro suffrage. Mr. Stevens says:

> Every loyal Southern man came to me and asked me to put it in the bill. There was not a loyal man, from Governor Hamilton to Governor Holden, Chief Justice Powell and Governor Sherwood—there were twenty of these men driven from their homes who dare not go back for fear of being murdered. They came to help me fabricate the bill. It was not the rebels that did it; it was of the loyal men that said give us that bill; and the vote of the loyal white men, added to that of the loyal black men, can carry every State but Virginia. I was in a caucus one night, when Governor Hamilton told us "to give them that law, and although we are now in the minority, and I dare not go home, for I should be murdered, give us that bill, and we can carry Texas on the side of the Union by twenty-five thousand majority." Governor Holden told me the same, and so did everybody except the Virginians.

We were in Washington in June and July last. We saw and conversed with the President four times. We saw Messrs. Seward,[2] Stanton,[3] McCulloch,[4] Welles,[5]

Speed,[6] Randall,[7] and Harlan,[8] of the Cabinet, each once. We saw Mr. Stevens twice, Mr. Sumner[9] twice, and Messrs. Clark,[10] Doolittle,[11] Kelly,[12] Boutwell,[13] Trumbull,[14] and others frequently, at the Capitol and at the hotels. We conversed with all of these gentlemen freely on the state of the country. We did not stop specially to inquire whether they were Radicals or not, as our object was to obtain information, and to do what we could to restore North Carolina to the Union. We did not see Gov. Hamilton.[15] We called at his boarding-house, and found him absent. We were not present at any caucus or consultation of Republicans or Radicals, nor were we invited to attend any such caucus or consultation. We heard not one word from Mr. Sumner, or Mr. Stevens, or Mr. Boutwell, or Mr. Kelly, or any one else, about negro suffrage. Mr. Sumner, for instance, conversed for one hour on the state of the country in general terms, speaking kindly of the Southern people, and expressing a desire that the Union should be restored; but that he made no allusion to negro suffrage. We saw Mr. Stevens in the room of the Clerk of the House, in presence of Dr. Powell,[16] Dr. Sloan,[17] Gen. Banks,[18] and others. The conversation was hurried, as the House was in session, and Mr. Stevens was called off once to vote. He said, among other things, that the whole work of reconstruction under the President was a usurpation, and null anf void. Of course we could not agree to that, as we had been an actor in this work ourself. He said he would see to it that this work should not stand. In this it is well known he agrees with Judge Ruffin[19] of this State. He spoke of an enabling act, but we did not see it. Negro suffrage was not mentioned by any one during the conversation. We have not, to this day, seen Mr. Stevens' enabling act. It was introduced at the heel of the session, and we looked for it in vain in the Washington papers. Just as we were about to leave, Dr. Powell handed Mr. Stevens a new test-oath, to be adopted in the place of the present test-oath. We do not remember the words of this oath sufficiently well to repeat them, but this oath had our approval, as a milder and better one than that which now exists. Before we went to Washington, while we were there, and since our return, negro suffrage has not been in all our thoughts as a measure to be voluntarily adopted by our people. We saw and heard enough, however, to convince us that if the Howard amendment should not be accepted by the Southern States, reorganization would follow, with negro suffrage, confiscation of property, and many other evils. This is the extent of our *Radicalism*, and of our "complicity" with Mr. Stevens.

We have no idea that Mr. Stevens intended to misstate our position. We do not believe him capable of falsehood or intentional misrepresentation. It is natural that he should include us with other Southern loyalists in his general statement as to what they desired. Gov. Hamilton is known to be in favor of negro suffrage. He attended the Republican caucus, and spoke to that effect. We did not. We told Mr. Stevens and others, *as we told the President*, in substance what we have said in our Address in relation to the condition of things in this State. We told them that loyalty in North-Carolina was at the bottom and disloyality on top; that our State government was in the hands of the secessionists; that supreme devotion to the Union was neither a passport to office nor a badge of respectability; and that the

Unionists of the State were depressed and disheartened, and the cause of restoration obstructed by this condition of things. We said this then, we set it out in full in our Address, and we stand on it now.

We differ with Mr. Stevens not only in regard to negro suffrage, but as to the Howard amendment. We wish the South to take that amendment to avoid further and greater evils; Mr. Stevens does not want the South to take it, as her refusal to do so will give him grounds to force upon us confiscation, executions for treason, and negro suffrage.

The *Sentinel* asks, "did Mr. Holden intimate to Mr. Stevens that he had been driven from home, and was afraid to go back, for fear of being murdered?" *We did not*. We are not afraid to live in North-Carolina. Whatever may happen, we expect to lay our bones in the "good old North State." Since the close of the rebellion, there has been no time when we have not been treated by all classes and all parties with personal courtesy and respect. But we feel we are under the ban, because of our Union sentiments, and that, if those who now control the State government and control society could have their way, they would indelibly stamp us and our posterity with a "hideous mark," because we were not true to the Confederacy. We want the word *Tory* written on the back of no man. But if the contest be forced upon us as to who shall be honored now and hereafter—the traitor to the Confederacy or the traitor to the Union— we wish it distinctly understood that our lot has been cast with the former. What we complain of is, that our opponents do not cultivate as they should, and as they agreed to do when they surrendered, *a spirit of nationality*; and that they seem to think more of the memories of the dead Confederacy than of the glories of the living Union. We shall not be able to agree with them, or act with them, as long as they pursue this course.

But we tell the *Sentinel* that we have evidence in our possession of the most undoubted character, that it is not safe for Union men in certain localities west of this, to announce their views from the stump. We *know* that one of our worthiest public men has been driven from the stump and silenced by armed ex-rebels; and we apprehend that the election will not be free at some boxes in that portion of the State. We *know* the fact that the American flag was pulled down by armed ex-rebels at Jefferson, Ashe County, a week or two since, and we sincerely believe, that if the State were now in the Union under present auspices, and if all the troops were removed, and there was no fear of consequences before the eyes of a certain set in this State, every unconditional Union man would be either driven from the State, or compelled, from fear for himself or his family, to be silent in relation to public affairs. That is our belief.

But "W. W. Holden's complicity with Thad. Stevens?" Nothing is too bad to be charged against Holden. Holden was responsible for the rebellion; he was responsible for peace; he was responsible for every thing bad and for nothing good under the provisional government; he was *not* responsible for negro suffrage under Mr. Johnson, when the latter advised it, but he *is* responsible for it now, by complicity with Mr. Stevens; he is responsible for the Howard amendment, though he did all he could to restore the State before this amendment was adopted; and if the people will not take his advice and accept this amendment, and the *only* course left them to escape future and greater evils, he will then be responsible for all these evils, including confiscation and negro suffrage! Such is Holden. Was there ever such a person before in the tides off time? Mr. Stevens is a traitor, a liar, a villain, a hideous monster on his own merits, in the estimation of the *Sentinel*; but when it is thought that some chance expression by Mr. Stevens will injure Holden, why then Mr. Stevens is a gentleman, a scholar, and a paragon of truth and honesty. Anything to destroy Holden! Ah, brother Pell[20] so-called-ah Seaton,[21] lover of the flag, Holden will not destroy. He stands on the rock of TRUTH, against which the petty whitecaps of your passions dash in vain.

[1] Radical Republican Thaddeus Stevens, member, U.S. House of Representatives, 1849-1853 as a Whig; 1859-1868 as a Republican. *Biographical Directory of the American Congress, 1774-1979*, s.v. "Stevens, Thaddeus."

[2] William Henry Seward, secretary of state.

[3] Edwin McMasters Stanton of Ohio; unionist; secretary of war, 1861-1868. *Dictionary of American Biography*, s.v. "Stanton, Edwin McMasters."

[4] Hugh McCulloch of Maine; secretary of the treasury. *Dictionary of American Biography*, s.v. "McCulloch, Hugh."

[5] Gideon Welles of Connecticut; secretary of the navy, 1861-1869. *Dictionary of American Biography*, s.v. "Welles, Gideon,"

[6] James Speed, attorney general.

[7] Alexander Williams Randall of Kentucky; postmaster general, 1865-1869. *Dictionary of American Biography*, s.v. "Randall, Alexander Williams."

[8] James Harlan of Iowa; secretary of the interior, 1865-1866. *Dictionary of American Biography*, s.v. "Harlan, James."

[9] Radical Republican Charles Sumner of Massachusetts; member, U.S. Senate, 1851-1874. *Biographical Directory of the American Congress, 1774-1979*, s.v. "Sumner, Charles."

[10] Daniel Clark of New Hampshire; member, U.S. Senate, 1857-1866; U.S. district court judge, 1866-1891. *Biographical Directory of the American Congress, 1774-1979*, s.v. "Clark, Daniel."

[11] James Rood Doolittle of Wisconsin; member, U.S. Senate, 1857-1869. *Biographical Directory of the American Congress, 1774-1979*, s.v. "Doolittle, James Rood."

[12] William Darrah Kelley of Pennsylvania; member, U.S. House of Representatives, 1861-1890. *Biographical Directory of the American Congress, 1774-1979*, s.v. "Kelley, William Darrah."

[13] George Sewell Boutwell of Massachusetts; member, U.S. House of Representatives, 1863-1869; secretary of the treasury, 1869-1873; member, U.S. Senate, 1873-1877. *Biographical Directory of the American Congress, 1774-1979*, s.v. "Boutwell, George Sewell."

[14] Lyman Trumbell of Connecticut; member, U.S. Senate, 1855-1873. *Biographical Directory of the American Congress, 1774-1979*, s.v. "Trumbell, Lyman."

[15] Probably Andrew Jackson Hamilton; unionist leader; member, U.S. House of Representatives, 1859-1861; provisional governor of Texas, 1865-1866; justice, Texas Supreme Court, 1866-1868. *Dictionary American Biography*, s.v. "Hamilton, Andrew Jackson."

[16] Robert James Powell.

[17] William Sloan.

[18] Probably Nathaniel P. Banks of Massachusetts; speaker U.S. House of Representatives, 1856-1858; governor of Massachusetts, 1858-1861; major general of volunteers, 1861-1865; member, U.S. House of Representatives, 1866-1878. Ezra J. Warner, *Generals in Blue: Lives of the Union Commanders* (Baton Rouge and London: Louisiana State University Press, 1964) s.v. "Banks, Nathaniel Prentiss."

[19] Thomas Ruffin, Jr.

[20] William E. Pell, publisher of the *Daily Sentinel*. Murray, *Wake: Capital County of North Carolina*:I, 565.

[21] Seaton Gales, publisher of the *Daily Sentinel*.

Holden to Louisa Holden A&H:Holden

Washington, Sunday 9th Dec. 1866.

My dear Wife: I reached here last evening, after an agreeable trip. I am feeling quite well.

Mr. Pool,[1] Col. Harris,[2] Mr. Taylor[3] and myself called on Mr. Stevens[4] to-day and laid our plans before him. He heard us patiently, and after the interview was over he asked us to draw a bill embodying our views. That will soon be done. I have good ground to hope that Congress will take prompt and proper action. We find loyal Unionists here from all the Southern States urging Congress to reorganize and sustain them in their rights. Our delegation, however, seems to be ahead of all of them in soundness of views, such as appear most likely to prevail. One thing seems to be certain, and that is, the present State governments will be obliterated. It is only a matter of time.

I heard Madame Ristori[5] last night. How I wished you were present. It would be impossible to describe her acting. I had never conceived any thing equal to it. She is certainly a person of transcendant genius. Though the tragedy is in Italian, and no one understood it unless it was read at the time in the translation in books handed round containing it, yet from the first she held the audience spell-bound, and in some of the closing scenes the effect was grand and impressive. I will tell you more about it when I get home.

Mr. Taylor, Mr. Jenkins,[6] Col. Harris, and Mr. Pool and myself have rooms close together at the Ebbitt. We are hard at work, but the time passes pleasantly. I can not say what time I will be at home. You smile at the idea of our being hard at work, but it is so. To see and talk with every body, and explain, and urge, and denounce, and plan, is no easy thing. There is so much to do, and so many different views, that at times I am almost ready to despair.

I will write you again to-morrow or next day. Please let Joseph[7] know what I have written, so that he can inform others. Tell Mr. Harrison[8] and other friends that we have strong hopes of success.

I have thought about you a great deal since I left home. You cannot tell how glad I would be to receive only a few lines from you.

With love to all, and especially to my dearest Wife, for the present,

Good-Bye,
W. W. Holden.

[1] John Pool, one of the organizers of the Republican party in North Carolina. *Dictionary of North Carolina Biography*, s.v. "Pool, John."

[2] Ceburn L. Harris.

[3] Probably James Fauntleroy Taylor, lawyer; A.B., U.N.C., 1841; A.M., 1844; state librarian, 1843-1854. *Dictionary of North Carolina Biography*, s.v. "Taylor, James Fauntleroy."

[4] Thaddeus Stevens.

[5] Adelaide Restori, Italian actress on her first tour of the United States. *Encyclopaedia Britannica*, 1968 ed., s.v. "Ristori, Adelaide."

[6] David Aaron Jenkins, opponent of secession; member, House of Commons, 1866-1868; state treasurer, 1868-1876. *Dictionary of North Carolina Biography*, s.v. "Jenkins, David Aaron."

[7] Joseph William Holden.

[8] William H. Harrison.

Holden to Louisa Holden DU:Holden

Washington, D.C., Feb. 11, 1867

My dear Wife:

We reached here yesterday, Sunday morning, after a somewhat fatiguing trip. We found when we reached Richmond that the Potomac was closed with ice, and we had therefore, to remain there all day. We stopped at the St. Charles Hotel, and at seven in the evening we took the cars to go by Gordonsville and Alexandria to Washington. The distance to Gordonsville is 76 miles from Richmond, and from Gordonsville to Alexandria about 90 miles. We reached the latter place about eight on Sunday morning and had to go thence 8 miles to Washington in a steam tug. We were two hours making the trip. It was intensely cold, and we had no fire on the tug. The ice at some points was so thick that the boat would be brought to a stand, and would then run back some distance, and gathering momentum, would crash throught, jarring every plank in the boat. So far as the eye could see the ice was rifted in great boulders in the river; yet if the boat had gone down the ice was compact enough to have borne our weight to the shore. We found the Ebbitt House very much crowded, and did not get a room until Sunday night. I am now writing in the fourth story, in the room which we occupy of Mr. Brandige,[1] a member of Congress from Connecticut, who is temporarily absent. Mr. Willard[2] is very polite and attentive to us.

We have thus far seen but few persons, we expect to make the rounds to-day and to-night. We have heard nothing really new. For my part, I am determined to press my own private business. I am encouraged from a conversation with Mr. Goodloe[3] to hope that Congress will pass a law giving the printing to the loyal papers, and the Standard will be one.

Mr. Settle[4] was here with a son of Judge Douglas,[5] but left before we arrived. He will probably return the latter part of the week. Gen. L.[6] and Mr. Harrison[7] get along very well. The latter is a little irritable, and reminds me of the old soldier, Dragonbert, in the Wandering Jew.

Mr. H. and Gen. L. expect to call on the President. I do not think of doing so.

My dear Wife and home are all the time on my mind. I feel I am working mainly for them. I know you think of me with equal affection, and count the hours of my absence. I am feeling very well, though I suffered a good deal on Sunday morning from the cold.

And now, good-by. My love to all. Kiss the children for their father, and believe me, as ever, your devoted and most affectionate husband.

W. W. Holden

P.S. The mail is so irregular I cannot tell when you will get this. I have written to Jo[8] at the same time.

[1] Augustus Brandegee, Connecticut; A.B., Yale, 1849; member, U. S. House of Representatives, 1863-1867. *Biographical Directory of the American Congress, 1774-1971*, s.v. "Brandegee, Augustus."

[2] Probably Henry A. Willard, identified in the 1870 U.S. Census as a "Retired Hotel Keeper." 1870 U.S. Census Population Schedule, District of Columbia: Ward 1, 258.

[3] Daniel Reaves Goodloe, abolitionist and journalist; assistant editor and editorial writer for the *National Era* in Washington, D.C.; employee in various federal agencies during the Civil War; federal marshal in North Carolina, 1865-1869; independent candidate for governor, 1868; Washington correspondent for the *News and Observer*. *Dictionary of North Carolina Biography*, s.v. "Goodloe, Daniel Reaves."

[4] Thomas Settle, Jr.

[5] Probably Robert Martin Douglas; private secretary to Governor Holden, 1868; private secretary to President Grant, 1869-1873; associate justice, North Carolina Supreme Court, 1896-1905. *Dictionary of North Carolina Biography*, s.v. "Douglas, Robert Martin."

[6] James Madison Brown Leach, lawyer; member, House of Commons, 1848-1857; member, U.S. House of Representatives, 1859-1861; lieutenant colonel, Twenty-first Regiment North Carolina Troops, 1861; member, Confederate House of Representatives, 1864-1865; member, state Senate, 1865-1868; 1879-1880; major general, state militia. *Dictionary of North Carolina Biography*, s.v. "Leach, James Madison Brown."

[7] William H. Harrison.

[8] Joseph William Holden.

Kemp P. Battle to Holden *Standard*
February 16, 1867

Raleigh, N.C.

My attention has been called to some comments in your paper on my late reports to the General Assembly.[1] It is stated that there will be during this year a large surplus in the Public Treasury. This is a great mistake. The error arises from not remembering that the taxes of one year are collected for the purpose of paying *the expenses of the following year*. Hence, if no taxes are collected in the fall and winter of 1867, the treasury will assuredly become empty during 1868. And so the taxes of 1868 are to meet the expenses of 1869.

The Revenue bill reported by me to the General Assembly was formed to raise probably, provided good crops are raised, a sum which added to the other receipts into the Treasury would provide a surplus somewhat exceeding $200,000. This was intentionally done.

1st, Because I thought it probable some of my recommendations would not meet with favor of the General Assembly, as such a general *ad valorem* taxation on property, as seemed to me just, has not heretofore been the policy of the State.

2d. I feel sure extraordinary appropriations would be made, for which I had no right to render estimates for.

In both predictions I was correct. Some items were struck from the reported bill, in the Committee on Finance, others in the House of Commons, while extraordinary appropriations have already been made, amounting to many thousands dollars. The combined effect of these causes is decidedly unfavorable to any considerable surplus.

As I have no banks such as the Banks of North-Carolina and Cape Fear once were, from which the Treasury can be supplied, when empty, it is eminently proper, that care should be taken that no deficiency shall exist. Besides, the Revenue Bill is exceedingly reasonable. Ten cents on the $100 value of land, money, &c., and fifty cents on the poll, the rates on other things in proportion, are taxes which give entire satisfaction to the people, even in this hour of distress.

Kemp P. Battle, Pub. Treas.

[1] In the *Standard* of February 9, 1867, Holden had commented editorially under the heading "Enormous Taxation," that the pending revenue or tax bill before the General Assembly would raise $500,000 more than would be needed for the ordinary expenses of state government.

Holden to John Sherman NCHR

RALEIGH, N.C., Feb. 23, 1867

Hon John Sherman.[1]

Dear Sir: As the bill recently passed to reconstruction the Southern States is likely to become a law, and as the loyal people of this State propose to take action immediately under it, there are some points to which I would be glad to have your opinion.

The present State governments are, I take it, illegal and can have no binding effect on their people. Do they cease at once to exist, or are they simply tolerated, the military commander "allowing" their local civil tribunals to take Jurisdiction, &c.? Or are the governments to be hereafter formed by the people to be deemed provisional?—and are the local civil tribunals of those governments the ones referred to?

I would be much obliged to you, Sir, for your construction of the act at the earliest moment convenient to you. The loyal people of this State desire to act immediately. They believe that they can call a Convention, frame a Constitution, and elect members of Congress in time to be admitted next December.

With high respect, Yours
W. W. Holden

[1] John Sherman, Ohio; member, U.S. House of Representatives, 1855-1861; member, U.S. Senate, 1861-1877, 1881-1897; secretary of state, 1877-1881, 1897-1898. *Biographical Directory of the American Congress, 1774-1971*, s.v. "Sherman, John." This letter was taken from James A. Padgett, ed., "Reconstruction Letters from North Carolina," *North Carolina Historical Review* 18 (July 1941):292-293.

Dr. W. D. Whitted to Holden *Standard*
April 9, 1867

Hendersonville, Henderson County
March 22nd, 1867

There is nothing that would afford me more pleasure than that of being present on the 27th, at your meeting and contribute my mite towards restoring our State to her normal and original position in the Union.–She has been dislocated long enough—I earnestly desire to see the luxation reduced, (surgically speaking,) and the erudite physician (the U.S. Congress) has proposed or indicated the appliances that are to be used for the reduction of the dislocated limb, and it only remains for us less distinguished as surgeons or physicians to make these appliances, and the old North State will be herself again both in body and limb.

I am now, as I ever have been, in favor of a restoration of the Union on the best terms that we can get. I was in favor of all compromises offered by the government during the war, looking towards returning to the Union. I was in favor of a State Convention during the war, hoping thereby to make our escape from Confederate rule and tyranny. I was in favor of the Constitutional amendment proposed in 1866, voted for it, &c. And I am now in favor of the military bill as passed by the 39th congress, although it deprives many good and true Union men from voting for delegates to the State Convention. You, I have no doubt, will represent as nearly as any one man could the sentiments of the Union men of Western North-Carolina, and we hope that you will stand square on the question as you have always done heretofore. Let us have no backing down at this late day, after so much suffering and privation on account of the perverseness of the rebellious portion of the country.

[Dr. W. D. Whitted[1]]

[1] W. D. Whitted, Henderson County; Hendersonville pharmacist and physician. Sadie Smathers Patton, *The Story of Henderson County* (Asheville: Miller Printing Company, 1947), 101, 193.

R. M. Henry to Holden *Standard*
April 11, 1867

Franklin, N.C., March 26, 1867

Hon. W. W. Holden

My dear Sir: Information of the meeting of the loyal Unionists, at Raleigh, on the 27th, reached me late on the 27th, too late by the means of travel, for me to reach Raleigh before Friday morning, however much I may desire to be there and participate with our friends in the consultations proposed. This I regret for many reasons. I would rejoice if it was in my power to be there and mingle with our true loyal friends from the different parts of the State, and receive from them counsel and advise them of the state of things in this faroff mountain home.

I must, however, content myself by assuring them by means of this short letter of my full concurrence in what was done in the meeting of the loyal Unionists of the Legislature, and of my willing acceptance of the terms proposed in the act of Congress "to provide for the more efficient government of the rebel States."

The secessionists and latter-day war saints persuaded the people to reject the Howard amendment, on the prejudice existing against impartial suffrage, which they insisted would be the necessary result of its ratification. What will they say now, that their leaders are bound and disfranchised, and the colored men are permitted to participate with the loyal whites in the work of reconstruction? Is this the hell that Crawford[1] of Rowan built? If so, I say well done Crawford.

Suffrage is the prerogative of the people in all free governments. It is usually confined to free male citizens of the age of twenty-one years and over. It is either a valuable right or it is worthless; if a valuable right why withhold it from the poor and illiterate? If it is worthless; why confer it on any? or do the learned and wealthy desire it? If the opinion commonly prevailing in America is true, that the right of suffrage is the means by which the citizen protects himself against wrong and oppression from the government, why withhold it from any? I am clear for every man to have the same power to protect himself from wrong oppression, that I am enjoying myself. I hold this to be the true doctrine of the Republicans and Unionists of the United States. It is a principle of human liberty and right that I am willing to stand or fall by.

Believing it to be the duty of Congress to guarantee to each State a "Republican form of government," and that sound policy requires that they should require the rebel States to be organized on a thorough loyal basis, it is becoming in us who have felt the proscriptive hand of traitors to look well to the future, in securing the State against a recurrance of such evils as she has just passed through under the iron hand of rebels and traitors.

I trust that our friends shall do nothing in their meeting with which I cannot heartily agree, and I hope in the future, when we shall return to the old family building of our fathers, that we may all be found side by side *knocking at the right door*.

I am most respectfully, yours truly,

R. M. Henry[2]

[1] William H. Crawford, Rowan County; member, House of Commons, 1864-1867, 1870-1872; member, state Senate, 1876-1877. Cheney, *North Carolina Government*, 1585-1979, 1260-1261.

[2] Robert M. Henry, Macon County attorney. 1860 U.S. Census Population Schedule, North Carolina: Macon, 588.

Geo. S. Boutwell to Holden *Standard* July 9,1867

Groton, Mass., June 18, 1867

My Dear Sir:

If it were possible for me to consult my personal wishes I would be with you at Raleigh on the 4th proximo. A session of Congress is called for the 3rd of July, and I feel it to be my duty to aid, as far as possible, in making a quorum for business. Never has it been more important to secure a session of Congress.

It is now plain that the work of reconstruction cannot go on under the lead of Mr. Johnson. Congress must again and constantly assert its power, or the South will be given up once more to the domination of those who ruled during the war, and after the war, previous to the legislation of last March.

The opinions of the Attorney General[1] have robbed the legislation of Congress of all its benign and healing qualities.

It is due to the South and the North that such perversity in law and morals should be controlled by the Legislative Department of the Government.

Very respectfully,
Geo. S. Boutwell

To W. W. Holden, Chairman, &c

[1] Henry Stanbery, lawyer; elected attorney general of Ohio, 1846; U.S. attorney general, 1866-1868. *Dictionary of American Biography*, s.v. "Stanbery, Henry."

Benj. F. Butler to Holden *Standard*
July 9, 1867

Lowell, Mass., June 19, 1867

Dear Sir:–Nothing would give me greater pleasure than to accept your kind invitation to meet my fellow citizens of Raleigh in their celebration of the anniversary of our nation's birth. Imperative public duties forbid.

Nothing can more awaken patriotic memories or strengthen the attachment of every true American to the Union than the reverent but joyful observance of that day.

Now that the waves of war have rolled by, it is an earnest of returning love to the Government in those who have faltered in the past, and a renewal of the holiest vows of those who have never changed in their devotion, to unite in such celebration.

Let us, then, all unite on that day in reviving the glorious memories of our fathers, in burying all that has separated us in the past, and, as one people, give heart and hand in carrying forward our beloved land in her glorious path of civilization, education and liberty under the law.

Most truly yours,
Benj. F. Butler[1]

To. Gov. Holden

[1] Benjamin F. Butler, Massachusetts; lawyer; brigadier general, Union army, 1861; promoted to major general; member, U.S. House of Representatives, 1867-1875, 1877-1879; governor of Massachusetts, 1882-1884. *Biographical Directory of the American Congress, 1774-1971*, s.v., "Butler, Benjamin Franklin."

Petition A&H:Harris

Petition to the Congress of the U. States of America:

We, the Officers, for and on behalf of the North Carolina State Equal rights League, representing the entire colored population thereof, do petition the Congress now in session to remove the disability of voting and holding office imposed on W. W. Holden by the Constitutional Amendment and Reconstruction Acts now in force:

For these reasons: That Mr. Holden has been especially conspicious and indefatigable in his efforts in behalf of the Union, the cause of Liberty, humanity and justice. His name and sufferings have become dear to us all because of the persecution which he has undergone and still receives at the hands of disloyalists; and we feel that the great influence which he has acquired by an unflinching advocacy and unfaltering defence of the rights of man would be enhanced to our benefit and that of all loyal men by removing from him the said disability imposed by said laws. Indeed, our necessities imperatively command that we petition for the relief of such a true and tried friend. We deem *his* aid in any and every manner of the utmost importance; and confess that we are hampered in our efforts at reconstruction by the action of a law of Congress, which prevents Mr. Holden from holding an office when there so few in whom we can place confidence, or who have been tried in the furnace and withstood the test.

In 1846, twenty-one years ago, Mr. Holden held a seat in the N.C. Legislature. At the beginning of the rebellion without canvassing for votes he was chosen to office. His defence of the Union had already put his life in immenent danger. Without friends, he was then forced to yield to the implacable spirit of slavery and rebellion in order to preserve his own, and the lives of his innocent family. But all the Nation knows that during the war he alone struck blow after blow at the rebellion from *within*; for which his life was sought, his office mobbed and his property and family imperilled by the fury of his enemies. Only the early advent of Gen. Sherman's vicorious army preserved him to us; and he breathed the air of freedom again only when the federal flag floated from the Capitol of North Carolina.

Therefore we pray, &c.
Jas. H. Harris,[1]
Pres. State Equal Rights League
W.H. Anderson[2]
Recording Secretary

At Office
in Raleigh
this 8th day of
July, A.D. 1867

[1] James Henry Harris, politician; teacher, New England Freedmen's Aid Society; member, 1865 Freedmen's Convention; president, 1866 Freedmen's Convention; charter member, North Carolina Republican Party; member, state House of Representatives, 1868-1870, 1883; member, state Senate, 1872-1874. *Dictionary of North Carolina Biography*, s.v. "Harris, James Henry."

[2] William H. Anderson, Wake County schoolteacher. 1870 U.S. Census Population Schedule, North Carolina: Wake, 270.

T. J. Candler to Holden *Standard*

February 26, 1868

Editors of the Standard:—

Gentlemen:–Allow me, in advance of the proceedings of the Republican meeting held in Buncombe, to say that I have received a letter from the Chairman of the meeting, in which he states that W. W. Holden was unanimously nominated for Governor; T. R. Caldwell,[1] for Lieutenant Governor, W. W. Rollins[2] for Superintendent of Public Works; A. H. Jones,[3] for Congress; and W. G. Candler,[4] for the Commons.

They have instructed G. W. Gahagan,[5] J. H. Duckworth,[6] and myself to represent the county of Buncombe in the State nominating Convention on the 26th instant.

Yours, etc.
T. J. Candler[7]

Raleigh, Feb. 22. 1868

[1] Tod Robinson Caldwell.

[2] W. Wallace Rollins, Madison County attorney. 1870 U.S. Census Population Schedule, North Carolina: Madison, 398 (microfilm).

[3] Alexander Hamilton Jones, editor; editor Hendersonville *Times*; opposed secession; member, 1865 convention; member, U.S. House of Representatives, 1868-1871. *Dictionary of North Carolina Biography*, s.v. "Jones, Alexander Hamilton."

[4] William Gaston Candler, Buncombe County; member, House of Commons, 1865-1866, 1868-1870, 1874-1875. Cheney, *North Carolina Government, 1585-1979*, 1071.

[5] G. W. Gahagan, Madison County farmer. 1870 U.S. Census Population Schedule, North Carolina: Madison, 378 (microfilm).

[6] James H. Duckworth, Transylvania County; delegate to 1868 convention. Cheney, *North Carolina Government, 1585-1979*, 845.

[7] Thomas J. Candler, Buncombe County; delegate to 1868 convention. Cheney, *North Carolina Government*, 1585-1979, 845.

William Gibbins to Holden A&H:Holden

Forsyth Coty NC. May the 4th 1868

Mr W W Holden

Sir Permit me to congratulate you upon your Glorious Triumph over the Rebels to the office of Governor of N. C. Forsyth spoke to be understood for the Constitution for you State & County offices. Forsyth is all right & no mistake. Permit me Sir, to make some Enquiries of you if it is not out of Place, to answer them [.] Some misunderstanding exists in regard to Justices of the Peace, as I understand it, as soon as the Constitution is Ratified by Congress their offices becomes vacant & then the Governor has to appoint a sufficient number to serve untill provisions are made for Election. others think the ones that is now in office Still continue to hold their offices untill others are elected. the Reasons why I make these Enquiries is some 3 or 4 men in our District (to wit Broadbay), speakes of petitioning you to appoint them when some of them did not vote, while the others Scrachd your Name off of the Ticket. if you have the appointing Power Beware of these Wolves in Sheeps Clothing You Cannot be too carefull in guarding against such men, telling the weak nees & Freedman that Holden Wont do to tie too, & many other things I could mention, & does Constables hold their offices untill Election. there is some fishing for that office, that did not vote at all or Scrachd their ticket The Republicans of my district wants a man to fill the Lowest office that voted the whole ticket, I will not mention names but will if needs be. I could mention various things that occurd Previous to the Election but do not wish to exhaust your Patinece.

Yours Respectfully
William Gibbins[1]

[1] William Gibbins, Forsyth County farmer. 1870 U.S. Census Population Schedule, North Carolina: Forsyth, 297 (microfilm).

Will B. Rodman to Holden A&H:Holden

Washington 5 May 1868

My dear Sir.

I suppose it is entirely too late to congratulate you on your election—but it is not too late to rejoice over the very gratifying majority by which the ticket is carried. Considering the perfect organization of the Conservatives and the leverage which they had in the passions and prejudices of our people, I confess I think the vote to be a remarkable one. We do certainly know that many white men earnestly desirious of the reconstruction of the Union,—not prejudiced against the personel of our ticket—were prevented form voting for the Constitution and the ticket, by lies as to what the Constitution contained, and by a system of terrorism unparalled in our history. The loss of power is a dreadful blow to the Conservatives. Under one name and disguise or another they have substantially held it during and since the war. It is like the expulsion of the Bourbons. Whatever the leaders may do, I hope the masses will settle down in contented acquiesence, at least, if not complete satisfaction. It is to the interest of the Republican party to conciliate and win over the white men of the Country. Indeed I think the very existence of the party at the South will depend on our success in such an effort. I do not doubt about the Presidential election—the colored people will continue to go with us in mass on that—and a great many whites will vote for the Republican nominee (if we give them a fair chance to do so) who were against us in the last election. We shall certainly carry N.Ca. for the nominee by a large majority. But *after that*—I am inclined to think it will be difficult if not impossible to prevent the splitting up of the colored vote. A white vote will then be needed to supply the loss. Now in my opinion it will be easier to get this vote from the Confederate sentiment of the State than any where else, and for these reasons. 1st The Democrats went into the war more generally than the Whigs—& of the two they are much more inclined to friendly co-operation with the Republicans than the Whigs—who mostly were "latter day war men"—are.

2nd the Democrats who went into the Conservative organization feel that they have not been received on an equal footing—& may be easily detached from the opposition. 3rd the men who actually served in the army appreciate more justly the true condition of things and the absolute necessity of submission to the government, than those who stayed at home. I think therefore our policy should be to conciliate this sentiment. I speak only of this section of the State—say the whole Tar River valley from Hyde up.

I suppose Cowles[1] has duly attended to sending to Congress a certified copy of the Constitution, which I hope they will act on so promptly that the Legislature may meet about 1 June. There is a inst deal for that body to do.

I shall be unable properly to attend to the duties of Code Commissioner—beyond the preparation with the others of a Code of practice & procedure which may serve until the experience of our Courts enable them to amend it. I hope you will consider the matter of the appointment of some proper person to succeed me, after that much is done, when I shall send you a formal resignation. Indeed I can hardly afford the time and labor necessary for the preparation of the practice part of the Code, but so many of the profession urge me to undertake that—that I mean to attempt it if possible.

Very truly
Yours &c
Will B. Rodman[2]

Hon. W. W. Holden

[1] Calvin Josiah Cowles. Cowles had served as president of the 1868 convention.

[2] William Blount Rodman, lawyer and jurist; A.B., U.N.C., 1836; 1862, appointed presiding judge of military court by Jefferson Davis; delegate to 1868 convention; associate justice, North Carolina Supreme Court, 1868-1878; 1868, he and two other commissioners drafted codes of criminal and civil procedure and a penal code. *Dictionary of North Carolina Biography*, s.v. "Rodman, William Blount."

John Pool to Holden A&H:Holden

E. City, May 9, 1868

Private

Hon. W. W. Holden.

My dear Sir:

Matchet Taylor,[1] Esqr., the defeated republican candidate for the Legislature, in Camden, is in my office, & requests me to write you. He was defeated by about 35 votes, & there is no doubt that very unfair means were resorted to defeat him. Threats, violence & interference with the polls keepers at South Mills precinct, & turning out of imployment &c have all been verified by affidavits taken before Capt. Doherty,[2] of the Freedman's Bureau of this place. I think, these affidavits have been forwarded to Genl. Canby.[3] It may not be necessary to the party, but it is a matter of personal justice to Mr. Taylor & his fire-tried friends in Camden, that this matter should receive attention. Relying upon the promise of Genl. Canby to order a new election in case of unfairness, Mr. T. & his friends submitted to the imposition rather than produce a disturbance of the peace at the election. Their good conduct allowed his defeat by unfair means. It is the duty of the General to see that right is done him. He is very anxious, & feels deeply on the subject—& insists that I now write you to use your influence with the Commanding General in his behalf. I hope you will do so without delay. I am satisfied that Camden would give 150 republican majority upon a fair vote. Mr. Taylor believes it would be larger. Our friends then need to be encouraged by some show of authority in their behalf.

I notice with hearty approbation your positions in the "Standard" of the 5th inst,[4] in reply to the infamous programme of the "Sentinel" of 2nd inst. Many ultra republicans, who did not vote for you, in this place, say, since seeing your issue of the 5th inst. that they regret not having voted for you. They feared you would allow yourself to be again imposed on by the impudence & fanning of Secessionists. allow me to say, my dear Sir, that we must all now see that no reliance can be placed upon the words, the honor or the position of any man thoroughly imbued with the fanaticism of sectionalism. Their infamous abuse, threats & personal insolence, during the late canvass, must convince us all that the hatred to the white Union men of the State is positivily infernal in its intensity & malignity. It is implacable. It cannot be appeased by any kindness or conciliation on your part. They will have war & hatred. They will allow but one alternative, viz: to be the *gross* or the *truth* that nips it. We must accept it, & act accordingly. I recommend no spasmodic, revengeful action. But with firm & dignified persistence, they must be made to feel that loyal men *will* be the masters in this State. Your only reliable friends look to you to hold a strong & unflinching hand. If you do, your administration will be sustained by us to the last extremity. But, if you suffer your natural exuberance of kind feeling, & personal generosity, to betray you into the errors that became so soon apparent in your administration as provisional governor, it will result in your own destruction as well as ours. Such is the universal feeling among the republicans here—& they are in high spirits at the manifestation of the right purpose in the "Standard" of the 5th inst. I have, all the time, told them that you could not be deceived & betrayed a second time. I shall be in Raleigh about the time of the meeting of the Legislature, & will confer with you on other points of vital importance to our future safety.

I could not quietly submit to be again placed under the government of Secessionists. They ought to be made to understand that the Union men would resort to force & violence before they would be again tyranized over by men whose morality was not shocked by robbery, whose humanity was not aroused by either murder, or the most atrocious cruelty, & whose insane hatred can now be neither appeased nor limited.

Yours very truly,
John Pool

P.S. I would have been glad to have gone to Washington, this week, but I have been suffering greatly, for several days, with erysipelas of the face, & get no better. My respect to Deweese,[5] Coleman,[6] Harris[7] & other friends.

[1] Matchet Taylor, Camden County; farmer. 1870 U.S. Census Population Schedule, North Carolina: Camden, 160 (microfilm).

[2] William H. Doherty, agent of the Bureau of Refugees, Freedmen and Abandoned Lands in Elizabeth City. Roster of Officers and Civilians on Duty in Bureau of Refugees, Freedmen and Abandoned Lands in North Carolina, November 1, 1868.

[3] Edward Richard Sprigg Canby, Indiana; graduate, U.S. Military Academy, 1839; brigadier general of volunteers, 1862; major general, 1864; brigadier general, U.S. Army, 1866; brevet major general, commanding Second Military District [North And South Carolina]. Francis B. Heitman, *Historical Register and Dictionary of the United States Army* (Washington: Government Pronting Office, 1903), s.v. "Canby, Edward Richard Sprigg."

[4] An editorial in the *Weekly Standard*, May 5, 1868, stated "*All political power in this State will soon pass into Republican hands*." It further stated that "No man who is not an open and avowed Republican must be permitted to eat a crust of bread from Town, County, or State Treasury."

[5] John Thomas Deweese, congressman; officer in Union army, serving finally as lieutenant colonel, Fourth Indiana Cavalry; appointed second lieutenant, Eighth

Regiment, U.S. Infantry, July, 1866, and assigned to North Carolina; resigned to accept appointment as commissioner in bankruptcy for North Carolina; member, U.S. House of Representatives, 1868-1870, resigning in latter year. *Dictionary of North Carolina Biography*, s.v. "Deweese, John Thomas."

[6] William Macon Coleman, lawyer; A.B., U.N.C., 1858; A. M., 1892; attorney general of North Carolina, 1868-1869. Grant, *Alumni History*, 123.

[7] Probably Ceburn L. Harris.

Louis V. Caziere to Holden DU:Holden

HEADQUARTERS SECOND
MILITARY DISTRICT
Charleston, S.C., May 16th, 1868

Sir:

I have the honor to transmit herewith your Certificate of Election as Governor of North Carolina.

You will please acknowledge the receipt of the Certificate, and take and subscribe the enclosed oaths of office, transmitting one copy to these Headquarters, and the other to the Secretary of State of the State of North Carolina.

Very Respectfully, sir,
Your Obedient Servant,
Louis V. Caziere
Aide-de-Camp,
Actg. Asst. Adjt. Genl.

To William W. Holden

TELEGRAM *Byron Laflin To Holden* A&H:Holden

Washington, June 15, 1868

To Hon. W. W. Holden

Senators and Genl Rawlings[1] advise you as Govr Elect to issue call for Legislature to convene June 29th.

Byron Laflin[2]
Natl Hotel

[1] John Aaron Rawlings, Illinois; captain, volunteers, 1861; major, 1862; brigadier general, 1863; chief of staff to General Grant, 1865-1869; secretary of war, March 11-

September 6, 1869. Heitman, *Historical Register and Dictionary of the United States Army*, s.v. "Rawlings, John Aaron."

[2] Byron Laflin, Pitt County; member, 1868 convention; member, state House of Representatives, 1868-1870. Cheney, *North Carolina Government, 1585-1979*, 846, 448, 450

PROCLAMATION *Standard* June 17, 1868

By W. W. Holden *Governor Elect of North Carolina*

In pursuance of authority vested in me by an act passed by the Congress of the United States, entitled "an act to admit the States of North-Carolina, South Carolina, Louisiana, Georgia, Arkansas, and Florida to representation in Congress," the members elect to the Legislature of North-Carolina, chosen under and by authority of the law of the United States of March 2d, 1867, "to provide for the more efficient government of the rebel States," and the laws supplementary thereto, are hereby notified to assemble in the City of Raleigh on Wednesday, the 1st day of July, Anno Domoni, 1868.

W. W. Holden,
Gov. Elect of North Carolina

Raleigh, June 15, 1868

J. W. Stephens to Holden A&H:Holden

Yanceyville NC
June the 20th 1868

Hon Gov W. W. Holden

Dear sir I wish to know of you if it is nessary for W. Cary[1] & myself to be in Raleigh on the 1st of July the time appointed by you for the convening legislature as you know Bedford Brown & Wm Long[2] are banded by the Howard amendment. I wish to call your particular attention to the condition I have placed myself in by coming out & standing up for the Republican party in this Co. & ask your support & protection in the matter. before I taken this stand (whitch I did becaus I thought it was rite & have never yet Regretted and hope I never Shall.) I had many friends & credit for any thing I wanted but now I have neither the trouth is that I have not means to buy what I actualy kneed for the support of my family. my crediters have pushed on me and taken every thing that the law would *allow* & I can look to know source but the Republican party if thaire is any thing that you can do for me in this hour of kneed pleas let me know what it is hoping to here from you soon

I remain your most obt Servt
J. W. Stephens[3]

[1] Wilson Carey, Caswell County; member, state House of Representatives, 1868-1870, 1874-1879, 1889; delegate to 1868 and 1875 conventions: seated in 1868 session of state House of Representatives when William Long was removed. Cheney, *North Carolina Government, 1585-1979*, 845, 874, 1089.

[2] William Long, Caswell County; member, House of Commons, 1852-1857, 1862-1864, 1868; removed from seat and Carey replaced him. Cheney, *North Carolina Government, 1585-1979*, 1089.

[3] John Walter Stephens, Caswell County; following quarrel with neighbor over chickens who strayed onto his property, identified as "Chicken" Stephens; member, state Senate, 1868; murdered in Caswell County courthouse May 21, 1870, by members of the Ku Klux Klan. *Dictionary of North Carolina Biography*, s.v. "Stephens, John Walter."

Friends of the U.L.A. to Holden A&H:Holden

Taylorsville Alexander Co. N.C.
June 24th 1868

To the Governor of N.Carolina

We the Republicans of Alexander Co. we would most Respectfully Communicate to Your Honor a fiew lines after being informed By Your Orders The representativs are to asemble in the city of Raleigh on the First of July next We the Republicans of Alexander Co. Petition to you the Honorable Governor of The State that we are utterly opposed to the Admittance of the Representative[1] who was Elected on the Conservative ticket who denounced the constitution in the Most bitter terms and swore that he would not live under such a Negro Government that he intended to leave the State if the constitution was Ratified that he was Perfectly Reckless and denounces the Present Congress and calls it Radical Congress sayse that thair laws whitch they make are not fit for white men to live under and that the Reconstruction Plan is an imposition upon the People and he further Denounces you the governor and sayse that you are a worse traitor than Benedick Arnold and Denounced you on the stump all over the county and also denounced the lieuten Governor and also all the State officers and calls the Republicans Negro Equality Men and now we suppose that this same man is going down to Raleigh to asquire thease same men whom he Denounced So bitterly to permit him To Take an Oath to support the same constitution whitch he so bitterly opposed but we the petitioners sincerely hope that his request will not be granted that whilest him and all others who took the same Position that he did will like, the sinners was around Noah's ark while claiming admitance we hope that they will be immediately sent sent [*sic*] back home likewise on there own expenses for we think that if Such men are Permitted to take there seats after saying that it wood be more Tolerable for Sodom and Gomorrah than the Republicans if they got in Power in conclusion we will say that the representative is allso opposed to General Grant being our candidate for President Now after all there threats whitch they have made against our Party if they permitted to take there seats we think it useless to take any Part in any Election hereafter we thing this suffise for the Present we will decline signing our names only as your republican Friends of the U.L.A.[2]

[1]Robert P. Matheson, Alexander County, merchant; member, state House of Representatives, 1868-1870, 1883, 1889; member, state Senate, 1879. Cheney, *North Carolina Government, 1585-1979*, 1044.

[2]Union League of America, secret society supporting the Republican Party; Governor Holden was first president of the Union League in North Carolina. Hugh Talmage Lefler, ed., *North Carolina History Told by Contemporaries*, 4th ed. (Chapel Hill: University of North Carolina Press, 1965). 318-321.

Ed. R. Canby to Holden A&H:Holden

Hdqtrs 2 Mil Dist
Charleston, S.C. June 29, 1868

Hon. W. W. Holden
Gov. elect of North Carolina
Raleigh, N.C.

Sir:

The Chief Justice elect[1] of the Supreme Court, will take and subscribe his oath of office at once before the US Comr. at Raleigh.

The Chief Justice will then administer the oath of office to the Associate Justices and also, at the inauguration to the State executive officers elect.

Sgd. Ed. R. Canby
Bvt. Maj. Gen'l
Commanding

[1] Richmond Mumford Pearson.

Jonathan Worth to Holden A&H:GP

State of North Carolina
Executive Department
Raleigh, July 1st, 1868

Gov. W. W. Holden
Raleigh, N.C.

Sir:—

Yesterday morning I was verbally notified by Chief Justice Pearson[1] that, in obedience to a telegram from Genl. Canby,[2] he would to-day, at 10 O'Clock A.M., administer to you the oaths required, preliminary to your entering upon the discharge of the duties of *Civil Governor* of the State; and that, therefore, you would demand possession of my office.

I intimated to the Judge my opinion that such proceeding was premature even under the reconstruction legislation of Congress, and that I should probably decline to surrender the office to you.

At sundown, yesterday evening, I received from Col. Williams,[3] commandant of this Military Post, an extract from the general orders, No. 120, of General Canby, as follows:–

Headquarters 2nd Military District.
Charleston, S.C., June 30th, 1868.
General Orders,
No. 120.

(Extract)

"To facilitate the organization of the new state governments, the following appointments are made. To be governor of North Carolina, W. W. Holden, Governor elect, vice, Jonathan Worth removed. To be Lieutenant Governor of North Carolina, Tod R. Caldwell, Lieutenant Governor elect, to fill an original vacancy. To take effect July 1st 1868, on the meeting of the General assembly of North Carolina."

I do not recognize the validity of the late election under which you, and those co-operating with you, claim to be invested with the civil government of the State. You have no evidence of your election, save the certificate of a Major General of the United States army. I regard all of you as, in effect, appointees of the Military power of the United States—and not as "deriving your powers from the consent of those you claim to govern." Knowing, however, that you are backed by Military force here, which I could not resist, if I would, I do not deem it necessary to offer a futile opposition, but vacate the office without the ceremony of actual eviction, offering no further opportunity than this my protest. I would submit to actual expulsion in order to bring before the Supreme Court of the United States the question as to the constitutionality of the legislation under which you claim to be the rightful Governor of this State, if the past action of that tribunal furnished any hope of a speedy trial. I surrender the office to you under what I deem military duress, without stopping, as the occasion would well justify, to comment upon the singular co-incidence, that the present state government is surrendered, as *without legality*, to him whose own official sanction, but three years ago, declared it *valid*.

I am, very Respectfully
Jonathan Worth
Governor of North Carolina.

[1] Richmond Mumford Pearson.

[2] Major General Edward Richard Sprigg Canby.

[3] George Angustus Williams, New York; 1852, graduate U.S. Military Academy; captain, 1861; brevet lieutenant colonel, 1863; commanded Raleigh military post; retired, 1870. Heitman, *Historical Register and Dictionary of the United States Army*, s.v. "Williams, George Augustus."

TELEGRAM *Ed. R. S. Canby to Holden* A&H:GP

Charleston, July 3, 1868

His Excellency
W. W. Holden, Govr. N.C.
Raleigh, N.C.

Your telegram announcing the ratification of the Constitutional Amendment[1] by the Legislature of No Ca has been recd., and instructions will be sent to-day to the Military Commanders in No Carolina to abstain from the exercise of any authority under the Reconstruction laws, except to close up unfinished business, and not to interfere in any civil matters unless the execution of the laws of June 25/68,should be obstructed by unlawful or forcible opposition to the inauguration of the new State Govt.

The RRd appoinments made by Gov. Worth have been annulled.

Ed. R. S. Canby

[1] The General Assembly ratified the 14th Amendment to the U.S. Constitution by a vote of 34 to 2 in the state Senate and 82 to 19 in the state House of Representatives.

Inaugural Address of Governor W. W. Holden A&H:GLB

(Delivered July 4th, 1868)

Fellow Citizens: The unity of government, which constitutes us one people, has been restored. The great rebellion is suppressed. The will of the majority, from which there will be no further appeal, has been pronounced. Although the passions which the rebellion engendered and evoked may disturb us for a season, they can neither afflict us hereafter nor retard the progress of free principles on this continent. The Union has been preserved. It has been preserved not only on its former basis of liberty for one race, but its foundations are how broad enough for the whole people, of whatsoever origin, color or former condition.

We have assembled to day to begin anew the work of self government. The congress of the United States, properly charged with the reconstruction of the lately insurgent States and their restoration to their Constitutional relations to the general government, has proceeded upon principles which have their basis in the rights of man; and it has so guarded those principles by enactments, and by amendments to the Constitution, as to render them Safe for the future in the hands of the people of the respective states. We believe that the work thus begun for the whole people, by the whole people of the State, will be prosecuted to fortunate results. We trust that the foundations which have been laid, and which we this day dedicate to Liberty and Union in North Carolina, will remain solid and firm for all time to come beneath the edifice of general prosperity and happiness to be erected thereon.

We feel sure that a government "of the people, by the people, and for the people" will outlast any other form, and will confer greater benefits than any other on those who are destined to live under it; and we are, therefore, confident that all that is valuable and perfect in whatsoever is merely human in its character, must flow from the form we have adopted.

The People of this State have formed and ratified a Constitution of government, which contains all the great principles of liberty contended for in past ages by the wise and good of England and America. The Constitution has been considered and approved by the Congress of the United States as "republican in form" and with this approval North Carolina has been restored to her former position and privileges in the Union.

The Constitution holds, Fellow Citizens, as a self-evident fact, that all men are equal in their political and civil rights. It declares that all governments originates from the people, is founded upon their will only, and is instituted solely for the good of the whole.

It declares "that the State shall ever remain a member of the American Union"—that there is no such right as that of secession, and that any attempt at secession "ought to be resisted by the whole power of the State."

It provides for the freedom of the press, for freedom of speech, and declares that the "privilege of the writ of *habeas corpus* shall *not* be suspended."

It guards every citizen's house as his castle, against general warrants not supported by proper evidence; and it guards personal liberty as of chief value to the citizen.

It declares that "as political rights and priveleges are not dependent upon, or modified by property, therefore no property qualifications ought to affect the right to vote or hold office."

It secures religious freedom.

It provides for education as a "*right*" which it is "the *duty* of the State to guard and maintain."

It declares that perpetuities and monopolies, heritary emoluments and privileges, and *ex post facto* laws are contrary to the genius of a free State, and ought not to be allowed.

It declares that human Slavery is "forever prohibited within this State."

It declares that all property shall be taxed "according to its true value in money" thus establishing the only just system of taxation; and for the protection of both the poll and the lands, it provides that for State and county purposes the poll tax shall never exceed two dollars, and that this tax shall be "equal to the tax on property valued at three hundred dollars in cash"—thus balancing the land against the poll tax and preventing injustice or oppression to either.

It makes the most stringent provisions for maintaining State credit.

It provides for a homestead for every head of a family, and as far as it was possible to do so, secures such homestead against all debts or obligations.

It very tenderly provides for the rights of married women, by exempting all their property from the debts of their husbands, and giving them power, with the assent of the husband, to convey such property as they may choose.

It provides for the poor, for the orphan, for the deaf and dumb and blind, for the Insane, for Idiots and inebriates, and in fine, for all who are benighted, wretched and forlorn.

It separates from each other the great departments of the Government, legislative, executive and judicial; and it makes them all dependent on the people as the only rightful source of power.

It provides that every male citizen shall be a voter; and every voter, with few exceptions, shall be eligible to office. Suffrage has thus been bestowed upon all. The colored man has the same right with the white man to vote and hold office. I do not inquire whether it was necessary to do this to accomplish reconstruction.

It is sufficient that Justice is always a necessity in forming governments that are to operate upon all, and that without it no government can be expected to endure. The ballot, thus bestowed upon our recently enfranchised people will remain with them. There is no power than can deprive them of it, without plunging us into a protracted and terrible civil war.

Four millions of human beings who have once tasted the blessings of freedom, would not surrender these blessings without a struggle. They would find powerful friends here and elsewhere in the country. Greater calamities and sufferings than those endured by our people in the late rebellion would come upon us with such a struggle, but the result though long delayed, would not be doubtful. Liberty for all would again triumph. Those who had provoked such a "war of races" would disappear from the earth, and their possessions would pass from their children to the conquerors. There can be no danger of such a conflict if every one will faithfully submit to the Constitution and laws, and follow the things that make for peace and good will among the people. The friends of reconstruction will prevail hereafter, as heretofore, not only in the State but in the nation, and the colored people will therefore, retain the right of suffrage, and exercise it as it is, in common with the white race, with no qualification save that of manhood. There is no reasonable ground to fear that it will not operate beneficially for all. The repugnance to it, which exists among many of our people, will gradually subside, when they shall be convinced by actual experience that none of the evils they anticipate have resulted from it.

This Constitution, fellow Citizens, must be administered by its friends and supporters. The people have so decided.

The interests it guards are too precious to be committed to any extent to unfriendly hands. Every office and every appointment under the State from the most inferior to the most exalted, must be filled by the friends of reconstruction and of the new State Constitution. So far as the Executive is concerned this purpose will be inflexibly maintained, not only from a sense of propriety and justice but as indispensable to a full and fair trial of the principles contained in the Constitution.

These principles are dear to the friends of liberty and of the government of the United States; and no opportunity should be afforded to those who are opposed to them to occupy official positions or to have employments, in which they would be tempted, as they certainly are disposed, to pervert, distort or misapply them. The friends of the Government must conduct the government in all its departments. Yet it does not follow that others will be singled out to be wronged or oppressed. The people do not oppress or wrong any one when they say that certain persons shall not have office, on account of their political opinions. Office is a privilege, which may be bestowed or withheld without infringing any right. Every Citizen of the State will be free. The laws will be made for all, and will operate equally upon all. Every Citizen will enjoy, in equal measure the protection of the courts. There will be no social proscription. No effort will be made to blacken the names of even unrepenant rebels, as was the case with the tories of the revolution; but it will be left to history to assign to their appropriate places all the actors in the late tragedy of rebellion. In fine, those who will conduct the government are not the enemies of any portion of the people of the State. They desire to do justice to all, and as far as may be, to be the friends of all. If the administration of public affairs shall bring peace, prosperity and hapiness [*sic*], all will share in these blessings; if on the contrary, it shall produce disorder, and further suffering and misery, none will be exempt from these calamities. The injunction of the Constitution regarding education should be faithfully observed.

Colleges, high schools, Normal schools for the education of teachers, and public schools for all, should be established at the earliest practicable period, and liberally sustained from the public Treasury. We should so conduct our Public Schools as to render them superior to all others of a similar kind in the State, and thus make it the interest, as well as the duty of parents to regard them as common to all, the rich and the middle classes as well as the poor. The first duty of a free State is to educate its children. It cannot be too often repeated that the structure and perpetuity of free institutions depend on the intelligence and virtue of the people. We must either prepare to educate thoroughly the rising generation of both races, or abandon the hope that we shall continue a free, self-governing State. It does not follow, nor does the Constitution require that the white and colored races shall be educated together in the same schools. It is believed to be better for both, and more satisfactory to both, that the schools should be distinct and separate. But they should be equally calculated to impart instruction, and the schools for the two, thus separate and apart, should enjoy equally the fostering care of the State.

The Constitution provides for organizing and arming the Militia to "execute the law, suppress riots or insurrections, and to repel invasion." The opinion of Washington, uttered in 1790 that a "free people ought not only to be armed but disciplined" and that a well organized militia "is certainly an object of primary importance, whether viewed in reference to the national security, to the satisfaction of the community, or to the preservation of order" is not less weighty or important now than it was then. The militia should be organized at once. It is the duty of the Executive to see that the laws are faithfully executed and to preserve peace among the people. This duty will be performed promptly, fearlessly, and firmly. Every citizen must submit to lawful authority, or refusing to do so, must expect the penallties of the violated law. In the language of our great general, second only to him who was "first in war, first in peace, and first in the hearts of his countrymen" "Let us have Peace." The sword, which would not have been drawn but for the criminal folly of the recently insurgent States, should never again be wielded by American against Americans. Every interest that is dear to us, and every hope that we may indulge for the future, is indissolubly bound up with peace and tranquility among ourselves. But there can be no peace without law, and there can be no efficacy in law without obedience. The law is over all. The poor and the humble should be protected to as full an extent as others. They need more than others this protection. Every one must be free to use what is his own, not trespassing on the right of others; to follow his particular calling or employment; to labor, and to enjoy the fruit of his labor, to speak freely his sentiments and to vote as he pleases, and not be injured or questioned by any for doing an of these things. The people of North Carolina are proverbial for their law abiding disposition. It is not apprehended that disturbances will arise, or that combinations will be formed to resist the laws; yet it is known that many hold the opinion that the reconstruction laws of the United States are unconstitutional, and therefore null and void; and it may be that this may lead, if not to open resistance, to a forcible denial in some localities of the rights guaranteed by the constitution of the state, formed and adopted in pursuance of said laws. It is also known that a disposition exists among an inconsiderable portion of our population, to oppress the poor whites and the colored race, on account of their political opinions.

The Magistrates and the Courts will be sustained by the whole power of the State, in such action as may be deemed necessary to protect those who may be thus wronged or oppressed; and the magistrates and the Courts will be sustained by the whole power of the State in giving effect to the Constitution itself, as having been fairly, justly and properly adopted, and as binding in all respects on every citizen until changed or modified in the mode prescribed in the instrument itself. Differences in political sentiments are to be expected, and are not calculated in themselves to endanger the state; but a purpose to subvert the Government, on the assumption that it is not properly derived, has not been constitutionally adopted, and is illegitimate and not binding, should be narrowly watched and promptly checked, on the first manifestation of any overt act on the part of those cherishing such purpose.

The Constitution of this State is, under the Constitution of the United States, the Supreme organic law. The government which it establishes, and the laws passed in pursuance of it, will be maintained and enforced. To render resistance, therefore, impracticable, if not impossible, and to maintain the peace by executing the laws in a Spirit of Justice to all, it is deemed essential that a portion of the Militia should be well discipled and armed, and should be thus ready at any moment, under the orders of the Commander-in-chief, for active duty.

It is not proposed, or is it required by the Constitution that the two races should be mustered and drilled in the same companies and regiments.

Following the example of the government of the United States, they may be divided into separate companies and regiments; but it is due to the colored race that they should have, whenever they desire it, officers of their own color for their own companies and regiments. In this, as in all other things concerning our white and colored fellow citizens, absolute civil and political equality should be maintained. The public burdens should fall equally on both, and there should be no distinction between them in their political and civil rights.

The Constitution provides that to "maintain the honor and good faith of the State untarnished, the Public debt regularly contracted before and since the rebellion, shall be regarded as inviolable and never be questioned." It would be difficult to overstate the value of character to individuals or to States.

A State which deliberately says "this is my seal—the debt is just, but I will not pay it" proclaims that there is no virtue in moral obligation, and sinks at once to the level of savage races whom no treaty or obligation can bind. States flourish and prosper, and are respected in proportion as they adhere to the eternal principles of Justice.

North Carolina when fully herself, uninfluenced by the passions of the rebellion, would have felt any stain upon her credit as a wound and would have submitted to any sacrifice to avert even the suspicion that our honor could be sullied by any act of her own. North Carolina is again a State, in the full sense in which she was before she rebelled, and her obligations and duties are as binding as they formerly were. These obligations and duties cannot be evaded or avoided. The payment of the interest on her debt, as provided for in the Constitution, would at once place her Credit on a secure footing. A debt ceases to affect credit injuriously when the interest is promptly paid, and when it is seen that an accumulation of valuable property and general prosperity is the result of the indebtedness. The credit of England is equal to that of any country, yet the English debt is the result of the accumulations of ages, and is of enormous magnitude. The secret of the credit of England is the unswerving punctuality with which her interest is paid, and the fact that she is constantly adding to her wealth and power by the use of what she has borrowed. I do not doubt that the General Assembly, responding to the general wish of our people, will make prompt and ample provision for meeting the interest of the State debt.

By meeting promptly the interest on her debt the state will be enabled to borrow money to prosecute internal improvements, which are essential to the development of her resources. Money thus expended, and money expended for education will constitute the very best investment the State could make. A vigorous and well-directed system of Internal Improvements, from the seashore to the Tennessee line, thus placing us in direct communication with the Mississippi valley, with cheap rates of freight and travel, would stimulate agriculture and the mechanic arts, build up our sea ports, increase our commerce both foreign and coastwide, draw thither immigrants from the Northern States and from Europe, arrest emigration from the State, give employment to thousands of our people, and thus place us at no very distant day in the front rank of American States. No state in the Union has superior advantages to North Carolina, whether we consider the extent of her seacoast, the value of her harbors, her geographical situation, the salubrity of her climate, or the nature and variety of her resources and productions. She is exempted on the one hand from the protracted and vigorous winters of the North, and on the other from the blasting heats of the South. Favored thus with climate and soil, extending from Currituck to Cherokee five hundred miles, and one hundred and eighty miles in width at one point with fifty thousand square miles of territory, and a population of not more than twenty to the square mile, it is obvious that a great and prosperous future is before her, if her people should prove true to themselves. What we need is capital and mind, to bring out these resources—to render them convenient and useful and available for wealth and power. We need skilled labor. We need educated, thinking, investigating, enterprising minds, on our farms, in our workshops and manufactures, in our mines, on our railroads, at the head of our schools and presses, and indeed in every industrial enterprise or pursuit.

Fellow Citizens. Let us come out of the caverns of the past, and forgetting whatever is not worthy to be remembered, let us resolve to do our duty in our day and time, as North Carolinians, as Americans. In a climate and with a soil which providence has done so much, let us resolve to do something for ourselves and our children. Let us devote ourselves to the arts of peace. Let us improve this great inheritance. Let our children and our children's children, when they shall come to take our places, say of us, "Our ancestors remembered and did what was wise, and what was good for us. Behold, the beautiful country they have left to us!— the just and equal laws that are over us, and the hope that their work has made strong in us that we can do even more for our children than they have done for us." Let us at least unite upon the one great object of improving and building up the State. Let us welcome capital and immigration, furnishing as they will the indispensable means to our progress and prosperity. Prejudices growing out of nativity, or out of the rebellion, are nor worthy to be cherished.

Let us discard such prejudices. We are once more Americans all. Let us receive with courtesty and kindness every citizen of the Northern or Eastern States who may cast his lot among us, and measure him as we measure others, according to his personal and moral worth. We cannot hope to improve our condition if we repel capital and immigration, either by so acting as to produce the belief that it is not safe to settle among us on account of the want of law and order, or unpleasant, because of rude or uncivil treatment to the immigrant. It should be remembered that our ancestors were, originally, as much "adventurers" as others. Of the three signers of the Declaration of Independence for this State neither was a native. Richard Caswell, one of our greatest Governors, and sometimes called the Washington of North Carolina, was not a native, nor was Joseph Caldwell, who built up our University and led the way with Murphy, Yancey, Stanly, Saunders and others in internal improvements and public instruction. We want the best people from Europe, and from all parts of the United States to settle among us. It is *men* that make a State. Let them come with their enterprise and money, their muscle and intelligence; and when they get here let the only rivalry be as to who shall do most for the good and the glory of our beloved State.

The government of the United States, in the prosecution of the war to suppress the rebellion, and in the measures it has adopted to reconstruct the Union, has exhibited extraordinary clemency and magnaniunity. It has taken no vengeance for the past, but has required only security for the future. It has deprived no man of his properity save for war purposes during the progress of the war; it has exiled no man; it has punished no man for the crime of rebellion. It has simply required that those who have been in rebellion should renew their allegiance, and that such guards should be placed in the organic laws of the States and the nation as to prevent future rebellion. Instead of defining or restricting suffrage permanently, it has left it with the respective States, to be determined and settled as the may choose; and this State, following in full measure the example of the national government, has made suffrage free to all. But the war to suppress the rebellion has, in its results, necessarily changed as it has settled the theory of construction previously held by a large portion of the people. Our liberities have been consolidated, and the Union can, in no event, be dissolved. It is to endure always. It must increase, but never decrease. For all great national purposes the government of the United States is over the States, and paramount to the States, and the allegiance of the citizen is first due to it. There is no appeal from the will of the nation expressed by a majority. Armed resistance to the national authority, whether by individuals of their own accord, or by individuals acting under supposed state authority or command is *treason*, and must be so held and treated. The doctrine of State's rights, as held by Mr. Calhoun and his followers, has ceased to have validity or vitality; and the teachings and doctrines of *Washington*, *Hamilton*, *Webster*, *Jackson*, *Clay*, and *Lincoln*, now constitute the true, and the only safe theory of construction.

This has been settled, under Providence, by the result of a solemn appeal to arms among brethren; and he who would unsettle this theory; thereby rendering it possible that secession should ever again be attempted, is no friend to his species, to his state, or to the general government of his country. The government of the United States is no longer a feeble luminary, receiving and dispensing light to surrounding planets; but it is a full sun, burning with a supreme splendor, pervading and holding up to itself the entire system and kindling new planets into life and motion. How beneficent, how glorious, how far reaching, will be the light it will dispense when it reaches its meridian, we shall not live to see, but the generations to come after us will walk in that light, and be contented, prosperous and happy. In the fullness of their gratitude they will thank God as we do, that the government of the United States, delivered from the perils of rebellion, and reconstructed on the basis of equal rights of all, is as indestructible as the earth itself, and as secure in its position and in the exercise of all its great powers, as

"The Northern Star
Of whose true, fixed and resting quality
There is no fellow in the firmament"

I have thus, fellow Citizens, stated briefly and plainly the great principles contained in our State Constitution, and I have frankly announced the policy which will characterize my administration. Cherishing neither malice nor resentment for anything that has occurred in the past, I shall endeavor to do my duty. I shall keep constantly in view the welfare of North Carolina. I love the Union, because it is the first, the last, the only hope of my State; and I love my State, because her people have been good and kind to me, and because her sky is above my home, as it will be above my grave. If I have enemies, that does not make me an enemy to my State, nor move me to a course of action based on resentment or revenge. I follow the principles of *Washington*, who founded, and of Lincoln, who saved the Republic; and when these principles cease to lead, I shall cease to follow.

May the God of our fathers have us in His holy keeping; may He govern, and not we; and may the future of our beloved state be as bright and as glorious as the last last seven years have been disastrious and unhappy.

Holden to the President A&H:GLB

Executive Chamber
Raleigh No C July 4th 1868

To the President of the United States

Sir

I am directed to transmit to you the accompanying resolution ratifying the fourteenth article to the Constitution of the United States.

You will see that it passed the House of Representatives and Senate of the General Assembly of North Carolina on the 2nd inst, and is signed by the presiding officers and clerks of both houses according to law.

Very Respectfully
W. W. Holden
Governor of the State of North Carolina

C. *Dewey to Holden* A&H:GP

Bank of the State of No. Caro
Raleigh 7th July 1868

His Excellency
W. W. Holden Governor

At a meeting of the Stockholders of this Bank held on the first Monday of July instant, the following Gentlemen were elected Directors on the part of the Individual Stockholders, Viz:

Geo: W. Mordecai,[1] Jno. H. Bryan[2]
B. F. Moore[3] Chas Manly
D. M. Barringer[4] Jno Devereux[5]
& W. H. Holleman[6]

Two Directors are to be appointed by the Governor, Secretary of State & Comptroller, on the part of the State; they are required to be Stockholders

I have the honor to be
Yr Mo Obt.
C Dewey Agt.[7]

[1] George Washington Mordecai, lawyer and railroad and banking executive; incorporator and first president of Raleigh and Gaston Railroad; 1849, president of the

Bank of the State of North Carolina; 1859, president of Bank of North Carolina; 1869, incorporator and first president of Oakwood Cemetery, Raleigh. *Dictionary of North Carolina Biography*, s.v. "Mordecai, George Washington."

[2] John Herritage Bryan, lawyer; A.B., U.N.C., 1815; A.M., 1820; member, state Senate, 1823-1824; member, U.S. House of Representatives, 1825-1829; U.N.C. trustee, 1823-1868. Grant, *Alumni History*, 81

[3] Bartholomew Figures Moore.

[4] Daniel Moreau Barringer.

[5] John Devereux, Jr.

[6] William H. Holleman, Wake County grocer and farmer. 1870 U.S. Census Population Schedule, North Carolina: Wake, 227 (microfilm).

[7] Charles Dewey, banker; cashier of the Bank of North Carolina and its successor, the Bank of the State of North Carolina; cashier and later president, Raleigh National Bank. *Dictionary of North Carolina Biography*, s.v. "Dewey, Charles."

Benj. W. Ivey to Holden A&H:GP

Fort Macon, N.C.
July 7th 1868

To his Excellency
Govr W. W. Holden of N.C.
Raleigh N.C.

Sir

Will you allow the honor of addressing you I wish to call your attention to A Matter deeply concerning me I was Tried by A Military commission convened at Willmington N.C. on or about the 8th of January 1866 on A Charge of Assault attempt to kill A Freedman at Lumberton N.C. on or about the 1st of December 1865 I was Tried without A Witness in my behalf and on those grounds the court found me Guilty And I am now undergoing Sentence at this place for Ten years I was Sentence to Albany Penetensuary by good luck I got Sent here instead of there I will give you A full Statement of my case Showing that Predjudice was the cause of my getting Such A Sentence on Such a Small offence On the 11th of December 1863 I belonged to the fifth N.C. Regt I laid down my Arms under Presedent Lincolns Proclamation of the 8th December 1863 And I Taken the oath of allegience at that time under the promises of having protection I then went north and Remained there untill after Genl Lees Surrender then I returned home at Lumberton N.C. I had not Been at home but A Short time and I was playing with Several Freedmen around Lumberton N.C. at the same time I had my gun in my hand not knowing it was loaded it accidently went off and Slightly wounded him in the legs he propose to appear in My behalf on the day of My Trial but court would not allow him to appear for nor against Me Since I have been here My

Mother and Friends has raised Two petitions and Sent one to the Presedent the other to Genl Canby I have not heard from neither one You can refer to Mr. E. Proctor[1] A Member of the legisture sitting Raleigh he is from Lumberton N.C.

I hope you Take this Matter into your consideration Please Let me hear from you Soon

I Am Sir Verry Respectfully
Your Obedient Servnat
Benj. W. Ivey[2]
Prisoner at
Fort Macon N.C.

[1] Edward K. Proctor, Robeson County; member, state House of Representatives, 1868-1870, 1883. Cheney, *North Carolina Government, 1585-1979*, 1255

[2] Benjamin W. Ivey, Robeson County; Company A, Fifth Regiment North Carolina Troops; enlisted 1862; promoted to corporal; absent without leave, January 1-August 31, 1863; returned to duty, September, 1863; deserted to the enemy, December 10, 1863; released from prison when took oath of amnesty, March 15, 1864. Manarin and Jordan, comps., *North Carolina Troops, 1861-1865: A Roster*, 4:137.

C. B. Mallett to Holden A&H:GP

Fayetteville N.C.
July 8th 1868

To His Excellency W. W. Holden
Gov of North Carolina

Dear Sir

By an Ordinance of the late Convention (a copy of which I enclose) The Public Treasurer was directed to issue to the Western R. R. Co five hundred thousand (500 000) dollars of the Bonds of the State in exchange for a like amount of the Bonds of the W. C. & R. R. R. Co[1] which had been paid to this Company, by the State, in liquidation of a subscription made to the Capital Stock of the Co.

I beg leave respectfully to call your attention to the matter and ask that you will give the necessary orders to have the Bonds prepared and delivered to this Company as contemplated by the Ordinance of the Convention.

Yours very Respectfully
C. B. Mallett[2]
Prest Western R. R. Co

[1] Wilmington, Charlotte and Rutherfordton Railroad Company.

[2] Charles Beatty Mallett, Fayetteville merchant; owner of spinning and weaving mills in and around Fayetteville; interested in and participated in railroad enterprises; president, Western Railroad Company. *Dictionary of North Carolina Biography*, s.v. "Mallett, Charles Beatty."

E. L. Pemberton to Holden A&H:GP

Fayetteville July 8 1868

Gov Holden

My dear Sir

Permit me to tender you my sincere congratulations, and for the privelige of saying in the language of Judge Reade "We are at home"

The impression prevails here that a batch of Magistrates will be appointed for each County in a very short time. I have just learned that a recommendation of persons for that position have been forwarded to you from this place I have not seen the list but learn that one of the names is that of A. G. Thornton,[1] which I most respectfully suggest to you *Not to appoint*, for reasons no doubt you are familiar his appointment would add no strength to the party, besides giving the opposition something to feed on for the lord knows how long.

Yours Truly
E. L. Pemberton[2]

[1] Alvin G. Thornton, Cumberland County; special justice of revenue. 1870 U.S. Census Population Schedule, North Carolina: Cumberland, 202 (microfilm).

[2] Edmund L. Pemberton, Cumberland County; hardware merchant. 1870 U.S. Census Population Schedule, North Carolina: Cumberland, 37 (microfilm).

Ed. R. S. Canby to Holden A&H:GP

Headquarters Second Military District
Charleston S.C. July 9 1868

His Excellency
The Governor of North Carolina
Raleigh N:C.

Sir

A number of complaints have been made to these Hd. Qrs. of illegality in the conduct of the recent elections in your State, or of frauds practised upon voters and of intimidation and violence offered, in order to prevent voting. Some of these complaints are trivial in character, while others are more serious and may possibly involve grounds for the contest of the election by the parties interested.

In the investigations ordered by me I have limited the inquiry to such facts as under the law and the orders for the conduct of the election would invalidate the election by reason of the illegal conducting it, by the distinction of the poll lists or ballot boxes, or by such force and intimidations as prevented a fair election.

The subordinate questions affecting the personal rights of individuals, either as electors or as candidates for election to office, concern more directly the civil authorities; and all questions of that character should be passed upon by them.

I have therefore directed that the poll lists, ballots &c from the several election districts in your State be transferred to the custody of the Secretary of State for North Carolina, and they will be accordingly forwarded tomorrow to the care of the Commanding Officer at Raleigh to be transferred by him to the Secretary of State.

I have the honor to transmit also as germain to the same subject, all papers in this office that relate to contested elections in your State, for such disposition as Your Excellency may think proper to make of them.

A copy of the registration for each County in your State will be furnished as soon as it can be prepared, and in the meantime any information from the registration books that may be required, will upon application, be promptly furnished.

Very respectfully
Your obdt. Servt.
Ed. R. S. Canby
Brt. Maj. General
Commanding

George Dixon to Holden A&H:GP

82 Lafayette Street
Salem, Mass
7 Mo. 12, 1868

To Governor Holden

Esteemed Friend,

I read with much interest thy Inaugural address, and would like a few copies of the Standard containing it, to forward to my Friends in Europe. I wish to keep them interested in North Carolina. I shall be glad to pay the cost of what are sent. I have arranged to return at the end of 9th month and reopen our 20 Freedmen's schools, then proceed to Jamaica to spend the winter, returning again to North Carolina in the Spring of 1869, make a short stay, and then proceed to Europe. It has occurred to me, if an emigration Society was organized, I might be useful in Great Britain, Ireland, and on the Continent of Europe, in inducing emigrants to locate in North Carolina. The Rebels are forming such a Society in Virginia. They will not effect much without a reliable agent on the other side of the Atlantic. I should like thy opinion on this subject. I purpose eventually settling down in your State, and should there be any position I could fill in thy giving, I should be glad to be remembered. Having given the Freedmen nearly 3 years of my life, without fee or reward, perhaps I have a little claim on my adopted State. I do not wish for any *permanent* position till my return from Europe—only 9 days are required to recross the Atlantic. So that should any thing arise I should return immediately. I shall keep thee informed of my movements—Knowing the multiplicity of thy engagements, I shall not encroach further on thy valuable time. With kind regards and best wishes for thy welfare spiritually and temporally—

I am thy obliged Friend
George Dixon[1]

[1] George Dixon, assistant superintendent of education, Danville, Virginia, for the Bureau of Refugees, Freedmen, and Abandoned Lands; later agent of the Friends Association in Greensboro. Records of Assistant Commissioner for the State of North Carolina, Bureau of Refugees, Freedmen, and Abandoned Lands: Letters Sent, 1865-1867, 423; Endorsements Sent, 77. National Archives Record Group 105 (microfilm copy in North Carolina State Archives).

Standard
July 13, 1868

TO THE PATRONS AND FRIENDS OF THE NORTH CAROLINA STANDARD.

I have disposed of the *Standard* establishment to Messrs. N. Paige & Co., and the paper will be hereafter conducted by them. I have entire confidence in these gentlemen, and bespeak for them the warm support of my friends.

In retiring from the *Standard* I feel as if I were parting with an old and valued friend. I do so with some reluctance, but my duties are such as to imperatively require it. The *Standard* will continue the same outspoken, fearless and unflinching Republican paper it has heretofore been.

I took charge of this paper when quite a young man, a quarter of a century ago. I have passed with it through many labors and trials. That I have committed errors as an Editor I very freely admit, but I can say with truth that during all this period my leading object has been the welfare and happiness of the people of the State.

I feel very grateful to friends who have sustained me in the discharge of my duties. I shall always remember them with affection, and I trust I shall never prove unworthy of them.

To the Republicans of the State I would say, *stand by your principles*. Let nothing move you to abandon these principles, or induce you to become lukewarm in their support. See to it especially that the old "Standard" is liberally sustained in the hands of the worthy gentlemen to whom I now transfer it.

Very truly yours,
W. W. Holden

Holden To Col. G. A. *Williams* A&H:GP

State of North Carolina
Executive Department,
Raleigh July 14 1868

Col. G. A. Williams
Commdg Military Post
At Raleigh

Sir

By virtue of authority vested in me by the Constitution of North Carolina, I proceeded to make the following appointments for Mayor and Commissioners of the City of Raleigh For Mayor

Wm H. Harrison
For Commissioners
Wm. R. Richardson
J. P. Adams[1]
A. L. Lougee[2]
John R. Harrison[3]
Jefferson Fisher
James H. Harris
E. A. Whitaker
Andy Lockart[5]
John T. Williamson[6]

W. W. Holden, Govr.

[1] James Adams, Wake County; Raleigh boot and shoemaker. 1870 U.S. Census Population Schedule, North Carolina: Wake, 205 (microfilm).

[2] Augustus L. Lougee, Wake County; Raleigh printer. 1870 U.S. Census Population Schedule, North Carolina: Wake, 195 (microfilm).

[3] John R. Harrison, Wake County; farmer. 1870 U. S. Census Population Schedule, North Carolina: Wake, 391 (microfilm).

[4] Edward Whitaker, Wake County; steward at the asylum. 1870 U.S. Census Population Schedule, North Carolina: Wake 254 (microfilm).

[5] Handy Lockhart, Wake County; black cabinet maker. Murray, *Wake: Capital County*:1, 568.

[6] John T. Williamson, Wake County; black farmer. Mortgage, John T. Williamson to Madison C. Hodge, Wake County Deed Book 39, 380-381 (microfilm copy in North Carolina State Archives).

William D. Haywood to Wm. H. Harrison A&H:GP

Mayors Office
City of Raleigh N.C.
July 14, 1868

Wm. H. Harrison Esqr
Raleigh, N.C.

Sir

I have submitted to the Board of Commissioners of this City, your demand upon me to surrender this Office, and the records, papers, property &c. belonging thereto, to yourself and other gentlemen named by you, who claim to be the appointees as Mayor and Commissioners of this city, of his Excellency Gov. Holden, upon due consideration, and under the advice of Counsel, it is the opinion of the Board of Commissioners, that the appointments purporting to be made by Gov. Holden are without the sanction of law, and we are advised, that it is both our right, and duty, to continue in the exercise of our offices, respectfully to decline to surrender the office, and to comply with the demand by you made upon me, I address you this letter by order of the Board of Commissioners

I am &c Your obt. Servt
William D. Haywood[1]
Mayor of the City of Raleigh, N.C.

[*Enclosure*]

It having been submitted to us, as Counsel for the City of Raleigh, whether W. W. Holden Governor of North Carolina, who has assumed the right to appoint and commission, a Mayor and Commissioners for the City of Raleigh, has any right, under the existing law, to make such appointments and issue such commissions; and also, to advise the Present Mayor and Commissioners now exercising said offices, as to their rights and duties in the premeses.

We unhesitatingly give it as our opinion, that Governor Holden has no such rights as he assumed in this behalf, that his appointments & commissions issued & made to those claiming to be Mayor and Commissioners of the City of Raleigh, are invalid, null, & void, and that it is the duty of the present incumbents of said offices, now exercising their functions, as well as their right, to continue in their offices, and in the performance of their official duties. July 14th 1868

B. F. Moore[2]
A. S. Merrimon[3]
Ed. Graham Haywood[4]
Attys at Law

[1] William Dallas Haywood, Wake County; clerk in the Secretary of State Land Office. 1870 U.S. Census Population Schedule, North Carolina: Wake, 301 (microfilm).

[2] Bartholomew Figures Moore.

[3] Augustus Summerfield Merrimon, lawyer and jurist; member, House of Commons, 1860-1861; judge, Eighth District, 1866-1867; 1872, unsuccessful candidate for governor; member, U.S. Senate, 1872-1873; justice, North Carolina Supreme Court, 1883-1889; chief justice, 1889-1892. *Dictionary of North Carolina Biography*, s.v. "Merrimon, Augustus Summerfield."

[4] Ed. Graham Haywood (Edward Haywood), Wake County; lawyer. 1870 U.S. Census Population Schedule, North Carolina: Wake, 263 (microfilm).

Holden to Maj. Genl. E. R. S. Canby A&H:GP

Raleigh July 14. 1868
Executive Office

To Maj. Genl. E. R. S. Canby
Commanding at Charleston—

Sir, I have recd your despatches to Col Williams[1] relating to Mayor and Commissioners of Raleigh

In the absence of a militia force I find myself unable to discharge my duties as governor of the State without federal military aid. I call upon you to sustain me in putting in operation the new government of this State

Very Respectfully
W. W. Holden
Gov. of NC.

[1] Lieutenant Colonel George Augustus Williams.

TELEGRAM *J. W. Schenck, Jr., To Holden* A&H:GP

Wilmington July 15 1868

To Gov. W. W. Holden

I have qualified and commissioners have accepted my bond. Old Sheriff refuses to turn over Office. Will you call on military to assist me?

J. W. Schenck, Jr.[1]

[1] James W. Schenck, New Hanover County; sheriff. 1870 U.S. Census Population Schedule, North Carolina: New Hanover, 498 (microfilm).

TELEGRAM *Holden to J. W. Schenck, Jr.* A&H:GP

Executive Office
Raleigh July 15 1868

To Maj. J. W. Schenck Jr. Sheriff of New Hanover

Sir: I have applied to Gen. Canby for the necessary military aid to place you in office.

Respectfully
W. W. Holden

TELEGRAM *Holden to Maj. Genl. Ed R. S. Canby* A&H:GP

Executive Department of N. Car.
Raleigh July 15th 1868

Maj. Genl. Ed. R. S. Canby Charleston

Sir: J. W. Schenck, Jr., the Sheriff of New Hanover, has qualified and given his Bonds, but the former Sheriff refuses to turn over the office. Please extend the necessary aid to place the new Sheriff in office.

Very Respectfully,
W. W. Holden

TELEGRAM *Ed. R. S. Canby to Holden* A&H:GP

Head Quarters 2nd Military District
Charleston S. C., July 15th, 1868

His Excellency
W. W. Holden
Govr of No. Ca.

Your dispatch of the 14th has just been received. The Governor of the State will be fully sustained in the inauguration of the new State Government under the laws of the United States, and the Constitution and laws of the State.

The 12th section of Article 7 of your Constitution provides that all charters, Ordinances and provisions of municipal corporations shall remain in force until legally changed, unless inconsistent with the provisions of this Constitution; and the 5th section of Article 14, provides that "in the absence of any provisions to the contrary, all officers in this State, whether heretofore elected or appointed by the Governor shall hold their positions only until other appointments are made by the Governor, or, if the officers are elective, until their successors shall have been chosen and duly qualified under the provisions of this Constitution."

I do not find an provisions in the Constitution which authorized the Governor to appoint Mayors or other officers (except Justices of the Peace) that are elective and I have asked the Attorney General to cite the Article under which the authority for these appointments is claimed, and have postponed any action until I am more fully advised of the merits in the case.

Ed. R. S. Canby
M. G. C.

E. R. S. Canby to Holden A&H:GP

Head quarters 2nd. Military District
Charleston S. C. July 15th 1868.

His Excellency
The Gov. of No. Carolina
Raleigh N.C.

Sir: I have the honor to State that the authority to defray the expenses of the quarantine, established under military authority in North Carolina, will cease when article 14 becomes a part of the Constitution of the United States and the quarantine officers in your State will accordingly be notified to day, that their compensation will cease on the 31st. of this month, unless the Legislature of the

State should make provision for continuing the quarantine and defraying its expenses which now amounts to $250 per month. The aid of the Military in the enforcement of a quarantine by the State authorities will of course be given if it should be necessary.

I enclose copies of the quarantine regulations and a list of the officers employed with the rate of compensation to each[1]

Very Respy
Your obt. Svt.
E. R. S. Canby.
Brt. Maj. General.
Commanding

[1] The regulations and list of officers have not been found.

Holden to Maj. Gen. E. R. S. Canby A&H:GP

Executive Office
Raleigh July 16, 1868

To Maj. Gen. E. R. S. Canby, Commanding &c

Sir: I felt sure that I would be "fully sustained in the inauguration of the new State government, under the laws of the United States and the constitution and laws of the State."

It is conceded that according to section 12 of article 7 of the Constitution, "all charters, ordinances and provisions relating to municipel corporations shall remain in force until legally changed, unless inconsistent with the provisions of this Constitution." But it is maintained as entirely clear that section 5 of article 14 confers on the Governor the power "in the absence of any contrary provision," To appoint "all officers in this State, whether heretofore elected or appointed by the Governor"—those thus appointed to office heretofore filled by the Governor to hold until new appointments are made; and those thus appointed to "elective" offices, as in the case of the towns and cities to hold "until their successors shall have been chosen and duly qualified according to the provisions of this Constitution." The first clause of section 5, to the word "or," was intended to confer, and does confer on the Governor this power, both as to "elective" offices and those filled by appointment; and that part of the section beginning with the word "or," was intended to provide that the Governor should not permanently or regularly fill these "elective" offices, but that this Executive power should operate only until such time as the law-making power should provide for elections by the people. Indeed, Sir, this conclusion seems almost too plain to require argument. The Convention which framed the Constitution had in view, as the primary object in this respect, the immediate removal by the Government of these officers, who were then holding, some by military appointment, some by election by the rebel element, and all of them by permission of, and responsible to the military. This was the object, as I happen to know, of the gentlemen in that body who framed section 5 of article 14.

It is true that the Governor would not have the power "to appoint Mayors and other officers," after the constitution had gone into full effect, and the election of these officers had been once made by the people; but, as preliminary to this, the power may certainly be exercised as provided in section 5 of article 14. The power to appoint Justices of the Peace conferred on the Governor, is also preliminary, and was intended to operate only until sections 4, 5 and 6 of article 7 could be put in operation.

Under section 5 of article 14, I have appointed State Directors in the North Carolina Railroad Company, and a State proxy. These Directors have gone forward, have exercised the powers thus conferred upon them, and, with the stockholders, now have full control of this Road. If resistance had been offered to Executive action in relation to this corporation, the same ground of appeal to you for aid would have existed that now exists in relation to the Mayor and Commissioners of Raleigh. I have also appointed Directors on the Atlantic and North-Carolina Railroad, and on the Wilmington and Weldon Road. I have also appointed a Mayor and Commissioners for the City of Charlotte. Whether further resistance will be offered to my appointments depends on your decision in relation to the Mayor and Commissioners of Raleigh. If you could have felt it your duty to sustain me when I called upon you for aid, and had done so promptly by putting out the old officers and installing the new, I am sure no riot or commotion of any kind would have taken place, and that no further resistance would have been attempted to the full and thorough inauguration of our new State government. I do not propose at this time to discuss the extent of your powers and duties. I am satisfied that it is your purpose to do your whole duty in maintaining peace, and in inaugurating the new State government; but I ask that it be borne in mind that the Governor of the State must necessarily be the Judge of his own powers under the Constitution; and furthermore, that the only disturbance of the peace in the City of Raleigh, since the appointments referred to were made, proceeded from the late Mayor[1] and his Police officers. By permission, or most probably by direction of this officer, his Police officers armed surrounded the City Hall in a defiant and threatening manner, and the result was several affrays occurred, in which a colored man was fired upon by a Police officer without provocation and one of my appointees as Commissioner was assailed and beaten with a bludgeon by the Chief of Police.[2] An unusually large number of special Police have been on duty, ostensibly to preserve order, but really to intimidate the friends of the government, and to rally around the late Mayor and Commissioners a force which they may deem sufficient to defy the civil power in the event you should decline to sustain my appointments.

I have the honor to be, Sir, with highest respect, Your obt. Servant.

W. W. Holden
Governor &c

In conclusion, I respectfully invite your attention to the opinion of W. M. Coleman Esq herewith enclosed.[3]

[*Enclosure*]

July 16/68

The Constitution of North Carolina makes the Attorney General the legal advisor of the Executive Department . The Attorney General holds that the Governer has the right under the Constitution to appoint the Mayor and Commissioners of the city of Raleigh He holds further that the action of the Governor under his advice must be *presumed* to be in conformity with the law until a court of Competent jurisdiction shall have decided otherwise.

As a matter of information, however, the Attorney General submits the following reasons for his opinions.

Section 5, Art. XIV of the Constitution reads as follows: [text not quoted.]

In this case it is clear that the second sentence would be held to be insensible and repugnent and in no wise affecting the Governor's power of appointment defined in the first sentence.

But the punctuation is immaterial. Take the section just as it stands in the Constitution and it positively declares that "no... Governor" if the following clause be construed so as to mean that the Governor has no power of appointment when "the officers are elective," why then this clause is repugnant to the body of the statute which expressly declares that the Governor shall have such power, and the latter clause being thus repugnant and inconsistant is consequently void.

But there is another rule of law equally as well established as the foregoing which is that a statute shall be construed if possible so that the whole shall stand, ut res magis voleat quam pereat. And there is no difficulty in construing this section so that the whole shall stand. The first clause rests the power of appointment in the hands of the Governor and the second clause provides that these appointees shall hold untill their successors shall have been &c. It is in this sense that the gentleman who drew up this section in it original form understands; it is in this sense the gentlemen understands it who proposed to amend by providing that if "the officers were elective," the Governor's appointees should only hold until their successors have been elected. In short, whether we take the maxim that a clause repugnant to the body of a statute is void or whether we construe the statute so that the whole stands, it is the opinion of the Attorney General that the power of appointment which the Governor claimes to exercies is rightfully vested in his hands.

[1] William Dallas Haywood.

[2] E. E. Harris, chief of police. For an account of the "riot," see *Daily Standard*, July 15, 1868. The freedman fired upon was not identified.

[3] William Macon Coleman, attorney general.

TELEGRAM *Ed. R. S. Canby to Holden* A&H:GP

Headquarters Second Military District
Charleston S.C. July 16th 1868

His Excellency
W. W. Holden
Gov. N.C.
Raleigh, N.C.

The Commanding Officer Wilmington has been instructed to install the Sheriff of New Hanover, if he has properly qualified under the law.

Ed. R. S. Canby
M. G. C.

Holden to the General Assembly of North Carolina A&H:GP

Executive Office July 17, 1868

To the Honorable The General Assembly of North Carolina

Gentlemen:–I desire respectfully to call your attention to the importance of the immediate organization of the militia, and especially to the organization of an adequate police force in each of the Counties of the State.

North Carolina is now a State of and in the Union; and it is proper in itself and expected by the people that provision should be made by which the Executive will be able, at all times, in whatsoever locality, promptly and faithfully to execute the laws.

The work of reconstruction will not have been fully accomplished until every officer provided for under the new order of things shall have been installed. When the State government is thus in complete operation in all its departments under the Constitution, it is not apprehended that any opposition to its authority will be encountered which may not be easily met and overcome by the militia and the local police.

It is the avowed purpose of the enemies of the government of the United States, and of the government of this State, to disregard the authority of these governments, and to subvert the latter, on the pretext that it is not constitutional in its origin and character. It is not apprehended that any collision will occur, or that the peace will be seriously disturbed, in any quarter of the State; but, in the judgment of the Executive it is deemed important, as a measure of peace and security for the future, that he should be clothed by law with the necessary powers to maintain the authority of the State Government against all assaults, to preserve the peace, to secure to the people the rights of free elections, and to so act as to aid in bringing to condign punishment all who may violate the law. The government of the State should be made "a terror to evil-doers and a praise to them that do well." The interests of society are too precious to be put in jeopardy by allowing even grounds for apprehending that the authority of the government may be successfully resisted or questioned.

By virtue of authority clearly vested in me, as I conceive, by the State Constitution, I have recently appointed Justices of the Peace, Mayors and Commissioners of towns, and Directors in various corporations. The organization of the militia and of an adequate police force would enable me at once to execute the law in this respect by installing these and other officers where resistance is offered, and in sustaining them in the performance of their duties.

It is scarcely necessary that I should repeat to the Genl. Assembly the views contained in my Inaugural Address in relation to the character of persons to be appointed to office. The people have decided that the new State government shall not be committed, to any extent, to unfriendly hands. Every office and every employment under the State, from the most inferior to the most exalted, should be filled by the known friends of the government of the United States and the government of North Carolina. It will not be safe or expedient, in my judgment, to deviate to any extent from this rule. It is my fixed purpose to maintain this rule, and to administer the government in such manner as to secure to all their right of life, liberty and prosperity.

Very Respectfully
W. W. Holden

W. F. Henderson to Holden A&H:GP

Lexington N.C.
July 17, 1868

Gov W. W. Holden

Dear Gov.

to Carry out Justice and orders I have issued—I am Compeled to have some assistance from the U.S. troops pleas to have sent to Lexington some 3 or 4 men. The rebles trid defiance to the Bureau and for the good of the Republican Party, I want assistance sent to Lexington Friday night I am here alone but am determined to sustain the great Cause of Liberty at the hazard of my Life.

I am yours Gov
W. F. Henderson[1]
Agent B R F & A L

P. S. the rebles say they will not submit to the Helish desires of Holden & his negro folowing

W F H

[1] W. F. Henderson, Lexington agent of the Bureau of Refugees, Freedmen, and Abandoned Lands. Roster of Officers and Civilians on Duty in Bureau of Refugees, Freedmen, and Abandoned Lands in North Carolina, November 1, 1868.

Holden to Col. Williams A&H:GP

State of North Carolina
Executive Department
Raleigh July 17th 1868

Col. Williams[1]
Post Commdr
Raleigh N.C.

Sir:

Information has been received at this Dept. that Wm. A. Philpot[2] late Sheriff of Granville refuses to surrender the papers and effects of the office to James I. Moore[3] the newly elected Shff of the county.

Mr. Moore having been elected according to Law and his bond having been tendered and received I call upon you to install him in office as has been done in the case of the shff of N. Hanover and as has been ordered by General Canby in the case of the Sheriff of Randolph.

Very Respy
W. W. Holden

[1] Lieutenant Colonel George Augustus Williams.

[2] William A. Philpott, appointed sheriff of Granville County September 1, 1865. Names of Magistrates Appointed by W. W. Holden Provisional Governor of North Carolina (GO 109), North Carolina State Archives, Raleigh.

[3] James I. Moore, elected sheriff, 1868. See Sheriffs' Bonds, Granville County (044.103.4), North Carolina State Archives, Raleigh.

Geo. A. Williams to Holden A&H:GP

Headquarters Post of Raleigh
Raleigh N.C. July 18, 1868

To His Ex: W. W. Holden Governor of North Carolina

Sir:

In reply to your communication of July 17, I have the honor to state, that last evening Lieut. Craft[1] Act: Adgt: of this Post, (accompanied by Sheriff Moore) bore an order from me to to Wm. A. Philpot late Sheriff of Granville County to surrender the papers and effects of his Office to Moore.

Wm. Philpot, who was in town, agrees to surrender them without further trouble and Moore expresses himself satisfied, that the promise will be fulfilled; however, if it is not, he is instructed to inform me, and I will send a force, that will execute it.

Very Resptfully, Your obedient servant
Geo. A. Williams
Brt Lt. Col U.S.A. & Maj. 6th Infty
Commanding

[1] Probably David L. Craft, Pennsylvania; Signal Corps, 1863; Second Lieutenant, 6th Infantry, 1867; brevet first lieutenant for bravery at battle of Petersburg. Heitman, *Historical Register and Dictionary of the United States Army*, s.v. "Craft, David L."

Ed. R. S. Canby to Holden A&H:GP

Headquarters Second Military District
Charleston So. Ca. July 22nd, 1868

His Excellency
The Governor of North Carolina
Raleigh N.C.

Sir:

I have the honor to acknowledge the receipt of your communication of the 16th inst, and the accompanying papers from the Attorney General of the State, and to state in reply, that all the conditions imposed by the laws of the United States as precedent to the restoration of your State, have practically been complied with.

The proclamation of the President of the United States of the 16th inst. gives legal notice to all departments of the Government that the Constitutional Amendment, known as Article fourteen, has been duly ratified by the Legislature of your State, and in consequence its people are by law, entitled to representation in the Congress of the United States, and, in fact, is now represented in that Congress. Under the 6th section of the law of March 2nd 1867 to provide for the more efficient government of the Rebel States, the provisional government of North Carolina has ceased to exist and with it the power to exercise, by the District Commander, any judicial functions in the determination of any questions arising under the new Constitution, which is now the fundumental law of your State, has also ceased to exist.

I have not, therefore, considered it proper to inquire further into the merits of this case than to ascertain whether it comes clearly and conclusively within the scope of the laws of the Unites States, which would authorize the District Commander to take the action which he is asked to take. I find that it is not. That it is a question involving the legal construction of the Constitution, and that it is subject to Judicial determination, in the manner provided by law, or of legislative remedy, if the subject be within the province of the Legislature. I have neither judicial nor legislative powers, and however clear my own opinion might be, as to the intent of the constitution, any decision that I might make would be without force, for the reason that it would be without authority to make it.

The duties remaining to the District Commander under the Reconstruction laws, are ministerial in their character, and so far as the new State Governments are concerned relate almost exclusively to giving necessary aid in the inauguration of the State officers "duly elected and qualified under the Constitutions thereof" and not ineligible by the Constitutional amendment. By natural and necessary implications, this will apply also to the officers, who, under the same conditions are duly appointed. But in this case, the grant of power to appoint must be clear and explicit, or if doubtful, the doubt must be resolved by other authority, than the District Commander.

Very Respectfully
Your Obedt. Svt.
Ed. R. S. Canby
Brevt. Maj. Genl. commanding

Holden to G. A. *Williams* A&H:GP

Executive Department of North Carolina
Raleigh July 25 1868

To Col. G. A. Williams, Commanding, &c.

Sir: I respectfully request that you order a file of men, or a sufficient number in your judgment, to proceed to Chapel Hill with the Superintendent of Public Works,[1] to protect the property of the University of this State.

Very Respectfully
W. W. Holden

[1] Ceburn L. Harris.

Jonathan Worth to Holden A&H:Worth

Raleigh, July 29th 1868

Govr Holden

Dear sir

It is known to you and the public that upon the occupation of this city by the military forces of the United States, the Governor's mansion was made the Head Quarters of Genl. Sherman:[1] and that his successors at this military post, continued to occupy the same until the latter part of the year 1867: and that during this occupation the furnishings all disappeared, and the property was otherwise very greatly damanged.

Immediately after the Genl. Assembly in 1867 made an appropriation of $5000. to repair the mansion & supply needful furniture, nearly all of which had disappeared, I applied to Genl. Sickles[2] for possession of the property. After much delay it was surrendered to me in July 1867.

The Genl. Assembly contemplated that I would make the mansion my residence as soon as it could be made habitable by needful repairs, and proper furniture should be supplied. It was supposed that the Government of the United States would pay rent for its occupation, at least after the President's proclamation that peace was restored; and as the law provided that the Governor, in addition to his salary, should be supplied with a residence, the Governor was authorised to apply for such rent, and to apply the same, when received, to his own use, to reimburse him for supplying his own residence.

My efforts to get rent have however, been thus far ineffectual. The Quarter Master here upon my application reported what would be a reasonable rent, but the Quarter Master Genl. refused to pay rent for State property occupied by the military. From this decision I appealed to the Secretary of War.[3] This appeal was made preceding the efforts of the President to remove Mr. Stanton as Secretary of War, and I have had no response. My correspondence on the subject will be found on file. I have received nothing for rent.

The repairs required consisted of the building a new barn which had been entirely destroyed while in possession of the military—the re-fencing of the grounds, new roofs over the principal buildings, re-papering the interior walls, re-painting, masonry, &c. I could make no discreet contract by the job for this various work. I therefore employed M. B. Royster[4] of this city,—a gentleman every way competent, to buy material, hire labor & execute the repairs under my direction. I agreed to pay him $2.50 per day. He has performed his duties, as I think, with remarkable judgment, fidelity & economy, and I am now ready to exhibit his account accompanied by vouchers, to any committee of the Genl. Assembly appointed to receive the same. The whole appropriation has been expended in repairs; leaving nothing for the purchase of new furniture.

The wall paper was purchased at wholesale prices in New York—and Mr. W. T. Clemson,[5] of this city, employed to paper the walls. Towards the wind up of the papering, Mr. Clemson informed me there was a small deficiency of paper, which, upon my request, he supplied, amounting, as by his bills filed with me, to $29.10—and Mr. Royster's acct, also filed with me, with accompanying vouchers, shows a balance in his hands of $7.75. which I have directed him to pay over to Mr. Clemson, which will reduce the amount due to Mr. Clemson to $21.35 for the payment of which I hope the Genl Assembly will make provision.

I collected & preserved what furniture I could find, which I will surrender to you on application.

I drew the $5,000. as follows—

For repairs of furniture	$ 69.30
For purchase of wall paper	668.86

Drafts in favor of M. B. Royster as follows:

Sept. 5th 1867	1000.00
Oct. 25 "	1500.00
Jan. 17 1868	1761.84
	5000.00

I have the honor to be

Yours very respectfully.
Jonathan Worth[6]

[1] William Tecumseh Sherman.

[2] Daniel Edgar Sickles, member, U.S. House of Representatives, 1857-1861, 1893-1895; Union army, colonel, 1861-1863; major general, 1863; military governor of Carolinas, 1865-1867. *Dictionary of American Biography*, s.v. "Sickles, Daniel Edgar."

[3] Edwin McMasters Stanton.

[4] Madison B. Royster, Wake County; farmer. 1870 U.S. Census Population Schedule, North Carolina: Wake, 34 (microfilm).

[5] Not identified.

[6] Governor Holden forwarded Jonathan Worth's letter to the General Assembly on July 29, 1868. See Holden to Joseph W. Holden, July 29, 1868, in A&H:GLB.

Holden to the General Assembly A&H:GLB

Executive Department of No Ca
Raleigh Aug. 4th, 1868

To the General Assembly of North Carolina

Gentlemen.

I would respectfully call your attention to the fact that there is no provision in the existing law by which the Governor can be officially notified of vacancies in the office of County Commissioners in cases in which the entire Board of Commissioners elect are disqualified by the 14th Article of the Federal Constitution. I would suggest some Legislation to remedy this defect. I would also call attention to the fact that in a few of the counties of the State there are tax collectors who have been elected or appointed under special acts and that in one county at least the Tax collector is holding over and insists on collecting the taxes. It is not clear that the Governor has the power to remove these officers, or that their functions have ceased. I would therefore respectfully recommend that the office of Tax Collector be abolished by Act of the Legislature and that those who are assuming to exercise the functions of the office be required to turn over their papers and the monies in their hands to the Sheriffs of their respective Counties.

I have the honor to be
Very Respectfully
W. W. Holden

John H. Everitt to Holden A&H:GP

South Gaston
Halifax Co N.C.
Aug 5 68

To His Excellency Gov W. W. Holden
Governor of N.C.

Your Excellency.

It is being reported to me hourly by various persons—that there is being formed in this District No 6 near this place a Company of Consertiv white men & three Conservitive Negroes for the purpose of resisting the newly appointed Civil Officers & for the purpose of waylaying & shooting the Civil Officers & heads of the League. They make threats—open in the public. They have already up to this time had two Colored men, Republicans, shot & severely wounded. One was shot by a white man son of the late Sheriff Snow[1] of this County—young Snow[2] is still here & says he defies the Civil authorities The other man was shot by a Conservitive (Negro) who was hired by this Same Company. No Republicans life is safe just in this vicinity at this time And as I am a newly appointed Justice of the Peace in this District, I appeal to you to know which course to pursue in such cases.

The names of the officers & men of this company can be given you if desired Please withhold my name in this matter as my life is threatened day by day—and I am verily in danger

I hope your Excellency will duly consider this matter & give me directions soon to act.

I am Sir very Respectfly your oblg Servant

John H. Everitt J.P.[3]
Dist No 6
Halifax Co N.C.

[1] Probably James S. Snow, wealthy Halifax County farmer and sheriff. 1860 U.S. Census Population Schedule, North Carolina: Halifax, 881 (microfilm).

[2] Henry A. Snow, farmer; enlisted as private, 1861; captured Winchester, Virginia, 1864; confined at Cape Lookout Prison until June 3, 1865, when took oath of allegiance. Manarin and Jordan, compilers, *North Carolina Troops, 1861-1865: A Roster* 5:203.

[3] John H. Everitt, Halifax County merchant. 1860 U.S. Census Population Schedule, North Carolina: Halifax, 788 (microfilm.)

Wm H. Porter to Holden A&H:GP

Fayetteville N.C.
Aug. 13th 1868

His Excellency W. W. Holden
Governor of North Carolina

Dear Sir,

The commission issued by you dated Aug 5th 1868, whereby I was appointed Mayor for the town of Fayetteville has been received. I have had an interview with Thomas J. Curtis[1] Esq. acting Mayor and was informed by him that he would without hesitation vacate the office and turn over to me all books papers &c belonging to the same as soon as a new board of Commissioners is qualified. With a view to having the Commissioners qualified I notified them on yesterday to meet for that purpose when the following named gentlemen refused to serve as Commissioners -viz - Robert Mitchell[2] Ambrose Overbaugh,[3] J. W. Welsh[4] & WH. Tomilson[5] —The Commissions of Messrs Overbaugh & Tomilson are herewith inclosed and at their requests returned. The refusal of the above named gentlemen to serve leaves the newly appointed Board of Commissioners without a quorum and consequently unable to transact business—and places me in rather an unpleasant position—as without a Board of Commissioners I am unable to perform the duties of Mayor. For the purpose of organizing The Board of Commissioners I respectfully suggest the following gentlemen as suitable persons to fill the vacancies caused by the resignations herein before mentioned, viz—John Riley,[6] Alvin G. Thornton, John W. Hopkins[7] & John Watson.[8]

As soon as I can get a Board of Commissioners properly qualified to act—I will be prepared to enter on the discharge of the duties of Mayor. Hoping that your Excellency will attend to this matter as soon as the pressure of your official duties will permit, and hoping that you will give me any instructions that the nature of the case may require, I must patiently await your action.

With many thanks for the confidence you have exhibited towards me by appointing me to the office of Mayor and with many wishes for your success in administering the affairs of State

I am Yours Very Respectfully
Wm H. Porter[9]

P. S. Messrs Mitchell & Welsh will return their commissions directly to you, Pressure is heavy

W. H. P.

[1] Thomas J. Curtis, mayor of Fayetteville, 1867-1868. John A. Oates, *The Story of Fayetteville and the Upper Cape Fear* (n.p., n.d.), 240

[2] Robert Mitchell, Cumberland County; wholesale grocer. 1870 U.S. Census Population Schedule, North Carolina: Cumberland, 41 (microfilm).

[3] Ambrose Overbaugh, Cumberland County; hotel keeper. 1870 U.S. Census Population Schedule, North Carolina: Cumberland, 187 (microfilm).

[4] J. W. Welsh, Cumberland County; blacksmith. U.S. Census Population Schedule, North Carolina: Cumberland, 38 (microfilm).

[5] W. H. Tomilson, Cumberland County; farmer. 1870 U.S. Census Population Schedule, North Carolina: Cumberland, 202 (microfilm).

[6] John Riley, Cumberland County; farmer. 1860 U.S. Census Population Schedule, North Carolina: Cumberland, 321 (microfilm).

[7] John W. Hopkins, Cumberland County; millwright. 1870 U.S. Census Population Schedule, North Carolina: Cumberland, 45 (microfilm).

[8] John Watson, Cumberland County; drayman. 1870 U.S. Census Population Schedule, North Carolina: Cumberland, 200 (microfilm).

[9] William H. Porter, Cumberland County; machinist. 1870 U.S. Census Population Schedule, North Carolina: Cumberland, 199 (microfilm).

S. Pool to John [Pool] A&H:GP

Chapel Hill,
Aug. 15, 1868

Bro. John,[1]

I find upon my return home that there is considerable dissatisfaction & complaint among the Republicans of the county. The suspension of the college for probably twelve months casts a gloom over our friends as well as the opposition. Many Republicans here are dependent upon its continuance for support, & the Conservatives are imposing upon the negroes & ignorant whites, by telling them that all is due to their voting the Radical ticket. I think it would be well to have the college property strongly guarded, & by citizens of the County as soon as the soldiers are withdrawn. This Col. Harris[2] intends shall be done. I shall advise him to employ about five negroes in & about the college who have always been there. They can be had for one half what an equal number of whites will cost. These should not be armed but held in readiness if needed to aid the eight or ten white armed men, with some extra arms, to be used in an emergency.

If it were not so difficult to get any appropriation from the Legislature at present, I should hope to see a rail-road from this place to Hillsboro. The cost of such a road, the coaches to be drawn by horses (no engine used), would not exceed $50,000. It would give employment to many Republicans, & probably secure to us this county in the next election. It would pass through a section of country desirable for summer residences to such as would educate their sons at the University, & desire to live on the road near the University, & thus have their sons board in their own families. It would increase the value of the land to an amount almost equal to the road, & I think the travel on such a road in a few years would be considerable & make it pay well. I simply throw out the suggestion. We are likely to lose in this county unless something is done. The Conservatives are charging that we have closed the University without taking any step looking to its resuscitation, & that we have thus injured the Republicans of the County who are those poorer classes whose support was derived directly or indirectly from the institution. As the Legislature are afraid to consider the University bill on account of its probably involving the questions of mixed schools, I think it would be well at once to pass the bill making a rail-road, to be run over by horses, from this place to Hillsboro. Such a step must at some time be taken. The work can now be done more cheaply than in future, & by Republicans only. The Conservatives could not utter a syllable against it. Unless something can be done, they will carry the county by an increased majority. By proper steps I believe the County of Graham,[3] Turner,[4] Cameron,[5] Battle[6] & Swain[7] could be carried against them. I find my child better & all well. Love to all.

Truly &c.
S. Pool[8]

[1] John Pool.

[2] Probably Lieutenant Colonel William Hamilton Harris, New York; graduate, U. S. Military Academy, 1861; brevet major and lieutenent colonel, 1864, for gallantry and meritorious service at Petersburg, Virginia. Heitman, *Historical Register and Dictionary of the United States Army*, s.v. "Harris, William Hamilton."

[3] William Alexander Graham.

[4] Josiah Turner, Jr.

[5] Paul Carrington Cameron.

[6] Kemp Plummer Battle.

[7] David Lowry Swain.

[8] Solomon Pool, educator and clergyman; A.B., U.N.C., 1853; member of the U.N.C. faculty, 1861-1867; became president of the university, 1869, but removed when university closed in 1871. *Dictionary of North Carolina Biography*, s.v. "Pool, Solomon." John Pool forwarded this letter to Governor Holden.

John A. Griswold to Holden A&H:GP

Washington Aug 17th 1868

His Excellency
Gov. Holden
Raleigh N.C.

Dr Sir

Having induced some friends of mine to invest in bonds of your state, I take the liberty of requesting from you information in regard to the prospect of the payment of the October & January interest, which I notice the Legislature has voted to pay, but has not yet provided the means by passage of a tax bill; can you inform me by return mail of the prospect of the passage of such a provision as shall ensure the prompt payment at the time specified?

We shall give "the enemy" a lively fight in N.Y. this fall with every indication in our favor of a Republican victory.

Yours truly & respectfully
John A Griswold M. C.[1]

[1] John Augustus Griswold, New York; president of several small railroads; member, U.S. House of Representatives, 1863-1869. *Biographical Directory of the American Congress, 1774-1971*, s.v. "Griswold, John Augustus."

E. L. Pemberton to Holden A&H:GP

Fayetteville Aug 17/68

His Excellency W. W. Holden

My dear sir

I feel it due our mutual friend Mayor Lee[1] that you should be truthfully informed in reference to Curtis[2] and his board of commissioners getting possession of the Mayors office of this town. Mr Lee as you are aware was in Raleigh at the time, and when leaving requested me as one of the board to look after the town affairs until his return. It is the custom here for the town Constable to Keep the Key of the Mayors office, and on learning that Curtis comtemplated holding a meeting with his board, I immediately went to see the Constable, and forbid him to give the Key up or to have the office opened under any pretext until Mr Lees return, which he readily promised me to obey, though afterwards he surrenderd the Key under threats as I am informed of their taking possession by force. After ascertaining what had been done and knowing that Mr Lee would be back in a day or two I thought it best to let the matters rest until his return. After Mr Lees return he saw Curtis and he Curtis expressed his perfect readiness to vacate as soon as appointments were made by you and as he momentarily expected to recieve your appointments, he was advised by Judge Buxton[3] & other friends to rest quiet until you were heard from. Judge Buxton also informed him that he had spoke to you on the subject before he left Raleigh and that you comtemplated appointing the old board with perhaps one or two exceptions.

I can assure you that Mr Lee acted in good faith in this whole matter and can also assure you (backed if it were necessary by every man in the town of Fayetteville) that you have no truer friend in this State than your friend Lee. As regards the little caucus held here, composed of fifteen persons Mr Lee nor any of your genuine supporters indorsed their proceedings Mr Porter who has been appointed Mayor has never been considerd nor does he express himself as one of your true friends.

Yours Truly
E. L. Pemberton

[*Endorsed*] Write him that J. R. Lee, Esq. and others are Mayor and commissioners. During his absence his powers were usurped by Rebels—that on his return he neither attempted to oust these Rebels nor did he report the facts to me. After waiting a reasonable time I acted. I could not appoint the old Board, for if I had I would have given Countenance to their tame submission to the Rebel usurption. If Curtis and his co-traitors had the right to pursue the course they did, then the present State government is null and void, &c.

That I regretted to be obliged to omit in the new Board all the old; that I am still their friend, and especially so of Lee and Pemberton, who must feel that upon the whole I did right.

[1] James R. Lee, Cumberland County; Fayetteville merchant. 1870 U.S. Census Population Schedule, North Carolina: Cumberland, 201 (microfilm).

[2] Thomas J. Curtis.

[3] Ralph Potts Buxton.

Henry W. Paschall to Holden A&H:GP

Summit N.C. Augest 18th 1868

Gov. Holden,

Dear Sir,

I take the present opertunity to say to you, that the people in Halifax & Warrington Co. need help from the loyal people of the State of N.C. When I arived at this place a few days ago, I found from the return of the Conservitive party at Raleigh, that they were very much disappointed, in not having carried out their points as they wished to. all they could do was to get as many conservitive nigers togeather as posiable in Halifax & Warrinton co. where the superstition and ignorance abounds amoung the people, and where they think they can easily deseve the people by their, poletical, rebellious, and treson proceedings.

We therefore appeal to you Gov., for the most inteligent, water proff. and fired tried republicans speakers, to be with us on the second Saturday in Sep., at Littlenton dopot N.C. let every loyal man in the orgination at Raleigh turn out for the purpose of Cheering up his brothers, while they appear to be sunct down in despair, and the Conservitive party striving to keep them the Same, there has been as I have learned this morning, Sir a great deel of shooting by those who are hired by the ku-klan-kluck, and I believe they intend to kill or at least shoot every man that will cast a vote for Collfax or Grant. Wheather it is best to take the steps which we perpose, we leave that Gov. for you to exercise your Judgment on, but we think if the Royal people of the S.V. are to supported the people of this State must be protected.

We now call your attention Gov. to the X chap. of Matt. 5 virse These twelve Jesus sent forth, and commanded them saying, go not into the way of the Gentiles, and into the city of the samaritans enter ye not. But go ye rather to the lost sheep of the house of Isruel.

I had a conversation with a gentleman who has reseved a severe wound from the ku-klan-kluck, and from what the rebbles have said to him Since, go to show that they endend to destroy every loyal man. they asked him was he a lig, he told them know, & they Ans. I am supprised at you being Shot, but that is nothing to what you will Sea in a few days. And for this cause I am deeply interrested, being the presendent of the orginaton of Warrington Co. No 3 Please do what you can for us in our destress, and write as soon as poseable Address Henry W. Paschall

Warrington co. N.C. Manson Post

S. Pool to John [Pool] A&H:GP

Chapel Hill
Aug. 19, 1868

Bro. John,

I had a letter from Charley[1] today saying Mr. Ashley[2] had requested him to attend a meeting of the Trustees on Monday next, the 23d inst. I presume there must be some mistake, as I have had no notice of any such meeting.

Judge Alden[3] & Col. Deweese[4] addressed the people here on Monday last. W. H. Craig[5] also spoke. He graduated at the late Commencement, & has but recently declared himself a Republican. Was heretofore claimed by the Conservatives. He had a school of about 15 children. The day after his speech all were withdrawn but two or three, whose parents were the only Republicans who sent to him. His school is closed therefore in consequence of his speech. Yesterday a colored woman was beaten here by the Messrs. Carr,[6] Conservatives, on slight provacation, I am told. I think she has brought her case today before the Bureau at Hillsboro. We have no magistrates — the Commissioners elect are generally understood to be banned, & are not doing their duty I suppose on account of the impression among them that they will be superseded by others shortly. I think if such is to be the case, it should be done at an early day.

We are all well & unite in love to all.

Truly &c
S. Pool

[1] Probably Charles Carroll Pool, nephew of Solomon and John Pool; superior court judge, 1868-1872. Cheney, *North Carolina Government, 1585-1979*, 578.

[2] Samuel Stanford Ashley, educator; delegate to 1868 convention; superintendent of public instruction, 1868-1871. *Dictionary of North Carolina Biography*, s.v. "Ashley, Samuel Stanford."

[3] Not identified.

[4] John Thomas Deweese.

[5] William Harrison Craige; A.B., U.N.C., 1868; teacher and planter. Grant, *Alumni History*, 138

[6] Not identified.

Pinkney Rollins to Holden A&H:GP

Marshall N.C
21st Aug 1868

Gov W. W. Holden
Raleigh N.C

Dear Sir

By reference to the proceedings of the Legislature of North Carolina, we were made to rejoice to know that the Capital Stock of the Western North Carolina Rail Road had been increased to twelve millions of dollars, and futher, that the restrictions imposed by former Legislation upon the Greenville and French Broad Rail Road had been removed. The people of this hill country are proud of the Legislature of N.C. Composed of "Scallawags" and "Carpet baggers." Gov, we have the honor to request, that in making the appointment of the Board of Directors, for the *Western Division* of the *Western North Carolina Rail Road* that you *remember* our *noble little county* (Madison) as the line from Asheville to the Paint Rock runs directly through this county.

You will hear a good report from us in Nov. for Grant & Colfax

I am very Respectfully

Pinkney Rollins[1]
Marshall NC

[1] Pinkney Rollins, Madison County; lawyer. 1870 U.S. Census Population Schedule, North Carolina: Madison, 397 (microfilm).

John W. Hofler to Holden A&H:GP

Sunsberry Augt 22/68

To his Excellency W. W. Holden Govenor of North Carolina Greeting

My Dear Sir

Permit me to inform you of the Condition of things in Gates County, we are here those of us who profess to be friends of the Republican party we are looked upon as the filth of Creation and are called Negroes and friends of that old Villian of a negro spoiler old Bill Holden I heard some express themselves the other Day and Say that if they could Get some to assist them they would go to Raleigh and take old Holden out and hang him to the first limb as they would another negro—and any thing they call you and your friends but Gentlemen Those who have been Elected to fill the office of Commissioners say that They will never take the office if they are compelled to take the oath as the law Requires and I heard one Say myself that he would not qualify and hold no office under no such a Damned Rascal as Bill Holden a Damnd Negrofied son of a Bitch We are here in a State of confusion I write you my Dear friend to inform you that should any fail to qualify and take the oath of office as Commissioner I suppose it will be in your hands to appoint others if it is I would be Glad and ask of you as a friend to confer on me the appointment of one I will take the oath and can take it with as clear Conscience as any man living I am your friend and has always been and expect to Remain one if you cant appoint Commissioners if there is any office that you can confer on any individual please Remember me my Dear friend I have written you the truth and nothing but the plain truth I wish I could See you face to face and could tell you all that I could tell you we are in the way of the opposite party and would be by them Exterminated and with the Rest of us yourself and the freedmen but thank God they have not Got it in theire power

Some make theire brags and say that if Seymore and Blair are Elected they will have a chance to Get Rid of the Damnd Radicals and Negroes but if that is thire hope they will be ere long Deluded and my prayer is that they may be please to Remember me if any fail to Comply and you have the power to appoint others please Give me one appointment for Gates County any Refference can be Given that is Required

Respectfully yours
John W. Hofler[1]

[1] John W. Hofler, Gates County; farmer. 1870 U.S. Census Population Schedule, North Carolina: Gates, 141 (microfilm).

J E Cook to Holden A&H:GP

Yanceyville NC August the 22 1868

thire was a meeting in yanceyvill on the (21) of august a dinner Gaveen By the Democratic and just at night the croud got in a fight and I went up to Command Peace and I could not the Democratic Rush in on the Republicans and they had to gave Bak for thir was But a few of Republican there one Nat Johnson[1] who come to up and sade Boy Let us mak Georg Bow[2] Leve the Place and in the House and Brought him at and made him the town the other Colored man stud up as Long as he coud and tell they Bet him down abought teenty of them Sir there will not any saying in Caswell Execpt we have some forest of the union Army we Can not stay hear —Sir my Life was in Danger I had to mak my escapt out of the PlaCe for fear of them

J E Cook[3]

[1] Not identified.

[2] George W. Bowe, member, state House of Representatives, 1872-1874. Cheney, *North Carolina Government, 1585-1979*, 1089.

[3] John Cook, Caswell County; minister of the Gospel. 1870 U.S. Census Population Schedule, North Carolina: Caswell, 477 (microfilm).

J. Pace to Holden A&H:GP

[Pittsboro]

Governor Holden

Dear Sir believing that it is the duty of every good Citizen to keep you well informed as to the condition of our unhappy Country I have concluded to drop you a few lines stating Publick feeling &c in our County.

The Malitia Bill give great satisfaction to Republicans so far as we understand —The great difficulty will be in Organiseing with Loyal Men to controll Without something of the kind we could not have held a full Election in Nov next For the sake of Civilization Religeon & free goverment—To organize our goverment that loyal honest men will controll We are persecuted in the western part of Chatham than at any time since the Surrender It is true that we have 600 majority but they are mostly colloured Person The white Republican are the most virturest honerest & Poorest potion of our people They have been but little in publick life, are peace men & deplore all disturbances They have canlcil the Colloured population to keep the peace & I am proud to say that the Black men is dispose to do it The

Special Malitia should be organize immediately They should be white men. They will have white Rebels to deal with. The Collored population will need no restraint There is was a mistake in the Certificate appointing Dr Gorrel magistrate they name is written J Gorrel, it should have been R W Gorrel[1] there is but one Gorrel in the county You will please correct the mistake by sending a new Certificate to my care at Pittsborough you would confer a favour on the neighbour—hood by appointing George Pitts[2] a magistrate he is a good loyal man living in the midst of rebels Aug 22nd 1868

Your Respectfully
J Pace[3]

[1] R. W. Gorrel, Chatham County; appointed justice of the peace, July, 1868. William W. Holden, Appointments of Justices of Peace (G.O.7) (original in North Carolina State Archives).

[2] Not identified.

[3] James Pace, Chatham County; county commissioner, 1868-1870; chairman, 1868-1869. *Chatham County, 1771-1971* (n.p.: Moore Publishihng Company, n.d.), 442; Chatham County, Minutes of the Board of County Commissioners, 1868-1874 (original in North Carolina State Archives).

W J. Dawes to Jacob F. Chur A&H:GP

Yanceyville N.C. August 22, 1868

Colonel Jacob F Chur[1]
A. A. A. Genl. Raleigh N.C.

Colonel

I arrived at home yesterday noon in time to witness the proceedings of a County Mass Meeting & Barbecue of the Democratic party of this County. The attendance was very large & till a late hour quiet & orderly—I felt all during the day extremely well pleased & gratified that at such a time as this when party feeling and evil passions are so greatly excited a democratic mass meeting could be held here & largely attended by the blacks of the oposite party & all go off so well. This was the condition when I left to go to supper. Some liquor was being sold but I did not discover that it was doing particular injury & did not interfere—Before finishing my supper word was brought to me that a fight had commenced. I immediately went to the ground—found a great excitement & loud noise. No blows were struck after I arrived—the Sheriff[2] was in the middle of the melee & had the only black man who was engaged under his protection There were a great number of blacks on the ground & near by fully equal in numbers I should judge to the whites, but they kept aloof from the quarrell. I can not too highly commend their good conduct & their readiness in complying with my directions. The chief participants in the affair were about a dozen young men who were inflamed with liquor & one black man. All the older citizens of the place were active in using every exertion to stop the melee & in no instance that came to my knowledge did they do any thing to aid or encourage its continuance. The moment I could leave the parties with safety I had the liquor saloons all closed & the excitement soon subsided. I do not deny that the present situation of political afairs & the equality of the negro is distasteful to this peoples, ie. the whites, but that they are disposed to any unlawful designs I do deny. These evils are liable to occur in any comunity at any election or canvass Whiskey is more commonly the cause as in this instance. I send you this hasty & unofficial account in order to vindicate the blacks who behaved so well as well also the citizens here who not only discountenanced the whole thing but used every exertion to suppress it, as well also myself for allowing such a thing to happen in my district after making you so many assurances that my people would behave. Active measures are being taken this morning to bring all the offending parties to speedy justice.

I will see that this is effectually done & trust it may prevent a recurrence of such a thing—

very respectfully (& hastily for the mail
is closing) your obet Servant
W J. Dawes[3]
Lt. &c
Raleigh Aug 24/68

[*Endorsed*] Respectfully referred to His Excellency W. W. Holden Gov &c for his information By Command of Col Bt Maj. Genl. N.A. Miles.

Asst Com
Jacob F. Chur
Bt. Lt Col A A A

[1] Jacob F. Chur, captain and brevet lieutenant colonel; acting assistant adjutant gerneral, Bureau of Refugees, Freedmen, and Abandoned Lands. Records of the Bureau of Refugees, Freedmen, and Abandoned Lands, NARS Microfilm Publication 843 (microfilm copy in North Carolina State Archives.)

[2] Jesse C. Griffith, sheriff of Caswell County, 1860-1879. William S. Powell, *When the Past Refused to Die: A History of Caswell County* (Durham: Moore Publishing company, 1977), 544.

[3] William Jason Dawes, Ohio; second lieutenant, 43rd Infantry, July, 1866; first lieutenant, 1867. Heitman, *Historical Register and Dictionary of the United States Army*, s.v. "Dawes, William Jason."

John H. Everitt to Holden A&H:GP

South Gaston N.C
Aug 24 1868

His Excellency Gov. W. W. Holden
Gov of North Carolina

Sir Yours of 21st ult was receive the 22nd, And as soon as I can get the names of that organization I will forward it with any other information I can get.

There is to be a large meeting of the republican party here next Saturay the 29 Inst. And I have herd from Several Sources that there will be a demonstratin on the part of Said organization on that day to prevent the Republican party from Speaking on the Stand. They have even threatened to Shoot any Republican that should take the Stand. will it be necessary or not for me to call out 10 or 15 men to keep peace & order, on that day. Please let me know without delay.

and sir very Respectfully

Your Obbt Servt
John H Everitt J. P.

Holden to C. B. Mallet A&H:GLB

Executive Department of North
Carolina
Raleigh Aug. 25th 1868

C. B. Mallet Esq[1]
Presdt Western Rail Road Co.
Fayetteville No Ca

Sir

I would suggest in accordance with the 3d Section of an "Act to amend the charter of the Western Railroad Company" that a meeting of the Stockholders of the Road be held in Fayetteville on Saturday the 12th day of next month. This will be within the thirty days prescribed by law, and will I think afford ample time.

Very Respectfully
W. W. Holden
Governor

[1] Charles Beatty Mallett.

Affidavit of Duncan Holmes A&H:GP

State of North Carolina
County of New Hanover

Duncan Holmes being duly sworn, deposes and says, That on Saturday August 22d 1868, he went to Clinton Sampson County North Carolina by appointment to speak to a meeting of Republican and Union Men which had been called there for that day. That he arrived at Clinton about 12 1/2 noon and proceeded to the Court House, in front of which the meeting was to be held. That on arriving there he found about Two hundred people present, half of whom were whites. That he took his place in the piazza in front of the Court House; and proceeded to address the people. That his speech was continually interrupted by the Whites who were present by threats to drag him from the piazza if he did not cease his speech and immediately leave the place. That the White portion of the crowd appeared to be armed, and this deponent noticed Pistols passed from one to another. That Several parties (White) in the crowd said to this deponent, that he could not speak there "unless he spoke as he ought to." That in consequence of the actions and threats made by the white men present this deponent was in fear of his life and Expected that he would be killed. That the colored people present were completely subjected, and so great was their fear of death in Consequence of the threats made by the whites that none of them dared say a word. That large members of Colored People were prevented from attending said meeting in Consequence of the threats made by the whites. And the deponent was informed and verily believes that at time of said meeting was in progress, Colored men were taken against their will into the Room of the Democratic Club and there Compelled by threats to swear they would vote for Seymour & Blair, and this deponent further says that over thirty colored citizens of Sampson County came to him privately after the meeting was over, and asked him for Gods sake to represent their miserable condition to the Governor of the state, and that to say to him that in said County of Sampson there was no protection for the life or property of any union man either Black or White. That the condition of the Colored Citizen of said County was miserable beyond description. That many have been taken from their homes and Killed and that no men dared make any remark, or enquiry into the matter, and that their condition as slaves was preferable to that they now suffer, that they have no rights and no protection from the law or any source and they pray for help from the state Government to protect their lives and the little property their masters have allowed them to retain. And this deponent further says that from his own experience and from what was told him by others, who came to him in fear and trembling, and with tears in their eyes, he verely believes that said County of Sampson is in an utterly lawless condition, and this deponent believes that his own life was only saved by his going twenty (20) miles out of his usual way and Striking the Rail Road at a station not in the direct road

Sworn and Subscribed to before me this 25th day of August 1868

(sd) Duncan Holmes[1]

J. C. Mann Clerk Superior Court

[1] Duncan Holmes, New Hanover County; mulatto wheelwright. 1870 U.S. Census Population Schedule, North Carolina: New Hanover, 380 (microfilm).

Holden to Maj. Gen. George G. Meade A&H:GLB

Executive Department of N.C.
August 25th, 1868

To Maj. Gen. G. G. Meade,
Commanding, &c.,
Atlanta, Ga.:

Sir:

Allow me to express my gratification at the assignement of troops to this State, and their location, with one exception. It is important to have some troops in the Salisbury and Charlotte region of the State, and I would be glad, if it meets your approval, if the two companies of cavalry ordered to Raleigh could be stationed at Salisbury. Four Companies of Gen. Miles[1] regiment of infantry, the 40th, would be sufficent in Raleigh. I am especially gratified, as our loyal people are, at the appointment of Maj. Gen. Miles to the command of this State.

Very Respectfully,
W. W. Holden,
Governor

[1] Nelson Appleton Miles, Massachusetts; 1862, colonel; brevet brigadier general, 1864; major general of volunteers, 1865; colonel, regular army, 1866; later noted Indian fighter in American west. *Dictionary of American Biography*, s.v. "Miles, Nelson Appleton."

John W. Stephens to Holden A&H:GP

Yanceyville NC
Aug the 29 1868

his Excelency
Gov W. W. Holden

Dear Sir, I arrived at home on last thursday evening. Should hav written sooner had it not bin for a meeting of the Republicans that came off here yestoday. I will give you a full detail of matters here if you will bare with me, and leave you to judge as to whether trups are kneeded here or not, though allow me to suggest if you should deem it necessary to send trups send (Col) in preferance to white, if you can.

On friday the 21 was the first out break since I left home that is while I was in Raleigh. this affray as you have hurd befor was on the day of a democratick meeting and Barbecue. the riot was brought on by the democrat party, & resulted in the beating a Republican by the name Jim Graves[1] very severley. thaire was some fifteen or twenty on him he knocked down several before they got him down. Lieut Dawes[2] says if a half doz would have fought as he did that they would have whwiped out the crowd if they had used nothing but sticks. Lieut Daws says that the (Col) Republicans deserve all the credit of Stopping the riot with as little damage being don as was don that is by not partisapting. thaire has not bin the first man arrestd as yet for enguaganeing in that riot. if the parties had bin arrested on the next day as Lieut Daws wrote you they was making arrangements to do, it would have saved a second riot on Sunday the 23 inst. commenced by the leder of the first, Nat. D. Johnson[3] a perfect outlaw a boye or rather a young man some 22 or 23 years old whitch his own father Thos. D. Johnson[4] has no controll over. he on Sunday evening an hour or two by Sun was on the st. and sent some two or three times for a (Col) man by the name of Eligha Swepson[5] to cum to him but he refused to go to him knowing that a short time before that he Johnson had beaten his bro very severly with a stick and had shot at him then Johnson went over across the St. and called Eligah to him and said to him I understand that you are carying Rocks for me. S. replyed that he had no rocks for any body. Johnson then struck him several blows across the head with a hevy club and then Sweepson struck Johnson he then drew a pistol and shot Sweepson whitch wounded him severley in the thy, and seeing the other Col. men was enraged broak and run for his farthers' house with the Col men after him & by that time Lieut Daws came up and he allso followed after Johnson ording the Col men to stop that he would arrest him & put him in jail and at this time called on a Col man by the name of John Lawson[6] to assist him in keeping the (Col) men frome committing violance on Johnson. Lawson Succeeded by telling them to stop and remember what Mr Stephens has allways told you that is not to take the law in your own hands but let the Law take its course. Johnson ran into his farthers' house seeing the crowd so near on him passed through the house out at the back dower Lieut Daws having orded him to jaile, he Johnson finding the only place of reffuge for him at that time made his escape for the jaile about 200 yds distance ran in and closed the dower after him Lieut Daws cuming then locked the dower and taken the Key in his own posesion, he remained in untill next morning when he was brought out before John E. Cook a (col) magistrate appointed by you and two white magistrats A. A. Pattillor[7] & Thos J. Brown[8] old J.P.'s who sat together on the case they allowed him to give bail in a sum of $500^{00} for his appearance at court. Lieut Daws thinks that trupes is not kneeded and allso advises that it will be best not to organise the malitia at all as the Rebles ar so mutch opposed to it they Sware that they will not submit to Negros being armed as detail Malitia as I came through the village the K.K.K.s raised sutch a yell of oustrasism after me that they was hurd over a mile from the village I have not bin on the St. since I got home yet. Dr N. M. Roan[9] & Lieut Daws has bin down to see me they boath tell me that the Citizens are all allarmed at the condition of affares in this Co. they say that the old and most respectable citizens are opposed to the proceedings of the wild and reckless men and boyes, & that will be stoped I have not bin on the St. as I remarked to see if this is so they told me that the report had gottan out by some means that I entended to turn the (Col) men loos on them as soon as I got home whitch was without foundation my replay to them was that if they would make the whites behav themselves and the the (col) men alone that I would pledge my life for the good behavior of them. Cook with the rest of the Col men thinks that that trups are indispencable here for the protection of themselvs I will say that I do not believe that the malitia can be organised without trups here unless things very mutch change that is at any while the Rebbles hold the Co. offices as they now have them Allow me to subscribe myself your most Obt Servt.

John W Stephens

[1] James Graves, Caswell County; black farmer. Caswell County Tax List, 1867, 82 (original in North Carolina State Archives).

[2] William Jason Dawes.

[3] Nathaniel D. Johnson, Caswell County; farmer. Caswell County Tax List, 1867, 84 (original in North Carolina State Archives).

[4] Thomas D. Johnson, Caswell county; retail merchant. 1870 U.S. Census Population Schedule, North Carolina: Caswell, 471 (microfilm).

[5] Not identified.

[6] Not identified.

[7] A. A. Patillo, Caswell County; member, County Court of Pleas and Quarter Sessions, 1866-1868. Minutes of Caswell County Court, 1866-1868 (original in North Carolina State Archives).

[8] Thomas J. Brown, Caswell County; Yanceyville postmaster; former member, County Court of Pleas and Quarter Sessions, 1866-1868. 1870 U.S. Census Population Schedule,

North Carolina: Caswell, 473 (Microfilm); Minutes of Caswell County Court, 1866-1868 (original in North Carolina State Archives).

[9] Nathaniel M. Roan, Caswell County; physician. 1870 U.S. Census Population Schedule, North Carolina: Caswell, 492 (microfilm).

Tod R. Caldwell to Holden A&H:GP

Morganton N.C
30th Aug 1868

Gov Holden

Dear Sir

You have no doubt been posted by Mr. Cowles[1] with regard to the proceedings at the late meeting of the Stockholders of the W. N C R road at Statesville. all the interests of the State were sacrificed to suit the whims & caprices of Vance[2] & Merrimon[3] & Tate[4]. The Charter violated & treated as worthless paper. I cannot do justice to the subject on paper and will not attempt it. It was necessary for one to be present in order to appreciate fully their *damnable rascality* —Swepson[5] was there in full communion with the destructives and I am sorry to believe that Genl. Littlefield[6] gave his influence to them privately and to some extent publicly in the meeting. The two State Directors from Buncombe[7] were weak kneed & did not stand up as they should have done. My particular friend Corpening[8] did not fill the bill. All together the State was badly sold and I trust that you will call upon the Secretary for a correct report of the proceedings both of the Stockholders meeting & that of the Directors and submit them to the Atto Genl[9] & Judge Rodman[10] or some other good lawyer and if their usurpation can be overthrown do it at once. Judge Henry[11] won't begin to do to trust —no dependence to be put in him.

In haste yours truly
Tod R. Caldwell

[1] Calvin Josiah Cowles.

[2] Zebulon Baird Vance.

[3] Augustus Summerfield Merrimon.

[4] Samuel McDowell Tate, railroad official and legislator; commanded Sixth North Carolina Regiment from Gettysburg to end of the Civil War; 1865, elected president of Western North Carolina Railroad, removed by Governor Holden in 1865 but restored by Governor Worth and removed again by Holden in 1868; member state House of Representatives, 1874-1875, 1881-1885; state treasurer, 1892-1894. *Dictionary of North Carolina Biography*, s.v. "Tate, Samuel McDowell."

[5] George William Swepson; president, Raleigh National Bank; president, Western North Carolina Railroad; indicted but never convicted of embezzeling $4 million in bonds of the railroad. *Dictionary of North Carolina Biography*, s.v. "Swepson, George William."

[6] Milton Smith Littlefield; brevet brigadier general of the Union Army to recruit black troops; purchased *North Carolina Standard* from Governor Holden, 1868; officer and agent of western branch of Western North Carolina Railroad. *Dictionary of North Carolina Biography*, s.v. "Littlefield, Milton Smith."

[7] William Gaston Candler and James Love Henry. James Love Henry, Buncombe County; superior court judge, 1868-1878. Cheney, *North Carolina Government, 1585-1979*, 578.

[8] Probably William Corpening, Burke County; farmer. 1870 U.S. Census Population Schedule, North Carolina: Burke, 332 (microfilm).

[9] William Macon Coleman.

[10] William Bount Rodman.

[11] Robert M. Henry.

C. B. Mallett to Holden A&H:GP

Office of the Western Rail Road Co.
Fayetteville Sept. 1st, 1868

To His Excellency
W. W. Holden
Gov. of No.Ca.

Governor.

The important matter stated in your letter of last week has been deliberately considered. I have been influenced by a serious and anxious desire to preserve the present organization of the Western Rail Road company of which I am the Chief Officer, & to avoid as far as I could the adoption of a course, which promises in my judgment, no good to the public nor to the parties who placed me in my present position. I am advised that no officer of this Company who has been elected for a term & who is entitled to fees or to a Salary during such term can be displaced during its continuance except it be for good cause. The office may be abolished & then the incumbent goes out because he has nothing to hold, but if the office be left the incumbent has during his term an estate or property therein. The purpose of the Act of July 21st 1868 as is apparent upon its face is to undo what was done a few months ago by a full meeting of the Stockholders the State being present and concurring through her representative. I am not aware that any reason can be shown why this arrangement should be disturbed so suddenly. Certainly none which is connected with the interests of this company. I have heard no complaint of remissness or of unfaithfulness to the State or individuals, no imputation of injustice nor any satisfactory cause assigned why I should contribute so extreme a change on the affairs of this Company as might result from the meeting which you propose. I have resolved therefore not to call the meeting for the reasons assigned, viz., that one of the main provisions of the Act of July is against the Constitution; that the making of this extreme change now is against the good faith of the State as pledged at the last annual meeting & because I cannot see that the public interest or any private interest (which this Company ought to regard) is to be at all promoted.

With respect I am Yours,
C. B. Mallett, Prest.
Western Rail Rd. Co.

Lewis Johnson to Holden A&H:GP

City of Washington Sept 7th 1868

His Excellency
Gov. W. W. Holden
Raleigh N.C.

Dear Sir:

We have some customers largely interested in the bonds of your State, at their request we beg to propound the following questions for which we would ask your kind indulgence, and when convenient a reply.

Has the State passed the tax law to provide for payment of the interest in the debt of the State maturing on the 1 Oct. & 1st Jany. proxenios; and if so, is the same in process of collection?

When will the past due coupons due respectively, Apl & Oct, & Jany & July be funded?

Does the Constitution & existing legislation provide for the prompt payment in the future of maturing interest?

With great respect we have the honor to be

Your obedient servant
Lewis Johnson[1]

[1] Lewis Johnson, Washington, D. C., banker. 1870 U.S. Census Population Schedule, District of Columbia: Ward 2, 293 (microfilm).

W. J. Dawes to Jacob F. Chur A&H:GP

Office Bureau R. F. & A. L.
Yanceyville N.C. Sept 8, 1868

Col Jacob F Chur A. A. A. G.
Bureau R. F. &. A. L.
Raleigh N.C.

Colonal

I have the honor respectfully to report that a delegation of the citizens of Milton waited upon me yesterday & represented that a serious riot had occured in their village & that my presence was desired by many of all parties.

In accordance I immediately went to Milton, & in company with a black man named George Bow who is a leading man in this County among the Colored people.

He was to have a meeting in the evening for the purpose of forming a Grant Club. I found everything quiet & orderly & heard the accounts of the affair from various persons white & colored none of which disagreed in any important particular—

I requested the Mayor to give me a written Statement which he did & which you will please find enclosed—I desired George Bow to inform himself particularly of the version of the affair given by the blacks. He did so & states that their statement corresponds with that prepared by the Mayor which I read to him. I am of the opinion the whole trouble is the consequence of the use of whiskey & not attributable to any antagonism of feeling between the races.

I spoke to a large & respectable collection of blacks last evening Several whites being present Affairs in this County are in a more satisfactory condition than they have been at any time since I have been here.

Personal difficulties have occurred & no doubt will occur again & if one or both of the parties are drunk may become very disgraceful & important, while at the same time the public feeling & Sentiment of both races is in favor of the maintanence of the law & of good order.

Very respectfully
Your obt Servant
W. J. Dawes
Lt 43 Inf. A. S. A. C.
Sept 8, 1868

[*Endorsed*] Respectfully forwarded to His Excellency, W. W. Holden, Governor, for his information.

Jacob F. Chur

[*Enclosure*]

Milton N. Ca. Sept 7th 1868

To Lieut. Dawes,
Agent Freedman's Bureau,

Sir,

In accordance with your request, I submit the following report of the riot in this place on Saturday night Sept. 5th 1868.

On last Saturday night the town constable, Mr. Staten[1] and myself went to John Barnett's[2] house to arrest him for refusing to work on the streets or pay a fine as ordered by the town commissioners: he resisted and had to be arrested by force. While we were trying the warrant a crowd of negroes collected around the door. John still refused to pay the costs and we carried him to a house used to confine the town prisoners. The crowd of negroes followed us, the number increasing every minute till it reached about one hundred. As soon as we reached the house the crowd began to threaten to rescue John, to tear down the house, to charge on the constable and myself with stones and to set fire to the town.

By declaring our intention to shoot the first one that attempted to rescue John we kept him in custody till his fine was paid. While we had him in custody two or three negroes who appeared to be indifferent to John's confinedment came up and began to threaten to kill any man that should arrest Kinkade Walker,[3] for whom a warrant had been issued, he being guilty of the same offence.

The rioters remained in the streets till 12 o'clock that night cursing the officers of the country, including the President of the U.S. the Gov. of the state and all local authorities. The oaths and threats were so loud that they were heard a quarter of a mile and were a great annoyance to the citizens of that part of the town. One shot was fired into Mr Wilsons dwelling without any provacation.

The pretext for these riotous proceedings was, that we had no right to have the streets worked on and that the law was not executed on whites and blacks alike. The most of the white men had paid their fines before we began to enforce the law, only one white man at that time refusing to pay and he was put under arrest before a single warrant was issued for any negro. No one who can read and has read the law doubts our authority. At this time there are about two or three whites and double as many negroes who have not complied with the law on account of absence and other causes over which we had no control.

Justice to the negroes requires that I should state that some of them have informed me that they were led into this riot mainly by a false report made to them by a white man, but we have not been able so far to collect evidence against him sufficiently strong to bring him to trial.

The leaders of the riot have been arrested and bound over to appear at the next term of the Superior Court.

During these demonstrations the white men were personally insulted in a most shameful manner and they deserve great credit for their forbearance; they made use of no menacing words to the negroes, not a blow was struck and no one sustained any injury of any kind.

One of the leaders of the riot was not long since appointed a magistrate by Gov. Holden, Kinkade Walker (republican candidate for the Legislature at the last election) as before stated refused to pay his fine, but did not engage in any restistance to the authorities.

The law has been executed, the town is quiet and no more trouble expected.

Very Respectfully
Henry A. Walker
Mayor of Milton

We the undersigned certify that the above statement is in accordance with our knowledge of the outbreak on last Saturday night and believe it does justice to all the parties concerned.

J. L. Staton Town constable
Samuel Watkins[4]
J. Wilson[5]
Wm M Broocks[6]
Charles Watkins[7]
NM Lewis[8]

[1] John L. Staton.

[2] John Barnett, black farm laborer. 1870 U.S. Census Population Schedule, North Carolina: Caswell, 399 (microfilm).

[3] Charles Walker, Caswell County justice of the peace, appointed July 17, 1868. W. W. Holden, Appointments of Justices of Peace, 1868-1870, G.O.7 (original in North Carolina State Archives), 59.

[4] Samuel Watkins, Caswell County; clerk in store. 1870 U.S. Census Population Schedule, North Carolina: Caswell, 398 (microfilm).

[5] John Wilson, Caswell County; Milton dry goods merchant. 1870 U.S. Census Population Schedule, North Carolina: Caswell, 399 (microfilm).

[6] William M. Brooks, Caswell County; Milton physician. 1870 U.S. Census Population Schedule, North Carolina: Caswell, 398 (microfilm).

[7] Charles Watkins, Caswell County: Milton dry goods merchant. 1870 U.S. Census Population Schedule, North Carolina: Caswell, 398 (microfilm).

[8] Nicholas M. Lewis, Caswell County; mayor of Milton, 1869-1870. 1870 U.S. Census Population Schedule, North Carolina: Caswell 400 (microfilm).

Miles Welch to Holden A&H:GP

September 12th 1868

From the League Society at Thornberry North Carolina Northampton County, at Henry K. Burgwyns[1] plantation, from A flag Raising at Halifax N. C. Meeting on our Way Back home the Democratic Conservative Party, formd a line a cross public Road with gun and pistle to prevent us from going Home to our Residents where We belongs to George P. Burgwyn.[2] was the head Commander of that Democratic Company. Commanding 10 or 15 men. that was to prevent the League men from going Home in the Co. Of Halifax when we came over into this said Co. John Long[3] of Northampton Co. drew his pistle upon one of our League men and made a pretind to Shoot him on the River shore We was invited over there to insists them in putting up the flag pole for grant and Colfax this was as we came over with about one Hundred men that it in my Council and now i Laid this before you gov to Justified the meddest and gov. this is what we want Satisfaction form this which is now Laid before you gov. Gov i had my men under good Command and Also Remaining the Same i will Close this By Saying i am Yours truly Humble Servant Miles Welch the president of this Council, at thornberry on H. K. plantation Northampton co N.C. post office at Jackson N. C. northampton County

[1]Henry King Burgwyn plantation "Thornbury," Northampton County on the Roanoke River.

[2] George P. Burgwyn, Northampton County; farmer. 1870 U.S. Census Population Schedule, North Carolina: Northampton, 580 (microfilm).

[3] John Long, Northampton County; farmer. 1870 U.S. Census Population Schedule, North Carolina: Northampton, 579 (microfilm).

TELEGRAM *Holden to Maj. General G. G. Meade* A&H:GLB

September 14th 1868
Executive Department of N.C.

To Maj. General, G. G. Meade, Atlanta, Ga.;

Sir:

I would be glad if you would immediately authorize Maj. Genl. Miles so to locate the troops under his command as to aid the civil power in bringing offenders to justice and enforcing the law. Troops are needed immediately in Halifax county to assist the civil authority. There are three localities especially in which the presence of a small number of troops would be of service. The Sheriff could at once execute any precept, and a salutary terror, by the mere presence of troops would be occasioned to the disaffected and disloyal. Please answer.

With much respect,
W. W. Holden
Govr

TELEGRAM *R. C. Drum to Holden* A&H:GLB

Atlanta, Georgia, Sept. 15th, 1868

To Governor W. Holden:

Maj. Genl. Meade instructs me to say that he will not change the disposition of troops for the purpose indicated in your telegram of yesterday. If any actual resistance to law which you cannot suppress occurs the Genl will promptly use the troops but until overt acts occur he shall keep them ready for emergencies in any part of the State the civil authorities must attempt at least to preserve the peace.

R. C. Drum,
A. A. A. Genl.

Robert M. Douglas to C. M. Farris A&H:GP

Raleigh Sept 21, 1868

C M Farris Esqr[1]
Keeper of the Capitol

Sir

I have the honor of informing you, that at a meeting of the Heads of Departments, held Sept 21, 1868, it was ordered,

That the Keeper of the Capitol be directed to reduce the expenses for work on the Capitol grounds, and to employ, if at all practcable, not more than two hands on the same.

Very Respectfully
Robert M. Douglas
Private Secretary

[1] Charles M. Farris, Wake County; keeper of the Capitol but subsequently identified as a tailor. 1870 U.S. Census Population Schedule, North Carolina: Wake, 263 (microfilm).

F. W. Liedtke to Holden A&H:GP

Office Bureau R. R. and A. L.
Company Shops N.C. Sept 22, 1868

To
His Excellency W. W. Holden
Governor of North Carolina
Raleigh N.C.

Sir

Some time ago Peter Summers,[1] Colored, Complained to me that last year he cropped with Bentley W. Page[2] of Caswell County, who now refuses to give up to him his Share of Tobacco. I made out his account and advised him to go to a Magistrate in that County. Today Mr. J. L. Borland,[3] a citizen of Caswell County applies to me, stating that he can not find a Magistrate who dares to take up any Case against any of the Enemies of the present State Government; that the old Magistrates, the old Sheriff, Jesse C.. Griffith, altho' the latter is debarred by the XIV Article, and his Deputies, are still claiming and exercising the authority and duties of their respective Offices, and that the two loyal Magistrates appointed by Your Excellency for Caswell County do not dare to act.

I have on several occasions been informed by loyal men that there is no lawful Sheriff, Constable or Magistrate to be found in that County and that a poor man has no chance of obtaining justice. I respectfully report this to your Excellency, praying that the complaint be enquired into.

I understand that the loyal Citizens of Williamson and Andersons Districts, Caswell County, forwarded to Your Excellency, about two months ago, thro' the Andersons Store Post office, a petition, praying the appointment of James Torrel[4] Zacharias Bryntle,[5] Richard Maynard,[6] John T. Rooney,[7] Wm F. Davis[8] and Jas L. Borland as Justices of the Peace, but having heard nothing more of it, they fear that the petition did not reach Your Excellency. I know nothing of the character of the men recommended in that petition.

Pardon me for addressing your Excellency personally on this Subject, which perhaps does not properly belong to my Office. I have done it from a desire to aid poor honest people who apply to me and whom I have no means of assisting myself.

I have the honor to be Your
Excellency's
obedient Servant
FW Liedtke
Lieut. 43d U.S. Infantry
Asst. Sub Asst. Comr F. B. and Justice
of the Peace for Alamance County

[*Endorsed*] Write to two justices at Yanceyville urging them to the performance of duty. State the facts, omitting name of this writer. Inform them that Co. Commissioners who are banned will be removed in due time.

[1] Peter Summers; in 1870 a domestic servant in Alamance County. 1870 U.S. Census Population Schedule, North Carolina: Alamance, 73 (microfilm).

[2] Bentley W. Page, Caswell County; white farmer. 1870 U.S. Census Population Schedule, North Carolina: Caswell, 459 (microfilm).

[3] James L. Borland, Caswell County; white farmer. 1870 U.S. Census Population Schedule, North Carolina: Caswell, 454 (microfilm).

[4] James T. Terrell, Orange County; white farmer. 1870 U.S. Census Population Schedule, North Carolina: Orange, 195 (microfilm).

[5] Zacariah Brindle, appointed Caswell County justice of the peace, October 10, 1868. W. W. Holden, Appointments of Justices of Peace, 1868-1870, G.O.7 (original in North Carolina State Archives), 60.

[6] Richard Maynard, Caswell County; white farmer. 1870 U.S. Census Population Schedule, North Carolina: Caswell, 459 (microfilm).

[7] John T. Roney, appointed Caswell County justice of the peace, September 17, 1868. W. W. Holden, Appointments of Justices of Peace, 1868-1870, G.O.7 (original in North Carolina State Archives), 59.

[8] William F. Davis, appointed Caswell County justice of the peace, September 17, 1868. W. W. Holden, Appointments of Justices of Peace, 1868-1870, G.O.7 (original in North Carolina State Archives), 59.

Speech By Gov. Holden *Standard*
September 23, 1868

Friends and Fellow-Citizens:

We are glad to see you all on this occasion. When the rebels have their convocations they meet by hundreds; but when the true men of the country rally together for the preservation of their liberties, they come by thousands. You "come as the winds come when forrests are rended; you come as the waves come when navies are stranded." You are here, my friends, on the present occasion with the clear notes of the bugle, the hoarse rumble of the drum and the thunders of artillery. You are here, under that glorious ensign, which is at once the idol and the admiration of all true hearts. More than all that, you are here, stalwart, determined, free men, resolved under that flag by the blessing of God, having strong arms to maintain your rights at all hazards.

I shall not attempt anything like a speech. There so many present who are better qualified to address you than I am, that I shall confine myself to only a few observations.

I owe it to you and to myself to make an allusion personal to myself. I have the honor to be, at this time, as I expect to be, God willing, for the next four years, the legal lawful, constitutional Governor of North Carolina. My friends, the rebels say that this State Government, organized under the law making power of this nation, is null and void, but they forget at the same time to state that they themselves, under the very same acts of Congress, from the 2nd day of March, 1867, to the 4th day of July, 1868, held office and governed this people under the very acts which they now say are unconstitutional. I mean the reconstruction acts of Congress, because those acts recognized those men in power and continued them. The difference is that in that case they held the offices, and in this case we hold them. That is a very fair specimen of rebel consistency and honestly. It is said that the bare election of the rebel Democratic candidates for the Presidency and Vice Presidency will vacate these offices; that those of us who have been invested with power by the votes of 92,000 of the freemen of North Carolina, will have to retire, sneak away from these mighty rebel Democratic candidates if they should be elected. Gentlemen, they never made on any occasion, a greater mistake. I say to you here, and now, that it is the fixed purpose of the present Government of North Carolina, sustained as that Government will be by the Congress of the United States, and sustained also, simply and solely because he cannot help himself, by Andrew Johnson—because even he is forced to do it—I say sustained even by Andrew Johnson himself in his late orders to the Generals in these States, that at all hazards, and under all circumstances, these governments, erected under the authority of Congress in these Southern States, *will be maintained.* It is useless to say how they shall be maintained. If war shall again occur in this country, if there be in these councils of Heaven a purpose again to rain down upon the people the calamities of civil strife, all of who are here assembled, the whole Republican people of this country, North and South, when that strife shall be upon us, will raise their heads to heaven, and solemnly affirm before God who sits in judgment upon the world, that they are not responsible. If war comes, it will come from "turbulent mutterers of stifled treason." It is now but three years since traitors were beaten to the earth and compelled to beg for quarter by the legions of Sherman and Grant and other great men. These foul traitors now come forward, put on airs, and assume that they are the persons in whom is to be vested the control of the people in these States, white and black.

Fellow-citizens, I do not see, you do not see it, our Republican allies in Vermont did not see it, and the result was thirty thousand majority for Grant and Colfax. And the news from glorious old Maine is still better, for I counted on only about five thousand gain, but the result is a clear gain of about 14,000 votes. The majority last year was 11,000; it is now 25,000, showing a clear gain of 14,000. But it is not so much as a comparative gain, and that is the best point for us, as that is an actual additon to the vote. The people, the soldiers, the glorious battle-scarred veterans who followed Grant and Sherman to victory, are coming out and casting their votes for themselves, for the country, for you, and for posterity.

I thank them for it—we all thank them for it; but the best requital we can make will be, as I have no doubt we shall, on the 3d day of November, to go to the ballot box and cast our vote for Grant and Colfax by not less than 30,000 majority. That will settle the question for us and our children, and for the rebels and their children, world without end.

My friends, I shall not detain you long. I desired in the first place to call your attention to the conditions of North Carolina, and in the second place, to the bright prospects all around us. I want my fellow-citizens here assembled, and especially my colored fellow-citizens, to carry with them the declaration I have just made, as your Governor, aided as I shall be by all true Republicans in the State, by the Congress, by the Supreme Court, and of necessity by Andrew Johnson, because he cannot do other wise, that under all circumstances the existing State government will be maintined. Why, gentlemen, all over the State the benefits felt in restored confidence, in renewed and stronger protection to the weak against the proud and the wicked. That is the true object of all governments to protect the weak against the strong—to prevent the powerful and the wicked from trampling on the weak, and that is the glory of the Republican party in this country. It is the party of the poor men, because the poor man needs more sympathy and more protection than the rich man does, and this is the party that gives him that protection.

We are prospering. Good crops are pouring in. The Good Lord himself is looking down benificently upon us. We will have next year no suffering for bread. The people everywhere will have enough to eat, and suppose they do turn you out because you vote against them, it is only about eight weeks. Only eight weeks. Recollect, that for more than four long years the forces of the national government toiled and struggled and labored, and 500,000 died on fields of battle and in hospitals to secure your liberty. Recollect those sacrifices made by the freemen of the Northern States, and a portion of the freemen of the Southern States, who crossing the lines, as my friend Gen. Bryan and others did, bared their bosoms in definance of their country.

If at this time throughout the entire country the best people, North and South, are incurring reproach, and obloquy and denunciation because as white men they will stand up for your rights as well as their own—I say if they do that, the best, the bravest, the most virtuoeus, and the most accomplished gentlemen and ladies in the whole land; if they endure all these things on your account, cannot you also endure it for eight short weeks? Then, my friends, I want you all to go to the polls and vote for the party of freedom. Any colored man who does not vote for Grant and Colfax is no man at all. Do not hurt him. Let him stand as a monument of folly to the the nineteenth century, and as evidence of the fact that men are free in North Carolina. Give equal protection and justice under the law and by the law to all the inhabitants of the State, white and black, rich and poor, and this same protection to all the people of the State, whether they be rebels or whether they be Republicans. This is the true doctrine.

Meanwhile, see to it, on your own account, and on account of those gallant dead who sleep in graves all over this land, fallen in defence of your rights and mine; by your regard for unborn posterity, while we regard the rights of rebels so long as they demean themselves as they should—see to it that in no event does one rebel get a single "bite" at a public office. The past has shown and the present shows that it is a most dangerous thing to trust one of those men in power.

Now, my friends, before I close I will say one or two things, to you, which the rebels never hear of. They never hear of the returns of the elections from Maine and Vermont. They cannot hear that, it is too serious for them; and another thing is they never see Frank Blair's letter, breathing treason. They never see it, never publish it; but at the election they will find it.

Allow me, my friends, to express my gratification, in the first place, as seeing so many of you here, and in the second place at observing the excellent order which prevails, the respect for law, and the respect even for the feelings of rebels, for you show even respect for them. That is all well. This country is free. The best evidence of our improved condition is that our people meet everywhere, in daylight, at midnight, under all circumstances, rebels and Republicans, and no man molests them. Even rebels may plot against the nation, and nobody says nay, except at the ballot box; but they are very careful to commit no overt act; very careful to avoid that, and, so long as they avoid that, they are free from arrest and punishment. Beyond that no one answers.

Now, my friends, we shall have to do a great deal of speaking. A number of of our friends who are present will be heard from. We shall have a rousing procession and speaking nearly all night. I tell you this to assure you that you will be well entertained all day and nearly all night. When the speaking is over at this stand and another stand, the marshalls will conduct the people to a fine barbecue.

In conclusion, asking your pardon for these broken and desultory remarks, I do myself the honor and you the pleasure of introducing to you on this occasion the Hon. Joseph R. Hawley, of the State of Connecticut. Governor Hawley is present by invitation. He was here in 1865, under a somewhat different capacity, in a capacity in which all true men were glad to meet him, at the head of his command, and flag hang in his hand his true, good sword, fighting in behalf of the nation. He is a man who, by his own industry and indomitable will , has made a national reputation. He is as true a man as ever drew a sword or raised a voice in defence of his country.[1]

[1] Governor Holden gave this speech to a Republican Party mass meeting in Raleigh, September 16, 1868, and was used to introduce Joseph Roswell Hawley, former governor of Connecticut.

Affidavit of Henry Baker A&H:GP

State of North Carolina
New Hanover County

Henry Baker[1] being duly sworn deposes and says that there is now concealed in the Democratic Club room Twenty five Hundred Carbines with belts, accoutrements &c. That the said arms all appeared new and in perfect order. That he was employed to clean them and carefully counted them. That the said arms are destined for various clubs in this County and others and will soon be shipped.

Subscribed and sworn to
before me this 24th day
of September A D 1868
D. C Mann
Clerk Superior Court

[1] Henry Baker, New Hanover County; Wilmington merchant. 1860 U.S. Census Population Schedule, North Carolina: New Hanover, 382 (microfilm).

John Patterson to Holden A&H:Holden

Hayesville Clay Co
No Ca
Oct the 3rd 1868

To His Excellency
Gov W W Holden
Raleigh N.C.

Dear Sir

As Sheriff of Clay County I have failed to get up the State Tax owing to the hard times and scarcity of moneys in this part of the State I went into office the Last of August and everything was in a confused state so you see that I did not have time to collect the Tax and get to Raleigh with it at the time set a part-money being so scarce here it is impossible to sell property for money here If your Excellency can possibly offer me any Relief I will certainly consider it an everlasting favor I think that I will be there shure with the Tax by the 20th November &c.

Very Respectfully
John Patterson Shff Clay Co N.C.

Jacob F. Chur to Holden A&H:GLB

Bureau of Refugees, Freedmen and
Abandoned Lands.
Raleigh No. Ca 5th October 1868

His Excellency W. W. Holden, Governor
Raleigh No. Ca

Sir

I am directed by the Asst Comm to transmit the enclosed copy of a communication from General Howard[1] for your information and to enquire whether there cannot be some action taken by the civil authorities to assume the care of the sick and helpless freedmen

Instructions will be immediately issued to close as rapidly as possible all dispensaries, and to admit no more patients to the Hospital. The Orphan's Asylum near Wilmington is under charge of the American Missionary Association, but that Society will probably not be able to continue its benefits after the assistance of the Bureau is withdrawn. Early attention should be given to this matter as but a short time yet remains for the action of the Bureau

I have the honor to remain

Very Respectfully
Jacob F. Chur
Bvt. Lt. Col
A. A. A. G.

[*Enclosure*]

War Department. Bu. R. F. & A. Lands.
Washington October 1. 1868.

Bervt Maj. Genl. Miles
Asst Commissioner
Raleigh N.C.

General

I am directed by the commissioner to your attention to the imperative necessity of breaking up the Hospital and dispensaries and the withdrawal of aid from Orphan Asylums in your State. After the 1st. of January next no further support by this Bureau can according to Law be extended to these Institutions. You will therefore exert yourself to induce the State, County, or municipal authorities, to assume the care of the sick and helpless freedmen, as also the inmates of the asylums. For the latter, if possible, interest the sympathies of private benevolent associations The commissioner desires to gradually withdraw the care of these people, heretofore exercised by the Bureau, and in the manner to occasion the least possible suffering

Please report your action in this matter

Very respectfully
Your Obt Svt
F. D Sewall
Acty. Asst. Adj. Genl.

[1] Oliver Otis Howard, Maine; brevet major general; commissioner, Bureau of Refugees, Freedmen, and Abandoned Lands, 1865-1869. *Dictionary of American Biography*, s.v. "Howard, Oliver Otis."

P. Ridenhour to Holden A&H:GP

Albemarle Stanly County N.C
To His Excellency Governor W W Holdin

Sir We the Commissioners for Stanly County being at a Loss to Know what to do as to Laying off the county into Townships & School districts forth with or not as it is stated by some that it is postponed until the first of January 1869—pleas Write to us and Instruct us in the matter whether we shall proceed at once or or [*sic*] wait until January n[e]xt

October the 6th 1868
Yours Respectfully
P. Ridenhour, Chairman

Jno. V. Sherard to Holden A&H:GP

Newberne, October 7, 1868

Gov Holden

I will drop you a few lines from this place to inform you that a box made in the shape of a coffin was found at a church in this place last evening containing enfields riffles. it is supposed the box was shiped here from the City of New York. The grand jury have this day undertook to have the matter investigated but cannot come to any definite conclusion about the matter I think a very strong effort is being made at this time by a certain party to arm themselves between this & the Presidential election. I have been instructed to inform you of this fact, officially on my part. So I hope you will be prepared to meet any emergency.

Yours
Jno Sherard[1]

[1] John Vickar Sherard, Goldsboro; A. B., U.N.C., 1846; member, House of Commons, 1848-1851; solicitor, Third Judicial District. Grant, *Alumni History*, 558.

Holden to Nelson A. Miles *Standard*
October 9, 1868

Executive Department
Raleigh, October 7, 1868

Gen. Nelson A. Miles, Commanding, &c.

Sir.—I have information that arms have been imported into this State, and distributed among members of a certain political organization. These arms are not of the ordinary character for sporting or hunting purposes, but repeating rifles, such as are used in war.

I have official information that a box of Enfield rifles has been found, secreted in Newbern. I learn also that boxes of arms have been shipped to Charlotte, and to points west of that place.

I have also learned that arms have been received and distributed in and around Wilmington. It is known that arms are in the hands of persons in that city and the surrounding country, of a character to leave the impression that they are to be used for the purposes hostile to the Government and to the peace of society.

I have deemed it my duty to inform you of these facts, and to request you so to distribute the troops under your command as to afford the greatest aid practicable to the civil authorities in sustaining the peace. I trust that troops will be at once sent to Wilmington, and to other points in the State. It is my fixed purpose to maintain the peace and to protect and maintain the State Government by all the means I can command. The people were surprised and hurried into the war in 1861, against their will. The authorities owe it to the people, to the Government, and to themselves to see to it that similar steps are not allowed to be taken now. The great body of our people are averse to violence and war. They want peace. They must have it. Those who may engage in war, or who may resort to violence to gain political ends, or to take vengenance on any portion of their fellow citizens, will be held to strict account and severely punished.

In the event of a conflict the civil authorities having first exhausted their power to preserve the peace, will call at once on the Federal military; and I have written this to notify you in advance of my purpose in this respect. I feel sure of your aid in any emergency to the extent to which it can be given under the orders you have received.

I have the honor to be, very respectfully,

Your obedient servant,
W. W. Holden

Nelson A. Miles to Holden *Standard*
October 9, 1868

Headq's District of North Carolina
Raleigh, N.C., Oct. 9th, 1868

Governor W. W. Holden

Sir:—I have the Honor to acknowledge the receipt of your communication of the 7th inst., requesting that troops may be sent to Wilmington, N.C., and stating that you have official information that a lot of Enfield rifles has been secreted in Newbern, also that you have reason to believe that arms have been sent to Charlotte, N.C., and several other points, &c. I have forwarded your letter to Gen. Meade for his information.

I have received reliable reports, legally substantiated, that several hundreds of Henry and Spencer rifles (many of them sixteen shooters) with accouterments, &c., complete, have been received at Wilmington and thence distributed to organizations in this State, styling themselves "Seymour and Blair" Clubs, and "K.K.K.'s." From other points officers report similar movements, the object of which has as yet not been made public. These facts have also been reported to the Department Commander and I have no doubt he will take proper action in the matter. While, therefore, these occurrences give rise to questions which may possibly produce serious results, still, actions in the first instance should be taken by the civil authorities, which, in my opinion can be done under the Act of the General Assembly of this State ratified August 24th, 1868, forbidding the conspiring of persons, by force or otherwise, to prevent the execution of laws of the state, and making it a high crime to engage in rebellion or insurrection against the authority thereof.

The Constitutional right of all citizens to the possession of arms for proper purposes, does not extend to the perfecting of organizations, armed with weapons of a purely military character, such as those reported as having been received in such unusual quanities at Wilmington and other points, otherwise batteries and regiments may be formed with equal propriety, inimical to the government, while it calmly awaits the fate intended by those who in 1860 pursued a similar course.

It will undoubtedly be claimed by those parties that their motives are perfectly good and as indicating no intention to forcibly resist the law or otherwise interfere with the peace and quiet of their respective localities. This cannot be granted. In 1861, professions of intense loyality to the Constitution and laws went hand in hand with concealed preparations for war. Many of these men are paroled prisoners who have sworn to obey the laws in force where they reside and not to bear arms against the government, &c. This State has been reorganized under acts of Congress, the sequence of the rebellion, and any attempt to disturb its laws and prevent the re-establishing of the authority is in my opinion an act of hostility and a violation of their solemn obligations, which may justly excite action on the part of the general government. Their rights in asserting and maintaining hostile positions towards the government, prompts condemnation on the part of all good citizens should follow.

This "apparent purpose and readiness" to appeal to arms, after the experience of the past seven years, is inexplicable. It is strange that many of the citizens of this State should so far forget their interests as to court another collision which cannot but be more disastrous than that recently ended. There is nothing in the present political contest to excite apprehensions on the part of any class or party. Two elections have quietly occurred here within the past twelve months as important as any that have taken place in the history of North Carolina, and with a degree of good order creditable to all concerned, and any attempts to excite distubrances by any parties, under any pretence whatsoever, are alike foolhardy and criminal. It probably requires no discussion to prove the entire futility of attempting any resistance of the Government in its efforts to perfect and complete the questions arising from the late war. Its whole power is guaranteed for the maintainance of the laws is at present constituted, and until legally changed, they should and must be respected.

Yours respectfully,
Your obedient servant,
Nelson A. Miles
Bvt. Maj. Gen., U.S.A., Comd'g. Dist.

J. W. Schenck, Jr., to Holden A&H:GP

Wilmington N.C. Oct 10th 1868

To his Excellency
W W Holden

I have the honor to request information in the following matter—During the year 1865 a reward was offered (I think by Gov Holden)[1] $500 for the arrest of one Berry Lowery[2] for the murder of J. P. Barnes[3]—Is that bounty still to be paid for the arrest and delivery of this man?

Most Respectfully your Obt Servant
J W Schenck Jr
Sheriff NH County

[1] The reward was offered by Governor Worth December 6, 1866. Governor Jonathan Worth Letter Book, 1865-1867, 330 (original in North Carolina State Archives).

[2] Henry Berry Lowry (Lowrie), outlaw; leader of a band originally engaged in guerilla warfare with Confederate Home Guard; arrested for the Barnes murder, but escaped and remained at large; jailed in Lumberton, December, 1868, but again escaped; reportedly died about 1872. *Dictionary of North Carolina Biography*, s.v. "Lowry, Henry Berry."

[3] James P. Barnes, postmaster at Clay Valley, Robeson County; scout for Home Guards; murdered December 21, 1864. *The Lowrie History as Acted in Part by Henry Berry Lowrie, the Great North Carolina Bandit*, 4th ed. (Lumberton: Lumbee Publishing Company, 1909), 42.

Silas L Curtis et al. to Holden A&H:GP

[Granville County]
Oct 11th 1868

Mr Govenor

Dear Sir

I take the privilige or writing to you—on this occasion—for this reason not because we are scared out—but in the first place. You are our State Executive—and when we are haveing outrages committed among us—You are our only Refuge to which we have to flee for advice and Protection—there for I take the privelige to inform You of some outrages comitted among us—and it is not onley now and then—it is geting to be a genrel thing, on Saturday Night last the KuKulx wer raging in oxford and tally ho—they first formed them selves in line in front of the Colored School Room—thinking the leagues were at lodge in there—and failing to find them went off to other places and don the same—tho as it happon the leagues had adjoined before they came out. And they watched them. and they now say they intend to brake up the Leagues before the Election. Col. Avery[1] in a speech on friday lat at oxford—thot if we would stop the Leagues he would stop the kukulx. and if not he could not do nothing with them on Thursday night last they went to a Colored mans house and got him out and Beet him Cruley beet his wife and cut her dress open and tied her to a tree—then if ever they told it or told who it was they would kill them—they then went to another ones house and comence tarring the top of his house off and some of them at the door & broke in Got hold of his wife he got out of the way—and got her out and she got loose and ran and they shot her in the back and by side of the face and She now lies in a low state of helth. and a few nights ago they went to another Colored Mans house and treated him the same. *I will now give you the Colored mens names Ned Mallory*[2] Passon Jones and Pressley *Herndon*. those white *men was* John C. Hugen, Wm Stem, John Wheeler, John Day, Wm Boles, Hay Stem, and one by the name of Bishop, Jack Boothe, Telay Moon, Sam Boothe, Henry Hasken, Flucher Moon, Tom Jones, Wm Jones, and others—that are comiting These out Rages and I have not told near All they have and are doing. and we appeal to you for some protection in some way. Surch men oght to be stoped in their out Rages.

Sir I hope to hear from you soon We dont want a malissia here among us. But God in heaven knows we must have somthing—otherwise we Will have to give up. Gen. Grant and take Seymore. and if I have to do that I am going to take a Rope and go to the woods.

Your obedant Servant
Silas L Curtis[3]

Cuffee Mayo[4]

[1] Probably Robert Avery, first lieutenant, 44th Infantry Regiment, brevet lieutenant colonel, inspector, Bureau of Refugees, Freedmen, and Abandoned Lands in Raleigh. Records of Assistant Commissioner for the State of North Carolina, Bureau of Refugees, Freedmen, and Abandoned Lands (National Archives Record Group 105) (microfilm copy in North Carolina State Archives).

[2] Edward Mallory was the man whipped. In 1870, he was a laborer in Raleigh township, Wake County. 1870 U.S. Census Population Schedule, North Carolina: Wake, 315 (microfilm).

[3] Silas L. Curtis, Granville County; Oxford shoemaker. 1870 U.S. Census Population Schedule, North Carolina: Granville, 317 (microfilm).

[4] Cuffee Mayo, Granville County; Oxford blacksmith. 1870 U.S. Census Population Schedule, North Carolina: Granville, 176 (microfilm). The letter was signed by fourteen additional men.

A Proclamation A&H:GLB
by W. W. Holden Governor of N.C.

Executive Department of No. Ca.
Raleigh, October 12, 1868

Information has been received at this department that military weapons, such as repeating rifles of various kinds, have been imported into this state, and have been distributed with ammunition and equipments to citizens in several localities.

It is believed that boxes containing arms, ammunition and equipments are concealed in divers places, ready to be distributed as opportunity may offer. The object of the persons thus engaged must be either to subvert the government, to resist the constituted authorities, or to prevent a free election in this State on the third day of next month The government of North Carolina has been lawfully and constitutionally established. This government has been freely and voluntarily formed by a majority of the Citizens, in pursuance of acts constitutionally passed by the Congress, under which my immediate predecessor held office from the 2d day of March, 1867, to the first day of July, 1868. The constitutionality of these acts if questioned during this period, were nevertheless subscribed to and maintained by him, and by every department of the government, from the said 2d day of March, 1867, to the said 1st day of July, 1868; and now that they have been executed by the common consent of the whole people voting under them at the polls for members of a Convention, for the new Constitution, and for members of Congress and State officers, the result which has been effected closes the discussion in relation to them, and renders the present Constitution of government as valid and binding as were the Constitutions of 1776 and 1835.

This government will be maintained for the following, among other reasons:

1st. It has been lawfully and constitutionally established by the whole people of the State. It is operating smoothly and harmoniously. Under it the people are quiet and peaceable, and are just entering anew on a career of prosperity. It must not be upset or even assailed, because the colored people have been allowed to vote; or because they will vote with a certain party; or because a few public men are out of office and a few are in.

2d. Senators and Representatives have been admitted by the Congress to seats in that body. The State is, therefore, *of* as well as *in* the Union. It is as much of the Union as New York or any other State. No state can secede, nor can Congress push a state out, or sever its relations with the common government. If Congress should, therefore, do what is exceedingly improbable, repeal the reconstruction acts, such repeal would have no more effect than a repeal of the act admitting Texas or Kansas to representation. The reconstruction acts have been executed, and are, therefore, beyond the reach of Congress.

3d. The Supreme Court has no jurisdiction of the subject. Its powers are expressly defined by the Constitution to be "judicial," and not political. It has already decided that the question of admission to representation is a political question, and that when determined by Congress as it has been in relation to North Carolina, the court will not interfere.

4th. The President would have no more power to declare the reconstruction acts null and void, with a view to the extinguishment of the government of this state, than I would have to declare that a certain County or Counties in this State should cease to exist.

The government of North Carolina is, therefore, as firmly established as that of any other state. It has the same control of the right of suffrage, and of its own internal affairs, as the other States have; and it possesses equal power with the other states to protect and perpetuate itself. The right of the people to have arms in their houses, and to "bear" them under the authority of law, is not questioned. On the contrary, it is claimed as a constitutional right sacred to freemen. The use of arms by the male population, for peaceable and lawful purposes, should rather be encouraged than otherwise; but when, in time of peace, weapons of an extraordinary character are imported into the State by political organizations, and deposited and distributed in a secret manner among persons whose spokesmen deny the authority of the existing government, and who publicly declare that all government, to be authoriative and binding, must proceed alone from one race of our people, a state of affairs is at once constituted which renders it the duty of every officer and every citizen to be more than usually vigilant. It cannot be pretended that these arms are intended for hunting or sporting purposes. It cannot be justly assumed that they are necessary for the protection of those who have them, since the whole power of the state and general governments is pledged to protect the peaceable and the law-abiding, whoever and wherever they may be.

If it be the purpose of any portion of the people in any event to resist the laws or to subvert the government, they should bear in mind that *TREASON* is the highest crime that can be committed; that they are liable to arrest and punishment under the "act to punish conspiracy, sedition and rebellion," which will be enforced, if necessary, with a firm hand; and they should reflect that the magnanimity of the government, which spared the lives and estates of those who engaged in the late rebellion, may not be extended a second time to save them from the consequences of their crimes.

If it be the purpose of any portion of the people, by the use of arms, or by threats or intimidation, to prevent the people from going to the polls and voting as they may choose to vote on the third day of the next month, it is my duty to inform them that force will be met with force, and that every person who may thus violate the law will be punished.

Every race of men in this State is free. The colored citizen is equally entitled with the white citizen to the right of suffrage. The poor and the humble must be protected in this right equally with the affluent and exalted. The election must be absolutely free.

In view, therefore, of the condition of affairs, I have deemed it my duty to issue this Proclamation, admonishing the people to avoid undue excitement, to be peaceable and orderly, and to exercise the right of suffrage firmly and calmly, without violence or force of any kind. Every good Citizen is gratified that North Carolina is at present as quiet and peaceable as any state in the Union. Let us maintain this good name of our State. Let us frown indignantly on the use of brute force, or bribes, or threats, to control the election; and let every officer of the State, civil and military, be prepared to check instantly any incipient step to sedition, rebellion or treason.

The flag of the United States waves for the protection of all. Every star upon it shines down with vital fire into every spot, howsoever remote or solitary, to consume those who may resist the authority of the government, or who oppress the defenceless and the innocent. The State government will be maintained; the laws will be enforced; every citizen, whatever his political sentiments, will be protected in his rights; the unlawful use of arms will be prevented, if possible, and if not prevented, will be punished; and conspiracy, sedition and treason will raise their heads only to be immediately subdued by the strong hand of Military power. The General commanding this department has instructed the district and post commanders to "act in aid and co-operation, and in subordination to the civil authorities," in maintaining the peace and in securing a free election. The power of both governments is thus pledged to peace, order and tranquility.

It is specially enjoined on all officers of the detailed Militia to observe the "act to organize a militia of North Carolina," and to act in strict subordination to the civil power. And all Magistrates, Sheriffs and other peace officers are also specially enjoined to be vigilant impartial, faithful and firm in the discharge of their duties, magnifying and enforcing the law, ferreting out offenders, protecting the weak against the strong who may attempt to deprive them of their rights; to the end that the wicked may be restrained, the peace of society preserved, the good name of the State maintained, and the government perpetuated on the basis of freedom and Justice to all.

Done at our city of Raleigh, on the 12th day of October, in the year of our Lord one thousand eight hundred and sixty-eight, and in the ninety-third year of our Independence.

W. W. Holden, Governor.

By the Governor
R. M. Douglas, Private Secretary

Holden to J. I. Moore *Standard*
October 15, 1868

Executive Department
Raleigh, October 14th, 1868

To J. I. Moore,[1] Esq., *Sheriff of the County of Granville.*

Sir: Edward Mallory,[2] a colored man, has complained to me that on Thursday night last a number of white men, armed, went to his house near Tally Ho, Granville county, took him and his wife out of their bed, tied them and whipped them severely. One of the men also with a knife mutilated his right ear. Edward Mallory has reported himself in person to my office, and I have seen the lashes and bruises on his body, and his mutilated ear. I learn also that on the same night the same body of men inflicted injuries on several other inoffensive colored people. In one case they dragged a colored woman from her bed, thinking no doubt they had a certain colored man who is an active Republican, and the woman, breaking loose from them, they fired upon her, wounding her seriously in the shoulder and head.

It is the duty of the Sheriff, the Magistrates, and all peace officers to maintain the law and see that the people are protected in their persons and property. When process properly issues to you from a Magistrate, you have at your command the whole power of the county to execute it. The civil power must first be tried and executed before the military can be called in. Your authority and power are ample for this purpose. You are hereby directed to proceed to the neighborhood in which these outrages occurred, with proper process issued by a Justice of the Peace on the oath of Edward Mallory, arrest these desperadoes, and see that they are properly bound to answer for their crime. I have heard that some of the Magistrates in Granville are not prompt to act when cases like these are laid before them. Edward Mallory informs me that a Magistrate declined to act in his case, but referred him to me. If I should have clear proof that any Magistrate declines to do his duty, but allows such outrages to be committed and the criminals to go at large, I will at once revoke his commission, and have it known of record that he is unworthy of his place. A good Magistrate is a public blessing, but a hesitating, compromising, cowardly officer is an obstruction to justice and right. If you are not certain that you can have all the necessary process in the neighborhood of Tally Ho, it would be well to get a Magistrate from some other part of the county to accompany you.

I deem it important that the detailed militia of your county should be called for. If they were organized at this time, I would not hesitate to send fifty of them to that part of the county to act under your orders in ferreting out those criminals, and impressing certain evil-minded traitors in that locality with a salutary dread of State authority. It is unnecessary to remind you that the colored people have the right to be secure in their houses as the white people, and that the law protects them equally with the whites. If one race can be thus outraged with impunity, there is but one step more which such desperadoes have to take to the white race to punish each of them as are Republican in the same manner. These colored people must be protected. I will not sit here unmoved, and inactive when they cry for justice and protection against men whose treatment, as in the case of Edward Mallory, is a disgrace to civilization. If, in enforcing the law, you should need aid let me know it. I have full confidence in your firmness, discretion and judgment. Magnify the law in the neighborhood referred to, and teach those who have thus violated it, a lesson they will not soon forget.

Very respectfully,
W. W. Holden,
Governor.

[1] James I. Moore, sheriff of Granville County. Granville County Official Bonds, Sheriffs, 1848-1887 (originals in North Carolina State Archives).

[2] Edward Mallory in 1870 was a laborer in Raleigh, Wake County. 1870 U.S. Census Population Schedule, North Carolina: Wake, 315 (microfilm).

E. M. Rosafy to Robert M. Douglas A&H:GP

Summerville, Brunswick Co
October 15th 1868

Robert M Douglas Esqr

Dear Sir,

Your letter of no date, in regard to Commission dues and fees, just received. In reply I respectfully beg to return to you my Commission as Commissioner for Brunswick County. You will please to express for same my humble thanks to His Excellency Governor W. W. Holden.——

The County of Brunswick is as yet unreconstructed, for owing to supineness and collusion on the part of some of our socalled leaders with the men of the old order of things, we are at the mercy of the latter, and the Constitution and new laws are administered not by its friends and supporters, but by its bitter ennemies, some of them but lately appointed to offices of trust and emolument. The Commission respectfully returned, would have enabled me to become "a comtemptible republican minority of one" in our County Board, but said board ignoring and disregarding my appointment by the Executive,—I can not but gratefully and respectfully return the same.

Your obedient servant
E. M. Rosafy[1]

Wilmington, Box 274

[1] Mathias Rosafy, later a Wilmington mail agent. 1870 U. S. Census Population Schedule, North Carolina: New Hanover, 354 (Microfilm).

A. W. Fisher to Holden A&H:GP

State of Vermont,
Representatives Hall,
Montpelier, Oct. 16, 1868

His Excellency
W. W. Holden
Governor N.C.

Dear Sir

I can get three thousand Springfield Rifled Muskets &c. and start them by Wednesday morning next.—I am assured now.

Gov. Page[1] sympathizes with us fully, and at first interview thought, in the absence of any law forbidding, that he would assume the responsibillity of loaning the arms, if certain promiment men approved of such a course: Upon consultation with them he has asked me to wait till he can get a resolution through the General Assembly which would not be every where understood and still give him authority to loan the arms.

The General Assembly adjourned yesterday till Monday P.M.

Tuesday will be the earliest day the matter can be acted upon, but there will not be the least trouble in getting the Resolution passed.

I have not decided whether to send by Steamer from N.Y. to Portsmouth Va. or to New Berne. Would like instructions.

Shall probably leave here on Wednesday next and be in N.Y. City Thursday. Any communications will find me at the Astor House.

If the number of arms mentioned is not sufficient, please telegraph. I hope the recent elections will quiet down the turbulent a little, and we shall have no use for arms

I have the honor to be Very Respectfully your obt. Sevt

A. W. Fisher[2] Adjt. Gen N.C.M.

P. S. Your letter, orders and draft received last night A. W. F

[1] John B. Page, governor of Vermont, 1867-1869. *World Book Encyclopedia*, s.v. "Vermont: Government."

[2] Abiel W. Fisher, Bladen County; member, 1868 convention; member, state House of Representatives, 1870-1872; Adjutant General, 1868-1871. Cheney, *North Carolina Government, 1585-1979*, 430, 845, 451.

R. M. Martin to Holden A&H:GP

Martindale, N.C., Oct 16th 1868

To his Excellency
Gov. W. W. Holden

Dear Sir. I write a note of inquiry—have the Registers any right to reject men because they have been convicted of Larceny and other petty thefts—I see nothing in our New Constitution, neither in the Registration acts to prohibit them—The K K Ks have a printed list at every precinct in this county containing in all about *200 voters*, they challenge and keep all of them from the polls—You will please inform me at once for you well know the desperate kind of people that we have to contend with in this county

I am Enrolling the Militia at Long Creek precinct. Any Documents you may see proper to send me will be distributed. If you have any of Hon Boydens[1] letters send a few—

Yours &c.
R. M Martin, J. P.[2]

Please address me at Charlotte N.C. care City Marshall

[1] Probably Nathaniel Boyden; member, U.S. House of Representatives, 1867-1869. Cheney, *North Carolina Government, 1585-1979*, 693.

[2] Robert M. Martin, Mecklenburg County; stencil maker. 1870 U.S. Census Population Schedule, North Carolina: Mecklenburg, 177 (microfilm).

Sam. McD. Tate to Holden A&H:GP

Raleigh
Octo: 19, 1868

His Excellency
Govr. Holden

Dear Sir

I had hoped to have had an interview with you today in relation to the Bonds due our Company, of the old appropriation, but heard you were engaged.

On the 26th or 27th of August last I made the certificate required by the old law to yourself and the Board of Internal Improvements, since which I have had no information in regard to the matter. There are three hundred and forty (340) bonds due and the contractors are clamorous about the work. I have ventured to assure them the delay was owing to press of other business.

I make mention of it because I feel sure you do not desire it to be understood as any intentional slight to the Buncombe people.

I have the honor to be

Your obt: Servt
Saml. McD. Tate Financial Agt.
WNCRR Co

V. C. Barringer to Holden A&H:GP

Concord N.C.
Oct. 20, 1868

Dear Sir:

Let me remind you that is would be well to advertise the next meeting of the Trustees for, at least, a month before the time of meeting.

It is desirable to have as many trustees present as possible, & thus infuse a general interest, in behalf of the University, all through the State. We may be sure of one thing. We must lay again the foundations of that institution & rebuild it, not only without the co-operation, but in spite of the effort of all the old family's in & so-called culture of the State. Succeed in whatever else we may, they mean to make us fail here, if failure is possible.

Everything looks well for G. & C. up here.

Yours faithfully
&c. &c.
V. C. Barringer[1]

Gov. Holden:
Raleigh, N.C.

[1] Victor Clay Barringer, lawyer; A. B., U.N.C., 1848; member, state Senate, 1860-1861; major, First North Carolina Cavalry, 1861; faculty member, Davidson College, 1861-1865; judge, International Court, Alexandria, Egypt, 1874-1894. *Dictionary of North Carolina Biography*, s.v. "Barringer, Victor Clay."

[Holden] to Sheriff of Cumberland County A&H:GP

State of North Carolina
Executive Department,
Raleigh October 24th 1868

To the Sheriff of Cumberland County[1]

Sir

I have received information that there is much lawlessness and disorder in the town of Fayetteville. It is your duty as Shff of the county to execute all process to you directed, and generally to preserve the peace. This duty must be performed at all hazards. If you meet with resistance you are commanded to use the necessary force to overcome it , and if after having tried and exhausted the power of the whole County, you find yourself unable to enforce the law and maintain order you will notify me at once of the fact and I will take the necessary steps to sustain you.

I am determined that "life, liberty and property" shall be protected in the town of Fayetteville. Those who may assail either, or resist the laws that are over us all, will certainly be brought to condign punishment.

Very Respectfully
Govr[2]

[1] John Reilly, sheriff of Cumberland County. 1870 U.S. Census Population Schedule, North Carolina: Cumberland, 187 (microfilm).
[2] This is an unsigned copy of a letter in Holden's handwriting.

John Reilly to Holden A&H:GP

Fayetteville N.C.
Oct. 27th 68

To His Excellency
W. W. Holden

Governor
I have the honor to acknowledge the receipt of yours of the 24th Inst. informing me of your having received information that there is "much lawlessness and disorder in the Town of Fayetteville"—I beg to state in reply that you have been grossly missinformed with regard to the present condition of this community. It is true that some two months since, this community was greatly excited by the holding of a boisterous Democratic Congressional Convention, also by wild and inflamatory Democratic Speeches—and at that time some outrages were committed in parts of the County. But for the last Six weeks perfect *order* has been restored in this Town and County.

Very Respectfully Yours &
John Reilly Sheriff Cumberland
County

Nelson A. Miles to Holden A&H:GP

Headquarters District of North
Carolina,
Raleigh, N.C. Oct 27th 1868.

Gov. W. W. Holden,

Sir
Referring to the letter of Lt. Gov. T. R. Caldwell,[1] of the 26th inst. requesting that troops be stationed at Morganton until after the election, I have to state that

it is practicable to send a detachment to that point from Salisbury, where a Company of the 40th Infantry, is stationed, should you consider it advisable to send Coloured troops to that victory,

Very respectfully,
Your obedient Servant,
Nelson A Miles
BV Maj Genl
Comd Dist.

[1] Not extant.

John Robinson to Holden A&H:GP

Goldsboro 30th Oct. 1868

His Excellency W. W. Holden,

My Dear Governor,

This morning two men from the neighborhood of Dudley brought the following report. —That one *night* this week, Six white men in a body, visited several negro houses searching—*they would not say for what!* but said they had a search warrant. The negroes, thinking (and justly, as it was in the night) that these men were acting without authority, collected a body of their own color with guns and made them desist. There was no collision, they parted peaceably; but Dr Hay[1] and myself have advised them (the colored men) to cause the parties whose houses thus were illegally entered, to have warrants taken out against these nocturnal marauders.

I beg to lay this matter before you for instruction. Under the new state of affairs, and as yet being without *legal forms*, we wish to act with caution. Could you forward, by return mail, such direction as you might think advisable

Registration is going on here very actively. Wayne Co. is exerting herself energetically *pro* and *con*; but I am of opinion our republican vote will exceed that of the last election.

I am, my dear governor
faithfully yours
John Robinson[2]

[1] Probably John H. Hays, Goldsboro physician. Wayne County Estate Files, Hays, John H. (originals in North Carolina Dtate Archives).

[2] John Robinson, Wayne Ccounty; white farmer. 1870 U.S. Census Population Schedule, North Carolina: Wayne, 96 (microfilm).

Wm. Cawthorn et al. to Holden A&H:GP

Warrenton N.C.
Oct 31th 1868

Excellency W. W. Holden
Gov. of North Carolina

Dear sir

We have descovered somthing in the Whites that we cannot account for by have their full Secret Meetings Night after Night for the last ten days—We have also learned from a reliable Source that boxes have been Received in this place containing sixteen Shooters we are fearful that their object is to raise a riot on the day of the Speaking which is to be Nov. 2d. thereby to defeat the Republicans on Tuesday. We have Convassed this County thurly and we think that the Colored people will Vote for the Republicans Canidates as heretofore unless they are overpowered by force of arms their numbers have increast so much for the last two Nights that they had to devide them in to two Halls as Nearly all the Men from the County have Come in and joined them we think that it is best for us to have Some protection on the day of Election as if they are defeated on the attempt on Monday we dont know what they might do on Tursday they have become quiet in Speaking but are acting loudly. You Will please with hold this from the public print, as their is danger of being assasinated by the K.K.K.

Yours obedient servants
Wm. Cawthorn[1]
Richard Faulkener[2]
Albert Burgess Per W. C.[3]
H. H. Plummer[4]

[1] William W. Cawthorne, Warren County; member, state House of Representatives, 1868-1872. Cheney, *North Carolina Government, 1585-1979*, 1300.

[2] Richard Falkner, Warren County; member, state House of Representatives, 1868-1872. Cheney, *North Carolina Government, 1585-1979*, 1300.

[3] Albert Burgess, Warren County; Littleton house carpenter. 1870 U.S. Census Population Schedule, North Carolina: Warren, 656 (microfilm).

[4] Harry H. Plummer, Warren County; clerk in dry goods store. 1870 U.S. Census Population Schedule, North Carolina: Warren, 687 (microfilm).

J.H. Everitt to Holden A&H:GP

Norfolk Va Nov 1st 1868

To His Excellency Gov W. W. Holden
Gov of North Carolina

Dear Sir

Being drove from my home[1] before I had the time or oppitunity to give in my Tax List or pay my taxes is the cause now of my wife & seven children to have to have to suffir. The Depty Sherriff has been & levied on what little support my wife & children did have & in a few days they will be left entirely destitute of everything to Sustain life & surrounded by a Sett of heartless brutes, that would strip their Cloths from their backs & leave them nude in the world—This much is what I have gained by doing & adhering to a cause that I thought was right I could probably raise the money to pay my Taxes & keep what little stuff I have for the support of my family from being sold But the Depty Sherriff has given no time even working & is now ready to sacrifice my property & leave my wife & little children entirely destitute. Gov if you have any Sympathy in this world for Suffering humanity please order the Sale Stoped until I can make arrangments to Settle the matter. I know you have denounced me from my being wrongly represented to you in many Cases—But for Gods Sake donot let innocent little children suffer for what is supposed to be my wrongs—I have three children now confined to sick bed No one to aid or comfort them But my wife, & she in very delicate health, & I Am actually forbiddedn by a Sett of Assassins to visit my wife & children under the penalty If I do shall be taken out & hanged to the nearest tree. No law to call them to Justice they bound together, by oath to Swear each other out of all & any difficulty. Now dont any one know that mine is bound to be a life of misery & for what

Hoping you will have some compassion on my wife & little children I remain ever a true friend to you & the cause.

J H Everitt

[*Endorsed*] Write to Sheriff to give him time, if possible, on his taxes, and write to him to return, as the whole power of the Courts is pledged to protect him. He is in no danger.

[1] See his letter to Holden of August 5, 1868.

Benjamin Satterfield to Holden A&H:GP

Roxboro Pr. Co NC

Nov 3, 1868 Govner

Dir Sir I tak the previlig of droping you a few Lines Sir we hav lorst Pr Co[1] by one 100 I am very Sory mr Josph holden[2] did not com hir I think he wold of done great Good hir the colerd pepol hir is all Right but the whites was influnc't by Joh Turner[3] and others our men wasn't working as tha ought to hav bin I must say ther was one act in the Legslationd in Congress that was not Right and I sas will rezalt in our Ruin Giving strong pour to all men who had Leed the cuntry to Ruin giving them Pour to Ruin it again Tha ar the saim an no beter if eney thing these fols wose tho I hop others Stats will do betr I have worked very hard night and Day to sav Person Conty an don well with the Colerd Popel I hav sav all but one of them that advocated an worked for the Dimocrat Party all the time befor hav come and voted the Republican if the whit Popol had of the county had bin as well awaken as the colerd we would of givn a larg majority in favor of Republican I have worked to the last moment

Benjamin Satterfield[4]

I am sory to think that we have Lorst our election but I hop we will not lose the Stat

[1] The vote for president in Person County in 1868 was 1,054 for Seymour (Democrat) and 953 for Grant (Republican). Cheney, *North Carolina Government, 1585-1979*, 1333.

[2] Joseph William Holden.

[3] Josiah Turner, Jr.

[4] Not identified.

R M Henry to Holden A&H:GP

Asheville N.C.
Nov 4 1868

Gov W. W. Holden,

My Dear Sir,

We had a big riot here yesterday, one negro killed and eight (8) wounded. The negroes came to the polls unarmed. The democratic party is responsible for the riot. The vote here falls short 130 of the Registration. The vote is about even in the County.

There is an investigation going on before the Coroners Jury.

Yours truly
R M Henry

W. J. Laird to Holden A&H:GP

November the, 9, 1868

To His Excelencey the Govenor

Sir by request of the Commissioners of the County I submit the following question to your honor

that is whether or not the Homested laid down in the Constitution has any baring on debts mad prior to its rattification or not Thear has become to be some dissatisfaction among the Republican party with regard to that one thing thay ar told by the demacrats and Lawyers of that party that the Homested has nuthing to do with any debts only new and that has bin made since its rattification

Sir your opinion on that point will give grate satisfaction to the citisans of this county

address me at Wadesboro Anson County NC

Your with Respect
W. J. Laird[1]

[1] William J. Laird, Anson County farmer. 1870 U.S. Census Population Schedule, North Carolina: Anson, 353 (microfilm).

Speech of Gov. W. W. Holden *Standard*
November 9, 1868

Friends and Fellow Citizens[1]: I thank you for the compliment you have paid me by calling upon me on this occasion. I rejoice with you in this impressive celebration of the triumph of the great principles of Liberty and Union. The day of our complete triumph, so long hoped and looked for, has arrived. After long years of struggles, trials and misfortunes, illustrated by deeds of indomitable valor on the sea and on the land, the Republic emerges into the full light of day, every star flashing on its ensign, and its foundations laid so deep and so securely on the principles of Freedom and Justice that hereafter we may fear nothing for it from any power that may assail it, whether from without or within.

"The flag still floats towards the sun,
The Union fears no traitor now;
Freedom for all at last is won,
And glory crowns the nation's brow."

Fellow-citizens, we have won everything. We have carried the election by at least two to one in the Electoral vote. We have given about the same number for Gen. Grant which was cast four years ago for the immortal Lincoln. Grant and Colfax are elected. Grant, like Washington, "first in war, first in peace, and first in the hearts of his countrymen," has been called by the people to the chief position, in which he will compose discordant elements, re-establish a genuine and generous feeling of nationality, secure freedom of speech to all, and so administer the government generally as to make respect for and obedience to the law the source out of which will proceed renewed confidence and general prosperity. But Mr. Seymour, poor, dear good man, is now afloat amid storms and tempests, on that "sea of troubles," the prospect of which so much afflicted him during the late campaign. And that interesting young man, Francis P. Blair, who fought at one time to suppress the rebellion, and then ran as a candidate for the Vice-Presidency to encourage it—of him it may be pathetically said:

"Hang up the fiddle and the bow,
Lay down the shovel and the hoe,
There's no more office for Francis P. Blair
He's gone where the "bad" darkies go."

Gentlemen, I am not surprised at the result. I felt all the while very much like Mr. Girard did in relation to one of his vessels richly laden from the Indies. The vessel was thought to be lost. At last some friend heard that the vessel had arrived, and running to Mr. Girard in breathless haste he was the first to inform him of his good luck. Mr. Girard was in one of his warehouses hard at work, and looking down at this friend said, "I knew she would come in, for she had a Captain who never lost a vessel." And I knew the old ship of State, freighted as she is with the most precious hopes of mankind, was safe, for Grant himself was the commander; Grant, who never lost a battle, and who is always coolest and most self-possessed when a great work is to be done.

North Carolina, fellow-citizens, has done her share to swell this great victory. The Ku Klux—nobody is afraid of them now. The truth is, we never were afraid of them here in North Carolina—the Ku Klux and the good white folks did all they could to defeat....have failed. We have carried the State by a handsome majority, and elected six out of the seven members of Congress. The Republican members elect are all good and true men, but we have special cause for rejoicing over the election of our friend Col. Deweese in this district, when we consider the unscrupulous manner in which he was assailed, and the exertions made here at the centre to defeat him.

And now, fellow-citizens, what in this crisis is the duty of all good citizens? I thought, a few days since, that the enemies of the government, under the stunning blow they had received, might submit themselves in good faith and give the Republican party a fair trial. Their organ in this city was very sick and very pious a day or two after the election; but to-day it bristles up and talks in a defiant tone, as if it might get well again under the inspiring news from New York and from the Ku Klux regions of Georgia and Louisiana. It reminds me of the old couplet,

"When the Devil was sick the Devil a Monk would be,
When the Devil was well the devil a Monk was he."

I fear, my friends, we cannot trust them, sick or well. That paper, gentlemen, the organ of the enemies of the government in this city, advises the people to hesitate before they trust their lives and property to our courts—in other words, it suggests an appeal to lynch law; and it also says, "there must be a change,"—it advises an "organization" to effect this change, and it speakes of a proposed meeting of "State delegates" with this view. Now, gentlemen, we have a Constitution, and a government, and laws in this State. That Constitution and these laws are over all. They bind and controll all. Under Republican rule no man is so high or so proud that the laws cannot reach him and pull him down, when he does wrong, and no man is so humble or so neglected that the laws cannot succor and protect him, when he does right.

Honest people do not fear the law. Honest Conservatives, who were obliged to swear and who did swear to support this Constitution before they could vote in the late election, will keep their oath; but the dishonest and the bad will still plot against the public peace—will stir up strife and ill will among the people, and all the time they will see defects in the law, but not in themselves, thus verifying the adage,

"No rogue e'er felt the halter draw
With good opinion of the law."

Now, my friends, the law will be enforced in North Carolina. These people, who advise lynch law, and who speak of "organizations" and "State delegates" to effect any change not warranted by the Constitution and the laws, will be made to respect the Courts and to obey the law. This law is as much for the colored man as the white man, as much for the poor man as the rich man. Next to the Divine Word, it is the law that governs every one, every where. There is no appeal from it but to the sword, and they who advise appeal from it advise the sword. Let them beware lest "they perish by the sword." I told you when you nominated me for the place I now hold, unworthy as I was, there were but two things I feared. I feared to do wrong, and I feared God Himself, in whom "we live, and move, and have our being." Beyond this I fear nothing in the performance of duty. The enemies of the government know this, or if they do not, they will know it, if they should resist the law or attempt any change in our affairs by force. I go further and say, that without regard to prejudice, or passion, or political feeling, I do not fear to do them justice, and I will do it. I will protect them in their lives, in their liberties, and in their property as I will protect you, as long as they obey the law., but beyond that, so far as I am concerned they will get nothing. They are entitled to get nothing in the way of honors or offices at the hands of the people.

Fellow-citizens, a large majority of the white people of the State have sinned against the nation to a greater or less extent by rebellion. Though my sin has not by any means been as great as that of others, I have acknowledged it, and I am sorry for it. Thousands of my fellow-citizens, brother Republicans, are similiarly situated with myself. Others sinned not. Others threw themselves into the fires of war, and fought and died for the nation. Their blood is sacred, because it was shed in a holy cause. It cries no longer from the ground for vengeance, but it calls for peace. For incorrigible, unrepentant traitors I have no favor and no respect. I could weep for their innocent children, and for the inheritance of infamy they will transmit to them, even the infamy of the tories of the Revolution, unless they repent and "do their first works" of fealty and affection for the union; but to the repentant, the honest, and the true, who accept the situation cordially, and stand by the government in good faith, and cultivate those things that make for peace and good will among us, I say, "friend, give me your hand." "The past is forgotten, except for good to all of us.—Let us now go forward with one accord as the children of Washington, into the great future that is opening before us." But the incorrigible and the impenitent, who still hate the government and the flag, must be made to know their place—must be governed until they become better men and better citizens.

And now, to my colored friends I would say, what has been the lesson taught you since you became men? It is, that your salvation as a self-governing people in common with the white race, depends not partly, but entirely on your standing together as one man. Your advancement in education, in manhood, in material strength, in good citizenship, is involved in this. Compact yourselves around the Republican banner in solid mass, like the iron wedge when it bursts the oak or the hickory. Be the iron wedge—never divide. You owe everything under Providence to the Republican party. This party has saved the country and saved you, and it can alone make the country what it ought to be. This election for the first time has given you practical assurance of your freedom. If it had gone against us, you might not have been reduced to the condition of persons called and known as slaves, for the sentiment of the civilized world would not have allowed that; but you would have been peons, serfs, with no substantial rights as citizens, and you last state would have been worse than your first. Some of you know how difficult it is now, even in this State, with a Republican Governor, a Republican Legislature, and loyal Judges and Justices of the Peace, to get justice against the influences that surround and seek to wrong you; but how would it be if you were divided, or floated from party to party, the football and the victim of each? Stand together! If you divide, now or hereafter, you are a lost people. I do not believe that the Republican party will ever desert you. It is a great party, and keeps its pledges. But it is falible, because it is human. If ever it does what is highly improbable—shows a disposition to abandon you—then you must look to yourselves, and in no event cease to stand by your rights and your liberties with that portion of the white race, no matter by what party named called, who will stand by, and succor and protect you.

We have lost nothing by the late election, fellow-citizens, but secession, and the probability, not to say certainity, of another war; and Mr. Seymour, in his "den of troubles," and that interesting young man, Gen. Blair, who wanted to trample things in the wrong time and place—and a few Ku Klux masks, and some charges of powder and shot that were to have been fired. We have lost everything bad and have gained everything that promises good to the country. In a word, we have gained a free, united, consolidated country. We have had an election which has "established justice, ensured domestic tranquility, and secured the blessings of liberty to ourselves and our posterity." Let us, therefore, rejoice and be glad.

Allow me, in conclusion, to express my gratification at the generally quiet and peaceable election we have had in this State. With the exception of a few localities it was the most peaceable election ever held in North Carolina. All classes and colors deserve credit for this, and it gives me pleasure to say so. The Republicans were governed by a stern purpose to ask nothing that was not right, and to submit to nothing that was wrong and hence the result. We owe much in this respect to the aid which the civil authorities received from the gallant commander of the national troops in this State, Gen. Miles. And I cannot help saying that if, in my judgment, we had such men as Miles in command in all the States south of us, the people of these States would have enjoyed a free and fair election, without riot or bloodshed.

And now, my friends, I will detain you no longer, but ask you to join me in three rousing cheers for the flag of the Union, and for the gallant officers and men of the army and navy who uphold and defend it.

[1] This speech ws delivered November 6, 1868, at a mass meeting celebrating the election of General Grant as president of the United States.

Hanibal D. Norton to Jacob F. Chur A&H:GP

Bu. R. F. and A. L.
Office of Agt. Sub Dist. of Morganton
Morganton, N.C. Nov. 12, 1868

Bvt. Lt. Col. Jacob F. Chur.
Asst. Comr.
Raleigh, N.C.

Colonel:

I have the honor to acknowledge receipt, on the 9th inst. of your letter of the 6th—in relation to the closing of the General Hospital, and disposal of the pauper patients there (one of whom, Adolphus Patton[1]—not "Daulphas Sutton"—came from Morganton) and to report that I have conferred with the Wardens of the Poor for Burke Co.,—thro' Mr. W. C. Erwin,[2] their chairman—and they decline to take any action in Patton's case, alleging that they, the old Board of Wardens, are "out of office," and cannot act unless re-appointed by the present Governor of the State. Mr. Erwin says: "there is a Poor House" (several miles out of town) "where the Freedman can live, if the Bureau will carry him there."

No provisions have been made for the poor, white or black—in this County, under the new *regime*. If the Governor of the State would appoint a new Board of Wardens of the Poor, for Burke Co., several sad cases of destitution might be ameliorated. The old ("Confederate") Board have been appealed to in vain.

Very respectfully
Your obdt. svt.
Hanibal D. Norton[3]
Agent, Bu. R. F. & A. L.

[*Endorsed*]

Bu. R. F. and A. Ld.
Hd. Qrs Asst. Comr. N.C.
Raleigh, N.C. 14th Nov. 1868.

Official copy respectfully furnished for the information of His Excellency, W. W. Holden, Governor, State of North Carolina.

Jacob F. Chur.
Bt. Lt. Col.
Asst Comr.

[1] In 1870, Adolphus Patton was listed as a "pauper" in the Rowan County Poor House. 1870 U.S. Census Population Schedule, North Carolina: Rowan, 574 (microfilm).

[2] William C. Erwin, Burke County; Morganton merchant. 1870 U.S. Census Population Schedule, North Carolina: Burke, 360 (microfilm).

[3] Hanibal D. Norton, Morganton agent of the Bureau of Refugees, Freedmen, and Abandoned Lands. Rosters, Records of the Assistant Commissioner for the State of North Carolina, Bureau of refugees, Freedmen, and Abandoned Lands (National Archives Record Group 105). (Microfilm copy in North Carolina State Archives.)

Affidavit of Jacob Pass A&H:GP

State of North Carolina
Caswell County

Personally appeared before me John W. Stephens, one of the Justices of said County, Jacob Pass,[1] Cold. who being duly sworn according to Law deposeth and saith that in the fall term of 1867, in the County Court of Caswell County he was fined in the sum of fifteen Dollars and ninety Cents (fine and costs) for a misdemeanor, and that on Tuesday last Sheriff Griffith[2] of said county came to Deponents house, levied on his Tobacco and Corn, nailed up the Corn crib and forbid the opening of said Crib by anyone on pain of arrest, that Deponent is a poor man, has much less than five hundred Dollars worth of personal or Real Estate, has a family of wife, daughter and Mother in Law dependant upon him for support, that much suffering is caused to him and his family by the action of said Sheriff Griffith, that Sheriff Griffith did not ask Deponent whether or not he owned property above the amount allowed and exempted from Execution by the Constitution, that Deponent told Sheriff Griffith of the amount of his property which consists of "7 1/2" Bbls of corn and about 400 lbs of Tobacco one fourth of a Stack of Oats besides some clothing and household furniture, all together of the value of about Eighty five dollars and nothing more; and that Defendant now craves protection from the unlawful proceedings of said Sheriff Griffith.

Sworn to and Subscribed before me this fourteenth day of November 1868

Jno W. Stephens J. P.
Jacob Pass

[*Endorsed*] Respectfully forwarded to Col. J. F. Chur. A. C. Jesse C. Griffith the present sheriff of Caswell County is, I believe, debarred from holding office, he having been Sheriff before, during and since the Rebellion. I respectfully request that this matter be brought before the proper authority for investigation.

F W Liedtke
Lieut 43d Infty
A.S.A.C.

[*Endorsed*] Respectfully referred to His Excellency, Gov. *W. W. Holden* for such action as the circumstances of the case require, or such suggestions as may tend to relieve the party named within

Jacob F. Chur,
Bvt. Lt. Col.
Asst. Commissioner

[1] Jacob C. Pass, Caswell County farmer. Caswell County 1867 Tax List (original in North Carolina State Archives).

[2] Jesse C. Griffith.

Oscar Eastmond to Holden A&H:GP

Asheville N.C.
November 14th 1868

Hon W. W. Holden
Gov. of N.C.
Raleigh N.C.

Dear Sir

I deem it proper to inform you that six persons have been arrested and bound to court in the sum of Three Thousand dollars for the killing of the colored man on the 3rd inst, Since which time, I caused the rearrest of these parties and several others, for violation of the Corporation ordinances, and as Mayor fined each one the sum of five dollars, which was the extent to which I could go, or I would have fined greater sums. A night police is now organized for the safety of the town, as there has been one attempt to burn the town, out of revenge. so long as I am in office, which will be but a short time longer, I shall do my whole duty, without partiality.

I have the honor to be Very
Respectfully
Your Obdt Servant
Oscar Eastmond
Mayor of Asheville

John H. Everitt to Holden A&H:GP

Norfolk Va Nov 15 68

Gov. W. W. Holden
Gov of NC

Dear Sir

Your Kind letter was recvd today. I hasten to reply. Enclosed you will find a letter from one of my Halifax friends.[1] You will See from the last part of it what Kind of Safety & on what conditions I Can return to my home & family—I have possitive proof now against the parties that Shot me. There was man from Halifax in Norfolk a few days ago & told me who the whole party was & who was Killed & Said he would have warned me of my danger But was warned if he did he would face my fate—He told me with the promise that I never reveal his name. He is a white man of good Standing of undoubted Veracity & a Strict member of the Church—He advises me to stay away from there by all means—& he further stated that If I had remained there one day longer when I was at home a few days ago I would have been taken from my House & hung—He reveals this to me through pure motives of friendship. Now these are plain naked facts of my condition. Not predicated by Partisan or party feeling

Now what say you I am to do—of course there is nothing but to remain in exile. There is no protection for a Republican in that County.

I remain your obt Servt
John H. Everitt

[1] Not extant.

Holden to the General Assembly A&H:GP

Executive Department of N. Carolina
Raleigh November 17th 1868

To the Honorable the General Assembly of North Carolina

Gentlemen

It is proper that at your first regular session under the new constitution, I should lay before you "information of the affairs of the state" and recommend to your consideration such measures as may be deemed expedient. The people of the state have reconstructed their government on the basis of the equal right of all. The state is quiet and tranquil. There is no ground for apprehending that secession will be again attempted, or that the peace of the country will be disturbed.

The year now closing has been richly crowned with harvests. The seasons have been propitious. A plentiful supply of bread has been produced for our whole population, so that want in this respect will not be felt during the coming year by any who will labor for a living. Fruits of all kinds have been gathered in abundance. The staples of cotton and tobacco are affording fair profits to those who have produced them, while from lumber and naval stores a considerable portion of our people are realizing good returns, as in former years. Our commerce is increasing. Our mineral resources are once more in process of development. Our Rail Roads are recovering from the depression under which they formerly labored, and promising better returns than heretofore to the State and Stockholders; while new lines of communication are being laid out, destined to penetrate and develop the great natural resources of portions of the State heretofore untouched by the hand of improvement. The State credit has been re-established on a solid basis, thus giving promise that at no distant day the bonds of the State will command as much in the market as those of the most favored and prosperous States. We have great cause to be thankful to Almighty God for the manifold blessings which He is bestowing upon us; and we can confidently look forward, under His protection and guidance, for a condition of prosperity and happiness which we have not heretofore enjoyed.

STATE DEBT AND FINANCES

The State debt and finances will doubtless receive the thoughtful and careful consideration of the General Assembly.

The amount of the State debt on the 1st of October 1868 was nineteen millions, two hundred and nine thousand nine hundred and forty five dollars ($19,209,945). This includes estimated amount of past due interest to be funded under Act of August 20, 1868 of two millions of dollars ($2,000,000). The above amount ($19,209, 945) is inclusive of bonds issued for internal improvement purposes since May 20, 1861 and prior to the year 1866. The amount of these bonds is one million, one hundred and twenty eight thousand dollars ($1,128,000) and the estimated interest therein due and unpaid is one hundred and eighty thousand five hundred and ten dollars ($180,510).

The amount of interest which has matured October 1st 1868 and been paid in cash, is one hundred and twelve thousand one hundred and one dollars ($112,101).

The interest maturing at subsequent dates during the present fiscal year is as follows: January 1st, 1869 three hundred and eight thousand one hundred and ninety seven dollars ($308,197). April 1, 1869 three hundred and four thousand one hundred and one dollars ($304,101). July 1, 1869 three hundred and eight thousand one hundred and ninety seven dollars ($308,197). Total for fiscal year ending September 30 1869, one million and thirty two thousand five hundred and ninety six dollars ($1,032,596). The amount of interest above stated as falling due April 1, 1869, includes interest on bonds four millions five hundred thousand dollars ($4,500,000) yet to be issued, bearing date October 1st, 1868.

The balance remaining in the hands of the Public Treasurer[1] October 1st, 1868 was one hundred and fifty thousand thirty four dollars eighty four cents ($150,034.84). The amount from taxes, including payments in October, is two hundred and twenty six thousand seven hundred and six dollars and forty two cents ($226,706.42). The taxes from several counties remain unpaid, but we cannot expect more than seventy five thousand dollars ($75,000) from this source.

The estimated probable expenses of the State government during the present fiscal year will be, three hundred and seventy five thousand two hundred and thirty dollars ($375,230). Add interest falling due during fiscal year of one million and thirty two thousand five hundred and ninety six dollars ($1,032,596) will leave the amount to be provided for one million four hundred and seven thousand eight hundred and twenty six dollars ($1,407,826).

To meet this the Treasurer will have fifty thousand thirty four dollars eighty four cents ($50,034.84) after paying one hundred thousand dollars ($100,000) temporary loan; taxes received since October 1st, 1868 ninety five thousand one hundred and ninety six dollars and thirty seven cents ($95,196.37) estimated taxes due seventy five thousand dollars ($75,000) proceeds of sale of north Carolina Rail Road bonds, one hundred and seventeen thousand six hundred dollars ($117,600) making a total of three hundred and thirty seven thousand eight hundred and thirty one dollars and twenty one cents ($337,831.21) leaving the amount of one million and sixty nine thousand nine hundred and ninety four dollars and seventy nine cents ($1,069,994.79) to be provided for by taxation during the present fiscal year.

The Stocks and bonds held by the State in corporations, and interest due from said corporations, is as follows: Stocks eight million five hundred and thirty four thousand five hundred dollars ($8,534,500). Bonds, four million two hundred and thirty four thousand dollars ($4,234,000). Interest four hundred and seventy two thousand five hundred dollars ($472,500). Making a total of thirteen million, two hundred and forty one thousand dollars ($13,240,000).

I recommend that some mode be provided to ensure the payment of this interest, and of such interest as may be due the State in future from corporations.

The report of the Public Treasurer will contain full details of the public debt, with recommendations as to the best means for providing for interest. I have full confidence in that officer, and respectfully commend his statements and views to the consideration of the General Assembly.

The estimated value of all the property in the State, lands and their improvements included, is two hundred and fifty millions of dollars ($250,000,000). I do not regard this as an extravigant estimate, but assuming that it is, and putting it at two hundred millions ($200,000,000) it is clear that the people of the State are fully able to carry on their government and at the same time provide for the payment of the interest on their debt. An *ad valorem* tax of one per cent on two hundred millions would raise two millions. At a half per cent it would be one million. A citizen worth five thousand dollars clear of debt would pay twenty five dollars to the State, in order to raise the million that will be necessary and so on in proportion. The interest on the State debt should be met promptly and in good faith, and the taxes necessary to meet it should be levied. The Constitution which we have sworn to support, provides that the public debt "shall never be questioned." If we hesitate to meet the interest of the debt, or if we fail from any cause to make due provision to meet it we thereby "question" the debt, and do violence to our solomn obligation. I believe that the General Assembly will impose and that the people of the State will cheerfully pay whatever amount may be necessary to meet the interest of the debt. I believe it will be popular to make such provision, but whether popular or not, it should be done. The great question for a statesman is, what is right? What does duty require under the circumstances? If the answer is, do a certain thing, do it, and leave it to time, events, and a just public judgement to vindicate and sustain the doers.

INTERNAL IMPROVEMENTS

The people of the State are so fully committed to internal improvements that I deem it necessary to say but little on the subject. Since the close of the rebellion, state aid has been extended to the Wilmington, Charlotte and Rutherford Road—to the Fayetteville and Western Road—to the Chatham and Coalfields Road—to the Tarborough and Wilmington Road and to the Western North Carolina Road. The work on the latter road is being vigorously prosecuted between Morganton and Asheville. A company has been organized under an act of the General Assembly at its last session, for the Western Division of this road, and it is expected that during the coming year the routes will be surveyed, and much of the work put under contract, While I would properly estimate the importance of the other improvements referred to I could not overstate the value of the extension west of the Blue Ridge.

These Roads, one to Paint Rock and the other to Ducktown, will open to immigration, and will greatly improve and benefit a region of the State which has heretofore been neglected, and is equal to any in the world in natural resources.

There is no work to which the people of the State are more fully committed, both by interest and inclination; and I have every confidence that it is in hands that will press it to speedy completion.

IMMIGRATION

The Constitution provided that "there shall be established, in the office of the Secretary of State,[2] a Bureau of Statistics, Agriculture, and immigration, under such regulations as the General Assembly may prescribe."

The attention of the General Assembly is especially invited to that portion of the report of the Secretary of State herewith transmitted, which refers to this subject. No state in Union presents greater inducements than our does to immigrants. I feel sure the General Assembly concurs with me as to the importance of encouraging immigrations; and I trust that body will at once adopt such measures on the subject as it may deem practicable and effective in their operation. We have a salubrious climate, a varied and fertile soil, an abundance of the most valuable minerals, inexhaustable water power, fine grazing lands, vast forrests of timber of all kinds, a long sweep of sea coast; and, in fine, every thing material and physical, which in a country in some respects almost new, can attract immigrants and fill the measure of their expectations. Our government is now settled on a solid basis. The laws are over all alike, and are faithfully and honestly administered. Society is peaceable and tranquil. Immigrants, therefore, will not only be welcomed by our people, but will be protected and respected and a fair field will be opened to them, in common with those who are here, to improve their condition.

EDUCATION

The attention of the General Assembly is respectfully invited to the report of the Superintendent of Public Instruction,[3] herewith transmitted. That officer is diligently engaged in his duties. I am satisfied, from my knowledge of his character and qualifications, that he will be able to put in operation, at an early period, under the sanction of the General Assembly, a system of "Schools and means of education" in all respects better and more extensive than any heretofore in existence in the State. The University of the State is inseparably connected with the free public schools. Both should be fostered. Education in agriculture, mechanics, mining, engineering, and in all the useful arts and sciences, should be encouraged. Normal instruction should be provided for at once, that we may have well educated teachers of our own for our public schools.

Nearly all the State School fund, the proceeds for the most part of the funds deposited with this State by the general government in 1836 has been lost. It is unnecessary to show how it was lost, or to dilate upon the advantages thus snatched from us. Regrets are vain for what is past. Let us improve the present and address ourselves to the future. We must have free public schools for all the children of the state, at whatever cost. This is a duty which can neither be postponed or evaded. So thoroughly am I impressed with this duty, and so earnestly am I committed to every feasible measure to render its full performance certain, that but for the assurance that it will be thus performed I would despair of free popular government in North Carolina.

"Education is the cheap defence of nations" not only from without but within. It is that light which distinguishes refined and civilized from barbarian races. It forms and compacts the only society among men which is worthy of the name. It touches the earth and it blossoms with luxuriance; its soil yields its choicist fruit, its mines open and pour out their varied treasures, and its rivers and seas are whitened with commerce, which carries with it not only exchangable wealth, but ideas in government, literature, science and art. It is the only sure basis of good morals, for without it the Divine Word, the fountain of all truth, would be a sealed book. It is the strongest bulwark that can be erected to protect the rights of property. Property holders are, therefore, especially interested in promoting education. Taxes for such a purpose should be cheerfully and promptly paid. The affluent and the enlightened can afford to care in this respect for the poor and ignorant, since it is not merely their duty, but their highest interests are thus best subserved. But little, if any of the money expended for education is sent out of the State. It remains with us, and while our people are thus enriched with knowledge, they are not rendered poorer even in money, as the latter is collected from the citizens by one hand of the State and immediately disbursed to them by the other.

The people of the State are anxious that industries and worthy immigrants should come hither and settle among us. It is a primary question with all such immigrants whether in the communities or states in which they are invited to settle, there are facilities for educating their children? If we do not put in operation as good public schools as there are in other portions of the country, we cannot hope to attract to the State any considerable number of immigrants. They will continue to turn their steps towards other regions, not more inviting than ours, it is true, in climate, soil and material resources, but in which they can secure for their children, at the public charge, a system of schools to fit them to become intelligent and useful citizens.

The people of North Carolina have long been a unit in favor of education. From the days of Yancey, Murphy, Stanly, Cameron, Gaston, Caldwell, and others, to the present, their enlightened statesmen of all parties have enjoined this as the first duty of the State. I am persuaded that the purpose to educate the rising generation is as firmly fixed now as at any former period. This is a subject upon which all can agree. A rivalry can exist in this respect which will be generous in its nature, which will violate no sacred rule of charity, and which, honoring those who may engage in it, will confer immeasurable benefits and blessings on this and future generations.

I recommend, in the most earnest terms, that the General Assembly during its present session provide for a general and uniform system of public schools. The schools for the white and colored children should be separate, but in other respects there should be no difference in the character of the schools, or in the provision made to support them.

The Board of Education and the Trustees of the University will doubtless make reports to the General Assembly at an early day as to the condition of the educational interests confided to them. Both these Boards are fully organized, and have transacted some important business.

PROTECTION TO LABOR

The Constitution provides that "the General Assembly shall provide by proper legislation, for giving to Mechanics and laborers an adequate lien on the subject matter of their labor." In the conflict going on between capital and labor the latter is more likely to suffer than the former; first, because money or capital is power; and secondly, because capital is generally controlled by a greater degree of intelligence than that which characterizes labor. Labor cannot afford to combine against capital to enforce its rights for the reason that it cannot, like capital, retire within itself and await results. Both should be protected in such manner as to prevent either from encroaching on the rights of the other. Contracts in writing should be encouraged, and should be strictly enforced. The mechanic or laborer should be required to perform his contract with scrupuilous fidelity; and on the other hand, no opportunity should be afforded to the contractor or employer to evade payment when the contract has thus been performed. The life of labor is steady employment at compensating wages, and the certainity of payment. The life of capital is steady enterprise and investment, unembarrassed by idleness, inattention, non-performance, or slack performance of contracts by those employed. I can perceive no difference, in a legal or moral point of view, between a contract broken by a mechanic or laborer, and an obligation disregarded by a capitalist or employer. The mechanic and laborer should be protected but not to the detriment of the employers when the latter has fully complied with his obligation. The former should be assured while laboring, that the reward of his labor will be realized; and to ensure this, there should be a lien in every case until he is paid. The remedy should be plain, speedy and cheap. As a general rule the mechanic and laborer cannot afford to engage in suits at law and pay fees. This is a subject which excites no small interest among the people. Those especially who live by their labor will continue to press the subject upon the attention of the General Assembly until suitable laws for their protection are enacted. A working man myself, I feel a deeper interest in whatever concerns the working men of the State. Our present and future prosperity must be based on labor. Labor should not only be honored, but it should be protected and promoted by every practicable means.

But while Labor should be protected and honored, idleness should receive no countenance or favor. Everyone should be required to pursue some honest calling for a living; and the presumption should be, as it fairly and justly is, that an habitual idler with no known or visible means of support, is in a condition to be tempted to the commission of crime. It is idlers and loungers who, for the most part, fill our jails and workhouses, as they will fill the Penitentiary. There is work of some kind for all to do, and all should be employed.

STAY LAWS

The law of Creditor and Debtor is of the first importance. The relations of those two classes should be plainly and carefully defined, and contracts should be promptly enforced. Our State government will not be in complete operation until every impediment to the collection of debts is removed. Stay Laws which give indulgence beyond the usual dilatory plea, or beyond the ordinary stay of execution on sufficient security, are, under any circumstances, of doubtful utility. The "evil day" of payment, as it is termed, is postponed in most cases to be felt with added force by the debtor.

A sound and judicious credit system should not be discouraged, but should rather be fostered and maintained; but such a system is impaired, if not destroyed, by general laws which may be said to place the creditor for years in the hands of the debtor, with the certainity in many cases of the loss of the debt. The debtor may plead for indulgence and levity as long as it is reasonable to do so, or as long as there is a well grounded assurance that he will be able to pay; but complaint may justly proceed from the creditor, who has certainly wronged no one by first extending credit for his property or goods, and by subsequent indulgence and forbearance. Stay Laws of various kinds have been in operation in this State for years. I say nothing of their constitutionality; but even when the unfortunate condition in which we have been placed during this period is considered, it cannot be assumed that the debtor will be harshly treated if now required to meet his obligations. The losses incurred by the rebellion are not confined to particular cases. They were general, affecting the whole people of the State in every walk of society. If a debtor cannot pay in the last resort, after reasonable indulgence has been extended to him, he is a Bankrupt. What rendered him a Bankrupt—whether the rebellion, or his own improvidence, or want of economy or foresight—is not material to the argument. We may lament his misfortunes and sympathize with him, but still the fact remains that he is still in possession of property which justly belongs to his creditors, some of whom may have been reduced to his condition by his failure to meet his obligations. The only refuge of such a person is to compromise with his creditors, or to enter a court of bankruptcy, or to make such an exhibit and disposition of his property and effects as will satisfy his creditors that he is fixed in an honest purpose to do them justice.

I do not by any means concur in the opinion that an honest bankrupt has incurred any serious loss of character as a business man, or that he should be distrusted or avoided. Such a man, on the contrary, has displayed honesty, moral courage and candor which entitle him to the respect and confidence of his neighbors, especially when we remember that we have just emerged from a condition in which nothing was solid, and in which nearly every one was involved in pecuniary disaster and distress. Failure in business or loss of property should but stimulate to renewed exertion.

The honest, industrious and upright citizen, however reduced or depressed by misfortune, will always find friends to aid him in his efforts to improve his condition.

I recommend that the Stay laws be repealed, and that debtor and creditor be placed on a footing similar to what which they occupied previous to the rebellion.

The homestead exemption provided in the Constitution, even if not good against former debts, will nevertheless operate benefically in the future. It will secure a home for the family in any event; and it will have a salutary effect to a certain extent in checking extravagance in the credit system.

THE MILITIA

Attention is invited to the Report of the Adjutant General,[4] herewith submitted. The views and suggestions of the Adjutant General have my entire approval. The opinion of Washington uttered in 1790, that a "free people ought not only to be armed, but disciplined" and that a well organized Militia "is certainly an object of primary importance, whether viewed n reference to the national security, to the satisfaction of the community, or to the preservation of order" is not less weighty or important now than it was then.

The expenditure incurred thus far on account of the Militia is quiet small. I did not deem it expedient or necessary to avail myself of the powers confered upon me to purchase arms. A considerable quanity of arms, with necessary equipment and ammunition, has been procured without cost, save for transportation. It is important that the Militia should be enrolled, but it is not deemed essential that the entire body should be disciplined or drilled. The recommendations of the Adjutant General on his subject seems to me to be such as should meet, as I trust they will, the approval of the General Assembly.

It is estimated that the expenses of the Adjutant General's Office for the ensuing year, including his salary, will not exceed five thousand dollars ($5,000). I recommend an appropriation sufficient to cover that amount.

ECONOMY IN PUBLIC EXPENDITURES

I cannot too earnestly commend to the attention of the General Assembly the importance of enforcing economy in the public expenditures. Public officers who disburse the public moneys should be required to be as careful and economical as they would be as individuals in their business transactions. The State is in debt, the people are for the most part poor, and it is, therefore, especially important that economy should be observed. I recommend that the duties of the State Auditor[5] be clearly and fully defined, and that it be made his duty to examine rigidly every account or claim against the State, of whatever character, before the Governor is required by law to issue his warrant for the same.

DUTIES OF PUBLIC OFFICERS AND THEIR SALARIES

Attention is respectfully invited to the fact that the duties of Secretary of State, Auditor, Treasurer, Superintendent of Public Works,[6] Superintendent of Public Instruction and the Attorney General,[7] have not yet been prescribed by law. It is important that the duties of these officers be at once prescribed.

It is also recommended that just and reasonable salries be allowed these and all other public officers. A public officer is expected to devote his whole time to his duties, and he should be well paid for his services. A government which pays extravagant salaries sets an injurious example of extravangance and waste to its citizens; but one that doles out a bare living to an officer who conscientiously and sedulously devotes himself to its service, is not only unjust to the officer and it itself, but it loses respectability in the eyes of the world, and will not long command that efficiency and peculiar fitness in its officials which is so desirable in the administration of public affairs.

PENITENTIARY

It will be seen by the Report of the Commissioners herewith transmitted, that they have located the Pententiary near Lockville, on Deep River, in Chatham County. The situation is deemed an excellent one in all respects. Arrangements are in progress to erect a stockade on the site, and convicts will be employed in grading the foundations and quarrying stone for the building. I have addressed a letter to each of the Sheriffs of the State, inquiring the number of prisoners, the crimes for which they are imprisoned, and the time for which they have been sentenced, so that, after the necessary information is obtained such as them as should be put to hard labor in the Penitentiary may be turned over to the Superintendent.

INSANE ASYLUM

The report of Dr. Eugene Grissom, Superintendent of the Asylum, is herewith transmitted. I am gratified to state that a decided improvement has been made in the management of the Asylum, under Dr. Grissom, whose zeal and fidelity, with the same qualities on the part of his Assistant, Dr. F. T. Fuller, and his subordinates generally, are deserving of commendation. The recommendations of the Superintendent in relation to the institution are commended to your attention. I do not doubt that the General Assembly will adopt every measure necessary to sustain this indispensable and noble charity.

INSTITUTION FOR THE DEAF AND DUMB AND THE BLIND

Attention is invited to the report of Willie J. Palmer Esq, Principal of this institution, and to the report of W. M. Coleman Esq. President of the board of Directors.

This institution is in a flourishing condition under the excellent management of its Principal. The suggestions in his report in relation to further improvements and the extension of the advantages of the institution are worthy of consideration.

THE UNION INDISSOLUBLE AND PERPETUAL

The suppression of the rebellion by the Government of the United States: the reconstruction of the Union on the basis of suffrage for all in the recently insurgent States, with the prospect that in due time suffrage will be conferred upon all in all the States; and the election to the Presidency of Ulysses S. Grant, and to the Vice Presidency of Schuyler Colfax, have rendered the union of the States indissoluble and perpetual. We now have, indeed, a free Republic, in which every man in nearly every state is fully the equal of every other man in political and civil rights. We have no distinctions founded on color or race, save those which are social in their character, but every one is free under the law to make his own way in life, and to win a good name for himself and his children. The Union is over all, States as well as people. There can be no appeal from its authority. Its action in any event, and in matters howsoever grave or vital, is irreversible and final. This will ensure stability in the government and confidence in it by the people, without which no section can be prosperous and powerful. This stability on the one hand and confidence on the other, will render certain the payment of the national debt, and the completion of every work of improvement which the government may project or foster. The Union extends with a vast breadth from the Atlantic to the Pacific seas. It is stretching itself out along the shores of both oceans, carrying with it the germs of free principles which will speedily spring into new States, to cluster in due time, as the old States are clustering, around one common centre. It would be impossible to set bounds either to the progress or the duration of the Republic.

We know only that it is a great, beneficent, constitutional government, stronger than it was when it was founded that its benefits and blessings are immeasurable to those who live under it; and that our children and our children's children will take a just pride in the fortitude, courage and wisdom of their ancestors, and partake in larger and fuller measure than we do of the elevating and refining influences of religion, liberty and law, which must spring from such a government. This government is in the hands of its friends, and will be administered by them. The government of North Carolina is in the hands of its friends, and of the friends of the National government, and will be administered by them. It should not be our aim to use it for proscription or oppression to any, but for the protection and benefit of all. Its very safety, without reference to the importance of maintaining and carrying out in good faith the great principles on which it is founded, absolutely requires that its friends should continue to administer its affairs. In no other way can harmony be maintained in those relations between the State and National government, surrendered for a time by rebellion, but now happily restored.

I have the honor to be gentlemen
Very Respectfully
Your obedient servant
W. W. Holden
Governor of N.C.

[1] David Aaron Jenkins.

[2] Henry J. Menninger, secretary of state, 1868-1873. Cheney, *North Carolina Government*, 1585-1979, 425

[3] Samuel Stanford Ashley.

[4] Abiel W. Fisher

[5] Henderson Adams, Davidson County; member, state Senate, 1862-1865; auditor of state, 1868-1873. Cheney, *North Carolina Government*, 1585-1979, 425, 1121.

[6] Ceburn L. Harris.

[7] William Macon Coleman.

[8] Eugene Grissom, physician; member, House of Commons, 1862-1865; superintendent, North Carolina insane asylum in Raleigh, 1868-1889. *Dictionary of North Carolina Biography*, s.v. "Grissom, Eugene."

Holden to Hanibal D. Norton A&H:GP

State of North Carolina
Executive Department
Raleigh Nov. 17th, 1868

Hanibal D. Norton Esq.
Agent Bu. R. F. & A. L.

Sir.

Your letter of the 12th Inst. addressed to Bvt. Lt. Col. Chur, has been referred to me. In reply I have the honor to state that care of the poor belongs entirely to the Board of County Commissioners.

Respectfully
W. W. Holden. Gov

W. D. McCallum et al. to Holden A&H:GP

Shoe Hill Robeson Co Nov 25th 1868

To His Excellency Gov Holden

Dear Sir

We the undersigned Citizens of Robeson County NC appeal to your Excellency to take some steps to relieve this section and adjacent Counties of a *desperate band of thieves and robers* with which we have been ifested more or less now for years. —They make frequent raids out into the surrounding Country going some times into South Carolina always taking advantage of the night-time and then returning to their places of concealment before day light. Some of the party are well known but from their surroundings and locality it is quite dificult to arrest them:—they live in a section inhabited principally by Mulattoes (of their own colour and kin) Many of whom it is believed give them aid and comfort and we are led to this belief from the fact that when any attempt is made to arrest them or search for stolen goods, they rally to their aid and defense biding difiance to all law—one of the Gang who is supposed to be one of the main leaders is a man by the name of Lowry[1] for whom Gov Worth had offered a reward for his apprehension being guilty of the murder of one of our best Citizens[2] and now owing to this and the numerous Cases of robery Charged to his account and his accomplices it is not believed they would submit to a peaceble arrest but would defend themselves to the death, and this has somewhat detered our Citizens from rising in their stregth and slaying the last one of them in self defense:—& for the protection of our homes our lives and our property, and so great is the terror they spread throughout the Country that many of our people say *a state of war would be preferable* for we have no peace nor protection, notwith standing we are able to protect ourselves if we were disposed to take the law into our own hands but the better part of our people here have always been disposed to be lawabiding and submission to the *powers* that be, and would not like to be misrepresented—and should we in self defense take the law into our own hands we believe that there are some that would accuse us of disloyalty and of killing loyal Citizens, therefore we have concluded to appeal to your Excellency hoping and trusting that you can do something for our relief for we assure you that we desire nothing more than the suppression of Crime the restoration of peace and the protection of our homes against the depredations of midnight robers and to effect this we would much prefer having it done by the strong arm of law and having it done promptly decently and in a way that will make an example of these Men and a terror to all such violators of law—and good order, and we would therefore suggest to your Excellency that we know of no more speedy and efficient mode than to declare all such as may be guilty of such crimes as outlawed and have them arrested dead or alive but we commit our cause into your hands trusting to your better judgment and wisdom to relieve us from the evils Complained of trusting that you will act promptly in the matter we subscribe ourselves with much respect your most obt Servts

W. D. McCallum[3]
& others

P.S. Since signing the above we learn from reliable sources that Mr Alexander McKenzie[4] who lives a near neighbor to this man Lowry above alluded to was shot this morning by some person concealed in the woods while Mr McKenzie was out feeding hogs inflicting a serious wound in the leg.

[*Enclosure*]

Raemont Robeson Co Nov 25th 1868

Col James Sinclair[5]

Dear Sir

There is a reign of Terror prevailing through the County in consequence of a band of Robers or thieves from the vicinity of *Scuffletown* who are now makeing frequent raids in diferent sections and even some times into S Carolina they disguise themselves by blacking their faces and trying up their heads so that their hair can not be seen. Maj J. H McQueen[6] was Robed last Monday night weeke and since that I hear that Mr Alex Purcell[7] was visited by them besides various other persons. We are sending up a communication to Gov Holden on the subject and I though I would take the individual responsibility of droping you a few lines that you might also see the Gov and have something done people cant rest at night it is as bad as Shermans Raid—You are now our Representative and we will expect you to make some effort to relieve us of this horrible scourge they rob white folks negroes and every body without respect to Colour Nothing more of interest

Most Respectfully
M McRae[8]

PS I would suggest that these men be declared as out lawed and a reward offered for their apprehension and have them taken dead or alive any communication can be addressed to me or any other person you may choose

Yrs M McRae

[1] Henry Berry Lowry.

[2] James P. Barnes.

[3] William D. McCallum, Shoe Hill physician. 1870 U.S. Census Population Schedule, North Carolina: Robeson, 2 (microfilm). The letter was signed by more than fifty persons.

[4] Alexander McKenzie, by 1870 a farmer in Moore County. 1870 U.S. Census Population Schedule, North Carolina: Moore, 543 (microfilm).

[5] James Sinclair, Robeson County; member, state House of Representatives, 1868-1870. Cheney, *North Carolina Government, 1585-1979*, 1255.

[6] James H. McQueen, Shoe Hill farmer. 1870 U.S. Census Population Schedule, North Carolina: Robeson, 121 (microfilm).

[7] Alex Purcell, Robeson County farmer. 1870 U.S. Census Population Schedule, North Carolina: Robeson, 110 (microfilm).

[8] Murdic McRae, Shoe Hill farmer. 1870 U.S. Census Population Schedule, North Carolina: Robeson, 8 (microfilm).

G. W. Swepson to Holden A&H:GP

Raleigh, N.C.
Novbr: 27th 1868

His Excellency
W. W. Holden
Raleigh, N.C.

Sir:

I have the honor to acknowledge receipt through you of letter of the Sheriff of Buncombe County in reference to parties employed in the corps of Engineers who took part in the late riot at Asheville.

I take the liberty to enclose copy of letter written this day to Major Turner[1] on the subject and hope the same will meet your approval.

Very Respectfully
G. W. Swepson
Prsds: West: div: W. N. C. R. Rd Co:

[*Enclosure*]

Raleigh, N.C.
November 27/68

Major J. C. Turner, chief Engineer
Asheville, N.C.

Dr. Sir:

I enclose copy of letter of the Sheriff of Buncombe county to Gov. Holden with the endorsement of the Governor on it.

I must request you to at once discharge every man who was connected with the late riot at Asheville, no matter what political party he belongs to; and in making up your different corps you will please give employment to men of all political parties, to wit: Old Whigs, Democrats and Republicans, so that nobody can make political capital out of it and neither side injure the Road.

Very Respectfully
(Sigd) G. W. Swepson
West: div: W. N. C. R. Rd Co.

[1] James C. Turner, chief engineer of the Western Division of the Western North Carolina Railroad Company. Cecil Kenneth Brown, *A State Movement in Railroad Development* (Chapel Hill: University of North Carolina Press, 1928), 195.

Holden to the General Assembly of North Carolina A&H:GP

STATE OF NORTH CAROLINA
Executive Department
Raleigh, November 28th, 1868

To the Honorable, the General Assembly of North Carolina:

Gentlemen: By an act passed by your honorable body at its last session, the sum of ten thousand dollars was appropriated for the purpose of furnishing the Executive Mansion, and making necessary repairs for the same.[1]

I beg leave respectfully to say that I would prefer, under the circumstances, not to expend this money for the purpose indicated. I am comfortably situated in my own private residence, where I will be as happy to receive my friends as I would be in the Executive Mansion.

The Mansion and grounds are, therefore, subject to such disposition as your body may choose to make of them. It would be very expensive to render the Mansion fit for a comfortable private residence; but it might, at small expense, be rendered suitable for school purposes or for public offices. I have expended a small portion of the appropriation on the Mansion, and on the furniture belonging to it. I will account for this with the Public Treasurer, and leave the remainder of the appropriation in his hands, subject to your order.

I have the honor to be, gentlemen, with great respect,

Your obedient servant,
W. W. Holden
Governor

[1] *Public Acts and Resolutions passed by the General Assembly of North Carolina, special Session of July, 1868*, c. 30.

Holden to the Sheriff of Warren County A&H:GP

Executive Department of North
Carolina
Raleigh November 30th, 1868

To the Sheriff of the County of Warren[1]

Sir:

I have received information in relation to a recent murder in your county, which renders it my duty to address you this letter. It seems that Lynes[2] was shot and killed by Suit[3] without due provocation; and that the jury of inquest was composed entirely of white men.

Mr. Suit admits the killing. I doubt if the crime is bailable at all, and if so, I am sure the bail taken is not sufficent. A Jury of white and colored men should be empaneled, and their verdict should be had. The habit which some of our people have of taking their guns, to be used against colored people, for offences, or supposed offences which inflamce their passions, must be put down. The life of Lynes was as sacred and as valuable in the eye of the law, and in the sight of God, as that of Suit or any other man. I am determined that in this and all other like cases, Justice shall be done. violent men like Mr. Suit, who resort to deadly weapons, without cause, must be made to feel in some way the power of violated law.

I trust, sir, that you will give the matter immediate attention. If any Justices of the peace are not disposed to do their duty, such will be removed and just and fearless men appointed in their places.

Very Respectfully
W. W. Holden
Governor

[1] Nathaniel R. Jones, sheriff of Warren county. 1870 U.S. Census Population Schedule, North Carolina: Warren, 663 (microfilm). For another version of the incident, see Jas. W. Alston to Holden, December 3, 1868, in this volume.

[2] Probably Howell Lines, otherwise not identified.

[3] William H. Suit, Nutbush Township farmer. 1870 U.S. Census Population Schedule, North Carolina: Warren, 538 (microfilm). On March 1, 1869, Suit was tried for manslaughter, and was found not guilty. Warren County Minute Docket, Superior Court, 1868-1874, February, 1869 Term (original in North Carolina State Archives).

Holden to the Sheriff of Robeson County A&H:GLB

State of North Carolina
Executive Department of N.C.
Raleigh Nov. 30th, 1868

To the Sheriff of Robeson County:[1]

Sir:

I have received information that bands of armed men, variously disguised, are breaking the peace, robbing and plundering, and causing terror to many of the good citizens of Robeson.

This lawlessness must be repressed and the criminals brought to Justice. The people of Robeson have the right to be secure in their persons, houses and property, and this right will be made good to them by the whole power of the State, if necessary.

It is especially your duty to preserve the peace, and to protect the honest and the law-abiding against robberies and violence. You have at your disposal for this purpose the whole power of the county. You are hereby commanded to use this power prudently and judiciously, but with the utmost determination and firmness. If any Justices of the Peace should refuse to cooperate with you in the performance of this duty, report them to me, and they will at once be removed. If you need more Justices to aid you, inform me of it and I will appoint them. In dealing with robbers and outlaws, such as those referred to, do not embarrassed by technicalities or State or County Lines; but see to it that you act with such vigilance, promptness and vigor as at once to deliver the good people of Robeson from the danger of being thus outraged and put in terror for their lives. This can be done only by pursuing and capturing these outlaws, and confining them to be tried for their crimes. *Herein fail Not.*

Very Respectfully
W. W. Holden
govr.

[1] Benjamin A. Howell, Robeson County; sheriff and Lumberton hotelkeeper. 1870 U.S. Census Population Schedule, North Carolina: Robeson, 98 (microfilm).

Baltzer & Taaks to Holden A&H:GP

New York Dec. 2 1868

Hon. W. W. Holden
Governor State of North Carolina
Raleigh N.C.

Your Excellency
Will permit us to enclose herein No 2951 $1000.
North Carolina State bonds
With all Coupons attached
Dated 1. Oct. 68.

which is one of a series of Nos. 1200 to 3200 that has been as we are informed declared not a good delivery by our Board of Stock brokers until certain charges of illegality preferred against that issue by parties in your State could be investigated and disproved.

We have bought of these Bonds for foreign account and upon our recommendation to introduce them into the London market; your Excellency will therefore readily perceive that it is of the utmost importance not only to us but also and preeminently to the credit of the State of North Carolina that these impediments be as promptly removed as Your Excellency will be able of sending proofs forward to the Board; in the meantime these Bonds remain on our hands.

We ask Your Excellency therefore very urgently that in returning us the Bond we now send you also by express to add your own confirmation of our belief that these Bonds are in every way fully as legally issued and valid as any other issue of the State of North Carolina and further if not encroaching too much on your convenience to add the concurrent opinion of the highest legal authority of the State.

These communications when received will be for our own private satisfaction independent of the paper which we trust you have already upon the advice of parties here sent on to the Stock Board

We are
Your Excellencys
Very obdt Servants
Baltzer & Taaks[1]

[1] In the original record of the North Carolina Supreme Court case of *Baltzer v. The State*, *North Carolina Reports* 104 (1898): 265, the complaint identified Herman R. Baltzer and William G. Taaks as partners engaged as bankers and brokers and negotiators of securities in New York (North Carolina Supreme Court Original Case No. 16001, North Carolina State Archives).

Holden to the Sheriff of Robeson County A&H:GLB

Executive Department of N.C.
Raleigh Dec. 2nd, 1868

To the Sheriff of Robeson County:[1]

Sir:

It having been represented to me by a committee of the citizens of your county, that the Public Peace is being disturbed, I have deemed it proper to issue a proclamation, and herewith enclose to you one hundred copies of the same, and look to you for the prompt execution of the order.

Very Respectfully
W. W. Holden
Governor

[1] Benjamin A. Howell.

Jas W Alston to Holden A&H:GP

Mansen N.C.
December 3d 1868

To His Excellency
Gov. W. W. Holden

Dear Sir

I expect ere this reaches you, you will have heard of another shooting in this County, and in my neighborhood. On Friday night last, I was called to see a

Colored man by the name of Howell Lines, who had been shot by a Mr. Wm. Suit. I hurried to the scene Professionally, as soon as I could. I found upon examination that the man was bound to die. I then as a Magestrate, went forthwith after Suit, and found him temporarily arrested by some Colored man. I immediately issued a warrant against him, appointed an Officer, and placed him in the Custody of the Law. I then went myself that night after the Sherriff,[1] and Coroner,[2] had an inquest fairly and legally held, we then had a Magestrates court of Three, John H. Bullock,[3] John Paschall,[4] Colored and myself. Upon the Testimony, it appeared that the deceased had a Pig of Suits. Suit hailed him in the dark, and without answering, the deceased, rushed upon Suit, when he shot him. Suit was in his house when he heard the Pig squall, caught up his gun, and went in pursuit of the Thief; as he supposed, when the unfortunate Occurrence took place as above stated.

I wrote to you to let you know, that I did my duty Professionally, and Officially, There seems to be much dissatisfaction among the colored Men, from what cause I do not know. Dr. Vogel.[5] was to see me on the Sunday, after this occurrence, and stayed with me until Monday Noon. I gave him all of the particulars, and he saw enough to assure you of my full compliance with my official duty.

In haste I remain Yours Truly &c
Jas W Alston[6]

Turn over

I will mention that Suit is an aged man, and has always been an unexceptionable character

JWA

[1] Nathaniel R. Jones

[2] John E. Jones, Warren County farmer and coroner. 1870 U.S. Census Population Schedule, North Carolina: Warren, 577; Warren County Officials' Bonds, Coroners, 1866 bond for John E. Jones.

[3] John H. Bullock, Nutbush District farmer and justice of the peace. 1870 U. S. Census Population Schedule, North Carolina: Warren, 534 (microfilm); W. W. Holden, Appointments of Justices of Peace, 1868-1870 (original in North Carolina State Archives).

[4] John M. Paschal, Warren County Tax List for Nutbush District, 1867; W. W. Holden, Appointments of Justices of Peace, 1868-1870 (original in North Carolina State Archives).

[5] Henry C. Vogells, agent of Bureau of Refugees, Freedmen, and Abandoned Lands in Raleigh. Records of Assistant Commissioner for the State of North Carolina, Bureau of Refugees, Freedmen and Abandoned Lands (National Archives Record Group 105). (microfilm copy in North Carolina State Archives).

[6] James W. Alston, Warren County; Nutbush District physician and justice of the peace. Warren County Tax List for Nutbush District, 1868; W. W. Holden, Appointments of Justices of Peace, 1868-1870 (original in North Carolina State Archives).

W. J. Doughty to Holden A&H:GP

Newport N.C. Decr. 5th 1868

Hon W. W. Holden
Governor of N.C.

Dear Sir"

Mr W F. Bell[1] a citizen of this (Carteret) County, who is present at this writing and who has come over the country fifteen miles to request me to write you and give a statement of his grievances about a certan steam saw mill formerly the property of F DeWitt & co[2] is very desirous that you should know the true situation of the affair as he is informed by Mrs Moore[3] that she has been to see you for the purpose of getting the assistance of the military to put her in possession if the property

I am of the opinion Governor that you would like a statement other than Mrs Moore's since you have been appealed to in the matter and I therefore yield to Mr Bell's solicitations, and inasmuch as I have had some connexion with the matter in the capacity of an attorney I think I shall be able to state the material points of the case and satisfy Mr Bell without doing injustice to any other party

F. DeWitt & Co in 1867 erected a steam mill upon the lands of W. F. Bell in this county. They bought of him a piece of land (or rather took a receipt in the nature of a bond to make title) supposed to be Twenty-five acres on the East side of a certain public road. the mill however was erected on the west side of the road with a verbal agreement that F DeWitt should have the use of the ground at the nominal price of ten cents per year as long as the mill was worked. Upon the first piece to wit 25 acres for which bond to make title was given F DeWitt & co erected certain dwelling houses and other houses.

In the spring of 1868 F. DeWitt & Co mortgaged or Deeded to H. B. Claflin & Co.[4] of New York the entire Mill property to secure a debt due them by said Co amounting to about Twenty Five hundred Dols.

With a few months past Mr De Witt has died his death resulting from a scald or burn received while working said mill

Recently a Judgment was obtained in the County Court of this County against F DeWitt & Co for which the said mill property was sold by the sheriff and Messrs Rieger Davis & Bro.[5] of Beaufort became the purchasers at one Hundred Dols.

Now the Mill & property & fixtures is claimed by four parties to wit Messrs Rieger Davis & Bro by virtue of a sheriffs Deed or bill of sale, 1stly-2ndly by Messrs H B Claftin & Co of new York by virtue of a Deed to them in the early part of this year being duly recorded.

3rdly by Mrs Moore as surviving partner of F De Witt & Co and 4thly by Mr W. F. Bell who claims by virtue of the mill being on and incorporated in his soil but only to indemnify him for a debt of Six Hundred and fifteen Dollars due from F. De Witt & Co for timber and provisions furnished said Mill & Co

Mr Bell who is present at this writing desires me to say that he contends that said mill should not be removed from his premises until he is paid the said sum above named. That, He has been advised by his attorneys that a steam mill so far partakes of the nature of real property being incorporated in the soil that he may object to its being removed before he is paid the said sum of Six Hundred and fifteen dollars due him for timber and provisions furnished said mill and said F. Dewitt. & Co

He further desires me to state that he has never objected since or before the death of Mr De Witt to said mill being worked by this Co. or any other Company and that he agreed that the said mill should be erected on his property as aforesaid upon the nominal verbal lease of ten cents pr year upon the consideration that the mill was a convenience to the public.

He wishes you also to know that yesterday Mrs. Moore, an agent of H. B. Claftin & Co and Capt Granger[6] of the Freedmans Bureau summoned him to a conference upon the premises which was unsatisfactory to all parties, and further he is induced to make this statement of facts because of the assurance on their part that they should again complain to you and believing Governor that upon a proper representative of the facts you will refer the matter to the courts where he is advised by his attorneys the case properly belongs under the present posture of affairs

He desires me also to state in order to rebut any statement to the contrary if any has been made that He has acted with all parties as if they were citizens of the state and only desires protect his own interest

He further desires me to say that he is very desirous of settling the matter amicably and in pursuance of this idea has offered to compromise the matter by buying their interest for one Thousand Dollars, or scaling his account to Five Hundred Dollars and giving them a Deed according to the tenor of the bond to make title upon their complying with the requirements and stipulations therein

In conclusion governor I desire for myself to say that I wish you a peaceful and prosperous administration and have the honor to subscribe myself

With much respect your Friend
W. J. Doughty[7]

[1] William F. Bell III, Carteret county; Newport merchant. 1870 U.S. Census Population Schedule, North Carolina: Carteret, 239 (microfilm).

[2] Francis DeWitt, native of Massachusetts, trader; later established a steam sawmill on Pettiford Creek, Carteret County, North Carolina. 1850 U.S. Census Population Schedule, Massachusetts: Hampshire County, Town of Ware, 382 (microfilm).

[3] Harriet J. Moore, Massachusetts native who participated with DeWitt in operating a steam sawmill at or near Pettiford Creek. 1870 U.S. Census Population Schedule, Massachusetts: Middlesex, Cambridge Ward 1, 312 (microfilm). See also Mrs. H.J. Moore to Gen. Miles, December 31, 1868, in this volume.

[4] H. B. Claflin and company, New York merchants, importers and distributors of merchandise. *Biographical Dictionary of American Business Leaders*, s.v. "Claflin, Horace Bingham." See also warranty deed from Francis Dewitt of Pettiford Creek and Mrs. Harriet J. Moore of Boston to Horace B. Claflin of New York, dated April 15, 1868, for a parcel of land on Pettiford Creek upon which was located a steam sawmill, and fifteen acres west of the highway upon which was located two tenement houses, as well as the steam mill and the machinery. Carteret County Deeds, Book CC, 307 (microfilm copy in North Carolina State Archives).

[5] In August, 1867, Term, Carteret County Court, John C. Garner brought action against Francis DeWitt for recovery of a $109.82 promissary note, and the jury found for the plaintiff. Carteret County Court Trial Docket, 1849-1868, August, 1867, Term (original in North Carolina State Archives). November 18, 1868, the Carteret County sheriff siezed the steam sawmill owned by Francis DeWitt and sold it to H. Rieger, James C. Davis, and J. H. Davis, Beaufort merchants, as execution in the name of John C. Garner. Carteret County Deeds, Book DD, 37 (microfilm copy in North Carolina State Archives).

[6] L. E. Granger, Second Lieutenant, Brevet captain, 40th U.S. Infantry, Assistant Sub-Assistant Commissioner, Bureau of Refugees, Freedmen, and Abandoned Lands in Beaufort. Roster. Records of the Assistant Commissioner for the State of North Carolina, Bureau of Refugees, Freedmen & Abandoned Lands (National Archives Record Group 105).

[7] William J. Doughty, Carteret county lawyer. 1870 U.S. Census Population Schedule, North Carolina: Carteret, 216 (microfilm).

William H. Doherty to Holden A&H:GP

Elizabeth City, N.C.
December 8th 1868

To His Excellency
W. W. Holden
Governor of N.C.

Sir,

Senator John Pool, who has just gone to Congress, has been consulting with me, and others of our true friends here, about the hasty, if not fraudulent, sale of the Land Script granted to the University for the endowment of an Agricultural school

He thinks that prompt & energetic measures should be taken, by the Atty Genl. of this State, to set aside the agreement & obtain full value for our Scrip. Now is the proper time when our Senators & Representatives are in Washington, & can co-operate in having justice done & this fraud defeated.

Senator Pool is very anxious to have something done. And I am very much interested in the matter

Please *remember my papers, applying for a position in the University*, & present them at the right time. Mr Pool left them with you With sincere respect & esteem,

William H Doherty

A. H. Jones to Holden A&H:GP

Fortieth Congress, US
Washington, D. C.
December 9, 1868

Governor Holden
Raleigh N.C.

Dear Sir: I this day received a statement from Asheville that the Inspectors of election in Transylvania county had forwarded a sworn statement to the Secretary of State that they ignorantly threw out and did not count in the returns first made *Thirty five votes* of legal registered voters who voted for me. I trust that the Secretary has received and will count these votes; for if he and you informed me right there were other returns sent in after the limit had expired. Every friend of yours and mine and of the party with which we act appear to be very much interested in my success in procureing the commission for a seat in the 41st Congress.

I have shown Judge J. L. Henry's[1] Statement to one or two friends in confidence. They say there can no longer be any room for doubting my right to the certifficate of election, and that it would be shameful to put me to unnecessary trouble to obtain a seat which I am justly entitled to, and will be certain to obtain in the end.

The evidence of fraud which is now reaching me by every mail is overwhelming. I have received letters from two persons who say they voted against me, but declare that I am clearly entitled to the seat for the reason that they know of more frauds in Haywood county alone than would cover three times 18 votes, and have put me in possession of facts in regard to facts and persons. They say the conduct of their own party at two precincts in the county should disgust every well disposed man in the country, and that they are disposed to see me have fair play and justice.

This days proceedings in Congress go to show that it has more back-bone than ever, and will not swerve one inch from the execution and enforcement of its own enactments, as regards reconstruction.

Very Respectfully
Yours Truly
A. H. Jones[2]

[1] James Love Henry

[2] Alexander Hamilton Jones.

Jere Smith et al. to Holden A&H:GP

Taylorsville Alexander Co
N. C. Decr 10th 1868

To His Excellency, W W Holden Gov of N.C

Dear sir: we the undersigned citizens of said County, would respectfully represent to your Excellency, that Daniel Mathison[1] a citizen also of the County aforesaid is a man considerably advanced in age and is the owner also of a small tract of land situate in said County or which he is yet indebted. The greater portion of the purchase money being still due, and that he has no other property of much value we would further show unto your Excellency that said Mathison has ever been the steadfast friend of the Union—That during the late Rebellion his house was a place of refuge for the distressed prisoners of the Union Army who made their escape from Salisbury and other Southern prisons and who made his house a stoping place on their route across the lines. That he not only fed and concealed them for weeks—but aided them in many ways to make good their escape which the Certificates of Capt Abercrombie[2] & others would fully show—We would further state that Mr Mathison has never asked the Government for remuneration in any way—That during the rebellion as before stated he gave cheerfully much of his little substance for the cause of the Union, and his Country—and that he is still intensely devoted to the Old flag of his Country and too Gov permit us to say to you that he has been and is yet an ardent supporter of yours—That he had two Sons who were not only Union men but were Union soldiers

That by his course during the war & since its close has incured the displeasure of the opposition party—That he battled for the Union almost solitary and alone in his county—when it was considered treason here almost to speak or talk of the old flag.

We earnestly ask your Excellency for the reasons set forth—on account of Mr Mathisons advanced age and on account of his impovrished condition & for his many sacrifices for his Country, for his great devotion for the same to use our influence with the proper authorities at Washington City to allow him to distill any damaged corn he may be able to get in this county into Whiskey—and to relieve him from paying the special tax of $400.00 (Distillers tax) he is more than willing to pay the tax on the gallon—but is wholy unable to pay the $400.00 tax—

We sincerely hope the Government will will [*sic*] appreciate his past services and give him the aid asked if such thing can be done, we would earnestly ask you Gov to use your influence in the matter at as early a date possible —& please write to Mr Mathison at his P.O. in Taylorsville and let him what can be done for him—

Respectfully &c
Jere Smith[3]
John M. Carson[4]

WM Bogle[5]
NA Moose[6]
AG Marshall[7]
J. J. Teague[8]

P. S.
We should have stated that there is large amount of damaged corn in this County which is unfit for bred

[1] Daniel Matheson, Taylorsville farmer. 1860 U.S. Census Population Schedule, North Carolina: Alexander, 159 (microfilm).

[2] Not identified.

[3] Jere Smith, Taylorsville teacher and student. 1870 U.S. Census Population Schedule, North Carolina: Alexander, 228 (microfilm).

[4] John M. Carson, Taylorsville physician. 1870 U.S. Census Population Schedule, North Carolina: Alexander, 223 (microfilm).

[5] Washington M. Bogle, farm laborer. 1870 U.S. Census Population Schedule, North Carolina: Alexander, 225 (microfilm).

[6] N. A. Moose, Taylorsville tailor. 1860 U.S. Census Population Schedule, North Carolina: Alexander, 136.

[7] A. G. Marshall, farmer. 1860 U.S. Census Population Schedule, North Carolina: Alexander, 113 (microfilm).

[8] James J. Teague, farmer. 1870 U.S. Census Population Schedule, North Carolina: Alexander, 225 (microfilm).

Wm. M. Coleman to Holden A&HGP

State of North Carolina
Attorney General's Office,
Raleigh Dec 10 1868

To His Excellency
W. W. Holden:

I have examined the Acts of 1848-9, of 1850-1 and of 1860-1 in relation to the McDowel and Yancey Turnpike Company, with special reference to the question whether said Company is entitled to receive any further moneys from the State.

An Act ratified the 29th of January 1849 provided that the state should pay to the Company three thousand dollars from sales or entries of the wild and untenanted lands in McDowel & Yancey counties, upon the performance of certain conditions.

An Act ratified Jan. 15th 1851 provided that when three thousand dollars was subscribed or secured to the Board &c "that then it shall and may be lawful for the Internal Improvement Board and they are hereby directed and empowered to pay over to said Com under the direction of the Governor three thousand dollars, the Governor being empowered to appoint a director on the part of the State &c."

The Turnpike Company has received this three thousand dollars.

An act ratified the 19th day of February 1861 provides that "in addition to the subscription already made on the part of the State" &c "the Internal Improvement board are hereby authorized in the manner provided by section third of said Act of 1850 and 51, to make an additional subscription on behalf of the State of three thousand dollars to said Road."

I take it that the words "measures provided" in Sec. 3 Act of 1850 & 51, mean that the money is to be paid by the Internal Improvement Board, under the Direction of the Governor and that if the said money has not yet been paid that the said Turnpike Company is entitled to it.

Respectfully
Wm. M. Coleman
Attorney Genl.

Holden to the General Assembly of North Carolina A&H:GLB

Executive Department of No. Ca.
Raleigh Dec. 11th, 1868

To the Honl. the General Assembly of North Carolina

Gentlemen:

I herwith transmit a communication from the Public Treasurer[1] in relation to the importance of some immediate provision to supply the deficiency in the Public Treasury; together with a bill for that purpose, which that officer has proposed. I beg leave most respectfully to commend the suggestions and views of the Public Treasurer to the favorable consideration of the General Assembly.

I have the honor to be Gentlemen,
With great respect Your Obt. Servant.
W. W. Holden

[1] David Aaron Jenkins.

John Pool to Holden A&H:GP

Ebbitt House
Washington Decr 13 1868

Gov Holden
Raleigh N.C.

My dear Sir: I hear from our North Carolina delegation, something said in regard to your desiring a place in the Cabinet. I hardly think any place will be given us, but if we can get a place for our State, I wish to know, *confidentially*, your wishes on the subject. Last Summer, I mentioned Genl. Dockery's[1] name in connection with a Cabinet appointment, to Hon. O. H. Dockery,[2] & the same has been again mentioned, since my arrival here. If you desire the place, I wish to know it, at once. I will not disclose your answer, if you desire me not to do so.

The present pay is not sufficient to support the Cabinet officers in the style they are required to maintain. But it will be recommended to Congress to increase the pay, & I think it will be increased. I wish to see some citizen of our State in the Cabinet, if for no other reason, to secure our people a fair share of patronage under the government. I cannot, at present, advise you whether it would be well for you to accept such a place. But I shall be informed better, before long, & will cheerfully give you the result of my best & unbiased judgement. It would be unfortunate to resign your present position, & find that you could not remain in the Cabinet, without splitting from your friends. I have no personal fears on this point, but some things are said, which I wish more fully to understand.

If possible, stop the progress of certain parties in North Carolina, who are reported to be putting in jeopardy the interests of the State & life of our party, for their private, pecuniary gains. There is great danger ahead & parties seem blind to the risk they are incurring. Let the investigation take its course. It is but the beginning. I fear much injury & perplexity to some of our party friends from it. But more would result from its suppression. Try to prevent the necessity for such things, hereafter. I feel that you can do much to check the wrong, if any has been done, & to save the disgrace to man & injury to the State. I hope, they misinform me, & that no corruption has existed, & none contemplated. But active & acute minds are upon the subject, & facts are known that need explanation. I hope you will act in the whole matter, so as to command the approbation of all good men, & give our enemies no advantage over you. If you find friends involved, do not compromise your administration, with their defense. I am in ignorance of what it all means, in the past, but it seems to me that the future is not safe – if half I hear be true.

I hope, you will be able to give Hon. A. H. Jones[3] his certificate, rightfully. If possible do it, & give him the benefits of honest doubts. I would not go further. He feels on the subject & thinks that he has been defrauded of his election – which, I think, is true.

There is nothing beyond what you see in the papers, worth writing you from this place. Whenever anything transpires, I will inform you.

Let me know as far as is proper from you, what all the trouble is in Raleigh— & what is threatened, & how & whether there are any corrupt plans for the future— We cannot sustain, nor wink at corruption.

Very truly respectfully your friend,
John Pool

[1] Alfred Dockery.

[2] Oliver Hart Dockery, congressman; A. B., U.N.C., 1848; member, House of Commons, 1848; lieutenant colonel, Confederate army; member, U.S. House of Representatives, 1867-1871; unsuccessful candidate for governor, 1888. *Dictionary of North Carolina Biography*, s.v. "Dockery, Oliver Hart."

[3] Alexander Hamilton Jones.

R H Bennett to Holden A&H:GP

Lockvill N. C
Dec. 17th/68

Hon. Gov. Holden

Dear Sir

I have the honer very respectfully requesting that you would be so kind as to rember me when you are about to Establish the Guard I thought it would be best for me to speak in time and by so doing you will confer a great favor on me, I am Sir very Respectfully you Humble Servant

R H Bennett[1]

[1] Richard H. Bennett, Chatham County; Pittsboro farm laborer. 1870 U.S. Census Population Schedule, North Carolina: Chatham, 186 (microfilm).

Certified Statement A&H:GP

Raleigh No Ca. Decr 19 1868

It is hereby certified that at a meeting of the Board of Internal Improvement held in the office of the Governor on the 20th day of October 1868 it was decided to subscribe to the stock of the Western Division of the No. Ca. Rail Road, on behalf of the state, the sum of Four millions of dollars, and in behalf of the eastern division of said road, the sum of ($340,000.) three hundred and forty thousand dollars, the same being the amount to which said road is entitled, on certificate of the President that the terms of the charter has been complied with

W W Holden Govr

Baltzer & Taaks to Holden A&H:GP

New York Dec. 20. 1868

His Excellency
W. W. Holden
Governor North Carolina
Raleigh.

We had the honor of receiving your Excellency's letter dated the 9 inst. With Chatham R. R. Bond returned in which you promise to send us the Attorney General's opinion on that issue in a few days. Fearing this may have been overlooked in the pressure of more important business we would take the liberty of recalling the matter to your Memory. We have been told the whole difficulty had been overcome and adjusted by an act of both Houses of your Legislature but are not aware of any official copy thereof having reached this city. Until then the whole thing remains in Statu Quo, Which is not desirable for holders of the tainted Bonds

We remain

Your Excellency's
Obdt Servt
Baltzer & Taaks

[*Endorsed*] Write and send copy of the Act.

J. T. Schenck to Holden A&H:GP

Charlotte NC.
Dec 20th 1868

His Excellency
W W Holden
Governor &C
Raleigh N.C.

Dear Sir

On my arrival I found that things had assumed a very serious aspeck resulting from the death of Mr Gleason[1] —the disposition for lynch was very strong on the part of the Conservatives—but so far the prisoners have been protected and the jail unmolested. All good citizens of all parties and races have exerted themselves to the utmost to prevent any disturbance and we think now we will be successful in preserving order

We enclose a ticket which will satisfactory to each wing of our party – and we desire you to make the appointments at once as and forward them by tomorrow's mail or by special conveyance as it is all important for the Board to be organized at once All parties have been consulted and agrees to Serve

Your Obt Servant
J. T. Schenck[2]

[1] James A. Gleason, formerly of Portsmouth, Virginia, where he was a wheelwright; 1st Lieutenant, Company H, 61st Virginia Infantry. In a report of the incident, the *Standard* on December 24, 1868, in a letter signed by "VERITAS," identified him as a "leading desperado of the Ku Klux organization." 1860 U.S. Census Population Schedule, Virginia: Norfolk, 131 (microfilm); Janet B. Hewett, ed., *The Roster of Confederate Soldiers 1861-1865* (Wilmington, N.C.: Broadfoot Publishing Company, 1996), 6:345.

[2] John T. Schenck, Mecklenburg County; Charlotte carpenter. 1870 U.S. Census Population Schedule, North Carolina: Mecklenburg, 073 (microfilm).

W. D. Whitted to Holden A&H:GP

Hendersonville No Ca
December 20th 1868

His Excellency Gov. W. W. Holden.

My dear Sir.

I have just recd a letter from our mutual friend A. H. Jones who as you are apprised is in Washington City. He appears to be in trouble about the result of the Congressional election in this District, he thinks that every conceivable manner of fraud, that could be resorted to, was practiced to defeat him, he says that every mail brings him evidences of this kind, and that all intelligent & prominent Republicans in Congress believes that he is entitled to a certificate of election, he desires all the help that he can get, and requested me to drop you a line on the subject, which I do cheerfully—I have no doubt that there was fraud practiced against him, and I hope that you will investigate the Matter, and if you can Concientiously & Consistently do so that you will give him a certificate. Jones sometimes get throwed off of his balance, and I am afraid that he is Suffering too much Solicitude about his matter, but we must do all we can for him. I hope that you will pardon me for taking the liberty of addressing you on this subject, I have done so from the best motives both towards yourself & Mr Jones. Our County is quiet – Crops good &c. accept my kindest wishes for your Success in office, Your good health and happiness. I

am Very Respectfully
& Truly yours,
W. D. Whitted

Holden to Lewis Bond A&H:GLB

Executive Department of North Carolina
Raleigh December 22nd, 1868

Lewis Bond Esq.
Sheriff of Bertie

Sir

You will find herewith enclosed a letter from G. M. Mitchell[1] of your county complaining of lawlessness and violence committed on on [*sic*] offending citizens. With the entire force of the county at your command it seems to me that you should make every effort to arrest and bring to Justice all persons engaged in these disgraceful proceedings. It is your *Sworn* duty to preserve the public peace, and to secure this, you should if necessary call to your assistance all good citizens of the county. The public peace shall be preserved, and no position however exalted shall shield offenders. Let me hear from you immediately

Very Respectfully
W. W. Holden
Govr.

[1] Giles M. Mitchell, Windsor merchant. 1860 U.S. Census Population Schedule, North Carolina: Bertie, 001 (microfilm).

F W Ahrens to Holden A&H:GP

Charlotte No Ca Decbr 24, 1868

To his Excellency
Gov. W W Holden
Raleigh N.C.

Sir

Your communication relative to the appointments of Mayor and Aldermen for our City was duly received, in relation to the present state of feelings here, I have the pleasure to state that everything now seems to be as quiet as usual, and it is thought that no further attempts at mob law, which was seriously threatened a few days ago, will be made. I shall however follow your advice, and use every precaution and all the means in my power to prevent any further disturbances.

It is a hard matter to give the facts in the Gleason[1] case, but it seems that when a cold policeman attempted to arrest a man who was or had been beating a cold man or boy, this man Gleason interfered in the arrest, and attempted to release the prisoner from the Officer, when Lee Dunlap[2] also interfered, and insisted that the cold policeman should arrest this man, in the mean time a white police officer took charge of the Prisoner, and took him before the Mayor, during the examination Gleason asked Mr Bissell[3] (acting Mayor) if he allowed any body in his office to call another a Son of a bitch, to which Mr. Bissell replied No, I will have any man arrested who uses profane language in my office, and asked who is the man? Upon which Gleason replied, pointing to Lee Dunlap, here is the man, when immediately thereafter, two shots were fired, there seems to have been fired by Lee Dunlap the result of which proved fatal in a few minutes afterward.

Gleason had made himself during the former election and registration very obnoxious, he was very abusive in his language towards republicans, and particularly towards the colored people, and is said to have made threats against republicans, generally and although it is very much to be deplored that the affair happened, I hope it may be a lesson to some other evil disposed, noisy persons in this community.

I have the honor to be

Very respectfully
Yr mst obdt Sevt
F W Ahrens
Mayor

[1] James A. Gleason.

[2] Lee Dunlap, Mecklenburg County; he was tried, found guilty, and remanded to jail. Mecklenburg County Superior Court Minute Book, 1869-1872, 42-43 (original in North Carolina State Archives).

[3] Edward H. Bissell, mining engineer and farmer; appointed alderman of Charlotte July 29, 1868. 1870 U.S. Census Population Schedule, North Carolina: Gaston, 800 (microfilm); Governors Commission Book 1858-1864, 1866-1877 (G.O.5.1) (original in North Carolina State Archives).

Mrs. H. J. Moore to Gen. Miles A&H:GP

Pettiford. Dec 28. 1868

Gen. Miles[1]

Dear Sir.

Your favor of the 21st inst. came duly to hand. Allow me to thank you for so promptly replying to my letter, and for the interest you are pleased to take on my behalf. I did not write you any details in my communication to you, for the reason that Capt. Granger[2] wrote down *from the lips of sworn* witnesses all the facts in the case, and told me that he would report everything to you. He expressed himself strongly on the subject of my having protection, and promised to see me again in a few days, so that I had no manner of doubt you were in full possession of all the facts.

I confess I am surprised and *hurt* at his negligence. He obtained *strong* proof that Maj. DeWitt[3] was murdered—also, that my life has been threatened and is in danger. Furthermore, that in my absence much of my moveable property was taken from here, making it almost impossible for me to renew my business, &.c. &c

Altho' as you say, the military power is second to the civil in the state, yet the sight of U.S. Muskets or *Straps*, is sufficient to bring these rebs. to terms at once, without any trial. Had Capt. Granger remained here even a few days, much good would have been accomplished in securing for me, life and property. I cannot appeal to the *civil* authorities for the officers in this County are all in sympathy with the rebs, and would enjoy driving a *Yankee woman* out of the region, and *confiscating* her property. There is not a magistrate that would decide against their neighbors. And here I would suggest that gov. Holden might, if he pleased appoint as magistrate in this place, *Oliver B. Bidwell*,[4] a northern gentleman, who has recently come here to reside, and who would, I think aid me somewhat. If you would have the kindness to get the Gov. to do this, I would be very glad. I am greatly at a loss what to do—if Col. Chur[5] complies with your request so I should suppose he would at once, and Capt Granger comes here, I think it would be of great service—but if he does not, I see no other way but to leave my property to these *plundering* murderers, wretches, and go North. If an example could be made of one of the most violent of these rebs, by arresting him, and making him give *heavy bonds* to keep the peace. it would have a great effect in keeping the others quiet. As at present situated, I cannot pursue my business, niether is my life safe for a moment. Capt. Granger suggested to me that he would get you to loan me a *needle gun*—can you do so?

I am very sorry to trouble you with my private affairs, but, it seems necessary that someone should aid me now. I do not see how the Legislature can reach the matter, but if it be not too much trouble to you, I should like to have you see the report which Capt. Granger made out, and judge for yourself about it. Is there any way by which I can get back my stolen property? Can you inform me whether there is to be any change in the appointment of magistrates after Jan 1st If so, what?

With thanks for your courtesy and kindness, I am

Very respectfully yrs
Mrs. H. J. Moore

Have you prepared that *Obituary* yet? If so, please forward.

Head Qrs. Dist. North Carolina.
Raleigh, N.C. Dec. 31, 1868

[*Endorsed*]

[Private] Respectfully referred to His Excellency, W. W. Holden, Governor of N.C.—with the request that steps be taken to insure safety of person and property to Mrs. Moore, and that some Civil Authority at Pettisford, N.C. be instructed to see that such steps are carried out.

I am unable to assist Mrs. Moore as I am not authorized to make any change in the present disposition of the troops in this command.

Nelson A. Miles
Col. and Bvt. Maj. Genl. U.S.A.
Commanding District

[1] Nelson Appleton Miles.

[2] L. E. Granger.

[3] Francis DeWitt.

[4] Oliver B. Bidwell, native of New York; Cayuga County farmer; in testimony before Magistrate Thomas Hill recorded in the governor's letter book, he identified himself as an agent of H. B. Claflin & Co. 1850 U.S. Census Population Schedule, New York: Cayuga County, Town of Mentz, 128 (microfilm); Thomas Hill to Holden, January 11, 1869, in A&H:GLB.

[5] Jacob F. Chur.

G. T. F. *Gannaway to Holden* A&H:GP

December 28th 1868

Gov Wm. W. Holden

Dire Sir

I shall Endevor to make the Repotes to you about the out rage and the Desterbance that has Been Done in Caswell County North Carolina in the last week past by the ku klux Clan. Thay have come in on some of the colard people whare was at thare Homes in peace and a bed a Sleep, and took him out of his Bed and Beat him so that he will not be able to Do any more work this winter if ever, and he has a large family and one is not able to help the other Surch outrage will not Do the civel officers which has Been appointed are in dainger at thare homes of a night on account of Surch thereats as has been made by this ku klux murderess Band. The Collard man thay beet his name is Jacob Brannock[1] and he was beet because he was a republican and had a fight with a white man on account of his principles the man that he fought his name is Andy Brinsfield[2] and is said to be one of the head men in this outrage and some more of particular one Jacob Summers[3] is the President of the Club Ezecael Paschall[4] vice President and Henderson Robertson[5] the Captain ku klux clan there some more adjudged of this Club of robbers and the way they Disguise that we canot tell corect who they are by being coverd with there ku klux heads

I hope that there will be some way to sop the Desturbance they have caused the Country if not I beleave that it will create war unless it is stop fourwith

Your obedint Servnat
G. T. F. Gannaway[6]

Post office Rockingham Lenox Castle

[1] Jacob Brannock, Caswell County farmer. *Senate Reports, 42nd Congress, 1st Sess., No. 1*, "Condition of Affairs in the Southern States," 66.

[2] Andy Brinsfield, Caswell County; Locust Hills frmer. 1870 U.S. Census Population Schedule, North Carolina: Caswell, 460 (microfilm).

[3] Jacob Summers, Caswell County farmer. 1870 U.S. Census Population Schedule, North Carolina: Caswell, 102 (microfilm).

[4] Eziecal Paschall, Caswell County farmer. Caswell county Tax List, 1867, 67 (original in North Carolina State Archives).

[5] Not identified.

[6] G. T. F. Ganaway, appointed Caswell county justice of the peace, October 10, 1868. William W. Holden Appointments of Justices of Peace, 1868-1870 (original in North Carolina State Archives).

R. Beverly Frayser to Holden A&H:GP

Point Caswell Newhanover county
N.C.
28th December 1868

To His Excellency
W. W. Holden Gov of NC

Sir

As I am the only white man *of this vicinity*, who ventured to declare his sentiments frankly and openly in favor of Gen Grant in the late election, and at the same time, in a public speech avowed my determination to do all I could to better the condition of the colored man, because the interest of the white race demanded it, I feel that it is my duty to communicate with you freely on the subject of our present condition here.—You are greatly censured most bitterly and mercilessly denounced by many extremeists of the opposite party, but I have always felt and believed that it was attributable to partisan prejudices and that your true history would demonstrate your high moral and intellectual worth as well as your fidelity to your country's interest and prosperity: and it is therefore, that I shall the more confidently proceed with what is now passing as a part and parcel of our history.—We today occupy a critical and an alarming position—men here without character and without qualification in any one particular are aspiring to and pressing their claims for *positions* upon mere party grounds, *which* require and will call into exercise all the energies of the most highly cultivated and best gifted minds of the country.—There is not a more important and responsible position in the gift of the people than the one of magistrate, and yet men who can scarcely write their names—whose conduct (*not upon political grounds*) has been obnoxious, are pressing their claims as superior and entitled to the support of the poor deluded colored man—

One word from you would put this whole confusion at rest—I may be in error, but my honest convictions are, that the best means to perpetuate party power would be to disarm the opposite party, by dealing fairly and justly with them—by showing to them that we will not inflict a wrong upon them to gratify party spleen or revenge—but with a generosity and true magnanimity which ever characterize the conduct of the honorable and ingenuous, we will exclude them from no *position* which the *public good demands* they *should* occupy—nor give them any which it suggests would *be perilous to the country*. We have not a man of the republican Party in Lower Black River Township or District who is qualified for either of the offices now soon to be filled by the suffrages of the people.—This Sir is a fair and honest statement—Then why jeopardize the public good, by empowering men to do business for which they are utterly and hopelessly disqualified? The Republican party, both in strength and character will have every thing to lose and nothing to gain by it—My policy would be in the election of magistrate, *Constable* and Clerk to select the most honorable intelligent and commendable men of the country, regardless of their political opinions and by that means you can add strength to your party, which I *assure you today*, (owing to the inefficiency and oppression as exhibitted and practised by some of the appointees, on some of the colored people here) has depreciated at least 50 per cent since the last election—The more intelligent colored men here say they have none of their color qualified for these positions; and they are willing to take good men from any party in order to restore peace, harmony and prosperity to the country—They are annoyed to death by the low and debased white man who has seized upon this, as his only opportunity to get position—you know Sir, such men are dangerous; that they cannot be trusted—In the name of justice and for the sake of our prople's welfare and happiness aid us with your influence to the end proposed—You *never were more of a union man than I have always been*—I spoke and maintained my position in direct opposition to the Rebellion during the *entire war* am the same now—ever expect to be—and a John Minor Botts[1] Man—with whom I have corresponded ever since I was 18 years of age; am now 46 years old write me if you can immediately most respectfully, your obt svt R. Beverly Frayser[2]

[Direct your letter to Point Caswell Newhanover Co. N. C. I never asked the *people* for a political office *in* my life—and never expect to do so which I name to relieve me of the charge of selfishness in writing this communication—

[1] John Minor Botts, Virginia; member, U.S. House of Representatives, 1839-1843, 1847-1849; opposed Mexican War and secession; presided over organization meeting of Union Republican Party of Virginia. *Dictionary of American Biography*, s.v. "Botts, John Minor."

[2] R. Beverly Frayser, New Hanover County; Point Caswell lawyer. 1870 U.S. Census Population Schedule, North Carolina: New Hanover, 179 (microfilm).

INDEX

A

Abolition of slavery, 250, 293
Adams, Henderson, 416
Adams, James, 333
African Americans: emancipation of, xix; Holden's response to emancipation of, 177; suffrage for, 287, 399; as troops, 196, 213, 216, 224, 232. *See also* freedmen and slavery
Ahrens, F. W., 439-440
Alamance County, 237
Albemarle Land Company, 66
Albright, William R., 237
Alexander County, 315
Allen, W. A., 63
Alston, James W., 426
Ammunition, 204
Amnesty oath, 205-206, 220, 228, 247, 281. *See also* pardons
Anderson, William H., 307
Anderson, William S., 214
Antietam, Battle of, xix
Arms (weapons), xxvii, 379, 381-383, 386-389, 391-392, 387, 397
"Army Convention," 144
Arrington, Archibald H., 159, 247
Ashe, Thomas S., 139
Ashe, William S., 50, 69, 104
Asheville (N.C.), 399, 407, 422
Asheville News, 31
Ashley, Samuel S., 355, 412
Atkinson, Thomas, 88
Atlantic and North Carolina Railroad, 184, 209
Attorney General (U.S.), 201, 219
Atwell, James W., 182
Avery, Robert, 385
Avery, William W., 36, 71, 87, 104, 106, 117

B

Badger, George E., 21, 52, 134, 164
Badger, Richard C., 121, 242, 256
Baines, A. B., 247
Baker, Henry, 379
Baltzer and Taaks, 425, 437
Bank of North Carolina, 192, 302, 327
Bankrupt Law of 1841, 83
Banks, Nathaniel P., 296
Barnes, James P., 385, 419
Barnett, John, 370
Barnett, Sam C., 222
Barringer, Daniel M., 14, 116, 153, 327
Barringer, Edmund G.L., 135
Barringer, Victor C., 394
Baskerville, George D., 23
Battle, Kemp P., 126, 302, 352
Bauman, John G., 214
Bayne, William H., 35
Beaufort (N.C.), 95, 234
Bell-Everett ticket, 111
Bell, William F., III, 428
Bennett, Henry, 93
Bennett, Richard H., 436
Benning, Henry L., 142
Benton, Thomas H., 29
Berry, John, 60
Bertie County, 439
Bidwell, Oliver B., 441
Biggs, Asa, xvii, 18, 25, 26, 42, 52, 91, 93, 98
Bissell, Edward H., 440
Blacks. *See* African Americans
Blount, George W., 168, 169-172
Bogle, Washington M., 433n
Bond, Lewis, 439
Bonds, 329, 352, 393, 425
Borland, James L., 374
Botts, John M., 445
Boutwell, George S., 296, 305
Bowe, George W., 358, 369
Bower, George, 71
Boyd, Andrew J., 209
Boyd, George D., 69
Boyden, Nathaniel, 269, 393
Bradford, Edmund, 146
Bragg, Thomas, xvii, 44, 52, 93, 98, 142, 153

Branch, Lawrence O'B., 79, 93, 98
Brandegee, Augustus, 300
Brannock, Jacob, 443
Breckinridge, John C., xviii, 55, 104, 105, 107, 112
Bridgers, Robert R., 106, 226, 235
Brindle, Zacariah, 374
Brinsfield, Andy, 443
Brooks, George W., 219
Brooks, William M., 371
Brown, Bedford, 106, 269, 314
Brown, Joseph E., 154
Brown, Thomas J., 365
Browne, William Carl, Jr., 44
Brunswick County, xxvi, 391
Bryan, John H., 327
Buchanan, James, xvi, xvii, 23, 47, 50, 52, 56, 57, 58, 83, 104
Bullick, William J., 169
Bullock, James M., 19
Bullock, John H., 427
Buncombe County, 308
Burgess, Albert, 397
Burgwyn, George W., 372
Burgwyn, Henry K., 372
Burke County, 405
Busbee, Perrin, 2, 26, 34, 45, 70
Busbee, Quentin D., 70, 121
Butler, Benjamin F., 306
Butler, William O., 26, 48, 55, 56
Buxton, Ralph P., 61, 353
Bynum, John G., 34

C

Caldwell, David F., 86
Caldwell, Greene W., 15, 29, 58
Caldwell, Tod R., 232, 395, 308, 366
Cameron, Paul C., 87, 352
Canby, Edward R. S., xxiv, 120, 311, 316-318, 330-331, 335-338, 341, 345
Candler, Thomas J., 308
Candler, William G., 308, 367n
Cantwell, Edward, 209
Cape Fear Bank, 86, 302
Capitol grounds (Raleigh), 373
Carey, Wilson, 314
Carson, John M., 433n
Carter, David M., 280n
Carver, Henry, 222
Cass, Lewis M., 26, 48, 50, 52, 56, 57
Caswell County, xxvi, 358, 359-360, 369, 374, 442-443
Catawba County, 13-14
Cawthorne, William W., 397
Caziere, Louis V., 313
Census printing, 53
Chapel Hill (N.C.) , xxvii
Charlotte (N.C.), 97, 382, 437-438, 440
Chatham and Coalfields Railroad, 411
Chatham County, 358-359
Chatham Railroad, xxvii, 437
Cherokee Battalion (N.C.), 127
Christian, Samuel H., 139, 159
Chur, Jacob F., 359, 369, 380, 404, 441
Claflin, Horace B., 430n
Clark, Daniel, 296
Clark, Henry S., 13
Clark, Henry T., 28, 92
Clarke, William J., 36, 43, 70
Clay County, 379
Clay, Henry, 24, 91
Clemens, Jeremiah, 55
Cleveland County, 218
Clingman, Thomas L., xvii, 50, 60, 72, 74, 91, 93, 98, 114, 269
Clinton (N.C.), 362
Coal fields, 86
Cobb, Howell, 54, 55, 93
Coffield, Cornelius H., 126
Cole, Christopher C., 88
Coleman, William M., 312, 340, 416, 433-434
Collins, William F., 43
Colored troops. *See* African Americans
Colquitt, Alfred H., 148
Common schools, 85, 88, 185, 239
Compromise of 1850, 47
Congressional Reconstruction. *See* Reconstruction
Conservative Party: during Civil War, 132, 154, 157-161, 163; during Reconstruction, 310
Constitution (N.C.), 279, 292
Conventions (N.C.): of common schools, 85, 88; of 1848, 20; of 1852, 57; of

1865, 187, 218, 244, 245, 247, 250-252; of peace 152; of Unionists, 173-176, 280-294
Cook, John, 358
Cooke, George T., 98
Cooke, William D., 78
Corpening, William, 366
Corwin, Thomas, 21
Cotten, Richard C., 42
Cotton, 190
County Commissioners, 348
Courts: civil, 221-224; county, 203; military, 221, 223, 245
Courts, Daniel W., 92
Cowles, Calvin J., 153, 162, 310, 366
Cox, Jacob D., 200, 204, 227
Craft, David L., 344
Craige, William H., 355
Crawford, William H., 304
Croom, William A., 183
Crudup, Edward A., 219
Cuningham, John W., 10
Curtis, Silas L., 385
Curtis, Thomas J., 350, 353
Cushing, Caleb, 107

D

Dancy, William F., 23
Daniel, John R. J., 24, 45, 51, 61
Daniel, Junius, 121
Daniel, Willie, 169
Davidson County, 343
Davis, Jefferson, 55, 143, 153, 173, 248, 256, 270
Davis, John M., 234
Davis, William F., 374
Dawes, William J., 364, 359, 369
Dawson, John, 131
Debt: of N.C., xxii, xxv, 248, 252-253, 255, 260, 270, 283, 293, 368, 409; of U.S., 4, 289
Democratic Party: conventions of, 6-8, 13-14, 58, 97, 104-105, 109, 110-111; Holden's relationship to, 90-91, 97-100, 101-102; state committee of, 16-17
Dennison, William, 235
Destructives, 132, 153, 155, 156, 158, 163-164, 167, 247
Devereux, John, Jr., 195, 327
Deweese, John T., 312, 355
Dewey, Charles, 327
DeWitt, Francis, 428, 441
Dick, Robert P., xx, 44, 57, 58, 107, 166-167, 178, 206, 207, 209, 219, 269
Dickinson, Daniel S., 107
Dixon, George, 331
Dixon, Thomas, Jr., xv
Dobbin, James C., 23, 24, 25, 27, 34, 52, 57, 58, 70
Dockery, Alfred, 21, 71, 435
Dockery, Oliver H., 435
Doherty, William H., 311, 430
Donnell, Richard S., 267
Doolittle, James R., 296
Doughty, William J., 428-429
Douglas, Robert M., 301, 373, 391
Douglas, Stephen A., xvi, xviii, 25, 47, 50, 52, 55, 56, 57, 58, 93, 104, 107, 109, 110, 115
Drum, R. C., 373
Duckworth, James H., 308
Duke, W. Greene, 78
Dunlap, Lee, 440

E

Eastmond, Oscar, 407
Eaton, William, Jr., xxi, 19, 177n
Eddins, William H., 182-183, 191
Education, xxv, 412-413
Educational Association of Wake County, 108
Edwards, Weldon N., 21-22, 38, 58, 81
Elections: certificates of, 313; for convention of 1865, 228-231; of county officials, 203,348; districts for, 57; of 1848, 26-27; of 1850, 42-43; of 1852, 62-63; of 1856, 83; of 1858, 96-97; of 1860, xviii, 102, 111-112; of 1864, 155, 163-167; of 1865, 250-251, 259-260, 264; of 1868, 399; fraud in, 330, 438; validity of, 317; voters rejected in, 392; white basis for, 39-40. *See also* suffrage

Ellis, John W., xvi, xvii, 49, 51, 58, 70, 72, 74, 85, 90- 94, 96
Emancipation, xix, 177
Equal Rights League, 307
Equal suffrage, 26-27, 31
Erwin, Marcus, 65, 117
Erwin, William C., 405
Evans, Clement A., 148
Everitt, John H., 349, 361, 398, 407

F

Falkner, Richard, 397
Farris, Charles M., 373
Fayetteville (N.C.), 350, 353, 394-395
Fayetteville and Western Railroad, 411
Ferebee, Dennis D., 264
Fillmore, Millard, xvii, 37, 83
First Regiment North Carolina Volunteers (U.S.), 182-183, 191-192
Fisher, Abiel W., 391, 415
Fisher, Charles, 14
Fisher, Jefferson, 219, 333
Foote, Henry S., 46, 54, 55
Fourteenth Amendment, xxv, 285-286, 318, 327, 345
Frayser, R. Beverly, 443-445
Free Suffrage, 26-27
Freedmen: convention of, 294; Holden's relationship to, 189-190; homicide of, 223; laws relating to, 267; sick and helpless among, 380-381; trials of, 240, 242. *See also* African Americans
Freedmens Bureau, 311
Fremont, John C., xvii, 84
French, Benjamin B., 21, 59
Friends, Society of, 205-206
Fries, Francis L., 95
Fugitive slave law, 56, 59
Fulton, Samuel, 35

G

Gahagan, G. W., 308
Gales, Seaton, 35, 78, 121, 298
Gales, Weston R., 21
Gannaway, G. T. F., 442-443
Gant, Jesse, 237
Gates County, xxvi, 357
Gettysburg, Battle of, xix
Gibbins, William, 309
Gilliam Robert B., 10, 131
Gilmer, John A., 247
Gleason, James A., 437, 440
Glenn, David C., 107
Goodloe, Daniel R., 301
Gorrel, R. W., 359
Governor's Mansion, 346-347, 422-423
Graham, William A., 18, 19, 27, 125, 153, 164, 244, 247, 256, 260, 263, 265, 268-70, 279, 352
Granger, L. E., 429, 441
Grant, U. S., xxvii
Granville County, xxvi, 227, 343-344, 385-386, 389-390
Graves, Calvin, 23, 44
Graves, James, 364
Great Seal (N.C.), 227
Green, James S., 93
Green, Thomas J., 104
Green, William F., 95
Greenville and French Broad Railroad, 356
Griffith, Jesse C., 359, 374, 406
Grissom, Eugene, 417
Griswold, John A., 352
Gulick, William B., 35
Guns. *See* Arms

H

H. B. Claflin and Company, 428, 442n
Habeas Corpus, 154, 156
Hale, Edward J., 134, 141, 150
Halifax County, xxvi, 27, 204, 349, 361, 372
Hamilton, Andrew J., 296
Hamilton, J. G. de Roulhac, xv
Hanes, Lewis, 227
Hargrave, Jesse, 121
Hargrove, Samuel, 106
Harlan, James, 296
Harmon, L. W., 225-226
Harrington, James S., 279
Harris, Ceburn L., xxiv, 154, 299, 312, 346, 416

Harris, E. E., 339
Harris, James H., 307, 333
Harris, William H., 351
Harrison, John R., 333
Harrison, William H., xix, 121, 141, 299, 301, 333, 334
Hartsfield, Jacob A., 183
Haryse, Julie D., 104
Hassell, Cushing B., 34
Haughton, John H., 153
Hawkins, William J., 81
Hawley, Joseph R., 196
Hays, John H., 396
Haywood, Edward G., 52, 334-335
Haywood, William D., 334, 339
Haywood, William H., 2
Haywood, William H., Jr., 52
Heartt, Dennis, xvi
Heaton, David, 190, 243
Hedrick, Benjamin S., 234, 248
Helper, Hinton R., 103
Henderson, W. F., 343
Henry, James L., 367n, 431
Henry, Louis D., 10-11
Henry, Robert M., 197, 203, 304, 399
Henson, Jefferson M., 121
High, William, 96
Hill, Daniel H., 184
Hill, Joel F., 63
Hill, John H., 21
Hines, Richard, 21
Hinton, Charles L., 43
Hofler, John W., 357
Hoke, John F., 52
Hoke, Michael, 14, 27
Holden, Ann A. Y., xvi, 59, 60
Holden, Henrietta, 62
Holden, Joseph W., 130, 299, 399
Holden, Laura, 88, 95
Holden, Louisa, 95, 103, 115, 116, 120-121, 122, 299, 300
Holden, Mary, 95
Holden, Thomas W., xv, 1
Holden, William W: addresses mass meetings, 173-176, 375-378, 400-404; appointed provisional governor, xxi; breaks with Governor Vance, xx, 157-161; candidacy of, 1858, xvii, 1864, 152-153; declines to canvass, 1864, 155; and Democratic Party, 97-100, 101-102; elected to Commons, xvi; elected state printer, 131; and emancipation, 177; and freedmen, 189-190; gubernatorial nominations of, xxiii, 251-252, 308; inaugural address of, 319-326; memoirs of, xv; and peace, xxix, 135-138, 146-148, 153-154; political defeat of, 1864, xx, 1865, xxiii; political disabilities of, 307; presidential endorsement denied, 256; proclamations by, 186-190, 228-231, 272-273, 314, 386-389; as provisional governor, 178, 180, 210, 259, 273-274, 277-278; refers to origins, 98; requests presidential endorsement, 255; seeks cabinet position, 435; speeches of, 173-176, 280-294; supports Reconstruction, xxiii, 177-178, 280-294; and Thaddeus Stevens, xxiv, 295-298
Holleman, William H., 327
Holmes, Duncan, 362
Homestead law, 400
Homicide. *See* Murder
Hood, George A., 121
Hopkins, John W., 350
Houston, Sam, 25, 48, 52
Howard Amendment, xxiv, 296, 314
Howard, Oliver O., 380
Howell, Benjamin A., 424, 426
Humphrey, Lott W., 106
Hunter, Robert M. T., xviii, 93, 104, 105, 107, 111

I

Immigration, 411
Ingersoll, Charles J., 8
Insane asylum, 417
Institution for deaf and blind, 417
Internal improvements, xxvi, 411
Internal revenue districts, 248
Ivey, Benjamin W., 328
Ivey, Stendon, 40

J

Jeffreys, William A., 2, 6
Jenkins, David A., xxiv, 299, 409, 434
Johnson, Andrew, xx, xxiii, 171-172, 176, 179-181, 190, 204-206, 208, 217, 220, 227, 231-234, 236, 244-247, 249-250, 252-253, 255- 256, 259, 264, 268-272, 275-278, 327
Johnson, DeWitt C., 103
Johnson, L. J., 63
Johnson, Lewis, 368
Johnson, Nathaniel D., 264
Johnson, Thomas D., 364
Johnston, Joseph E., 148
Jones, Alexander H., 308, 431, 435, 438
Jones, Alfred, 44
Jones, Edmund W., 178
Jones, John E., 427
Jones, Nathaniel R., 423, 427
Joyner, Andrew, 21, 194, 218

K

Kansas, 93
Kelley, William D., 296
Kerr, John, 62, 151
Kerr, John, Jr., 56, 92
Kidder, Edward, 211
King, Richard W., 183
King, William R. D., 59
Kittrell (N.C.), 11
Know Nothing Party, 78, 79, 84
Kossuth, Lajos, 47, 52
Ku Klux Klan, xxv, xxvi, 354-355, 383, 385-386, 392, 437-438, 442-443

L

Lacy, Drury, 70
Laflin, Byron, 313
Laird, William J., 400
Land Bill, 93
Land distribution question, 70, 72, 91
Land script sale, 430
Lander, William, 23, 106, 159
Lane, Joseph, xviii, 57, 104, 107
Lane, William B., 29
Lane, William K., 151
Lankford, Menalcus, 95
Latham, Charles, 67
Lawrence, Edward, 211
Lawrence, J. J., 169
Leach, James M. B., 301
Leach, James T., 159, 164
Leake, Walter F., 17, 24, 69
Lee, James R., 353
Legislature, 264-265, 313
Lemay, Thomas J., 19
Letcher, John, 103
Lewis, Augustus M., 69, 118
Lewis, Nicholas M., 371
Liedtke, F. W., 374
Lincoln, Abraham, 109, 111, 120, 171
Lines, Howell, 423, 427
Literary Board, 44, 48, 65-67, 87, 98, 193
Literary Fund, 186, 239
Little, George, 39, 158, 163
Littlefield, Milton S., xxv, 366
Lockhart, Handy, 333
Locofoco Party, 74, 75
Logan, George W., 159
Long, John, 372
Long, Nicholas M., 104
Long, William, 314
Lougee, Augustus L., 333
Lowry Band, 419-420, 424
Lowry, Henry B., 385, 419

M

Macon, Nathaniel, 39
Magistrates, 182, 183-184, 197, 203
Mallett, Charles B., 329, 361, 367
Mallory, Edward, 386, 389
Mangum, Addison, 212
Manly, Charles, 23, 26, 27, 31, 35, 38, 40, 41, 87
Marshall, A. G., 433n
Martin, Alfred, 214
Martin, Robert M., 392
Mason, William S., 178, 206, 220, 267
Masten, John, 95
Matheson, Daniel, 432
Matheson, Robert P., 315
Maynard, Richard, 374

Mayo, Cuffie, 386
McAden, Rufus Y., 260, 265
McCallum, William D., 419-421
McCulloch, Hugh, 243, 295
McDowell and Yancey Turnpike Co., 433
McDowell, Thomas D. S., 95
McDuffie, Malcolm J., 126
McGowan, Patrick, 70
McKay, Allmand A., 246
McKay, James I., 24
McKay, William M., 125
McKenzie, Alexander, 420
Mclean, Archibald D., 43
McLean, James R., 168
McMannin, Charles T., 212
McMannin, John A., 212
McNair, Malcom, 121
McPheeters, A.M., 227
McQueen, James H., 420
McRae, Duncan K., 23, 26, 34, 52, 58, 91, 92, 93, 94, 159
McRae, Murdic, 421
Meade, George G., 236, 245, 363, 372, 373
Meek, Alexander B., 109
Mendenhall, Nereus, 205-206
Menninger, Henry J., 411
Merrimon, Augustus S., 334-335, 366
Mexican War, 19
Miles, Nelson A., 363, 372, 382-384, 395, 441
Militia, xxvi, 341-342, 390, 415-416, 436
Mills, Columbus, 63
Milton (N.C.), 369-371
Missouri Compromise, 35
Mitchell, Anderson, 240-241
Mitchell, Giles M., 439
Mitchell, Robert, 350
Montgomery County, 135
Moore, Bartholomew F., xxi, 157, 177n, 267, 327, 334-335
Moore, Harriet J., 428, 441
Moore, James I., 343-344, 389-390
Moore, William A., 106
Moose, N. A., 433n
Mordecai, George W., 327
Morehead, James T., 168
Morehead, John M., 151
Morganton (N.C.), 395
Morganton General Hospital, 404-405
Morrill, Justin S., 93
Mountain Banner, 31
Murder, 223, 423-424, 426-427
Murray, Albert, 238
Murray, Eli, 225

N

Nags Head (N.C.), 127
National debt, 4, 289
Naval blockade, xix
Nebraska bill, 75
Negroes. *See* African Americans
Neuse (ram), 243
New Bern (N.C.), 234, 381
New Hanover County, 336, 379, 443-445
Nixon, Jere, 34, 36
North Carolina Railroad, 30, 31, 51-52.
North-Carolina Reader, 48-49
North Carolina Standard, xvi, xix, xxv, 3, 332-333
North Carolina Volunteers (U.S.), 182-183, 191-192
Northampton County, 27, 204 ,372
Northwestern Railroad, xxvii
Norton, Hanibal D., 404-405, 419

O

O'Hara, James., 294-295
Ogburn, Edmund B., 88
Orange County, xxvii
Oregon Territory, 35
Orphan Asylums, 380
Outlaw, David, 29, 61
Overbaugh, Ambrose, 350

P

Pace, James, 358
Page, Bentley W., 374
Page, John B., 391
Page, Rufus H., 98
Palmer, Willie J., 134
Pardons, xxii, 185, 201-202, 247-248, 284. *See also* Amnesty oaths

Paroled soldiers, 198-199
Paschal, John M., 4427
Paschall, Eziecal, 443
Paschall, Henry W., 354
Pass, Jacob C., 405-406
Pasteur, Thomas J., 64
Patillo, A. A., 365
Patterson, John, 379
Patterson, Rufus L., 104, 181, 194
Patton, Adolphus, 405
Peace movement, xxix, 135-140, 146-148, 153-154, 158-159
Pearson, Richmond M., 246, 316, 317
Pell, William E., 298
Pemberton, Edmund L., 330, 353
Penitentiary, 416
Person County, 221, 399
Person, Samuel J., 29, 117
Pescud, Peter F., 131
Pettiford Creek steam mill, 428, 441
Pettigrew, James J., 130
Phelps, Charles, 62
Phelps, John T., 67
Phillips, Samuel F., 70, 264
Philpott, William A., 343, 344
Pierce, Franklin, xvi, 59, 62, 70
Plummer, Harry H., 397
Poisson, William W., 215
Polk, James K., 14, 29
Pool, Charles C., 355
Pool, John, xxiv, xxviii, 269, 271, 299, 311, 351, 355, 430, 435
Pool, Solomon, 351, 355
Poor relief, 272-273, 405, 419
Porter, William H., 350
Powell, Robert J., 178, 220, 247, 249, 250, 255, 263, 270, 296
Presidential Reconstruction. *See* Reconstruction
Printing contracts, 78, 131, 301
Proctor, Edward K., 329
Provisional governor: *See* Holden, William W.
Pungo Road, 67-68
Purcell, Alex, 420
Puryear, Richard C., 69

Q

Quakers, 205-206
Quarantine, 337
Quitman, John A., 55

R

Railroads, xxvi, 318, 352
Raleigh (N.C.), 333, 339
Ramsay, James G., 159
Rand, Nathaniel G., 118
Randall, Alexander W., 296
Rawlings, John A., 313
Rayner, Kenneth, 21
Reade, Edwin G., 221, 247, 254
Reconstruction: congressional plan of, 285, 304-305; presidential plan of, xx, 285; Holden's position on, 177-178, 280-294. *See also* Restoration of Union
Reid, Ansolem, 95
Reid, David S., xvi, 12-13, 17, 20, 24-26, 30, 32, 34-35, 37, 40, 42-43, 46, 49, 52, 56, 57, 59, 62, 65, 73, 74, 82-84, 98, 151
Reilly, John, 394-395
Rencher, Abraham, 57
Republican Party, xxiv, xxvi, 308, 315
Restoration of Union, 266, 275-278, 291. *See also* Reconstruction
Restori, Adelaide, 299
Revenue bill, 302
Richardson, William R., 178, 333
Richmond Enquirer, 137
Ridenhour, Phillip, 381
Riley, John, 350
Riots, xxvi, 339, 358-360, 364-365, 369, 399, 407, 422
Rives, Robert E., 70
Roan, Nathaniel M., 36
Roanoke Island, 126
Roanoke Republican, 20
Robbins, George R., 93
Robertson, Henderson, 443
Robeson County, 419-421, 424, 426
Robinson, John, 396
Robinson, William, 35, 123-125
Rodman, William B., 309

Rogers, Sion H., 121
Rollins, Pinkney, 356
Rollins, W. Wallace, 308
Roney, John T., 374
Root, Charles B., 123
Rosafy, Mathias, 391
Rountree, Charles J., 169
Royster, Madison B., 3347
Ruffin, Thomas, Jr., 35, 39-40, 296
Ruffin, Thomas, Sr., 35, 37n, 39-40, 296
Ruger, Thomas H., xxii, 217, 222, 227, 232, 240-241
Rushing, Darling, 70
Russ, John P. H., 178

S

Salisbury (N.C.), 363
Sampson County, xxvi, 362
Sanders, Willis H., 96
Satterfield, Benjamin, 399
Saunders, Romulus M., l, 6-7, 34, 42, 57, 58, 63
Saunders, William L., 113, 114
Schenck, James W., Jr., 336, 384
Schenck, John T., 437
Schofield, John M., 172, 191
Scott, Winfield, 75
Seago, Eli M., xix, 140
Secession, xviii, 120, 249, 282, 293, 311
Settle, Thomas, Jr., 69, 82, 152, 264, 301
Settle, Thomas, Sr., 61
Seward, William H., 52, 86, 103, 109, 179, 199, 210-211, 259, 261-262, 273, 295
Shackelford, James, 214
Shaw, Henry M., 69
Shepard, James B., xvi, 2, 16-17, 19, 34, 36, 45
Sheperd, William S., 143
Sherard, John V., 381
Sheriffs, election of, 203
Sherman, John, 303
Sherman, William T., 168, 270, 346
Short, Richard, 169
Sickles, Daniel E., 346
Sinclair, James, 420
Slavery, xvi, 43,49, 59, 106, 170, 174, 248, 250, 261-262
Sloan, William, 261, 296
Smith, Benjamin B., 34
Smith, Jere, 432
Smith, Samuel P., 159
Smith, Sidney, 52
Smith, William N. H., 150, 159
Snow, Henry A., 349
Snow, James S., 349
Soule, Pierre, 59
Speed, James, 198-199, 296
Spelman, John, 123, 151, 158
Spruill, Hezekiah G., 65
Stallings, Whitmel, 73
Stanbery, Henry, 306
Standard. See *North Carolina Standard*
Stanly County, 381
Stanly, Edward, 13, 34
Stanton, Edwin M., 295, 347
Starbuck, Darius H., 248
State Journal, 144
State Bank, 86
State rights, 170
Staton, John L., 370
Stay laws, 414-415
Steele, Walter L., 151
Stephens, Alexander H., 147, 156
Stephens, John W., 314, 364
Stevens, Thaddeus, xxiv, 295-299
Stewart, Charles, 8
Stokes, Montford S., 36
Stone, Jonathan M., 19
Strange, Robert, Jr., 26, 34, 52, 56
Suffrage: for African Americans, 287; extension of, 38; for paroled soldiers, 198-199; for loyal Unionists, 304-305; question of, 26. *See also* Elections and Free Suffrage
Suit, William H., 423, 427
Summers, Jacob, 443
Summers, Peter, 374
Sumner, Charles, 296
Swain, David L., xxi, 29, 177n, 352
Swamp lands, 65-68
Swann, Reubin, 218
Swepson, George W., 366, 421-422
Syme, John W., 98

T

Tarborough and Wilmington Railroad, 411
Tariff, 4
Tate, Samuel M., 366, 393
Taxes, 4, 273, 348
Taylor, James F, xxiv, 299
Taylor, Matchet, 311
Taylor, Zachary, 26, 29, 34, 36, 37
Teague, James J., 433n
Terrell, James T., 374
Test Oath Ordinance, 125
Texas, 8
Thirteenth Amendment, 261-263, 267-268
Thomas, William H., 71, 127
Thornton, Alvin G., 330, 350
Tomlinson, W. H., 350
Toole, Henry I., 13
Toombs, Robert A., 61
Transylvania County, 431
Treasurer (N.C.), 43, 434
Trumbull, Lyman, 296
Tucker, Thomas G., 109, 115
Turner, James C., 422
Turner, Josiah, Jr., 100, 159, 260, 247-249, 255, 260, 352, 399

U

Union conventions, xxiii, 168-169, 173-176, 279-294, 304
Unionists, 118
Union League, xxv, 213, 316
Union Party, xxiv
University of North Carolina, 87, 274, 346, 351

V

Van Buren, Martin, 4
Vance, Harriette E., 208
Vance, Zebulon B., xviii, 128-130, 133-134, 141, 143, 152-153, 155, 158, 162, 195, 208, 221, 247, 256, 263, 265, 270, 366
Venable, Abraham W., 11, 23, 29,45-47, 50, 53, 55-57, 60, 64 , 69-70, 99
Vermont, 391-392
Vicksburg, Battle of, xix
Violence, xxvii, 223, 423, 426-427. *See also* Ku Klux Klan; Murder; Riots
Vogells, Henry C., 427
Voters. *See* Elections

W

Waddell, Alfred M., 195
Wake County, 27
Walker, Charles, 370
Walker, Henry A., 370-371
Walker, John, 104
Walker, Robert J., 8
Wallace, Stephen D., 209, 214
Walsh, William A., 98, 184
Ward, Joseph D., 7-9
Warren County, 39, 397, 423, 426-427
Warren, Edward J., 159
Warrenton News, 98
Washington Union, 53-54
Waters, Hardy H., 67
Watkins, Charles, 371
Watkins, Samuel, 371
Watson, John, 350
Watson, John W. B., 104
Wayne County, xxvi, 396
Weapons. *See* Arms
Webb, Thomas, 209
Webster, Daniel, 21
Welch, Miles, 372
Welles, Gideon, 295
Welsh, J. W., 350
Western North Carolina Railroad, xxvii, 329, 356, 366, 393, 411, 436-437.
Western Railroad Company, 361, 367
Wheeler, John H., 13-15, 21, 24, 43, 49, 58
Whig Party, 4, 20, 31
Whitaker, Edward, 333
Whitaker, Wesley, Jr., 78
White, John, 195
Whitford, John D., 209
Whitted, William D., 303, 438

Wilder, Gaston H., 34, 45, 63, 70, 118
Wiley, Calvin H., 48, 85, 88, 108, 185, 239, 243
Willard, Henry A., 300
Williams, George A., 317, 333, 343-344, 346
Williams, John G., 178
Williamson, George, 63
Williamson, John T., 333
Williamston and Tarboro Railroad, xxvii
Wilmington (N.C.), xxvi , 131, 195-197, 212-215, 224, 382
Wilmington Commercial, 20
Wilmington and Weldon Railroad, 226, 235, 236
Wilmington to Goldsboro Railroad, 209
Wilmington, Charlotte and Rutherfordton Railroad, xxvii, 329, 411
Wilmot Proviso, xvi, 28, 34
Wilson (N.C.), 168
Wilson, Frank I., xvii, 76, 101, 104, 110
Wilson, John, 371
Wilson, Thomas, 63
Windley, Jacob D., 67
Winslow, Warren, 125
Winstead, Charles S., 64
Winston, Patrick H., 70
Winthrop, Robert C., 21
Wise, Henry A., 56, 59, 127
Wood, Fernando, 48
Woodfin, Nicholas W., 153
Woods, Priscilla, xv
Woody, Tinsley A., 222
Wooley, Calvin W., 135
Wooten, Council, 247
Worth, Jonathan, xxv, 155-157, 192, 221, 254, 261, 265, 270, 272, 274, 278, 317, 346-347

Y

Yadkin County, 238-239
Yancey, William L., 107, 109
Yanceyville (N.C.), 358-360, 364-365
Yarborough Hotel, 52